The Story of God Bible Commentary Series Endorsements

"Getting a story is about more than merely enjoying it. It means hearing it, understanding it, and above all, being impacted by it. This commentary series hopes that its readers not only hear and understand the story, but are impacted by it to live in as Christian a way as possible. The editors and contributors set that table very well and open up the biblical story in ways that move us to act with sensitivity and understanding. That makes hearing the story as these authors tell it well worth the time. Well done."

Darrell L. Bock
Dallas Theological Seminary

"The Story of God Bible Commentary series invites readers to probe how the message of the text relates to our situations today. Engagingly readable, it not only explores the biblical text but offers a range of applications and interesting illustrations."

Craig S. Keener
Asbury Theological Seminary

"I love The Story of God Bible Commentary series. It makes the text sing and helps us hear the story afresh."

John Ortberg
Senior Pastor of Menlo Park Presbyterian Church

"In this promising new series of commentaries, believing biblical scholars bring not only their expertise but their own commitment to Jesus and insights into today's culture to the Scriptures. The result is a commentary series that is anchored in the text but lives and breathes in the world of today's church with its variegated pattern of socioeconomic, ethnic, and national diversity. Pastors, Bible study leaders, and Christians of all types who are looking for a substantive and practical guide through the Scriptures will find these volumes helpful."

Frank Thielman
Beeson Divinity School

"The Story of God Bible Commentary series is unique in its approach to exploring the Bible. Its easy-to-use format and practical guidance brings God's grand story to modern-day life so anyone can understand how it applies today."

Andy Stanley
North Point Ministries

"I'm a storyteller. Through writing and speaking I talk and teach about understanding the Story of God throughout Scripture and about letting God reveal more of his story as I live it out. Thus I am thrilled to have a commentary series based on the story of God—a commentary that helps me to Listen to the Story, that Explains the Story, and then encourages me to probe how to Live the Story. A perfect tool for helping every follower of Jesus to walk in the story that God is writing for them."

Judy Douglass
Director of Women's Resources, Cru

"The Bible is the story of God and his dealings with humanity from creation to new creation. The Bible is made up more of stories than of any other literary genre. Even the psalms, proverbs, prophecies, letters, and the Apocalypse make complete sense only when set in the context of the grand narrative of the entire Bible. This commentary series breaks new ground by taking all these observations seriously. It asks commentators to listen to the text, to explain the text, and to live the text. Some of the material in these sections overlaps with introduction, detailed textual analysis and application, respectively, but only some. The most riveting and valuable part of the commentaries are the stories that can appear in any of these sections, from any part of the globe and any part of church history, illustrating the text in any of these areas. Ideal for preaching and teaching."

Craig L. Blomberg
Denver Seminary

"Pastors and lay people will welcome this new series, which seeks to make the message of the Scriptures clear and to guide readers in appropriating biblical texts for life today."

Daniel I. Block
Wheaton College and Graduate School

"An extremely valuable and long overdue series that includes comment on the cultural context of the text, careful exegesis, and guidance on reading the whole Bible as a unity that testifies to Christ as our Savior and Lord."

Graeme Goldsworthy
author of *According to Plan*

1-2 SAMUEL

The Story of God Bible Commentary

1–2 SAMUEL

Paul S. Evans

Tremper Longman III & Scot McKnight
General Editors

ZONDERVAN

1–2 Samuel
Copyright © 2018 by Paul S. Evans

This title is also available as a Zondervan ebook.

Requests for information should be addressed to:
Zondervan, *3900 Sparks Dr. SE, Grand Rapids, Michigan 49546*

ISBN 978-0-310-49093-7

Cover design: Ron Huizinga
Cover image: iStockphoto ®
Interior composition: Kait Lamphere

Printed in the United States of America

18 19 20 21 22 23 24 25 26 27 28 /DHV/ 15 14 13 12 11 10 9 8 7 6 5 4 3 2 1

To My Parents, Randy and Sandy,
Who took me to church,
Modeled faith,
And still show God's love to me.
I am blessed in a Proverbs 20:7 sort of way.

Old Testament series

New Testament series

Contents

Acknowledgments

"The greatest part of a writer's time is spent in reading, in order to write: a man will turn over half a library to make one book."

Samuel Johnson

The writing of this commentary depends in large part on the works of authors who wrote before me. The footnotes throughout will evince my chief conversation partners for my study of 1–2 Samuel, many of whom I have never met but from whom I have benefited immensely. Yet mention should be made of the interlocutors of whom I have first-hand knowledge and for whom I am very grateful. First, I would thank Tremper Longman and George Athas, the editors of this commentary, for their patient reading of my work and their generous comments, critiques, and queries which have definitely improved the final product. As well, I thank Nancy Erickson for her careful editorial eye and helpful suggestions and remarks on late drafts of my work.

I would also thank the exceptional students at McMaster Divinity College who took my "Life of David" courses and contributed to this commentary through stimulating questions and lively interactions during our time in class together. I am also indebted to Keith Bodner for both times of discussion regarding key passages of Samuel, as well as memorable times of fellowship together. Other valuable conversations surrounding Samuel involved various ecclesial gatherings over the past several years where I was able to put parts of this commentary through a test-run in sermons at Shushwap Community Church (Sicamous, B.C.), Gateway Church (Caledonia, ON), Church on the Rock (Hamilton, ON), Hamilton Chinese Alliance Church, as well as chapel services at McMaster Divinity College. At Gateway Church, I learned much from Steve Kerr, both through his excellent sermon series on David and through engaging conversation about Samuel over good coffee. At Church on the Rock, a chance to teach a summer small group on Samuel further helped me focus my thinking on several aspects of the book and I learned much through interaction with participants of that group.

I must also acknowledge my thankfulness for McMaster Divinity College's generous one-year research leave from course work, which allowed time for

11

in-depth study and the actual writing of this commentary. At McMaster Divinity College, I am also grateful for my excellent graduate assistants, Joshua Gardner, Alex Stewart, and Dustin Burlet, who have contributed to my research through procuring books and articles for me as well as assisting in editing, proofreading, and many other tasks.

Of course, I cannot overstate the debt I owe my wife of twenty-two years, Caitlin Evans, for her love and support, and thanks must be expressed for continued patience during the writing of this commentary, even when, near the end of its composition, my writing cut into some of our time off in the summer with our precious children, Chaim and Talyah.

Finally, I express my thanks to my first Bible teachers, my parents, Randy and Sandy Evans, who brought me up in the nurture and admonition of the Lord and infused in me an enduring love for the Bible. Their selfless love, vibrant faith, and godly examples have left an indelible mark on my life, and I dedicate this commentary to them in honor of their 50th wedding anniversary on May 18, 2018.

The Story of God Bible Commentary Series

Why another commentary series?

In the first place, no single commentary can exhaust the meaning of a biblical book. The Bible is unfathomably rich and no single commentator can explore every aspect of its message.

In addition, good commentary not only explores what the text meant in the past but also its continuing significance. In other words, the Word of God may not change, but culture does. Think of what we have seen in the last twenty years: we now communicate predominantly through the internet and email; we read our news on iPads and computers. We carry smartphones in our pockets through which we can call our friends, check the weather forecast, make dinner reservations, and get an answer to virtually any question we might have.

Today we have more readable and accurate Bible versions in English than any generation in the past. Bible distribution in the present generation has been very successful; more people own more Bibles than previous generations. However, studies have shown that while people have better access to the Bible than ever before, people aren't reading the Bibles they own, and they struggle to understand what they do read.

The Story of God Bible Commentary hopes to help people, particularly clergy but also laypeople, read the Bible with understanding not only of its ancient meaning but also of its continuing significance for us today in the twenty-first century. After all, readers of the Bible change too. These cultural shifts, our own personal developments, and the progress in intellectual questions, as well as growth in biblical studies and theology and discoveries of new texts and new paradigms for understanding the contexts of the Bible—each of these elements work on an interpreter so that the person who reads the Bible today asks different questions from different angles.

Culture shifts, but the Word of God remains. That is why we as editors of The Story of God Bible Commentary, a commentary based on the New International Version 2011 (NIV 2011), are excited to participate in this new series of commentaries on the Bible. This series is designed to speak to this generation with the same Word of God. We are asking the authors to explain what the Bible says to the sorts of readers who pick up commentaries so they can understand not only what Scripture says but what it means for today.

The Bible does not change, but relating it to our culture changes constantly and in differing ways in different contexts.

As editors of the Old Testament series, we recognize that Christians have a hard time knowing exactly how to relate to the Scriptures that were written before the coming of Christ. The world of the Old Testament is a strange one to those of us who live in the West in the twenty-first century. We read about strange customs, warfare in the name of God, sacrifices, laws of ritual purity, and more and wonder whether it is worth our while or even spiritually healthy to spend time reading this portion of Scripture that is chronologically, culturally, and—seemingly—theologically distant from us.

But it is precisely here that The Story of God Commentary Series Old Testament makes its most important contribution. The New Testament does not replace the Old Testament; the New Testament fulfills the Old Testament. We hear God's voice today in the Old Testament. In its pages he reveals himself to us and also his will for how we should live in a way that is pleasing to him.

Jesus himself often reminds us that the Old Testament maintains its importance to the lives of his disciples. Luke 24 describes Jesus' actions and teaching in the period between his resurrection and ascension. Strikingly, the focus of his teaching is on how his followers should read the Old Testament (here called "Moses and all the Prophets," "Scriptures," and "the Law of Moses, the Prophets and Psalms"). To the two disciples on the road to Emmaus, he says:

> "How foolish you are, and how slow to believe all that the prophets have spoken! Did not the Messiah have to suffer these things and then enter his glory?" And beginning with Moses and all the Prophets, he explained to them what was said in all the Scriptures concerning himself. (Luke 24:25–27)

Then to a larger group of disciples he announces:

> "This is what I told you while I was still with you: Everything must be fulfilled that is written about me in the Law of Moses, the Prophets and the Psalms." Then he opened their minds so they could understand the Scriptures. (Luke 24:44–45)

The Story of God Commentary Series takes Jesus' words on this matter seriously. Indeed, it is the first series that has as one of its deliberate goals the identification of the trajectories (historical, typological, and theological) that land in Christ in the New Testament. Every commentary in the series will, in the first place, exposit the text in the context of its original reception. We will interpret it as we believe the original author intended his contemporary audience to read it. But then we will also read the text in the light of the death and resurrection of Jesus. No other commentary series does this important work consistently in every volume.

To achieve our purpose of expositing the Old Testament in its original setting and also from a New Testament perspective, each passage is examined from three angles.

Listen to the Story. We begin by listening to the text in order to hear the voice of God. We first read the passage under study. We then go on to consider the background to the passage by looking at any earlier Scripture passage that informs our understanding of the text. At this point too we will cite and discuss possible ancient Near Eastern literary connections. After all, the Bible was not written in a cultural vacuum, and an understanding of its broader ancient Near Eastern context will often enrich our reading.

Explain the Story. The authors are asked to explain each passage in light of the Bible's grand story. It is here that we will exposit the text in its original Old Testament context. This is not an academic series, so the footnotes will be limited to the kinds of books and articles to which typical Bible readers and preachers will have access. Authors are given the freedom to explain the text as they read it, though you will not be surprised to find occasional listings of other options for reading the text. The emphasis will be on providing an accessible explanation of the passage, particularly on those aspects of the text that are difficult for a modern reader to understand, with an emphasis on theological interpretation.

Live the Story. Reading the Bible is not just about discovering what it meant back then; the intent of The Story of God Bible Commentary is to probe how this text might be lived out today as that story continues to march on in the life of the church.

Here, in the spirit of Christ's words in Luke 24, we will suggest ways in which the Old Testament text anticipates the gospel. After all, as Augustine famously put it, "the New Testament is in the Old Testament concealed, the Old Testament is in the New Testament revealed." We believe that this section will be particularly important for our readers who are clergy who want to present Christ even when they are preaching from the Old Testament.

The Old Testament also provides teaching concerning how we should live today. However, the authors of this series are sensitive to the tremendous impact that Christ's coming has on how Christians appropriate the Old Testament into their lives today.

It is the hope and prayer of the editors and all the contributors that our work will encourage clergy to preach from the Old Testament and laypeople to study this wonderful, yet often strange, portion of God's Word to us today.

TREMPER LONGMAN III, general editor Old Testament
GEORGE ATHAS, MARK BODA, AND MYRTO THEOCHAROUS, editors

Abbreviations

AB	Anchor Bible
ABD	*Anchor Bible Dictionary.* Edited by David Noel Freedman. 6 vols. New York: Doubleday, 1992
ALASP	Abhandlungen zur Literatur Alt-Syren-Palästinas und Mesopotamiens
AnBib	Analecta Biblica
ANE	Ancient Near East
ANET	*Ancient Near Eastern Texts Relating to the Old Testament.* Edited by James B. Pritchard. 3rd ed. Princeton: Princeton University Press, 1969
Ant.	Josephus, *Jewish Antiquities*
ARAB	*Ancient Records of Assyria and Babylonia.* Daniel David Luckenbill. 2 vols. Chicago, 1926–27
ARM	Archives royales de Mari
ASV	American Standard Version
BAR	*Biblical Archaeology Review*
BDB	Brown, Francis, S. R. Driver, and Charles A. Briggs. *A Hebrew and English Lexicon of the Old Testament*
Bib	*Biblica*
BO	Bibliotheca Orientalis
BSac	*Bibliotheca Sacra*
BTCB	Brazos Theological Commentary on the Bible
BZAW	Beihefte zur Zeitschrift für die alttestamentliche Wissenschaft
CANE	*Civilizations of the Ancient Near East.* Edited by Jack M. Sasson. 4 vols. New York, 1995. Repr. in 2 vols. Peabody, MA: Hendrickson, 2006
CBQ	*Catholic Biblical Quarterly*
ConBOT	Coniectanea Biblica: Old Testament Series
COS	*The Context of Scripture.* Edited by Willian W. Hallo. 3 vols. Leiden: Brill, 1997–2002
FOTL	Forms of the Old Testament Literature
HBM	Hebrew Bible Monographs
JBL	*Journal of Biblical Literature*
JCS	*Journal of Cuneiform Studies*

JETS	*Journal of the Evangelical Theological Society*
JHNES	The Johns Hopkins Near Eastern Studies
JPS	Jewish Publication Society
JSOT	*Journal for the Study of the Old Testament*
JSOTSup	Journal for the Study of the Old Testament Supplement Series
JSS	*Journal of Semitic Studies*
KJV	King James Version
KUB	*Keilschrifturkunden aus Boghazköi.* Berlin: Akademie, 1921–
LHBOTS	Library of Hebrew Bible/Old Testament Studies
LQ	*Lutheran Quarterly*
LXX	Septuagint, or Old Greek version
MT	Masoretic Text
NAB	New American Bible
NAC	New American Commentary
NEB	New English Bible
NICOT	New International Commentary on the Old Testament
NIV	New International Version
NIVAC	NIV Application Commentary
NLT	New Living Translation
NRSV	New Revised Standard Version
OEANE	*The Oxford Encyclopedia of Archaeology in the Near East.* Edited by Eric M. Meyers. 5 vols. New York: Oxford University Press, 1997
OTL	Old Testament Library
RIMA	Royal Inscriptions of Mesopotamia Assyrian Periods
RSV	Revised Standard Version
SAAB	*State Archives of Assyria Bulletin*
SBLDS	Society of Biblical Literature Dissertation Series
SHCANE	Studies in the History and Culture of the Ancient Near East
SOTSMS	Society for Old Testament Studies Monograph Series
SR	*Studies in Religion*
TOTC	Tyndale Old Testament Commentary
VC	*Vigiliae Christianae*
VT	*Vetus Testamentum*
VTSup	Vetus Testamentum: Supplement Series
WAW	Writings from the Ancient World
WBC	Word Biblical Commentary
WTJ	*Westminster Theological Journal*
ZABR	*Zeitschrift für altorientalische und biblische Rechtgeschichte*
ZAW	*Zeitschrift für die alttestamentliche Wissenschaft*

Introduction to 1–2 Samuel

The book of Samuel is one of the great literary works in human history. Its masterfully told stories have captured the imagination of readers for millennia: Hannah's heartfelt pleadings for a child; the fall of the Elide house; the calling of young Samuel and his establishment as a prophet without peer; the young shepherd boy David's musical talent and his defeat of the giant; the manic King Saul's fall from grace and his eerie visit to a witch; David's adultery with Bathsheba and the cunning murder of her husband; the sad decline of David's fortunes and the tragic family deaths and turmoil. The story is laced with high drama, intrigue, theological insight, and mystery. Of course, the book is more than a great literary work. It is also a historical account of both individuals and a nation. More than this, Samuel is also Scripture and was written to teach its reader about God and his workings in the world, both in the past in ancient Israel as well as in the future with the coming of Jesus Christ to fulfill the Davidic promises.

Composition, Transmission, and Canonicity

The Division and Naming of the Book

Though 1–2 Samuel are two books in modern Bibles, they originally were one book. Due to their length, they were divided into two books in the Greek translation called the Septuagint (also known as the LXX). The Septuagint named the books 1 and 2 Kingdoms (or Reigns), along with what we now know as 1–2 Kings being 3 and 4 Kingdoms (Reigns). The Hebrew book of Samuel was first divided into two books in AD 1517 with the first Rabbinic Bible, and eventually this became the norm.

The name for the book can cause some confusion. Due to the practice of naming books after their author in other instances in the Bible, some may think that the prophet Samuel was the author of the book. This is not the case, however, as Samuel dies in the first half of the book (1 Sam 25:1). The book may have been named after him because he was the first main character in the book and was clearly a significant figure in Israelite history. His ministry formed a transition from the era of judges to that of kings. Samuel uniquely served as judge, priest, and prophet. He looms large in political events, religious proceedings, and military exploits. Following Samuel's tenure, others did not multitask in this way: prophets served as prophets, priests as priests, etc. Samuel not only occupies the central role for the beginning of the book, his statements and actions set out the plan of what follows. He anointed the first two kings of Israel (1 Sam 9; 16), expounded on the role and character of kingship (1 Sam 12), and prophetically announced the end to Saul's kingship and God's special choosing of David as king (1 Sam 13:14). Thus, the naming of the book after Samuel is appropriate.

Authorship

Like many other Old Testament books, the book of Samuel is anonymous and does not name anyone as its author. Some early Jewish traditions held that several prophets contemporary with the events wrote the book. This opinion was likely based on the book of Chronicles which refers to sources for David's reign written by the prophets Samuel, Gad, and Nathan (1 Chr 29:29). While it is indeed possible that prophets contributed to the book, the book itself makes no such claim, and even Chronicles does not suggest the book was written totally by one of these prophets.

Regarding sources for the book, Samuel itself notes "the book of Jashar" as a written source employed by the author (2 Sam 1:18), and the administrative lists clearly reflect reliance on a written source as well (2 Sam 8:15–18; 20:23–25; 23:8–39). Scholars have further posited some hypothetical source material that was utilized by the author, including larger literary blocks often referred to as the ark narrative (1 Sam 4–7:1); the history of David's rise (1 Sam 16–2 Sam 5); and the succession narrative (2 Sam 9–20; 1 Kgs 1–2).[1] Similarly, the beginning of 1 Samuel is often thought to rely on early Shiloh traditions (esp. 1 Sam 1–3), and the end of 2 Samuel relies on other materials forming concluding appendices (2 Sam 21–24). Some scholars have further suggested that some of the sources were characterized by their pro-kingship stance (e.g., the story of Saul's anointing and his deliverance of Jabesh Gilead in 1 Sam 9; 11:1–11), while other sources were anti-kingship (e.g., Samuel's warnings about kingship in 1 Samuel 12).[2] While the exact demarcation of different sources in Samuel is debated (and resists a scholarly consensus), it seems clear that a later author used a variety of older sources in writing the book, though most of these sources are no longer available to us.

---

1. L. Rost, *Die Überlieferung Von Der Thronnachfolge Davids*, BWANT III/6 (Stuttgart: W. Kohlhammer, 1926).

2. E.g., M. Noth, *The History of Israel* (New York: Harper & Row, 1960).

Occasion for Writing

Determining the occasion for the writing of Samuel must consider the fact that the book is part of a larger, continuous storyline recounting the history of Israel from the time Israel entered the land to the time they were expelled from it (Joshua, Judges, 1–2 Samuel, and 1–2 Kings). Together these books form a grand, connected narrative of Israel's history that evaluated that history in light of the teachings and theology of Deuteronomy. For this reason, scholars often refer to this larger story as the "Deuteronomistic History." The occasion for the writing of this history was the traumatic experience of the Babylonian exile, when much of the population of Judah was taken to Babylon after Jerusalem and its temple were destroyed in 586 BC by Nebuchadnezzar. The beleaguered exilic community had a crisis of faith at this time and wrestled with fundamental questions. How could this happen? Why were they in exile? What about God's promises to David and the patriarchs? What does this mean for their faith and religion? During this crisis of faith, God inspired the author of Joshua–2 Kings to compose an epic narrating Israel's story.

Though the author is anonymous, scholars refer to this author as "the Deuteronomist" (or "Dtr" for short) because the history he compiled was informed by the theology of Deuteronomy. Deuteronomy addresses "all Israel" (Deut 1:1; 5:1; 11:6; 13:12[11]; 18:6[5]; 21:21; 27:9; 29:1[2]; 31:1, 7, 11; 32:45; 34:12) as a single people of God in covenant with a single God—Yahweh. Furthermore, Israel is to worship at a single sanctuary—"the place the LORD your God will choose" (e.g., Deut 12:5; 14:24; 16:6; 18:6; 26:2; 31:11)—which later is revealed as Jerusalem. Though not a great focus in the book of Samuel, the choosing of this place *is* initiated with David's conquest of Jerusalem (2 Sam 5) and the securing of the Temple Mount (2 Sam 24).

Another important aspect of the theology of Deuteronomy is its theology of "retribution" which became a guiding principle for the author of this history of Israel. This retribution theology maintains that obedience to God's covenant will result in blessing, while disobedience will result in punishment. This can especially be seen in the list of blessings and curses in Deuteronomy 28.

> If you fully obey the LORD your God and carefully follow all his commands I give you today, the LORD your God will set you high above all the nations on earth. All these blessings will come upon you and accompany you if you obey the LORD your God: (Deut 28:1–2)

On the other hand, "if you do not obey the LORD your God and do not carefully follow all his commands and decrees I am giving you today, all these curses will come upon you and overtake you" (Deut 28:15). This perspective is summed up well near the end of the book:

This day I call heaven and earth as witnesses against you that I have set before you life and death, blessings and curses. Now choose life, so that you and your children may live and that you may love the LORD your God, listen to his voice, and hold fast to him. For the LORD is your life, and he will give you many years in the land he swore to give to your fathers, Abraham, Isaac and Jacob. (Deut 30:19–20)

With Deuteronomy's theological principles in place at the beginning of the history, Israel's story unfolds and the reader is left to see whether Israel will be faithful and experience blessing in the land or whether they will be unfaithful and experience expulsion from the land. Thus, the book of Deuteronomy "appears as the hermeneutical key and the ideological basis for reading and understanding the following history."[3] Deuteronomy's theology is clearly reflected in Samuel's statements: "If you are returning to the LORD with all your hearts, then rid yourselves of the foreign gods and the Ashtoreths and commit yourselves to the LORD and serve him only, and he will deliver you out of the hand of the Philistines" (1 Sam 7:3); and "do not turn away from the LORD, but serve the LORD with all your heart. . . . But be sure to fear the LORD and serve him faithfully with all your heart; consider what great things he has done for you. Yet if you persist in doing evil, both you and your king will perish" (12:20, 24–25).[4] This theology is expressed not only in speeches of the prophet but in the events that unfold within the story. Thus, the history as a whole answers the questions of the exilic community based on Deuteronomy's theology: the exile occurred because of their disobedience to God's covenant; God's promises have not failed; the people have failed and Israelite kings failed; and God is true to his word and he will bring his eternal covenant to fulfillment.

The Date of Samuel's Composition

The most likely date for the writing of the larger history of Joshua–Kings—and thus the final composition of the book of Samuel—is during the exile. The end of the larger story (2 Kings) concludes with the destruction of Jerusalem in 586 BC and the beginning of the Babylonian exile, with the last event narrated (the freeing of Jehoiachin to eat with the Babylonian king) dating to around 560 BC (2 Kings 25). Therefore, the book of Kings as we know it could not have been composed *prior* to these events. It is unlikely that the book was written *after* the exile, or the author would have referred to

---

3. Thomas Römer, *The So-Called Deuteronomistic History: A Sociological, Historical and Literary Introduction* (London; New York: T&T Clark, 2005), 24.

4. Robert D. Bergen, *1, 2 Samuel*, NAC 7 (Nashville: Broadman & Holman, 1996), 45.

their return to Jerusalem. This puts the date of the final composition of the conclusion to the larger history of Israel (Joshua–Kings) to the period when Judah was in Babylonian exile and probably between 560–539 BC. The book of Samuel was compiled as part of this history and likely was completed during this time.

Literary Analysis

Genre
A. Historiography

A clear purpose of the book of Samuel is to depict and interpret historical events.[5] However, since the literary genre of "history" in the modern sense did not exist in the ancient world, some caution should be taken in describing its genre as "history." Furthermore, the English word "history" is ambiguous and can mean either the *events* of the past or *verbal accounts* of these events. For the sake of clarity, it is better to use the word "historiography" to refer to verbal accounts of the past, and to refer to the actual events themselves as history. Historiography is a genre wherein a nation or group attempts to render an account of its collective past, and the book of Samuel qualifies as such. The author engaged in research, gathering information from oral or written sources, then recorded his findings in a unified narrative. This process set apart ancient historians from storytellers; however, ancient historiography *was* closer to storytelling than modern history writing.

Though writing before their time, the author of Samuel used techniques similar to those of ancient Greek historians. Greek historiography was often organized thematically, using genealogies, speeches, or narrative formulas as structuring devices, instead of strictly following chronological order. Speeches were largely the creative work of the historian rather than being drawn from transcripts in his sources. Also, both the overall content and particular details of the narrative were subject to the historian's interpretation of the events. This same historical method can be seen in Samuel.

For example, 1 Samuel 29–30 is out of chronological order with 1 Samuel 28:3–25 and is a flashback of sorts. After all, 1 Samuel 29 begins with David marching out with the Philistines on their way to Jezreel (29:11), which is where the Philistine army was in 1 Samuel 28:4 (Shunem is on the north side of the Jezreel valley). Further, in the last chapter Samuel had predicted that

---

5. This discussion of biblical historiography relies on my article "History, Historiography," in *The Baker Illustrated Bible Dictionary*, ed. Tremper Longman, Pete Enns, and Mark Strauss (Grand Rapids: Baker, 2013), 787–88.

Saul would die the next day, but several days are narrated in 1 Samuel 29–30 (e.g., 1 Sam 30:1). As well, the events of 2 Samuel 21 and the Gibeonite slaying of Saul's sons appears to have taken place prior to Absalom's rebellion (2 Sam 15–18), as Shimei's curse on David seems to assume David as responsible for the death of Saul's house (though it was really the Gibeonites). Similarly, the story of David's census (2 Sam 24) took place at an unknown time but likely earlier in David's reign.

In the larger history of Israel (Joshua–Kings), speeches are used as structuring devices, emphasizing the central theological points of the author at key points in his story (e.g., Josh 1; 1 Sam 12; 2 Sam 7; 1 Kgs 8:14–61). All of these speeches use distinctive vocabulary, suggesting the same author composed them. Since the writer was not present at the occasion of these speeches (as they occurred long before his birth), he composed the speech (inventing much of the wording) according to what he thought appropriate to the given situation. The creative contributions of each historian can be clearly seen when a speech is recorded in two or more biblical books (e.g., 2 Sam 7 and 2 Chr 17). This is not to say that the speeches are historically misleading but that they were necessarily composed to present a narrative of the past. All historiography, ancient and modern, involves creative writing, selectivity, and interpretation of sources.

When dealing with Old Testament historiography it must be remembered that it is loaded with interpretation and does not attempt to merely recount what happened as objectively as possible. For example, 2 Kings 15:37 records an attack against Judah by foreign kings; however, the author does not describe any reasons for the attack other than saying, "In those days the LORD began to send Rezin king of Aram and Pekah son of Remaliah against Judah." While no doubt there *were* political reasons for the attack, the author does not comment on these reasons but instead gives a theological interpretation to explain it. In fact, theological reasons for past events and their relevance for the present and future are what characterize biblical historiography. The ultimate explanation for historical events is God and his providential mastery of history. The authors often referred to divine causation to the exclusion of any human factors. Conversely, modern historiography would focus solely on the human reasons for an event and exclude any possible divine causation. In this way biblical historiography does not follow the standards of modern history writing, though as ancient history writing it is an exemplar.

One historian has said "History . . . is all fictionalized, and yet history."[6] That is, all history writing necessitates adapting historical events to the literary

---

6. Baruch Halpern, *The First Historians: The Hebrew Bible and History* (San Francisco: Harper & Row, 1988), 68.

form of historiography. Writing a representation of the past in a text involves a "fictionalizing" aspect.[7] Historiography is "fictional" in that it "employs the devices of all narrative presentation."[8] However, in another sense historiography is the opposite of fiction since it attempts to tell what really happened (i.e., historical events). Historiography has been helpfully compared with "representational art" that, although constrained by historical facts, is an artistic representation of events similar to how a painting represents reality.[9] It is important to recognize that historical narratives of the Bible are not the exact events and words from the past. While there is a correspondence to reality, historical narratives are not to be equated with it. Historiography is written in a literary form similar to fiction, though it functions in an entirely different manner. Since recognizing the genre (e.g., parable, poem) of any biblical passage is crucial for interpretation, realizing the differences between ancient and modern history writing is vital for understanding the genre of the book of Samuel.

B. Apology for David

Some scholarship has suggested that the book of Samuel also functioned as an apology for the Davidic monarchy, as it defends David against charges that he usurped the throne from Saul, killed off his heirs, and unlawfully became king. As an apology, the story has a defensive attitude toward David and answers actual or possible charges leveled against him. The charges are not explicitly stated in the story, but by reading between the lines we can see accusations that were likely made against David by Saulide supporters: (1) David ambitiously advanced himself in Israel at the expense of Saul; (2) David was a deserter (leaving Saul's court) who joined with the enemy (the Philistines); (3) David forced prominent religious leaders to join him in his conspiracy; (4) David was an outlaw who led a pack of rebels against the state; (5) David had a hand in the deaths of Saul, Abner, and Ishbosheth.

Reading the David story, it is easy to see how such charges could have arisen. The book of Samuel, however, answers these charges by asserting: David was widely popular among the people, and his early military victories (e.g., Goliath) on behalf of Israel showed his loyalty and ability to serve as king; David did not attempt to take the throne by force; David showed great restraint against Saul and was blameless in his dealings with him; Abiathar the priest only joined David after Saul had all the priests of Nob killed; David's band of men made no moves against Saul but functioned only defensively and

---

7. V. Phillips Long, *The Art of Biblical History* (Grand Rapids: Zondervan, 1994), 62.
8. Halpern, *First Historians*, 269.
9. Long, *Art of Biblical History*, 67–69.

fought for Israel's benefit; David only fled to Philistia because Saul was out to kill him; David was never loyal to the Philistines but covertly used his position there to help Israel; David played no part in the deaths of the Saulides (Saul, Abner, Ishbosheth) but instead punished those who killed them; what is more, David's ascension to the throne was Yahweh's doing.

In this way it does seem that Samuel's accounts of David's rise to the throne function apologetically and this apologetic function may have been one of the original purposes of some of the literary sources of the book (assuming they were written during the early Davidic monarchic period). But this does not mean that the reader should not trust the stories. While they are written from their own perspective and emphasize David's innocence in his rise to the kingship, they are not for that reason false. While some view the story skeptically due to their (at least partial) function as an apology, such skepticism is unwarranted. In fact, David is not whitewashed in the story but is portrayed in a multi-faceted way from the beginning. As the commentary will show, David's flaws are not hidden from view even early on in his story.

Historical Context

Setting of the Contents of the Book

The book of Samuel follows the books of Judges and Ruth not only in canonical order but in historical context. First Samuel 1 begins its story in the period of the judges. From its inception Israel was a theocracy, that is, they had no human king. Instead, Yahweh was their king (cf. Judg 8:23). Originally led by such great figures as Moses and Joshua, after settling in the promised land Israel was led by various "judges" whom God would raise up in Israel's time of need. During this period the people struggled and Israel cycled through intervals of apostasy, oppression by foreigners, and deliverance through the hand of the judges. Throughout the period of the judges, things continued to worsen. While initially the judges faithfully fulfilled their calling (e.g., Othniel in Judg 3), later judges were less pious and less successful, with Samson apparently unaware of his calling and instead spending most of the time looking to satiate his own lusts (Judg 14–16). The book of Judges concludes with the notable absence of any judge and some terrible events that take place as a result: the gang rape and murder of the Levite's concubine (Judg 19), the near slaughter of the entire tribe of Benjamin (Judg 20), and the abduction of virgins from Shiloh to be forced into marrying the surviving Benjamites (Judg 21).

One of the main purposes of the book of Judges is to show why Israel needed a human king. A key phrase repeated in the book of Judges is "In those days Israel had no king; everyone did as they saw fit" (Judg 17:6; 21:25), with the narrator noting four times that there was no king in Israel at times when terrible things happen (Judg 17:6; 18:1; 19:1; 21:25). The dark events that close off the book of Judges set the stage for the creation of Israel's monarchy and the introduction of Israel's last judge, Samuel. It is in this context that the story of Samuel begins. There is no king in Israel despite the obvious need for one.

The Historicity of the Book of Samuel

In biblical scholarship there are a wide range of opinions regarding the historicity of the events depicted in the books of Samuel. While most of the twentieth century maintained an academic consensus on the historicity of the united monarchy of Saul, David, and Solomon, this eventually eroded with some radically skeptical scholars,[10] often called "minimalists" (due to their believing only a *minimal* amount of history is to be found in biblical narratives), casting doubt on their veracity. Some went so far as to say that Israel was never a united nation (but only two nations, Israel and Judah) and that these three kings never existed. Since this introduction does not provide room enough to deal with their arguments at length, a short summary will have to suffice. Much of the skepticism about the veracity of biblical historiography is concerned with: (1) the late date in which it was written; and (2) a lack of archaeological (specifically epigraphic or inscriptional) evidence.

1. Regarding the late date of Samuel's final composition (ca. 560–539 BC), the skeptics argue that this casts doubt on whether the book could accurately depict events that occurred in 1000 BC. However, this concern is answered with the recognition that its author relied upon early literary sources (as noted above). He did not fabricate the history but relied on sources in composing the book. As far as ancient historiography goes, the books of Samuel *are* a good example of ancient history writing. In fact, prior to the writing of the larger history of Israel (Joshua–Kings), there was really nothing that can be properly be called "historiography" in the ancient world. Since the writing of Joshua–Kings predates Greek historiography, many scholars view it as the first historiography ever written.

2. Regarding the lack of archaeological (epigraphic or inscriptional) evidence, since the time the minimalists first declared that David was not a historical person, two important archaeological inscriptions have been

---

10. E.g., Philip R. Davies, *In Search of 'Ancient Israel'*, LHBOTS 148 (Sheffield: Sheffield Press, 1992); Niels Peter Lemche, "David's Rise," *JSOT* 10 (1978): 2–25; Niels Peter Lemche and Thomas L. Thompson, "Did Biran Kill David? The Bible in the Light of Archaeology," *JSOT* 64 (1994): 3–22.

found to mention David. Discovered in 1993, the Tel Dan inscription dates to the ninth century BC and commemorates the victory of an Aramean king over both the "king of Israel" and "the house of David." "House of David" is a standard way of referring to the dynasty of David and the Tel Dan inscription was the first epigraphic reference to David discovered. Shortly thereafter, French scholar Andre Lemaire reexamined the Moabite Stone, an inscription originally found in 1868 (and also dating to the ninth century BC), and discovered that it too referred to the "house of David."[11] Though the Tel Dan inscription and the Moabite Stone date to over one hundred years after David, they suggest that David was a historical person who established a royal dynasty in Israel. Thus, we have two ancient Near Eastern extrabiblical inscriptions that reference David and imply David was a historical person. While archaeology can never prove the details of his life story as recorded in Samuel, we have every reason to trust its story.

Historical Dates for Saul and David

While exact dates for the reigns of Saul and David are debatable, there is a general consensus that David's first year as king (over Judah only) was around 1011–1007 BC and that he began his reign over all of Israel around 1004–1000 BC. The length of Saul's reign is disputed, however, as the verse stating its length is textually corrupt, with Hebrew manuscripts omitting Saul's age and only giving two years as the length of his reign (and the number "two" is misspelled). The Hebrew reads "Saul was ___ years old when he began to reign and two years he reigned over Israel" (1 Sam 13:1). What is more, the Greek translations omit the verse entirely so we are only left with much later texts (like the Latin Vulgate) to supply the information. Most do not follow the Hebrew at this point, as a two-year reign is not long enough for all the events narrated in 1 Samuel to occur. The New Testament, on the other hand, lists the length of Saul's reign as forty years. If a forty-year reign for Saul is assumed, then he was anointed king around 1050 BC.

Theological Message

The book of Samuel develops theological concepts that are important not only for reading in the context of the Old Testament but also for reading from a New Testament context and a twenty-first century context. The most prominent theological themes are the fulfillment of the prophetic word, trust

---

11. André Lemaire, "'House of David:' Restored in Moabite Inscription," *BAR* 20 (1994): 30–37.

in God, the seriousness of sin, the importance of true repentance, the Davidic covenant, and the anointed one/Messiah.

The Fulfillment of the Prophetic Word

Prophets are important figures in the story of Samuel with both named (Samuel, Nathan, Gad) and anonymous prophets (e.g., 1 Sam 2:27–36) playing important roles as bearers of the prophetic word of God. Many short-term prophecies are fulfilled in the story (e.g., 1 Sam 2:34, fulfilled in 1 Sam 4:11), while others are not fulfilled for a great deal of time. For example, God's prediction that he will give Saul's kingdom to one of his "neighbors" (1 Sam 15:28) is not fulfilled until 2 Samuel 5:3. What is more, the prophecy of 1 Samuel 2:36 is not fulfilled until 1 Kings 2:26–27, 35. The way a prophecy is fulfilled is often surprising or takes multiple stages before it is ultimately fulfilled. For example, Saul's horrific slaughter of the priests of Nob (1 Sam 22) facilitates the fulfillment of the prophecy that no one in Eli's "family line will ever reach old age" (1 Sam 2:32). Yet, it is only one stage of the many that will finally displace the Elide house as priests.

This emphasis on the prophetic word continues in the latter prophets of the Old Testament and the New Testament Scriptures as well. Furthermore, Samuel is a valuable witness to the church today of the character of God's word. It is utterly reliable and will not fail—even when present circumstances may cause doubt as to its veracity. It is causative and powerful—it not only spoke the universe into existence, it irresistibly instigates and directs events as God sees fit. God's word is also fulfilled in complex and multifaceted ways. His word is often fulfilled in stages, with partial fulfillments followed by ultimate fulfillments. The book of Samuel itself is only ultimately fulfilled in Christ and the new covenant.

Trust in God

One of the themes that surfaces throughout the story of Samuel concerns issues of trust in God. In the larger story characters frequently show their trust to be misplaced, trusting in religion (religious ritual) or their own strength (e.g., armies) rather than God. Faith is placed in the ark of the covenant, which is used by Israel in a failed effort to win a battle with their enemies (1 Sam 4). Sacrifices (1 Sam 13:9; 15:15), oaths (1 Sam 14:24), lot-taking ceremonies (1 Sam 14:41–42), and even séances (1 Sam 28) are undertaken by Saul in an attempt to get what he wanted, showing a misplaced trust in ritual.

Opposing this trend are instances of people trusting not in ritual, or using ritual to manipulate God, but simply trusting in God. On the basis of their knowledge of God's character risks are taken, but no demands are made.

Jonathan ventures a heroic attack on the enemy based on his belief that God *could* save him, saying "*Perhaps* the LORD will act in our behalf. Nothing can hinder the LORD from saving, whether by many or by few" (1 Sam 14:6, emphasis added). David bravely confronts Goliath based on his belief that God saves "not by sword or spear" (1 Sam 17:47). The theological ethic of fully trusting God can be seen in the actions of David, who, when given opportunities to avenge himself on Saul (2 Sam 24, 26), resists taking matters into his own hands but instead trusts his future to God, waiting on God to deliver the kingdom to him. Later in life David falters in his trust, putting his faith in the number of soldiers at his disposal instead of in God, causing a national disaster (2 Sam 24). David quickly repents of his actions and again throws his complete trust in Yahweh, trusting in God's mercy in regard to the punishment for the census (2 Sam 24:14).

This emphasis on trust in God rather than manipulation of the deity is developed and reiterated in its Old Testament context (e.g., Exod 20:1–3; Jer 7:1–15) as well as in the New Testament (e.g., Matt 12:38–39). However, in the book of Samuel we find a more detailed treatment of some of these issues, making the book of Samuel an important resource for the church today regarding seeking God's will and living by faith rather than relying on signs for direction or attempting to divine his will.

The Seriousness of Sin

The stories in the book of Samuel underscore the utter seriousness of sin. Early on Eli and his sons are judged for their sin, dying on the same day (1 Sam 4). Due to their sin, Israel itself suffers a terrible defeat by the Philistines until they repent (1 Sam 7:6). Saul's dynasty is sentenced to end with him (1 Sam 13:13–14) due to his sin in refusing to wait for Samuel for the sacrifice (1 Sam 13:9). Subsequently, Saul's sin in sparing Amalekite animals for sacrifices (and sparing their king) results in his utter rejection as king altogether (1 Sam 15:23). Sin has serious consequences. David's life also showcases the deadly cost of sin as his adultery with Bathsheba and the murder of Uriah (2 Sam 11) bring to a halt what had been a reign of virtually non-stop success. After his sin David's life is a mess, with persistent family problems and tragedies and personal powerlessness with his children and those under his command (e.g., Joab). The book of Samuel is a sobering example that the wages of sin is death (Rom 6:23), though that is not the end of the story.

The Importance of True Repentance

Coupling the theme of the gravity of sin is the importance of repentance. After the loss of the ark to the Philistines, the prophet Samuel calls on Israel to repent: "If you are returning to the LORD with all your hearts, then rid yourselves of the foreign gods and the Ashtoreths and commit yourselves to the LORD and serve him only, and he will deliver you out of the hand of the Philistines" (1 Sam 7:3). The people obeyed, performing rituals of repentance (e.g., pouring out water, fasting) and confessing their sin (1 Sam 7:6). Furthermore, the prophet interceded for them (1 Sam 7:5) and offered a burnt offering (1 Sam 7:10). Later, at Samuel's prompting the people again repent of their sin of asking for a king and ask the prophet to intercede again (1 Sam 12:17–19). Samuel does so but also calls the people to obey the Lord and turn away from idols (1 Sam 12:20–21).

The connection of the importance of renewed obedience accompanying true repentance can be seen in Saul's disobedience regarding the Amalekites in 1 Samuel 15. Saul is very slow to admit wrongdoing and initially denies it point-blank (1 Sam 15:13, 20). Eventually, after Samuel calls him on his lie, Saul eventually confesses his sin (1 Sam 15:25, 30), but he refuses to obey the prophet. Though God has rejected him as king (1 Sam 15:23), Saul disobediently and stubbornly holds on to the kingship. Though Saul would perform ritual, he would not obey (1 Sam 15:22).

Unlike Saul, however, David quickly repents of his sin (2 Sam 12:13; 24:10). Furthermore, when God sends a prophet to David, David obeys him (2 Sam 24:18–25). The importance of repentance, coupled with the fruit of obedience, is highlighted in the example of Israel's greatest king.

The theme of repentance in the book also speaks to Yahweh's character as a God who forgives and redeems. Throughout the story we see that God is gracious and forgiving. Yahweh takes away the sin of the repentant (1 Sam 12:19–25; 2 Sam 12:13) and can even expectantly withdraw punishment for sin (2 Sam 24:16). Thus, the story demonstrates the gracious character of God highlighted throughout the Old Testament (e.g., Exod 34:6–7; 2 Chr 30:9; Neh 9:17; Ps 86:15; Joel 2:13) and developed further in the New Testament (Eph 2:8–9; 4:32; Titus 3:5; 1 John 2:12). Furthermore, Samuel is a great resource for the church today for theological reflection both on the importance of repentance and the gracious character of God.

The Davidic Covenant

One of the key moments in David's story is when God establishes his covenant with him (2 Sam 7). Covenant refers to God's act of establishing a relationship with humankind and is the most common analogy used in the Bible for the relationship between Yahweh and his people (e.g., previous covenants are made with Noah, Abraham, Moses). The Davidic covenant finds partial fulfillment first in Solomon (1 Kgs 8:19), who reigns after David and builds the temple. However, its promises are not fully realized in Solomon but only in the later Son of David, Jesus (Heb 1:5). Furthermore, elsewhere the New Testament uses the language of the Davidic promise—"I will be his father, and he will be my son" (2 Sam 7:14)—in reference to the church itself, saying "I will be a Father to you, and you will be my sons and daughters" (2 Cor 6:18) as "the apostle Paul considers this Davidic hope fulfilled in the Christian community as whole."[12]

Through Yahweh's covenant with David, God granted unconditional and eternal blessings to David and his descendants (2 Sam 7:16; Ps 45:6). In fact, 2 Samuel 7:14–16 makes clear that Yahweh will never remove the Davidic covenant even if David's descendants prove disobedient. It is the radically gracious nature of the Davidic covenant that becomes the basis for Israel's future hope, even when they found themselves in exile (e.g., Ps 89; Isa 55:3). What is more, God's gracious commitment to the Davidides becomes the seedbed for both later messianism and the gospel of grace proclaimed in Jesus' name in the New Testament.

The Anointed One/Messiah

Probably one of the most significant theological themes in Samuel is that of the "anointed one," *mashiah* in Hebrew and usually rendered Messiah in English. The anointed one is the leader who had been anointed by the prophet and designated by God to be Israel's leader. The term eventually becomes one that denotes the coming ideal anointed one—the Messiah.

The origins of the hope for an anointed one who would save Israel begin in Samuel. The need for a king was underscored in the book of Judges, where terrible events took place because "Israel had no king" (Judg 17:6; 18:1; 19:1; 21:25). The need is also displayed at the beginning of the book of Samuel, where the priesthood had been corrupted with the wicked sons of Eli ministering at the tabernacle with the ark of the covenant. Eli himself is also culpable for the deplorable state of the religious establishment in Shiloh and implicated by the prophet due to his partaking in the choice pieces of meat (1 Sam 2:29) that were unlawfully and malevolently taken from the worshipers (1 Sam 2:14–16). Due to this failed leadership, the institutions of priesthood, tabernacle, and ark were not fulfilling their functions in Israel's religious life nor serving God as intended.

As the story proceeds, Shiloh falls from prominence as Eli and his sons die and the ark is taken by the Philistines (1 Sam 4). Though Saul is initially

---

12. Mark J. Boda, "Biblical Theology and Old Testament Interpretation," in *Hearing the Old Testament: Listening for God's Address*, ed. C. Bartholomew and D. Beldman (Grand Rapids: Eerdmans, 2012), 139.

called to deliver them from the Philistines (1 Sam 9:16), due to his failure the situation is not remedied until David conquers Jerusalem (2 Sam 5:7), defeats the Philistines (2 Sam 5:17–25), brings the ark to Jerusalem (2 Sam 6), and the faithful priest Zadok ministers before it. At that point Israel's most prominent institutions—the monarchy, the priesthood, and the primary worship site (with the ark of the covenant)—are all tied to David in Jerusalem. Thus, David's role in putting things to right in Israel becomes a type of the future anointed one. However, the clear failures of David's descendants undermined even the role of the anointed one (the king). Kings after David proved sinful and unfaithful. They often neglected Israel's institutions and worshiped foreign gods. They "did not follow the LORD completely, as David [their] father had done" (1 Kgs 11:6, 33; 14:8; 15:3; 2 Kgs 14:3; 16:2).[13] Thus a tension is introduced in Israel's story between the ideal anointed one and the miserable failures of later anointed ones.

Surprisingly, this failure in leadership did not lead them to abandon the idea of ideal anointed leadership but instead led them to look for an anointed one who would be faithful and again restore Israel. The tenacity of the faith in a coming anointed one cannot be attributed solely to David's example. After all, David himself failed miserably at times, treating people as his possession and taking a loyal servant's wife and murdering her husband to cover it up (2 Sam 11). It seems clear that the persistent belief in a coming anointed one is highly dependent upon the prophetic word and thus on Israel's faith in God. Though kings failed them, they held fast that their God would not. The faithfulness of God gave them hope for the future. God had acted on Israel's behalf in the past (e.g., the exodus) and would do so again. God had promised an anointed one who would reign forever, and he would deliver on that promise.

Before even David's time, Jacob prophesied that David's tribe, Judah, would rule, saying, "The scepter will not depart from Judah, nor the ruler's staff from between his feet, until he to whom it belongs shall come and the obedience of the nations shall be his" (Gen 49:10). The prophecy of Nathan to David in 2 Samuel 7 promises that a son of David would rule forever (2 Sam 7:12–16; cf. 2 Sam 23:5). This promise is reiterated and elaborated in the royal psalms, which talk of the Davidic king as ruler not only of Israel but of all the nations, despite opposition (Pss 2:1–3, 5–12; 110:1–2). As David defeated the Philistines, so the coming Messiah would defeat the enemy (Pss 2:9; 110:1). Like David, he will rule in Jerusalem (Ps 2:4–6; 110:2). The Davidic king's rule will never end (Pss 21:4; 45:6; 72:5). The anointed

---

13. Only three kings are said to be like David in this: Asa (1 Kgs 15:11), Hezekiah (2 Kgs 18:3), and Josiah (2 Kgs 22:2).

one defends the poor, delivers the powerless, and destroys the oppressor (Pss 72:2–4, 12–14). He is the inheritor of David's covenant (Pss 89:28–37; 132:11–12) and all the Davidic promises. The coming anointed one is even said to be God's son (2 Sam 7:14; Pss 2:7; 89:27), and Psalm 45:6–7 even labels the messiah divine.

Israel's prophetic literature perpetuates the messianic themes with Davidic figures featured prominently. As God is said to be "with David" frequently in Samuel (1 Sam 16:18; 18:28; 22:17), so God will be with the coming Davidic ruler, who will be called Immanuel, "God with us" (Isa 7:14). As the anointed one is referred to as a son (2 Sam 7:14; Pss 2:7; 89:27), so Isaiah looks forward to a son to be born who will be given fantastic names:

> For to us a child is born, to us a son is given, and the government will be on his shoulders. And he will be called Wonderful Counselor, Mighty God, Everlasting Father, Prince of Peace. (Isa 9:6)

As David was Jesse's son, the messiah will be a branch from Jesse's stump (Isa 11:1) who, like David (1 Sam 16:13), will permanently have the spirit of the Lord on him (Isa 11:2). As David ruled "doing what was just and right for all his people" (2 Sam 8:15), so the messiah "with righteousness … will judge the needy, with justice he will give decisions for the poor of the earth" (Isa 11:4). As David was a shepherd, so the messiah will shepherd Israel. Ezekiel prophesies that God "will place over them one shepherd, my servant David, and he will tend them; he will tend them and be their shepherd" (Ezek 34:23).

As David established his kingdom, so will the messiah. Significantly, David's kingdom is equated with God's kingdom in the story of David in Chronicles. While 2 Samuel 7:16 promises that "Your house and your kingdom will endure forever before me; your throne will be established forever," in Chronicles Nathan's oracle proclaims about David's offspring, "I will set him over my house and my kingdom forever; his throne will be established forever" (1 Chr 17:14). The kingdom of the coming Davidic anointed one will be nothing less than God's kingdom.

All of these themes and messianic prophecies are drawn together in the New Testament in the person of Jesus of Nazareth. Reading the Gospels we quickly realize that the term "son of David" is a messianic title (e.g., Matt 9:27; 12:23; 15:22; 20:30), and in the Epistles Jesus' qualifications as Messiah are tied to his familial relationship with David (e.g., Rom 1:3–5; 2 Tim 2:8). Prenatal prophecies about Jesus draw on Nathan's oracle in 2 Samuel 7 and claim Jesus will inherit David's throne and have an eternal kingdom (Luke 1:32–33). Jesus is born in David's hometown of Bethlehem (Luke 2; cf. 1 Sam 16). As David's righteous rule built the kingdom of God in Israel, so Jesus, as David's heir, establishes the kingdom of God (Mark 1:14, 15). In Jesus all the hopes set out in the books of Samuel are fulfilled. God's kingdom is established; the Messiah is on the throne, and he has defeated the enemy and is friend to the needy. Jesus is the culmination of the Davidic hope and the goal and purpose of not only the story of the book of Samuel but of all Old Testament stories.

Resources for Teaching and Preaching

M any excellent monographs and commentaries have been written on the books of Samuel. Within the footnotes of this commentary one will find frequent reference to commentaries by Anderson, Alter, Arnold, Bodner, Brueggeman, and Klein. In addition to these great commentaries, I would recommend the following resources:

Alter, Robert, *The Art of Biblical Narrative*. London: G. Allen & Unwin, 1981.

Fokkelman, J. P., *Narrative Art and Poetry in the Books of Samuel: Vow and Desire (1 Sam. 1–12)*. Assen: Van Gorcum, 1993.

Fokkelman, J. P., *Narrative Art and Poetry in the Books of Samuel: A Full Interpretation Based on Stylistic and Structural Analysis: Vol. 1, King David (II Sam. 9–20 & I Kings 1–2)*. Studia Semitica Neerlandica. Assen, The Netherlands: Van Gorcum, 1981.

Goldingay, John, *Old Testament Theology: Israel's Gospel*. Downers Grove, IL: InterVarsity Press, 2003.

Hamilton, Victor P., *Handbook on the Historical Books*. Grand Rapids: Baker, 2001.

Long, V. Philips, *The Reign and Rejection of King Saul: A Case for Literary and Theological Coherence*. Edited by David L. Peterson. SBLDS, 118. Atlanta: Scholars Press, 1989.

Polzin, Robert, *Samuel and the Deuteronomist: A Literary Study of the Deuteronomistic History: Part Two: 1 Samuel*. Indiana Studies in Biblical Literature. San Francisco: Harper & Row, 1989.

Polzin, Robert, *David and the Deuteronomist: A Literary Study of the Deuteronomistic History. Part Three: 2 Samuel*. Indiana Studies in Biblical Literature. Bloomington; Indianapolis: Indiana University Press, 1993.

LISTEN to the Story

¹There was a certain man from Ramathaim, a Zuphite from the hill country of Ephraim, whose name was Elkanah son of Jeroham, the son of Elihu, the son of Tohu, the son of Zuph, an Ephraimite. ²He had two wives; one was called Hannah and the other Peninnah. Peninnah had children, but Hannah had none.

³Year after year this man went up from his town to worship and sacrifice to the LORD Almighty at Shiloh, where Hophni and Phinehas, the two sons of Eli, were priests of the LORD. ⁴Whenever the day came for Elkanah to sacrifice, he would give portions of the meat to his wife Peninnah and to all her sons and daughters. ⁵But to Hannah he gave a double portion because he loved her, and the LORD had closed her womb. ⁶Because the LORD had closed Hannah's womb, her rival kept provoking her in order to irritate her. ⁷This went on year after year. Whenever Hannah went up to the house of the LORD, her rival provoked her till she wept and would not eat. ⁸Her husband Elkanah would say to her, "Hannah, why are you weeping? Why don't you eat? Why are you downhearted? Don't I mean more to you than ten sons?"

⁹Once when they had finished eating and drinking in Shiloh, Hannah stood up. Now Eli the priest was sitting on his chair by the doorpost of the LORD's house. ¹⁰In her deep anguish Hannah prayed to the LORD, weeping bitterly. ¹¹And she made a vow, saying, "LORD Almighty, if you will only look on your servant's misery and remember me, and not forget your servant but give her a son, then I will give him to the LORD for all the days of his life, and no razor will ever be used on his head."

¹²As she kept on praying to the LORD, Eli observed her mouth. ¹³Hannah was praying in her heart, and her lips were moving but her voice was not heard. Eli thought she was drunk ¹⁴and said to her, "How long are you going to stay drunk? Put away your wine."

¹⁵"Not so, my lord," Hannah replied, "I am a woman who is deeply

troubled. I have not been drinking wine or beer; I was pouring out my soul to the LORD. [16]Do not take your servant for a wicked woman; I have been praying here out of my great anguish and grief."

[17]Eli answered, "Go in peace, and may the God of Israel grant you what you have asked of him."

[18]She said, "May your servant find favor in your eyes." Then she went her way and ate something, and her face was no longer downcast.

[19]Early the next morning they arose and worshiped before the LORD and then went back to their home at Ramah. Elkanah made love to his wife Hannah, and the LORD remembered her. [20]So in the course of time Hannah became pregnant and gave birth to a son. She named him Samuel, saying, "Because I asked the LORD for him."

[21]When her husband Elkanah went up with all his family to offer the annual sacrifice to the LORD and to fulfill his vow, [22]Hannah did not go. She said to her husband, "After the boy is weaned, I will take him and present him before the LORD, and he will live there always."

[23]"Do what seems best to you," her husband Elkanah told her. "Stay here until you have weaned him; only may the LORD make good his word." So the woman stayed at home and nursed her son until she had weaned him.

[24]After he was weaned, she took the boy with her, young as he was, along with a three-year-old bull, an ephah of flour and a skin of wine, and brought him to the house of the LORD at Shiloh. [25]When the bull had been sacrificed, they brought the boy to Eli, [26]and she said to him, "Pardon me, my lord. As surely as you live, I am the woman who stood here beside you praying to the LORD. [27]I prayed for this child, and the LORD has granted me what I asked of him. [28]So now I give him to the LORD. For his whole life he will be given over to the LORD." And he worshiped the LORD there.

Listening to the Text in the Story: Genesis 11:27–23:30; Genesis 25; Genesis 30; Judges 13

The story of Samuel begins with the story of his mother's infertility. In the Old Testament, the motif of an infertile woman is quite common. Sarah (Gen 11:27–23:30), Rebekah (Gen 25), Rachel (Gen 30), and Samson's mother (Judge 13) all struggled with infertility. The sons born to these women, however, turn out to be key figures in the story of God's redemption. In fact, another barren woman in the New Testament, Elizabeth (Luke 1:7), alludes to Hannah's story (Luke 1:25) in her celebration of the birth of her significant son, John the Baptizer.

To help us listen to the story, it is important to know that in ancient Israel children were crucial for both preserving and developing their largely agricultural society. Children were necessary as heirs (male children especially) and as labor for both agricultural and household duties. Also, in order to understand the story of Hannah's predicament one has to understand that in the ancient Near East fertility was associated with divine blessing (e.g., Ps 127:3) and infertility was understood largely to be a divine curse (cf. Job 15:34). While today some may choose not to have children, such a choice would have been inconceivable to a woman of the ancient Near East. In the ancient mindset, having children was close to the very reason for a woman's existence. The well-being of women was attached directly to their children who could look after them after the death of a husband. Further, children linked women into the family kin structure, providing them with security.

On a personal level, fertility was a matter of honor for these women, and persistent infertility shamed them. Furthermore, the broader society was not sympathetic toward infertility or accepting of those suffering on that account. Even though Hannah was likely Elkanah's first wife, her status in the family would be precarious due to her infertility. In that culture, a barren wife could easily be given a lower status if not divorced altogether.

EXPLAIN the Story

The story of Samuel's birth is a highly structured narrative involving a difficult situation, prayers, and answers to prayer. As the opening to the book of Samuel it also provides central themes that will be developed throughout the rest of the book. In this chapter the unique circumstances surrounding the birth of Samuel are narrated. Samuel's mother, Hannah, dejected and persecuted for her barrenness, entreats Yahweh to give her a son, whom she promises to give to the Lord's service in return. God grants her request and she gives birth to Samuel. Samuel's special destiny and connection with Israel's first king is emphasized in his naming (see below). Eventually Hannah brings Samuel to the service of the Lord at the temple in Shiloh with the priest Eli.

Samuel's Parents (1:1–8)

As the story begins we are first introduced to Samuel's father, Elkanah, who, we are told, had two wives. This is not atypical in the biblical period, where polygamy was accepted and legal in Israelite law (see Deut 21:15–17). One of the main reasons for the taking of a second wife in that culture was the first wife being infertile. In this instance, infertility seems likely to be the case, as we are told that one wife, Peninnah, had children but that the other wife, Hannah, had none.

Elkanah is presented as a pious Yahweh worshiper from the northern tribe of Ephraim. His devout character is evident in his yearly trips to worship and sacrifice at Shiloh (a 15-mile trip or a two-day journey for a family like this). Shiloh was an important worship sanctuary in Israel from the early days of the settlement of the land. The tent of meeting was set up there in Joshua's day (Josh 18:1), and it appears to have been the primary sanctuary for Israel during the period of the Judges (Judg 18:31).

In Judges 21:19, reference is made to an annual feast of Yahweh that took place at Shiloh, and it could be this festival to which Elkanah and his family journeyed each year. (It is possible the festival was the Feast of Tabernacles, which would have been at the end of the summer.) Since no festival is mentioned in the text, however, it could be simply a family ritual, which would again highlight Elkanah's piety. This piety is explicitly contrasted by the impiety of the priests at Shiloh. In verse 3, where it describes Elkanah's practice of worshiping the Lord, it mentions that Hophni and Phineas were the priests at Shiloh. In the next chapter we learn that these sons of Eli were wicked priests (cf. 2:12–17, 22).

Despite Elkanah's piety, his family is not an altogether happy one. In verse 6 we are given a glimpse of the bitter hostility that existed between Elkanah's wives. Hannah is tormented not only by the personal shame of infertility on account of her cultural context, but to add insult to injury she is also tormented by her "rival," Penninah, who continually provokes Hannah about the fact she has no children (cf. Gen 30:14–15).

Elkanah clearly loves Hannah (nowhere does it state that he loved Penninah) and even gives her a "double portion" in light of her predicament (1:5). Hannah, however, is continually misunderstood in this story. Even in Elkanah's attempt to console her (1:8) her predicament is misunderstood. Elkanah seems oblivious to Penninah's treatment of Hannah and clearly does not really *get* Hannah's situation regarding her infertility. The idea that the husband would be worth "ten sons" (1:8) shows his lack of understanding of the importance of bearing children for women in the ancient Near East. It is even possible that it shows a measure of Elkanah's self-importance or self-interest and desire to have his wife value him higher.

Hannah's Request (1:9–18)

Finally, after years of suffering this disgrace, when the family pilgrimaged to Shiloh, Hannah stood (1:9) and prayed silently to the Lord. Again Hannah is misunderstood, this time by the priest at Shiloh, Eli. When Hannah poured out her heart to God, Eli mistook her prayer for inebriation. Perhaps drunkenness was *not* uncommon at Shiloh, given his sons' despicable behavior (see 2:12). More likely, sincere, earnest, emotional prayer *was* uncommon at Shiloh, leading Eli to make this misdiagnosis. Eli's mistake also alludes to the lack of perception of this priest. After Hannah explains that she was not under the influence of alcohol but earnestly praying, Eli finally blesses her that the Lord might grant her request.

The Birth and Naming of Samuel (1:19–20)

Upon returning to their home God "remembers" (1:19) Hannah and she conceives and gives birth to a son whom she names Samuel (1:20). The naming of Samuel actually brings out a lead motif for the story and hints at his destiny. In Hebrew Samuel's name (*shemuel*) means something like "His name is El (God)."[1] In naming Samuel, Hannah connects the meaning of her son's name to the fact that she "asked" (Hebrew *shaul*) for him from the Lord. The Hebrew word for "asked" here is identical to the name of Israel's first king, Saul (whose name means "asked"). Even the later Hebrew phrase, which is translated in the NIV as "he will be given over" (1:28), could be literally translated as "he is Saul" (1:28). It seems odd that Samuel's name is connected to this verb since it is identical to Saul's name and Samuel's name does not have this verb at its root. In fact, this clear connection with Saul's name has led some critical scholars to suggest that this birth story was originally about Saul and only secondarily applied to Samuel.[2] However, more recent commentators have pointed out how this wordplay allusion to Saul foreshadows the future connection between Samuel and Israel's first king.[3] Furthermore, this birth narrative about the "asking" for a son introduces the story of Israel's "asking" for a king. In fact, besides Hannah's request of God here, the only other request of God in 1 Samuel 1–8 is the request of the people for a king (1 Sam 8:10 uses the same Hebrew verb *shaul*), so this initial "asking" may foreshadow the people's later request.[4]

---

1. Cf. P. Kyle McCarter, *I Samuel*, AB 8 (Garden City, NY: Doubleday, 1980), 62–63.

2. E.g., McCarter, *I Samuel*, 13–14; Michael D. Coogan, *A Brief Introduction to the Old Testament: The Hebrew Bible in its Context* (New York: Oxford University Press, 2009), 194.

3. E.g., Keith Bodner, *1 Samuel: A Narrative Commentary*, HBM 19 (Sheffield: Sheffield Phoenix, 2008), 8; Robert Polzin, *Samuel and the Deuteronomist: A Literary Study of the Deuteronomistic History: Part Two: 1 Samuel*, Indiana Studies in Biblical Literature (San Francisco: Harper & Row, 1989), 18–26; Moshe Garsiel, *The First Book of Samuel: A Literary Study of Comparative Structures, Analogies, Parallels.* (Ramat Gan: Revivim, 1985), 73–75.

4. Polzin, *Samuel and the Deuteronomist*, 25.

The Giving of Samuel (1:21–28)

The rhythms of family life return and the family again pilgrimages to Shiloh, only this time Hannah remains at home with her new baby boy. Hannah explains this delay in that she intends to wean the child before giving him up. In the ancient Near East children were usually not weaned until the age of three, so the child likely lived with his mother for several years.[5] When Hannah demurred from attending the yearly sacrifice, Elkanah agrees but says, "only may the LORD make good his word" (1 Sam 1:23). This is the first mention of the word of Yahweh in the books of Samuel, and it will be a central player in the larger story. What is curious about Elkanah's statement is that in the narrative so far there has been no explicit "word of the Lord" given. Therefore, many think that Elkanah's statement probably means something like "the Lord's will be done."[6] However, in the context of the larger story his statement means much more than this, as it also expresses the author's conviction that regardless of people's actions, God's word *will* come to pass.

After weaning young Samuel, Hannah fulfilled her vow and brought him to Shiloh to live. At that time Hannah and her husband offered generous sacrifices and, ironically, brought a skin of wine with them to Eli. She, whom the priest had once accused of drunkenness, now brings both her son and her wine in dedication to the Lord.

When Hannah presents Samuel to Eli, she again makes a connection between Samuel's name and the Hebrew verb "to ask" (*shaul*). As noted above, this allusion to Israel's first king inextricably links Samuel to Saul and the story of Samuel's birth to the story of the rise of kingship in Israel. In fact, this allusion to Saul is not the only royal allusion in Samuel's birth narrative. Other plays on words evoke royal overtones as well. In verse 9 when Eli is first mentioned, two words that often have royal meanings are used. The NIV translates the verse as "Now Eli the priest was sitting on his chair by the doorpost of the LORD's house," and this is a fine translation, but when read in Hebrew, royal allusions are also seen in that the word for "chair" (Hebrew *kisse*) is also the word for "throne." In fact, besides references to Eli's "chair," every other time the word appears in the Hebrew Bible (as it does here) as "the *kisse*," that is, with the definite article, it means "throne" (e.g., Gen 41:40; Judg 3:20; 1 Kgs 7:7; Ezek 1:26). Royal connotations are also seen in the word for "temple" in

---

5. Though lacking in the traditional Hebrew text (MT) and the Greek translation (LXX) of v. 22, Josephus (*Ant.* 5.347) puts an additional phrase in Hannah's mouth concerning her dedication of Samuel saying, "I will give him as a Nazirite forever." This appears to be a later addition to the text in order to make explicit the sense of Hannah's words back in 1:11 where she vowed that her future child's hair would never be cut (Ralph W. Klein, *1 Samuel*, WBC 10 [Waco, TX: Word, 1983], 1).

6. David Toshio Tsumura, *The First Book of Samuel*, NICOT (Grand Rapids: Eerdmans, 2007), 129.

verse 9 (Hebrew *heykal*), as it is also the word for "palace" (e.g., 1 Kgs 21:1; 2 Kgs 20:18; Isa 13:28; 39:7; Hos 8:11; Nah 2:16; Ps 144:12; Prov 30:28; Dan 1:4). In fact, given that this was not the *temple* of the Lord (which is not built until the time of Solomon) but a *tent* sanctuary, the use of the word strengthens the likelihood of a play on words here.

Because the matter of kingship in Israel is one of the main concerns of the larger narrative, these royal allusions are understandable. The opening chapters of Samuel begin the story of the rise of kingship in Israel and the fall of the priesthood in Shiloh. Eli is sitting on the "throne" in the "palace," but a change in leadership is coming—a divinely inspired regime change. Shiloh will be replaced as the epicenter of worship and Eli's house replaced as the spiritual leaders in Israel. Moreover, the royal overtones with which Eli is associated (throne and palace) may foreshadow the fate of the royal dynasty (the house of Saul) chronicled in the chapters to come.

Thus, the opening story of the book prepares the reader for what is to come. Hannah's request for a son foreshadows Israel's request for a king (1 Sam 8). The etymology given for Samuel's name here prefigures Israel's first king, Saul, and "the story of Samuel's birth is the story of Saul's birth as king of Israel."[7] As God had mercy on Hannah and answered her request, so God will concede to Israel's request for a king. While this first chapter ends with Hannah's fortunes changed, the reader is theologically prepared for the change of Israel's fortunes in the narratives that lie ahead.

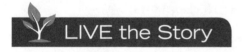

LIVE the Story

The God of the Needy and the Powerless

While the saying (which does not come from the Bible though frequently is attributed to it) goes, "God helps those who help themselves," the Bible itself largely contradicts this and instead suggests that "God helps those who *cannot* help themselves." The story of Hannah serves as a great reminder of how God comes to the aid of those truly in need. As noted above, in the ancient Near East, a woman who could not have a child was nearly an outcast. Hannah's situation was worsened by Elkanah's other wife, Peninnah, who tormented her in that regard. On top of all this, her husband, while loving, did not seem to understand her predicament. Hannah was alone with her pain. Yet this pain drove her to the house of the Lord.

Scholars have coined the phrase, "God's preferential option for the poor,"

---

7. Polzin, *Samuel and the Deuteronomist*, 26.

to describe a perceived phenomenon throughout the Bible: that God appears to be partial toward the poor and the needy.[8] This is not to suggest that God does not love all people. Many people of God in Scripture were not poor. God showed mercy on rich people like Abraham, tax collectors, and fishermen (Levi and Peter), as well as the poor, the blind, and the lame. Throughout Scripture, however, we see God taking special interest in the weak, the downtrodden, and the vulnerable. This theological theme can be seen in the New Testament as well. In Mary's *magnificat* she states:

> "[God] has performed mighty deeds with his arm; he has scattered those who are proud in their inmost thoughts. He has brought down rulers from their thrones but has lifted up the humble. He has filled the hungry with good things but has sent the rich away empty." (Luke 1:51–53)

James similarly writes:

> Listen, my dear brothers and sisters: Has not God chosen those who are poor in the eyes of the world to be rich in faith and to inherit the kingdom he promised those who love him? (Jas 2:5)

Jesus's commission is stated in similar terms, drawing on the book of Isaiah:

> "The Spirit of the Lord is on me, because he has anointed me to proclaim good news to the poor. He has sent me to proclaim freedom for the prisoners and recovery of sight for the blind, to set the oppressed free, to proclaim the year of the Lord's favor." (Luke 4:18–19)

One aspect of being poor that is spiritually beneficial is that poverty leads a person to depend on God in a way that one who has plenty can easily forget to do. A poor person has only God to look to in times of need, whereas the rich can rely on their material possessions and forget God. This is not to say that poverty is an ideal state. As the proverb reads:

> Keep falsehood and lies far from me; give me neither poverty nor riches, but give me only my daily bread. Otherwise, I may have too much and disown you and say, "Who is the LORD?" Or I may become poor and steal, and so dishonor the name of my God. (Prov 30:8–9)

Furthermore, it is not only the poor who are vulnerable or powerless. Hannah was not necessarily poor. While the text doesn't explicitly describe Elkanah's economic state, the fact that he has two wives may indicate he is a person of some means (after all, he had to provide for two wives). Furthermore,

---

8. God's preferential option for the poor was initially articulated by Gutierrez Gustavo Gutierrez, *A Theology of Liberation: History, Politics, and Salvation* (New York: Orbis Books, 1973).

the family's frequent pilgrimages and the gifts they bring to Shiloh may also suggest Elkanah was well-to-do. Yet, despite earthly provisions, Hannah is not privileged. She is needy. She was powerless to change her situation and God heard her cry and answered her prayer.

Rather than understanding that God has a "preferential option for the poor," a more biblical view would be that the God of the Bible has a preferential option for those who *acknowledge their poverty*. This "poverty" may be material or otherwise, just as Jesus states, "Blessed are the poor in spirit" (Matt 5:3). It is about those who realize they are in total reliance upon God and his grace. Here in our story, we have a great example of God moving to answer the prayer of one who acknowledged her need and desperate reliance upon God.

LISTEN to the Story

¹Then Hannah prayed and said:

"My heart rejoices in the LORD;
 in the LORD my horn is lifted high.
My mouth boasts over my enemies,
 for I delight in your deliverance.
²"There is no one holy like the LORD;
 there is no one besides you;
 there is no Rock like our God.
³"Do not keep talking so proudly
 or let your mouth speak such arrogance,
for the LORD is a God who knows,
 and by him deeds are weighed.
⁴"The bows of the warriors are broken,
 but those who stumbled are armed with strength.
⁵Those who were full hire themselves out for food,
 but those who were hungry are hungry no more.
She who was barren has borne seven children,
 but she who has had many sons pines away.
⁶"The LORD brings death and makes alive;
 he brings down to the grave and raises up.
⁷The LORD sends poverty and wealth;
 he humbles and he exalts.
⁸He raises the poor from the dust
 and lifts the needy from the ash heap;
he seats them with princes
 and has them inherit a throne of honor.
"For the foundations of the earth are the LORD's;
 on them he has set the world.
⁹He will guard the feet of his faithful servants,

but the wicked will be silenced in the place of darkness.
"It is not by strength that one prevails;
¹⁰those who oppose the LORD will be broken.
The Most High will thunder from heaven;
   the LORD will judge the ends of the earth.
"He will give strength to his king
   and exalt the horn of his anointed."

¹¹Then Elkanah went home to Ramah, but the boy ministered before the LORD under Eli the priest.

¹²Eli's sons were scoundrels; they had no regard for the LORD. ¹³Now it was the practice of the priests that, whenever any of the people offered a sacrifice, the priest's servant would come with a three-pronged fork in his hand while the meat was being boiled ¹⁴and would plunge the fork into the pan or kettle or caldron or pot. Whatever the fork brought up the priest would take for himself. This is how they treated all the Israelites who came to Shiloh. ¹⁵But even before the fat was burned, the priest's servant would come and say to the person who was sacrificing, "Give the priest some meat to roast; he won't accept boiled meat from you, but only raw."

¹⁶If the person said to him, "Let the fat be burned first, and then take whatever you want," the servant would answer, "No, hand it over now; if you don't, I'll take it by force."

¹⁷This sin of the young men was very great in the LORD's sight, for they were treating the LORD's offering with contempt.

¹⁸But Samuel was ministering before the LORD—a boy wearing a linen ephod. ¹⁹Each year his mother made him a little robe and took it to him when she went up with her husband to offer the annual sacrifice. ²⁰Eli would bless Elkanah and his wife, saying, "May the LORD give you children by this woman to take the place of the one she prayed for and gave to the LORD." Then they would go home. ²¹And the LORD was gracious to Hannah; she gave birth to three sons and two daughters. Meanwhile, the boy Samuel grew up in the presence of the LORD.

²²Now Eli, who was very old, heard about everything his sons were doing to all Israel and how they slept with the women who served at the entrance to the tent of meeting. ²³So he said to them, "Why do you do such things? I hear from all the people about these wicked deeds of yours. ²⁴No, my sons; the report I hear spreading among the LORD's people is not good. ²⁵If one person sins against another, God may mediate for the offender; but if anyone sins against the LORD, who will intercede for

them?" His sons, however, did not listen to their father's rebuke, for it was the LORD's will to put them to death.

²⁶And the boy Samuel continued to grow in stature and in favor with the LORD and with people.

²⁷Now a man of God came to Eli and said to him, "This is what the LORD says: 'Did I not clearly reveal myself to your ancestor's family when they were in Egypt under Pharaoh? ²⁸I chose your ancestor out of all the tribes of Israel to be my priest, to go up to my altar, to burn incense, and to wear an ephod in my presence. I also gave your ancestor's family all the food offerings presented by the Israelites. ²⁹Why do you scorn my sacrifice and offering that I prescribed for my dwelling? Why do you honor your sons more than me by fattening yourselves on the choice parts of every offering made by my people Israel?'

³⁰"Therefore the LORD, the God of Israel, declares: 'I promised that members of your family would minister before me forever.' But now the LORD declares: 'Far be it from me! Those who honor me I will honor, but those who despise me will be disdained. ³¹The time is coming when I will cut short your strength and the strength of your priestly house, so that no one in it will reach old age, ³²and you will see distress in my dwelling. Although good will be done to Israel, no one in your family line will ever reach old age. ³³Every one of you that I do not cut off from serving at my altar I will spare only to destroy your sight and sap your strength, and all your descendants will die in the prime of life.

³⁴"'And what happens to your two sons, Hophni and Phinehas, will be a sign to you—they will both die on the same day. ³⁵I will raise up for myself a faithful priest, who will do according to what is in my heart and mind. I will firmly establish his priestly house, and they will minister before my anointed one always. ³⁶Then everyone left in your family line will come and bow down before him for a piece of silver and a loaf of bread and plead, "Appoint me to some priestly office so I can have food to eat."'"

Listen to the Text in the Story: 1 Samuel 1; Genesis 11:27–23:30; Genesis 25; Genesis 30; Judges 13

Following the miraculous birth of Samuel, his mother, Hannah, prays a heart-felt prayer of thanks to God for his provision. Though several stories of God giving a child to a barren woman are found in Scripture, this is the first time that the new mother is said to offer such a thanksgiving. As will be seen in the Explain the Story section, the story not only looks back in thanks but also prophetically foreshadows the story to come.

EXPLAIN the Story

This chapter begins with Hannah offering a prayer of thanksgiving to God for his provision of a son. This prayer resonates not only with her situation but also looks forward to the larger story of David as well. Following Hannah's prayer, the second half of the chapter details the wickedness of the sons of Eli, priest at Shiloh, which is set in comparison with the righteous life of the boy Samuel who served in the LORD's presence faithfully. Finally, an anonymous prophet brings a word from the LORD concerning the end of the Elide line and the future establishment of a new priestly line.

Hannah's Prayer (2:1–10)

As is common in biblical literature (e.g., Gen 49; Exod 15:1–18; Deut 32), we now are given a poetic section within a prose narrative, recording Hannah's prayer praising God for his provision of a son. Much of the poem resonates with Hannah's situation. She speaks of boasting over "enemies" (1 Sam 2:1), which likely refers to her "rival" wife (1 Sam 1:6) Penninah, who tormented her about her infertility. Hannah's references in 1 Samuel 2:5 to the "hungry" who "are hungry no more" may refer to Hannah's going hungry in her grief (1:7) and then her eating (1:18). Similarly, her reference to God raising "the poor from the dust" and "the needy from the ash heap" (1 Sam 2:8) likely refers to her powerless situation of infertility, which she compares to literal poverty.

Other parts of the prayer do not seem to fit with Hannah's story. Hannah references "The bows of the warriors" (1 Sam 2:4), being seated "with princes," and inheriting a "throne" (1 Sam 2:8). Most odd for her context is the concluding line: "He will give strength to his king and exalt the horn of his anointed" (1 Sam 2:10). If we remember, however, the royal allusions we saw in 1 Samuel 1—Eli sitting on a "throne," reference to the shrine in Shiloh as a "palace" (1 Sam 1:9), and the naming of Samuel pointing to the name of Saul (1 Sam 1:20)—the allusions and references in this poem should not be too surprising. The royal allusions in chapter 1 brought to the fore the issue of the rise of kingship in Israel. Now Hannah's prayer adds further allusions to God's victorious anointed king. The prayer addresses two situations: Hannah's now fruitful womb and the coming monarchy in Israel.

Hannah's prayer has many similarities to the closing prayer of David in 2 Samuel 22 (cf. Pss 18; 113). Remembering that originally these books were one composition, these two poetic compositions serve as bookends to the story. Hannah's prayer almost reads like an abbreviation of David's psalm. Just as David's psalm looks back on his rise to kingship from his now triumphant perspective, the prayer of Hannah looks forward to these same events from the same triumphant perspective.

Take a look at the clear parallels between these two psalms:[1]

1 Samuel 2:1–10	2 Samuel 22
v. 1 "My mouth boasts over *my enemies*"	v. 4 "saved from *my enemies*"
v. 1 "my *horn* is lifted high . . . I delight in your *deliverance*"	v. 3 "the *horn* of my *salvation*"
v. 2 "there is no *Rock* like *our God*"	v. 32 "who is the *Rock* except *our God*"
v. 4 "those who stumbled are *armed with strength*"	v. 40 "You *armed me with strength*"
v. 6 "he brings down to the *grave*"	v. 6 "the cords of the *grave* coiled around me"
v. 7 "he *humbles* and he exalts"	v. 28 "you save the *humble*, but your eyes are on the haughty to bring them low"
v. 9 "He will guard the feet of his *faithful* servants"	v. 26 "to the *faithful* you show yourself faithful"
v. 10 "The Most High will *thunder from heaven*"	v. 14 "the LORD *thundered from heaven*"
v. 10 "he will . . exalt the horn of *his anointed*"	v. 51 "he shows unfailing kindness to *his anointed*"
v. 10 "He will give strength to *his king*"	v. 51 "he gives *his king* great victories"

Further connections with David's story can also be seen. Hannah's words in 1 Samuel 2:3 "Do not keep talking so proudly" are literally translated "Do not increase your speaking 'O Tall One, Tall One!'" As the story progresses we find that Saul is said to be taller than anyone else in all of Israel (1 Sam 10:23), and David's most famous enemy, Goliath, is a giant of a man (1 Sam 17:4). Hannah's words could be placed on the mouth of David and make perfect sense. Furthermore, reference to the "horn" (1 Sam 2:1) could allude to the "horn" of oil with which David is anointed (1 Sam 16:1, 13). By contrast, Saul is anointed with a "flask" of oil (1 Sam 10:1).

In other words, Hannah's song is appropriate for more than one context.

---

1. This chart is adapted from a similar chart in Polzin, *Samuel and the Deuteronomist*, 33–34.

In the context of the larger story of the books of Samuel, it not only prophetically looks forward to the rise of kingship in Israel but alludes to the fall of
the house of Saul (O Tall One) and the establishment of David (anointed
with a horn of oil). In fact, some early church fathers thought of her prayer
as evidence of her prophetic status. Augustine wrote: "are these words going
to be regarded as simply the words of one mere woman giving thanks for the
birth of her son? . . . The words poured out by this woman transcend the limit
of her own thoughts."[2]

The Corruption of Shiloh (1 Sam 2:11–17)

With the return of his parents to Ramah, the boy Samuel ministered in Shiloh
under Eli. His ministry is then contrasted with that of Eli's sons. The sons
of Eli are described by the narrator as "scoundrels" (1 Sam 2:12). Literally
in Hebrew they are called "sons of Belial." Ironically, in chapter 1 Hannah
claims that Eli thinks her a "daughter of Belial" (1:16) when he mistakes her
sincere prayer for drunkenness, yet it is Eli's own sons who rightly bear such a
designation. The wickedness of the priests is described in some detail. Under
Mosaic law, priests received a specific portion of the sacrifices offered to God
as their sustenance, though the fat was to be burned to Yahweh (Lev 7:30–36).
Eli's sons, however, would take the best portions of the meat, *including* the
fat. This was a serious cultic offense. First of all, a principle of sacrifice was to
offer the best to God. Even before the law, Cain in Genesis 4 seems to have
displeased God for this reason, as only his brother Abel is said to offer the
best ("fat" of the "firstborn"), while Cain offers only "some" of the fruit of
the ground (Gen 4:3). Second, in Mosaic law the fat is explicitly reserved for
Yahweh himself (see Lev 3:16; 7:25). Furthermore, when worshipers resisted
these wicked priests and demanded that the fat be burnt for the LORD, Eli's
sons would threaten the worshiper with violence (1 Sam 2:16). The narrator
condemns their actions in no uncertain terms as "treating the LORD's offering
with contempt" (1 Sam 2:17).

The Boy Priest (2:18–21)

In contrast to Eli's sons, the boy Samuel served God faithfully at Shiloh. It is
noted he is wearing a "linen ephod," a garment that only priests wore. The reference may indicate that it was unusual for a boy so young to be an apprentice
priest like this and may also contrast Eli's sons further as the boy Samuel was
careful to serve correctly, even in the case of how he dressed.

Eli blesses Samuel's parents when they come visit and asks God to give

---

2. John R. Franke, ed. *Joshua, Judges, Ruth, 1–2 Samuel*, Ancient Christian Commentary on
Scripture, Old Testament (Downers Grove, IL: InterVarsity Press, 1998), 202.

Hannah more children to take the place of her son whom she dedicated to the service of Yahweh. The narrator then describes the blessed fruitfulness of Elkanah and Hannah as she gives birth to five more children. However, none of these children are named in the story, showing that Samuel is the one who will be the focus going forward. This is clearly affirmed in the description of Samuel growing up in God's presence (1 Sam 2:21b).

Eli Rebukes His Sons (2:22–25)

In contrast to the admirable parenting displayed by Hannah and Elkanah, Eli's failures as a parent are underscored in his response to news about his sons' extensive sins. Not only did they forcibly help themselves to the sacrificial meat offered to God, they unlawfully had sexual relations with the women who served God at Shiloh (v. 23). Eli confronts his sons about their sin, warning them of the seriousness of their offenses. Eli, however, does not command his sons to stop (though this may be implicit), demonstrating the truth of the prophet's words in 2:29 that Eli honored his sons more than God. Sadly, Eli's rebuke has no effect on these priests. Strikingly, the narrator ascribes their lack of penitence to God's wish to have them killed (v. 25).

The sins of the sons of Eli are further contrasted with the continued development of Samuel. While wicked reports of Eli's sons circulate "among the LORD's people" (v. 24), Samuel earns favor with not only the people but with God himself (v. 26). The contrast could not be any clearer.

An Ominous Prophecy (2:26–36)

After Eli's ineffective rebuke of his sons, God sends a prophet who berates Eli for scorning the high calling of the priestly office and the generous provision made for his family (v. 28). Eli has "honored" his sons above God and has "fattened" himself on the best portions of the offerings. Although Eli did not physically take the offerings from the worshipers, as did his sons, he partook of their meat. This may explain the fact that Eli is only said to rebuke them after hearing about their sexual sins at the sanctuary. He may have known or perhaps turned a blind eye to taking the best of the meat since he himself enjoyed feasting on it (so much so he is described as very overweight in 1 Sam 4:18). In the Hebrew there is a clear wordplay here. The Hebrew word for "heavy/overweight" (*kbd*) can also mean "honored." Eli became "heavy" (*kbd*) on the illegal portions of the sacrifice and honored (*kbd*) his sons but failed to honor (*kbd*) God (v. 30).

The prophet declares that Eli will be the last old man in his line (v. 32), that his sons will die on the same day (v. 34), and that those in his family line who survive will be reduced to poverty (v. 36). Ironically, the priestly line who fattened themselves on stolen sacrificial meat will one day beg for bread from the new priestly line. This future situation fits the description Hannah gave in her prayer where she stated, "Those who were full hire themselves out for food" (2:5), again connoting a prophetic aspect to her poem.

Finally, the unnamed prophet declares that God will raise up for himself a faithful priest (v. 35). In the immediate context one cannot help but think of young Samuel who already ministers before the Lord faithfully. However, looking forward into the ongoing story, the prophetic word is finally fulfilled in the appointment of Zadok and his line to the priesthood in 1 Kings 2:26–27, 35.

While it is easy to miss, the monarchy is once again brought into view with the reference that this faithful priest will "minister before my *anointed one*" (v. 35, emphasis added). The connection between the priest and the king is again emphasized. Priest and king together serve God in their distinct roles. But the Elide priesthood is not to last. Regime change is coming. The royal imagery associated with the Elide line and the imagery in Hannah's prayer anticipates the fall of both the Elide priestly line and the Saulide dynasty.

We are not told how Eli reacts to this prophecy. Was he shaken by this word? Was he brought to tears? Did Eli see this coming? Or were his dim eyes as blind to his own sins as they were to his own sons' wickedness, which he did not discover until his old age? Yet one more prophetic word for Eli is coming where we are explicitly told Eli's reaction (3:18). Perhaps that reaction to the second word of God is more understandable given that it is not the first time he has heard such an indictment.

LIVE the Story

Abuse of Power

The Elide priests were appointed by God. They were specially chosen to represent Israel in the sanctuary and given not only a high calling but a high privilege as well. Yet they failed to see the high responsibility that came with this privileged position. This is a sobering message to those of us in ministry today. Pastors, teachers, and ministers in any area of ministry need to see not only the privilege of their calling but the gravity and seriousness of their responsibility as well. Likely all involved in church life will have seen or heard stories of ministers who have fallen, not unlike the Elides, to greed, lust, or simply to power and notoriety. The word of the anonymous man of God in 1 Samuel 2 is ever relevant today. Like the Elides, we can honor ourselves above God (2:29). We can use our position to our favor instead of God's favor. Monetarily, some pastors have fallen due to abuse of finances in their appropriation of church funds. Yet these funds are offerings to God. Sometimes familiarity allows us to forget that these offerings are holy, dedicated to the Lord's work, and not to be spent on our own honor, enjoyment, or pleasure. Some pastors have fallen into adultery with parishioners, often beginning with a subtle abuse of the influence that comes with the ministering person. The example of Eli's sons who slept with women who came to serve God at Shiloh may seem shocking when first read, but it is a sin that continues to rear its ugly head in today's church. While it "takes two to Tango" and sexual promiscuity involves two people, when one party is in a position of power over the other there is no true consent by the weaker party. Even outside the church, sexual consent is not understood to be present when it is due to pressure by one in a position of trust, influence, or authority.[3] God does not turn a blind eye to sin, as did Eli. The prophetic word here reminds us of the high calling of the minster and warns that abusing the ministerial office is to "treat the LORD's offering with contempt" (2:17).

Contempt for Spiritual Things

Eli's sons are said to "treat the LORD's offering with contempt" (2:17). It is sometimes said that "familiarity breeds contempt." That is, in long-standing relationships over time the familiarity that comes with intimacy eventually causes one of the partners in a relationship to lose respect and even feel contempt for the other. Eli's sons grew up in the priesthood and were familiar with the sacrificial system and the inner workings of the tabernacle. Eventually, their familiarity led to taking spiritual things for granted and a lack of respect for these things with which they had become intimately familiar.

Similar dangers exist today where the familiarity of church and the gospel leads those in ministry (or their children) to develop a level of contempt for spiritual things. However, just as in a marriage familiarity with one's spouse need not provoke contempt but instead can pave the way for even deeper intimacy, so familiarity with spiritual things does not *need* to breed contempt. At the beginning of marriages, actions and symbols of intimacy such as a tender kiss, an embrace, or kind words can actually evoke love and lead to greater love. If *these* are the things that become familiar, then this familiarity of support, kindness, and respect can sustain love. Relationships often become disrespectful, however, and what becomes familiar are dishonoring actions and words. When these negative actions and feelings become familiar, contempt is bred.

---

3. Marie Marshall Fortune, *Is Nothing Sacred: When Sex Invades the Pastoral Relationship* (San Francisco: Harper & Row, 1989). Peter Rutter, *Sex in the Forbidden Zone: How Therapists, Doctors, Clergy, Teachers and Other Men in Power Betray Women's Trust* (Los Angeles: J P Tarcher, 1989).

In relationships, contempt is an emotional reaction to not feeling respected or cared for. If a spouse feels their partner values them, their marriage will thrive, but if a spouse feels devalued by their partner, it is a breeding ground for contempt. Sadly, spouses sometimes feel devalued due to a selfish attitude, so that they feel their partner is not meeting their needs. Similarly, we can be selfish in our spiritual relationship with God and begin to be "me-centered," focusing on ourselves rather than God. Regular worship helps prevent this "me-first" perspective from developing into contempt for God. Worship is not about us but all about God. Regular participation in worship helps realign our perspective and keeps us from our self-absorption. Worship of God reminds us of his worth and his value. Reading God's word reminds us of the goodness of his character. Familiarity in human relationships can breed contempt because the more we get to know our spouse, the more flaws we will see in them. This can lead us to lose some of the respect we previously had for them. In the case of our spiritual relationship with God, however, the more we get to know him the more we will see his value and his worth. True familiarity with God should lead to greater respect and a desire for intimacy, not contempt. Contempt comes from a selfish perspective. Honoring God comes from a worship perspective.

Pointing to Jesus

The story of Samuel's birth and childhood has many connections with the gospel story in the New Testament. Hannah's poetic prayer has many connections with the prayer of Jesus' mother Mary, often referred to as her Magnificat (Luke 1:46–55).

Hannah's Prayer (1 Sam 2:1–10)	Mary's Magnificat (Luke 1:46–55)
v. 1 "My heart rejoices in the LORD . . . I delight in your deliverance"	vv. 46–47 "My soul glorifies the Lord and my spirit rejoices in God my Savior"
v. 2 "There is no one *holy* like the LORD"	v. 49 "*holy* is his name"
v. 3 "Do not keep talking so *proudly* or let your mouth speak such arrogance, for the LORD is a God who knows"	v. 51 "he has scattered those who are *proud* in their inmost thoughts"
v. 8 "He raises the poor from the dust and lifts the needy from the ash heap; he seats them with princes and has them inherit a *throne* of honor"	v. 52 "He has brought down rulers from their *thrones* but has lifted up the humble"
v. 5 "Those who were full hire themselves out for food, but those who were *hungry* are hungry no more"	v. 53 "He has filled the *hungry* with good things but has sent the rich away empty"

Both prayers speak of God turning the tables on the rich and powerful in favor of the poor and vulnerable (1 Sam 2:8; Luke 2:52). Both speak of the rich going without but the hungry being fed (1 Sam 2:5; Luke 2:53). Furthermore, in the next chapter Jesus' development to adulthood is described in terms borrowed directly from the description of Samuel's development from a child to a young man: "And the boy Samuel continued to grow in stature and in favor with the LORD and with people" (2 Sam 2:26). Similarly, Luke writes of Jesus' maturation that "Jesus grew in wisdom and stature, and in favor with God and man" (Luke 2:52).

Why does Luke make this connection with Samuel? The early church father, Cyprian, considered Samuel to be a type of Christ.[4] Considering the significance of Samuel in these opening narratives provides us with an understanding as to this connection. As we have seen, the birth of Samuel hailed the era of the kings (anointed ones/*messiah*) in Israel. Similarly, the birth of Jesus begins a new era of the Anointed One (*messiah*) as the true King of Israel. Furthermore, as we have seen, Samuel's birth foreshadowed the fall of both the Elide dynasty and Shiloh's role as Israel's religious epicenter. Similarly, Jesus' ministry heralded the end to the official priesthood in Jerusalem. As Samuel denounced Israel's religious leaders, so Jesus denounced the leadership of his day for their corruption (Matt 23:1–36). Just as Samuel will prophesy the end of the priestly dynasty (1 Sam 3:11–14, 18), so Jesus prophesied the destruction of the temple itself (Matt 24). Just as Samuel replaced Eli, so Jesus replaces temple and the *entire temple system* with himself (e.g., Jesus forgives sin without the temple system; cf. Mark 2:5).[5] Just as the fall of Shiloh (Ps 78:60; Jer 7:12, 14; 26:6, 9) prepared the way for a new sanctuary in Jerusalem, so the fall of the temple from Jesus' day signaled the end of the old covenant and the beginning of the new. So, the Gospel of Luke's verbal allusion to the story of Samuel's birth is appropriate. Samuel was a transitional and unique figure. He served as a prophet, priest, and, until the king was anointed, as the temporal ruler of Israel. Jesus similarly but more comprehensively fulfills all three roles as a prophet (Luke 1:76; 13:33; 24:19; Acts 3:23), priest (Heb 3:1; 4:14–15; 5:5–6, 10; 6:20), and king (Matt 21:5; 27:11; Luke 19:38; John 12:13, 15; 18:36; Rev 17:14; 19:16).

---

4. Franke, *Joshua, Judges, Ruth, 1–2 Samuel*, 193.
5. N. T. Wright, *Jesus and the Victory of God*, Christian Origins and the Question of God, Volume 2 (Philadelphia: Fortress, 1996), 438, 553–63 (esp. 553–54).

CHAPTER 3

1 Samuel 3:1–21

 LISTEN to the Story

¹The boy Samuel ministered before the LORD under Eli. In those days the word of the LORD was rare; there were not many visions.

²One night Eli, whose eyes were becoming so weak that he could barely see, was lying down in his usual place. ³The lamp of God had not yet gone out, and Samuel was lying down in the house of the LORD, where the ark of God was. ⁴Then the LORD called Samuel.

Samuel answered, "Here I am." ⁵And he ran to Eli and said, "Here I am; you called me."

But Eli said, "I did not call; go back and lie down." So he went and lay down.

⁶Again the LORD called, "Samuel!" And Samuel got up and went to Eli and said, "Here I am; you called me."

"My son," Eli said, "I did not call; go back and lie down."

⁷Now Samuel did not yet know the LORD: The word of the LORD had not yet been revealed to him.

⁸A third time the LORD called, "Samuel!" And Samuel got up and went to Eli and said, "Here I am; you called me."

Then Eli realized that the LORD was calling the boy. ⁹So Eli told Samuel, "Go and lie down, and if he calls you, say, 'Speak, LORD, for your servant is listening.'" So Samuel went and lay down in his place.

¹⁰The LORD came and stood there, calling as at the other times, "Samuel! Samuel!"

Then Samuel said, "Speak, for your servant is listening."

¹¹And the LORD said to Samuel: "See, I am about to do something in Israel that will make the ears of everyone who hears about it tingle. ¹²At that time I will carry out against Eli everything I spoke against his family—from beginning to end. ¹³For I told him that I would judge his family forever because of the sin he knew about; his sons blasphemed God, and he failed to restrain them. ¹⁴Therefore I swore to the house

of Eli, 'The guilt of Eli's house will never be atoned for by sacrifice or offering.'"

[15]Samuel lay down until morning and then opened the doors of the house of the LORD. He was afraid to tell Eli the vision, [16]but Eli called him and said, "Samuel, my son."

Samuel answered, "Here I am."

[17]"What was it he said to you?" Eli asked. "Do not hide it from me. May God deal with you, be it ever so severely, if you hide from me anything he told you." [18]So Samuel told him everything, hiding nothing from him. Then Eli said, "He is the LORD; let him do what is good in his eyes."

[19]The LORD was with Samuel as he grew up, and he let none of Samuel's words fall to the ground. [20]And all Israel from Dan to Beersheba recognized that Samuel was attested as a prophet of the LORD. [21]The LORD continued to appear at Shiloh, and there he revealed himself to Samuel through his word.

Listen to the Text in the Story: Exodus 27:21; Leviticus 24:1–4

According to Exodus 27:21, the lamp in the tabernacle was to be lit from evening until the morning (cf. Lev 24:1–4), so when verse 3 says "the lamp of God had not yet gone out," it would seem to indicate the events of this chapter took place during the night. On the other hand, the phrase "lamp of God" is elsewhere used in Samuel (2 Sam 21:17) to refer to hope (cf. 1 Kgs 11:36; 2 Kgs 8:19), leading some to suggest that it should be similarly interpreted here.[1] That is, there was still hope for Israel, as God was about to call Samuel and use him in mighty ways for Israel's sake.

EXPLAIN the Story

This chapter recounts the calling of Samuel to be a prophet. Though already an apprentice-priest who has been dedicated to service at Shiloh by his mother, now God himself calls Samuel and he delivers his first prophecy (against Eli and his house). The chapter ends noting how Samuel's prophetic status is recognized throughout Israel. While the chapter began with a note that the word of the LORD was uncommon in those days, it ends declaring that things

---

1. John H. Walton and Victor Harold Matthews, *The IVP Bible Background Commentary: Genesis–Deuteronomy* (Downers Grove, IL: InterVarsity Press, 1997), 284–85.

have changed and that now God was revealing his word regularly through Samuel, his chosen prophet.

Scarcity of the Word (3:1)

The setting for the story that unfolds in this chapter is important. Before Samuel becomes a prophet, the word of the LORD was "rare" (3:1), and there were also few visions from God. Since prophets were the ones who received words from the Lord or revelatory visions, this reveals that there were few prophets in Israel. This situation could be the result of God's displeasure, as is the case later when God does not provide prophetic guidance to Saul (1 Sam 14:37; 28:6). Given that Israel was still involved in idolatry (1 Sam 7:3–4), the lack of prophetic revelation being given is likely due to this disobedience (cf. Amos 8:11).

What is more, the fact that prophetic revelations were rare in those days explains why Eli and Samuel are taken by surprise when the word of Yahweh comes to Samuel. Furthermore, it makes the event of great significance. God was once again sending prophetic guidance for his people.

The Call of the Lord (3:2–14)

In the context of discussing spiritual insights (words, visions, etc.) we are told that Eli's eyes were becoming weak. As we saw previously, his spiritual insight was also poor. Now we are told that Eli is sleeping in "his usual place" (v. 2) but Samuel was sleeping "in the house of the LORD, where the ark of God was" (v. 3). The different locations for the characters in this drama are significant. While we are not told exactly where Eli's "usual place" for sleeping was, it is clear it was not in the temple itself. Samuel's choice to camp out in the temple underscores his dedication to God and contrasts Eli's apathetic and indifferent attitude toward holy things.

During the night, the LORD calls Samuel three times. The first two times both Samuel and Eli are oblivious to the fact that it is God calling young Samuel. Here the narrator reminds us that Samuel "did not yet know the LORD" (v. 7), which serves to excuse the young man to an extent.[2] However, the fact that Eli, the seasoned priest, fails to perceive that God is calling the youth does not speak well of his spiritual sensitivities. We have already seen that he misdiagnosed Hannah's piety for drunkenness and apparently did not perceive his sons' sinful failings until his old age. It is only the *third* time that Samuel comes to him claiming he called him that Eli perceives it is God and advises Samuel how to respond.

---

2. Samuel's slowness to perceive God's revelation, however, is a trait we will see displayed later in the prophet's life. E.g., Samuel seems to need step-by-step guidance in his choosing of Saul (1 Sam 9), is slow to accept God's rejection of Saul (1 Sam 15:11), and thinks that David's elder brother, Eliab, is God's anointed one (1 Sam 16:16).

The fourth time God calls Samuel there is a sense in which God shows his frustration. Rather than just saying "Samuel" as he did at first, he now says his name twice "Samuel, Samuel!" (3:10). As well, this time there is reference to God's presence, as it says God "came and stood there" (3:10). Previously, in the other three instances of God's calling of Samuel, it only notes the call with no reference to God's presence. One gets the feeling that even if Eli failed to advise his apprentice properly, God was not going to let Samuel mistake his call the fourth time. Later in verse 15 we are told that this was indeed a "vision" that Samuel saw.

The word of the LORD given to Samuel is very similar to the word spoken by the anonymous prophet in the previous chapter (2:27–36). The previous prophecy predicted the fall of Eli and his house, but now God informs Eli that the wait is over, judgment is at hand. Now God explicitly declares that Eli "knew about" his sons' sins but "he failed to restrain them" (3:13). What is more, there is no opportunity given for his sins to be atoned. This harsh statement is *just deserts* for the house of Eli: they stole from God's sacrifices; therefore no sacrifices will atone for them.

God's Word in the Light of Day (3:15–18)

Samuel stays lying down in the house of the Lord until morning. Imagine what it must have been like for young Samuel at this point! Here he is an apprentice of Eli and his first prophecy is railing against his master. To say this was awkward does not do the situation justice. He, a youth, is called to level judgment against what was most likely the most powerful family in Israel.[3] Samuel lies there all night without returning to Eli. Of course, Samuel is not the first prophet to hesitate to become the LORD's messenger (cf. Exod 3; Judg 6).

We could also wonder about Eli's actions, or lack thereof. Did Eli stay up waiting for Samuel to return? The text says that Eli realized it was the LORD calling Samuel (3:8). Why did he not go see Samuel to find out what happened? Did he fall asleep? Was he unconcerned about God's word? Or perhaps Eli sensed the type of word this might be. Given that the last word from God was an indictment against him and that there were not many words from God in those days, Eli may have surmised that the word was again against him and his house. If this was the case, Eli may have been dying to know what the word was but hesitant to go into God's presence where Samuel was (before the ark and the lamp—symbols of God's presence) to query about it. Or although he wanted to know—he did not want to know.

---

3. Bergen, *Samuel*, 85.

Whatever the reason for Eli's lack of inquisitiveness during the night, when morning came Eli demands (threatening him with a curse) that Samuel tell him what God had said. Samuel proceeds to tell him all that God had revealed to him. Eli appears to accept God's word humbly (3:18)—though it could also signal his apathy. Eli does not repent in response to the prophetic word, which would seem like the appropriate response to the indictment. Eli's response shows again that God's indictment on him is correct. Eli is a "blind" leader who cannot perceive what is expected of him.

A Prophet Established (3:19–21)

With his first prophecy, Samuel's career as Israel's prophet begins and the text declares that Yahweh was with him. In fact, God's word through Samuel was reliable. During the period of the judges most of Israel's leaders were local in nature rather than national, but Samuel's impeccable reputation became known across the entire land of Israel (from Dan in the north to Beersheba in the south). God continues to reveal himself at Shiloh—through the prophet Samuel—but Shiloh's days are numbered.

Spiritual Blindness

Eli's physical features tell the story of his spiritual state. While the priest is not described as wicked himself, the anonymous prophet in chapter 2 indicted Eli for getting fat on the choice pieces of offering meat that were supposed to be offered to God (2:29). Eli's obese state is explicitly referenced in the next chapter as he is described as very "heavy" (1 Sam 4:18). Here in chapter 3 we are told of Eli's loss of sight (3:2). Just as Eli's physical weight told of his sin, so his physical blindness evinced his spiritual sightlessness. Eli's lack of spiritual discernment is first hinted at when he misdiagnosed Hannah's earnest prayer as drunkenness (1 Sam 1:14). Now in chapter 3 he fails to perceive that God is speaking to his young apprentice until the third time. In Luke 6:39 Jesus warns "Can the blind lead the blind? Will they not both fall into a pit?" Yet this is exactly what the situation in Shiloh was like. Eli was spiritually blind, yet he was the spiritual leader of Israel.

Throughout Scripture, blindness is often a metaphor for lack of spiritual sight (Isa 6:10; 42:18–19; 43:8; 56:10; Matt 15:14; Luke 6:39; John 12:40; Rom 2:19; 2 Cor 4:4; 2 Pet 1:9; 1 John 2:11; Rev 3:17). Spiritual blindness refers to an inability to recognize truth. Jesus referred to religious teachers in his day as blind (Matt 15:14; 23:16–17, 19, 24, 26), though they claimed to see clearly. This blindness is not limited to the religious teachers in Jesus' day. Apart from Christ all people are spiritually blind, as Paul writes:

> The god of this age has blinded the minds of unbelievers, so that they cannot see the light of the gospel of the glory of Christ, who is the image of God. (2 Cor 4:4)

The good news, however, is that Jesus came for the blind. He came not only to heal physical blindness but to restore sight to the spiritually blind (Matt 13:17; John 9:39). As Paul writes:

> For God, who said, "Let light shine out of darkness," made his light shine in our hearts to give us the light of the knowledge of God's glory displayed in the face of Christ. (2 Cor 4:6)

In Acts 26:18, the apostle Paul views his God-given mission in terms of making blind eyes see: "to open their eyes and turn them from darkness to light, and from the power of Satan to God."

To be healed from spiritual blindness, we must first admit we are blind. The religious leaders of Jesus' day refused to admit their need and so were declared guilty. The Pharisees denied their need, saying "What? Are we blind too?" (John 9:40), to which Jesus replied, "If you were blind, you would not be guilty of sin; but now that you claim you can see, your guilt remains" (John 9:41). Similarly, the church at Laodicea claimed to be in need of nothing, but Jesus tells them, "But you do not realize that you are wretched, pitiful, poor, blind and naked" (Rev 3:17).

We must also trust God and his vision. In this chapter Eli accepts the prophetic word of judgment, saying, "He is the LORD; let him do what is good in his eyes" (3:18). This is the first step in the right direction for the old priest: affirming his blindness and trusting in God's eyesight. Though Eli's days are numbered, his submitting to the divine will shows the humility required to receive God's healing mercy. Sadly, those who reject God's word are not so positioned. Remember in the last chapter Eli's sons refused to listen to their father's rebuke because "it was the LORD's will to put them to death" (1 Sam 2:25). Those who refuse to admit their blindness reap what they sow. Those who refuse to submit to God end up permanently blind (John 12:40), like Israel (Rom 11:10).

Sin That Cannot Be Atoned?

The statement that the sin of Eli will "never be atoned for by sacrifice or offering" (3:14) is harsh. It is blunt. It is frightening. Yet it is in line with the broader biblical revelation concerning atonement and the effectiveness of sacrifices. In Mosaic law, willful, intentional sin was *not* covered by sacrifices. The sin and guilt offerings legislated in the Old Testament only covered accidental and non-deliberate sins. For example, Numbers 15:27–31 states:

> But if just one person sins *unintentionally*, that person must bring a year-old female goat for a sin offering. The priest is to make atonement before the LORD for the one who erred by sinning *unintentionally*, and when atonement has been made, that person will be forgiven. One and the same law applies to everyone who sins *unintentionally*, whether a native-born Israelite or a foreigner residing among you. But anyone who sins *defiantly*, whether native-born or foreign, blasphemes the LORD and must be cut off from the people of Israel. Because they have despised the LORD's word and broken his commands, they must surely be cut off; their guilt remains on them. (emphasis added)

Similar laws are found in Leviticus 5:14–19. However, Leviticus 6:1–7 and Numbers 5:6–8 indicate that a deliberate sin requires the guilty party to confess the sin and make restitution. If this is done, the sin seems to switch to a category of inadvertent sin and atonement can be made at that point. There is *no* sacrificial atonement to a sinner who does not confess and repent.

This is consistent with New Testament revelation regarding atonement, even in light of Christ's finished work on the cross. In the book of Hebrews we read: "If we deliberately keep on sinning after we have received the knowledge of the truth, no sacrifice for sins is left" (10:26). Just as under Old Testament law, a sinner is barred from restoration if there is no confession and repentance of sin (cf. Heb 6:4–6).

LISTEN to the Story

¹And Samuel's word came to all Israel.

Now the Israelites went out to fight against the Philistines. The Israelites camped at Ebenezer, and the Philistines at Aphek. ²The Philistines deployed their forces to meet Israel, and as the battle spread, Israel was defeated by the Philistines, who killed about four thousand of them on the battlefield. ³When the soldiers returned to camp, the elders of Israel asked, "Why did the LORD bring defeat on us today before the Philistines? Let us bring the ark of the LORD's covenant from Shiloh, so that he may go with us and save us from the hand of our enemies."

⁴So the people sent men to Shiloh, and they brought back the ark of the covenant of the LORD Almighty, who is enthroned between the cherubim. And Eli's two sons, Hophni and Phinehas, were there with the ark of the covenant of God.

⁵When the ark of the LORD's covenant came into the camp, all Israel raised such a great shout that the ground shook. ⁶Hearing the uproar, the Philistines asked, "What's all this shouting in the Hebrew camp?"

When they learned that the ark of the LORD had come into the camp, ⁷the Philistines were afraid. "A god has come into the camp," they said. "Oh no! Nothing like this has happened before. ⁸We're doomed! Who will deliver us from the hand of these mighty gods? They are the gods who struck the Egyptians with all kinds of plagues in the wilderness. ⁹Be strong, Philistines! Be men, or you will be subject to the Hebrews, as they have been to you. Be men, and fight!"

¹⁰So the Philistines fought, and the Israelites were defeated and every man fled to his tent. The slaughter was very great; Israel lost thirty thousand foot soldiers. ¹¹The ark of God was captured, and Eli's two sons, Hophni and Phinehas, died.

¹²That same day a Benjamite ran from the battle line and went to Shiloh with his clothes torn and dust on his head. ¹³When he arrived, there

was Eli sitting on his chair by the side of the road, watching, because his heart feared for the ark of God. When the man entered the town and told what had happened, the whole town sent up a cry.

[14]Eli heard the outcry and asked, "What is the meaning of this uproar?"

The man hurried over to Eli, [15]who was ninety-eight years old and whose eyes had failed so that he could not see. [16]He told Eli, "I have just come from the battle line; I fled from it this very day."

Eli asked, "What happened, my son?"

[17]The man who brought the news replied, "Israel fled before the Philistines, and the army has suffered heavy losses. Also your two sons, Hophni and Phinehas, are dead, and the ark of God has been captured."

[18]When he mentioned the ark of God, Eli fell backward off his chair by the side of the gate. His neck was broken and he died, for he was an old man, and he was heavy. He had led Israel forty years.

[19]His daughter-in-law, the wife of Phinehas, was pregnant and near the time of delivery. When she heard the news that the ark of God had been captured and that her father-in-law and her husband were dead, she went into labor and gave birth, but was overcome by her labor pains. [20]As she was dying, the women attending her said, "Don't despair; you have given birth to a son." But she did not respond or pay any attention.

[21]She named the boy Ichabod, saying, "The Glory has departed from Israel"—because of the capture of the ark of God and the deaths of her father-in-law and her husband. [22]She said, "The Glory has departed from Israel, for the ark of God has been captured."

Listen to the Text in the Story: Genesis 35:16–18; Exodus 25:16, 21; 40:20; Numbers 10:33–35; Deuteronomy 10:1–5; Judges 20:26–27; The Sumerian King List; The Black Obelisk; Naram-Sin; Sennacherib's Seige of Jeruslem (The Taylor Prism)

In this chapter we meet the Philistines for the first time in the story. The Philistines were not indigenous to Canaan but were a largely sea-faring people from the Aegean region near Greece who settled along the southern coast of Canaan around 1190 BC, where Gaza, Ashkelon, Ashdod, Ekron, and Gath became well-known Philistine cities. Although relatively new to Canaan, the Philistines adopted local deities with temples to Dagon in their major cities (Judg 16:21–23; 1 Sam 5:2–3; 1 Chr 10:10–12), as well as a temple to Astarte in Beth Shan (1 Sam 31:10). The Philistines were largely the dominant power in the region from 1150–1000 BC, even dominating Israelite areas (cf. 1 Sam 4; 10:5; 13:23–14:16; 2 Sam 23:13–17).

Also referenced for the first time in the story is the ark of the covenant (often called the ark of God). The ark is probably the most well-known object in the Bible thanks to its role in the blockbuster film *Raiders of the Lost Ark* by Steven Spielberg (1981). The ark was a sacred rectangular wooden box about three to four feet long and two-and-a-quarter feet both in width and height and covered in gold both inside and out. The box contained the two tablets of the Ten Commandments, a pot of manna from Israel's wilderness wanderings, and Aaron's rod that budded (Exod 25:16, 21; 40:20; Deut 10:1–5). The box's golden lid, called the mercy seat, had two statues of cherubim with wings outstretched to cover the ark. Yahweh is said to be "enthroned between the cherubim" (1 Sam 4:4; cf. 1 Chr 28:2; Pss 99:5; 132:7). Thus, the ark represented God's presence and was kept in the inner sanctuary of the tabernacle.

Most important for understanding the story in 2 Samuel 4 is the military role the ark played. Since it represented God's presence, it was sometimes believed to ensure victory in battle. This tradition can be seen in Numbers 10:35, which reads:

> Whenever the ark set out, Moses said, "Rise up, LORD! May your *enemies* be scattered; may your *foes* flee before you." (emphasis added)

Similarly, Numbers 14:44 implies that entering into battle without the ark resulted in defeat. Furthermore, the ark was often where Israel's elders would seek an oracle regarding holy war (Judg 20:26–27; 2 Sam 5:19, 23).

In this chapter we see that some in Israel in Samuel's day viewed the ark of the covenant as a sort of guarantee to military victory. Israel's idea of a sacred object guaranteeing victory is not unique in the ancient world. In ancient Greece, the city of Troy was said to have a wooden statute of the goddess Pallas Athena, often referred to as the Trojan Palladium, which was thought to guarantee the city's safety. The Trojans believed the image had fallen from heaven in response to the prayer of Troy's founder, Ilus. At one point Ilus was said to have been struck with blindness for touching the statue in his attempt to rescue it from a fire (similar to the story in 2 Sam 5:1–8 of Uzzah who was struck dead after touching the ark in his attempt to stop it from falling off a cart). In the story of the fall of Troy, the only reason that the city became vulnerable to defeat was because Odysseus and Diomedes stole the statue from the city.[1]

---

1. The story is recorded in Virgil's *Aeneid*, which can be found online: http://classics.mit.edu/Virgil/aeneid.html.

The term palladium has come into usage to figuratively mean something that is believed to provide protection or safety.

In the ancient Near East, deities were often pictured as divine warriors who fought the nation's battles and defeated their enemies' deities. Popular war deities included Baal (Canaan), Nergal and Ishtar (Assyria), and Marduk (Babylon). Often idols or standards of deities were carried to war to symbolize the god's presence with the army.[2] For example, the Mesopotamian king, Naram-Sin, is said to have slain "Arman and Ibla with the 'weapon' of the god Dagan."[3] Ancient Assyrian kings often refer to the standard of their god that goes before them and their victory is regularly attributed to the "weapon of the god Ashur."[4] Similar to the taking of the ark, the Sumerian King List mentions that En-men-barage-si, a king who defeated Elam, "carried away as spoil the 'weapon' of Elam," probably referring to Elam's idol.[5] Similarly, the Assyrian King Shalmaneser explicitly mentions having his gods/images with him on his military campaign.[6]

These ancient parallels help us to understand the popular belief system in the ancient world. Just as Greek tradition viewed the efficacy of a palladium as due to its magical or sacred qualities, so many Israelites mistakenly viewed the ark in this way. Israel was not alone in this misguided superstition.

EXPLAIN the Story

This chapter narrates a difficult time in Israelite history. Under the thumb of Philistine aggression, the Israelites suffer a terrible defeat to their perennial enemy. In response, the elders of Israel decide to bring the ark of the covenant with them into battle, thinking that its power would turn the tide against the Philistines and result in an Israelite victory. Tragically, this does not occur. The Israelites suffer an even worse defeat, with the ark being captured by the enemy and the Israelite priests being killed. When word of the tragedy reaches Shiloh, the old priest Eli falls back off his chair and breaks his neck, ending his forty-year tenure as Israel's leader (4:18). The closing scene of the chapter is of Eli's pregnant daughter-in-law, who goes into premature labor as a result of hearing the tragic news of the defeat of Israel and the capture of the ark. The woman subsequently dies in childbirth, but not before naming her new son Ichabod, or "where is the glory?"

---

2. Walton and Matthews, *IVP Bible Background Commentary*, 286.
3. *ANET*, 268.
4. E.g., *ANET*, 287, 288.
5. Ibid., 265.
6. Ibid., 278.

Samuel's Word to All Israel (4:1a)

The chapter begins with Samuel's word coming to all Israel. Some interpreters think this part of the verse actually belongs with chapter 3, which ended with God's word coming to Samuel (3:21). However, it has been counted as part of chapter 4 in both Hebrew and Christian traditions of versification. While the note does fit with chapter 3, it is easy to see its relevance to chapter 4. Reading this notice of Samuel's word to Israel as the beginning of chapter 4 suggests either that it is Samuel's word that initiates the battle with the Philistines or that the events that followed are the fulfillment of Samuel's words of judgment (3:11–13, 18). Alternatively, it could be both. Samuel gives the word to attack the enemy and this action results in the fulfillment of the word of judgment given in the previous chapter. Either way, we see the word of the LORD carried out in this story, making this notice of Samuel's word to all Israel an integral part of the chapter.

War with the Philistines (4:1b–5)

Israel sets out to fight its archenemy—the Philistines. Since the enemy is said to be located in Aphek, an Israelite city, it seems clear that the Philistines have been the aggressors in the conflict. Sadly, the Philistines win a great victory over Israel with 4,000 Israelites dying on the battlefield. When the troops return home with their tails between their legs, the elders of Israel ask, "Why did the LORD bring defeat on us today before the Philistines?" (4:3). Yet, surprisingly, they are not said to seek a prophetic oracle or the word of the LORD. This is in spite of the fact that the previous chapter ended noting the availability of the prophetic word through Samuel (1 Sam 3:21).

Instead of seeking the prophetic word, they choose to bring the ark of the covenant to the camp. As noted above, one role of the ark in Israel's history had been as the place where oracles were sought (Judg 20:26–27). While ignoring (or forgetting) that aspect of the ark's military role, the elders here rely on the tradition of the ark functioning as God's presence and guarantor of victory. This approach is typical of this period under the judges, as the people were unfamiliar with the word of the LORD (3:1) and were quite superstitious in their religious sensibilities. Examples of this can be seen in Gideon's demand for signs for guidance and insurance of success (Judg 6:17, 36, 39) and Jephthah's vow to ensure victory (Judg 11:30–31).

When the ark is brought to the battlefront, Eli's wicked sons accompany it (4:4). While the loud celebration (4:5) over the decision to bring the ark to battle indicates the wholehearted approval of the people, any who knew of Samuel's prophecy regarding the fate of Eli's sons may have had second thoughts when they saw Hophni and Phineas show up at the front lines.

The Philistine Response (4:6–11)

When the Philistines hear that the ark had come to the Israelite camp, they are afraid, as they had heard of its power. Their knowledge of Israel's God and the ark, however, are flawed. They initially say that "a god" is in their camp and then they refer to the "mighty gods" of Israel, clearly revealing the Philistine's polytheistic worldview. Furthermore, their knowledge of salvation history is not very accurate, either, as they claim that these are the "gods" who plagued the Egyptians "in the wilderness" (4:8). In reality, the plagues on Egypt were not in the wilderness, but in Egypt itself, and there is only one God—Yahweh—not several "mighty gods." Furthermore, they seem to think that the ark *is* a god and therefore its presence is reason for fear. Ironically, this flawed, pagan perspective may derive from some flawed Israelite traditions regarding the ark, as the elders of Israel also view the ark's presence as magically guaranteeing victory.

The Philistines respond with one of the best "half-time pep talks" in the Bible. The imperative "Be strong!" recalls Moses's words to Joshua in Deuteronomy (Deut 31:6, 7, 23) and Joshua's words to Israel (Josh 1:6, 9, 18, 10:25; 23:6). The speech seemingly works wonders as the Philistines again rout the Israelites, this time resulting in 30,000 dead, the capture of the ark, and the death of Israel's priests (4:11). However, the notice of the deaths of Eli's sons reminds the reader that the hand of Yahweh was in on this Philistine victory as his word to Eli through the prophets are fulfilled (cf. 2:30–31; 3:12–15). The Philistines capture the ark and take it to their territory.

Reaction in Shiloh (4:12–18)

News of the horrific Israelite defeat reaches Shiloh as a Benjamite messenger runs from the front lines with dirt on his head—a sign of mourning—to report the defeat. In Shiloh, Eli is again "sitting" on his seat (or throne—in Hebrew they are the same word, *kisse*), waiting anxiously and worried about the ark (4:13). The messenger initially reports the bad news to the townspeople but when Eli hears the uproar and inquires about it, the messenger then tells the tale to the old priest. Again, reference is made to Eli's diminished eyesight, which at this point has rendered him virtually blind (4:15). In verse 16 the NIV translates Eli's query to the messenger as "What happened, my son?" which communicates the gist of his request but misses something at the same time. Literally, in the Hebrew, Eli asks "what is the word, my son?" This question recalls the prophetic "word" spoken about Eli's house in the previous chapters (2:27–36; 3:11–14). Furthermore, Eli calling the messenger his "son" recalls the "word" of the Lord concerning the imminent death of his own "sons" (2:34).

The messenger reports the losses in an apparent ascending order of tragedy from Eli's perspective. (1) Israel fled from the enemy, (2) the army has taken casualties, (3) Eli's sons have been killed, and (4) the ark has been captured. It is the last mentioned loss that most distresses Eli—surprisingly more so than the loss of his children—as at the mention of the loss of the ark Eli falls off his seat (throne), breaks his neck, and expires.[7]

The text notes that at his death Eli had "led Israel forty years" (4:18). This seems to connect him with the judges era, as similar notices are given about leaders in the book of Judges (e.g., Judg 10:2, 3; 12:7, 8, 11, 13; 15:20; 16:31). Since Eli's tenure is said to have been over the last forty years, he would appear to have been leading Israel during the tumultuous and chaotic times depicted in Judges 17–19.[8] This concluding notice, then, functions as a final stain on Eli's record and completes his characterization as the unknowing priest and ineffective leader of Israel.

An Ominous Birth (4:19–22)

Eli's daughter-in-law provides yet another shocking reaction to the news of the capture of the ark of God. Being great with child, she goes into premature labor and begins to deliver her child. The midwife attempts to encourage the woman by telling her that she's given birth to a boy, but this does not console her and she despairingly named her baby Ichabod, which is literally translated "where is the glory?" The woman dies in childbirth, not an uncommon incident in the ancient world. This particular incident, however, closely parallels another fatal labor that also resulted in another despairing name given to a newborn. In Genesis 35 Jacob's wife, Rachel, endures a very difficult and fatal labor. As in the story of Eli's daughter-in-law, Rachel's midwife attempts to encourage the laboring mother by telling her she is giving birth to a son (Gen 35:17). Similarly, the dying mother names her child a despondent name— Benoni or "son of my sorrow" (Gen 35:18). In this case Jacob renamed the child Benjamin or "son of the right" (Gen 35:18), while in 1 Samuel 4 no positive name change is made. Ironically, in 1 Samuel 4 it is a Benjamite who gives the bad news, which results in the untimely death of the laboring mother and the delivery of a baby whose birth and naming resembles that of Benjamin. Here the Elide dynasty falls, and it will be a Benjamite, Saul, who will head up Israel's first royal dynasty. However, just as Eli's grandson, Ichabod,

---

7. Eli's concern for the ark (over the safety of his children) may show his piety and concern with God's honor, or it may indicate that he, like the people, had a misplaced faith in the ark, thinking that the ark was what safeguarded Israel. Given that Eli was the spiritual leader of Israel and the Israelites had this flawed understanding of the role of the ark, the latter seems like a distinct possibility.

8. Bodner, *1 Samuel*, 49.

is not given a promising future, so too the future of Israel's first king will be less than stellar.

If we recall the royal imagery surrounding Eli in the first chapter of Samuel (see commentary above) and the twice referenced "throne" here in this chapter (4:13, 18), we can see that the story of the exile of the ark to enemy lands and the fall of the "dynasty" of Shiloh from its "throne" has been told to foreshadow the Babylonian exile. As noted in the introduction, the original audience of the complete story of Israel's history was probably living in exile. At the end of the story in 2 Kings 24–25, Judah was exiled to a foreign land (Babylon) and their last king, Zedekiah, similar to Eli, was not only spiritually blind but physically blinded (2 Kgs 25:7), and his sons were also killed (2 Kgs 25:7). The image of the dynasty at Shiloh falling from the throne foreshadows the fall of the Davidic dynasty under the Babylonians. Furthermore, the loss of the ark of the covenant foreshadows the loss of the Jerusalem temple to the Babylonians.

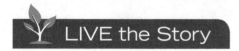

LIVE the Story

The Word of the LORD

The events of this chapter begin the pattern of promise and fulfillment in the book of Samuel. The word of the LORD delivered by both the anonymous man of God (2:27–36) and Samuel himself (3:11–14) begins to be fulfilled in this story. Appropriately the chapter begins noting Samuel's word to the people. The battle with the Philistines is enjoined seemingly in response to Samuel's word. In other words, the prophetic word not only *predicts* what will happen, it *facilitates* its own fulfillment by sending Israel into battle. While it may be surprising that the prophetic word sent Israel into a battle it will lose, this is not a unique occurrence in Scripture. In 1 Kings 22 when the evil king of Israel, Ahab, is debating whether to go to battle God sends a "deceiving spirit" (22:23) into the mouths of his prophets to encourage the wicked king to go to battle where he will be killed (cf. Ezek 14:9–10). Similarly, in the New Testament God is said to send "a powerful delusion so that they will believe the lie" (2 Thess 2:11), which is a bit disturbing, but it must be noted that the reason is so that those "who have not believed the truth but have delighted in wickedness" (2 Thess 2:12) may be condemned. Here it is the house of Israel, with its wicked priests (the Elide house) and their participation in pagan worship (remember Judg 18:30–31!), that is given a word to go to battle where it will be judged. The word of the LORD will accomplish what God wants it to (Isa 55:11). Even in the New Testament, one's perspective on the word of the LORD depends upon the recipients. In Paul's words, what may be the "aroma of Christ among those who are being saved" may be "the aroma that brings death" to "those who are perishing" (2 Cor 2:15–16). Regardless of this perspective or human disposition towards it, "the word of our God endures forever" (Isa 40:8).

Putting God in a Box

It is easy for us to put people in a "box," that is, to categorize them or label them based on first impressions, their appearance, or something we know about them. Putting someone in a box is to prejudge a person and to limit their potential in your mind. This not only causes hurt feelings but can cause significant problems as you refuse to see the potential in other people because you have categorized them inaccurately or prejudiciously. Putting God in a box can result in similarly negative consequences, but to an even greater degree, and this is exactly what Israel does in this story. By equating the ark (which *is* a wooden box) with God, they thought they could bring God on their side by carrying the ark with them to the battle. But try as you might, you can not put God in a box.

Israel's decision to use the ark of the covenant to make God save them results in an even worse defeat, serving as an apt reminder that God cannot be manipulated. The ark was an orthodox, sacred object, ordained by God to help Israel—but it was *not* God himself.

In a scene in the famous Spielberg movie, *Raiders of the Lost Ark*, Indiana Jones and his colleague Marcus Brody explain to army intelligence why Hitler was seeking the ark. Brody ominously states: "An army that carries the ark before it is invincible." However, the tragic events of 1 Samuel 4 show this was not the case. The ark was *not* a palladium. Possession of it did not guarantee victory at all. Victory is not due to a sacred object, but "victory rests with the LORD" (Prov 21:31). God "will not be captured, contained, assigned or managed by anyone or anything for any purpose."[9] As we will see throughout the story, God acts in his own way, in his own time, and cannot be limited in any way by a human agenda.

Trusting in Religion Rather Than God

As noted above, this story in 1 Samuel 4 of the fall of the Elide dynasty and the loss of the ark foreshadows the fall of the Davidic dynasty and the loss of the Jerusalem temple to the Babylonians. The parallel between these events actually helps to underscore the theological message against trust in religion instead of trust in God. In our story the Israelites thought the ark guaranteed victory, and

---

9. Walter Brueggemann, *Theology of the Old Testament: Testimony, Dispute, Advocacy* (Philadelphia: Fortress, 1997), 184–85.

in the story of the fall of Jerusalem to the Babylonians, the Jerusalemites thought similarly about the Jerusalem temple. In Jeremiah 7 we see the prophet warning the people not to trust in the temple to save them from Babylon. He writes:

Do not trust in deceptive words and say, "This is the temple of the LORD, the temple of the LORD, the temple of the LORD!" (Jer 7:4)

Instead Jeremiah tells them what they need to do.

If you really change your ways and your actions . . . then I will let you live in this place, in the land I gave your forefathers forever and ever. But look, you are trusting in deceptive words that are worthless. (Jer 7:7–8)

Jeremiah spoke against those who viewed the temple as a palladium or magical guarantee of their city's safety. Here the lessons Jeremiah would try in vain to teach the generation of the Babylonian exile are already present in the story of the fall of Shiloh and the exile of the ark.

God does not want us to trust in religious objects; he wants us to trust in him. Furthermore, the reasons for the Israelite defeat by the Philistines in 1 Samuel 4 and the reasons for the Babylonian exile are clear—sin. In 1 Samuel 4, Hophni and Phineas despised Yahweh and sinned grievously against him, resulting in their death, the loss of the ark, and the defeat of Israel. Similarly, the reasons for the destruction of Jerusalem and the loss of the temple in Jeremiah's day are clearly explained in 2 Kings 24:3–4.

Surely these things happened to Judah according to the LORD's command, in order to remove them from his presence because of the sins of Manasseh and all he had done, including the shedding of innocent blood. For he had filled Jerusalem with innocent blood, and the LORD was not willing to forgive.

When sin is not dealt with and trust in the LORD is replaced by trust in religion, judgment awaits. The only hope in that situation is repentance, as Jeremiah explained in the quotation above (Jer 7:5–8).

In the New Testament, Jesus came up against this same problem of trust in religion instead of trust in God. In the temple courts Jesus saw a similar situation where the temple became an object of religious trust apart from repentance of sin. Jesus actually quotes from Jeremiah 7 when he declares that the temple has become a "den of robbers" (Mark 11:17; Luke 19:46). Those who would interpret Jesus' words here as barring churches from bake sales or selling anything at church (for a fundraiser, etc.) misunderstand Jesus' quotation. As noted, Jesus quotes Jeremiah at this point, and a closer look at the context in Jeremiah makes its relevance clear. Jeremiah 7:9–11 states:

"Will you steal and murder, commit adultery and perjury, burn incense to Baal and follow other gods you have not known, and then come and stand before me in this house, which bears my Name, and say, 'We are safe'—safe to do all these detestable things? Has this house, which bears my Name, become a den of robbers to you?"

A "den of robbers" is a safehouse where criminals go to hide. Jeremiah (and Jesus after him) accuses the Israelites of turning the house of prayer into a hideout for criminals. They somehow believed that they could go all week sinning and worshiping other gods, but then show up at the temple on Sabbath and believe they were "safe." In Jeremiah's day, Judah had perverted the purpose of the temple, just as in our story in 1 Samuel 4 Israel was perverting the purpose of the ark, and just as the religious were perverting the purpose of the temple in Jesus' day. All were trusting in a religious object to save them rather than repenting of their sin and trusting in God.

Jeremiah 7 actually seems to be a theological reflection on the events of 1 Samuel 4, as can be seen in how Jeremiah 7:12–14 references the story as an example:

"Go now to the place in Shiloh where I first made a dwelling for my Name, and see what I did to it because of the wickedness of my people Israel. While you were doing all these things, declares the LORD, I spoke to you again and again, but you did not listen; I called you, but you did not answer. Therefore, what I did to Shiloh I will now do to the house that bears my Name, the temple you trust in, the place I gave to you and your ancestors."

Shiloh is used as an example of the results of trust in sacred objects rather than in Yahweh himself. The priests trusted in the tabernacle while grievously sinning; the people trusted in the ark without paying heed to the word of Yahweh.

Sadly, these scriptural lessons, reiterated in both testaments, were often forgotten, and in church history there are many instances where Christians ended up trusting in sacred relics or icons. In medieval times a part of a saint's body or something that belonged to them unfortunately became objects of trust and faith for some believers. In other instances such items were trusted for protection in military conflicts as people would carry a palladium (an icon or relic) into battle or parade them around the walls of besieged cities.[10]

---

10. E.g., In 1402 the Sacra Cintola, which was thought to be the belt of the virgin Mary, was said to be paraded around a city near Florence when it was surrounded by an enemy. https://en.wikipedia.org/wiki/Girdle_of_Thomas#Legend.

Lest we think this is just a problem for the ancient world, it is worth considering how even in today's church we struggle with misguided trust in religion versus trust in God. Just as in ancient Israel, today orthodox, God-given traditions and practices of the faith can become objects of trust and faith rather than God. A good example is the Lord's Supper (Communion or the Eucharist). It is an orthodox practice, instituted by Jesus himself, with physical elements used to remember Christ's death on the cross. Even this practice, however, can be misused when partakers view it as an almost magical religious rite which functions to forgive their sins. Just as the ark of the covenant reminded Israel of God's presence among them and their sacred past, so communion functions to remind Christians of Christ's death on our behalf. Other examples could be enumerated as well (water baptism, church attendance, tithing, etc.). All of these are God-ordained practices and traditions, but can become objects of misguided trust.

The antidote to this superstitious trust in religious things is hearing and obeying the word of God. In 1 Samuel 4, those who were attentive to God's word would have known that the plan to bring the ark was foolhardy, as the prophets had already spoken of the doom of Hophni and Phineas, the very ones bearing the ark. Those in Jerusalem in Jeremiah's day who listened to Jeremiah's prophetic word would have realized that trust in the temple to save them was foolishness. Similarly today, daily reorientation to the truth in Scripture will prevent misguided trust in religion and instead lead believers to trust in God, not religion.

LISTEN to the Story

¹After the Philistines had captured the ark of God, they took it from Ebenezer to Ashdod. ²Then they carried the ark into Dagon's temple and set it beside Dagon. ³When the people of Ashdod rose early the next day, there was Dagon, fallen on his face on the ground before the ark of the LORD! They took Dagon and put him back in his place. ⁴But the following morning when they rose, there was Dagon, fallen on his face on the ground before the ark of the LORD! His head and hands had been broken off and were lying on the threshold; only his body remained. ⁵That is why to this day neither the priests of Dagon nor any others who enter Dagon's temple at Ashdod step on the threshold.

⁶The LORD's hand was heavy on the people of Ashdod and its vicinity; he brought devastation on them and afflicted them with tumors. ⁷When the people of Ashdod saw what was happening, they said, "The ark of the god of Israel must not stay here with us, because his hand is heavy on us and on Dagon our god." ⁸So they called together all the rulers of the Philistines and asked them, "What shall we do with the ark of the god of Israel?"

They answered, "Have the ark of the god of Israel moved to Gath." So they moved the ark of the God of Israel.

⁹But after they had moved it, the LORD's hand was against that city, throwing it into a great panic. He afflicted the people of the city, both young and old, with an outbreak of tumors. ¹⁰So they sent the ark of God to Ekron.

As the ark of God was entering Ekron, the people of Ekron cried out, "They have brought the ark of the god of Israel around to us to kill us and our people." ¹¹So they called together all the rulers of the Philistines and said, "Send the ark of the god of Israel away; let it go back to its own place, or it will kill us and our people." For death had filled the city with panic; God's hand was very heavy on it. ¹²Those who did not die were afflicted with tumors, and the outcry of the city went up to heaven.

Listen to the Text in the Story: Exodus 6–8; Judges 16; Inscription of Tiglath-pileser I; Fall of Nineveh Chronicle

In the ancient world, the kidnapping of idols and religious objects was commonplace (e.g., 2 Kgs 25:13–17). The capture of idols symbolically meant gaining the power of the enemies' gods or signified the defeat of their gods. This demonstrated that the enemy's deity was subordinate to their own. For example, the Neo-Babylonian king Nabopolassar states: "In the month of Ab the king of Akkad and his army . . . plundered them, sacked them extensively, (and) abducted their gods. In the month of Elul the king of Akkad and his army returned and on his way he took (the people of) Hindanu and its gods to Babylon."[1] In fact, the statue of the Babylonian god, Marduk, was taken from Babylon by several successive conquerors of Babylon: the Hanaeans (seventeenth century BC), the Elamites (thirteenth century BC), and the Assyrians (seventh century BC).[2]

Idols were usually taken to the victor's own temples. For example, an inscription from the Assyrian King Tiglath-pileser reads: "I conquered the entire land of Sugu. I brought 25 of their gods, their booty, their possessions, (and) their property. . . . At that time I donated the 25 gods of those lands, my own booty which I had taken, to adorn the temple of the goddess Ninlil, beloved chief spouse of the god Ashur, my lord."[3]

In this chapter the ark is taken to a Philistine temple for Dagon in Ashdod. The Philistines had at least three different temples dedicated to Dagon, with others likely in Gaza (Judg 16:21–23) and Beth Shan (as suggested by 1 Chr 10:10–12 in light of 1 Sam 31:10). Dagon was an important ancient pagan deity who was worshiped by the Canaanites before the Philistines invaded their territory and adopted him as one of their deities. Dagon was widely worshiped by Semitic peoples in Mesopotamia and Syria. Though the god Baal is more widely known from biblical literature, in the northern town of Ugarit the temple of Dagon was actually bigger than that of Baal, and in Ugaritic literature Dagon is the father of Baal.

The backbone of Philistia was the so-called Philistine Pentapolis, which

1. Albert Kirk Grayson, *Assyrian and Babylonian Chronicles* (Locust Valley, NY: Augustin, 1975), 91.

2. Walton and Matthews, *IVP Bible Background Commentary*, 287.

3. Albert Kirk Grayson, *Assyrian Royal Inscriptions* (Wiesbaden: Harrassowitz, 1972), 2.28:11–12.

was a league of five cities: Gaza, Ashkelon, Ashdod, Ekron, and Gath. Each of these cities was a city-state with its own rulers (cf. 1 Sam 6:18), and each royal city ruled "country towns" (e.g., 1 Sam 27:5). In this story of the ark's sojourn in Philistia, we see reference to three of these royal cities of Philistia: Ashdod, Gath, and Ekron.

EXPLAIN the Story

This chapter gives an interesting and somewhat comical picture of the Philistines in their own land and their experience with the ark of the covenant, which they had captured in battle from the Israelites. The Philistines put the ark in the temple of their god, Dagon, probably to show that their god had overpowered the Israelite god. However, the next morning it appeared that Dagon did not even have power over his own idol as his statue is found on the ground prostrate before the ark. Despite their putting the idol back in its place, the following morning it is again on the ground before the ark, and this time it has been dismembered and decapitated! If these events did not make the Philistines realize that Yahweh was behind them, the tumors that God sent on the Philistines did. In response, they sent the ark to Gath and then to Ekron, with the inhabitants of both cities suffering from tumors as a result. These outbreaks incited widespread panic and caused the Philistines to utter a cry that even reached heaven.

The Ark in Ashdod (5:1–7)

After the tragic and ominous events in the last chapter, the story now has a somewhat comical interlude. This chapter is unique in the book of Samuel in regard to its absence of Israel; the scene is populated purely by Philistines and takes place only in Philistine cities. Having captured the ark of the covenant in their victory over Israel (1 Sam 4), the Philistines put their prize in the temple of their god, Dagon. The Philistines particularly have a habit of taking trophies of war to their temples. In Judges 16, Samson is brought to a Philistine temple as something of a war trophy, and in 1 Samuel 31:10, Saul's armor is brought to another Philistine temple.

As it turns out, bringing God's ark to their temple was as bad an idea as was bringing God's judge, Samson, to another temple of Dagon in Judges 16. The Philistines thought bringing Samson to their temple would benefit them (i.e., enhance their entertainment! [see Judg 16:25]), but their war trophy actually caused them great trouble.[4] As chronicled in 1 Samuel 5–6, bringing the ark to Dagon's temple will similarly cause great trouble in Philistia.

---

4. Bodner, *1 Samuel*, 51.

After putting the ark in their temple, the next morning the Philistines find that Dagon is prostrate before the ark. That is, he is in a position of obeisance and worship to the Israelite God (recalling that the Philistines considered the ark a god in 1 Sam 4:7). This is ironic given that the capture of an enemy's deity(ies)/ idols was thought to show that the victor's god had vanquished the god of the defeated army. Yet here was their god bowing to the god of the defeated Israelites.

Perhaps hoping it was simply an unfortunate accident, the Philistines dutifully replace Dagon on his stand, but the next morning they again find their deity on the ground. And this time matters are worse. Dagon has been decapitated and dismembered. The severed body parts were lying on the threshold (at the doorway to the temple), while his body remained on the ground. As Bodner comments: "the decapitated Dagon seems to have made it as far as the threshold of the temple. It is as though Dagon was attempting to flee (from his own house!)."[5] This would have proven awkward for the priests of Dagon, as they would have had to step over around these pieces to enter the temple. So traumatic was this event that 1 Samuel 5:5 tells us that this led to a superstitious practice of the Philistines not to step on the threshold when entering Dagon's temple in Ashdod.

The comic nature of these events would not be lost on an Israelite reader, yet the situation was anything but lighthearted. Yahweh proceeded to inflict the Philistines with tumors on account of the ark (5:6). What exactly these "tumors" were has been a matter of scholarly debate. Some[6] have suggested that they might be swollen lymph glands (buboes) as a symptom of bubonic plague, while others[7] think they are hemorrhoids. The reference to rats in the next chapter (6:5) may support the bubonic-plague interpretation since rats are carriers of the plague. Regardless of the specifics, the Philistines suffered greatly on account of the ark.

At this point the Philistines began to understand what was going on. The God of Israel was afflicting them on account of their having kidnapped the ark. They now even understand that the prostration and dismemberment of Dagon's statute was also due to Yahweh's actions, stating: "[the God of Israel's] hand is heavy on us and on Dagon our god" (5:7).

The Ark in Gath and Ekron (5:8–12)

In an attempt to fix their problem, they gather all the Philistine leaders to decide what to do, and the collective wisdom is to move the ark to another Philistine city. This is interesting as it was not only the leaders of Ashdod who

---

5. Ibid., 52.

6. Klein, *1 Samuel*, 50; P. D. Miller and J. J. M. Roberts, *The Hand of the Lord: A Reassessment of the "Ark Narrative" of 1 Samuel*, JHNES (Baltimore: Johns Hopkins University Press, 1977), 49.

7. Bodner, *1 Samuel*, 53. See KJV, which renders "emerods in their secret parts" (1 Sam 5:9).

made this decision but "all the rulers of the Philistines" (5:8). This body politic would have included leaders from Gath, which was one of the biggest cities in Philistia. Perhaps they thought that the problem only lay in having the ark at Dagon's temple. They may have still thought retaining the ark would be a benefit to the nation if it were only at Gath instead of Ashdod. Either way, one gets the sense that they do not want to give up their war trophy.

Gath fared no better than Ashdod, however, with the whole city being thrown into a "great panic" and sustaining an "outbreak of tumors" (5:9). This time no national assembly is called to decide an appropriate action. Instead, Gath sends the ark to Ekron. The people of Ekron cry out in protest even as the ark is arriving, postulating that the Gathites are plotting to kill them. Therefore, they call a second national assembly with "all the rulers of the Philistines" (5:11) and demand that "the ark of the god of Israel" be sent away from Philistia, thinking that it would otherwise decimate their population.

The final verse in this chapter notes that the "outcry" of the city of Ekron "went up to heaven" (5:12). This phrase is nearly identical to the phrasing of the "outcry" of the Israelites in bondage in Egypt which similarly "went up to God" (Exod 2:23), as the following table shows.

Exodus 2:23	1 Samuel 5:12
their *cry for help* (*shavah*)	the *outcry* (*shavah*) of the city
went up (*alah*)	*went up* (*alah*)
to God	to heaven

As indicated in the table, the Hebrew terms used in each verse are identical. This leads the reader to anticipate a reaction from God in the following chapter. Given the nearly identical phrasing here as in Exodus, the similarity or dissimilarity of God's reaction may tell us something of the special place the Israelites have in God's plan.

LIVE the Story

A God of Awe-ful Power

Lest any reader think that the ark was captured due to Yahweh's powerlessness, here this chapter makes clear that nothing could be further from the truth. While the ark did not guarantee victory for the Israelites, it was still the symbol of God's presence and a sacred object through which he chose to work. Both the Israelites and the Philistines misunderstood the ark and had to find out the hard way. Israel thought bringing the ark with them to battle would bring victory as it brought God with them. The Philistines thought capturing the ark and bringing it home would either bring the power of that god under their control or that the Israelite God was defeated by their god, Dagon. Both nations suffered immensely from their trifling with the holy things of God and thinking they could control or manipulate him by doing so.

The Revelatory Purpose of the Plagues

This story of the travels of the ark underscores the mysterious power of God. In light of this dangerous power emanating from the ark, one might question why God would let the ark be captured in the first place. Surely if he can plague a nation with tumors, he could have prevented this. Israel could have still been defeated in battle to show them that God cannot be manipulated and that sin has its consequences without the ark being lost to a pagan nation. While one can never know fully the reasons for God's actions, perhaps there is a redemptive purpose in the loss of the ark to the Philistines. Through their experience with the ark the Philistines are led to know that Yahweh is *really* God. In the previous passage we saw that the Philistines had heard the story of the exodus (even if some of the details were slightly skewed) and of the plagues on the Egyptians as they said: "We're doomed! Who will deliver us from the hand of these mighty gods? They are the gods who struck the Egyptians with all kinds of plagues in the wilderness" (1 Sam 4:8). Now, due to their firsthand experience with the ark, the rumors they have heard are confirmed. There is a God in Israel, and he is real.

This purpose is very similar to the plagues of the exodus itself. Throughout the story of the exodus the plagues are not simply a punishment on the Egyptians for their enslavement of the Israelites. In fact, God explicitly states that the purpose of the plagues is revelation. The plagues are to bring knowledge of Yahweh not only to Israel but to the Egyptians as well. Consider the following verses:

Exod 6:7—God's mighty acts	"You will know that I am the LORD your God"
Exod 7:5—God's hand against Egypt	"The Egyptians will know that I am the LORD"
Exod 7:17—Plague of Nile to Blood	"By this you will know that I am the LORD"
Exod 8:10—Plague of Frogs	"So that you may know there is no one like the LORD our God"
Exod 8:22—Plague of Flies	"that you will know that I, the LORD, am in this land"

Similarly, in 1 Samuel 5 the tumors and afflictions that plague the Philistines are not God's revenge on these pagans. His purpose is not to punish them for defeating Israel or taking the ark. The purpose is that the Philistines will know him. Not knowledge based on hearsay, like they already had of the exodus—but knowledge based on their own observation and experience. In the Bible, knowledge of God means not only to have knowledge of his existence but to recognize and submit to him. In Proverbs, the "knowledge of God" is coupled with a corresponding "fear of the LORD" (cf. Prov 2:5). The plagues on the Philistines, like the plagues on the Egyptians, brought the fear of the Lord upon them (cf. 1 Sam 5:11), and the fear of the Lord is necessary for people to begin to know him (Prov 1:7; Ps 111:10).

In our contemporary culture the fear of the Lord is usually not something often talked about. Modern Christianity often talks about God's love, God as father, or God as my buddy. When contemporary praise music speaks of the Christian's relationship with God, it is often compared to a romantic relationship, with one chorus even stating, "Jesus I am so in love with you."[8] However, the analogy between a romantic relationship and relationship with God misses something. Of course, all analogies break down at some point, but there seems to be no room for "fear" in a romantic relationship. Fear of God is an integral part of our relationship with God. Loss of this aspect of relationship leads to one taking for granted their salvation. It accounts for our shallowness and the self-centeredness of our faith. Only when one remembers the holy character of God and our unholiness can we realign our thinking properly. Only when the wrath of God is remembered and his righteous, fearful judgment upon sin recalled can we have a proper perspective and understanding of life and the faith. Only then can we understand the cross of Jesus Christ and make sense of it. Lack of the fear of God leads to sinful living, selfishness, and trifling with the holy things of God.

---

8. "Let My Words Be Few," Matt Redman and Beth Redman, ThankYou Music, 2000.

LISTEN to the Story

¹When the ark of the Lᴏʀᴅ had been in Philistine territory seven months, ²the Philistines called for the priests and the diviners and said, "What shall we do with the ark of the Lᴏʀᴅ? Tell us how we should send it back to its place." ³They answered, "If you return the ark of the god of Israel, do not send it back to him without a gift; by all means send a guilt offering to him. Then you will be healed, and you will know why his hand has not been lifted from you." ⁴The Philistines asked, "What guilt offering should we send to him?" They replied, "Five gold tumors and five gold rats, according to the number of the Philistine rulers, because the same plague has struck both you and your rulers. ⁵Make models of the tumors and of the rats that are destroying the country, and give glory to Israel's god. Perhaps he will lift his hand from you and your gods and your land. ⁶Why do you harden your hearts as the Egyptians and Pharaoh did? When Israel's god dealt harshly with them, did they not send the Israelites out so they could go on their way?

⁷"Now then, get a new cart ready, with two cows that have calved and have never been yoked. Hitch the cows to the cart, but take their calves away and pen them up. ⁸Take the ark of the Lord and put it on the cart, and in a chest beside it put the gold objects you are sending back to him as a guilt offering. Send it on its way, ⁹but keep watching it. If it goes up to its own territory, toward Beth Shemesh, then the Lᴏʀᴅ has brought this great disaster on us. But if it does not, then we will know that it was not his hand that struck us but that it happened to us by chance." ¹⁰So they did this. They took two such cows and hitched them to the cart and penned up their calves. ¹¹They placed the ark of the Lord on the cart and along with it the chest containing the gold rats and the models of the tumors. ¹²Then the cows went straight up toward Beth Shemesh, keeping on the road and lowing all the way; they did not turn to the right or to the left. The rulers of the Philistines followed them as far as the border of Beth

Shemesh. [13]Now the people of Beth Shemesh were harvesting their wheat in the valley, and when they looked up and saw the ark, they rejoiced at the sight. [14]The cart came to the field of Joshua of Beth Shemesh, and there it stopped beside a large rock. The people chopped up the wood of the cart and sacrificed the cows as a burnt offering to the LORD. [15]The Levites took down the ark of the LORD, together with the chest containing the gold objects, and placed them on the large rock. On that day the people of Beth Shemesh offered burnt offerings and made sacrifices to the LORD. [16]The five rulers of the Philistines saw all this and then returned that same day to Ekron.

[17]These are the gold tumors the Philistines sent as a guilt offering to the Lord—one each for Ashdod, Gaza, Ashkelon, Gath and Ekron. [18]And the number of the gold rats was according to the number of Philistine towns belonging to the five rulers—the fortified towns with their country villages. The large rock on which the Levites set the ark of the LORD is a witness to this day in the field of Joshua of Beth Shemesh.

[19]But God struck down some of the inhabitants of Beth Shemesh, putting seventy of them to death because they looked into the ark of the LORD. The people mourned because of the heavy blow the LORD had dealt them. [20]And the people of Beth Shemesh asked, "Who can stand in the presence of the LORD, this holy God? To whom will the ark go up from here?"

[21]Then they sent messengers to the people of Kiriath Jearim, saying, "The Philistines have returned the ark of the LORD. Come down and take it up to your town."

Listen to the Text in the Story: Genesis 20; Psalm 24:3–4; Ritual against Pestilence; Pulisa's Ritual against Plague

In the ancient Near East plague and sickness were often attributed to an angered god of an enemy people. Some ancient texts describe rituals to deal with such instances, such as a text from ancient Hatti which says:

These are the words of Uhha-muwas, the Arzawa man. If people are dying in the country and if some enemy god has caused that, I act as follows: They drive up one ram. They twine together blue wool, red wool, yellow wool, black wool and white wool, make it into a crown and crown the ram with it. They drive the ram on to the road leading to the enemy and while doing so they speak as follows: "Whatever god of the enemy land has caused this plague—see! We have now driven up this crowned ram to pacify thee, O god! Just as the herd is strong, but keeps peace with the ram, do thou, the god who has caused this plague, keep peace with the Hatti land! In favor turn again toward the Hatti land!" They drive that one crowned ram toward the enemy.[1]

Similar to the story in 1 Samuel 6, in this text the ritual entails taking a chosen animal and setting it on the road leading to the land of their enemy. In the text from Hatti, the chosen ram is to be "driven" to their enemy's land, whereas in 1 Samuel 6 the cart-carrying cows make their way to Israel without being diven there (1 Sam 6:12).

EXPLAIN the Story

Having attempted political solutions to the ark problem, the Philistines now attempt a religious solution and inquire of the priests and diviners. These pagan clerics determine that the ark must be sent back to Israel with "guilt offerings" in the form of golden models of the tumors and the rats that are plaguing the Philistine cities (6:5). Furthermore, in order to confirm it was Yahweh who plagued them they place the ark on a new cart pulled by two cows who have recently calved and have never pulled a cart before. Since the cows would naturally want to go to their young to nurse, if the cows take the cart toward Israel on their own they will know it was really Yahweh behind the plagues. Amazingly, the cows proceed directly to Israel. The ark again returns to Israelite territory, though God strikes down seventy Israelites from Beth Shemesh for looking into the ark.[2] Just as the ark threatened the Philistines, so it remained a threat to Israel.

The Priestly Plan (6:1–6)

After the failure of the plan of the elders of Philistia to remedy the suffering of the Philistines by transferring the ark to other cities (1 Sam 5:8–10), the people now inquire of their religious leaders what is to be done about the ark.

---

1. "Ritual against Pestilence," *ANET*, 347; cf. "Pulisa's Ritual against Plague," trans. B. J. Collins, *COS* 1.62:161.

2. The MT and LXX both read "seventy men, fifty thousand men" but the last three words are usually omitted from translations (e.g., NIV, NRSV, RSV, NEB, NAB) as they are understood to be a gloss with an obscure function. Cf. S. R. Driver, *Notes on the Hebrew Text and the Topography of the Books of Samuel with an Introduction on Hebrew Palaeography and the Ancient Versions and Facsimiles of Inscriptions and Maps* (Oxford: Clarendon, 1913), 58; Henry Preserved Smith, *A Critical and Exegetical Commentary on the Books of Samuel* (New York: Scribner's Sons, 1904), 49. John Mauchline, *1 and 2 Samuel* (London: Oliphants, 1971), 81. McCarter, *I Samuel*, 131.

In the ancient Near East priests were trained in the treatment of sacred objects and diviners were experts in magical rites, so consulting these experts would have made sense to them. We are told that the ark had been in Philistine territory for seven months at this point, so they had been suffering for a while. Though initially resistant to giving up the ark, instead attempting to relocate their war trophy, at this point the Philistines are ready to be rid of it.

Since the Philistines had now understood that the Israelite God was behind the plague, they sought to appease this deity. The experts' recommendation is to make golden models of both the tumors and rats that plague them (6:5). (Up to this point, there has been no mention of rats, though this may support the interpretation of the tumors as buboes of bubonic plague as rats are carriers of the plague.) While the making of models of tumors and rats to send with the ark seems strange to a modern reader, in the ancient world this would have been a logical approach. An angry deity must be appeased with appropriate gifts. In this case, the religious experts decide that golden replicas of the agents of their suffering—tumors and rats—are required. This superstitious approach is sometimes called sympathetic magic, where it is thought that one can influence something based on resemblance to another thing (like the use of a doll resembling a person to affect the actual person in Voodoo).

Interestingly, the priests make reference again to the exodus story, recalling the stubbornness of the Egyptians and the hardening of their hearts in refusing to let Israel go (6:6; cf. Exod 7:14; 8:32; 9:7, 35) and encouraging the Philistines not to follow the mistakes of the Egyptians. It seems that the little revelation they did have—God's deliverance of Israel in the exodus—which they probably heard secondhand, was confirmed by these plagues. However, although they voice the message of Moses, their advice is pure pagan superstition.[3]

Sending the Ark Back (6:7–12)

With a plan in place to return the ark, a superstitious test is devised to make sure that Yahweh is behind the plagues. They yoke two cows together who have never been yoked before (i.e., they weren't used to pulling a cart) and who have recently "calved," (i.e., recently given birth) which would mean that they naturally would want to return and nurse their young. If, however, the cows do not return to their young and instead pull the cart together and head toward Israel, this would be a sign that Yahweh truly was behind the calamities. If the cows do not head to Israel, then they would "know that it was not his [Yahweh's] hand that struck us but that it happened to us by chance" (6:9).

3. Francesca Aran Murphy, *1 Samuel*, BTCB (Grand Rapids: Brazos, 2010), 47–48.

After following the instructions of their religious experts, the cows remarkably headed straight to Israelite territory (6:12). However, this was not enough to convince the Philistines, who choose to follow them until the last minute. Perhaps the Philistines were hoping it was all coincidence so that they could keep their trophy of war.

The Ark in Beth Shemesh (6:13–21)

With the Philistine leaders covertly looking on, the ark enters the Israelite town of Beth Shemesh. The Israelites living in Beth Shemesh were in their fields harvesting when they saw the ark coming toward them. The ark conveniently stops by a large rock, making it a perfect place on which to set the ark. The people then chopped up the wood of the new cart that was carrying the ark and sacrificed the cows as a burnt offering to Yahweh (6:14). At this the Philistines who had followed the cart finally returned home (6:16).

Lest this seem to be the end of the matter, the fearful power of Yahweh continues to manifest itself, this time against Israel. Seventy Israelites from Beth Shemesh look into the ark and God strikes them dead for the offense (6:19). The people of Beth Shemesh mourn these tragic deaths and ask an important question: "Who can stand in the presence of the LORD, this holy God?" (6:20). It was not only the Philistines who needed to learn about the fear of the Lord. Looking into the ark revealed that the people of Beth Shemesh did not fear God. They did not understand the sanctity of the ark any more than the Philistines did.

The Philistine character of their faith can also be seen in the conclusion to the chapter. Both Israel and Philistia tried to solve their ark problem by shipping it to another city. In this case there appears to be an element of deceit involved when they simply say to the Israelite town of Kiriath Jearim, *the ark is back, come bring it to your town!* (6:21). While what they said is technically the truth, it is obvious to the reader that some extremely important details are left out. The drive for self-preservation outweighed the principle of full disclosure. Ironically, Kiriath-Jearim itself has a history of deception, as we read in Joshua 9 of how this city was Gibeonite and only joined Israel due to their deceiving Israel. As they say, "what goes around comes around."

LIVE the Story

God's Truth Communicated to Pagans

The pagan superstitious ways of ancient diviners are displayed in this passage quite clearly. These pagan clerics use sympathetic magic in an attempt to solve their problems. They set up a "test" of their own devising in order to determine whether Israel's God really was behind the plagues. They view the deity as needing gifts to appease his wrath and provide golden idols as "guilt offerings" to that end. None of these actions are remarkable in terms of the cultural environment of the ancient Near East. It displays an approach similar to shaman and superstitious diviners of many eras. What is most surprising, however, is the way in which God works through their superstitious approaches to communicate his truth. Even though the provision of golden idols was nothing more than sympathetic magic and the "test" with the previously unyoked cows was dreamed up entirely by the pagan clerics, God responded to these actions to reveal himself.

As noted in the commentary on the previous chapter, the purpose of the plagues on Philistia—like those on the Egyptians in the time of Moses—was revelation. As we saw in 1 Samuel 4, the Philistines had heard of the exodus, even if they did not get all the details right (1 Sam 4:8). The Philistines initially thought they had defeated Yahweh, explaining why they put the ark in Dagon's temple. But when Dagon was dismembered and decapitated by the ark, this probably challenged that belief. The addition of plagues on the Philistines would have also strengthened the belief that Yahweh is not defeated at all but very much in control. Given their previous knowledge of the exodus plagues in Egypt, these plagues on Philistia would have reinforced the truth that Yahweh is very real and powerful. It was probably this realization of the truth of the exodus that led the pagan religious experts to refer to the exodus once again here in 1 Samuel 6. In fact, the pagan clerics seem to speak the voice of Moses in warning their fellow Philistines not to harden their hearts like Pharaoh and the Egyptians did but to let the ark depart just as the Egyptians finally let the Israelites leave (6:6).

Despite the fact that they were the enemy of Israel, God's chosen people, God cared to reveal himself to these Philistines. God was at work among them, and the message of the exodus proclaimed through an unlikely mouthpiece—a pagan priest. Ironically it is the pagans who seem to understand God better by the end of this story. They are the ones who reference the exodus story and its lessons.[4] The Israelites, on the other hand, do not seem to remember such lessons or to have the same fear of Yahweh, as they fearlessly look into the holy ark of the covenant at Beth Shemesh (6:19).

What is more, these pagan priests and diviners act better than the Israelite priests of the Elide house in giving honor/glory to God. In 1 Samuel 6:5 they tell the people to "give glory (*kbd*) to Israel's god." In Hebrew, this is the

---

4. Bill T. Arnold, *1 & 2 Samuel*, NIVAC (Grand Rapids: Zondervan, 2003), 124.

same root "honor/glory" (*kbd*) that has been used so frequently in these early chapters of Samuel. In 1 Samuel 2:30 God warned Eli through the anonymous prophet that "Those who honor (*kbd*) me I will honor (*kbd*), but those who despise me will be disdained." In 1 Samuel 2:29, the prophet said that Eli "honored" (*kbd*) his sons more than God. Now, ironically, we have Philistine priests telling their people to "give glory to" (*kbd*) Israel's god (1 Sam 6:5), which functions to further highlight Israel's *dis*honoring of Yahweh.

This is not the only occasion in Scripture where God reveals himself to non-Israelites. In Genesis 20 when Abraham stayed with Abimelech, king of Gerar (who is also identified as a Philistine in Gen 26:1), God appeared to the pagan king in a dream (Gen 20:3) to warn him he was about to face judgment for taking Abraham's wife, Sarah. Abimelech protests his innocence to God since Abraham told Abimilech that Sarah was only his sister (Gen 20:5). To this protestation God remarkably replies:

> Yes, I know you did this with a clear conscience, and so I have kept you from sinning against me. That is why I did not let you touch her. (Gen 20:6)

In God's reply we learn that not only was Abimelech innocent in the matter but that God was already at work in Abimelech's life and he had kept him from touching Sarah on account of his innocence.

Other examples could be cited (Hagar and Ishmael in Gen 21; Rahab in Josh 2:10) to show that God has shown concern for non-Israelites throughout history. Significantly, in these examples of God revealing himself to non-Israelites a clear distinction is made between those who are in covenant with God and those who are not. For example, in Genesis 20 Abimelech acts uprightly in contrast to the deceitful Abraham (who lies about his relationship with Sarah), yet Abimelech still must ask Abraham to pray for him in order to avoid divine curse (Gen 20:7, 20). This pericope is an example of the working out of the promises to Abraham in Genesis 12:2–3, where God says:

> I will make you into a great nation, and I will bless you; I will make your name great, and you will be a blessing. I will bless those who bless you, and whoever curses you I will curse; and all peoples on earth will be blessed through you.

Due to Abraham's status as being in covenant with Yahweh, when Abimelech "cursed" Abraham by threatening his progeny through Sarah, God cursed him. When Abimelech blessed Abraham (giving gifts, etc.), God blessed Abimelech.[5]

---

5. Joel N. Lohr, *Chosen and Unchosen: Conceptions of Election in the Pentateuch and Jewish-Christian Interpretation*, Siphrut 2 (Winona Lake, IN: Eisenbrauns, 2009), 111.

God's concern with Gentiles and his promises to Abraham find their ultimate fulfillment in Christ. Through the new covenant inaugurated by Jesus Christ, "all peoples on earth will be blessed" (Gen 12:3). Now, "those who have faith are children of Abraham" (Gal 3:7; cf. 3:29). The covenant promises to Abraham are made available to all the families of the earth through the gospel of Christ (Rom 4:16–19).

God continues to reveal himself to non-Israelites, but now, through faith, non-Israelites can become children of Abraham in covenant with God. An important example can be seen in the New Testament where we are told how God revealed himself to Cornelius, a gentile, through an angel (Acts 10:3). In this instance God instructed this non-Israelite to call for Peter, who led Cornelius and his house to the Lord (Acts 10:44–48). Through the gospel of Jesus Christ, a gentile and his household are able to come into covenant with God (cf. 1 Thess 1:9). Praise God that while once we "were separate from Christ, excluded from citizenship in Israel and foreigners to the covenants of the promise, without hope and without God in the world. But now in Christ Jesus [we] who once were far away have been brought near through the blood of Christ" (Eph 2:12–13).

Who Can Stand in the Presence of the Lord?

As noted above, when seventy citizens of Beth Shemesh die as a result of looking into the ark, the remaining citizens ask an important question: "Who can stand in the presence of the LORD, this holy God?" (1 Sam 6:20). The tragic deaths instilled the fear of Yahweh in them and led the Israelites to ask the right questions. Who indeed can stand in his presence? In Psalm 24 the psalmist asks an analogous question and provides an important answer when he writes:

> Who may ascend the mountain of the LORD? Who may stand in his holy place? The one who has clean hands and a pure heart, who does not trust in an idol or swear by a false god. (Ps 24:3–4)

According to this psalm, clean hands and purity of heart are a prerequisite for standing in God's presence. This state is further defined as not trusting in an idol or swearing "by a false god" (Ps 24:4). Interestingly, Psalm 24 is ascribed to none other than David, the one who successfully brings the ark to Jerusalem in 2 Samuel 6. Despite David's foibles, faults, and sins, he never lifts his heart to an idol. As will be explicitly seen in the next chapter, at this point in its history Israel does *not* have clean hands in this regard, as Samuel has to call Israel to put away their "foreign gods and the Ashtoreths" (1 Sam 7:3).

From this story we can see that God desires holiness from his people, not just sincere worship. This message is brought out again and again in Scripture. In Amos, we see God's opinion of worship devoid of righteousness and holiness in the lives of the worshipers. God says:

> I hate, I despise your religious festivals; Your assemblies are a stench to me. Even though you bring me burnt offerings and grain offerings, I will not accept them. Though you bring choice fellowship offerings, I will have no regard for them. Away with the noise of your songs! I will not listen to the music of your harps. But let justice roll on like a river, righteousness like a never-failing stream! (Amos 5:21–24)

Harsh words from the God of love. He "hates" their worship services when the worshipers are living lives of sin. Similar words come from the book of Ezekiel which states:

> My people come to you, as they usually do, and sit before you to listen to your words, but they do not put them into practice. Their mouths speak of love, but their hearts are greedy for unjust gain. Indeed, to them you are nothing more than one who sings love songs with a beautiful voice and who plays an instrument well, for they hear your words but do not put them into practice. (Ezek 33:31–32)

Israel had God's words through Moses. They had the presence of God symbolically represented on the holy ark of the covenant. They had the sacred history of the exodus and God's deliverance and provision of the land. Yet they did not put Moses's words into practice. They did not obey even the first of the Ten Commandments (Exod 20:3) but instead combined the worship of Yahweh with the worship of other gods.

This is ever applicable in our context in the modern church. While the church has largely left behind the old gods of gold and silver molten idols, idolatry is still with us, with many different "gods" competing for dominance in providing meaning in life, fulfillment, and security. As it is sometimes said, idols today are not so much the type on the shelf but rather on the self. A famous saying attributed to the early church father Augustine states "Idolatry is worshiping anything that ought to be used, or using anything that ought to be worshiped."[6] Sex, work, and money are three of the most prevalent idols in

---

6. Though frequently attributed as a quote from Augustine, it appears he never said exactly these words but that this popular quotation paraphrases ideas from his work "On Christian Doctrine" where he distinguishes between "use" and "enjoyment." Cf. Augustine of Hippo, "On Christian Doctrine," in *St. Augustine's City of God and Christian Doctrine*, ed. Philip Schaff, trans. J. F. Shaw, vol. 2, A Select Library of the Nicene and Post-Nicene Fathers of the Christian Church, First Series (Buffalo, NY: Christian Literature Company, 1887), 523. Peter Sanlon discusses Augustine's distinction between "enjoyment" and "use" explaining that "Augustine's insight [is] that some things are to be used as a

the Western church today. The gospel of these idols is preached in various ways under the rubrics of self-expression, self-fulfillment, and self-actualization. These doctrines encourage us to make ourselves our own god.

In the story of 1 Samuel 6 God begins to bring his people back to whole-hearted worship through instilling the fear of God into them. In the next chapter, we will see that in response to the prophetic word delivered by Samuel, the people eventually do put away their idols and return to worshiping God alone.

Those of us who are Christians must pray that God would show us our idols. But through the conviction of the Holy Spirit, whether through the pricking of the conscience or tragic events, when a Christian realizes their idols, they must be dealt with. How? Deuteronomy provides some answers.

> This is what you are to do to them: Break down their altars, smash their sacred stones, cut down their Asherah poles, and burn their idols in the fire. (Deut 7:5)

> Break down their altars, smash their sacred stones and burn their Asherah poles in the fire; cut down the idols of their gods and wipe out their name from those places. (Deut 12:3)

The message here is to take radical action. Do not leave an idol standing (cf. 1 John 5:21). The good news is that as the Christian tears down the idols in their lives,

> They will receive blessing from the LORD and vindication from God their Savior. Such is the generation of those who seek him, who seek your face, God of Jacob. (Ps 24:5–6)

---

means and others are to be loved in themselves. In other words, God is not to be reduced to the same level as the creation, and creation is not to be enjoyed without due reference to God" (Peter Sanlon, "An Augustinian Mindset," *Themelios* 33 [2008]: 41–42).

LISTEN to the Story

¹So the men of Kiriath Jearim came and took up the ark of the LORD. They brought it to Abinadab's house on the hill and consecrated Eleazar his son to guard the ark of the LORD. ²The ark remained at Kiriath Jearim a long time—twenty years in all.

Then all the people of Israel turned back to the LORD. ³So Samuel said to all the Israelites, "If you are returning to the LORD with all your hearts, then rid yourselves of the foreign gods and the Ashtoreths and commit yourselves to the LORD and serve him only, and he will deliver you out of the hand of the Philistines." ⁴So the Israelites put away their Baals and Ashtoreths, and served the LORD only.

⁵Then Samuel said, "Assemble all Israel at Mizpah, and I will intercede with the LORD for you." ⁶When they had assembled at Mizpah, they drew water and poured it out before the LORD. On that day they fasted and there they confessed, "We have sinned against the LORD." Now Samuel was serving as leader of Israel at Mizpah.

⁷When the Philistines heard that Israel had assembled at Mizpah, the rulers of the Philistines came up to attack them. When the Israelites heard of it, they were afraid because of the Philistines. ⁸They said to Samuel, "Do not stop crying out to the LORD our God for us, that he may rescue us from the hand of the Philistines." ⁹Then Samuel took a suckling lamb and sacrificed it as a whole burnt offering to the LORD. He cried out to the LORD on Israel's behalf, and the LORD answered him.

¹⁰While Samuel was sacrificing the burnt offering, the Philistines drew near to engage Israel in battle. But that day the LORD thundered with loud thunder against the Philistines and threw them into such a panic that they were routed before the Israelites. ¹¹The men of Israel rushed out of Mizpah and pursued the Philistines, slaughtering them along the way to a point below Beth Kar.

[12]Then Samuel took a stone and set it up between Mizpah and Shen. He named it Ebenezer, saying, "Thus far the LORD has helped us."

[13]So the Philistines were subdued and they stopped invading Israel's territory. Throughout Samuel's lifetime, the hand of the LORD was against the Philistines. [14]The towns from Ekron to Gath that the Philistines had captured from Israel were restored to Israel, and Israel delivered the neighboring territory from the hands of the Philistines. And there was peace between Israel and the Amorites.

[15]Samuel continued as Israel's leader all the days of his life. [16]From year to year he went on a circuit from Bethel to Gilgal to Mizpah, judging Israel in all those places. [17]But he always went back to Ramah, where his home was, and there he also held court for Israel. And he built an altar there to the LORD.

Listen to the Text in the Story: Exodus 2:23; 32:11–13; Luke 19:1–10; Acts 26:20; A Hymn to Baal; Poems about Baal and Anat; Babylonian Libation Prayer

Baal was one of the most popular gods in Canaanite religion and mythology. In ancient Ugaritic texts Baal is described as sitting "enthroned like the sitting of a mountain . . . In the midst of his mountain, the divine Zaphon, On his [pleasant] mountain of victory. Seven lightnings [are in his hand], Eight storehouses of thunder—The shaft of lightning he [brandishes]."[1] Baal was the storm god often referred to as the "rider on the clouds."[2] As the bringer of rain, Baal was a fertility god who was believed to bring fertility to the land in the spring when he rose from the underworld but would then die in winter. Often in Scripture, reference is made to Baal in the plural (Baals or Baalim), not to indicate multiple gods named Baal, but to refer to the varied ways in which Baal was manifested in different localities.[3] Since Israelites lived in a land dependent on rain for the fertility of its crops, the worship of the fertility god Baal was the most enduring temptation for Israel (cf. Num 25:1–9; Deut 4:3; Ps 106:28; Hos 9:10).

Another pagan deity referred to in this chapter is Ashtoreth, which is actually a plural form of the name of a goddess called Astarte (Hebrew=*ashtoreth*). In Canaanite mythology, Astarte was a consort of the god Baal. The singular

---

1. Jack M. Sasson, *CANE*, 4 vols. (New York: Scribner's Sons, 1995), 4:2053–54.
2. E.g., "Poems about Baal and Anat" *ANET*, 130.
3. Day, "Baal," *ABD* 1:547.

form of the goddess' name is rarely used in Scripture (1 Kgs 11:5; 2 Kgs 23:13). The use of the term in the plural probably is due to the many different ways in which she is represented in different localities (cf. Judg 2:13; 10:6; 1 Kgs 11:5; 2 Kgs 23:13).[4] The vocalization of the name as Ashtoreth is likely due to the biblical author's replacing the actual vowels of the name with the vowels for the Hebrew word "shame" (Hebrew=*bosheth*) in order to disparage the false god Astarte. (See later discussion in commentary on 2 Sam 2:8 and 4:4).

The reference in 1 Samuel 6:6 to the pouring out of water before Yahweh is unparalleled in biblical literature. There is no priestly legislation in this regard, and nowhere else in the Old Testament does such a ritual occur. Pagan rituals of pouring out water were often for the dead or done to ward off evil spirits. For example, an ancient Babylonian text describes the worshiper as "pouring out water" to their god "for the family of Sin-nasir" so that in the afterlife the family "may eat his bread and drink his water."[5] However, given the context of the ritual in the Babylonian text, this parallel doesn't help explain the significance of the water pouring in 1 Samuel 6. Other instances in the ancient Near East concern the offering of water to the gods as a drink (similar to the way sacrifices were thought to feed the gods).[6] While this is unlikely to be the meaning of the practice here in 1 Samuel 6, its origins may have been in libation ritual practices of Israel's ancient neighbors. As Long notes, "In Israel . . . such practices appear to have been emptied of their literal significance even while being retained as ritual features."[7]

EXPLAIN the Story

As the last chapter ended with a call to the town of Kiriath Jearim to come take up the ark, so this chapter begins with them doing just that. They station the ark at Abinadab's house where it remains for two decades. As a result of the events surrounding the capture and return of the ark, however, Israel finally turns back to God (1 Sam 7:2). Under Samuel's leadership they put away their idols (7:4), confess their sin (7:6), and repent. Subsequently, the Philistines again move to attack Israel, but in response to Samuel's intercession God throws the enemy into a panic with "loud thunder" (7:10). The result is

---

4. Day, "Ashtoreth," *ABD* 1:492–94.

5. J. N. Postgate, *Early Mesopotamia: Society and Economy at the Dawn of History* (London; New York: Routledge, 1992), 100.

6. Sarah Iles Johnston, *Religions of the Ancient World: A Guide* (Cambridge, MA: Harvard University Press, 2004), 331–32.

7. V. Philips Long, "1 Samuel," in *Zondervan Illustrated Bible Backgrounds Commentary: Old Testament: Volume 2, Joshua, Judges, Ruth, 1 and 2 Samuel*, ed. John Walton (Grand Rapids: Zondervan, 2009), 304.

a great victory over the Philistines, the likes of which continued throughout Samuel's tenure as Israel's leader (7:15).

The Ark in Kiriath Jearim (7:1–2)

In response to the request of the people of Beth Shemesh (6:21), the men of Kiriath Jearim collect the ark from Beth Shemesh, installing it at the house of Abinadab. Not wanting to have the tragic events of Beth Shemesh repeated in their town, they set apart Abinadab's son to guard the ark. The word "guard" in Hebrew (*shmr*) can have both meanings of liturgical service (like that of a priest) or actual guarding, as in keeping others away (like that of a palace guard). Perhaps there is a double meaning here as having Eleazer "on guard" would likely prevent others from curiously peering into the ark, but doubtless Eleazer is meant to be taking care of the ark as a sacred object as well. Given that we are then told that the ark remained in Kiriath Jearim for two decades and no further casualties are mentioned, we can assume that Eleazer performed his duties well. The ark remains in this backwater Gibeonite town until eventually David brings it to his new capital of Jerusalem (2 Sam 6). In the meantime, the effect of the terrors of the ark is the return of Israel to their God.

Israel's Return to Yahweh (7:3–6)

Once again Samuel returns to the story after his noticeable absence in the story of the journeys of the ark. Seeing the people of Israel finally returning to the Lord, Samuel instructs them what they need to do. They must stop their pagan worship and get rid of their false gods, "their Baals and Ashtoreths" (v. 4). After Israel obeys Samuel's commands, the prophet assembles all Israel together and intercedes for them. At Mizpah "they drew water" from a well and "poured it out before the LORD" (7:6). As noted in the Listen to the Story section, this is a unique ritual in the Old Testament, and ancient Near Eastern parallels are not helpful here. Given that the context is repentance, perhaps the significance is that pouring out the life sustaining water was to show that they rely on God wholly. This would be similar to fasting (which the Israelites also do here in 7:6), where one gives up normal nourishment to focus on God. Though we may not know the exact significance of the ritual, it is clear that Israel repented and confessed their sin at Mizpah.

Rematch with the Philistines (7:7–17)

When the Philistines hear that Israel had assembled they set out to attack. Despite the difficulties the Philistines had with the ark, they had handily won the previous battle with Israel and were the dominant power in the region.

All Israel assembling together would have been interpreted as an act of rebellion or preparation for war. The Israelites are understandably afraid at the advance of the enemy (7:7). This time, with no ark to rely upon for help, they plead with Samuel to cry out to Yahweh for their deliverance. It would appear that Israel learned its lesson. They have repented of their sin and now rely wholly on God for deliverance. They implore Samuel to "not stop crying out" to God, (7:8) and Samuel sacrifices a lamb before "he cried out to the LORD" for Israel (7:9). This "crying out" to God reminds us of the "outcry" of the Philistines that reaches heaven in 1 Samuel 5:12. However, we do not read of God responding directly to the Philistine outcry in any way. Here in this chapter, God answers the cry of his prophet Samuel.

God sends thunder against the enemy and the Philistines panic. The use of thunder in this context may be significant, given the Israelites recent turning away from Baal (v. 4). As noted in the Listen to the Story section, Baal was believed to be the storm god who was in control of rain, thunder, and lightning, so Yahweh's use of thunder here could be sending a message to Israel that Baal is no god at all. Yahweh, not Baal, controls thunder.

The Philistines are routed by the Israelites and Samuel memorialized the victory by setting up a stone and naming it Ebenezer—literally "stone of help." Interestingly, the memorial does not presume upon God's deliverance or suggest that God is on their side from now on. Instead, the stone is named Ebenezer because "thus far the LORD has helped us" (7:12). This shows some change of attitude since the previous battle where they presumed upon God's deliverance due to the presence of the ark. Now they are just acknowledging God's deliverance thus far and not presuming upon his unconditional defense of Israel. A further significance of the name Ebenezer is that it is the name of the location of the last tragic battle with the Philistines (1 Sam 4:1; 5:1). While these two battles clearly have two different locations, the naming of this stone at the site of the victorious battle with the same name as the site of battle they had previously lost is obviously intentional. It is as if this new victory reverses the earlier defeat.

This part of the story concludes by noting the Philistine threat had been dealt with (7:13). In fact, we are told that this situation continued throughout Samuel's tenure as Israel's leader. What is more, Israel recovered cites they had previously lost to the Philistines and even had peace with the Amorites. Similar to the end of chapter 3, which noted Samuel's establishment as a prophet (3:20–21), this chapter concludes noting Samuel's establishment as Israel's leader.

It must be pointed out that the statement that "[t]hroughout Samuel's lifetime, the hand of the LORD was against the Philistines" (1 Sam 7:13) seems somewhat odd in light of the many battles with the Philistines that occur within Samuel's lifetime during Saul's reign (e.g., 1 Sam 10:5; 13:3). However, the statement may be emphasizing that this was the situation in Israel while Samuel led them as judge, but when Saul was king things changed. This summary statement of Samuel's judgeship directly contrasts with the characterization of Saul's reign in 1 Samuel 14:52, as can be seen in a literal translation given in the table below.

1 Samuel 7:13	1 Samuel 14:52
"all the days of Samuel"	"all the days of Saul"
"the hand of the LORD was against the Philistines"	"there was bitter war with the Philistines"

This juxtaposition does not speak well of Saul's effectiveness as ruler. Furthermore, noting the military dominance of Israel under Samuel and the peace his leadership established puts the people's request for a king in the next chapter in an interesting light. The people demand a king despite the lack of a military threat.

 LIVE the Story

The Need for Evidence of Repentance
After the ark is settled in Kiriath Jearim the Israelites are said to "turn back" to the Lord (7:2). The Hebrew word (*nhh*) in this verse translated "turned back" in the NIV is elsewhere rendered "wail" or "lament" (the NIV 1984 translated the phrase as "Israel mourned and sought after the LORD"). While lamentation, wailing, and seeking the Lord are all integral parts of repairing the broken relationship with their God, more tangible actions are also required. Samuel directs Israel toward necessary concrete actions. In some real sense, the lamentation of Israel in 7:2 showed their faith and sorrow, but not until they obey Samuel's instructions do we truly see biblical repentance. Emotion is not repentance. Sorrow in itself is not repentance. As Paul writes, "Godly sorrow brings repentance that leads to salvation" but not all sorrow; as Paul explains, "worldly sorrow brings death" (2 Cor 7:10).

Biblical repentance is a turning *away* from sin and turning *toward* God in obedience. The Hebrew word most often used to express repentance in the Old Testament is the verb *shub*, "to return." Used literally it means to turn around or turn back and usually is used in contexts of actual movement from one physical place to another. When used metaphorically, it refers to repentance from sin. In other words, repentance is not just sorrow or the feeling of regret. Repentance involves action. It requires turning away from actions, words, or beliefs that are offensive to God (cf. Jer 4:1; Ezek 14:6).

In the New Testament the Greek verb *metanoein*, "to change one's mind," is usually used for repentance. This indicates a change in a person's character, outlook, and temperament: a change of mind regarding one's sin and a change of mind in regard to what God demands of the sinner. It involves a mental transformation but does not end there. Like the Old Testament view of repentance as involving action, the changing of one's mind must result in tangible changes. As John the Baptizer said, "Produce fruit in keeping with repentance" (Matt 3:8). Similarly, Paul says he "preached that they should repent and turn to God and prove their repentance by their deeds" (Acts 26:20; cf. Jas 2:17).

Biblical repentance leading to salvation is illustrated memorably in Luke 19. When Jesus comes to the house of Zacchaeus, the people grumbled that Jesus was associating with a "sinner" (Luke 19:7). But then Zacchaeus states "Look, Lord! Here and now I give half of my possessions to the poor; and if I have cheated anybody of anything, I will pay back four times the amount" (Luke 19:8). Even though we don't read of Zacchaeus repenting through prayer, Jesus responds to Zacchaeus's actions by declaring, "Today salvation has come to this house" (Luke 19:9). His repentance was evident in his actions.

It is important to remember the central place of repentance in the gospel message. Hebrews 6:1 states that "repentance from acts that lead to death" is its "foundation." The story of the Israelites' repentance in 1 Samuel 7 can serve as a reminder of what biblical repentance truly is: faith in action—turning *away* from sin and turning *to* God.

The Cry That Is Answered

As noted last chapter, the Philistines' "outcry" due to the calamities brought by the ark is said to reach heaven (1 Sam 5:12). In the commentary on chapter 5 we noted that a nearly identical expression is used of Israel in bondage in Egypt (Exod 2:23). Yet God responds to Israel's cry but not to the Philistine cry. In Exodus it is clear that the response to Israel's cry is based on his covenant with their forefathers, as frequent reference to them is made (Exod 3:6, 15, 16). God responds to his people out of covenant loyalty—promises he made to Abraham and his offspring. He had no such covenant with Philistia.

In 1 Samuel 7, Israel "cries" once again to God (7:2). This time Israel shows their covenant loyalty to God through their repentance and forsaking their idols (7:4), thus fulfilling their obligations in this regard (cf. Exod 20:3–4). Therefore, Israel's cry to Yahweh was not just a cry of anguish (like the Philistine cry in 1 Sam 5:12), but a cry of desperate reliance on Yahweh alone.

No other gods are appealed to. No human means of victory are relied upon. No strategies of war or defense are drawn up. No religious relic is brought to the battlefield. The weapon of their warfare is prayer. Israel only appeals to Samuel, their spiritual leader and mediator, to "cry" to God on their behalf, much like Moses interceded for Israel (Exod 32:11–13). As James would later state: "The prayer of a righteous person is powerful and effective" (Jas 5:16), so God responds to Samuel's prayer. God is faithful to his covenant and responds to the needs of his people.

But we must not forget the lessons Israel learned from their earlier battle with the Philistines (1 Sam 4). God cannot be manipulated. God cannot be coerced into aiding Israel. So, we must avoid thinking of prayer in similarly magical terms. God is faithful and acts for his people, but his people cannot manipulate God through prayer. As Brueggemann writes of this story "The decisive answer of Yahweh to Samuel's prayer is not an automatic reaction to predictable religious gesture."[8] God is sovereign and will not be manipulated. While the Bible unashamedly speaks about the effectiveness and necessity of prayer, our petitions to God do not obligate him to answer in the way that we see fit. We are in the position to cry out to God and petition him, but the answer is up to him. When we pray we leave the rest up to God.

Nevertheless, from this story we again see how vitally important prayer is. It may have seemed absurd to some on that day with the Philistines closing in. Rather than plan military strategy, Israel instead simply "cried out" to their God. How many times in our lives have we forgot to pray and instead attempted to rely on our own wits and talents to succeed?

Often we forget to pray when we forget how reliant upon God we really are. When we think we have it all together, we forget that every good thing we have is from God (Jas 1:17). Then when things get rough, we forget to turn to the only One who can save us. In other words, our own misguided self-sufficiency ironically results in insufficient results. When we acknowledge our insufficiency and appeal to our Creator, he may act in all-sufficient ways.

---

8. Walter Brueggemann, *First and Second Samuel*, Interpretation (Louisville: John Knox, 1990), 53.

LISTEN to the Story

¹When Samuel grew old, he appointed his sons as Israel's leaders. ²The name of his firstborn was Joel and the name of his second was Abijah, and they served at Beersheba. ³But his sons did not follow his ways. They turned aside after dishonest gain and accepted bribes and perverted justice.

⁴So all the elders of Israel gathered together and came to Samuel at Ramah. ⁵They said to him, "You are old, and your sons do not follow your ways; now appoint a king to lead us, such as all the other nations have."

⁶But when they said, "Give us a king to lead us," this displeased Samuel; so he prayed to the LORD. ⁷And the LORD told him: "Listen to all that the people are saying to you; it is not you they have rejected, but they have rejected me as their king. ⁸As they have done from the day I brought them up out of Egypt until this day, forsaking me and serving other gods, so they are doing to you. ⁹Now listen to them; but warn them solemnly and let them know what the king who will reign over them will claim as his rights."

¹⁰Samuel told all the words of the LORD to the people who were asking him for a king. ¹¹He said, "This is what the king who will reign over you will claim as his rights: He will take your sons and make them serve with his chariots and horses, and they will run in front of his chariots. ¹²Some he will assign to be commanders of thousands and commanders of fifties, and others to plow his ground and reap his harvest, and still others to make weapons of war and equipment for his chariots. ¹³He will take your daughters to be perfumers and cooks and bakers. ¹⁴He will take the best of your fields and vineyards and olive groves and give them to his attendants. ¹⁵He will take a tenth of your grain and of your vintage and give it to his officials and attendants. ¹⁶Your male and female servants and the best of your cattle and donkeys he will take for his own use. ¹⁷He will take a tenth of your flocks, and you yourselves will become his slaves. ¹⁸When that day

comes, you will cry out for relief from the king you have chosen, but the
LORD will not answer you in that day."

[19]But the people refused to listen to Samuel. "No!" they said. "We want
a king over us. [20]Then we will be like all the other nations, with a king to
lead us and to go out before us and fight our battles."

[21]When Samuel heard all that the people said, he repeated it before
the LORD. [22]The LORD answered, "Listen to them and give them a king."

Then Samuel said to the Israelites, "Everyone go back to your own
town."

Listen to the Text in the Story: Deuteronomy 10:17; 16:19; 17; 18:1–8;
Exodus 3:1–22; Numbers 20:1–13; Instructions to Commanders of
Border Garrisons

The taking of bribes to pervert justice is a serious indictment against Samuel's
sons (1 Sam 8:3). Deuteronomy 16:19 commands "Do not pervert justice
or show partiality. Do not accept a bribe." Similarly, in Deuteronomy 10:17
Moses praises God as the "great God, mighty and awesome, who shows no
partiality and accepts no bribes." Of course, this condemnation of the taking
of bribes is not unique to Israel but has clear parallels in ancient Near Eastern texts. For example, an ancient Hittite text contains royal instructions to
"border governors" to judge "properly and make things right. . . . Let no one
take a bribe. He is not to make the stronger case the weaker, or the weaker the
stronger one. Do what (is) just."[1] The actions of Samuel's sons in accepting
bribes and withholding justice are serious offenses that rightly have angered
the Israelites, leading them to demand a change to the situation.

EXPLAIN the Story

Following the positive big-picture summary of Samuel's judgeship that concluded the last chapter, the text now slows down to highlight some other
important aspects of Samuel's judgeship and an unforeseen turn of events.
First, Samuel appoints his sons as his successors, a strange move, as prophets
and judges are God-appointed, not hereditary offices like those of priests or
kings. Second, his sons were corrupt judges and took bribes. This leads the
elders of Israel to demand that Samuel appoint a king to lead them. Samuel

---

1. "Instructions to Commanders of Border Garrisons" trans. B. McMahon, *COS* 1.84:221–25.

is deeply offended by this request, but God assures him it is not Samuel they are rejecting but God. What is more, God commands Samuel to give them a king. While Samuel proceeds to warn the people that a king would cause hardship for them (and seems to be trying to dissuade them from their request), the people have made up their mind and God is willing to grant their request. Things have irrevocably changed. Israel is going to have a king "such as all the other nations" (8:5).

Samuel's Sons (8:1–3)

After the thoroughly positive review of Samuel's leadership career that concluded the last chapter, Samuel's move to appoint his sons as Israel's leaders is somewhat surprising. While priestly roles were hereditary and dependent upon being a member of the tribe of Levi (Deut 18:1–8), the roles of both judges and prophets were not. Judges were appointed by God in times of need (Judg 2:16). Prophets were called by God directly (e.g., Exod 3:1–22; Amos 7:14–15; Jer 1:4–10). Having a son lead in place of his father is actually characteristic of a monarchy, which normally involved dynastic succession through one family line (cf. Deut 17:20). Samuel's actions here are closer to that of a king than a prophet or judge, giving some insight into why he took offense at the request for a king.

While installing his own sons in roles that normally depend upon God's initiative is troublesome enough, the fact that Samuel's sons are corrupt judges makes matters even worse. This is the first hint that Samuel is a more complex character than has been revealed thus far in the story. Though the big-picture assessment of his prophetic career was positive, in the following story the narrator is going to bring out other aspects of his character. Like the judges before him, his character is not pristine but infected with some selfishness and pride, which, as we will see, is a catalyst in some important events to follow.

We are told that these things happened in Samuel's old age (8:1), which provides an interesting parallel with Samuel's mentor, Eli, whose sons were corrupt in his old age as well (1 Sam 2:22). As we will recall, the corruption of Eli's sons merited prophetic indictments and resulted in the loss of the ark and defeat by the Philistines (1 Sam 4). Here the corruption of Samuel's sons leads the elders of Israel to demand a king.

The Demand for a King (8:4–22)

The elders of Israel are fed up with Samuel's sons' corrupt ways and realize that Samuel is rapidly aging. In their mind, this necessitates a change. Given their cultural environment, with all the "other nations" (8:5) having kings who lead them, the demand for a king makes sense. However, Israel is not to be just like all the "other nations." Instead, God had declared that Israel was to be "high above all the nations" (Deut 26:19). One thing that made Israel unique was that Yahweh was their king. This principle can be seen in the story of Gideon in Judges 8 when the people ask him to rule over them but he demurs, saying "I will not rule over you, nor will my son rule over you. The LORD will rule over you" (Judg 8:23). A picture of Yahweh as Israel's king can be seen earlier in our story when it stated that Yahweh was "enthroned between the cherubim" (1 Sam 4:4) on the ark (cf. 2 Sam 6:2; 22:11; 1 Chr 13:6; Pss 18:11; 80:2; 99:1). The situation in Israel is sometimes called a theocracy instead of a monarchy; that is, instead of a monarch on the throne, God (*theos*) was on the throne.

When Samuel hears the request for a king to "lead" them, he takes it personally. The text says this thing "displeased Samuel" (8:6). Literally in Hebrew this verse says, "this thing was evil in Samuel's eyes." This is a strong statement. In some ways taking this as a personal affront is understandable. First, when the people request a king to "lead" them, literally in Hebrew the text says "a king to *judge* them"—yet Samuel and his sons are the ones in the role of judge at present. Samuel is deeply offended and takes the request as a rejection of his role as their leader. This personal affront taken by Samuel is a hint that he is not without faults of his own. Not only are his sons judging corruptly (and he either did not realize it or has done nothing about it), but he also was holding to his power and influence more dearly than he should have.

God assures the prophet that he is not being rejected by the people—they are rejecting God's kingship over them. Interestingly, God does not seem to take the same amount of offense to the request as does Samuel. God quickly decides to accede to their request and agrees to grant them a human king. God does not seem to be as taken off guard by this request as is the prophet. God explains to Samuel that this is par for the course with his people. Ever since delivering them in the exodus, they continually forsook him and followed false gods (8:8). So, their wanting a king to rule in place of God is not surprising.

Of course, the law of Moses already anticipated this turn of events and gave specific instructions in this regard. Deuteronomy 17:14–15 reads:

> When you enter the land the LORD your God is giving you and have taken possession of it and settled in it, and you say, "Let us set a king over us like all the nations around us," be sure to appoint over you the king the LORD your God chooses.

Samuel, as prophet and judge in Israel, should have known this legislation. Perhaps he did but did not see this happening during his tenure as Israel's leader. Whether he knew of it or not, his deep offense at the request gives us a glimpse into a self-interested side of his character.

Although acceding to the people's request, God commands Samuel to "warn" the people what the ways of the king will be like (8:9). Samuel proceeds to do just that. Having a king will require a large entourage and workforce. Furthermore, a monarchy will cost the people monetarily (fields, tithes), both to provide for the king himself and for his officials (8:14–15).

Samuel goes even further to say that a king will, in fact, enslave the entire population (8:17)! Samuel then warns the people "you will cry out for relief from the king you have chosen, but the LORD will not answer you in that day" (8:18). At this point one wonders whether this was what God intended him to say. Will the king really enslave all Israel? Will they cry out to God but God will not listen? Clearly Samuel is attempting to dissuade them from requesting a king. This is confirmed by the people's reaction in the next verse, "But the people refused to listen to Samuel. 'No!' they said. 'We want a king over us.'" (8:19). Remember that God did not say "talk the people out of this" or "tell them how terrible it will be so they will change their mind about the request." Samuel, however, seems bent on talking the people out of their decision, while God had already agreed to it.

Some of what the prophet warns them is to be expected of a king (a king cannot rule without officials, armies, tithes, etc.). It is only in the concluding remarks that Samuel appears to go too far in claiming that the king will enslave them and that God will not answer them. This would seem to imply that God is the one who has taken such great offense at the request.

After Samuel's warning God simply tells him, "Listen to them and give them a king" (8:22). Surprisingly, in response to God's command, Samuel's immediate response is to send everyone back home (8:22). Does this show some reluctance in the prophet in following God's command? He does not tell the people what God said ("give them a king"). God said nothing about sending the people away. Perhaps Samuel's own offense and frustration at the request is coming to the fore in this action.

Talk of the faulty character of a prophet can strike a believer the wrong way at first blush. However, the text has already prepared us for this. First, at the beginning of the chapter we already were informed that Samuel had appointed his sons as his successors, in spite of the fact that the roles of prophet and judge are not dynastic or passed on through family lines (like that of a king). This could be a hint of why Samuel is so offended by the request for a king. Samuel somehow thought he had established a dynasty that would lead Israel for years to come. Second, we are told that Samuel's own sons were corrupt (8:3). We are not told what Samuel did about this or even whether he was aware of the problem. Did he, like Eli, know of his sons' sins and turn a blind eye? Or was he unaware? Both undermine his credibility to some extent. Samuel was the "judge" of Israel, but was he unable to judge his own sons? Samuel was the "seer" or "prophet" in Israel, but was he unable to see the sin of his own sons?

Samuel, of course, would not be the first judge to have subtle or even glaring flaws. One only has to read the book of Judges to see that most of the judges had problems. Gideon brought deliverance to Israel but was clearly of weak faith, demanding signs and reassurances from God (6:17; 6:36–37a) before he would obey. In fact, in the end Gideon turns to idolatry and leads Israel astray (Judg 8:27). Samson was judge over Israel, but clearly he had little interest in anything but foreign women (cf. Judg 14:1–3; 16:1, 4). He too brought some deliverance to Israel, but his character flaws are manifest throughout his story. Finally, Eli is said to have "led (literally *judged*) Israel forty years" (4:18), but his character flaws are evident (see commentary on chs. 1–4). Should character flaws in Samuel really be so surprising?

Even the prophet *par excellence*, Moses, took matters into his own hands due to his frustrations with the people when they challenged his leadership. In Numbers 20, the Israelites complained bitterly to Moses about the lack of drinking water available in the desert. They said: "Why did *you* bring the LORD's community into this wilderness, that we and our livestock should die here? Why did *you* bring us up out of Egypt to this terrible place?" (Num 20:4–5, emphasis added). When Moses brought this complaint to God, similar to the story here in 1 Samuel 8, God shows no sign of being offended at the Israelites. Instead he simply commands Moses, "Speak to that rock before their eyes and it will pour out its water. You will bring water out of the rock for the community so they and their livestock can drink" (Num 20:8). Moses proceeds to first scold the people, "Listen, you rebels, must we bring you water out of this rock?" (Num 20:10), then he struck the rock with his staff, and water flowed out (Num 20:11). Moses's actions not only fail to follow God's command exactly (he was told to speak to the rock, not strike it), but he also makes it sound like he is the one bringing the water out when he says, "must *we* bring you water out of this rock?" (Num. 20:10, emphasis added).

This incident has many parallels with the story in 1 Samuel 8. God commands Samuel to tell the people the ways of the king, but Samuel seems to go even further and tries to convince the people not to have a king. God commands Samuel to set a king over them, but Samuel does not tell the people God's answer and instead sends the people home. In both instances the prophets have obviously taken offense at the challenge to their leadership and shown their (understandable) frustration in their actions. In both instances God's prophets seem to have taken more offense than God to the people's words.

LIVE the Story

Qualities of Spiritual Leaders

This story speaks to the high calling of being a spiritual leader. While God worked mightily through Samuel and established him as his prophet (1 Sam 3:21), here in 1 Samuel 8 we begin to see some weakness in the prophet. First, Samuel's flawed perspective is seen, since in his old age he appoints his sons as his successors. It may seem a reasonable move at the human level, but Samuel's roles of both judge and prophet of Israel are ones appointed by God alone (cf. Judg 2:16; Exod 3:1–22; Amos 7:14–15; Jer 1:4–10). Second, we see that, like Eli's sons, Samuel's sons are corrupt and abuse the power of their position. Again, two issues come to the fore: the problem of the abuse of power and the high calling of spiritual leadership. Regarding the abuse of power, in the case of Eli and his sons, they abused the priestly role, taking the best of the sacrificial meat for themselves, and, in Eli's sons' case, committing immoral sexual acts with women who served in the temple (1 Sam 2:15–16, 22). In the case of Samuel, his sons are corrupt judges, taking bribes and perverting justice for their own gain (1 Sam 8:3). (For more on abuse of power see Live the Story in 1 Sam 2.)

In both the case of Eli and Samuel, their sons' actions reflect poorly on them. Given that both are in positions of spiritual leadership, this should not be surprising. In the New Testament, Paul asserts that a spiritual leader "must manage his own family well and see that his children obey him, and he must do so in a manner worthy of full respect. (If anyone does not know how to manage his own family, how can he take care of God's church?)" (1 Tim 3:4–5). While the behavior of children is due to their own personal sin, a disobedient child can also be the result of a permissive parent. Samuel appointed his children to their positions (1 Sam 8:1), adding to his responsibility for their actions.

These portrayals of children who turn away from faithfulness to God is in direct contrast to the emphasis placed in Israel on bringing up children in the faith. Deuteronomy reiterates the importance of teaching the faith to your children. For example, Deuteronomy 6:7 commands, "Impress them on your children. Talk about them when you sit at home and when you walk along the road, when you lie down and when you get up." Similarly, Deuteronomy 11:19 reiterates, "Teach them to your children, talking about them when you sit at home and when you walk along the road, when you lie down and when you get up" (cf. Deut 4:9, 10; 6:2, 20–21; 30:2; 31:13). Given that the story of Israel's history found in Joshua–2 Kings is clearly written in light of and greatly influenced by Deuteronomy, it is not surprising that the issue of faithful and faithless sons continues to be highlighted by the Historian.

Power Corrupts

Lord Acton's adage is well known: "All power tends to corrupt; absolute power corrupts absolutely." Here in this passage we see Samuel's sons allowing their power as judge to corrupt them by taking bribes and perverting justice for their own gain. While Samuel did not partake in such corruption but served God faithfully, here in this chapter we see the subtle temptations of power manifest in Samuel as well. Samuel was in a position of authority, but the authority was granted to the end of serving God by leading his people. Once God granted the people's request to give them a king, a servant leader should have stepped aside and allowed God's will to be done. But not Samuel. He was personally affronted by the request, but not because Samuel was wicked. He was not. As the previous chapter noted (1 Sam 7), Samuel was a faithful servant of God. Probably on this basis he rationalized his wish to keep his power as "what was best" for Israel. However, possibly subconsciously, for Samuel power had become an end in itself, as we can see by how Samuel failed to take God's word as priority. God twice declared that he would install a king, yet Samuel continued in his opposition to God's plan and attempted to talk the people out of their decision.

If the seductive nature of power can be a temptation for Samuel, we too are susceptible. For any who wield some form of power or influence, there is a danger that power can become an end in itself instead of a means to an end. Anyone in a role of some kind of authority is susceptible: parents, bosses, or anyone in a leadership role, including those in spiritual leadership. As was probably the case with Samuel, this can happen subtly without one realizing it is happening. Charles Colson writes of his involvement in the US government and his transition from seeing power as merely a means to an end to it becoming an end in itself. He writes:

> I entered government believing that public office was a trust, a duty. Gradually, imperceptibly, I began to view it as a holy crusade; the future of the republic, or so I rationalized, depended upon the president's continuation in office. But whether I acknowledged it or not, equally important was the fact that my own power depended upon it.[2]

Colson found this concern with his own power only subtly grew. He rationalized the need for power by viewing it as necessary to effect positive change. But gradually his fondness of his own power led to power becoming an end in itself.

Christian leaders today are just as susceptible to the lure of power as were spiritual leaders of the past. In fact, these temptations are not limited to leaders

---

2. Charles W. Colson, "The Power Illusion," in *Power Religion*, ed. M. Horton (Chicago: Moody Press, 1992), 26.

of mega-churches or television ministries, though the corruption of some such leaders is well known. Ministers of smaller ministries are also susceptible to the allure of power and notoriety. Pastors often become the subject of public adoration or come to be viewed as authoritative in unhealthy ways. While initially this type of treatment may be undesired, subtly it can become welcomed and eventually embraced as a goal or an end in itself. Such power can be rationalized as important in order to fulfill the pastoral office but can turn into a fondness for power that eventually corrupts.

Colson writes about the corrupting effects of power on spiritual leaders. He writes:

> Power is like saltwater; the more you drink the thirstier you get. The lure of power can separate the most resolute of Christians from the true nature of Christian leadership, which is service to others. It's difficult to stand on a pedestal and wash the feet of those below.[3]

It is important to keep in mind a Christian view of leadership as outlined in the Bible. When Jesus' disciples were succumbing to the allure of power— arguing about who would be the greatest among them—Jesus gave a great description of what Christian leadership should be like. The Lord said:

> The kings of the Gentiles lord it over them; and those who exercise authority over them call themselves Benefactors. But you are not to be like that. Instead, the greatest among you should be like the youngest, and the one who rules like the one who serves. (Luke 22:25–26)

It is vital that Christian leaders in any capacity remember this principle of servant leadership. If a leader remembers they are there to serve and not be served, then power will not corrupt. Remember, if Samuel was susceptible to the dangers of the corrupting side of power, so are you and so am I. Of course, on our own, sinners like us are unable to resist the seductive aspect of power, but through the empowering of the Holy Spirit, servant leadership is possible. On the cross Jesus took on himself all of our sin, including our pride and selfishness. Through the forgiveness granted through the gospel of Jesus Christ and through the empowerment of the Spirit, Christians (Rom 8:3–4) can realize true redemption from sin and realize the ethic of servant leadership (Gal 5:16).

---

3. Ibid., 26–27.

LISTEN to the Story

¹There was a Benjamite, a man of standing, whose name was Kish son of Abiel, the son of Zeror, the son of Bekorath, the son of Aphiah of Benjamin. ²Kish had a son named Saul, as handsome a young man as could be found anywhere in Israel, and he was a head taller than anyone else. ³Now the donkeys belonging to Saul's father Kish were lost, and Kish said to his son Saul, "Take one of the servants with you and go and look for the donkeys." ⁴So he passed through the hill country of Ephraim and through the area around Shalisha, but they did not find them. They went on into the district of Shaalim, but the donkeys were not there. Then he passed through the territory of Benjamin, but they did not find them.

⁵When they reached the district of Zuph, Saul said to the servant who was with him, "Come, let's go back, or my father will stop thinking about the donkeys and start worrying about us."

⁶But the servant replied, "Look, in this town there is a man of God; he is highly respected, and everything he says comes true. Let's go there now. Perhaps he will tell us what way to take."

⁷Saul said to his servant, "If we go, what can we give the man? The food in our sacks is gone. We have no gift to take to the man of God. What do we have?"

⁸The servant answered him again. "Look," he said, "I have a quarter of a shekel of silver. I will give it to the man of God so that he will tell us what way to take." ⁹(Formerly in Israel, if someone went to inquire of God, they would say, "Come, let us go to the seer," because the prophet of today used to be called a seer.)

¹⁰"Good," Saul said to his servant. "Come, let's go." So they set out for the town where the man of God was.

¹¹As they were going up the hill to the town, they met some young women coming out to draw water, and they asked them, "Is the seer here?"

¹²"He is," they answered. "He's ahead of you. Hurry now; he has just

come to our town today, for the people have a sacrifice at the high place.
¹³As soon as you enter the town, you will find him before he goes up to
the high place to eat. The people will not begin eating until he comes,
because he must bless the sacrifice; afterward, those who are invited will
eat. Go up now; you should find him about this time."

¹⁴They went up to the town, and as they were entering it, there was
Samuel, coming toward them on his way up to the high place.

¹⁵Now the day before Saul came, the LORD had revealed this to Samuel:
¹⁶"About this time tomorrow I will send you a man from the land of
Benjamin. Anoint him ruler over my people Israel; he will deliver them
from the hand of the Philistines. I have looked on my people, for their
cry has reached me."

¹⁷When Samuel caught sight of Saul, the LORD said to him, "This is
the man I spoke to you about; he will govern my people."

¹⁸Saul approached Samuel in the gateway and asked, "Would you
please tell me where the seer's house is?"

¹⁹"I am the seer," Samuel replied. "Go up ahead of me to the high
place, for today you are to eat with me, and in the morning I will send
you on your way and will tell you all that is in your heart. ²⁰As for the
donkeys you lost three days ago, do not worry about them; they have been
found. And to whom is all the desire of Israel turned, if not to you and
your whole family line?"

²¹Saul answered, "But am I not a Benjamite, from the smallest tribe of
Israel, and is not my clan the least of all the clans of the tribe of Benjamin?
Why do you say such a thing to me?"

²²Then Samuel brought Saul and his servant into the hall and seated
them at the head of those who were invited—about thirty in number.
²³Samuel said to the cook, "Bring the piece of meat I gave you, the one I
told you to lay aside."

²⁴So the cook took up the thigh with what was on it and set it in front
of Saul. Samuel said, "Here is what has been kept for you. Eat, because it
was set aside for you for this occasion from the time I said, 'I have invited
guests.'" And Saul dined with Samuel that day.

²⁵After they came down from the high place to the town, Samuel talked
with Saul on the roof of his house. ²⁶They rose about daybreak, and Samuel
called to Saul on the roof, "Get ready, and I will send you on your way."
When Saul got ready, he and Samuel went outside together. ²⁷As they were
going down to the edge of the town, Samuel said to Saul, "Tell the servant

to go on ahead of us"—and the servant did so—"but you stay here for a while, so that I may give you a message from God."

¹⁰:¹Then Samuel took a flask of olive oil and poured it on Saul's head and kissed him, saying, "Has not the Lord anointed you ruler over his inheritance? ²When you leave me today, you will meet two men near Rachel's tomb, at Zelzah on the border of Benjamin. They will say to you, 'The donkeys you set out to look for have been found. And now your father has stopped thinking about them and is worried about you. He is asking, "What shall I do about my son?"'

³"Then you will go on from there until you reach the great tree of Tabor. Three men going up to worship God at Bethel will meet you there. One will be carrying three young goats, another three loaves of bread, and another a skin of wine. ⁴They will greet you and offer you two loaves of bread, which you will accept from them.

⁵"After that you will go to Gibeah of God, where there is a Philistine outpost. As you approach the town, you will meet a procession of prophets coming down from the high place with lyres, timbrels, pipes and harps being played before them, and they will be prophesying. ⁶The Spirit of the Lord will come powerfully upon you, and you will prophesy with them; and you will be changed into a different person. ⁷Once these signs are fulfilled, do whatever your hand finds to do, for God is with you.

⁸"Go down ahead of me to Gilgal. I will surely come down to you to sacrifice burnt offerings and fellowship offerings, but you must wait seven days until I come to you and tell you what you are to do." ⁹As Saul turned to leave Samuel, God changed Saul's heart, and all these signs were fulfilled that day. ¹⁰When he and his servant arrived at Gibeah, a procession of prophets met him; the Spirit of God came powerfully upon him, and he joined in their prophesying. ¹¹When all those who had formerly known him saw him prophesying with the prophets, they asked each other, "What is this that has happened to the son of Kish? Is Saul also among the prophets?"

¹²A man who lived there answered, "And who is their father?" So it became a saying: "Is Saul also among the prophets?" ¹³After Saul stopped prophesying, he went to the high place.

¹⁴Now Saul's uncle asked him and his servant, "Where have you been?"

"Looking for the donkeys," he said. "But when we saw they were not to be found, we went to Samuel."

¹⁵Saul's uncle said, "Tell me what Samuel said to you."

¹⁶Saul replied, "He assured us that the donkeys had been found." But he did not tell his uncle what Samuel had said about the kingship.

¹⁷Samuel summoned the people of Israel to the LORD at Mizpah ¹⁸and said to them, "This is what the LORD, the God of Israel, says: 'I brought Israel up out of Egypt, and I delivered you from the power of Egypt and all the kingdoms that oppressed you.' ¹⁹But you have now rejected your God, who saves you out of all your disasters and calamities. And you have said, 'No, appoint a king over us.' So now present yourselves before the LORD by your tribes and clans."

²⁰When Samuel had all Israel come forward by tribes, the tribe of Benjamin was taken by lot. ²¹Then he brought forward the tribe of Benjamin, clan by clan, and Matri's clan was taken. Finally Saul son of Kish was taken. But when they looked for him, he was not to be found. ²²So they inquired further of the LORD, "Has the man come here yet?"

And the LORD said, "Yes, he has hidden himself among the supplies."

²³They ran and brought him out, and as he stood among the people he was a head taller than any of the others. ²⁴Samuel said to all the people, "Do you see the man the LORD has chosen? There is no one like him among all the people."

Then the people shouted, "Long live the king!"

²⁵Samuel explained to the people the rights and duties of kingship. He wrote them down on a scroll and deposited it before the LORD. Then Samuel dismissed the people to go to their own homes.

²⁶Saul also went to his home in Gibeah, accompanied by valiant men whose hearts God had touched. ²⁷But some scoundrels said, "How can this fellow save us?" They despised him and brought him no gifts. But Saul kept silent.

Listen to the Text in the Story: Numbers 11:16–25; Judges 19–21; El Amarna Letter 51

In the ancient Near East, anointment with oil was usually to formally recognize the elevated legal status of an individual such as a slave, a bride, or a vassal. Similarly, the anointing of a king was an ancient Near Eastern practice. Hittites anointed their kings, and Egyptians anointed their officials as well as their Syrian vassal kings.[1] For example, an El Amarna Letter (51:4–9) describes a

---

1. John Day, "The Canaanite Inheritance of the Israelite Monarchy," in *King and Messiah in Israel and the Ancient Near East: Proceedings of the Oxford Old Testament Seminar*, ed. John Day, LHBOTS 270 (Sheffield: Sheffield Academic, 1998), 80.

king (Addu-nirari) in Nuhasse (modern Syria) who was anointed king by his overlord, the Egyptian Pharaoh (it reads "Whom the king of Egypt has made a king, and on whose head he has put oil, no one shall . . .").[2] Some[3] have speculated the act of anointing a king derived from the Hittites or the Egyptians, though it seems more likely the practice was borrowed from the Canaanites.[4] In the Old Testament, the anointing of a chosen individual with oil was a significant symbolic act, designating a person for leadership in Israel. Oil was used ceremonially at the consecration of priests (Exod 28:41; 29:2) and the choosing of a prophet (1 Kgs 19:16; cf. Ps 105:15) but is most well known for its use to designate the chosen king (1 Sam 10:1; 16:13; 1 Kgs 1:39; 19:16), similar to the practice in the ancient Near East. In the Bible, oil is often associated with gladness (Isa 61:3; Ps 45:7), and in some Old Testament passages oil might represent God's spirit (Isa 61:1; Zech 4:14), which could suggest that being anointed represents being empowered by the spirit of God (Ps 89:20–21; cf. Isa 11:1–4) and God's favor (Pss 23:5; 92:10). Previous to the anointing of Saul, this practice was only used for priests and the tabernacle, so its use to designate the king indicates that the monarchy in Israel is, like the priesthood, divinely sanctioned.

EXPLAIN the Story

While the previous chapter ended leaving the reader somewhat in suspense, with God commanding Samuel to give the people a king and Samuel sending the people home, now the story of the new king begins. We are introduced to Saul, who is searching for his father's missing donkeys but finds the prophet Samuel instead. Samuel privately anoints Saul and provides three signs to confirm its legitimacy. The spirit of God comes on Saul and he prophesies, though people from his hometown question his validity. Finally, Samuel calls a national assembly and Saul is elected by casting lots and acclaimed king by the populace. Through all of these events, Saul appears not only humble but lacking confidence and perhaps entertaining doubt regarding his calling to the kingship.

Saul's Genealogy (1 Sam 9:1–2)

Similar to the opening of the book (that delineated Samuel's ancestry), here a new character is introduced with the listing of Saul's heritage. Interestingly,

---

2. W. L. Moran, *The Amarna Letters* (Baltimore: Johns Hopkins University Press, 1992), 122.

3. Noth argued for a Hittite origin. See Martin Noth, "Office and Vocation in the Old Testament," in *The Laws in the Pentateuch and Other Essays* (Edinburgh: Oliver & Boyd, 1966), 239. Roland de Vaux argued for an Egyptian origin. See Roland de Vaux, "The King of Israel, Vassal of Yahweh," in *The Bible and the Ancient Near East* (London: Darton, Longman & Todd, 1972), 299–300.

4. Day, "Canaanite Inheritance," 81.

both Samuel and Saul are the sixth sons in their respective genealogical lists. This, along with how Samuel's birth story connected his name to "asked" (Hebrew *shaul*) in 1 Samuel 1:28 and the introduction of the new main character as Saul (Hebrew *shaul*), connects the prophet and king once again.

Two features of Saul's genealogy are noteworthy. First, 1 Samuel 9:1 says Saul's father is "a man of standing." The Hebrew words behind this translation either refer to a person of "wealth" (so NRSV, NLT) or a "powerful warrior" (ASV, KJV). Probably here the descriptor refers to Saul coming from a well-to-do family. The second important feature of Saul's genealogy is that he is from the tribe of Benjamin. While the tribe descended from Jacob's son, Benjamin, and eventually becomes one of the most prominent and powerful tribes, at this point in the story the connotations of being a Benjamite were not great. Not long before the time of Samuel, as relayed in Judges 19–21, there was a terrible civil war in Israel wherein the tribe of Benjamin was nearly annihilated. The war began due to some horrific deeds (Judg 19) that occurred in the Benjamite town of Gibeah, which is actually likened to Sodom in the book of Judges (compare Gen 19 and Judg 19). As we will see in the next chapter, Saul is actually from Gibeah (1 Sam 10:10). While Saul himself is described as an imposing figure, standing a head taller than the rest of the Israelites (v. 2), Saul's association with this notorious village acts as somewhat of a stigma on his otherwise impressive pedigree.

In Search of the Lost Donkeys (9:3–14)
The story of Saul begins with his father losing his donkeys and Saul and his servant being sent to find them. In light of the behavior of other sons (Eli's sons, Samuel's sons) in the book of Samuel so far, Saul's immediate obedience to his father's request reflects well on him. Saul and his servant boy travel far and wide in search of the donkeys but fail to locate them, leading them to contemplate turning back (9:5). It is at this point that the servant boy has the idea to search for prophetic assistance. In fact, the young lad knows of a man of God in a nearby town who will be able to help them. What town exactly he is referring to is not stated; neither is the identity of the man of God. This provides some narrative suspense until we find out in 9:14 that the prophet is no less than Samuel himself.

As Saul and his young servant approach the town, they meet some young ladies who were coming out to draw water. This is not a unique occurrence in biblical literature, as scholars have pointed out a young man meeting a woman at a well is a betrothal "type-scene." A type-scene is a literary convention used by authors who present a scene that is very familiar to their audience. Though the details of the scene may change, the audience has a general idea of where it is going. For example, in the modern western when cowboys agree to meet in the street at high noon, the audience knows that a duel/shootout is going to take place. In the Bible when a man journeys away from home and meets a young woman (or women) at a well, it signals a romantic encounter. Usually, one of them draws water from the well, and the scene concludes with the confirmation of a betrothal. Robert Alter has identified this type-scene in the story of Isaac and Rebekah (Gen 24:10–61), Jacob and Rachel (Gen 29:1–10), and Moses and Zipporah (Exod 2:16–21). Alter points out that through the use of type-scenes a narrator usually communicates important aspects of the young man's character.[5] In the story in 1 Samuel 9, Saul is on a journey from home (looking for his father's donkeys) and meets a group of young women who are coming to draw water from the well. However, contrary to the reader's expectations, the scene does not end with Saul's betrothal. The type-scene comes to a halt before its happy conclusion. Instead of getting a wife, Saul meets the prophet Samuel. Instead of a betrothal feast, there is a sacrificial feast (vv. 22–24).

Some have suggested that this "aborted type-scene" symbolizes Saul's kingship, which also is "aborted," and the aborted betrothal-at-the-well scene "provides something of a miniature summary of Saul's career."[6] Robert Alter comments:

> The deflection of the anticipated type-scene somehow isolates Saul, sounds a faintly ominous note that begins to prepare us for the story of the king who loses his kingship, who will not be a conduit for the future rulers of Israel, and who ends skewered on his own sword.[7]

Though modern readers might miss this, ancient readers would not. Saul's aborted type-scene prefigures Saul's aborted regency as Israel's first king.

Samuel and Saul Meet (9:15–20)

After stopping to ask for directions, Saul and his servant approach Samuel. At this point the narrator flashes back (vv. 15–16) to the day before when Yahweh informed the prophet exactly when he would meet the one who he was to anoint as the leader of Israel. While up to this point it may have seemed like the lost donkeys and the meeting between Saul and Samuel that was about to take place was merely coincidence, the narrator now reveals that even before Saul started seeking the donkeys, God was directing his prophet to him.

---

5. Alter, *The Art of Biblical Narrative* (London: G. Allen & Unwin, 1981), 51–62.
6. Bodner, *1 Samuel*, 85.
7. Alter, *The Art of Biblical Narrative*, 81.

In this prequel to the present story, God's speech to Samuel is theologically significant. First, as you will remember, although God understood the people's initial request for a king as a rejection of his kingship (8:7), God quickly acceded to their request and commanded Samuel to give them a king. Why he reacted this way was not stated in the text, but now we see that God's concern is first and foremost for his people, as he says "my people" three times in verse 16 (though it is not evident in the NIV translation but can be seen, e.g., in ESV, CEB, NRSV, NASB, NKJV, JPS, KJV). God states that Samuel must anoint him over "my people" and that the king will save "my people" from the Philistines because the cry of "my people" has reached him. In contrast to Samuel's statement that kingship in Israel will be a reason that God will *not* answer them (8:18), here the kingship *is* God's answer to Israel's afflictions.

It is worth noting that God does not command Samuel to anoint Saul as king (Hebrew *melek*) but as "ruler" (Hebrew *nagid*, "prince" or "ruler"). This contrasts with the case of David, where Samuel is instructed to anoint David as "king" (1 Sam 16:1). In fact, when Yahweh says to Samuel upon seeing Saul, "This is the man I spoke to you about; he will *govern* my people" (9:17, emphasis added), the word used for "govern" is an uncommon term (literally meaning "restrain"), not one normally used for the rule of a king (like the Hebrew verb *malak*, "to rule"). Similarly, the narrator does not call Saul king (Hebrew *melek*) except for when he is referring to the people's perspective (cf. 1 Sam 11:15).

It is possible that the choice of "ruler" (Hebrew *nagid*) rather than "king" (Hebrew *melek*) could be due to the limited nature of Saul's office. Since Yahweh is Israel's true king, perhaps the term king is avoided and Saul's role is viewed as more limited. Even in the next chapter when the people acclaim him as king, Samuel does not use the term but only declares that Saul is "the man the LORD has chosen" (10:24). Perhaps this foreshadows the nature of Saul's rule. It is cut short and he never really fulfills the role of the king.

The story then returns to the present when Samuel first lays eyes on Saul, at which point God, taking no chances that the prophet might miss his target, speaks to Samuel saying, "this is the man" (v. 17). Samuel informs Saul that he is the prophet Saul was looking for (v. 19), and he proceeds to demonstrate this clearly with his uncanny knowledge of Saul's affairs (v. 20). Samuel then underscores the tremendous importance of Saul for Israel, about which Saul is quite baffled. Saul informs Samuel he is a Benjamite and (contrary to what is said in Saul's genealogy in v. 1) from the least of all the clans of his tribe. Saul was aware of the stigma that came from being a Benjamite at the time and is very humble about his pedigree. But despite his somewhat marginalized status as a Benjamite, God has chosen him. As can be seen elsewhere in Scripture, God often chooses the unlikely for his purposes.

A Pre-Coronation Meal (9:21–25)

Samuel invites Saul and his servant to a meal where a choice piece of meat had been set aside beforehand for Saul—again showing that their meeting that day was no accident. It is somewhat surprising, however, that Samuel does not choose this time to anoint Saul. This occasion looks similar to the one where Samuel later anoints David, with a meal and an audience, and is also similar to the coronation meal Adonijah holds (1 Kgs 1:41, 49), with both dinners having "invited guests" (1 Sam 9:22). This may show some further reluctance on the part of the prophet, just as he sent the people home after God had commanded him to give the people a king (1 Sam 8:22). This meal seemed like the perfect place to anoint Saul, but Samuel does not.

The delay in anointing continues as Saul and Samuel share some private time together on the roof of the house, but he still does not anoint him. In fact, it is not until the next morning when Saul is set to leave that Samuel acts. Yet at this point Samuel wants further privacy, getting Saul to send his servant boy on ahead. Why the secrecy?

Saul is Anointed and Commissioned by Samuel (10:1–8)

Samuel finally anoints Saul, kisses him, and declares him to be the leader (Hebrew *nagid*) over Israel. Interestingly, Saul is anointed not with a horn of oil, as is standard in other anointings of kings, like David and Solomon (cf. 1 Sam 2:10). Instead a "flask" or "vial" of oil is used. Only one other king is so anointed, Jehu, who reigns over the Northern Kingdom and who, like Saul, had a brief reign that was far from ideal, though initiated by Yahweh.

Similar to Samuel's show of prophetic power when introducing himself to Saul (9:19–20), Samuel provides proof of the legitimacy of this anointing by predicting three signs that will occur. The exact meaning of the signs (meeting two men by Rachel's tomb, three men at Bethel, etc.) is not clear, and they may chiefly function to simply show the predictive power of the prophet and legitimate the anointing in Saul's eyes (note that Moses is also given three signs in Exod 4:1–9). The most significant of these signs is the descent of the spirit of Yahweh upon Saul, causing him to prophesy with the company of the prophets he meets, and the promise he will be "changed into a different person" (10:6). Why exactly the new leader of Israel should join the company of the prophets is unclear. Part of the reason may be that Samuel, who was so offended that his leadership was called into question by the people, is the "leader" of the prophets (1 Sam 19:20), and Samuel is thereby seeking to maintain some significant influence over the fledgling king. Nevertheless, Saul's participation with the prophets leads to more questions over Saul's role (see 1 Sam 10:11).

Samuel's last directions to Saul (10:8) again underscore his authority over the new king but are fairly difficult to understand. Many scholars suggest they are out of place and fit better into other contexts in the book (perhaps 1 Sam 13).[8] As it is, they are potentially confusing to young Saul as Samuel urges him to "do whatever your hand finds to do" (10:7) but also cautions him to "wait seven days" until the prophet arrives and tells him what to do (10:8). This advice seems contradictory and might help explain Saul's actions later at Gilgal in 1 Samuel 13, where he chooses to offer the sacrifice (i.e., does "whatever his hand finds to do") when Samuel does not come at the appointed time to offer the sacrifice (13:8). One commentator has noted that 10:7 urges Saul to act "unconditionally" while 10:8 instead demands "acting conditionally" and suggests that it "must have had a slightly confusing or misleading effect on Saul."[9] Perhaps this is somewhat of a test for Saul, as he is given freedom to act but on specific occasions only within certain parameters. Regardless, this command regarding his future actions at Gilgal proves momentous for his reign as king.

The Signs Come to Pass (10:9–13)

Yahweh takes no time in working in Saul, as the narrator tells us that God changes his heart before he even leaves Samuel's presence (v. 9). This doesn't agree entirely with what Samuel predicted, as he said it would happen after the spirit came on Saul and he prophesied (10:8). Perhaps God was more eager than Samuel at this point. Nevertheless, all of the signs predicted by Samuel come to pass, though not all are narrated in the text. The main emphasis of the narrator is clearly on the work of the spirit in Saul's life, as he describes Saul's charismatic experiences with the powerful work of the spirit's descent on him. Interestingly, this takes place in Saul's hometown of Gibeah (v. 10), and those who knew him are perplexed by what they see (v. 11). Just like Jesus laments in the New Testament that a prophet has no honor in his own town (Mark 6:4; John 4:44), so here Saul's prophetic experiences are questioned by the locals. The question "Is Saul also among the prophets?" is likely an expression of amazement by the residents but also somewhat negative and implying a negative answer. It is kind of like saying, "What is going on here? Saul isn't a prophet!"

Another local resident questioned further, "Who is their father?" Seeing as such prophetic groups were sometimes called "sons/company of the prophets" (1 Kgs 20:35; 2 Kgs 2:3, 5, 7, 15; 4:1, 38; 5:22; 6:1; 9:1) and Samuel is said to be their leader (1 Sam 19:20), it could be a reference to Samuel. Whatever the

---

8. E.g., Klein, *1 Samuel*, 92.

9. J. P. Fokkelman, *Narrative Art and Poetry in the Books of Samuel: Vow and Desire (1 Sam. 1–12)* (Assen: Van Gorcum, 1993), 432.

precise meaning of these questions, we are told that the first question became a regular saying in Israel, perhaps questioning the nature of Saul's office. What type of leader was he?

Acclaimed King (10:14–27)

Saul refrains from telling his family about his anointing, perhaps thinking it was not meant to be public yet (as implied by the secretive nature of the anointing). The choice of Saul was soon to be made public, however, as Samuel calls a national assembly at the same place he had done following Israel's defeat by the Philistines (1 Sam 7:1). Samuel begins by reviewing salvation history and God's deliverance of his people in the past and reminds the people again that their demand for a king is tantamount to rejecting God. This is somewhat surprising seeing as God has been directing Samuel to provide a king for Israel and clearly was seeking to use the king to save Israel from the Philistines (10:16). Thus, it seems Samuel's speech (which omits the fact that the wickedness of Samuel's own sons actually instigated the request for a king) once again is born out of Samuel's personal affront taken at the people's request for a king (1 Sam 8:6). Perhaps Samuel's choice of Mizpah for the assembly was to remind the people that they did not need a king to be delivered from the Philistines. (The last assembly at Mizpah resulted in God's deliverance from their archenemy.)

Following his prophetic indictment of the people, Samuel oversees a lot-casting ceremony to choose the king. Interestingly, Samuel makes no mention of God's choice of Saul and his anointing. This seems like an odd procedure for electing a king, as usually in the Old Testament casting lots is to find a guilty party (Josh 7; 1 Sam 14; Jonah 1:7), not to determine an honored and chosen one. Nevertheless, the lot eventually singles out Saul, but to everyone's surprise he is nowhere to be found. In order to locate Saul they proceed to ask (of course Hebrew for "ask" here is *shaul*) Yahweh, who tells them Saul is hiding among the baggage. Why was he hiding? So far Saul has seemed very humble and lacking confidence, so this is not necessarily out of character. It is possible that Saul hid because lot-casting ceremonies are usually used to find guilty people. Whatever the reason, given that he had been anointed by the prophet (confirmed by no less than three miraculous signs) and empowered by Yahweh's spirit, Saul's continuing hesitancy does not bode well for him. His actions suggest a reluctance to obey God's calling.

When the people finally see Saul, they approve of the choice with enthusiasm. After all, Saul was a head taller than everyone else. At this point Samuel finally commends Saul (though he again avoids using the word "king"), and the people acclaim him as king.

Samuel proceeds to write down the job description for the king and deposits it before Yahweh. Interestingly, Deuteronomy 17:18 says the king himself is supposed to write down a copy of the law, but here Samuel does it. As one commentator observes, "Saul stands with his hands at his side as the prophet takes on a kingly task."[10] Following this Samuel dismisses the people, again showing that he is still in charge.

All the people return home, but some are not accepting of their new leader. Some "scoundrels" question Saul's appointment and his potential to save them. In response, Saul says nothing. Saul's restraint is probably admirable, though it may also showcase his lack of confidence and his doubts about his calling.

LIVE the Story

Divine Coincidences

How exactly Saul's father's donkeys got lost is not conveyed in the story. But this seemingly mundane occurrence led to a life-changing moment in Saul's life. In fact, the search for the donkeys was nearly abandoned were it not for the suggestion of Saul's young servant to seek prophetic help. Further, Saul's running into the prophet on his way into the city would seem like an amazing coincidence were the reader not told that God had told Samuel beforehand when he would meet the man to anoint as Israel's leader. Once this is revealed, one may suspect that God had orchestrated these events or at least worked within them to bring out his will. The Bible often showcases God's sovereign work behind seemingly coincidental events. The story of Joseph illustrates this clearly (Gen 37–50), as does the book of Esther. The Westminster Confession explains God's work behind seemingly coincidental events in that "God, the great Creator of all things, doth uphold, direct, dispose, and govern all creatures, actions, and things, from the greatest even to the least" (5.1). The exact nature of God's governance over the actions of people is the subject of considerable theological debate, but Paul makes it clear that "in all things God works for the good of those who love him" (Rom 8:28). Coincidence can often be a glimpse of God's sovereign providence.

Freedom to Obey

Samuel's final commands to Saul in 10:7–8 are, from one perspective, somewhat difficult to understand. Saul is given the freedom and license to do whatever "his hand finds to do" (1 Sam 10:7) but at the same time is given strict

---

10. Barbara Green, *How Are the Mighty Fallen?: A Dialogical Study of King Saul in 1 Samuel*, JSOTSup 365 (London; New York: Sheffield Academic, 2003), 213.

parameters in regard to what he must do at Gilgal (1 Sam 10:8). While these commands could have been confusing for the inexperienced king, they are not necessarily so. The situation is not dissimilar to the situation in the garden of Eden, where the first human couple are given freedom but are restrained as well. God first says, "You are free to eat from any tree in the garden" (Gen 2:16) but immediately afterwards states, "but you must not eat from the tree of the knowledge of good and evil" (Gen 2:17). Picking and choosing between different parts of God's word and ignoring other parts can lead to disaster. In the New Testament we are told that Christians are free (Gal 5:1) but our freedom is not meant for disobedience (Gal 5:13). James calls God's law the "perfect law that gives freedom" (Jas 1:25). Just as Saul was given freedom but was also called to obey the prophet, so we are given freedom in Christ but also called to obey his word.

The Work of Yahweh's Spirit

This story underscores the role of Yahweh's spirit. In fact, of the three signs predicted to happen to Saul, only the story of the spirit's work in Saul is narrated. The role of Yahweh's spirit in his prophesying is primarily to confirm Saul's role as leader in Israel. This is quite close to the spirit's role in the story of the Israelite elders whom Moses appointed to support him in his work in Numbers 11:16–25. In order to confirm their legitimacy, the spirit of God came on the elders and they prophesied temporarily. These elders, however, did *not* become prophets, as it was a temporary manifestation of God's spirit in order to validate their divine appointment for service (cf. the role of the coming of the Holy Spirit to confirm the legitimacy of the salvation of uncircumcised believers in Acts 10:44–47).

The story further highlights the spirit of Yahweh's role in personal transformation as Saul is "changed into a different person" (10:6). Also, the freedom and unpredictable nature of Yahweh's spirit is underscored here, as even Samuel himself failed to see Saul's divine change of heart occurring as soon as it did (the prophet predicted it would happen after his run-in with the prophets, but instead it occurred immediately as Saul turned to leave Samuel). Later in the story, after Saul's disobedience led to his rejection as king and the spirit of God had left him (1 Sam 16:8), the spirit again grips Saul and causes him to prophesy once again, this time in order to neutralize Saul while David escaped his grasp (1 Sam 19:23–24). The spirit blows where it will (John 3:8) and often catches its recipients off guard.

While the work of Yahweh's spirit in Saul's story anticipates the Holy Spirit's work in believers today, it is important not to equate the two or view the former as normative. All the occasions of Yahweh's spirit coming on individuals in the Old Testament are exceptional rather than normative. Drawing from this story, we could well see the principle that God does not call us to serve without first empowering for service. The empowerment here is primarily seen in God changing Saul "into a different person" (10:6); however, it never states that Yahweh's spirit now indwelt Saul (i.e., had continued residence in Saul). Therefore, while there are similarities between Saul's story here and Christian experiences of empowerment by the Holy Spirit (e.g., Acts 2), the two should not be equated. While the New Testament explicitly states that the Spirit indwells believers (1 Cor 3:16–17; 6:19–20; Rom 8:9), this is never said in the Old Testament. The continued indwelling of the Holy Spirit in the New Testament was something new made possible by Christ's work on the cross. The coming of Yahweh's spirit in the Old Testament usually was on an unlikely candidate (e.g., Gideon, Saul) who was chosen to deliver God's oppressed people. This was primarily brought on by God's concern for his people Israel rather than concern for an individual and their personal relationship to Yahweh. As Block writes: "We may conclude, therefore that the [spirit] functions as the agency/agent through which Yahweh arrests otherwise unqualified and resistant individuals and thrusts them out into his service."[11]

---

11. Daniel I. Block, *Judges, Ruth*, NAC 6 (Nashville: Broadman & Holman, 1999), 154.

LISTEN to the Story

¹Nahash the Ammonite went up and besieged Jabesh Gilead. And all the men of Jabesh said to him, "Make a treaty with us, and we will be subject to you."

²But Nahash the Ammonite replied, "I will make a treaty with you only on the condition that I gouge out the right eye of every one of you and so bring disgrace on all Israel."

³The elders of Jabesh said to him, "Give us seven days so we can send messengers throughout Israel; if no one comes to rescue us, we will surrender to you."

⁴When the messengers came to Gibeah of Saul and reported these terms to the people, they all wept aloud. ⁵Just then Saul was returning from the fields, behind his oxen, and he asked, "What is wrong with everyone? Why are they weeping?" Then they repeated to him what the men of Jabesh had said.

⁶When Saul heard their words, the Spirit of God came powerfully upon him, and he burned with anger. ⁷He took a pair of oxen, cut them into pieces, and sent the pieces by messengers throughout Israel, proclaiming, "This is what will be done to the oxen of anyone who does not follow Saul and Samuel." Then the terror of the LORD fell on the people, and they came out together as one. ⁸When Saul mustered them at Bezek, the men of Israel numbered three hundred thousand and those of Judah thirty thousand.

⁹They told the messengers who had come, "Say to the men of Jabesh Gilead, 'By the time the sun is hot tomorrow, you will be rescued.'" When the messengers went and reported this to the men of Jabesh, they were elated. ¹⁰They said to the Ammonites, "Tomorrow we will surrender to you, and you can do to us whatever you like."

¹¹The next day Saul separated his men into three divisions; during the last watch of the night they broke into the camp of the Ammonites

and slaughtered them until the heat of the day. Those who survived were scattered, so that no two of them were left together.

[12]The people then said to Samuel, "Who was it that asked, 'Shall Saul reign over us?' Turn these men over to us so that we may put them to death."

[13]But Saul said, "No one will be put to death today, for this day the LORD has rescued Israel." [14]Then Samuel said to the people, "Come, let us go to Gilgal and there renew the kingship." [15]So all the people went to Gilgal and made Saul king in the presence of the LORD. There they sacrificed fellowship offerings before the LORD, and Saul and all the Israelites held a great celebration.

Listen to the Text in the Story: Genesis 19; Numbers 22; Deuteronomy 2:19; 22:3–6; Judges 3:13; 10:7–9; 11; 19–21; 2 Samuel 16, 19; Annals of Tiglath-Pileser III; A Letter Reporting Matters in Kalah; Sennacherib's Seige of Jerusalem; Annals of Ashurbanipal; Mari Royal Archives

In this chapter we encounter another frequent enemy of Israel, the Ammonites. Outside of the biblical texts, the Ammonites are first mentioned in ancient Assyrian annals of the kings Tiglath-Pileser III,[1] Sargon II,[2] Sennacherib,[3] and Ashurbanipal.[4] Ammonite territory was across the Jordan River and south of the Jabbok. In Genesis 19 the Bible recounts the incestuous origins of the nation with the story of Lot, who unwittingly impregnated his daughters (an event orchestrated by his daughters), resulting in the birth of Ben-ammi and Moab, ancestors of the Ammonites and Moab respectively. The Ammonites were hostile to Israel (Judg 3:13; 10:7–9; 11) despite their being distant relations. God had commanded Israel to treat the Ammonites kindly (Deut 2:19), though the Ammonites were condemned for hiring Balaam the seer (Num 22) and were therefore barred from joining Israel's congregation (Deut 23:3–6).

Saul's dissection of the bodies of the oxen and his sending them around Israel in order to motivate the Israelites into joining the rescue mission has both biblical and extrabiblical parallels. An ancient Near Eastern text from ancient Mari contains reference to decapitating a prisoner then taking his head throughout the land in order to motivate reluctant warriors to ready themselves for battle, providing a similar scare tactic parallel to the story in

---

1. *ANET* 282b.
2. "A Letter Reporting Matters in Kalaḫ," trans. K. L. Younger Jr., *COS* 3.96:245.
3. "Sennacherib's Siege of Jerusalem" trans. Mordechai Cogan, *COS* 2.119B:302.
4. *ANET* 294b.

1 Samuel 11.[5] In the Bible, however, this is the second time that Gibeah was the source of severed pieces of flesh to be delivered to all Israel in order to provoke a military response. In Judges 19, when a Levite's concubine was raped and murdered by the residents of Gibeah, he cut her body into twelve pieces and sent them to all of Israel (Judg 19:29). It seems likely that the story of Saul's actions here is purposefully alluding to that dark day in the recent past. But this time, rather than Gibeah being the oppressive culprit, it is the city standing alongside the oppressed and opposing a foreign enemy.

EXPLAIN the Story

While the last chapter ended with some "scoundrels" questioning whether Saul is up to the challenge of saving Israel, the Ammonite threat provides an opportunity to answer this question. After hearing about the Ammonite king Nahash's plan to mutilate the men of Jabesh Gilead, Yahweh's spirit comes on Saul and he musters the troops to deliver the city. After the victory, some in the celebratory crowd suggest condemning to death those who had previously opposed Saul's leadership, but Saul intervenes on their behalf. Finally, Samuel leads the people to "renew" the kingship and crown Saul as king. Thus, the rise of Saul to the throne seems complete.

Background to the Ammonite Threat

One of the Dead Sea Scrolls copies of the book of Samuel (though only a portion of it survives) contains an extra paragraph that belongs between the end of 1 Samuel 10 and the beginning of 1 Samuel 11. Though not found in the traditional Hebrew (Masoretic) or Greek (Septuagint) textual traditions, this copy of Samuel (labelled 4QSam[a] by scholars) dates to before the time of Christ and is much older than any other copies of the book of Samuel we have, leading many scholars to view this extra paragraph as originally part of the story. In fact, many modern Bible translations include this missing paragraph in their English translations of the Bible (e.g., NRSV, NLT, NEB, NAB). In this missing paragraph, Nahash is introduced as the king of the Ammonites, and Nahash's victories against Israel's Transjordanian tribes (Gadites and Reubenites) and his policy of gouging out the right eye of each of his captives is described. Further, it notes that seven thousand Israelites escaped Nahash's attack and holed up at Jabesh Gilead, providing the background for understanding the Ammonite king's move against Jabesh Gilead, which is quite far north from the Ammonite capital.

---

5. *Archives Royales de Mari: Lettres Diverses*, vol. 2, trans. Charles Francois Jean (Paris: Impr. Nationale, 1950), 48. Cf. Long, "1 Samuel," 323.

The Threats of Nahash "the Snake" (11:1–3)

The Ammonite, Nahash (which in Hebrew is the word for "snake"), put the Israelite town of Jabesh Gilead to siege, causing the residents to negotiate terms of a surrender. Nahash's terms, however, are horrific, as he demands they allow him to gouge out their right eyes so that he can disgrace Israel. With little choice, the people of Jabesh Gilead contemplate agreeing to these terms but first send messengers around Israel to ask for assistance.

Significantly, Jabesh Gilead was the *one* town in Israel that refused to answer a similar call to arms in Judges 21, but now they are asking Israel to mobilize and come to their aid. Given their history of draft dodging, their expectations of receiving help from the Israelite military probably seemed slim (and perhaps this is why Nahash allows them time to send messengers to find help). In the infamous story in Judges 21, Jabesh Gilead was slaughtered by the other tribes due to their failure to respond to the call to arms. In fact, only four hundred virgin girls from the town were left alive. These survivors subsequently became wives for some of the Benjamites who had survived the Israelite slaughter of their tribe. In other words, were it not for the town of Jabesh Gilead, Benjamin would have been annihilated. Perhaps the towns-people are hoping that Israel remembers this fact and will move to rescue them, despite their failure to join the other tribes in battle in Judges 21.

Word of the Crisis Reaches Yahweh's Anointed (11:4–10)

When the messengers reach Saul's hometown of Gibeah, Saul is apparently working as a farmer and only hears about the crisis second hand, after the townspeople were already publicly weeping over the news. When Saul hears the news, however, rather than weeping, he gets extremely angry. While this emotion would make sense in light of Jabesh Gilead's supportive role in recent Benjamite history, it is clear that it is God's spirit that brings on the anger (11:6).

The coming of the spirit on Saul here is reminiscent of the language used for the coming of Yahweh's spirit upon Israel's past judges (e.g., Judg 3:10; 6:34; 11:29; 13:25; esp. 14:6, 19). Thus, Saul's new role shows continuity between Israel's past leaders who were filled with Yahweh's spirit and were raised up to lead a great deliverance for an oppressed people. Interestingly, at this point, rather than kingship appearing to be a tremendous break in the theocratic order (as implied in 1 Sam 8), it shows tremendous continuity with God's rule of Israel before the monarchy.

Inspired by God's spirit, Saul takes a pair of oxen (presumably his own, with which he was farming in v. 5) and slaughters them, cutting them into pieces, which he sends throughout Israel to demand assistance for the city. The oxen cutlets serve as a threat to non-participants. If they refuse to follow their leaders (Saul and Samuel) into battle, their oxen will be similarly cut to pieces.

Saul's call to arms is a remarkable success as Yahweh's "terror" falls on the people and they respond "together as one" (11:7). The messengers bring the good news of the coming help back to Jabesh (11:9), and in response the people of Jabesh deceptively report to the Ammonites that they will surrender to their terms the next day (11:10), presumably so that the Ammonites will be caught off guard by the approaching Israelite militia.

The Battle and Its Aftermath (11:11–15)

For the assault on the Ammonites, Saul strategically divides the army into three groups, a proven tactic also used by previous judges (7:16; 9:43). Under his leadership, Israel delivers Jabesh Gilead, with the battle ending in the heat of the day (11:11), just as Saul promised them (11:9). Having seen Saul's leadership abilities, the people then approach Samuel and demand that the ones who previously questioned Saul's abilities to save (the "scoundrels" of 10:27) be executed for their treasonous comments. Even though it was Samuel who was approached, it is Saul who takes the initiative and intervenes, granting amnesty to those involved. In fact, Saul rightly declares that it is God, not Saul, who has "rescued" Israel (11:13). He will let no executions of Israelites mar Yahweh's victory that day.

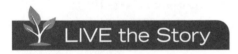

LIVE the Story

The Terror of Yahweh

As Saul acknowledged after the victory (11:13), the power behind this rescue mission was Yahweh, not the newly anointed king. It was God's spirit who came on Saul and moved the king to act (11:6). It was the "terror of the Lord" that moved the people to respond (11:7). What exactly was this terror? It could be they feared that Saul might do to them as he had done to the oxen (though Saul only threatens to do the same to their oxen). After all, fear of the king may be somewhat understandable, given the scathing predictions Samuel made in 1 Samuel 8 about what the king would be like. However, this terror would be better called the "terror of Saul," and it is not. Similarly, it is also clearly not the fear of Nahash, or it would be better called "the terror of Nahash" (or the Ammonites).

The "fear of Yahweh" is presented as one of the highest virtues in the Bible. This fear is called both the "beginning of wisdom" (Prov 9:10; Job 28:28) and the "beginning of knowledge" (Prov 1:7). In 1 Samuel 11, rather than the word "fear" (as found in the wisdom books: e.g., Prov 1:7; 9:10; Job 28:28; and Eccl 12:13) we find reference to the "terror" of Yahweh. This exact phrase is found repeatedly in the second chapter of Isaiah (2:10, 19, 21), where a day of Yahweh's judgment is envisioned and the "fearful presence of the LORD" causes people to hide in caves or holes in the ground. The Hebrew word for "fearful presence" used here in 1 Samuel 11:7 is also used as an epithet for God in Genesis, where Jacob refers to God as the "Fear of Isaac" (Gen 31:42, 53).

Christians today often want to avoid talking about the "fear" of Yahweh, as we want to emphasize God's love and grace. However, the Bible is very clear on the importance of fearing God. The fear of Yahweh involves being in awe of God and properly respecting him. Thus, fearing Yahweh ultimately requires observing his commandments and engaging in appropriate ethical behavior. Of course, these actions are the connotations of fear, not the meaning of fear itself. Fear really does mean an emotion of being afraid. There is good reason to be afraid of God, especially if you live in disobedience to him.

It is important to note the difference between godly and ungodly fear. In the New Testament, Jesus cautions us not to fear humans (Luke 12:4). Fear of humans divides us against each other, can create chaos in our lives, and can even create a paralyzed state of mind resulting in failure to take appropriate action. However, godly fear produces good fruit in a believer's life. Proverbs credits the fear of God with the gaining of knowledge (2:5), the hating of evil (8:13), living a long life (10:27; 14:27), and attaining prosperity (22:4). In our story here in 1 Samuel 11, this "terror of the LORD" bore good fruit in Israel. First, it resulted in obedience to the anointed one (Saul) as the people responded to his call. Second, it resulted in unity in Israel, for the text says, "they came out together as one" (11:7). Third, it resulted in engaging in appropriate behavior, as they participated in the rescue of the oppressed people in Jabesh Gilead. Thus, godly fear results in repentance, unity, and righteous action. Misplaced fear has the opposite effect. Here in 1 Samuel 11 the terror of God led the people to be obedient to the call of Yahweh's anointed one.

The Office of the Israelite King and the Office of the Messiah

The books of 1–2 Samuel are rife with contributions to the understanding of the anointed one or the Messiah (*mashiah* is the Hebrew word for "anointed one"). Primarily, David will become the central figure upon which messianic expectations are developed. However, even here in the initial stories of the first anointed king of Israel much can be discerned. In fact, both Saul and David, as God's anointed, are: chosen by God (9:16; 16:1); anointed by the prophet (10:1; 16:13); endowed with the spirit (1 Sam 10:6; 16:13); and subsequently deliver Israel from their enemy (1 Sam 11:6–10; 17:32–52). Some scholars have noted that these four elements are not found in any of the later kings of Israel and Judah but only reappear again in the case of Jesus himself.[6] From this beginning both the office of the king and the theology of messiah (the anointed one) are formulated.

In this high beginning for kingship and the origins of messianic expectations, contrary to what became the norm in the later monarchy, we see kingship showcased in an almost ideal form. Though Samuel earlier warned that the king would make others plow his own field (8:12) and even take the fields of others (8:14), Saul is humbly working his own field with his own oxen (11:4). Rather than taking the oxen of others as Samuel predicted (8:16), Saul sacrifices his own oxen (11:7) for the greater good—to muster Israel to rescue the oppressed. The king here is not selfish or power hungry but concerned to help the oppressed. Saul leads Israel to victory, but he does so humbly and does not take credit for it himself, instead attributing the victory to Yahweh (11:13). Finally, after the victory, Saul delivers those Israelites who treasonously opposed his kingship by granting them amnesty rather than meting out royal justice (11:13).

Similar to Saul's actions in this story, later messianic descriptions attribute a humility to the Messiah (Zech 9:9), an unselfish (and self-sacrificial) disposition (Isa 53), and a prominent role of the spirit and concern for the oppressed (Isa 61:1). Finally, the Messiah is the one who can grant amnesty to those who, by the law, would be condemned for their actions (John 8:11).

It is clear from its inception that the main role of the anointed king in Israel is to save. The primacy of salvation for the role of king can be seen in 1 Samuel 10:27 when Saul is elected by lot and his detractors question whether he could "save" them. This salvific role is accentuated here in Saul's first actions as king, as the main theme is clearly "salvation" (Hebrew *yasha*, "deliverance"). At the beginning of the chapter the oppressed (11:3) send out messengers, hoping for someone to "rescue/save" (Hebrew *yasha*) them. In 11:9 Saul sends the messengers back, assuring the city that they will be rescued (Hebrew *yasha*, "saved/delivered"). Finally, after the deliverance of Jabesh Gilead, Saul declares that Yahweh was the one who "rescued" (Hebrew *yasha*) Israel (1 Sam 11:13).

The primary role of the anointed one (Hebrew *mashiah*) being to save remained throughout its theological development in the history of Israel through to messianic expectations in Judaism and Christianity, as can be seen in the cry to Jesus repeated in the gospels, "Hosanna" (Matt 21:9, 15; Mark 11:9, 10; John 12:13), which literally means "Please save!" Furthermore, this role is accentuated by the very name of the Messiah. When the angels

6. E.g., William J. Dumbrell, "The Content and Significance of the Books of Samuel: Their Place and Purpose within the Former Prophets," *JETS* 33 (1990): 55.

announce the Messiah's birth to the shepherds in Luke 2:11, they declare that a "savior" has been born. When his birth is announced to Joseph in Matthew 1:21, the angel declares that his name will be called "Jesus" because he will "save," as the name Jesus (Joshua, transliterated from the Hebrew) literally means "Yahweh will save" (based on the same Hebrew word employed throughout 1 Sam 11, *yasha*). Jesus is the long awaited anointed one/Messiah who "will save" his people.

CHAPTER 11

1 Samuel 12:1-25

 LISTEN to the Story

¹Samuel said to all Israel, "I have listened to everything you said to me and have set a king over you. ²Now you have a king as your leader. As for me, I am old and gray, and my sons are here with you. I have been your leader from my youth until this day. ³Here I stand. Testify against me in the presence of the LORD and his anointed. Whose ox have I taken? Whose donkey have I taken? Whom have I cheated? Whom have I oppressed? From whose hand have I accepted a bribe to make me shut my eyes? If I have done any of these things, I will make it right."

⁴"You have not cheated or oppressed us," they replied. "You have not taken anything from anyone's hand."

⁵Samuel said to them, "The LORD is witness against you, and also his anointed is witness this day, that you have not found anything in my hand."

"He is witness," they said.

⁶Then Samuel said to the people, "It is the LORD who appointed Moses and Aaron and brought your ancestors up out of Egypt. ⁷Now then, stand here, because I am going to confront you with evidence before the LORD as to all the righteous acts performed by the LORD for you and your ancestors.

⁸"After Jacob entered Egypt, they cried to the LORD for help, and the LORD sent Moses and Aaron, who brought your ancestors out of Egypt and settled them in this place.

⁹"But they forgot the LORD their God; so he sold them into the hand of Sisera, the commander of the army of Hazor, and into the hands of the Philistines and the king of Moab, who fought against them. ¹⁰They cried out to the LORD and said, 'We have sinned; we have forsaken the LORD and served the Baals and the Ashtoreths. But now deliver us from the hands of our enemies, and we will serve you.' ¹¹Then the LORD sent Jerub-Baal, Barak, Jephthah and Samuel, and he delivered you from the hands of your enemies all around you, so that you lived in safety.

¹²"But when you saw that Nahash king of the Ammonites was moving

against you, you said to me, 'No, we want a king to rule over us'—even though the LORD your God was your king. ¹³Now here is the king you have chosen, the one you asked for; see, the LORD has set a king over you. ¹⁴If you fear the LORD and serve and obey him and do not rebel against his commands, and if both you and the king who reigns over you follow the LORD your God—good! ¹⁵But if you do not obey the LORD, and if you rebel against his commands, his hand will be against you, as it was against your ancestors.

¹⁶"Now then, stand still and see this great thing the LORD is about to do before your eyes! ¹⁷Is it not wheat harvest now? I will call on the LORD to send thunder and rain. And you will realize what an evil thing you did in the eyes of the LORD when you asked for a king."

¹⁸Then Samuel called on the LORD, and that same day the LORD sent thunder and rain. So all the people stood in awe of the LORD and of Samuel.

¹⁹The people all said to Samuel, "Pray to the LORD your God for your servants so that we will not die, for we have added to all our other sins the evil of asking for a king."

²⁰"Do not be afraid," Samuel replied. "You have done all this evil; yet do not turn away from the LORD, but serve the LORD with all your heart. ²¹Do not turn away after useless idols. They can do you no good, nor can they rescue you, because they are useless. ²²For the sake of his great name the LORD will not reject his people, because the LORD was pleased to make you his own. ²³As for me, far be it from me that I should sin against the LORD by failing to pray for you. And I will teach you the way that is good and right. ²⁴But be sure to fear the LORD and serve him faithfully with all your heart; consider what great things he has done for you. ²⁵Yet if you persist in doing evil, both you and your king will perish."

Listen to the Text in the Story: Deuteronomy 1–4; Joshua 23–24; Judges 17:6; 21:25; Assur Charter (L. 1349)

In this chapter Samuel gives a type of farewell speech to Israel, as he makes way for the leadership of the newly anointed king, Saul. Early in the larger story, Joshua made a similar speech near the end of his tenure. In the present chapter Samuel prefaces it with an admission that "I am old and gray" (1 Sam 12:2), just as Joshua had similarly acknowledged "I am very old" (Josh 23:2). As well, similar to Joshua, Samuel uses the occasion to remind the people of his accomplishments and good service to them (cf. Josh 23:3–4). What is

more, Samuel recites much of salvation history in his speech, similar to the
opening of Moses's last grand speech to Israel (Deut 1–4).

In leadership transition situations in the ancient Near East, it was unfortunately common for the new leader to smear the name of their predecessor. For
example, when the Assyrian King Sargon took the Assyrian throne in 722 BC
he undertook political propaganda against his predecessor, Shalmaneser V,
claiming that his predecessor had implemented taxes on the people of Ashur
but that he (Sargon) was going to remove them.[1] Sources show that these taxes
date from long before Shalmaneser,[2] so the claims of Sargon amount to a smear
campaign. Thus, it makes sense that Samuel sets out to clear his name before
Israel's new leader assumes power.

EXPLAIN the Story

After Saul's leadership was aptly shown in the rescue of Jabesh Gilead, Samuel
sees it a fit time to step aside somewhat so the new king can now rule. Samuel's farewell address reminds the people both of his own blameless service to
Israel and God's saving actions in Israelite history. Samuel's memory, however,
seems faulty in a self-serving way in his recitation of recent events. Nevertheless, Samuel commits to pray for them and faithfully delivers God's word,
exhorting them to obey God, else they (and their king) perish for their evil.

The Prophet's Clean Record of Service (12:1–5)
The last chapter ended with a celebration at Gilgal in coronation of the new
king. On this occasion Samuel sees fit to give something of a farewell speech.
Samuel begins by pointing out the great length of his term, from his "youth"
until his present old age. The prophet is also at pains to emphasize that he did
not use the office to his own personal gain. He did not take bribes or oppress the
people in any way. In response the crowd affirms the truth of Samuel's words.

Surprisingly, Samuel makes reference to his sons in this protestation of his
innocence (12:2). Given that his audience (and the reader) knows that his sons
in fact "accepted bribes" and "perverted justice" (1 Sam 8:3), this is surprising
and reveals a blind spot in the prophet's vision, as he seems unaware of his sons'
evil deeds. This blind spot would also explain Samuel's inaccurate recollection
of how it came about that the people asked for a king. In this farewell speech,

---

1. Assur Charter lines 31–33. See Vera Chamaza, "Sargon II's Ascent to the Throne: The Political
Situation," *SAAB* 6 (1992): 24–25.

2. A. T. Olmstead, *Western Asia in the Days of Sargon of Assyria, 722–705 B.C.: A Study in Oriental
History* (New York: Holt, 1908), 32, n.27. cf. Sung Jin Park, "A New Historical Reconstruction of
the Fall of Samaria," *Bib* 93 (2012): 98–106.

Samuel claims the context for the people's request for a king was the attack of
Nahash the Ammnonite (11:12). However, the real context for this request
was the sins of Samuel's sons (1 Sam 8:5).

Samuel's proclamation of innocence intentionally contrasts the way in
which he predicted the king would act (1 Sam 8). Samuel maintains that he
has not taken anyone's "ox" or "donkey" (12:3), though he earlier claimed an
Israelite king would do just that (1 Sam 8:16). Samuel points out he has not
oppressed the people (12:3), though he earlier claimed that the king would
make the people "slaves" (8:17) and cause them to "cry out for relief" from
oppression (8:18). Again we can see the prophet's personal affront taken at the
people's request for a king. Samuel is at pains to point out that his leadership
is superior to that of the king.

The people agree that Samuel has been innocent of these crimes.
Interestingly, the people do not bring up anything about his sons' evil deeds
or contradict the prophet regarding the real context for the demand for a king.

Salvation History Recited 12:6–15

After establishing his spotless record as Israel's leader, Samuel proceeds to
remind the people of how Yahweh had saved Israel in the past, starting with
the exodus and recalling the deliverers God raised up during the tenure of the
judges, including his own name along with them. Through this recitation of
history, Samuel seems to be pointing out that God's use of judges in the past
was sufficient for Israel and that kingship was not necessary. Of course, Samuel's revisionist history fails to note the many problems with the era of the judges
when "Israel had no king; everyone did as they saw fit" (Judg 17:6; 21:25).

As already noted, Samuel's recollection of the battle against Nahash as the
context for requesting a king is quite skewed. Clearly in the story a king was
demanded in response to the sins of Samuel's sons (1 Sam 8). God then agreed
to provide a king, whom Samuel anointed (10:1). This king was then chosen
by lot (10:21) and acclaimed by the people (10:24). Only after all of this did
Nahash attack (11:1–2), causing the anointed one to rally Israel into a rescue
mission (11:6–11).[3] Samuel's revisionist history is clearly self-serving in that
he highlights the positive aspects of God's use of judges and deflects any blame
for the request for a king from his own sons.

---

3. One way of harmonizing the prophet Samuel's presentation of events here with the narrative is to
take into account the extra verse at the end of 1 Sam 10 found in the Dead Sea Scrolls (see commentary
on ch. 10), which talks about Nahash's previous actions against the Gadites and the Reubenites *before*
his attacking Jabesh Gilead. If this was the case it is possible the request for a king *could* have taken
place in the context of ongoing war with the Ammonites. Nevertheless, the narrator clearly sets the
context of the request for a king as the sin of Samuel's sons who he had appointed as leaders (1 Sam
8:1–4). The narrator clearly did not see an Ammonite threat as the reason for the request for a king.

Nevertheless, Samuel's assertion to the people that Saul "is the king you have chosen, the one you asked for" proves significant going forward and helps explain David's uniqueness vis-à-vis Saul (cf. 1 Sam 13:14). As well, Samuel is clearly correct that the people have rejected God's rule in their request for a king. Samuel's admonition that the people must fear Yahweh "and serve and obey him" (v. 14) else they will fall under God's hands of judgment is spot on. Samuel's message of repentance and obedience is orthodox and becomes one of the main themes of the entire history. This is what makes Samuel's character so complex. While he was clearly personally offended at the request for a king and was blind to his sons' sin, he was also a faithful prophet of God who delivered his word faithfully and was a capable leader of Israel (as demonstrated in 1 Sam 7).

The Sign of a Thunderstorm (12:16–18)

After concluding his admonitions to obey Yahweh and not rebel, Samuel calls on God to send thunder and rain to confirm that asking for a king was evil. In Palestine it was very rare to get rain during the wheat harvest time (May and June), so a thunderstorm during this time would definitely look miraculous. Yahweh answers Samuel's call, bringing thunder and rain. Once again, we see God's endorsement of his prophet in that Yahweh "let none of Samuel's words fall to the ground" (1 Sam 3:19). Furthermore, the unseasonable weather could actually endanger their crops, which would ring a note of judgment regarding their sin in asking for a king. The story makes no comment about whether this freak weather brought any economic hardship on the people, but the possibility of such would have not been missed by the people (and it could explain their subsequent fear of death).[4]

The Prophet's Role and Closing Words (12:19–25)

The weather evoked both awe and repentance from the people, and they ask Samuel to intercede for them. In response Samuel encourages not fear but obedience and warns them about idolatry (12:20–21). Samuel then reassures the people God "will not reject his people" (12:22), even though they asked for a king. Further, Samuel promises to continue to pray for the people, characterizing failure to do so as nothing less than "sin" (12:23). What is more, far from indicating his retirement, Samuel commits to continue to teach the people "the way that is good and right" (12:23). In other words, Samuel

---

4. Longman has suggested that the untimely weather was "the outworking of a covenant curse which motivates the Israelites to repent of their past sin and to keep the sanctions which had just been presented to them by Samuel." T. Longman III, "1 Sam 12:16–19: Divine Omnipotence or Covenant Curse?" *WTJ* 45 (1983): 171.

may not be the political "leader" of Israel any longer, with Yahweh's anointed now among them, but he will continue to be the spiritual leader—Yahweh's prophet—who will pray for them and teach them. Some scholars see in this a description of the new role of prophets in light of the monarchy: prophets no longer served as political leaders (like Moses and Samuel) but remained the spiritual leaders and teachers of the people.[5]

Samuel concludes by again warning them of the perils of disobedience and exhorting them to fear and obey God. Persisting in evil, he warns, will mean the end of both them *and their king.* Since Samuel explicitly noted that Saul was present for his speech (12:3), his words can be seen as a direct warning to Saul and perhaps some flexing of his spiritual muscle to let Saul know that he is not above the prophet.[6]

LIVE the Story

Re-Telling the Old, Old Story

It is said that those who cannot remember the past are condemned to repeat it.[7] The idea is that if nations or individuals do not learn from their mistakes in the past, they will make the same mistakes again. The biblical authors appear to hold to a similar idea in that they frequently recite the main events of Israel's history, particularly Yahweh's acts on Israel's behalf. Here in 1 Samuel 12 the prophet reminds the people about their past mistakes and God's acts of both judgment and salvation in response. Despite the fact that, as we have seen, Samuel's recitation of salvation history was colored with his personal issues, it served a very important purpose: to remind them not to repeat their mistakes (forgetting Yahweh) and to inspire new generations to faith in God (by reminding them of his salvific acts). This retelling of the salvation story is commanded frequently in Scripture. For example, Exodus 10:2 states, "that you may tell your children and grandchildren how I dealt harshly with the Egyptians and how I performed my signs among them, and that you may know that I am the LORD" (cf. Deut 6:20–25). In the larger history of Joshua–2 Kings, similar recitations of Yahweh's acts on Israel's behalf are frequently found (e.g., Deut 1–4; Josh 23–24; 2 Sam 7; 1 Kgs 8). So today, Christians must continue this practice corporately and individually by reading the Bible and telling again the old, old, story.

5. McCarter, *I Samuel*, 219; Arnold, *1 & 2 Samuel*, 190.

6. Chrysostom similarly viewed Samuel's words here as directed to the new king "to take down his pride." Franke, *Joshua, Judges, Ruth, 1–2 Samuel*, 238.

7. The quote is usually attributed to George Santayana.

God Uses Flawed Humans

The 1997 movie *The Apostle*, which starred Robert Duvall as a charismatic Southern preacher, Euliss "Sonny" Dewey, portrayed a very complex character who, though flawed, was a good man. In the film Sonny is presented as an effective evangelist who loves God deeply and cares for people, though he is weak and imperfect, with serious anger management issues. In a jealous rage when Sonny confronted his wife's lover (the youth pastor at his church) on a baseball diamond, he swung a baseball bat at him, accidentally killing him. On the run from police, Sonny starts a new church, ministers to the poor, and wins many to Christ. In fact, the last scene of the film (spoiler alert) has him converting fellow prisoners on the chain gang as even in his incarceration he continues to win people for Christ. When the film was released some Christians criticized the film as mocking Pentecostal or Southern holiness churches and wished it had been a more positive portrayal of a Christian preacher. In an interview with *Christianity Today*, however, Duvall denied that he intended to mock in any way but simply was portraying a complex, complicated man with a deep faith.[8] Nevertheless, Christians differ as to whether Sonny's "humanity" portrayed in the film discounted his deep spirituality and clear spiritual gifts also showcased. My opinion is that the film shows that God works through deeply flawed individuals.

Can such a polarity exist in one spiritual leader? For some time now, my six-year-old son always categorizes each character in the toys he plays with as a "good guy" or "bad guy." This way of playing usually worked well with the relatively simple scenarios in his play (Star Wars, superheroes, or police). However, not too long ago we were watching a movie together and he asked about a character in the show, "Is he a good guy or a bad guy?" In response, I tried to explain that the character in question was a bit of both. He was a good guy overall but had done a bad thing in this instance. Since he was used to lumping all people into the categories of "good guy" or "bad guy," he had a pretty hard time with it. Similarly, Christians often have a hard time when the fallibility of the prophet Samuel is pointed out. Samuel is a good guy. How come you are saying he is a bad guy? What is more, Samuel is a prophet! Aren't prophets by definition good guys?

As we have seen so far in the story of Samuel, the prophet is a very complex character. We see his taking personal offense at the people's request for a king (1 Sam 8:6); his blindness to his son's sins (1 Sam 12:2); and now his biased description of recent history. Yet, this same prophet was faithful and *did* capably lead Israel. Samuel served with integrity and did not abuse his office in any way. Furthermore, Samuel faithfully delivered the word of God to the people (1 Sam 3:19).

---

8. Mark Morking, "The 'Low'-Down on Robert Duvall," *Christianity Today*, 27 July, 2010, http://www.christianitytoday.com/ct/2010/julyweb-only/lowdownrobert-july-10.html.

Throughout the Bible we see the heroes of the faith presented "warts and all." In order to save his own skin, Abraham lied (twice) about his wife being his sister (Gen 12:10–20; 20:1–18). Moses disobeyed God (Num 20:8–12); David killed a faithful soldier and committed adultery with his wife (2 Sam 11). Even in the New Testament, the apostle Peter took up with Judaizers (Gal 2:11–14) and the apostle Paul wrote off John Mark (Acts 15:38–39) because of his initial failure (Acts 13:13), though eventually Paul came to see the value of John Mark (2 Tim 4:11).

Throughout church history, great Christian leaders of the past have also shown similar complexity. Augustine of Hippo is one of the great theologians in church history whose writings continue to edify, inspire, and move many to greater faith. Yet Augustine is also the same person who saw the only value in women as for procreating, yet saw sex as sinful (and sexual desire the result of original sin)–even sex in marriage (though sex in marriage was a "forgivable fault").[9] Martin Luther is a giant in church history, as his actions and writings led to the Protestant reformation. However, regrettably, Luther also wrote influential anti-Semitic works (e.g., *On the Jews and Their Lies*) that exhibited outrageous racism. Another reformer and pastor, John Calvin, is famous for his theological writings to which many churches (Reformed, Presbyterian, Congregational) today still hold as foundational for their beliefs. Yet Calvin was also instrumental in the denouncing of Michael Servetus and supported his execution for the crime of heresy (the denial of the Trinity).

Therefore, we do a disservice to the gospel by treating Christian leaders as "saints" or heroes without weaknesses. This type of view of great Christians of the past led to their near worship in medieval times with the idolatrous practice of the "invocation of the saints," whereby believers would make direct requests (basically "pray") to dead saints for their intercession. It is important to learn from Christians who have gone before us, but we must realize that they were not perfect. Each Christian is both holy and sinful. There are no purely "good guys."

Samuel's legacy is an example of the dichotomy of every individual involved in Christian service. In the New Testament, "saint" (holy one) is one of the most common terms used of Christians: i.e., due to Christ's atonement, all believers are "saints" ("holy ones"). Yet at the same time, believers are sinners. Every believer is a complex character. Every Christian is fallible. God uses broken vessels to do his good work—treasures in jars of clay (2 Cor 4:7). The most encouraging aspect of the Bible's inclusion of such complex characters is that it shows how God uses flawed, broken people for his service—and I know I am such a person.

---

9. That is, "*venialis culpa*" or "venial fault." See Augustine, *On the Good of Marriage*, VI.6.

LISTEN to the Story

¹Saul was thirty years old when he became king, and he reigned over Israel forty-two years.

²Saul chose three thousand men from Israel; two thousand were with him at Mikmash and in the hill country of Bethel, and a thousand were with Jonathan at Gibeah in Benjamin. The rest of the men he sent back to their homes.

³Jonathan attacked the Philistine outpost at Geba, and the Philistines heard about it. Then Saul had the trumpet blown throughout the land and said, "Let the Hebrews hear!" ⁴So all Israel heard the news: "Saul has attacked the Philistine outpost, and now Israel has become obnoxious to the Philistines." And the people were summoned to join Saul at Gilgal.

⁵The Philistines assembled to fight Israel, with three thousand chariots, six thousand charioteers, and soldiers as numerous as the sand on the seashore. They went up and camped at Mikmash, east of Beth Aven. ⁶When the Israelites saw that their situation was critical and that their army was hard pressed, they hid in caves and thickets, among the rocks, and in pits and cisterns. ⁷Some Hebrews even crossed the Jordan to the land of Gad and Gilead.

Saul remained at Gilgal, and all the troops with him were quaking with fear. ⁸He waited seven days, the time set by Samuel; but Samuel did not come to Gilgal, and Saul's men began to scatter. ⁹So he said, "Bring me the burnt offering and the fellowship offerings." And Saul offered up the burnt offering. ¹⁰Just as he finished making the offering, Samuel arrived, and Saul went out to greet him.

¹¹"What have you done?" asked Samuel.

Saul replied, "When I saw that the men were scattering, and that you did not come at the set time, and that the Philistines were assembling at Mikmash, ¹²I thought, 'Now the Philistines will come down against me at Gilgal, and I have not sought the Lord's favor.' So I felt compelled to offer the burnt offering."

¹³"You have done a foolish thing," Samuel said. "You have not kept the command the Lord your God gave you; if you had, he would have established your kingdom over Israel for all time. ¹⁴But now your kingdom will not endure; the Lord has sought out a man after his own heart and appointed him ruler of his people, because you have not kept the Lord's command."

¹⁵Then Samuel left Gilgal and went up to Gibeah in Benjamin, and Saul counted the men who were with him. They numbered about six hundred.

¹⁶Saul and his son Jonathan and the men with them were staying in Gibeah in Benjamin, while the Philistines camped at Mikmash. ¹⁷Raiding parties went out from the Philistine camp in three detachments. One turned toward Ophrah in the vicinity of Shual, ¹⁸another toward Beth Horon, and the third toward the borderland overlooking the Valley of Zeboyim facing the wilderness.

¹⁹Not a blacksmith could be found in the whole land of Israel, because the Philistines had said, "Otherwise the Hebrews will make swords or spears!" ²⁰So all Israel went down to the Philistines to have their plow points, mattocks, axes and sickles sharpened. ²¹The price was two-thirds of a shekel for sharpening plow points and mattocks, and a third of a shekel for sharpening forks and axes and for repointing goads.

²²So on the day of the battle not a soldier with Saul and Jonathan had a sword or spear in his hand; only Saul and his son Jonathan had them.

²³Now a detachment of Philistines had gone out to the pass at Mikmash. ¹⁴:¹One day Jonathan son of Saul said to his young armor-bearer, "Come, let's go over to the Philistine outpost on the other side." But he did not tell his father.

²Saul was staying on the outskirts of Gibeah under a pomegranate tree in Migron. With him were about six hundred men, ³among whom was Ahijah, who was wearing an ephod. He was a son of Ichabod's brother Ahitub son of Phinehas, the son of Eli, the Lord's priest in Shiloh. No one was aware that Jonathan had left.

⁴On each side of the pass that Jonathan intended to cross to reach the Philistine outpost was a cliff; one was called Bozez and the other Seneh. ⁵One cliff stood to the north toward Mikmash, the other to the south toward Geba.

⁶Jonathan said to his young armor-bearer, "Come, let's go over to the outpost of those uncircumcised men. Perhaps the LORD will act on our behalf. Nothing can hinder the LORD from saving, whether by many or by few."

⁷"Do all that you have in mind," his armor-bearer said. "Go ahead; I am with you heart and soul."

⁸Jonathan said, "Come on, then; we will cross over toward them and let them see us. ⁹If they say to us, 'Wait there until we come to you,' we will stay where we are and not go up to them. ¹⁰But if they say, 'Come up to us,' we will climb up, because that will be our sign that the LORD has given them into our hands."

¹¹So both of them showed themselves to the Philistine outpost. "Look!" said the Philistines. "The Hebrews are crawling out of the holes they were hiding in." ¹²The men of the outpost shouted to Jonathan and his armor-bearer, "Come up to us and we'll teach you a lesson."

So Jonathan said to his armor-bearer, "Climb up after me; the LORD has given them into the hand of Israel."

¹³Jonathan climbed up, using his hands and feet, with his armor-bearer right behind him. The Philistines fell before Jonathan, and his armor-bearer followed and killed behind him. ¹⁴In that first attack Jonathan and his armor-bearer killed some twenty men in an area of about half an acre.

¹⁵Then panic struck the whole army—those in the camp and field, and those in the outposts and raiding parties—and the ground shook. It was a panic sent by God.

¹⁶Saul's lookouts at Gibeah in Benjamin saw the army melting away in all directions. ¹⁷Then Saul said to the men who were with him, "Muster the forces and see who has left us." When they did, it was Jonathan and his armor-bearer who were not there.

¹⁸Saul said to Ahijah, "Bring the ark of God." (At that time it was with the Israelites.) ¹⁹While Saul was talking to the priest, the tumult in the Philistine camp increased more and more. So Saul said to the priest, "Withdraw your hand."

²⁰Then Saul and all his men assembled and went to the battle. They found the Philistines in total confusion, striking each other with their swords. ²¹Those Hebrews who had previously been with the Philistines and had gone up with them to their camp went over to the Israelites who were with Saul and Jonathan. ²²When all the Israelites who had hidden in the hill country of Ephraim heard that the Philistines were on the run, they

joined the battle in hot pursuit. ²³So on that day the LORD saved Israel, and the battle moved on beyond Beth Aven.

²⁴Now the Israelites were in distress that day, because Saul had bound the people under an oath, saying, "Cursed be anyone who eats food before evening comes, before I have avenged myself on my enemies!" So none of the troops tasted food.

²⁵The entire army entered the woods, and there was honey on the ground. ²⁶When they went into the woods, they saw the honey oozing out; yet no one put his hand to his mouth, because they feared the oath. ²⁷But Jonathan had not heard that his father had bound the people with the oath, so he reached out the end of the staff that was in his hand and dipped it into the honeycomb. He raised his hand to his mouth, and his eyes brightened. ²⁸Then one of the soldiers told him, "Your father bound the army under a strict oath, saying, 'Cursed be anyone who eats food today!' That is why the men are faint."

²⁹Jonathan said, "My father has made trouble for the country. See how my eyes brightened when I tasted a little of this honey. ³⁰How much better it would have been if the men had eaten today some of the plunder they took from their enemies. Would not the slaughter of the Philistines have been even greater?"

³¹That day, after the Israelites had struck down the Philistines from Mikmash to Aijalon, they were exhausted. ³²They pounced on the plunder and, taking sheep, cattle and calves, they butchered them on the ground and ate them, together with the blood. ³³Then someone said to Saul, "Look, the men are sinning against the LORD by eating meat that has blood in it."

"You have broken faith," he said. "Roll a large stone over here at once." ³⁴Then he said, "Go out among the men and tell them, 'Each of you bring me your cattle and sheep, and slaughter them here and eat them. Do not sin against the LORD by eating meat with blood still in it.'"

So everyone brought his ox that night and slaughtered it there. ³⁵Then Saul built an altar to the LORD; it was the first time he had done this.

³⁶Saul said, "Let us go down and pursue the Philistines by night and plunder them till dawn, and let us not leave one of them alive."

"Do whatever seems best to you," they replied.

But the priest said, "Let us inquire of God here."

³⁷So Saul asked God, "Shall I go down and pursue the Philistines? Will you give them into Israel's hand?" But God did not answer him that day.

³⁸Saul therefore said, "Come here, all you who are leaders of the army, and let us find out what sin has been committed today. ³⁹As surely as the LORD who rescues Israel lives, even if the guilt lies with my son Jonathan, he must die." But not one of them said a word.

⁴⁰Saul then said to all the Israelites, "You stand over there; I and Jonathan my son will stand over here."

"Do what seems best to you," they replied.

⁴¹Then Saul prayed to the LORD, the God of Israel, "Why have you not answered your servant today? If the fault is in me or my son Jonathan, respond with Urim, but if the men of Israel are at fault, respond with Thummim." Jonathan and Saul were taken by lot, and the men were cleared. ⁴²Saul said, "Cast the lot between me and Jonathan my son." And Jonathan was taken.

⁴³Then Saul said to Jonathan, "Tell me what you have done."

So Jonathan told him, "I tasted a little honey with the end of my staff. And now I must die!"

⁴⁴Saul said, "May God deal with me, be it ever so severely, if you do not die, Jonathan."

⁴⁵But the men said to Saul, "Should Jonathan die—he who has brought about this great deliverance in Israel? Never! As surely as the LORD lives, not a hair of his head will fall to the ground, for he did this today with God's help." So the men rescued Jonathan, and he was not put to death.

⁴⁶Then Saul stopped pursuing the Philistines, and they withdrew to their own land.

⁴⁷After Saul had assumed rule over Israel, he fought against their enemies on every side: Moab, the Ammonites, Edom, the kings of Zobah, and the Philistines. Wherever he turned, he inflicted punishment on them. ⁴⁸He fought valiantly and defeated the Amalekites, delivering Israel from the hands of those who had plundered them.

⁴⁹Saul's sons were Jonathan, Ishvi and Malki-Shua. The name of his older daughter was Merab, and that of the younger was Michal. ⁵⁰His wife's name was Ahinoam daughter of Ahimaaz. The name of the commander of Saul's army was Abner son of Ner, and Ner was Saul's uncle. ⁵¹Saul's father Kish and Abner's father Ner were sons of Abiel. ⁵²All the days of Saul there was bitter war with the Philistines, and whenever Saul saw a mighty or brave man, he took him into his service.

Listen to the Text in the Story: Judges 6–7, 11; Annals of Tiglath-Pileser I; Annals of Shalmaneser III; The Babylonian Chronicle

The newly minted king of Israel is met with another military challenge, this time with the Philistines. The graveness of the threat is heightened by the reference to "three thousand chariots" (1 Sam 13:5) that, in addition to the immense size of the enemy's army, functioned to further terrorize Israel. Due to the difficulty of using chariots in the hilly terrain referred to in 1 Samuel 13, some earlier commentators have cast doubt on the historicity of the reference to chariots here.[1] One of the main functions of chariot use in the ancient world, however, was to put fear into the enemy.[2] This can be seen in how Assyrians would often bring chariots through rough terrain in order get them to the battlefront. For example, the annals of the Assyrian King Shalmaneser III reads "I smashed out with copper picks rough paths in mighty mountains which rose perpendicularly to the sky like the points of daggers (and) into which no one among the kings my fathers had ever passed. I moved (my) chariots (and) troops. . . ."[3] Another Assyrian King, Tiglath Pileser I, claims that "in the high mountains . . . which were impassable for my chariots, I put the chariots on (the soldiers') necks (and thereby) passed through the difficult mountain range."[4] Clearly the value of having chariots present at the battlefield outweighted the difficulties of transporting chariots through rough terrain.

This chapter contains the first predictions of a king who will replace Saul's royal dynasty. What is more, Samuel says this coming king (who will soon be identified as David) will be "a man after his own heart" (13:14). This has led many interpreters to question how David could be called a man after God's own heart when he commits adultery, murder, and displays other ungodly characteristics at times. Contrary to many interpretations, however, "after his own heart" does not really mean someone who has a heart similar to God's. In Hebrew the term "heart" really refers to the "will" or "choice." Basically the phrase "after God's own heart" means "after God's choice." The same phrase is found elsewhere in the Bible and in all instances the meaning is concerned with "desire," "will," or "choice." See the following texts:

1 Sam 13:14	"The Lord has sought out a man *after his own heart*"
1 Sam 14:7	"Do all that you *have in mind* [after your heart]"
Ps 20:4	"May he give you *the desire of your heart* [after your heart]"
Jer 3:15	"Then I will give you shepherds *after my own heart*"

---

1. E.g., Henry Preserved Smith, *A Critical and Exegetical Commentary on the Books of Samuel* (New York: Scribner's Sons, 1904), 95.

2. Long, "1 Samuel," 328.

3. Grayson, *Assyrian Rulers*, 8.

4. Grayson, *Assyrian Royal Inscriptions*, 2.21:10.

There is also a parallel use of the phrase in an ancient text called the Babylonian Chronicle where it says that Nebuchadnezzar installed a "king after his own heart" in Jerusalem, referring to appointing Zedekiah as king in 587 BC.[5]

What this phrase means in 1 Samuel 13 is that rather than Saul's son being the next king, Yahweh will choose the next king of Israel. As John Goldingay writes:

> Other occurrences of such phrases imply this need not suggest he is a king who shares Yhwh's priorities or way of thinking. It simply identifies David as the king whom Yahweh personally chose and made a commitment to.[6]

Nevertheless, since both Saul and David are chosen by God (8:22; 10:24), it may be asked what the difference is this time with David. Perhaps Saul's election was different due to it being in response to the sinful demands of the Israelites for a king. In contrast, David's election will be based entirely on God's choice. As Long writes: "David was Yahweh's choice in a way that Saul, given in response to the people's request, was not."[7]

A distinction between Saul and David may also be seen in the use of the word "king" (Hebrew *melek*) in relation to both. The people request a "king" (Hebrew *melek*) of Samuel (8:5–6). God initially told Samuel (9:16) to anoint Saul "ruler" or "leader" (Hebrew *nagid*). When Samuel anoints Saul (10:1) he does *not* use the word "king" (Hebrew *melek*) but again "ruler" (Hebrew *nagid*). However, as the story progresses, after Saul has been chosen by lot *the people* proclaim, "Long live the king!" (10:24), explicitly using the word "king" (Hebrew *melek*). Furthermore, after Saul delivers Jabesh Gilead *the people* make Saul "king" (using the Hebrew verb from the same root as *melek*). In other words, a clear distinction can be seen between Saul and David. God anointed Saul "leader" (Hebrew *nagid*), but the people installed him as "king" (Hebrew *melek*). In contrast, when God sends Samuel (1 Sam 16:1) to Jesse's house to anoint a new leader, God explicitly says, "I have chosen one of his sons to be king" (Hebrew *melek*). David is God's choice (i.e., *after God's own heart*).

In this chapter (v. 41) reference is made to the Urim and Thummim, which were evidently a type of Israelite lot-casting for gaining divine guidance. Etymologically, it is possible that Urim means "accursed" (related to the

---

5. The full text of this portion of the Babylonian Chronicle can be found online; http://www.livius.org/sources/content/mesopotamian-chronicles-content/abc-5-jerusalem-chronicle/. See A. Kirk Grayson, *Assyrian and Babylonian Chronicles* (Locust Valley, NY: Augustin, 1975), 102, chronicle 5, reverse 11–13; Arnold, *1 & 2 Samuel*, 199.

6. John Goldingay, *Old Testament Theology: Israel's Gospel* (Downers Grove, IL: InterVarsity Press, 2003), 557.

7. V. Philips Long, *The Reign and Rejection of King Saul: A Case for Literary and Theological Coherence*, SBLDS 118 (Atlanta: Scholars Press, 1989), 93.

Hebrew *arar* for "curse") and Thummim means "whole" or "perfect" (related to the Hebrew *tamam* for "perfect"). Thus, one gave the positive answer (Thummim) while the other gave the negative answer (Urim). Alternatively, the significance of the names may be in that Urim begins with the first letter in the Hebrew alphabet (*aleph*) and Thummim begins with the last letter (*taw*).[8] Mosaic legislation (Exod 28:30; Lev 8:8) mandated the Urim and Thummim be placed in the high priest's breastplate, which was apparently worn on top of the high priestly ephod (Exod 28:28). Thus, it could be that the ephod that Ahijah carried here (and that later Abiathar brings to David in 1 Sam 23:6) contained the Urim and Thummim (and was not just a normal ephod that priests wore).[9] Though we are not explicitly told this by the text, David's frequent use of the ephod for obtaining divine guidance (e.g., 1 Sam 23:9–12) might suggest this.

The actual process of gaining divine guidance through the Urim and Thummim is never detailed in Scripture. Some have speculated that they were two objects that could both give positive or negative answers. Thus, when both objects gave the same answer (either two "yes" or two "no"), divine guidance was gained.[10] But if the objects gave opposite answers, then no guidance was given. Thus, Urim and Thummim could not be compelled to give an answer, as we see later with Saul's inability to gain guidance through them (e.g., 1 Sam 28:6). Of course, given the lack of details provided in the biblical text, our understandings of the process of their use remains quite speculative.

EXPLAIN the Story

Faced with Philistine aggression, the new king subsequently musters the entire Israelite militia and then waits the required seven days for Samuel to arrive and offer the requisite pre-battle sacrifices. When Samuel is late to arrive, and the army is deserting Saul, Saul takes matters into his own hands and offers the burnt offering himself. Samuel arrives shortly afterwards and condemns Saul's foolish actions, announcing the end of his royal dynasty. What is more, Samuel declares that God has chosen a successor to the throne—a man of God's own choice. In the meantime, the Philistine threat continues. Initially, Jonathan spearheads an assault on the Philistines, leading Israel to a great victory. During the battle, however, Saul foolishly uttered a vow of fasting on

---

8. Klein, *1 Samuel*, 140.

9. J. Alec Motyer, "Urim and Thummim," in *New Bible Dictionary* (ed. Douglas; Leicester, England: InterVarsity Press, 1996), 1220.

10. H. H. Rowley, *The Faith of Israel: Aspects of Old Testament Thought* (London: SCM Press, 1965), 28–33.

his army. When the soldiers became weak from fasting they ate meat of the spoils of war without draining the blood. Saul then inquires of Yahweh but gets no answer. Saul, therefore, initiates a lot-casting ceremony to find out who is to blame for God's silence.[11] Unbeknownst to Saul, Jonathan, who was unaware of Saul's vow, had eaten honey during the battle and the lot falls on him. Though Saul swears that Jonathan must be executed, the people rescue him from his father owing to the fact that God brought a great deliverance that day through Jonathan.

Introducing Saul's Reign (13:1)

Throughout the books of Samuel–Kings there is a relatively standard way of introducing the reign of a king (often called regnal resumes) with both his age and the length of his reign being stated (e.g., 1 Kgs 14:21; 22:42). This chapter begins such a regnal resume for Saul but unfortunately in the original Hebrew it is missing some important information. Hebrew manuscripts do not list Saul's age and give the length of his reign as only two years (and the number "two" is misspelled). Other textual traditions aren't much help either, as the verse doesn't even appear in the Greek Septuagint. Since a reign of only two years, as recorded in the Hebrew manuscripts, doesn't seem to give enough time for the events described in 1 Samuel 13–31 or for Saul to have a grandson before his death (2 Sam 4:4), the correct number must be missing. Furthermore, shortly after Saul's death, his son, Ishbosheth, is forty years old (2 Sam 2:10) when he briefly reigns. Therefore, the NIV has chosen to follow Josephus (*Ant.* 6.387) and Acts 13:21, which give the length of his reign as "forty" years. Regarding Saul's age, the NIV likely follows a few later Greek manuscripts that give Saul's age as "thirty," though this may be too young seeing as in the very next verse (1 Sam 13:2) his son, Jonathan, is old enough to command an army. Regardless of the details, it is quite ironic that the king with such a flawed reign is given such a flawed introduction here.

War with the Philistines (13:2–7)

While in 1 Samuel 7 Samuel had led a decisive victory over the Philistines, the archenemy of Israel rears its ugly head once again here. This was of course

---

11. There is a significant variant in textual traditions for 1 Sam 14:41. The traditional Hebrew text (MT) only gives a brief prayer by Saul: "Give perfect things," or as the 1984 NIV translates, "Give me the right answer." However, the ancient Greek text (LXX) of 1 Sam 14:41 has Saul pray a longer prayer to God: "Why have you not answered your servant today? If the fault is in me or my son Jonathan, give Urim, but if the men of Israel are at fault, give Thummim." Most scholars believe the longer prayer was originally in the Hebrew as well but was missed by a copyist whose eye jumped from the first instance of the word "Israel" in the verse to the second instance, accidentally omitting everything in between. See Klein, *1 Samuel*, 132.

anticipated as God said that the new king was to "deliver [my people] from the hand of the Philistines" (1 Sam 9:16), but as we will see, the Philistines will continue to be a problem for Saul throughout his reign. Saul's first act as king following the coronation celebration and Samuel's farewell speech in chapter 12 is to create a standing army, drafting three thousand Israelites, and sending the rest of the men who were present at the coronation back home. At this point, some of Samuel's warnings about the king are coming true (cf. 1 Sam 8:11). Saul keeps two thousand soldiers with him and a thousand with his son Jonathan to their hometown of Gibeah.

Subsequently, Jonathan leads an attack on the Philistine outpost, which incites further conflict (and Israel's subsequent deliverance!). Realizing that the standing army would not be enough, Saul calls for the entire militia once again to assemble together (13:3–4). A big battle is brewing, and the Philistine military advantage is emphasized (13:5). Once gathered, the Israelites saw the odds were against them and started to hide (13:6) or leave altogether (13:7). Saul remained at Gilgal with his troops in quite a fright at their prospects.

A Late Prophet and a Premature Sacrifice (13:8–12)

This is where things, tragically, get very interesting. The narrator tells us that Saul waits seven days to act—the very time Samuel had set for him to wait (13:8). This seems to be a reference to 1 Samuel 10:8, when Samuel says to Saul: "Go down ahead of me to Gilgal. I will surely come down to you to sacrifice burnt offerings and fellowship offerings, but you must wait seven days until I come to you and tell you what you are to do." However, contrary to what Samuel declares there (he had said "I will surely come down to you," 1 Sam 10:8), here in chapter 13 the narrator notes that "Samuel did not come to Gilgal, and Saul's men began to scatter" (13:8). Therefore, Saul takes matters into his own hands and offers the pre-battle sacrifices himself. As stated earlier in the commentary, Samuel's advice to Saul in 1 Samuel 10:7–8 was potentially confusing. First, he is told to "do whatever your hand finds to do, for God is with you" (10:7), then he is told to wait for Samuel to tell him what to do (10:8). Here in chapter 13, Saul is in a bind. Samuel has not come when he said he would, and Samuel had told him that God was with him and that he had freedom to act. Therefore, Saul's offering the sacrifice might have seemed like the most reasonable option for him.

Ironically, the tardy prophet shows up just as Saul has finished offering the burnt offering (13:10) and has not even offered the fellowship offerings. Samuel incredulously questions Saul about his actions and Saul defends himself by pointing out Samuel's tardiness and the reality that the troops were abandoning him (1 Sam 13:11; cf. 13:8). Saul further explains his motivation: he felt he needed to seek "The Lord's favor" before the Philistines attacked so he "felt compelled to offer the burnt offering" (13:12). Here we begin to see the superstitious character of Saul come to the fore. Saul's concern was for the "good luck" that offering sacrifices might bring to their battle prospects. This move toward superstition and divination was noticed by the early church father Chrysostom, who insightfully writes:

> And mark it, he [the devil] desired to bring Saul into [the] superstition of witchcraft. But if he had counseled this at the beginning, the other would not have given heed; for how should he, who was even driving them out? Therefore gently and by little and little he leads him on to it.[12]

The Prophetic Rebuke (13:13–14)

Samuel first labels Saul's actions as "foolish" then berates him for disobeying Yahweh's command (13:13). Exactly what command from Yahweh Samuel is referring to is unclear, given that the only command we find that would fit here is Samuel's command to wait seven days for him to come (1 Sam 10:8). What is more, Samuel then claims that if Saul had obeyed then Yahweh would have "established [his] kingdom over Israel for all time" (13:13). At this point we must question whether this is Samuel's interpretation of God's choice of Saul or whether there was a divine word on this given to Samuel, which does not appear in our text. As is, we never find any indication that God made such a commitment to Saul. While in 2 Samuel 7 God makes just such a commitment to David, it is usually seen as something unique and exclusive to David's line. Are Samuel's words somewhat presumptuous? Did God really plan to have Saul and his line on the throne forever?

Samuel's words, however, are vindicated by the progression of the story and his declaration that God has appointed a man of his own choice to succeed Saul (13:14). (Though Saul's story continues for some time, David looms on the horizon already.) Samuel further declares that Saul's "kingdom will not endure" (13:14), though he does not say he is no longer king. Clearly, God was still planning on working with Saul in the interim, as can be seen in 1 Samuel 15 where he commands Saul to wipe out the Amalekites. Only after his disobedience there do we hear that God has now "rejected" him "as king over Israel" (15:26) or that now God has "torn the kingdom of Israel from [Saul] today and has given it to one of [his] neighbors" (15:28). This is the first transgression of Saul that revokes the dynastic succession of his line but not his present role as leader in Israel.

---

12. Franke, *Joshua, Judges, Ruth, 1–2 Samuel*, 242.

Troop Movements (13:15–18)

Following his prophetic rebuke, Samuel exits the scene and goes to Gibeah.[13] Licking his wounds, Saul counts how many men he has left and finds only six hundred soldiers remaining (13:15). This shows tremendous attrition given that he started with a standing army of two thousand (since one thousand were not with Saul but with his son) then called for the rest of the Israelite militia to come, which in chapter 11 numbered 330,000 (1 Sam 11:8). It seems clear that Saul's choice to offer the burnt offering did not engender the courage in the army that he hoped. Samuel's desertion likely caused even more to abandon the new king.

Furthermore, contrary to Saul's fears, which fueled his disobedient act, full-scale warfare does not arise immediately. No battle ensues. After Samuel left Gilgal and Saul counted his men, he moves his army to Gibeah while the Philistines camped at Mikmash (13:16), nearly five miles away. Seeing as we were just told that Samuel went to Gibeah, it could be that Saul was following him somewhat. Perhaps seeking out prophetic support or forgiveness? Hostilities resume, however, as the Philistines send out raiding parties to attack Israelite settlements, perhaps in an effort to cut off Saul's army from reinforcements.

The Philistine Metal Monopoly (13:19–22)

At this point in the story we are told about the Philistine monopoly on metalworking in the area, which means that no one in Israel besides the king and his son had a sword (13:22). This helps explain why the Israelites were so afraid of the Philistines and were abandoning the cause so quickly. Not only were they vastly outnumbered, they were at an extreme disadvantage in the area of weapons technology. This aside also shows the extent of Philistine power. If the Philistines could prevent Israel from even having a blacksmith, they were clearly the dominant power in the land.

Jonathan's Attack at Mikmash (13:23–14:15)

Chapter 13 concludes in noting some of the movements of the Philistine army near Mikmash. At this point Saul is waiting with his army at the outskirts of Gibeah (1 Sam 14:2) while Jonathan spearheads an assault against the enemy. The narrator notes that a priest from the Elide house is accompanying Saul (14:3). What is more, this priest is explicitly said to have an ephod with him. Perhaps this continues to highlight Saul's superstitious nature as he ensures that he has ready access to ritualistic guidance. Ironically, despite the presence of this religious expert, we are told "no one was aware that Jonathan had left" (1 Sam 14:3). Apparently there was no unique or prophetic insight present in this group.

---

13. Though the Septuagint does not have Samuel head to Gibeah and instead the people head there to join the army.

Jonathan's motivation for attacking the Philistine's superior military force is theological in nature, as he says to his armor-bearer, "Perhaps the LORD will act in our behalf. Nothing can hinder the LORD from saving, whether by many or by few" (14:6). Clearly Jonathan had a strong faith in God and was aware of Yahweh's previous acts of salvation wherein he saved Israel when the enemy had a clear numerical advantage (e.g., Judg 7). However, Jonathan also shows a bit of a superstitious side in that he acts in accordance with a self-proclaimed "sign" (1 Sam 14:10). Jonathan's motivation here appears quite different than Saul's (as seen later in this chapter).

First, Jonathan prefaces his sign with a faith statement (14:6). Second, his sign does not appear to be set up toward selfish ends that would help him to avoid taking risks. In fact, Jonathan's requested sign appears weighted toward his engaging the enemy in battle. Jonathan decides that when he reveals himself to the enemy if they say "come up to us" it is a sign he will succeed, but if they say "wait there until we come to you" (14:9) it is a sign he should not engage the Philistines because he will not succeed. It seems likely that an army sitting on top of a hill would rather have the fight come up to them (where they are stationed and have the high ground) rather than choosing to come down-hill to attack. So Jonathan's sign is not too difficult. This is in contrast to many popular uses of signs where usually the harder difficulty of the requested sign is in direct proportion to how much a person wants to *avoid* doing something. Here Jonathan is willing to go fight the enemy (if God will help him), and he makes the most likely reaction of the Philistines the sign that he should fight. Jonathan does not try to coerce God into helping. Contrary to his son, Saul *demands* signs of God and is paralyzed from action until he obtains one.

Jonathan's foray against the enemy is successful and he and his armor bearer defeat twenty Philistines (14:14). Immediately thereafter God sends a panic into the Philistine camp (14:15) and begins to deliver the Philistines into Israel's hands.

Saul's Response to Jonathan's Attack (14:16–46)

When Saul sees what is happening he is very slow to act. First he determines who initiated the attack on the enemy (14:17). Even when he realizes it is his son, he does not join in the battle. It seems that *Saul will not participate in God's deliverance until he gets ritualistic guidance.* Instead, Saul first says, "bring the ark of God" (v. 18).[14] At the very least, the ark was seen as something of a

---

14. Interestingly, the LXX reads "bring the ephod" instead of "bring the ark" at this point in 1 Sam 14:18. This also parallels David's request to the priest to "bring the ephod" right before inquiring of the Lord in 1 Sam 23:9. Thus it is possible that the LXX reflects the original reading.

good luck charm to Saul (as it was to the Israelites in 1 Sam 4). Furthermore, Saul then begins talking to the priest. Given the description of the priest as the one with the ephod (14:2), Saul was clearly trying to obtain an oracle. As the oracular process proceeded, the tumult in the Philistine camp increased to the point that it could no longer be ignored (14:19). The fact that God was giving the Philistines into their hands finally became so obvious that even superstitious Saul could not hold out any longer. Finally, even without ritual confirmation, Saul chooses to join in the deliverance that God was bringing and orders the attack on the Philistines. In order to do this he was forced to interrupt the oracular procedure he had initiated.[15] When Saul and the Israelites finally engage their enemy, they find the Philistines in confusion and killing each other (1 Sam 14:20).

In an aside by the narrator in 14:24, the superstitious characterization of Saul continues to be developed. We are told that in order to get some ritualistic insurance of success in battle Saul had bound the people under an oath saying, "Cursed be anyone who eats food before evening comes, before I have avenged myself on my enemies!" (14:24). The self-centered nature of the vow is worth noting: "avenged *myself* on *my* enemies." The superstitious nature of the vow is obvious, as is its contrary-to-good-sense nature. Forbidding your troops sustenance in the midst of a long battle in order to ensure success is foolhardy. Naturally, his army gets weak. What is more, Jonathan (unaware of the vow) eats some honey that he finds (14:27) and gets much-needed energy to continue the fight. When informed of his father's rash vow, Jonathan clearly voices his disapproval (14:29–30). Then, finally, due to their extreme hunger the Israelite troops (though aware of the vow) end up taking from the spoils of war and eating meat with the blood still in it (14:32). The people's culinary sin is reported to Saul (1 Sam 14:33), so he arranged a place for them to properly slaughter their meat and even built an altar to Yahweh (1 Sam 14:35). Again, in keeping with this superstitious aspect of his character, Saul attempts to deal with his problems through the use of ritual.

Subsequently, Saul decides to continue the attack on the Philistines, but before they go to battle Saul inquires of Yahweh (14:36). When God does not answer him, Saul extrapolates that God's silence must be due to sin, so he proceeds to draw lots—to demand a "sign" to help them find the "sinner." The casting of lots to determine the sinner had good biblical precedents. In the time of Joshua this very method was used to determine who the sinner in the Israelite camp was (Josh 7), though at that time Yahweh himself commanded it be done (Josh 7:13–15). In this story Yahweh does not initiate

---

15. Ordering the priest to "withdraw your hand" (1 Sam 14:19). Tsumura (*Samuel*, 366) suggests this meant for the priest to withdraw his hand from the ephod.

the process, and it was already clear who had sinned. Saul sinned by offering the burnt offering without Samuel (1 Sam 13), and the people had sinned against Yahweh by eating the blood (14:34). Also, Saul must have realized that this unfortunate situation was created by his rash vow that he imposed on the people. What did Saul need to know? Why did he need further ritual confirmation regarding who had sinned? Saul here is using an orthodox practice in a divinatory way.

Immediately before casting lots, Saul invokes Yahweh's name in swearing that the guilty party must die—even if it is his own son (14:39). Presumably, Saul does not think it is his son but is using him as an extreme example, so it is quite ironic. However, the ritualistic inquiry backfires as the lot falls on Jonathan, implicating him as the guilty party (14:42). This despite the fact that the people are guilty of eating meat with blood in it (14:33) and Saul himself is guilty of disobeying Samuel's command to wait and instead offering the burnt offering himself (13:13). Jonathan is the *least* guilty of all but is chosen clearly by lot. First, Jonathan did not know of the oath (14:27) when he ate the honey. Second, Jonathan did not eat of the meat with the blood in it, as did the people. Third, it was Jonathan who spearheaded the assault on the Philistines and through whom God was bringing his people victory.

Jonathan's response is telling in his emphasis that he only tasted a "little" honey but now must die. Given his earlier expressed opinion on the foolishness of his father's vow (14:29–30), Jonathan is clearly questioning the justice of this turn of events. Surely this crime does not fit the punishment of death (14:43). After all, since when is the punishment of death handed out like this for the infraction of someone else's oath of which they were unaware? Yet Saul's superstitious nature once again comes to the fore as he utters another oath, a self-imprecation, swearing that Jonathan will die for tasting the honey (14:44). Rather than showing remorse of any kind, Saul appears happy to execute his son. Luckily for Jonathan the people stand up for Jonathan and "rescue" (literally "ransom") him (1 Sam 14:45).

In response to the people's refusal to execute Jonathan, Saul stops pursuing the enemy (14:46). Before the ritualistic probe into the guilty party, Saul had planned to pursue the Philistines all night, and the people agreed to follow his lead saying, "Do whatever seems best to you" (14:36). Then, in the matter of how the casting of lots should proceed they also agreed to follow his lead, again saying, "Do what seems best to you" (14:40b). However, in the end the people do *not* follow Saul in the matter of the lots. Perhaps due to this turn of events Saul scraps his plan of an all-night pursuit, as the loyalties of the people are now suspect.

The Battles of the King (14:47–52)

Following this story of a somewhat mixed victory over the Philistines, we are given an overview of Saul's military exploits. Saul proved a capable military leader who had success against all of Israel's enemies (14:48–49). The king's family is also introduced, including not only his children but his cousin Abner, the commander of Saul's army, who will become an important character moving forward. Finally, the chapter concludes setting the scene for what follows, noting that the war with the Philistines was long and drawn out and that Saul's practice was to draft any man who he thought would be of service in the war (14:52). Again, we see some of Samuel's predictions coming true as he warned in 1 Samuel 8:11–12 that the king "will take your sons and make them serve with his chariots and horses, and they will run in front of his chariots. Some he will assign to be commanders of thousands and commanders of fifties . . . and still others to make weapons of war and equipment for his chariots."

LIVE the Story

Saving Faith—by Little or Few

Contrary to his father's doubting and superstitious ways, Jonathan displays a real faith in God. His statement to his armor bearer in 14:6, "Perhaps the LORD will act in our behalf. Nothing can hinder the LORD from saving, whether by many or by few," showcases some important aspects of faith. First, it makes no presumption that God has to act in the way Jonathan wishes. Yahweh is free to act as he sees fit. One cannot manipulate God into anything. Yet, at the same time, in faith, it also states a powerful "perhaps." This "perhaps" is an important part of faith (cf. 1 Sam 6:5; 9:6; 2 Sam 16:12). It is a vital part of prayer life. If we do not entertain that God may "perhaps" answer us, there is little motivation to pray. But acknowledging the possibility that God will indeed answer our prayers draws us to the throne of grace.

The second significant aspect of Jonathan's statement is an awareness of God's unlimited power. "Nothing can hinder the LORD from saving" (14:6). God's success does not depend upon the extent of assistance he secures from his people. Salvation comes from the LORD (Ps 3:8). As Paul states in Acts 17:25, God "is not served by human hands, as if he needed anything."

Taken together, Jonathan's statement provides great impetus for faith and prayer. God is free to act according to his will. Yet, there is a real "perhaps" involved. God *may* yet act on our behalf. Furthermore, God can do anything, regardless of the circumstances.

Superstition and Reliance on Signs for Decision Making

Making decisions is not always easy.[16] As a Christian, making decisions ultimately concerns discerning God's will. Most clearly, God's will is revealed in his word. Any decision that goes against God's explicit will, written in the Bible, would obviously be wrong. For example, a decision to steal, kill somebody, or commit adultery would obviously be against God's will. But Christians are often faced with decisions where no clear biblical precedent is given. In such instances it is worth exploring what processes are available to aid believers in decision making. The story of Saul and Jonathan in 1 Samuel 13–14 has clear implications in this regard. Here a clear contrast is made between the faith of Saul and that of his son, Jonathan. While Jonathan displays a laudable faith, Saul displays little but superstition in his decision making.

Similar to Saul, some Christians ask God for signs to aid in the decision-making process. It is like believers' attempt to assist God in communicating to them. They want to give God a mechanism whereby he can communicate to them in a way they will understand. Usually the difficulty of the requested sign is in direct proportion to how much a person wants to do or wants to avoid doing something. That is, one might say, "God, if there is an earthquake in my city today, I will take it as a sign for me to become your missionary to Pakistan." Or, "God, if the sun shines tomorrow I will take it as a sign for me to take the day off from work and relax."

Growing up in the church, I have heard many stories where a Christian would put out their "fleece" to find help in making a tough decision. There is ample anecdotal evidence for the effectiveness of this method. However, relying on anecdotes as a rationale for this method runs the risk of justifying superstition on the basis of unsubstantiated reports. Rather than relying on the authority of anecdotes, believers must first ask whether there is biblical support for such a method of obtaining direction from God.

Another popular practice among Christians is to make a vow to God in order to get God to do something for them. I remember as a Christian teenager when I wanted something really bad I would sometimes make a vow to God. I would vow to do a good thing if God would make something happen for me. For example, I would pray: "if that girl will just say yes when I ask her out, I will serve you whole heartedly, O God!" While this is pretty funny looking back now, I was quite serious at the time. Invariably, such vows are extremely self-centered. They are in reality an attempt to manipulate God into getting your own way.

---

16. Cf. Paul S. Evans "Living by Faith and Not by Signs: Seeking but Not Divining the Will of God," *McMaster Journal of Theology and Ministry* 12 (2010): 33–60; https://www.mcmaster.ca/mjtm/documents/MJTM12EvansLivingbyFaith.pdf.

Regarding the role of signs and vows to God in Christian decision making, it is important to determine whether there are biblical precedents for these methods of discerning God's will. The story of Saul in 1 Samuel speaks to this issue quite clearly. Saul is clearly obsessed with ritualistic insurance of signs of success. In fact, Saul inclines toward using orthodox Israelite ritual in ways close to sorcery and divination.[17] Saul's superstitious nature is evident in his decision to offer the burnt offering to gain Yahweh's favor (instead of obeying the prophet's command); his keeping the priest with the ephod nearby so that he has ready access to ritualistic guidance; his ordering the ark of the covenant to be brought; his foolishly swearing an oath that his troops fast during the battle; his decision to draw lots to find out who the sinner is (when it was already clear who had sinned); and his self-imprecatory vows to have the sinner killed when found. The problems with Saul's superstitious actions are clear in how his disobedient sacrifice backfired (rather than encouraging the people to fight, they abandoned him more) and how the lot actually fell on the only innocent party—his son, Jonathan. This last turn of events is very significant as the sign (the casting of lots) appeared clear but was clearly wrong. This is a perfect illustration of the problem with reliance on signs for decision-making.

The problem of Saul's failures is very relevant today. Saul's superstition is not that different from many people today. To greater or lesser degrees, parts of our culture can be quite superstitious. This is evidenced in the rise of metaphysical cults, the occult, the New Age movement, etc. Even in the secular West, we Westerners want to tap into the supernatural, especially if it will bring power or security into our lives. And *it is not just Christians who look for signs*. Many non-Christians do not believe in coincidence. The danger is that if we Christians rely on methods like signs or vows to discern God's will and we downplay the importance of biblical content, our faith degenerates into superstition and magic. The idea that supernatural signs are needed actually reflects a pagan spirituality quite similar to Saul's, and his misuse of orthodox practices in divinatory ways is relevant for the church today.

The popular book, *Experiencing God*, by Blackaby and King[18] lists four standard orthodox means for discovering God's will: the Bible, prayer, circumstances, and the church. While helpful guidelines, all of these means can also be used in "divinatory ways." For example, the Bible can be used as a divinatory tool by "Scripture flipping" (adherents will close their eyes, open the Bible to a random page, and look at the first word that their finger hits) or simply taking verses out of context as speaking directly to one's situation; prayer can

---

17. Polzin, *Samuel and the Deuteronomist*, 135.

18. Henry T. Blackaby and Claude V. King, *Experiencing God: How to Live the Full Adventure of Knowing and Doing the Will of God* (Nashville: Broadman & Holman, 1994).

be used as a bargaining tool with God, vowing or asking for arbitrary signs; circumstances can be used by viewing coincidence as divine guidance; and finally the church: hearing the opinion of someone else as infallible prophetic guidance can be used as a divinatory practice.

While the story of Saul provides an important caution against improper attempts at discerning God's will, this is not to say that the Bible says nothing about finding God's will. Deuteronomy 30:11–14 states:

> Now what I am commanding you today is not too difficult for you, or beyond your reach. It is not up in heaven, so that you have to ask, "Who will ascend into heaven to get it and proclaim it to us so we may obey it?" Nor is it beyond the sea, so that you have to ask, "Who will cross over the sea to get it and proclaim it to us so we may obey it?" No, the word is very near you; it is in your mouth and in your heart so you may obey it.

The point here is that Israel had the word of God—the law—and that law was all they needed. They were not told to seek additional revelation or signs but were to obey what had already been revealed. In the New Testament Paul quotes from this passage, saying that Christians also do not need an additional word (Rom 10:6–8). Paul concludes that Christians already have what they need: the gospel message being proclaimed by the apostles. Christians do not need to pursue signs in order to determine God's will. It has been laid out in the gospel itself.

While some might mistakenly think that asking for signs was appropriate in the Old Testament era though perhaps it is not appropriate today, the story of Saul would argue against any normative value for signs. This appears to be the general biblical perspective. This can be seen in the book of Isaiah when Isaiah orders the evil king, Ahaz, to request a sign from God. Ahaz piously rejects Isaiah's request to ask for a sign, saying, "I will not ask; I will not put the LORD to the test" (Isa 7:12). Though Ahaz is actually defying the divine will in his "pious" refusal, he is probably quoting the orthodox position that asking for a sign was a way of putting God to the test.

This negative view of requesting signs is carried on in the New Testament by Jesus. In Matthew 12:38–39 we read:

> Then some of the Pharisees and teachers of the law said to him, "Teacher, we want to see a sign from you." He answered, "A wicked and adulterous generation asks for a sign!"

When Jesus refers to an "adulterous generation" it is hard not to think of the generation of the judges. In a programmatic statement near the beginning of the book of Judges, the Israelites are described as a new "generation"

(Judg 2:10), which "prostituted themselves to other gods" (Judg 2:17). The syncretism of the judges period is characterized as adulterous. During this period we see judges who, like Saul, demand signs of God (e.g., Gideon in Judg 6:17, 36–39) or utter foolish vows in attempt to ensure their success (e.g., Jepthah in Judg 11:30–31). Jesus sees a similarity with what the Pharisees are requesting. In the context of Matthew 12, the request for a sign from Jesus was an evasion of the issue. They did not like what Jesus was saying to them, so they demanded a sign (a pagan/adulterous request). Again, the request for a sign is evidence of underlying resistance to God's revealed will.

In conclusion, what should Christians who are seeking to know God's will do? First, daily reorientation to the truth revealed in Scripture is required. Eugene Peterson has insightfully commented that Christians have an "ancient predisposition for reducing every scrap of divine revelation that we come across into a piece of moral/spiritual technology that we can use to get on in the world."[19] The Bible is not to be used as a tool of divination. We must resist reading the Bible selfishly. Instead, we must read to get to know God. The Bible is not meant to give us some mystical guidance to get us through the day. Paul lists the purposes of Scripture as chiefly salvific (2 Tim 3:15) and also useful "for teaching, for rebuking, for correcting, and for training in righteousness" (2 Tim 3:16). Note that "direct mystical guidance for daily decisions" does not appear on this list. When we read the Bible we should notice what it tells us about God and not try and pull out some indications of what specifically we should do today or what decision we should make in each situation we come across. As Walton has commented, "The paganism in each of us drives us to be self-absorbed, but God's revelation draws us to himself."[20] In other words, it's not about you—despite our culture's consumerist, self-centred orientation; it is about God.

---

19. Eugene H. Peterson, *Subversive Spirituality* (Grand Rapids: Eerdmans, 1997), 30.
20. John H. Walton, *Genesis*, NIVAC (Grand Rapids: Zondervan, 2001), 387.

CHAPTER 13

1 Samuel 15:1–35

 LISTEN to the Story

¹Samuel said to Saul, "I am the one the LORD sent to anoint you king over his people Israel; so listen now to the message from the LORD. ²This is what the LORD Almighty says: 'I will punish the Amalekites for what they did to Israel when they waylaid them as they came up from Egypt. ³Now go, attack the Amalekites and totally destroy all that belongs to them. Do not spare them; put to death men and women, children and infants, cattle and sheep, camels and donkeys.'"

⁴So Saul summoned the men and mustered them at Telaim—two hundred thousand foot soldiers and ten thousand from Judah. ⁵Saul went to the city of Amalek and set an ambush in the ravine. ⁶Then he said to the Kenites, "Go away, leave the Amalekites so that I do not destroy you along with them; for you showed kindness to all the Israelites when they came up out of Egypt." So the Kenites moved away from the Amalekites.

⁷Then Saul attacked the Amalekites all the way from Havilah to Shur, near the eastern border of Egypt. ⁸He took Agag king of the Amalekites alive, and all his people he totally destroyed with the sword. ⁹But Saul and the army spared Agag and the best of the sheep and cattle, the fat calves and lambs—everything that was good. These they were unwilling to destroy completely, but everything that was despised and weak they totally destroyed.

¹⁰Then the word of the LORD came to Samuel: ¹¹"I regret that I have made Saul king, because he has turned away from me and has not carried out my instructions." Samuel was angry, and he cried out to the LORD all that night.

¹²Early in the morning Samuel got up and went to meet Saul, but he was told, "Saul has gone to Carmel. There he has set up a monument in his own honor and has turned and gone on down to Gilgal."

¹³When Samuel reached him, Saul said, "The LORD bless you! I have carried out the LORD's instructions."

¹⁴But Samuel said, "What then is this bleating of sheep in my ears? What is this lowing of cattle that I hear?"

¹⁵Saul answered, "The soldiers brought them from the Amalekites; they spared the best of the sheep and cattle to sacrifice to the LORD your God, but we totally destroyed the rest."

¹⁶"Enough!" Samuel said to Saul. "Let me tell you what the LORD said to me last night."

"Tell me," Saul replied.

¹⁷Samuel said, "Although you were once small in your own eyes, did you not become the head of the tribes of Israel? The LORD anointed you king over Israel. ¹⁸And he sent you on a mission, saying, 'Go and completely destroy those wicked people, the Amalekites; wage war against them until you have wiped them out.' ¹⁹Why did you not obey the LORD? Why did you pounce on the plunder and do evil in the eyes of the LORD?"

²⁰"But I did obey the LORD," Saul said. "I went on the mission the LORD assigned me. I completely destroyed the Amalekites and brought back Agag their king. ²¹The soldiers took sheep and cattle from the plunder, the best of what was devoted to God, in order to sacrifice them to the LORD your God at Gilgal."

²²But Samuel replied:

"Does the LORD delight in burnt offerings and sacrifices
    as much as in obeying the LORD?
To obey is better than sacrifice,
    and to heed is better than the fat of rams.
²³For rebellion is like the sin of divination,
    and arrogance like the evil of idolatry.
Because you have rejected the word of the LORD,
    he has rejected you as king."

²⁴Then Saul said to Samuel, "I have sinned. I violated the LORD's command and your instructions. I was afraid of the men and so I gave in to them. ²⁵Now I beg you, forgive my sin and come back with me, so that I may worship the LORD."

²⁶But Samuel said to him, "I will not go back with you. You have rejected the word of the LORD, and the LORD has rejected you as king over Israel!"

²⁷As Samuel turned to leave, Saul caught hold of the hem of his robe, and it tore. ²⁸Samuel said to him, "The LORD has torn the kingdom of Israel from you today and has given it to one of your neighbors—to one

better than you. [29]He who is the Glory of Israel does not lie or change his mind; for he is not a human being, that he should change his mind."

[30]Saul replied, "I have sinned. But please honor me before the elders of my people and before Israel; come back with me, so that I may worship the LORD your God." [31]So Samuel went back with Saul, and Saul worshiped the LORD.

[32]Then Samuel said, "Bring me Agag king of the Amalekites."

Agag came to him in chains. And he thought, "Surely the bitterness of death is past."

[33]But Samuel said,

> "As your sword has made women childless,
>   so will your mother be childless among women."

And Samuel put Agag to death before the LORD at Gilgal.

[34]Then Samuel left for Ramah, but Saul went up to his home in Gibeah of Saul. [35]Until the day Samuel died, he did not go to see Saul again, though Samuel mourned for him. And the LORD regretted that he had made Saul king over Israel.

Listen to the Text in the Story: Exodus 17:8–14; Numbers 14:43, 45; Judges 3:13; 6:3–5, 33; 7:12; 10:12; Deuteronomy 25:17–19; Joshua 7; Mesha Stela

In this chapter the Amalekites first appear in the story. The Amalekites were a nation descended from Esau (Gen 36:12, 16) and attacked Israel during the wilderness wanderings (Exod 17:8–13). Following the exodus, the Amalekites frequently fought Israel (Num 14:43, 45; Judg 3:13; 6:3–5, 33; 7:12; 10:12). Due to their evil acts, Yahweh promised vengeance against the Amalekites: "I will completely blot out the name of Amalek from under heaven" (Exod 17:14; cf. Deut 25:17–19). Here in 1 Samuel 15, God orders Israel's first king to "totally destroy" the Amalekites, which brings up one of the most difficult practices mentioned in the Bible for modern readers to come to terms with: the practice of "devoting to destruction," often referred to as "the ban" (though the NIV only translates it as "the ban" once, in 1 Chr 2:7), or as *herem* (which is the Hebrew word for the practice). The ban meant to utterly devote something to God (i.e., devote it to destruction), to annihilate or exterminate. In practice it meant that for enemies placed under the ban no prisoners were to be taken, but all were to be killed. Furthermore, no spoils of war could be taken, as all the enemies' property was to be completely destroyed (Josh 7:7, 10–13).

When entering the land of Canaan after the exodus, Israel was commanded to apply the ban to all the Canaanites (Deut 20:16; cf. Josh 10:40; 11:11). The act of the ban has a religious sense in the Old Testament. Something that is devoted to destruction is consecrated to God as his exclusive possession.

The practice of *herem* was not unique to Israel. In an ancient inscription called the Mesha Stela (or Moabite Stone), the Moabite king claims he "devoted to destruction" (*herem*) an Israelite town to his own god, Chemosh.[1] However, it must be noted that the practice of *herem* in Israel is limited to cities and enemies that Yahweh himself designates. The Israelites could not decide on their own what was to be utterly destroyed and most of their enemies were *not* actually put under the ban for total destruction. Implementing *herem* required a direct divine mandate. Most of the time the rationale provided for the ban was to prevent the contamination of God's holy people (Josh 6:18; 7:1, 12; 22:20; 1 Kgs 20:42). For example, Deuteronomy 20:17–18 reads:

> Completely destroy them—the Hittites, Amorites, Canaanites, Perizzites, Hivites and Jebusites—as the LORD your God has commanded you. Otherwise, they will teach you to follow all the detestable things they do in worshiping their gods, and you will sin against the LORD your God.[2]

Since things devoted to destruction were the exclusive property of Yahweh, violations of the ban were taken very seriously. For example, Deuteronomy 7:26 warns that if you bring something under the ban into your house you will also be put under the ban (cf. Josh 7:1, 2:24–26). In 1 Samuel 15, the Hebrew word *herem* appears eight times (sometimes as a verb, other times as a noun), so understanding its meaning is vital if we are to understand the story here and why Saul is called to task for his disobedience of the ban.

EXPLAIN the Story

While the previous story signaled the end of Saul's dynasty, this story definitively ends Yahweh's endorsement of Saul's regency. Given the straightforward task of wiping out the Amalekites, Saul fails to carry out Yahweh's command,

---

1. You can read the entire Mesha Stele inscription online: https://en.wikipedia.org/wiki/Mesha_Stele.

2. It should be pointed out that on occasion people placed under the ban were in fact exempted when they submitted to, rather than resisted, Yahweh's claims. In the book of Joshua, the Canaanite Rahab (Josh 2) and the Gibeonites (Josh 9) stand as examples of such exemptions and contrast with the Canaanite kings' resistance of Yahweh's plan (5:1; 9:1–2; 10:1–5; 11:1–5), suggesting that the Canaanites died primarily due to their stubborn resistance of God. As Hubbard asserts, the survival of Rahab and the Gibeonites actually "affirms divine acceptance of foreigners like Rahab and the Gibeonites within Israel" (cf. Deut 10:18). Robert L. Hubbard, *Joshua*, NIVAC (Grand Rapids: Zondervan, 2009), 202.

sparing their king and the best of the animals. Yahweh informs Samuel and expresses regret over making Saul king. Samuel confronts Saul on his disobedience, but Saul denies the charge due to the fact he only spared the king, and the soldiers saved the animals to use in sacrifices. Samuel rebukes Saul, declaring that Yahweh desires obedience more than sacrifices. Furthermore, Samuel likens Saul's disobedience to divination and idolatry. Despite the prophetic condemnation of his actions, Saul begs Samuel to honor him before the people and help him repent. Surprisingly, Samuel concedes to do so and completes the task to which Saul was called—killing the Amalekite king, Agag. The chapter concludes noting that Samuel (though mourning Saul's demise) did not visit Saul again and that God regretted he had made Saul king.

A Mission from Yahweh (15:1–3)

The chapter begins with Saul being given a clear mission to carry out as God's anointed. Though Saul's dynasty has been revoked, he still serves as the current king of Israel, and here we see God's intent to continue to use Saul in that role. While in the last interaction between the prophet and king there seemed to be some miscommunication (see 1 Sam 13), this time Samuel seems at pains to make it clear what the mission is. Last time, though Samuel had told Saul to wait for him before offering the sacrifice (1 Sam 10:8), Saul proceeded with the sacrifice when Samuel was late. In his rebuke of Saul, Samuel claimed the king had "not kept the command the LORD your God gave you" (13:13), which, since the text contains no command from Yahweh, presumably referred to Samuel's own command to Saul in 1 Samuel 10:8. In other words, when Samuel commands Saul, he should be aware it is Yahweh commanding him. Here in 1 Samuel 15:1 Samuel makes this clear from the outset, emphasizing that what he is about to say is "the message from the LORD." There can be no appeal to ignorance or misunderstanding this time around. The mission Saul is to carry out is to completely destroy the Amalekites, placing them under the ban (see discussion of "the ban" above). Nothing was to be saved—no people, no animals.

Saul's Partial Obedience (15:4–9)

Once again Saul musters the Israelites, this time securing over two hundred thousand soldiers. Admirably, Saul warns the Kenites, who have proved friends of Israel in the past, of the coming attack on Amalek so they do not become collateral damage during the battle (15:6). Saul then attacked and prevailed against the Amalekites. However, against the clear word of Yahweh, Saul captured the Amalekite king alive, along with the best of the animals (15:9). Probably Saul spared the king to display him as a trophy of war, which fits with his subsequent setting up a "monument in his own honor" in Carmel (15:12).

God Rejects Saul as King (15:10–23)

When Saul disobeyed Yahweh's commands, Yahweh informs Samuel and expresses his "regret" (in Hebrew, *nhm*) over making Saul king in the first place. This is the first of four occurrences of the Hebrew root *nhm* in this chapter. The NIV translates the Hebrew word as "regret" both in 1 Samuel 15:11 and in 1 Samuel 15:35. However, the NIV translates *nhm* as "change his mind" twice in 1 Samuel 15:29. Traditional translations (KJV, RSV, ASV) translate the word as "repent" in all four instances in this chapter (while the ESV consistently translates all four occurrences as "regret"). "Repent" here does not indicate repentance from sin but a change of mind about something (similar to the meaning of "regret"). In order to see the significance of the word in this chapter, I would suggest that all four occurrences should be translated similarly.

After being told of Yahweh's change of mind or regret (*nhm*), the prophet responds in anger and "cries" out to Yahweh all night long. This anger might be due to the fact that Samuel had grown accustomed to the new arrangement wherein Saul was the king, but the king was to submit to the prophet. Since the arrangement was coming to an end, Samuel was angry. After all the work he put into molding the new king, it was all for naught. However, it seems most likely that the prophet was simply angry with God for changing his mind. Samuel would not be the only prophet to wish God would never change his mind. The prophet Jonah was given a mission to "preach against" (Jonah 1:2) Nineveh due to its wickedness, but in the end when God saw their repentance "he relented [repented/changed his mind (Hebrew *nhm*)] and did not bring on them the destruction he had threatened" (Jon 3:10). This made Jonah very angry, and in Jonah 4:2 he prays to God, "Isn't this what I said, LORD, when I was still at home? That is what I tried to forestall by fleeing to Tarshish. I knew that you are a gracious and compassionate God, slow to anger and abounding in love, a God who relents (*nhm*) [repents/changes his mind] from sending calamity." Similar to Jonah who became angry at God for changing his mind (*nhm*) and sparing Nineveh (Jon 3:10), Samuel is angry at God for changing his mind (*nhm*) about Saul.

Early the next morning, Samuel goes to meet the king but is told Saul had already departed and that he "set up a monument in his own honor" in Carmel (15:12). The text does not explain what exactly the monument was, but the fact that it was in his own honor tells us enough: the once humble king is humble no longer. When Samuel finds Saul, before even being asked the king immediately states that he has obeyed Yahweh's orders (15:13). Samuel is not fooled. Not only had God already told Samuel of Saul's disobedience, but he could hear the sound of the sheep and cattle that were spared from destruction.

Saul appears to subtly blame his soldiers in his response ("the soldiers brought them") and also emphasizes they will indeed be slaughtered—in a sacrifice to Yahweh (15:15). Saul may have thought of the plan to sacrifice the animals as fulfilling the command to kill them and thus it was just *delayed* obedience. The rationale for this disobedient delay is clear—the animals would be better put to use as sacrifices (1 Sam 15:15) than merely killed in battle. Clearly Saul believed ritual was the most important thing. It is best to please the deity with sacrifices. Samuel confronts these skewed values head on:

> Does the LORD delight in burnt offerings and sacrifices
>> as much as in obeying the LORD?
> To obey is better than sacrifice,
>> and to heed is better than the fat of rams.
> For rebellion is like the sin of divination,
>> and arrogance like the evil of idolatry.
>> (1 Sam 15:22–23)

It is no accident that Saul's rebellion and arrogance are likened to divination and idolatry. Saul's gradual descent into divination and witchcraft is clearly seen as the story progresses. From his initial attempt to inquire from the man of God regarding his father's donkeys (9:6–10) to his oath of fasting (14:24), his frustrated efforts to inquire of Yahweh (14:37), his casting of lots to seize the sinner (14:41–42), his willingness to perform ritual rather than obey (13:9; 15:21), and his oath to kill Jonathan (14:44), we see how Saul's superstitious ways moved him toward using orthodox Israelite practices in divinizing ways. Furthermore, the reference to "divination" here foreshadows the dark end to Saul's life when he goes all the way and consults a witch at Endor in an attempt to gain some insurance of his success (1 Sam 28).

Finally, Samuel informs Saul that since he rejected God's word, God has rejected him as king (15:23). Not only is his future dynasty canceled, but his current role as king is now revoked. While this punishment may seem harsh to some, elsewhere those who violate God's commands concerning the ban (devoting to destruction) are not just demoted, they are actually killed (cf. Josh 7).

Dramatically, Saul tries to prevent Samuel from leaving by grabbing his robe, causing it to tear. Samuel, like any good pastor, uses it as an illustration— just as this robe has torn, so God has torn the kingdom from Saul. Furthermore, Yahweh will give it to one of Saul's neighbors, who is better than him (15:28). Samuel further affirms that Yahweh's mind is made up and he will not change it. Significantly, the Hebrew root for "change his mind," *nhm*, is the very same word used to express God's (in)action. In 1 Samuel 15:11, God himself states that he regretted (*nhm*) that he made Saul king, and in the closing verse the narrator states that God regretted (*nhm*) that he made Saul king (15:35). At this point the reader must decide whom to believe. Whose statement is reliable? God's (and the narrator's) or Samuel's? It is a basic hermeneutical principle that in biblical narrative God is a reliable character. Furthermore, the narrator also is reliable (often referred to as a third-person omniscient narrator—in that the narrator knows everything about the story). Therefore, if there is contradiction between the words of a character and the words of God (or the biblical narrator), God is always right.

So, while Samuel says God doesn't change his mind (*nhm*), clearly God does and did regarding Saul's regency. In regard to Saul's case, however, Samuel asserts that God will not change his mind about the need to replace him, nor will he change his mind concerning the election of Saul's neighbor, who will reign in his place. History will prove Samuel correct in this regard, though the prophet is incorrect in altogether denying God the ability or disposition to change his mind.

Repentance for a Disobedient King (15:24–35)

Only when the prophet pronounces an end to his kingship does Saul finally admit to sin. What is more, Saul's confession is coupled with yet another excuse, explaining his action as due to his fear of the people (15:24; cf. 1 Sam 14:45). This hardly comes off as sincere repentance. It is reminiscent of the first sin in the garden of Eden where, when confronted with their sin, both the man and the woman blame someone else for their sin (Gen 3:12–13). Looking ahead in the story this is quite the contrast to the repentance of David when caught in sin (2 Sam 12:13–18; 2 Sam 24:10, 17).

Following this half-hearted confession, Saul begs the prophet to "come back" with him (15:25). However, it does not appear that the king and prophet have moved to a new location to which they should now return. Significantly, the Hebrew word here for "come back" (*shub*) can also mean "repent." How translators decide on which meaning to render into English depends on the context in which the word is found. In other words, when the text is clearly about physical movement, the meaning of the Hebrew root *shub* would clearly mean "return" or "come back." However, in a context where there is no movement from geographical locations but instead there is a context of sin and confession, the word usually means "repent." For example, in 1 Samuel 7:3 Samuel says, "If you are returning (*shub*) to the LORD with all your hearts, then rid yourselves of the foreign gods . . . ." Similarly, in 1 Kings 8:47 Solomon uses the root *shub* of repentance, noting, "if they have a change of heart (*shub*) in the land where they are held captive, and repent (*shub*) and plead with you in the land of their captors and say, 'We have sinned, we have done wrong, we have acted wickedly'. . . ." Elsewhere in the larger history of Israel, the verb *shub* is used of either acts of "turning away" from God (i.e., "sin"; cf. Josh 23:12; Judg 2:17; 8:33) or acts of "turning away" from sin (i.e., "repentance"; cf. 1 Kgs 8:48). Both senses are found here in 1 Samuel 15. In 1 Samuel 15:11 Yahweh describes Saul's sin as "turning away" (*shub*) from following him, and here in 15:25 Saul expresses a wish to "turn back" (*shub*) or "repent" from his previous sin.

While a geographical sense for the word is possible here in 1 Samuel 15 (that is, Saul and Samuel are "returning" to the place they had just left, though their initial departure was not expressed in the text), in the context of Saul's sin and his request for forgiveness (15:25), *shub* here has a repentant connotation. As Polzin writes:

> The tendency of commentators to understand *šûb* here as only a local affair (but where are Samuel and Saul supposed to be returning *from*?) has caused many to ignore the penitential meaning of Saul's request. The absence of any clear indication of where Samuel and Saul are supposed to be, before their "turning back" in verse 31, inclines one to conclude that the geographic sense of *šûb*, if present at all, is only a vehicle for its primary meaning here of "to repent."[3]

Considering for a moment that the word here should be translated "repent," the conversation between king and prophet would be rendered as follows:

15:25 (Saul): "Please forgive my sin and *repent* with me, so that I may worship the LORD."

15:26 (Samuel): "I will not *repent* with you. You have rejected the word of the LORD . . ."

15:30 (Saul): "I have sinned. But please honor me before the elders of my people and before Israel; *repent* with me"

15:31 (Narrator): So Samuel *repented* with Saul, and Saul worshiped the Lord.

When Saul asks Samuel to "repent with me," it is not as though the prophet had sin to repent from. Saul's request is more like asking the prophet to accept his repentance or help him by interceding for him. Given the well-known prophetic role of intercession (1 Sam 12:23), Saul's request makes sense. Supporting this understanding of Saul's request are the subsequent actions of Samuel. After turning back to repent with Saul, Samuel completes the

---

3. Polzin, *Samuel and the Deuteronomist*, 143.

repentance of Saul by killing the Amalekite king, Agag, and thereby righting Saul's wrongdoing (15:32–33). Perhaps Samuel hoped that God might have a change of heart after all.

Following this public show of repentance, Samuel and Saul part ways. Samuel leaves for Ramah and Saul for his hometown of Gibeah. Sadly, Samuel never again went to see Saul, though Samuel continued to mourn for him (15:35). Furthermore, God felt regret as well (15:35). Interestingly, the one character who expresses no sorrow or obvious regret over these events is Saul. It would seem the king remained unrepentant to the end.

LIVE the Story

An Immutable God Who Changes

First Samuel 15 has important implications for theological debates about God's being. Christian theology traditionally holds that God is immutable. That is, he does not change for either the better (he is already perfect!) or the worse. God is consistent and dependable and always acts according to his own principles. Building on this, some go on to state that God therefore cannot change his mind. However, in 1 Samuel 15 there is clear evidence that God does just that. As noted above, in this story both the narrator and God himself state that God regrets/changes his mind (*nhm*) about Saul (15:11, 29). Furthermore, this is not the only place in the Bible where God does so. In the story of the flood in Genesis, upon seeing the violence on the earth, God "regretted" (*nhm*) making humans on the earth (Gen 6:6). Another important instance is found in the book of Jonah, where God responded to the Ninevites repentance in Jonah 3:10 by "relenting/changing his mind" (*nhm*) and not destroying them. Jonah later throws this back in God's face in Jonah 4:2, where the prophet prays to God and complains about God's very nature: that God is "a gracious and compassionate God, slow to anger and abounding in love, a God who relents [*nhm*, repents/changes his mind] from sending calamity." This characteristic of God to change his mind/relent/repent is noted elsewhere in Joel 2:13, which repeats Jonah's phrase near verbatim, "Return to the LORD your God, for he is gracious and compassionate, slow to anger and abounding in love, and he relents (*nhm*) from sending calamity."

To some, however, talk of God's changing his mind appears incompatible with his immutability, and Samuel's statement in 1 Samuel 15:29 is often pointed to: "He who is the Glory of Israel does not lie or change his mind (*nhm*); for he is not a human being, that he should change his mind (*nhm*)." However, given the context where Samuel's statement contradicts both God's and the narrator's clear statements, this seems to be weak ground on which to build a theological argument.

In order to be faithful to Scripture's witness of God's character, it must be allowed that God is both immutable and can change his mind. As noted above, God's immutability means that he is consistent and dependable and always acts according to his own principles. However, as depicted clearly in the Bible stories, God acts in response to human actions. He is still consistent. His character does not change. He is always true, moral, and holy. But in response to human decision, God reacts, according to his perfect nature. God may mandate punishment for sin, but in response to human repentance he may relent from punishing. Praise God that he is not fairweather, unreliable, or inconsistent (like humans), but that he *can* and *often does* change his mind and relent from punishment in response to human repentance. As Brueggemann observes, the statements in 1 Samuel 15 "pose a theological problem about the character of God, who does not change and yet who changes."[4] Perhaps holding both of these in tension is closest to biblical faith.

Obedience Rather Than Sacrifice

Samuel's famous statement to Saul emphasizing obedience over ritual observance is not an isolated perspective in the Old Testament. Later prophets would similarly critique Israel's reliance on religious ritual and their neglect of obedience to God's commands (e.g., Amos 5:21–24). This prophetic perspective of the primacy of obedience over ritual sacrifice was not a rejection of the sacrificial system but a call to examine motives and actions.

Samuel's pronouncement to Saul is drawn on by Jesus in the New Testament in Matthew 9:11–13 and Matthew 12:3–7. In the Gospel it is rendered, "I desire mercy, not sacrifice" (interpreting "obedience" as showing "mercy"). In the Gospels, Jesus emphasizes that love for a neighbor is more important than religious ritual. This is similar to Jesus' response when asked about the greatest commandment, as he states, "To love him with all your heart, with all your understanding and with all your strength, and to love your neighbor as yourself is more important than all burnt offerings and sacrifices" (Mark 12:33).

This message has continued implications for Christians today. Sometimes it is easy to go through the motions as a Christian. We might attend church regularly, tithe, volunteer in some capacity, but still live in disobedience to God's word. We may somehow think that doing the right religious act, or saying (or singing) the right thing in worship, ensures right standing with God. However, this reliance on ritual or religious behavior is idolatrous.

---

4. Brueggemann, *First and Second Samuel*, 116.

The Sin of Divination and Idols

This takes us back to Samuel's statement to Saul in 1 Samuel 15:23. How is rebellion like divination/witchcraft and arrogance like idolatry? First, *divination desires an independence, not a submission.* Therefore, it is rebellion against God. Mosaic law forbids mediums, wizards, and those who consult the dead (Deut 18:11; Lev 19:31; 20:6, 27). Besides being a blatantly false religion, the art of mediums and spiritists was condemned because it attempted to circumvent Yahweh himself by seeking from other spirits what only Yahweh can legitimately provide. From a biblical point of view, God's freedom does not allow for divination. Saul's emphasis on ritualistic reassurance and his demand for signs showed his rebellion. Even today, a person wants divination when they do not want to submit to God's will. On the other hand, if rebellion is witchcraft, submission is faith in God. When we submit to God we put our faith in him and do not attempt to retain control for ourselves.

This brings us to the second half of Samuel's statement. How is arrogance like idolatry? The Hebrew word for "arrogance" here is found only seven times in the Old Testament.[5] Besides in our passage, all other appearances of the word mean "to pressure, to insist, persuade, or urge." This pairs well with the sin of rebellion. Rebellion will not submit to God, and "arrogance" demands its own way of God. That is, it attempts to force or manipulate God. This is why this sin is likened to idolatry.

Attempting to manipulate or use God is treating God like an idol. Idols are well taken care of (dressed in expensive garments, offered sacrifices, etc.) in the hopes that the god will take care of those who contribute to the care of the image. Saul attempted to force his will on God through his use of ritual. As noted above, prioritizing ritual over obedience evinces profoundly skewed values. In a way, this is worshiping the ritual rather than the creator.

Biblical law is diametrically opposed to idol worship. The first three of the Ten Commandments (Exod 20:3–7) are a guard against idolatry and the manipulation of Yahweh.

1. You shall have no other gods before me.
2. You shall not make for yourself an image
3. You shall not misuse the name of the LORD your God

The Bible shows throughout that God cannot be manipulated, and these commands forbid any attempts to do so. As Water Brueggemann writes,

> If it is correct, as P. D. Miller suggests, an imageless quality is Yahweh's distinguishing characteristic . . . we may see in the prohibition of images an

---

5. Gen 19:3, 9; 33:11; Judg 19:7; 1 Sam 15:23; 2 Kgs 2:17; 5:16.

assertion of the unfettered character of Yahweh, who will not be captured, contained, assigned, or managed by anyone or anything, for any purpose.[6]

At the heart of idolatry and divination is a refusal to submit to God and a rebellious attempt to manipulate him or conform him to our own will, though this is not always clear in the mind of the idolater. In outward appearances (and possibly in his own duplicit evaluation of himself), Saul was a practicing Yahwist. This can be seen in his use of orthodox Israelite rituals and his later expulsion of mediums and spiritists from Israel (1 Sam 28:3). While on the surface Saul was orthodox, underneath he was bent toward idolatry and divination. The story of Saul can give good cause for examining our own faith. While on the surface we may appear orthodox (faithful, church-attending, tithing Christians), below the surface are we submitting to God or hoping to manipulate him through our religious deeds into giving us what we want in life?

6. Brueggemann, *Theology of the Old Testament*, 184–85.

CHAPTER 14

1 Samuel 16:1-23

LISTEN to the Story

¹The Lord said to Samuel, "How long will you mourn for Saul, since I have rejected him as king over Israel? Fill your horn with oil and be on your way; I am sending you to Jesse of Bethlehem. I have chosen one of his sons to be king."

²But Samuel said, "How can I go? If Saul hears about it, he will kill me."

The Lord said, "Take a heifer with you and say, 'I have come to sacrifice to the Lord.' ³Invite Jesse to the sacrifice, and I will show you what to do. You are to anoint for me the one I indicate."

⁴Samuel did what the Lord said. When he arrived at Bethlehem, the elders of the town trembled when they met him. They asked, "Do you come in peace?"

⁵Samuel replied, "Yes, in peace; I have come to sacrifice to the Lord. Consecrate yourselves and come to the sacrifice with me." Then he consecrated Jesse and his sons and invited them to the sacrifice.

⁶When they arrived, Samuel saw Eliab and thought, "Surely the Lord's anointed stands here before the Lord."

⁷But the Lord said to Samuel, "Do not consider his appearance or his height, for I have rejected him. The Lord does not look at the things people look at. People look at the outward appearance, but the Lord looks at the heart."

⁸Then Jesse called Abinadab and had him pass in front of Samuel. But Samuel said, "The Lord has not chosen this one either." ⁹Jesse then had Shammah pass by, but Samuel said, "Nor has the Lord chosen this one." ¹⁰Jesse had seven of his sons pass before Samuel, but Samuel said to him, "The Lord has not chosen these." ¹¹So he asked Jesse, "Are these all the sons you have?"

"There is still the youngest," Jesse answered. "He is tending the sheep."

Samuel said, "Send for him; we will not sit down until he arrives."

¹²So he sent for him and had him brought in. He was glowing with health and had a fine appearance and handsome features.

Then the LORD said, "Rise and anoint him; this is the one."

[13]So Samuel took the horn of oil and anointed him in the presence of his brothers, and from that day on the Spirit of the LORD came powerfully upon David. Samuel then went to Ramah.

[14]Now the Spirit of the LORD had departed from Saul, and an evil spirit from the LORD tormented him.

[15]Saul's attendants said to him, "See, an evil spirit from God is tormenting you. [16]Let our lord command his servants here to search for someone who can play the lyre. He will play when the evil spirit from God comes on you, and you will feel better."

[17]So Saul said to his attendants, "Find someone who plays well and bring him to me."

[18]One of the servants answered, "I have seen a son of Jesse of Bethlehem who knows how to play the lyre. He is a brave man and a warrior. He speaks well and is a fine-looking man. And the LORD is with him."

[19]Then Saul sent messengers to Jesse and said, "Send me your son David, who is with the sheep." [20]So Jesse took a donkey loaded with bread, a skin of wine and a young goat and sent them with his son David to Saul.

[21]David came to Saul and entered his service. Saul liked him very much, and David became one of his armor-bearers. [22]Then Saul sent word to Jesse, saying, "Allow David to remain in my service, for I am pleased with him."

[23]Whenever the spirit from God came on Saul, David would take up his lyre and play. Then relief would come to Saul; he would feel better, and the evil spirit would leave him.

Listen to the Text in the Story: Judges 9; 1 Kings 22; 2 Corinthians 12:7; Tomb painting of Asiatic tribute bearers from the tomb of Sobekhotep (Eighteenth Dynasty); "The King and the Queen-Mother in the Matter of the Amurrite Princess"

Contrary to the "flask" of oil used in Saul's anointing back in 1 Samuel 9, here in 1 Samuel 16 the prophet is commanded to use a "horn" of oil to anoint the new king. This is likely an animal horn used as a container for oil. As noted in the commentary on 1 Samuel 9, anointing with oil was used in the ancient Near East on various occasions. However, anointing from a "horn" of oil appears to have been unique to ancient Syria-Palestine.[1] For example,

---

1. Othmar Keel, *The Symbolism of the Biblical World: Ancient Near Eastern Iconography and the Book of Psalms* (New York: Seabury Press, 1978), 258.

an envoy from Syria-Palestine carrying a horn of oil for anointing is depicted on a tomb of an Egyptian (dating to around 1420 BC).[2] An ancient Syrian (Ugaritic) text also refers to someone who "has also taken oil in a horn and poured it on the head of the daughter of the king of Amurru."[3] Given the symbolic meaning of a horn in the ancient Near East as indicating power, the use of a horn in anointing here suggests a superior anointing to that of Saul.

EXPLAIN the Story

With Saul's current reign now revoked, a new chapter in Israel's history begins as Yahweh sends Samuel to the house of Jesse to anoint Israel's new king. When Jesse's eldest son, Eliab, who is tall like Saul, comes before the prophet, Samuel concludes that Eliab must be the one to anoint. God, however, informs him of his error and explains that God does not look at outward appearances but at the heart. After considering seven of Jesse's sons, at God's command Samuel eventually anoints David, the youngest son. At this, Yahweh's spirit comes powerfully on David. As the story switches scenes to the rejected king, Saul, we are told God's spirit had departed from him and been replaced by a tormenting spirit. Saul's attendants suggest finding a musician to calm the king when the evil spirit comes on him, and they suggest bringing in David, whose reputation as both musician and warrior precedes him. Thus, David is not only chosen by God but by Saul himself.

Samuel's Last Prophetic Mission (16:1–3)

The chapter opens as the last chapter ended, with Samuel still mourning for Saul. Yahweh, however, is ready to move on (chiding Samuel for his mourning) and has a new mission for Samuel—to anoint Saul's replacement. Like in the case of Samuel's anointing of Saul, the prophet is not told exactly who the chosen one is until the last moment, but he is given explicit instructions on where to go. Samuel initially objects to the plan, afraid Saul would kill him if he found out. Clearly things have changed from the last scene where Samuel was firmly in charge and had informed Saul of his sin and rejection. Now their relationship had so deteriorated that Samuel (correctly) perceives that the king is capable of murdering him if he knew what Samuel was up to.

Regardless of the risky nature of anointing a new king while the other king lives, Samuel's hesitance to obey Yahweh's order here does not reflect well on him. Samuel, more than most, should be aware of the primacy of obedience to

---

2. Long, "1 Samuel," 341.
3. Ibid.

God. Yet his fear of Saul seemed to outweigh his fear of God here. God, however, alleviates Samuel's concerns, telling the prophet that rather than express his full intentions he is to simply state that he has come to sacrifice and to invite Jesse's house to the meal. Then Yahweh will indicate whom Samuel is to anoint.

The Anointing of David (16:4–13)

When Samuel arrived in Bethlehem, its inhabitants were nervous about the prophetic visit. Of course, the last thing Samuel did of late was slaughter the Amalekite king into pieces, so the prophet was no doubt an intimidating presence. Samuel reassures them that he comes in peace and expresses his intentions to sacrifice and invites Jesse and his sons to the meal.

When Jesse's family arrived, the eldest son, Eliab, impressed the prophet and Samuel thought that this son must be the one to anoint. Is this because Eliab was similar to Saul in that both are very tall? Samuel's snap judgment does not reflect well on the prophet. He was specifically told that Yahweh would indicate to him whom to anoint (16:3), yet he rushed to judgment on his own. Regardless, Yahweh sets the prophet straight and urges the prophet not to look on a candidate's height or external features. God does not look on things like people do, instead looking at the heart rather than outward appearances. In Hebrew, the words translated as "outward appearance" are literally "the eyes," which contributes to the irony of the description of David in 16:12 (see below).

Jesse proceeds to bring seven of his sons (he had quite a full quiver) before Samuel, but none were the chosen one. Eventually, Samuel inquires whether these were all of his sons. Jesse responds that there was one more, the youngest, who was out in the field shepherding the flock (perhaps symbolizing his royal career in shepherding Israel). Samuel demands he be brought and when he arrives, surprisingly, given Yahweh's claim that he doesn't look on the outward appearance, David's fine appearance is emphasized (16:12). In fact, literally in Hebrew it says David has "beautiful eyes" (16:12). Seeing as Yahweh just finished saying to Samuel that he doesn't look "to the eyes" (which is what "outward appearance" is literally in Hebrew), this is quite ironic.

David's appearance, however, was not what humans thought a king should look like. In fact, in the next chapter when Goliath first lays eyes on David he despises him for his looks (17:42), as he didn't look like a warrior. Clearly both Samuel and the people were impressed by a tall, imposing physique (cf. 1 Sam 10:24). Here God chooses the youngest (the Hebrew word used here can also mean "smallest") son, overlooked by his entire family as even deserving an invite to the sacrificial meal. David was attractive, but his physical prowess was not initially impressive. Though his height was apparently significantly less than Israel's present king or his older brother, David proves to be by far a superior warrior than either.

Yahweh informs Samuel that this is the one to anoint as king. In front of his brothers, Samuel then anoints David with a "horn of oil" (not the "flask" used for Saul), which resulted in Yahweh's spirit coming on David. While the spirit also came on Saul in 1 Samuel 10:10 (using the identical phrase in Hebrew), it was not directly connected to his being anointed. Furthermore, in David's case the spirit was on him from "that day on" (16:13), implying it was permanent. In contrast, Saul's experiences with the spirit appear more ad hoc, as the spirit rushes on him in 10:10 when he comes upon the company of the prophets and then again in 11:6 when he hears of the siege of Jabesh Gilead.

Unlike when Samuel anointed Saul, the prophet does not offer other advice or give predictions or signs to confirm the anointing. Instead, Samuel exits the scene. This might be the first indication that this time around things are going to be different. Unlike with Saul, Samuel does not foster a mentor relationship with the young king. In fact, Samuel will have almost nothing to with David from here on out. This really was Samuel's last mission.

Saul's Inner Demons (16:14–23)

The story then moves to the house of the current (though rejected) king, Saul. Just as the spirit had come on David, the narrator informs us that the spirit had now left Saul. In its place an "evil spirit" from Yahweh now tormented him. This is not the first time in the Deuteronomistic History that God had sent an evil spirit. In Judges 9, we read of God sending an "evil spirit" (Judg 9:23, ESV, NRSV) that sowed discord between the evil king Abimelech and the people of Shechem. Now an "evil spirit" from God will lead to similar results, but this time between Saul and David.

The presence of the evil spirit was evident to Saul's attendants who not only diagnose his problem but prescribe a remedy as well. Saul should find a musician who could play the lyre and alleviate Saul's symptoms. While Saul agrees to the plan and orders them to find such a musician, one of his servants knew of David's abilities on the lyre and recommends him to Saul. Furthermore, David's bravery, ability as a warrior, oratory skill, and his good looks are also noted by the servant (16:18). What is more, the servant states that Yahweh is with him. It would be hard to find a higher commendation! Who exactly this servant is and how he knew about these qualities of David is a mystery, but his placement there in Saul's court must have been providential.

This is the first mention of David's musical skills, but it is not the last. Later in the story we will see David involved in musical worship (2 Sam 6:5) and described as "the hero of Israel's songs" (2 Sam 23:1). Furthermore, biblical tradition ascribes 73 of the 150 psalms in the book of Psalms to David, and the book of Chronicles presents David as the founder of temple worship music (cf. 1 Chr 6:31–48; 15:16–22; 25:1–31; 2 Chr 8:14; 29:25–30).

After hearing the high commendation for David, Saul sends word to Jesse to give him his son "who is with the sheep." This reference to shepherding is a bit surprising since the servant's recommendation did not include any word of his shepherding skills. Nonetheless, Jesse agrees to the request (not that he had much choice since this was a demand of the king) and sends along a gift with his youngest son. I imagine Jesse must have been quite surprised to hear of the king requesting his youngest son, seeing as Jesse did not even deem it important to bring young David to the sacrifice when Samuel visited Bethlehem. On the other hand, given the recent anointing of David by the prophet, this turn of events may have hinted to Jesse that Yahweh's anointing was already coming into effect, with David now being brought into the center of political power in Israel.

Saul immediately took a liking to David (literally the Hebrew says he "loved him") and decided to keep him in his service permanently. The chapter concludes, noting that the plan of Saul's attendants worked better than they thought it would. Whenever the spirit would come on Saul, David's music would comfort the king, as the servants predicted (16:16). What is more, the evil spirit would *actually leave* Saul at David's lyre playing (16:23). Even Saul's perceptive servants did not predict that miracle.

LIVE the Story

God Looks Past Outward Appearances

As Aristotle reportedly said, "Personal beauty is a greater recommendation than any letter of reference."[4] In this story, the prophet Samuel is initially swayed by the stature and appearance of David's eldest brother, Eliab, so much so that he concludes that Eliab was the one he was sent to anoint. This is not the first time Samuel thought that impressive looks qualified one to lead Israel. In 1 Samuel 10:24, after Saul's election, Samuel declared: "Do you see the man the LORD has chosen? There is no one like him among all the people."

Samuel is not alone in his weakness for judging based on appearances. We are often swayed by what we see on the outside. Today there continues to be widespread discrimination based on outward appearance. Many studies[5] have

---

4. Attributed to Aristotle by Seneca in *On Tranquility of Mind*.

5. E.g., G. Busetta, F. Fiorillo, and E. Visalli, "Searching for a Job is a Beauty Contest," Munich Personal RePEc Archive, Paper No 49392, Aug 30, 2013; A. Feingold, "Good-Looking People Are

shown that attractive people get more call backs on job applications, are more likely to get promoted, and are consistently paid more than less-attractive workers, despite having equal training, performance, and competence.

Unfortunately, this type of discrimination occurs not only in the secular workplace but within Christian ministry as well. (Some churches even request a recent picture of the candidate when searching for a pastor.) Perhaps this is due to some churches continuing to follow secular trends and rationales in this regard. After all, many secular companies have determined that people are more likely to buy their product from an attractive person and purposefully hire to that end. Perhaps similarly, if you want a potential pastor to be influential or to successfully "sell" the gospel, from a human point of view attractive looks would be considered an asset.

Regardless, as the proverbial saying goes, "looks can be deceiving." In 1 Samuel 16, God sets Samuel straight and informs him that he has "rejected" Eliab, using the same word as God's rejection of Saul (see 1 Sam 15:23, 26; 16:1). God is *not* deceived by outward appearances but can look inside and see what someone is truly like. This is a recurring theme in Scripture (cf. 1 Kgs 8:39; Luke 16:15; John 5:24–25; 7:24; 2 Cor 5:16).

This story should caution us to not judge by outward appearances. The kingdom potential of a person cannot be determined based on outward appearances. Furthermore, rather than operating the church like a business and following secular principles, we must realize that God often takes the unlikely or the improbable candidate and transforms them into the leader Israel needed. God often uses a small army to defeat the larger army so that he gets the glory. As Paul writes in the New Testament,

> God chose the foolish things of the world to shame the wise; God chose the weak things of the world to shame the strong. God chose the lowly things of this world and the despised things—and the things that are not—to nullify the things that are, so that no one may boast before him. (1 Cor 1:27–29)

An Evil Spirit from God

One of the most disturbing aspects to the story of Saul's slow demise is God sending an "evil spirit" to the rejected king. Popular Christianity has largely viewed the devil and demonic activity as that of independent malevolent entities who are the archenemies of God. Yet here the "evil spirit" is sent from

Not What We Think," *Psychological Bulletin* 111 (1992): 304–41; B. Harper, "Beauty, Stature, and the Labor Market: A British Cohort Study," *Oxford Bulletin of Economics and Statistics* 62 (2000): 771–800; J. E. Biddle and D. S. Hamermesh, "Beauty, Productivity, and Discrimination: Lawyers' Look and Lucre," *Journal of Labor Economics* 16 (1998): 172–201.

God himself. It should be noted at the outset that the word "evil" in Hebrew (*ra*) has a range of meaning from "calamity," "disaster," or "injury" to "moral evil." So, the "evil" spirit from Yahweh here need not mean "morally evil" or "wicked" but could simply mean "harmful," "damaging," or "injurious."

Along these lines, some have interpreted this "evil" spirit as a psychological problem. In some ways Saul's behavior *does* fit with behaviors of those who suffer from paranoid schizophrenia or bipolar illness. Of course, the two interpretive options need not be mutually exclusive. Whether his problems were due to mental illness or demonic activity, the text makes it clear that his problems were from Yahweh! The text does not shy away from the fact that the "evil" (whether psychological, demonic, or both) that was overtaking Saul's life originated from the divine will.

While this is hard to fit with the popular understanding of God today, it is consistent with a biblical view of God. Both Isaiah 45:7 and Amos 3:6 view God as the cause of "disaster" or "evil" (the Hebrew word *ra*). Furthermore, God clearly uses a "deceiving spirit" in 1 Kings 22:19–22 to his own end. Even in the New Testament we see God giving the apostle Paul a "thorn in my flesh," which is also called a "messenger of Satan" sent to "torment" him (2 Cor 12:7). Clearly in both testaments, evil spirits have no independence except that allowed by God and God uses their evil intentions for his own purposes (cf. 2 Sam 24:1 and 1 Chr 21:1).

Furthermore, Saul's struggle with his inner demons only begins after his defiance of Yahweh's commands (1 Sam 15). As noted in the previous chapter, after his disobedience in the Amalek affair Samuel is in mourning, God is regretting (15:35), but nothing is said of Saul's grief or remorse. The disobedient and defiant king appears unrepentant and only interested in covering up his sin (being "honored" in front of the elders, 1 Sam 15:30). Modern psychology tells us that failure to feel guilt after doing something you know to be wrong is a sign of psychopathy. From this perspective, Saul's struggle with his inner demons after this episode is clearly linked to his disobedience, and the author's reference to Yahweh sending an "evil spirit" to torment Saul must be interpreted in this light.

Saul's tormented state serves as a sober warning of the consequences of continued disobedience. While Saul was free to make his own choices, he did not have similar control over the consequences of his actions. In many ways, choices make us who we are. Saul's disobedience led to his torment. As Motyer writes:

> Choices are the privilege and price of being human. Our privilege is that
> of being responsible beings, recognizing moral values, called to make

responsible choices, and given the opportunity and obligation to live in the light of the foreseeable consequences of our actions. The price we pay is that every choice, for good or ill, goes to fashioning our characters, and whether in the long or short term—or both—makes us answerable to the Judge of all the earth.[6]

---

6. Alec Motyer, *The Message of Exodus: The Days of Our Pilgrimage* (Leicester: InterVarsity Press, 2005), 122.

LISTEN to the Story

[1]Now the Philistines gathered their forces for war and assembled at Sokoh in Judah. They pitched camp at Ephes Dammim, between Sokoh and Azekah. [2]Saul and the Israelites assembled and camped in the Valley of Elah and drew up their battle line to meet the Philistines. [3]The Philistines occupied one hill and the Israelites another, with the valley between them.

[4]A champion named Goliath, who was from Gath, came out of the Philistine camp. His height was six cubits and a span. [5]He had a bronze helmet on his head and wore a coat of scale armor of bronze weighing five thousand shekels; [6]on his legs he wore bronze greaves, and a bronze javelin was slung on his back. [7]His spear shaft was like a weaver's rod, and its iron point weighed six hundred shekels. His shield bearer went ahead of him.

[8]Goliath stood and shouted to the ranks of Israel, "Why do you come out and line up for battle? Am I not a Philistine, and are you not the servants of Saul? Choose a man and have him come down to me. [9]If he is able to fight and kill me, we will become your subjects; but if I overcome him and kill him, you will become our subjects and serve us." [10]Then the Philistine said, "This day I defy the armies of Israel! Give me a man and let us fight each other." [11]On hearing the Philistine's words, Saul and all the Israelites were dismayed and terrified.

[12]Now David was the son of an Ephrathite named Jesse, who was from Bethlehem in Judah. Jesse had eight sons, and in Saul's time he was very old. [13]Jesse's three oldest sons had followed Saul to the war: The firstborn was Eliab; the second, Abinadab; and the third, Shammah. [14]David was the youngest. The three oldest followed Saul, [15]but David went back and forth from Saul to tend his father's sheep at Bethlehem.

[16]For forty days the Philistine came forward every morning and evening and took his stand.

[17]Now Jesse said to his son David, "Take this ephah of roasted grain and these ten loaves of bread for your brothers and hurry to their camp.

¹⁸Take along these ten cheeses to the commander of their unit. See how your brothers are and bring back some assurance from them. ¹⁹They are with Saul and all the men of Israel in the Valley of Elah, fighting against the Philistines."

²⁰Early in the morning David left the flock in the care of a shepherd, loaded up and set out, as Jesse had directed. He reached the camp as the army was going out to its battle positions, shouting the war cry. ²¹Israel and the Philistines were drawing up their lines facing each other. ²²David left his things with the keeper of supplies, ran to the battle lines and asked his brothers how they were. ²³As he was talking with them, Goliath, the Philistine champion from Gath, stepped out from his lines and shouted his usual defiance, and David heard it. ²⁴Whenever the Israelites saw the man, they all fled from him in great fear.

²⁵Now the Israelites had been saying, "Do you see how this man keeps coming out? He comes out to defy Israel. The king will give great wealth to the man who kills him. He will also give him his daughter in marriage and will exempt his family from taxes in Israel."

²⁶David asked the men standing near him, "What will be done for the man who kills this Philistine and removes this disgrace from Israel? Who is this uncircumcised Philistine that he should defy the armies of the living God?"

²⁷They repeated to him what they had been saying and told him, "This is what will be done for the man who kills him."

²⁸When Eliab, David's oldest brother, heard him speaking with the men, he burned with anger at him and asked, "Why have you come down here? And with whom did you leave those few sheep in the wilderness? I know how conceited you are and how wicked your heart is; you came down only to watch the battle."

²⁹"Now what have I done?" said David. "Can't I even speak?" ³⁰He then turned away to someone else and brought up the same matter, and the men answered him as before. ³¹What David said was overheard and reported to Saul, and Saul sent for him.

³²David said to Saul, "Let no one lose heart on account of this Philistine; your servant will go and fight him."

³³Saul replied, "You are not able to go out against this Philistine and fight him; you are only a young man, and he has been a warrior from his youth."

³⁴But David said to Saul, "Your servant has been keeping his father's

sheep. When a lion or a bear came and carried off a sheep from the flock, [35]I went after it, struck it and rescued the sheep from its mouth. When it turned on me, I seized it by its hair, struck it and killed it. [36]Your servant has killed both the lion and the bear; this uncircumcised Philistine will be like one of them, because he has defied the armies of the living God. [37]The LORD who rescued me from the paw of the lion and the paw of the bear will rescue me from the hand of this Philistine."

Saul said to David, "Go, and the LORD be with you."

[38]Then Saul dressed David in his own tunic. He put a coat of armor on him and a bronze helmet on his head. [39]David fastened on his sword over the tunic and tried walking around, because he was not used to them.

"I cannot go in these," he said to Saul, "because I am not used to them." So he took them off. [40]Then he took his staff in his hand, chose five smooth stones from the stream, put them in the pouch of his shepherd's bag and, with his sling in his hand, approached the Philistine.

[41]Meanwhile, the Philistine, with his shield bearer in front of him, kept coming closer to David. [42]He looked David over and saw that he was little more than a boy, glowing with health and handsome, and he despised him. [43]He said to David, "Am I a dog, that you come at me with sticks?" And the Philistine cursed David by his gods. [44]"Come here," he said, "and I'll give your flesh to the birds and the wild animals!"

[45]David said to the Philistine, "You come against me with sword and spear and javelin, but I come against you in the name of the LORD Almighty, the God of the armies of Israel, whom you have defied. [46]This day the LORD will deliver you into my hands, and I'll strike you down and cut off your head. This very day I will give the carcasses of the Philistine army to the birds and the wild animals, and the whole world will know that there is a God in Israel. [47]All those gathered here will know that it is not by sword or spear that the LORD saves; for the battle is the LORD's, and he will give all of you into our hands."

[48]As the Philistine moved closer to attack him, David ran quickly toward the battle line to meet him. [49]Reaching into his bag and taking out a stone, he slung it and struck the Philistine on the forehead. The stone sank into his forehead, and he fell facedown on the ground.

[50]So David triumphed over the Philistine with a sling and a stone; without a sword in his hand he struck down the Philistine and killed him.

[51]David ran and stood over him. He took hold of the Philistine's sword

and drew it from the sheath. After he killed him, he cut off his head with the sword.

When the Philistines saw that their hero was dead, they turned and ran. [52]Then the men of Israel and Judah surged forward with a shout and pursued the Philistines to the entrance of Gath and to the gates of Ekron. Their dead were strewn along the Shaaraim road to Gath and Ekron. [53]When the Israelites returned from chasing the Philistines, they plundered their camp.

[54]David took the Philistine's head and brought it to Jerusalem; he put the Philistine's weapons in his own tent.

[55]As Saul watched David going out to meet the Philistine, he said to Abner, commander of the army, "Abner, whose son is that young man?"

Abner replied, "As surely as you live, Your Majesty, I don't know."

[56]The king said, "Find out whose son this young man is."

[57]As soon as David returned from killing the Philistine, Abner took him and brought him before Saul, with David still holding the Philistine's head.

[58]"Whose son are you, young man?" Saul asked him.

David said, "I am the son of your servant Jesse of Bethlehem."

Listen to the Text in the Story: Genesis 6:4; Numbers 13:33; Deuteronomy 3:11; Egyptian Papyrus Anastasi I;[1] Writings of Alchaeus[2]

Several texts in the Bible refer to people of great height, sometimes translated as "giant(s)," though it is better to see them as *gigantic* rather than giants. These individuals were not "giants" in the fairy-tale sense but extremely large people. The Anakim, or sons of Anak (Num 13:22 and 13:28), encountered by Israel during the conquest (cf. Josh 15:14; Judg 1:20) are known for their gigantic size. The Anakim are said to have descended from the Nephilim in Numbers 13:33. However, Nephilim does not seem to be an ethnic term but rather a word used for a heroic or powerful individual. In Genesis 6:4 reference is made to the Nephilim, who are said to be "heroes of old, men of reknown" (Gen 6:4), but no reference is made to their stature or their being giants.

The Hebrew word most commonly translated "giant" is *raphah* (e.g., Deut 3:11, 13; 2 Sam 21:16, 18, 20). The tallest person mentioned in the Bible is likely King Og, whose bed was "about 14 feet long and 6 feet wide" (Deut 3:11,

---

1. Edmund S. Meltzer and Edward Frank Wente, *Letters from Ancient Egypt*, WAW 1 (Atlanta: Scholars Press, 1990), 108.

2. Andrew M. Miller, *Greek Lyric: An Anthology in Translation* (Indianapolis: Hackett, 1996), 38–50.

NIV note), suggesting he could have been ten–eleven feet tall (or otherwise
liked oversized beds), but his actual height is not listed. Og is said to have been
the "last of" the Rephaim (Deut 3:11). Large ancient human skeletons over
nine feet in length have been discovered in the ancient Near East.[3] Furthermore,
Egyptian Papyrus Anastasi I, dating from the thirteenth century BC, references
Canaanite warriors who were between seven and nine feet tall (it claims some
stood "five cubits (from) their nose to foot").[4] A sixth-century BC Greek text
by Alchaeus also references a warrior who stood around 8 feet 4 inches tall.[5]

While the biblical "giants" were extremely large people, most were actually
not *that* much taller than the largest individuals recorded in the modern era.
The Guinness World Records lists the American Robert Wadlow as the tallest
man ever recorded in the modern era, measuring 8 feet 11.1 inches.[6] The
tallest person alive today is Sultan Kosen from Turkey, who is 8 feet 3 inches.
In all, sixteen people have been recorded as over eight feet tall in recent history.
While many of the tallest people in the modern era had debilitating medical
conditions (such as acromegaly), this was not always the case. The Libyan
basketball player Suleiman Ali Nashnush was 8 feet 1.25 inches when he
played basketball for Libya's national team in 1962. Also, Edouard Beaupré
of Canada, known as the "Willow Bunch Giant," measured 8 feet 3 inches
tall and was renowned as a strongman for his feats of strength (lifting horses
weighing as much as nine hundred pounds) and wrestling abilities.

In 1 Samuel 17, Goliath is never referred to as a "giant," but his proportions
as outlined in the traditional Hebrew text certainly suggest he was a gigantic
man. The traditional Hebrew text (the Masoretic Text) states that Goliath is
about 9 feet 9 inches tall. However, Greek witnesses to the text along with the
oldest Hebrew text of this passage in existence (from the Dead Sea Scrolls)
peg him at about 6 feet 9 inches. Which text is correct is a matter of debate.

If the traditional text is correct, Goliath is indeed a "giant" of a man. If
the Greek manuscripts (and the Hebrew Dead Sea scroll manuscript) preserve
the correct height of this Philistine warrior, then he would have simply been a
large soldier by ancient standards. Furthermore, a height of 6 foot 9 may have
been similar to the height of the current king of Israel, Saul, who was a "head"
taller than anyone else in Israel. Some scholars have suggested that the average
height of a man in ancient Israel was around 5 feet to 5.5 feet tall.[7] If this was

---

3. Walton and Matthews, *IVP Bible Background Commentary*, 188.

4. Meltzer and Wente, *Letters*, 108. Cited in Richard S. Hess, *Joshua: An Introduction and Commentary*, TOTC 6 (Downers Grove, IL: InterVarsity Press, 1996), 218, n. 3.

5. Miller, *Greek Lyric*, 49.

6. *Guinness World Records, 2013* (New York: Guinness World Records), 78–79.

7. Clyde E. Billington, "Goliath and the Exodus Giants: How Tall Were They?" *JETS* 50 (2007): 494.

the case then we could expect Saul to be well over 6 feet tall—a pretty good matchup for the Philistine champion.

It seems unlikely, however, that the Greek and Dead Sea scroll reading of Goliath as only 6 feet 9 inches tall in this passage is correct since a taller Goliath seems to best fit with the literary context. The 125 pounds of armor Goliath is said to be wearing (1 Sam 17:5–7) implies a larger man. Furthermore, although Goliath is not called a "giant" in 1 Samuel 17, his coming from Gath fits with an understanding of him being such. The book of Joshua notes that all the Anakites in Judah and Israel were destroyed, except for in "Gaza, Gath and Ashdod" (Josh 11:22). So, Goliath comes from a town where the last of the Anakites, people renowned for their stature, settled. Goliath was clearly an abnormally large man and six feet nine doesn't seem to fit the literary context.

EXPLAIN the Story

Again, Israel's archenemies threaten God's people. This time a Philistine champion named Goliath offers an alternative to all-out war by suggesting that Israel send out a man to fight him in one-to-one combat, with the survivor winning the day for his nation. Due to Goliath's size and weaponry, the Israelites are too afraid to answer his challenge. Enter a young shepherd boy named David who had been sent to the battle lines to bring food to his older brothers. When David hears Goliath's challenge, he is incensed by the Philistine's defiance of Israel's God and offers to fight the Philistine. After convincing Saul that he is up to the challenge, David heads out to meet the Philistine with only his staff in one hand, a pouch with five stones over his shoulder, and a sling covertly held in the other. Despite the mocking of Goliath, David declares that he will defeat the Philistine and make it known that the God of Israel is real. David deftly slings a stone at Goliath's forehead, causing him to fall facedown on the ground, where David then decapitates the Philistine with his own sword. The Philistines flee and are pursued by the Israelite soldiers, who win the day. The chapter closes with a conversation between King Saul and his general, Abner, concerning David's identity. It seems that even at this early point in their relationship Saul has begun to view David as a threat to his kingship and wants Abner to be aware.

Battle Lines Are Drawn (17:1–3)

The chapter opens with the Philistines again showing military aggression by assembling their army near an Israelite town (Sokoh). They set up camp at a strategically important area that contained the main passage between Philistine and Israelite territories in the area. Saul led the Israelite army to meet the Philistine challenge with battle lines drawn on opposing hills and a valley between them.

Goliath's Challenge (17:4–11)

A gigantic man steps out from the Philistine lines to challenge Israel. He is a seasoned veteran of war and wears the latest high-tech gear available at the time. As an alternative to a full-scale war, Goliath suggests a one-on-one fight between himself and an Israelite soldier—winner take all. The arrangement to have two heroes fight instead of thousands battling was popular in that day. Interestingly, in his challenge Goliath explicitly calls out Saul: "Am I not a Philistine, and are you not the servants of Saul?" (17:8). Seeing as the tallest man in Israel was Saul (10:23), perhaps Goliath is mocking the Israelite king for not meeting his challenge himself. Regardless, both Saul and all of Israel were too afraid to go meet Goliath in battle.

Introducing David (17:12–16)

Although the reader was already introduced to David in the last chapter, he is reintroduced here. Most scholars view this as due to the author's reliance on different sources and their honoring the different traditions by utilizing them despite the apparent redundancy. However, this narratorial aside provides some important pieces of information for understanding the story here in chapter 17. First, we are told why David's father, Jesse, was *not* present at the war camp: he was very old (v. 12). Second, we are told that David's eldest brothers had "followed Saul" to the war. This is interesting in light of the events that occurred in the previous chapter. The prophet Samuel had anointed their baby brother as king over Israel, yet these same brothers loyally follow Saul. Thirdly, this background information explains David's current situation. Despite being called up by Saul for duty at the end of chapter 16, here the narrator informs us that David continued to shepherd his father's sheep in his hometown, going "back and forth" between his duties for the king and his father—sort of working two jobs. Evidently, Saul had not called for David's lyre playing in some time, given that Goliath had challenged Israel for forty days before David hears of it (17:16).[8]

---

8. Another possibility is that chs. 16 and 17 are not in chronological order but have been thematically structured to introduce David first as a musician and then as a warrior. Joyce Baldwin (*1 and 2 Samuel: An Introduction and Commentary*, TOTC 8 (Leicester, England; Downers Grove, IL: InterVarsity Press, 1988], 124) speculates that 1 Sam 16 may have originated in Bethlehem, while ch. 17 may have originated in the military archives of Jerusalem.

David's Mission (17:17–24)

David's father sends him to the front lines to check up on his sons, sending along some provisions for David's brothers and some cheese for their commanding officer (perhaps in an effort to secure good treatment for the sons; after all, keeping those sons alive would mean regular delivery of cheese). David secures interim care for the flock then goes to the front lines as his father ordered him. However, upon reaching the front lines, perhaps distracted by the sound of the "war cry," David does *not* deliver the bread to his brothers or the cheese to their commander but instead leaves "his things with the keeper of supplies" (17:22) and "ran" to the battle lines to speak to his brothers. As David talked with his siblings, Goliath came out and made his regular challenge, and "David heard it" (17:23). While other Israelites "fled" in fear of the Philistine champion, David's reaction sets him apart from the other Israelites.

David's Faith and Ambition (17:25–30)

The Israelites describe the available reward for the one who succeeds in defeating Goliath. David is interested. He turns to the men near him and inquires about said reward (v. 26). In his inquiry, we see a glimpse of David's theological perspective. While Goliath said he defied "the armies of Israel" (17:10), David interpreted this as nothing less than defying "the armies of the living God" (17:26). This perspective explains David's courage. While defying a human army is one thing, defying God's own army is folly. David's strong faith in God comes to the fore here.

At the same time, David's human ambition is also seen in his multiple inquiries into the reward. David first hears of the reward in verse 25, then inquires of the reward in verse 26, and is told once again in verse 27. Following Eliab's rebuke of David, he again inquires about the reward in verse 30 and receives the same answer once again. While David clearly has a strong faith, his interest in the reward is underscored here.

David's older brother, Eliab, whom Samuel was initially keen to anoint, hears David's inquiries into the reward and gets very angry. He accuses his little brother of abandoning the sheep and only coming from Bethlehem "to watch the battle" (v. 28). Most would interpret Eliab's tirade against David as unjust and inaccurate. After all, contrary to Eliab's accusations, David left a shepherd with the sheep and was there on his father's orders, not just for selfish reasons. Furthermore, the fact that Eliab loyally followed Saul (v. 13) despite Samuel's anointing of David as king may show some lack of faith in his baby brother, if not jealousy. However, as David's brother it is also possible that he knows a little something about David. After all, David did just abandon the supplies and run to the battle lines (v. 22), where he continually asked about the reward for slaying the giant. What is more, many of the words found in Eliab's critique here show up in 2 Samuel 11–12, where the worst of David's character is displayed with his sin with Bathsheba and the murder of her husband. For example, in Hebrew the words "see" (11:2), "battle" (2 Sam 11:7, 25), "sheep" (2 Sam 12:2, 4), "few" (2 Sam 12:8), and "evil" (12:9, 11) all appear in that later story. Also in 1 Samuel 17:28 we read that Eliab "burned with anger at him," which is the identical phrase found in 2 Samuel 12 when David "burned with anger against" the man who stole the ewe sheep in Nathan's parable (who was actually David himself). As Bodner writes:

> Even at this triumphal moment in the Davidic career, Eliab is used to sound a note of warning: David should always attend to matters of heart. . . . When Eliab accuses David of neglecting 'those few sheep', in this context it sounds like a rant. Later in the story, David will neglect his role as a 'shepherd' of God's people. There is 'one little ewe lamb' mentioned in 2 Samuel 12 that becomes an occasion of great stumbling and national disaster.[9]

So perhaps Eliab's critique is mixed. Like David's character, it is partly true, partly flawed. Still, in the present story one feels for David and his reply of "Can't I even speak?" (17:29). David, however, immediately proceeds to inquire once more about the reward. This continual inquiry into the reward could be in order to "get it on record"—kind of like saying "just so we are all clear, this is what I'll get if I do this—you guys are my witnesses."

David and Saul (17:31–39)

When Saul hears about David's statements and inquiries into the reward, he has David brought to him, where David makes his intentions to fight Goliath known. Saul objects to David's offer, saying, "you are only a young man, and he has been a warrior (Hebrew *ish milhamah*) from his youth" (v. 33). Saul's assessment of David shows the king's lack of perception, as it contradicts the description of David by Saul's attendant last chapter who said that David was "a brave man and a warrior (Hebrew *ish milhamah*)" (16:18). Whether or not Goliath was a "warrior (Hebrew *ish milhamah*) from his youth" is open to question (though it is likely), but David, a youth, *actually is* a "warrior" (Hebrew *ish milhamah*)!

To counter Saul's objection, David proceeds to argue that he is capable. He tells of his battles with both lions and bears, where he bested them in hand-to-hand combat. *Note that he doesn't give away his intention to use a sling*

---

9. Bodner, *1 Samuel*, 183.

in the battle. He doesn't say, "I shot lions and bears with my trusty sling." In fact, his description of his battle with the bear sounds like he means Goliath (he grabs it by its "beard" [ESV, v. 35], and bears don't have beards). One thing is for sure, David is not planning on fighting Goliath this way, but he *has to sell it* this way to Saul because those were the rules of the game. The challenge was a request for single-armed infantry combat. In the end, David's story of fighting the wild animals convinces Saul that David is a capable warrior and he gives his permission. In fact, Saul declares that "the LORD be with you" (17:37). The king was already told this when David was first recommended to him by his servants (16:18), now Saul acknowledges it as well.

Saul then puts his own armor on David. While this could be a generous act, perhaps the king thought that it would be helpful to have a soldier dressed in his armor defeating the giant so he could claim some responsibility for it. David initially tries out the armor but concludes he is not able to wear it (as he is not used to it), and he takes it off. Of course, as we will see, David's plan didn't require armor.

To understand David's plan to defeat Goliath, we need to understand a few things about ancient combat. In ancient warfare there were basically three divisions of arms: cavalry, infantry, and artillery. Cavalry consisted of soldiers on horses or with chariots. Infantry were men with swords and armor. The artillery were slingers and archers. While the deadly effectiveness of archers probably needs no introduction, it is important to realize the same about ancient slingers. Ancient historians wrote about the deadly accuracy of slingers. An ancient Greek historian named Thucydides, in his work *The Peloponnesian War*, described how Athens' infantry was decimated in the mountains by slingers (they failed to take Sicily as a result).[10] Within biblical history itself, the effectiveness of slingers is referenced. In Judges 20:16 seven hundred Benjamite slingers are mentioned, "each of whom could sling a stone at a hair and not miss" (cf. 1 Chr 12:2; 2 Chr 26:14).

Baruch Halpern has suggested that ancient warfare was something like a game of rock, paper, scissors.[11] When in formation, infantry could take out cavalry with pikes. Cavalry could take out artillery by their speed, which made them hard to hit and able to quickly close the distance between them. The artillery or projectile slingers and archers were most effective against infantry. In other words, instead of: rock beating scissors—scissors beating paper—and paper beating rock, in ancient warfare: infantry beats cavalry—cavalry beats slingers—and slingers beats infantry.

---

10. Thucydides, *Peloponnesian War*, 7.78.3–7.79.2.
11. Baruch Halpern, *David's Secret Demons: Messiah, Murderer, Traitor, King* (Grand Rapids: Eerdmans, 2001), 11.

Once this is realized, David's ingenious plan comes to light. While he sold Saul on his abilities by describing his talent in hand-to-hand combat, it was David's skill with the sling that he was planning to use in the battle. A close look at how David approaches Goliath hints at his plan. David then "took his *staff in his hand*, chose five smooth stones from the stream, put them in the pouch of his shepherd's bag and, *with his sling in his* [other] *hand*, approached the Philistine" (1 Sam 17:40, emphasis added). Why did David bring a staff with him? Probably a distraction (he had no plans to use the staff as a weapon!) so that Goliath would not notice the sling in his other hand. The ruse appears to work, as Goliath disparagingly yells at David, "Am I a dog, that you come at me with *sticks*?" (1 Sam 17:43, emphasis added).[12]

The Battle (17:40–54)

When David comes near Goliath, the warrior despised David because he did not look like a warrior (as the NIV translates, "a boy, glowing with health and handsome"). Clearly Goliath was unaware of the lesson God had driven home in the previous chapter about judging someone by their looks. No doubt playing to the Philistine crowd, Goliath cursed David by his gods and threatened to feed him to the birds and wild animals.

As you will recall in the last chapter, Saul's servant who recommended David so highly noted David's rhetorical skills (16:18), and here he is proved right as David gives one of the best speeches in the Bible. David's speech is theologically sound and rhetorically powerful. In response to Goliath's "religious language" in cursing him by his gods, David uses "religious language, but instead of cursing, he outlines the character of Israel's God specific to this situation."[13] While Goliath may have the best weapons technology ("sword and spear and javelin," v. 45), David has Yahweh on his side, and the battle is God's. David expresses an unshakable confidence not only that he will defeat Goliath, but that Yahweh will give "all" the Philistines into Israel's hands (17:46–47). David even declares that "the whole world will know that there is a God in Israel" (v. 46).

Furthermore, it will be a teaching moment not just for the Philistines but for "all those gathered here" (v. 47). Remember, Israel had rejected Yahweh's kingship in demanding a "king" like "all the other the nations" (1 Sam 8:5). In this speech David calls Israel back to its faith in God. As Brueggemann puts it, "this is a 'missionary speech,' summoning Israel and the nations to

---

12. Some have suggested that Goliath may have had poor eyesight, which is often the case with individuals with giantism. E.g., Diether Kellermann, "Die Geschichte Von David Und Goliath Im Lichte Der Endokrinologie," *ZAW* 102 (1990): 354–55.

13. Bodner, *1 Samuel*, 187.

fresh faith in Yahweh."[14] David declares that "the battle is Yahweh's"—not the army's and not the king's.

At David's words, Goliath moved to attack, but David "ran quickly" toward him (17:48), with his lack of armor allowing for quicker movements. After all, Goliath is described as wearing over a hundred pounds of metal! He could hardly be expected to be quick moving. Ending the ruse, David then pulls out his sling (doubtless now throwing down the staff) and Goliath suddenly realized David was not coming to fight with a stick after all. At this point, the onlookers may no longer have viewed David as an underdog. *After all, slingers beat infantry like rock beats scissors.* Still, it required a crack shot since only Goliath's forehead was not covered by armor (knowing this, David had picked not just one stone but five). David deftly strikes Goliath in the forehead. It must have traveled with tremendous force, as the text says the stone "sank" into his forehead and the giant fell face first to the ground (17:49).

It seems David was not going to take any chances that the stone may have only stunned Goliath (or knocked him unconscious), as we are told David "ran" to the fallen warrior and proceeded to take his enemy's own sword and "killed him" and then "cut off his head" (17:51). At this the Philistines flee, and the Israelites pursued them and won the battle that day. To the victor go the spoils, so David took Goliath's weapons for himself, placing them in his tent (17:54). The giant's head, however, he put in Jerusalem. This is surprising, seeing as Jerusalem was still ruled by the Jebusites and was not an Israelite city.[15] This may be a glimpse of David's ambition. Did he already have a plan to make Jerusalem his capital city one day? After all, that is exactly what he does immediately after he is crowned king over all Israel in 2 Samuel 5:5–9.

A Concluding Flashback (17:55–58)

Now the narrator takes us back in time to when David was about to go fight against Goliath, and Saul and his general, Abner, were looking on, at which point Saul asks his general who David's father is. This is quite surprising, given that in the previous chapter he was told David was the son of Jesse (1 Sam 16:18) and Saul twice sent messengers to Jesse (16:19, 22). Abner claims he does not know who David's father is, so the king commands him to find out. However, it is possible that Saul himself knows full well who David's

---

14. Brueggemann, *First and Second Samuel*, 132.

15. Or, perhaps Jerusalem was the *eventual* destination of Goliath's head (as David would one day rule from there). After all, we are told David put Goliath's weapons in his "tent" but at this point David didn't have a "tent" there as he was not camping with the army. Therefore, storing the giant's armor in his tent must mean that later David did so, and the same is obviously true of his story of Goliath's severed head.

father is but wants his general to be aware of David. Or perhaps his mental illness was causing memory lapses.[16]

Immediately after his victory over Goliath, Abner brought David before Saul, with David still holding on to the dead Philistine's head. Here Saul asks David directly who his father is. Given the context, where there was said to be a reward for killing the giant wherein one's family would be "exempt from taxes in Israel" (17:25), the inquiry into his family makes sense. However, more seems to be going on than that. Saul offers no congratulations or thanks to David. Saul's inquiry into David and his suggestion that his general, Abner, consider David suggest that Saul was already beginning to see David as a rival. Perhaps, as Bodner suggests, "Saul has been told on a couple of occasions that his 'friend/neighbor' will succeed him, and now he is wondering if this 'son' could be the one."[17]

LIVE the Story

Faith That Saves

David's faith-filled theological perspective allowed him a different vantage point on the grave situation in the valley of Elah. While the other Israelites cowered from the threats of mighty Goliath, David instead saw things from a theological perspective, wherein Goliath, by "defy[ing] the armies of Israel" (17:10), was actually "defy[ing] the armies of the living God" (17:26). While Saul and the Israelites were terrified by Goliath's size and appearance, David instead saw his vulnerability.

David's reliance on God for victory is a reminder to us of our own powerlessness without Christ. The victory over Goliath is the victory brought by God himself. As David puts it, "the battle is the LORD's" (17:47). So, we are reminded of Zechariah 4:6, which famously states: "'Not by might nor by power, but by my Spirit,' says the LORD Almighty." This is a powerful call to Christians to remember that victory is not of ourselves but due to the one in whom we put our faith. Just as Israel was trying to succeed by being like "the other nations" and demanding a king to lead them (1 Sam 8:5), so we often rely on human efforts for success. Jesus reminds us of our dependence on him in John 15:5, "I am the vine; you are the branches. If you remain in me

---

16. Of course, many would explain the problem of Saul not recognizing David as being due to this chapter coming from a different source than the previous chapter with its story of Saul and David's initial meeting. E.g., Klein, *1 Samuel*, 173; Robert Alter, *The David Story: A Translation with Commentary of 1 and 2 Samuel* (New York: Norton, 1999), 109–10.

17. Bodner, *1 Samuel*, 190.

and I in you, you will bear much fruit; apart from me you can do nothing." The gospel reminds us that we cannot make it on our own but that Jesus has provided all we need. After all, Jesus notes that even a small faith can move mountains (Matt 17:20).

God Uses Complex Characters

In these first glimpses of David, we begin to see a very complex character develop. David partially obeys his father, bringing provision to the battle-front, but he doesn't deliever the goods as requested and instead leaves them with "the keeper of supplies" (v. 22). David shows self-interest in his preoccupation with the reward on offer for slaying the giant, repeatedly asking about it (vv. 25, 26, 30). When convincing Saul he can defeat the giant, David misrepresents his intentions, instead describing hand-to-hand combat (vv. 34–36). David breaks the rules of combat in sneaking a sling onto the battlefield against Goliath by distracting him with his staff. Halpern characterizes David's battle tactic here as "a blow below the belt, a sucker punch, a man with a howitzer mowing down a peasant with a pitchfork."[18] David's storing of the head of the giant in Jerusalem shows his ambition to make Jerusalem his capital when king. While none of the above would be described as outright sin, it clearly shows that David is not a pristine character whose motivations were purely pietistic.

The point here is not simply to mar the good name of David or to sully his character, but to realize that despite his admirable qualities, David needed a savior, too. While David is a type of Christ in his role as Israel's anointed one, or messiah, the Old Testament still looks for God's perfect anointed one to come. Furthermore, it can be an encouragement to us that God works through flawed people, because we all are flawed. All of us are complex characters. Our best moments in service of God are doubtless tainted with selfish motives. None of us has "arrived" (Phil 3:12), and none of us are completely sinless. Yet thanks to Jesus' death and resurrection, our sin is not counted against us, and God works through us to continue to establish his kingdom.

David as a Type of Christ

Though David's flaws are evident, his words and deeds also set him apart from Saul. In the battle with Goliath, David proves himself to be a worthy successor to the throne of Israel. Though called to deliver Israel from the Philistines (1 Sam 9:16), Saul refuses to meet Goliath's challenge. In contrast, David does not hesitate to defend Israel and runs to the battle. In fulfillment of Samuel's

---

18. Halpern, *David's Secret Demons: Messiah, Murderer, Traitor, King*, 13.

words, David proves he is "better" than Saul (1 Sam 15:28) and is worthy to rule Israel. David relies on God and saves Israel in an unexpected way. In this David also functions as a type of the future anointed one, Jesus, who will also save Israel in an unexpected way. Both David and Jesus are Israel's messiahs, both their victories are against the odds, yet spectacular.

CHAPTER 16

1 Samuel 18:1-30

LISTEN to the Story

¹After David had finished talking with Saul, Jonathan became one in spirit with David, and he loved him as himself. ²From that day Saul kept David with him and did not let him return home to his family. ³And Jonathan made a covenant with David because he loved him as himself. ⁴Jonathan took off the robe he was wearing and gave it to David, along with his tunic, and even his sword, his bow and his belt.

⁵Whatever mission Saul sent him on, David was so successful that Saul gave him a high rank in the army. This pleased all the troops, and Saul's officers as well.

⁶When the men were returning home after David had killed the Philistine, the women came out from all the towns of Israel to meet King Saul with singing and dancing, with joyful songs and with timbrels and lyres. ⁷As they danced, they sang:

"Saul has slain his thousands,

and David his tens of thousands."

⁸Saul was very angry; this refrain displeased him greatly. "They have credited David with tens of thousands," he thought, "but me with only thousands. What more can he get but the kingdom?" ⁹And from that time on Saul kept a close eye on David.

¹⁰The next day an evil spirit from God came forcefully on Saul. He was prophesying in his house, while David was playing the lyre, as he usually did. Saul had a spear in his hand ¹¹and he hurled it, saying to himself, "I'll pin David to the wall." But David eluded him twice.

¹²Saul was afraid of David, because the LORD was with David but had departed from Saul. ¹³So he sent David away from him and gave him command over a thousand men, and David led the troops in their campaigns. ¹⁴In everything he did he had great success, because the LORD was with him. ¹⁵When Saul saw how successful he was, he was afraid of him. ¹⁶But all Israel and Judah loved David, because he led them in their campaigns.

¹⁷Saul said to David, "Here is my older daughter Merab. I will give her to you in marriage; only serve me bravely and fight the battles of the LORD." For Saul said to himself, "I will not raise a hand against him. Let the Philistines do that!"

¹⁸But David said to Saul, "Who am I, and what is my family or my clan in Israel, that I should become the king's son-in-law?" ¹⁹So when the time came for Merab, Saul's daughter, to be given to David, she was given in marriage to Adriel of Meholah.

²⁰Now Saul's daughter Michal was in love with David, and when they told Saul about it, he was pleased. ²¹"I will give her to him," he thought, "so that she may be a snare to him and so that the hand of the Philistines may be against him." So Saul said to David, "Now you have a second opportunity to become my son-in-law."

²²Then Saul ordered his attendants: "Speak to David privately and say, 'Look, the king likes you, and his attendants all love you; now become his son-in-law.'"

²³They repeated these words to David. But David said, "Do you think it is a small matter to become the king's son-in-law? I'm only a poor man and little known."

²⁴When Saul's servants told him what David had said, ²⁵Saul replied, "Say to David, 'The king wants no other price for the bride than a hundred Philistine foreskins, to take revenge on his enemies.'" Saul's plan was to have David fall by the hands of the Philistines.

²⁶When the attendants told David these things, he was pleased to become the king's son-in-law. So before the allotted time elapsed, ²⁷David took his men with him and went out and killed two hundred Philistines and brought back their foreskins. They counted out the full number to the king so that David might become the king's son-in-law. Then Saul gave him his daughter Michal in marriage.

²⁸When Saul realized that the LORD was with David and that his daughter Michal loved David, ²⁹Saul became still more afraid of him, and he remained his enemy the rest of his days.

³⁰The Philistine commanders continued to go out to battle, and as often as they did, David met with more success than the rest of Saul's officers, and his name became well known.

Listen to the Text in the Story: Exodus 15:20; Judges 11:34; 1 Samuel 15:27; Texts from Ugarit and Emar

Beginning this chapter we see Saul's son, Jonathan, bind himself to David in a covenant, offering him his royal robe and his weapons. Several commentators have noted the symbolic significance of the royal robe in the book of Samuel.[1] In chapter 15, when Saul tore Samuel's "robe," the prophet declared that it symbolized the kingdom being torn away from the rejected king (15:27). If a similar symbolism is present here, then Jonathan is in effect giving up his claim on the throne and willingly handing it over to David. This understanding is later expressed when Jonathan declares to David, "You will be king over Israel, and I will be second to you" (1 Sam 23:17).

Texts from the ancient Near East suggest that Jonathan's gift of royal clothing may have had legal implications. A text from Ugarit describes how a rebellious son is required to leave behind "his mantle" when he is kicked out of the family home.[2] In another instance, the king's son must choose between staying with the king or going with his divorced mother. If he chooses to go with his mother he is required to leave behind his robe on the royal throne.[3] This abandonment of the royal robe implied "that he has relinquished his legal status as prince."[4] Unlike Saul's offer of weaponry in the previous chapter, David accepts Jonathan's gift.

EXPLAIN the Story

Following the great victory over Goliath, David's success grows exponentially. Not only does he prove himself a powerful warrior, the king's son, Jonathan, becomes fast friends with David, symbolically acceding his line to the throne by his gift of his royal robe and weapons. After the Israelite women praise David more highly than Saul, however, the king views David as a threat and attempts to kill him. To this end, Saul offers his daughter, Merab, to David in marriage, on condition that David would fight the Philistines, hoping David would die in battle. Despite David's faithful service, Saul reneged on his promise and instead offered Merab to another man. Next, Saul similarly offered his daughter Michal to David, on condition that he kill a hundred Philistines and bring him their foreskins as a bride price. David fulfilled this macabre royal request by bringing home twice the required amount. At this, Saul followed through and gave Michal to David in marriage. As Saul saw

---

1. Bruce C. Birch, "The First and Second Books of Samuel," in *The New Interpreter's Bible* (Nashville: Abingdon, 1998), 1120. Cf. Bodner, *1 Samuel*, 193.

2. E.g., Ras Shamra 8.145, cited in Åke Viberg, *Symbols of Law: A Contextual Analysis of Legal Symbolic Acts in the Old Testament* (Stockholm: Almqvist & Wiksell, 1992), 132.

3. *Le palais royal d'Ugarit* IV, 17.159, cited in Viberg, *Symbols of Law*, 132. Cf. Stan Rummel, "Clothes Maketh the Man—An Insight from Ancient Ugarit," *BAR* 2 (1976): 6–8.

4. Long, "1 Samuel," 353.

David's great success and popularity his fear of David grew, and we are told Saul remained David's enemy for the rest of his life.

Jonathan and David (18:1–4)

The last chapter ended with David speaking with Saul and Abner, and now we find out that the king's son, Jonathan, was also present for the conversation. When David finished talking, Jonathan becomes fast friends with David and, like his father (16:21), he too loves David (18:1). The reasons for these feelings are not explained, but since David had just killed Goliath (and stood there with the giant's head in hand), it could be admiration for his heroics. After all, Jonathan had also fought the Philistines against great odds and based his confidence on Yahweh's ability to save (1 Sam 14:6). Jonathan found a kindred spirit in the son of Jesse.

As we were told last chapter, David had been working two jobs, being Saul's therapeutic musician and continuing to care for his father's flocks (1 Sam 17:15), but Saul now decides that David can no longer go back to his father's house. Perhaps Saul wants to keep an eye on David, but probably he plans to put him to use in the army, as we read before in 1 Samuel 14:52, "whenever Saul saw a mighty or brave man, he took him into his service."

David's Success and Saul's Jealousy (18:5–9)

In verse 5 we are told that David enjoyed continued success and was therefore promoted in the Israelite army. Then in verse 6 we get a narrative flashback to the time immediately after David killed Goliath and the Israelite women serenaded the victory.[5] It was customary for women to sing celebratory songs after a great victory (cf. Exod 15:20; Judg 11:34) and here the women's song celebrates both Saul and David. Saul takes great offense at the song, however, since David is ascribed with a greater number of kills than Saul. Many interpreters have pointed out that no qualitative comparison is implied in using the terms "thousands" and "ten thousand" as they are often simply synonymous terms for "many" in Biblical Hebrew poetry. For example, Psalm 91:7 states: "A *thousand* may fall at your side, *ten thousand* at your right hand, but it will not come near you" (emphasis added).[6] Or Micah 6:7, "Will the Lord be pleased with *thousands* of rams, with *ten thousand* rivers of oil? Shall I offer my firstborn for my transgression, the fruit of my body for the sin of my soul?" (emphasis added).[7] Thus, in light of the literary conventions of biblical poetry,

---

5. Every other instance of "the Philistine" in 1 Samuel refers to Goliath. See 1 Sam 17:8, 10, 11, 16, 23, 26, 32, 33, 36, 37, 40, 41, 42, 43, 44, 45, 48, 49, 50, 51, 54, 55, 57; 18:6; 19:5; 21:9; 22:10.

6. Klein, *1 Samuel*, 188.

7. Bodner, *1 Samuel*, 194.

the song is really "a non-partisan victory cry."[8] It should not be interpreted literally. After all, as Bodner points out, given the explicit context that this was sung after the slaying of Goliath, "Between them, Saul and David have killed but one enemy soldier, so the women's song is just popular music enshrining a happy moment."[9] However, Saul interprets it "in the worst possible sense" and becomes suspicious that David is after his throne.[10]

Prophesying Murder (18:10–19)

The very next day, the evil spirit sent from God again returns to torment Saul. What is more, Saul is said to be "prophesying" in his house as a result. As you recall, Saul was said to "prophesy" before in chapter 10 when he came upon the company of the prophets (10:10–13). Given the context of the evil spirit, however, this prophesying is clearly to be viewed negatively. Many interpreters have understood the word here to mean a type of ecstatic or unusual behavior, leading many translations to render the word "raving" here instead of "prophesying" (e.g., NLT, ESV, NRSV). In this frenzied state, Saul twice attempts to pin David to the wall with his spear, but the young musician managed to avoid his spear both times.

Saul continues to plot David's demise, but rather than killing David himself, Saul intends to have the Philistines kill him in battle. To this end he first appoints David as a commander over a thousand men (18:12), but the tactic backfires as David enjoys continued success and all of Israel grows to love him (18:15). Next, in order to keep David in harm's way, Saul offers his older daughter, Merab, to David, conditional on David's continued fighting against the Philistines. When the date set for the marriage came, however, Saul instead gave Merab to another man. The incident emphasizes Saul's lack of integrity. First of all, marrying the king's daughter was supposed to be part of the promised reward for his slaying of Goliath (17:25), yet Saul added another condition before he would allow it. Second, even when David fulfilled his obligations, Saul went back on his word and gave David's fiancée away to another man.

David and Michal (18:20–30)

When Saul learned that his younger daughter, Michal, was in love with David, Saul again took the same tack and attempted to put David in harm's way. Perhaps due to his reneging on the last marriage offer, Saul now sends word to David through intermediaries informing David of the offer. David's response

---

8. Klein, *1 Samuel*, 188.
9. Bodner, *1 Samuel*, 194.
10. Klein, *1 Samuel*, 188.

that he is "a poor man" is likely an allusion to Saul's failure to deliver on the reward for killing Goliath.[11] After all, the stated reward (which David confirmed three times! cf. 1 Sam 17:25, 26, 31) was "[t]he king will give great wealth to the man who kills him. He will also give him his daughter in marriage and will exempt his family from taxes in Israel" (17:25). David here declares he has not received "great wealth" at this point. Taking the reward as stated, it might appear that the giving of wealth was to precede the giving in marriage.

Saul's servants report David's words to him, but Saul does not address David's allusion to the lack of promised reward. Instead, Saul interprets David's remark as concern that he cannot afford to pay a bride-price to the father, which was required in the ancient world for a young suitor to marry a well-to-do daughter (in this case *a princess*). Saul magnanimously accedes to no bride-price besides one hundred Philistine foreskins (a very macabre request indeed). David agrees and, perhaps due to Saul's previous double-dealing ways, David brings back *double* the amount of required Philistine tokens and their "full number" are counted out before Saul (18:27). At this, Saul followed through and gave Michal to David in marriage. David was now the king's son-in-law, and this caused Saul to fear David even more. The chapter ends, noting the exponential growth of David's military success and accompanying fame.

LIVE the Story

If God Is for Us, Who Can Be Against Us?

In the New Testament the apostle Paul writes, "If God is for us who can be against us?" (Rom 8:31), and this truth is clearly demonstrated in the story of David. God is clearly *for* David. He is the one Yahweh chose ("after his own heart"). Yahweh's commitment to David is seen in the many references to Yahweh's presence with David. From his initial anointing by Samuel, Yahweh's spirit rushed on David (16:13), and the text repeatedly states that Yahweh was "with him" (16:18; 18:12, 28). Furthermore, God's presence with David got results. First, due to God's being "with" him, David was "successful" in whatever he undertook (18:5, 15, 30). Second, David is "loved" by all of Israel and Judah (18:16), including the king's own children, Jonathan and Michal (18:1, 3, 20). Third, each of Saul's actions against David, which he intended for evil, become opportunities for David. The king's attempts to get David killed in battle by making him a military commander result in greater military

---

11. Bodner, *1 Samuel*, 199.

success for David and greater notoriety. Saul's manipulative use of his own daughters against David results in his success against the Philistines and his becoming the royal son-in-law. David's success is reminiscent of Joseph's story, where the many actions that were intended to harm him "God intended ... for good" (Gen 50:20).

A famous messianic title, found in Isaiah 7:14 and applied to Jesus in Matthew 1:23, is Immanuel. Literally in Hebrew Immanuel means "God with us," indicating that just as God was with David, so God will be with the son of David, the Messiah. Therefore, as Christians, if we are in Christ, we are on God's side. God's presence is with us through the Holy Spirit (Eph 1:13; 1 Cor 3:16; cf. 2 Cor 13:5) and God's sovereign work is in our lives. And similar to God's work in David's (and Joseph's) life, "we know that in all things God works for the good of those who love him, who have been called according to his purpose" (Rom 8:28). In other words, just as David was carried along by God's powerful will and purpose, so we as Christians are similarly being carried. Our salvation and success does not depend on our own work and effort but on God's work on our behalf and God's powerful presence with us in Christ.

But just as God's presence and work on David's behalf make his rise to the throne irresistible, conversely Yahweh's opposition to Saul makes his demise unavoidable. That is, if God is against you, who can be for you? While Yahweh's spirit had previously come on Saul to empower him to lead Israel (10:10; 11:6), after his disobedience and rejection Yahweh's spirit left him (16:14). Yahweh was no longer "with him." Instead an injurious or evil spirit was sent to the rejected king. Saul was now on the wrong side of history. He has been rejected as king but was resisting this divine decree and stubbornly holding on to the throne.

During the American Civil War, President Abraham Lincoln is said to have been asked whether God was on his side of the conflict. Lincoln famously replied, "Sir, my concern is not whether God is on our side. My greatest concern is to be on God's side." Saul was told by Samuel that God was no longer on his side, but Saul hoped this would change. In the story we see Saul's attempts to manipulate God to be on his side in his disobediently offering sacrifices before battle (13:9); his saving the best cattle for sacrifice instead of destroying them as commanded (15:15); and in his frantic attempts during the last days of his life to receive divine assurance that God was with him (1 Sam 28:6), even consulting a witch (28:8). Saul's sad story is a reminder that God cannot be forced on to "our" side. Instead we must in faith join *God's* side and submit to his will, trusting in him to direct our lives for his purposes.

CHAPTER 17

1 Samuel 19:1-24

 LISTEN to the Story

¹Saul told his son Jonathan and all the attendants to kill David. But Jonathan had taken a great liking to David ²and warned him, "My father Saul is looking for a chance to kill you. Be on your guard tomorrow morning; go into hiding and stay there. ³I will go out and stand with my father in the field where you are. I'll speak to him about you and will tell you what I find out."

⁴Jonathan spoke well of David to Saul his father and said to him, "Let not the king do wrong to his servant David; he has not wronged you, and what he has done has benefited you greatly. ⁵He took his life in his hands when he killed the Philistine. The LORD won a great victory for all Israel, and you saw it and were glad. Why then would you do wrong to an innocent man like David by killing him for no reason?"

⁶Saul listened to Jonathan and took this oath: "As surely as the LORD lives, David will not be put to death."

⁷So Jonathan called David and told him the whole conversation. He brought him to Saul, and David was with Saul as before.

⁸Once more war broke out, and David went out and fought the Philistines. He struck them with such force that they fled before him.

⁹But an evil spirit from the LORD came on Saul as he was sitting in his house with his spear in his hand. While David was playing the lyre, ¹⁰Saul tried to pin him to the wall with his spear, but David eluded him as Saul drove the spear into the wall. That night David made good his escape.

¹¹Saul sent men to David's house to watch it and to kill him in the morning. But Michal, David's wife, warned him, "If you don't run for your life tonight, tomorrow you'll be killed." ¹²So Michal let David down through a window, and he fled and escaped. ¹³Then Michal took an idol and laid it on the bed, covering it with a garment and putting some goats' hair at the head.

¹⁴When Saul sent the men to capture David, Michal said, "He is ill."

¹⁵Then Saul sent the men back to see David and told them, "Bring him up to me in his bed so that I may kill him." ¹⁶But when the men entered, there was the idol in the bed, and at the head was some goats' hair.

¹⁷Saul said to Michal, "Why did you deceive me like this and send my enemy away so that he escaped?"

Michal told him, "He said to me, 'Let me get away. Why should I kill you?'"

¹⁸When David had fled and made his escape, he went to Samuel at Ramah and told him all that Saul had done to him. Then he and Samuel went to Naioth and stayed there. ¹⁹Word came to Saul: "David is in Naioth at Ramah"; ²⁰so he sent men to capture him. But when they saw a group of prophets prophesying, with Samuel standing there as their leader, the Spirit of God came on Saul's men, and they also prophesied. ²¹Saul was told about it, and he sent more men, and they prophesied too. Saul sent men a third time, and they also prophesied. ²²Finally, he himself left for Ramah and went to the great cistern at Seku. And he asked, "Where are Samuel and David?"

"Over in Naioth at Ramah," they said.

²³So Saul went to Naioth at Ramah. But the Spirit of God came even on him, and he walked along prophesying until he came to Naioth. ²⁴He stripped off his garments, and he too prophesied in Samuel's presence. He lay naked all that day and all that night. This is why people say, "Is Saul also among the prophets?"

Listen to the Text in the Story: Genesis 31:34–35; Exodus 15:23; 1 Samuel 15:23; El Amarna Letter 286; A Letter from Abdu-hepa of Jerusalem

In this chapter, David is forced into hiding due to Saul's malevolent intentions. Jonathan, however, moves on David's behalf and goes to his father and speaks "well of David" to him (19:4)—literally he spoke "good things" about David. Jonathan's speaking "good things" on David's behalf finds an interesting parallel in an ancient Near Eastern letter from El-Amarna wherein a man named Abdu-hepa finds himself falsely accused saying, "What have I done to the king, my lord? They blame me before the king, my lord (saying): 'Abdu-Heba has rebelled against the king, his lord."[1] In his letter Abdu-hepa asks the Egyptian scribes to speak "good things" to his king for him.[2] The parallel

---

1. *ANET*, 487
2. Ibid., 488.

implies the speaking was not simply about David's good character but that the speaking had political overtones, as Jonathan assured the king that David had shown the requisite loyalty due the crown.[3]

In this chapter, David's wife, Michal, utilizes a teraphim, or "idol," to help David escape from her father's grasp. Teraphim appear fifteen times in the Old Testament and appear to have been "household gods"[4] or perhaps statutes of ancestors.[5] They clearly varied in size as Jacob's wife Rachel hid teraphim beneath her saddle (Gen 31:19), but here in our story Michael uses a teraphim as a dummy for David's sleeping body, implying its size was close to that of a human. Biblical texts clearly condemned teraphim (Exod 15:23; 2 Kgs 23:24), though at other times, such as in 1 Samuel 19, they are referred to without any clear censure by the narrator. While not too much is known about teraphim, it is clear that they were not part of official religions or national cults but were prominent in popular or folk religion. In that capacity, it appears they were thought to be useful for divination (Ezek 21:21; Zech 10:2). In this respect, it is ironic that Saul is thwarted by (a disguised) teraphim when Samuel had warned Saul earlier that his rebellion was tantamount to teraphim use (1 Sam 15:23—translated as "idolatry" by the NIV).

EXPLAIN the Story

In this chapter, Saul abandons his plan to have David die at the hands of the Philistines (probably due to David's continued success against them) and begins taking direct measures to have David killed by his own men. First, he directly speaks to Jonathan and his servants about killing David, but Jonathan warns David to hide and then tries to convince his father not to kill David. Saul responds by swearing that David will not be executed, leading David to come back to Saul's court. However, when the evil spirit from God comes on Saul, he again attempts to kill David with his spear. David escapes to his own house, but Saul sends soldiers to guard it, planning to kill him the next morning. David's wife Michal helps him escape and he goes to stay with Samuel in Ramah. Three times Saul sends men to capture David, but each time the pursuers come upon a group of prophets and are unable to continue their

---

3. Klein, *1 Samuel*, 196.

4. Michael Heltzer, "New Light from Emar on Genesis 31: The Theft of the Teraphim," in *'Und Mose Schrieb Dieses Lied Auf': Studien Zum Alten Testament Und Zum Alten Orient: Festschrift Für Oswald Loretz Zur Vollendung Seines 70 Lebensjahres Mit BeiträGen Von Freunden, SchüLern Und Kollegen*, ed. Manfried Dietrich and Ingo Kottsieper (Münster: Ugarit-Verlag, 1998), 357–62.

5. Karel van der Toorn, "The Nature of the Biblical Teraphim in the Light of the Cuneiform Evidence," *CBQ* 52 (1990): 203–22.

search as God's spirit immobilizes them by forcing them to prophesy. Finally, Saul himself comes to Ramah, but the same thing happens to the king as well, allowing David to escape.

Orders to Kill David (19:1–7)

We are not told how much time had passed since the last chapter, but David's continued successes against the Philistines, summarized in the previous verse, have led Saul to abandon his plan to have David die at their hands. Now Saul directly speaks to his son and attendants about killing David. Due to his love for David, Jonathan warns David, who hides while Jonathan attempts to convince his father not to kill David by pointing out David's innocence and valuable service. Saul responds by swearing that David will not be executed, leading David to come back to Saul's court.

Saul Again Attempts to Kill David (19:8–17)

After swearing that David would not be killed, immediately following another notice of David's success against the Philistines (19:8), Saul returns to his murderous ways. Once again, the evil spirit from Yahweh comes on Saul, and while David is playing the lyre for the king, Saul attempts to kill David with his spear. Again, David dodges Saul's spear and escapes, but this time Saul is more resolute. Last time Saul missed with the spear, no overt follow up attempt was made (only Saul's plan to have David die in battle with the Philistines). This time Saul sends men to David's house to ensure he does not escape, planning to kill him in the morning. Once again, Saul's progeny intervenes to save David—this time, David's wife, Michal. Likely seeing the men stationed outside their home, Michal, evidently quite perceptive of her father's ways, correctly discerns that this can only mean one thing—David will be killed in the morning. She therefore urges her husband to run away that night.

Michal proves a capable ally as she helps David escape through the window (as the doors were being guarded) and creates a makeshift mannequin of her husband out of an idol, a garment, and goats' hair and puts it in their bed. Michal then covers for David by telling the guards he was sick in bed. The ruse works as the men do not attempt to take David but instead return to Saul. Evidently, the men did not understand that David was to be killed or David's illness would not have deterred them from their task. At this point, Saul explicitly states his intentions to kill David and orders them to bring him—even if it means bringing him *in his sickbed* (19:15). Of course, when the soldiers return they only find Michal's idolatrous dummy in the bed. When questioned about her actions, Michal claims that David had threatened her life.

David Flees to Samuel (19:18–24)

On the run from the king, David goes to see Samuel at Ramah, which was Samuel's home base of operations (1 Sam 7:17). This is the first time the prophet has made an appearance in the story since he anointed David in chapter 16. Samuel harbors the young fugitive. When word of David's whereabouts gets back to the king, Saul sends men to apprehend David, but they fail to get past the group of prophets as God's spirit immobilizes them by causing them to prophesy. When Saul is told of what happened he is undaunted. Despite his own experience with Yahweh's spirit and his power (1 Sam 10:12; 11:6), Saul attempts to fight against the divine will by sending more men. Even after the second attempt fails in the same way, he sends a third contingent, which also results in more prophesying.

Finally, the king himself goes to Ramah to take matters into his own hands. Predictably, the same thing happens to him as the spirit of God causes him to prophesy, preventing the king from completing his murderous task. What is more, the king removes his clothes and prophesies before Samuel "all that day and all that night" (19:24). The length of time the king is immobilized clearly left David plenty of time to make his escape. Furthermore, these strange incidents again perpetuate the saying about Saul being among the prophets (cf. 10:12).

The symbolic significance of these events cannot be overstated. Just as Saul's initial installation as king involved his prophesying with the prophets (10:10), now his rejection as king culminates once again in his prophesying with the prophets. What is more, just as garments are symbolic of the kingdom in this story, with Saul's tearing of Samuel's garment signifying the tearing away of his kingdom from him (1 Sam 15:27–28) and Jonathan's giving his garment to David signified his acceding the throne to David (18:4), so now Saul takes off his garments "implicitly, to divest himself of the kingship, just as the first episode of Saul among the prophets was an investment with kingship."[6] As Klein notes, "Prophetic ecstasy, which once offered confirmation of his anointing, is now used to certify him as a person from whom Yahweh had departed."[7]

LIVE the Story

The Spirit's Battle

When David is running for his life, his first stop is with the prophet who anointed him. Some commentators have wondered why David would not flee

---

6. Alter, *The David Story*, 122.
7. Klein, *1 Samuel*, 200.

to the south (Judah) where he was from, but instead he goes north to Samuel's home base of Ramah (1 Sam 7:17).[8] While we are not told exactly why this is the case, it fits with David's declared faith perspective back in 1 Samuel 17:47 where he stated, "it is not by sword or spear that the LORD saves." Thus, this theme comes to the fore again in this story as David takes cover with Samuel and the prophets against Saul's military power. Saul sends soldiers to apprehend David, but they are immobilized by Yahweh's spirit.

What is very interesting is the military imagery used in the description of Samuel poised over the prophets as their leader (19:20). As Alter writes:

> The image is implicitly military: the term for "poised" (*nitsav*) is cognate with the terms for garrison and prefect. Samuel . . . commands no divisions, but the band of ecstatics are his troops, and the infectious spirit of God that inhabits them and devastates Saul's emissaries acts as a defensive perimeter.[9]

Despite their military might, the soldiers and the king himself are helpless before their encounter with Yahweh's spirit. Again, we are reminded of Zechariah 4:6, which famously states: "Not by might nor by power, but by my Spirit,' says the LORD Almighty." This story is yet another reminder of the feebleness of human strength in the face of Yahweh's spirit. Furthermore, the military imagery here reminds us of the reality of spiritual warfare. As Christians, our real battle is not against "flesh and blood" (Eph 6:12) and "the weapons we fight with are not the weapons of the world" (2 Cor 10:4). Though the enemy appears to have superior temporal might, as Christians we can be encouraged that the "battle is the LORD's" (1 Sam 17:47; cf. 2 Chr 20:15). As God was with David, so he is with those who are in Christ.

---

8. E.g, Birch, "Books of Samuel," 1127.
9. Alter, *The David Story*, 121.

CHAPTER 18

1 Samuel 20:1–42

 LISTEN to the Story

¹Then David fled from Naioth at Ramah and went to Jonathan and asked, "What have I done? What is my crime? How have I wronged your father, that he is trying to kill me?"

²"Never!" Jonathan replied. "You are not going to die! Look, my father doesn't do anything, great or small, without letting me know. Why would he hide this from me? It isn't so!"

³But David took an oath and said, "Your father knows very well that I have found favor in your eyes, and he has said to himself, 'Jonathan must not know this or he will be grieved.' Yet as surely as the LORD lives and as you live, there is only a step between me and death."

⁴Jonathan said to David, "Whatever you want me to do, I'll do for you."

⁵So David said, "Look, tomorrow is the New Moon feast, and I am supposed to dine with the king; but let me go and hide in the field until the evening of the day after tomorrow. ⁶If your father misses me at all, tell him, 'David earnestly asked my permission to hurry to Bethlehem, his hometown, because an annual sacrifice is being made there for his whole clan.' ⁷If he says, 'Very well,' then your servant is safe. But if he loses his temper, you can be sure that he is determined to harm me. ⁸As for you, show kindness to your servant, for you have brought him into a covenant with you before the LORD. If I am guilty, then kill me yourself! Why hand me over to your father?"

⁹"Never!" Jonathan said. "If I had the least inkling that my father was determined to harm you, wouldn't I tell you?"

¹⁰David asked, "Who will tell me if your father answers you harshly?"

¹¹"Come," Jonathan said, "let's go out into the field." So they went there together.

¹²Then Jonathan said to David, "I swear by the LORD, the God of Israel, that I will surely sound out my father by this time the day after tomorrow! If he is favorably disposed toward you, will I not send you word and let you know? ¹³But if my father intends to harm you, may the LORD

deal with Jonathan, be it ever so severely, if I do not let you know and send you away in peace. May the LORD be with you as he has been with my father. ¹⁴But show me unfailing kindness like the LORD's kindness as long as I live, so that I may not be killed, ¹⁵and do not ever cut off your kindness from my family—not even when the LORD has cut off every one of David's enemies from the face of the earth."

¹⁶So Jonathan made a covenant with the house of David, saying, "May the LORD call David's enemies to account." ¹⁷And Jonathan had David reaffirm his oath out of love for him, because he loved him as he loved himself.

¹⁸Then Jonathan said to David, "Tomorrow is the New Moon feast. You will be missed, because your seat will be empty. ¹⁹The day after tomorrow, toward evening, go to the place where you hid when this trouble began, and wait by the stone Ezel. ²⁰I will shoot three arrows to the side of it, as though I were shooting at a target. ²¹Then I will send a boy and say, 'Go, find the arrows.' If I say to him, 'Look, the arrows are on this side of you; bring them here,' then come, because, as surely as the LORD lives, you are safe; there is no danger. ²²But if I say to the boy, 'Look, the arrows are beyond you,' then you must go, because the LORD has sent you away. ²³And about the matter you and I discussed—remember, the LORD is witness between you and me forever."

²⁴So David hid in the field, and when the New Moon feast came, the king sat down to eat. ²⁵He sat in his customary place by the wall, opposite Jonathan, and Abner sat next to Saul, but David's place was empty. ²⁶Saul said nothing that day, for he thought, "Something must have happened to David to make him ceremonially unclean—surely he is unclean." ²⁷But the next day, the second day of the month, David's place was empty again. Then Saul said to his son Jonathan, "Why hasn't the son of Jesse come to the meal, either yesterday or today?"

²⁸Jonathan answered, "David earnestly asked me for permission to go to Bethlehem. ²⁹He said, 'Let me go, because our family is observing a sacrifice in the town and my brother has ordered me to be there. If I have found favor in your eyes, let me get away to see my brothers.' That is why he has not come to the king's table."

³⁰Saul's anger flared up at Jonathan and he said to him, "You son of a perverse and rebellious woman! Don't I know that you have sided with the son of Jesse to your own shame and to the shame of the mother who bore you? ³¹As long as the son of Jesse lives on this earth, neither you nor your kingdom will be established. Now send someone to bring him to me, for he must die!"

³²"Why should he be put to death? What has he done?" Jonathan asked his father. ³³But Saul hurled his spear at him to kill him. Then Jonathan knew that his father intended to kill David.

³⁴Jonathan got up from the table in fierce anger; on that second day of the feast he did not eat, because he was grieved at his father's shameful treatment of David.

³⁵In the morning Jonathan went out to the field for his meeting with David. He had a small boy with him, ³⁶and he said to the boy, "Run and find the arrows I shoot." As the boy ran, he shot an arrow beyond him. ³⁷When the boy came to the place where Jonathan's arrow had fallen, Jonathan called out after him, "Isn't the arrow beyond you?" ³⁸Then he shouted, "Hurry! Go quickly! Don't stop!" The boy picked up the arrow and returned to his master. ³⁹(The boy knew nothing about all this; only Jonathan and David knew.) ⁴⁰Then Jonathan gave his weapons to the boy and said, "Go, carry them back to town."

⁴¹After the boy had gone, David got up from the south side of the stone and bowed down before Jonathan three times, with his face to the ground. Then they kissed each other and wept together—but David wept the most.

⁴²Jonathan said to David, "Go in peace, for we have sworn friendship with each other in the name of the LORD, saying, 'The LORD is witness between you and me, and between your descendants and my descendants forever.'" Then David left, and Jonathan went back to the town.

Listen to the Text in the Story: Numbers 28:11–15; 1 Samuel 19:1–3; 2 Samuel 9

As David continues to be estranged from Saul, the new moon feast becomes an occasion for David and Jonathan to test the waters and gauge the king's true disposition toward David. New moon feasts were festive occasions with sacrifices offered (Num 28:11–15) and other celebratory events (cf. Num 10:10; Ps 81:3). In ancient Mesopotamia, new moons were also occasioned by festivals and special events. In fact, some think the Israelite new moon festival may have correspond to the Babylonian *bubbulum*, which was the interlunium celebrated at the end of a month immediately preceding the new moon.[1] In the latter festivals the king served in a prominent role.[2] In fact,

1. K. van der Toorn, *Family Religion in Babylonia, Syria and Israel: Continuity and Change in the Forms of Religious Life*, SHCANE 7 (Leiden; New York: Brill, 1996), 211–18.

2. Postgate, *Early Mesopotamia*, 265.

Ezekiel 45:17 implies similarly important roles for Israelite royalty in these festivals and suggests that "David's absence from Saul's table may have had political repercussions."[3] David's excuse, however, that he had to be in Bethlehem, likely was believable since the new moon festival required the "entire clan" to be together for a "communal meal."[4] It was likely the eldest son's role to gather the clan together (acting as "the paterfamilias of his clan"),[5] which explains David's request to "let me get away to see my brothers" (1 Sam 20:29).

EXPLAIN the Story

David leaves Ramah to meet with his close friend Jonathan, who is unaware of his father's murderous intentions and initially thinks David must be mistaken in that regard. In order to prove Saul's intentions to Jonathan, David comes up with a plan wherein he will hide in a field during the new moon feast while Jonathan attends the banquet and gives his father an excuse for David's absence. Saul's over-the-top reaction to the excuse results in his verbally assaulting his son and attempting to kill him with his spear, making his homicidal intentions clear. Distraught, Jonathan meets up with David in the field and urges him to leave, but not before reaffirming their covenant of loyalty to each other. The two friends embrace and say a tearful goodbye. Jonathan heads back to town while David goes on the run and will remain a fugitive for the immediate future.

David Meets with Jonathan (20:1–23)

With Saul incapacitated by Yahweh's spirit in Ramah (19:24), David has a day's head start on the king, so David leaves Samuel and goes back to meet with Jonathan to inquire why his father is out to kill him. Jonathan denies his father's homicidal tendencies, believing his father would have confided in him if this were so. Clearly Jonathan is not as perceptive as his sister Michal, who quickly discerned that her father was out to kill David (19:11). After all, Jonathan had nearly been executed at his father's orders in 1 Samuel 14:44, and Saul had told Jonathan of his plans to kill David in 1 Samuel 19:1.[6] Of course, after the latter conversation, Jonathan managed to talk his father out of it and Saul had sworn that he would not kill David (19:6). Presumably, Jonathan had taken his father at his word. David now explains to his naïve friend that the king had not confided in him about his murderous plans because Saul knew of Jonathan and David's close friendship.

---

3. Long, *1 Samuel*, 355.

4. Van der Toorn, *Family Religion*, 213–14.

5. Ibid., 214.

6. Peter D. Miscall, *1 Samuel: A Literary Reading* (Bloomington: Indiana University Press, 1986), 107.

Willing to entertain the possibility, Jonathan agrees to do what David thinks is best in the situation. David therefore comes up with a plan that, like Jonathan's plan in chapter 19, once again involves David hiding in a field while Jonathan goes to investigate the truth of his father's intentions. This time, instead of Jonathan directly confronting his father on his treatment of David as he did before (19:3), a plan is made for Jonathan to judge his father's reaction to David's absence from the planned royal feast of the new moon (cf. Num 28:11–15; Ezra 3:5; Neh 10:33; Ezek 46:6). Evidently, David, perhaps due to his being a son-in-law or because of one of his other important roles (Saul's armor bearer, commander of a thousand, etc.), was required to participate in the feast. If Saul reacts well, it would indicate that David is not in danger. If Saul loses his temper, it will reveal his murderous intentions.

That is as far as David's plan got, however, and he was unsure of how exactly Jonathan would let him know if Saul loses his temper (20:10). Jonathan suggests they head to the field, perhaps for something like a dry run (20:11). Before the plan is rehearsed, however, Jonathan again swears his loyalty to David and his promise to do his best to protect him. Then Jonathan asks that David in return show Jonathan loyalty (20:14–15). As Miscall points out, Jonathan "apparently fears that David may betray him, that he may be using him for the moment and will turn against him in the future when he is in a less precarious situation."[7] In other words, though both David and Jonathan are committed to each other, each also harbors some doubts about the other. After all, David's statement to Jonathan, "If I am guilty, then kill me yourself! Why hand me over to your father?" (20:8), betrays some suspicion of his friend. David was likely baffled that Jonathan did not warn him of Saul's attempt to apprehend him, both at his own house (19:11–17) and in Ramah (19:12–24).

Jonathan is rightly concerned about his future. Usually in the ancient world, when one dynasty replaces another, all male descendants of the previous dynasty are slaughtered to ensure there is no challenge to the throne (e.g., 1 Kgs 15:29; 16:11; 2 Kgs 10:6–7). If David is to ascend the throne, Jonathan wants to make sure he and his descendants are not killed as a result. To solemnize these promises, Jonathan makes a covenant with him and makes David "reaffirm his oath." Later in the story David's vow to show kindness to Jonathan's descendants becomes an important factor (cf. 2 Sam 9:1, 3, 7).

With the covenant in place, Jonathan spells out the details of how he will secretly communicate about his father's reaction. If Saul did not intend to kill David, they would still need to communicate covertly lest it come to light that David was not really in Bethlehem with his brothers. If Saul did intend

---

7. Ibid., 114.

to kill David, obviously, secrecy was essential, lest the king locate his quarry. Therefore, Jonathan sets a signal in place for David. He will come to the field to practice his archery and shoot three arrows and then send his boy to collect them. The signal depended on what he would tell the boy.

The New Moon Feast (20:24–33)

While David hunkers down for a couple nights of roughing it in the field, Jonathan heads to the royal banquet. David's spot at the table was vacant, but Saul said nothing, thinking there must be a good reason for his absence— that he was ceremonially unclean. Given that the last time Saul knew David's whereabouts he was with the prophet Samuel, it is surprising that Saul thought David's ceremonial uncleanness was the most likely reason for his absence. This imagined excuse of Saul, however, fits with his character, as he has proved himself quite obsessed with cultic ritual thus far. Whatever it was, Saul felt confident that David's absence was a one-time thing with a good excuse. Of course, David really *did* have a good excuse for missing the banquet. Saul was out to kill him! Strangely, Saul does not consider his own behavior toward David to be the reason for his absence, probably due to his growing madness and sociopathic ways wherein he is blind to his own faults.

Regardless, on the next day of the festival, David's absence did not sit so well with the rejected king, leading him to query his son as to where "the son of Jesse" was. Saul's avoidance of using David's proper name here and in what follows (20:30, 31) shows his disdain for David, sort of like only calling someone by their last name.[8] In fact, "son of Jesse" is used throughout the books of Samuel as a term of derision for David (cf. 1 Sam 22:7, 8, 13; 25:10; 2 Sam 20:1). Jonathan provides the answer David had instructed him to give (20:7)—that he has gone to Bethlehem for a sacrifice—leading Saul to lose his temper. Saul realized Jonathan was covering for David and was infuriated that his son couldn't see that David's rise means that Jonathan will never be king. Saul is so angered he does not call Jonathan by name but instead uses an extremely vulgar reference to his mother. Then Saul outright declares that David "must die!" (20:31). As Jonathan attempted to defend David, Saul hurled his spear at Jonathan, as he had at David many times before. Seeing as a moment ago Saul appeared quite concerned about Jonathan's future kingdom, this attempt now to kill his son seems quite contradictory.[9] Saul is clearly not a reasonable person of sound mind. There could no longer be any doubt— even for the once naïve prince—"Jonathan knew that his father intended to kill David" (20:33). In anger, Jonathan left the meal without eating.

---

8. Alter, *The David Story*, 127.
9. Bodner, *1 Samuel*, 221.

Jonathan Warns David (20:34–42)

The next morning Jonathan proceeded with the plan and went to the field where David was in hiding. Curiously, he does not exactly follow the plan in detail. While he had said he would come to the field in the evening (20:19)—perhaps to avoid suspicion or make sure he wasn't followed—Jonathan now comes in the morning. While he said he would shoot three arrows then instruct his boy (20:20–22), instead Jonathan shoots only one arrow, instructs the boy, and sends him away. It seems Jonathan was panicked and couldn't bring himself to wait until the evening and couldn't even wait to shoot three arrows. What is more, abandoning the secrecy of the entire plan, Jonathan meets up with David in person. Both were emotionally distraught and say a tearful goodbye, with David crying the most. Jonathan reiterates his pact with David, then the two friends go their separate ways. Thus begins a new phase in David's story, that of an exiled fugitive on the lam.

The Demands of God's New Kingdom

As Saul explains to his son, because he was the heir to the throne, Jonathan's relationship with David is complicated. David's rise to the kingship means the demise of the royal claims of Saul's house. By supporting David, Jonathan is abdicating his right to rule. Jonathan, however, is not unaware of this fact. Jonathan knows David will rule Israel one day, and the incident at the new moon festival is a turning point in his life as he now had to definitively decide between his father and his best friend, David. It was a bold choice he made: to turn from his own father and his own rights to the throne to faithfulness to the son of Jesse. His faith in David was not without doubts, as our analysis has shown (cf. 20:14–15). He had no guarantee that David would protect him and his descendants when David took the throne, and it was normal procedure in those days during regime change to slaughter everyone else who might have a claim on the throne. Yet Jonathan makes the risky choice to put his faith in David and stake his (and his children's) future on God's anointed one. This is no easy believism. There was a real cost to Jonathan in choosing David. As Brueggemann points out, this text "invites us to reflect on the cost of loyalty and the terrible ambiguities within which loyalty must be practiced."[10]

These aspects of the text have implications for issues of faith and loyalty today. Just as Jonathan chose to honor David over his father, so Jesus calls for

---

10. Brueggemann, *First and Second Samuel,* 153.

ultimate loyalty to the extent that he even declares, "If anyone comes to me and does not hate father and mother, wife and children, brothers and sisters— yes, even their own life—such a person cannot be my disciple" (Luke 14:26). Jonathan displays such radical commitment here—putting his loyalty to the new king and kingdom above the commitments of his own father and even his own life. Jonathan could see that as God was bringing in his new kingdom, with a king of God's choosing (after his own heart), the old kingdom was passing away. The way to secure his future was in covenant with the new and future king, God's anointed one. So, for believers today, loyalty to the anointed one, Jesus Christ, and his kingdom takes precedence over all other commitments. The way to secure our future is in covenant with the son of David, Jesus Christ, who sealed the new covenant with his own blood (Luke 22:20).

CHAPTER 19

1 Samuel 21:1–15

 LISTEN to the Story

¹David went to Nob, to Ahimelek the priest. Ahimelek trembled when he met him, and asked, "Why are you alone? Why is no one with you?"

²David answered Ahimelek the priest, "The king sent me on a mission and said to me, 'No one is to know anything about the mission I am sending you on.' As for my men, I have told them to meet me at a certain place. ³Now then, what do you have on hand? Give me five loaves of bread, or whatever you can find."

⁴But the priest answered David, "I don't have any ordinary bread on hand; however, there is some consecrated bread here—provided the men have kept themselves from women."

⁵David replied, "Indeed women have been kept from us, as usual whenever I set out. The men's bodies are holy even on missions that are not holy. How much more so today!" ⁶So the priest gave him the consecrated bread, since there was no bread there except the bread of the Presence that had been removed from before the LORD and replaced by hot bread on the day it was taken away.

⁷Now one of Saul's servants was there that day, detained before the LORD; he was Doeg the Edomite, Saul's chief shepherd.

⁸David asked Ahimelek, "Don't you have a spear or a sword here? I haven't brought my sword or any other weapon, because the king's mission was urgent."

⁹The priest replied, "The sword of Goliath the Philistine, whom you killed in the Valley of Elah, is here; it is wrapped in a cloth behind the ephod. If you want it, take it; there is no sword here but that one."

David said, "There is none like it; give it to me."

¹⁰That day David fled from Saul and went to Achish king of Gath. ¹¹But the servants of Achish said to him, "Isn't this David, the king of the land? Isn't he the one they sing about in their dances:

> "'Saul has slain his thousands,
> 　　and David his tens of thousands'?"
>
> [12]David took these words to heart and was very much afraid of Achish king of Gath. [13]So he pretended to be insane in their presence; and while he was in their hands he acted like a madman, making marks on the doors of the gate and letting saliva run down his beard.
>
> [14]Achish said to his servants, "Look at the man! He is insane! Why bring him to me? [15]Am I so short of madmen that you have to bring this fellow here to carry on like this in front of me? Must this man come into my house?"

Listen to the Text in the Story: Exodus 19:15; 25:30; 35:13; Leviticus 15:18; 24:5–9.

On the run from Saul, David stops at Nob to secure some sustenance and a weapon. The only available food, however, is the consecrated bread of the Presence in the shrine. This bread was usually only to be eaten by the priests (Lev 24:5–9). The presiding priest, Ahimelek, agrees to give David the bread on condition that he and his men had "kept themselves from women" (v. 4; i.e., had not been sexually active. Cf. Exod 19:15; Lev 15). From an ancient Israelite legal perspective, sexual activity could open one up to becoming ritually unclean (Lev 15:18).[1] It was common in the ancient Near East for soldiers to be consecrated prior to a battle.[2] This need was heightened if they were to be partaking of consecrated bread.

EXPLAIN the Story

This chapter is divided into two scenes chronicling David's fugitive wanderings. The first describes David's stop in the priestly town of Nob, where he secures both food and a weapon from an apparent ally, Ahimelek the priest. His presence at Nob did not remain a secret, however, as one of Saul's servants, Doeg, was present for David's clandestine meeting with the priest, which will soon spell disaster for the priests of Nob (1 Sam 22). The second scene has David going outside of Israelite territory to a Philistine town in order to find refuge from Saul. However, David's reputation had preceded him and the anointed one was forced to act like he was insane in order to escape Gath.

---

1. Long, *1 Samuel*, 357.
2. Postgate, *Early Mesopotamia*, 265.

The Visit to Nob (21:1–9)

After his tearful goodbye with his best friend, David heads to the priestly town of Nob, where, we find out (21:9), he has stored the sword of Goliath. Presumably, in storing the weapon there, David must have had a prior relationship with Ahimelek, which also explains why, of all places, he went to Nob. When David arrives, however, the priest is inexplicably fearful of David's presence. Ahimelek's initial questions likely suggest the origins of his fear as he asks David, "Why are you alone? Why is no one with you?" (21:1). David's presence without other soldiers was a red flag for the priest and may have hinted at David's fugitive status. Given their prior relationship, however, evinced in that he was storing the sword for David, why the priest would be fearful for this reason is not altogether evident. Did the priest have doubts about David's character and think he was there to harm him in some way? Given the widespread admiration of David, I think this is unlikely. The key to explaining the priest's fear is most likely the presence of Doeg the Edomite, Saul's servant. David was clearly on the run, and the presence of Saul's servant meant that if the priest helped the fugitive it might get back to Saul and incur the fury of the king. David tells the priest he is in fact on a mission for the king and is not working alone, as his men are waiting for him at an undisclosed location. If David and Ahimelek had a prior understanding, David's lie here may have been as much to provide a cover for the priest as to provide one for David. Furthermore, David's explanation may have been meant for the ears of Doeg, so as not to arouse the suspicion of the servant of Saul. After all, in the next chapter David admits he knew Doeg was present during his interactions with the priest (22:22).

Having explained his cover story, David proceeded to ask for food from the priest. Ahimelek replied that there was nothing but the sacred "bread of the Presence" (Exod 25:30; 35:13), which was usually only to be eaten by the priests (Lev 24:5–9). However, torah laws were subject to interpretation in instances where straying from regulation was due to concern for the greater good. For example, in Leviticus 10:12–20, a violation of Leviticus 6:16 was allowed by Moses due to the extenuating circumstances of the death of Aaron's sons.[3] Furthermore, violations of the Sabbath were allowed for priests to prepare sacrifices (Num 28:9), circumcise babies (John 7:22), or for the rescue of one's animal or a person whose life was at stake (Luke 14:5).[4] Bergen sums up this well: "As a vested Aaronic priest, Ahimelech possessed authority to interpret and apply Torah guidelines to specific cases and could do so with

---

3. Bergen, *Samuel*, 221, n. 91.
4. Ibid.

some latitude."[5] Therefore, seeing David's need of food as a life and death situation, Ahimelek decided that eating the bread was permissible in the present circumstance and agreed to give David and his men the bread, provided they had "kept themselves from women" (21:4). David informed him that this was always the case with his soldiers (and of course, there were no other men with him in this instance). This acquiescence on Ahimelek's part reflects positively on his characterization, as does his concern for holiness (demanding they had kept themselves from women), which contrasts with the priesthood at Shiloh recounted in 1 Samuel 2–3.[6]

At this point in the story the narrator ominously reveals that Saul's servant, Doeg the Edomite, was present at the shrine (21:7). As we will sadly find out in the next chapter, Doeg will not only report what he saw to the king but will also be instrumental in carrying out Saul's murderous orders. Literally in Hebrew Doeg is described in verse 7 as "the mightiest of Saul's shepherds" (which the NIV interprets as the "chief" shepherd). Perhaps Doeg's description as "mighty" explains how he managed such prolific killing in the next chapter. The text says that Doeg was "detained before the LORD" (21:7), probably meaning he was cultically unclean for some reason.

Before he leaves, David has one more request of the priest: a weapon, by which David undoubtedly means Goliath's sword. Seeing as the last time we heard of Goliath's weaponry David had stored it in his own tent (17:54), David must have stored it in Nob for just such an occasion, and David and the priest likely had an understanding of some sort. Perhaps privy to the type of man Doeg was, and in case David's story of acting at the king's behest did not fool Doeg, Ahimelek does not just give David the sword but instead describes it as "The sword of Goliath the Philistine, *whom you killed* in the Valley of Elah" (21:9, emphasis added) as a reminder (to Doeg) that David is a powerful warrior.[7] Either way, David is happy to take the giant's sword off the priest's hands and then make his exit. Sadly, the events at Nob are far from over, as both Ahimelek and Doeg will appear again in the dreadful events of the next chapter.

David in Gath (21:10–15)

David then leaves Nob and heads to Philistine territory, and the hometown of Goliath—Gath. Given his close call at Nob, with Doeg's presence upsetting the secrecy of his meeting, David might have begun to think there was

---

5. Ibid., 221.

6. Bodner, *1 Samuel*, 226.

7. Keith Bodner, *David Observed: A King in the Eyes of His Court*, HBM 5 (Sheffield: Sheffield Phoenix, 2005), 228.

nowhere safe in Israelite territory for him to hide. However, going to Gath, with their late champion's own sword in his hand, was a brazen move. Upon arrival in Gath, the servants of the Philistine king, Achish, recognize David for who he is and even recall the serenade of the Israelite women that so angered Saul. Furthermore, they even refer to David as "the king of the land," giving further proof of David's widespread fame. Given that David's reputation was largely made in conflict with the Philistines, Achish's knowledge of David's identity did not bode well for his future in Gath. Therefore, David was understandably afraid and took drastic measures to make his escape, pretending to be insane. The Philistine king responds by sending him away but not before insulting his own servants by saying he already has enough "madmen" in his court, which perhaps hints at the later disagreements within Achish's court regarding what to do with David (cf. 1 Sam 29:1–9).[8]

LIVE the Story

Deception and Truth Telling

The narrator does not pause to reflect on the ethics of the many lies and deceptions that have occurred throughout the story thus far, and David's brief stop in Nob is no exception. David's wife, Michal, has lied in order to aid David's escape (1 Sam 19:13–14). Jonathan lied to Saul (1 Sam 20:28–29). Now in chapter 21 David himself lies about being on a mission from the king and having an accompanying group of men waiting for him (21:2). Furthermore, while not explicitly telling a lie, David deceptively pretends to be insane before the Philistines to secure his escape. While not the concern of the narrator, the text may cause many readers to question its ethics and whether lying and/or deception is justified on certain occasions.

Writing on 1 Samuel 21, the early church father John Cassian observed "that holy men sometimes lied in praiseworthy or at least in pardonable fashion" but argued that "in the light of the gospel, these things have been utterly forbidden, such that none of them can be committed without very serious sin and sacrilege."[9] On the other hand, Chrysostom, another early church father writing on Michal's deceit of chapter 19 concluded, "not in war only, but also in peace the need of deceit may be found, not merely in reference to the affairs of the state but also in private life."[10] Throughout church history there

---

8. A. Graeme Auld, *I & II Samuel: A Commentary*, OTL (Louisville: Westminster John Knox, 2011), 264; Bodner, *1 Samuel*, 229.

9. Franke, *Joshua, Judges, Ruth, 1–2 Samuel*, 292.

10. Ibid., 285.

have been divided opinions on the subject. Augustine famously held that it was never right to tell a lie, even to save an innocent life, arguing that it was better that the body of the innocent die than the eternal soul of the liar be jeopardized. Similarly, some moralists argue it is never moral to lie because the end does not justify the means. Other theologians, following Thomas Aquinas, often classify lies into three categories: a jocose lie, a falsehood told for amusement (i.e., a joke); officious lies, sometimes called "white lies," which hurt no one; and injurious lies that cause harm. Aquinas only held injurious lies to be a mortal sin (with the others being venial, or forgivable, sin).

It is important, however, to take into account the biblical evidence for a theology of truth telling and deception. The most famous prohibition of lying is found in the ninth of the Ten Commandments which bars giving "false testimony against your neighbor" (Exod 20:16), which technically is a reference to testifying in court. There are several instances, however, in biblical narrative where characters lie and the action is viewed positively. For example, the Hebrew midwives in Exodus 1:15–21 lie to the Egyptians in order to save the lives of the Hebrew baby boys whom the Pharaoh had ordered to be killed. The narrator in that instance explicitly voices approval of their deception (Exod 1:20–21). In the book of Joshua, Rahab lies to the king of Jericho in order to aid Israel in conquering the Canaanite city (Josh 2:4–6) and is thereby spared by Joshua (Josh 6:17, 23). Furthermore, Rahab's actions are clearly considered examples of faith in the New Testament (Heb 11:31; Jas 2:25).

In this story David claims he is on a mission from the king and that he has a band of men with him whom he has told to wait for him at an undisclosed location. Some interpreters, bothered by David's deception here, actually suggest that David *did* tell the truth in this instance. Usually this line of Davidic defense depends upon the conviction that it is never right to lie, though one is not obligated to tell everyone all the truth they know. When it is not desirable to tell someone the truth, one can refuse to speak, change the subject, or tell a white lie that is technically true though deceptive. Along these lines, some suggest that David proves adept at this mental sleight-of-hand when he claims he is on a mission from "the king." David actually speaks the truth as he really means "king Yahweh," not Saul.[11] Since David meant Yahweh when he said king, he was not deceiving the priest and Doeg or speaking a formal falsehood. This is what is often referred to as mental reservation, wherein David has a mental reservation about what he means by king that is not shared by his audience. Even if by saying king David meant Yahweh, he knew full well that king would mean "Saul" to his audience. Thus, this would be called a *strict* mental

---

11. Bergen, *Samuel*, 221. Bergen suggests this is probable "since David is elsewhere recorded referring to God as king (cf. Pss 5:2; 20:9; 24:7–10; 29:10; 68:24; 145:1)."

reservation where only the speaker's mind knows what was really meant. For an example of a strict reservation, let's say that I was playing catch with a baseball and I threw the ball and accidentally broke my neighbor's window. When asked whether I broke their window I could say "no" because in my mind the *ball* broke the window, *not me*. Still I think most would say that a strict mental reservation like this is, for all intents and purposes, a falsehood. Furthermore, this line of interpretation does not fully exonerate David. While it may explain David's claim of being on the king's mission, it does not explain David's claim to have told his men to wait for him at an undisclosed location.

Searching for a biblical ethic on truth telling would suggest that while the ninth commandment's prohibition against lying provides a general principle, there are exceptions during which truth telling is *not* the moral thing to do.[12] The Hebrew midwives, Jonathan, and Michal all serve as examples of deceiving to save an innocent life. These types of instances are what theologians call a "necessary lie," that is, a lie that is justified due to a conflict between truth telling and doing the right thing (e.g., saving a life). In other words, one's responsibility to tell the truth may conflict with one's duty to preserve life. Telling a lie in such an instance would be similar to killing in self-defense. Just as such an action would not be equated with the sin of murder, so a necessary lie told to save an innocent life should not really be equated with the sin of lying.

Of course, in the vast majority of instances in our own lives, the challenge is simply to speak the truth rather than lie to our own advantage. Our own intentions are not fully pure and rarely are we in such a situation where speaking the truth would result in someone committing an immoral act like murder. A biblical ethic is first and foremost to speak the truth, as Paul writes, "Therefore each of you must put off falsehood and speak truthfully to your neighbor, for we are all members of one body" (Eph 4:25). The Bible, however, gives clear examples where lying and deception are the moral thing to do in exceptional circumstances. In fact, similar to the way Rahab's deceptive actions are viewed positively in the New Testament (Heb 11:31; Jas 2:25), David's actions here in 1 Samuel 21 are affirmed, as Jesus defends David's taking the bread of the Presence (Matt 12:4; Mark 2:26; Luke 6:4) despite the fact David obtained the bread under false pretenses.

---

12. Arnold, *1 & 2 Samuel*, 285.

CHAPTER 20

1 Samuel 22:1–23

 LISTEN to the Story

¹David left Gath and escaped to the cave of Adullam. When his brothers and his father's household heard about it, they went down to him there. ²All those who were in distress or in debt or discontented gathered around him, and he became their commander. About four hundred men were with him.

³From there David went to Mizpah in Moab and said to the king of Moab, "Would you let my father and mother come and stay with you until I learn what God will do for me?" ⁴So he left them with the king of Moab, and they stayed with him as long as David was in the stronghold.

⁵But the prophet Gad said to David, "Do not stay in the stronghold. Go into the land of Judah." So David left and went to the forest of Hereth.

⁶Now Saul heard that David and his men had been discovered. And Saul was seated, spear in hand, under the tamarisk tree on the hill at Gibeah, with all his officials standing at his side. ⁷He said to them, "Listen, men of Benjamin! Will the son of Jesse give all of you fields and vineyards? Will he make all of you commanders of thousands and commanders of hundreds? ⁸Is that why you have all conspired against me? No one tells me when my son makes a covenant with the son of Jesse. None of you is concerned about me or tells me that my son has incited my servant to lie in wait for me, as he does today."

⁹But Doeg the Edomite, who was standing with Saul's officials, said, "I saw the son of Jesse come to Ahimelek son of Ahitub at Nob. ¹⁰Ahimelek inquired of the LORD for him; he also gave him provisions and the sword of Goliath the Philistine."

¹¹Then the king sent for the priest Ahimelek son of Ahitub and all the men of his family, who were the priests at Nob, and they all came to the king. ¹²Saul said, "Listen now, son of Ahitub."

"Yes, my lord," he answered.

¹³Saul said to him, "Why have you conspired against me, you and the son of Jesse, giving him bread and a sword and inquiring of God for him, so that he has rebelled against me and lies in wait for me, as he does today?"

¹⁴Ahimelek answered the king, "Who of all your servants is as loyal as David, the king's son-in-law, captain of your bodyguard and highly respected in your household? ¹⁵Was that day the first time I inquired of God for him? Of course not! Let not the king accuse your servant or any of his father's family, for your servant knows nothing at all about this whole affair."

¹⁶But the king said, "You will surely die, Ahimelek, you and your whole family."

¹⁷Then the king ordered the guards at his side: "Turn and kill the priests of the LORD, because they too have sided with David. They knew he was fleeing, yet they did not tell me."

But the king's officials were unwilling to raise a hand to strike the priests of the LORD.

¹⁸The king then ordered Doeg, "You turn and strike down the priests." So Doeg the Edomite turned and struck them down. That day he killed eighty-five men who wore the linen ephod. ¹⁹He also put to the sword Nob, the town of the priests, with its men and women, its children and infants, and its cattle, donkeys and sheep.

²⁰But one son of Ahimelek son of Ahitub, named Abiathar, escaped and fled to join David. ²¹He told David that Saul had killed the priests of the LORD. ²²Then David said to Abiathar, "That day, when Doeg the Edomite was there, I knew he would be sure to tell Saul. I am responsible for the death of your whole family. ²³Stay with me; don't be afraid. The man who wants to kill you is trying to kill me too. You will be safe with me."

Listen to the Text in the Story: Genesis 28; Exodus 2; Judges 11; Ruth 4:17; The Story of Idrimi, King of Alalakh

In this chapter, David, like Jacob (Gen 28) and Moses (Exod 2:15) before him, seeks refuge in a foreign land.[1] David's choice of Moab likely reflects his Moabite ancestry on his great-grandmother Ruth's side (cf. Ruth 4:17). A similar situation is found in an ancient Near Eastern text wherein the king of Halab (Aleppo), Idrimi, is forced to leave his land and seek refuge in a foreign land with relatives on his mother's side. The text reads "I am Idrimi. . . .

---

1. Long, *1 Samuel*, 358.

An evil deed happened in Halab, the seat of my family, and we fled to the people of Emar, brothers of my mother, and we lived (then) in Emar."[2] As in David's case, a band of men joined Idrimi in his exile. "They discovered that I was the son of their overlord and gathered around me."[3] Eventually Idrimi, like David, returns to become king and rule the land. David's story here also has parallels with the story of the Israelite judge, Jephthah, who was forced out of his homeland only to have a band of adventurers (Judg 11:3) join and follow him.

EXPLAIN the Story

The main scene in this chapter is a sequel to David's visit to Nob in the previous chapter. Bookending this scene are two brief scenes featuring David. David first flees from Gath to his homeland of Judah, where his family joins him. From there David attracts a ragtag group of followers, ending up with four hundred men under his command. Next, David journeys to Moab, the homeland of his great-grandmother Ruth, and secures asylum for his family before returning to Judah on command of the prophet Gad. The scene then changes to Saul in Gibeah, wherein Saul learns from Doeg the Edomite that Ahimelek has aided David. In response, Saul charges Ahimelek with treason and orders the execution of all the priests of Nob. When Saul's soldiers refuse the order, Saul orders Doeg the Edomite to kill them instead. Doeg takes to his work with relish, killing eighty-five priests as well as all the inhabitants of the priestly town of Nob. In the final scene we learn that one priest of Nob, Abiathar, escapes and meets up with David. Upon hearing the fate of the priests, David offers protection to Abiathar as they now have a common enemy in Saul.

At the Cave of Adullam (22:1–2)

David's first stop after escaping Gath is the cave of Adullam, located in his homeland of Judah (Josh 15:35). Hearing of his arrival, his family joins him there. More importantly for the ongoing story, a ragtag band of disenfranchised and marginalized people also joins David, forming a small army of the malcontent. At this point, David has a contingent of four hundred at his command, but soon their numbers will grow to six hundred (1 Sam 23:13). The large number of discontented or otherwise distressed people does not speak well for Saul's rule or his popularity.

---

2. *ANET*, 557.
3. Ibid.

David in Moab (22:3–5)

Aware that Saul's murderous intentions toward him put his family in Saul's crosshairs, too, David seeks to find refuge for his family. Interestingly, David takes them to Moab. While the reason for choosing Moab is not clear in the text, possibly the reasons stem from his great-grandmother Ruth having been a Moabite. Also, it is possible that as an enemy of Saul (1 Sam 14:47), David might have hoped that they would have an interest in supporting Saul's rival.[4] Having secured their safety, David is then commanded by a prophet named Gad to return to Judah. David and his men therefore go to "the forest of Hereth" a place not otherwise known, though several locations have been suggested.[5] This is the first appearance of the prophet Gad, but he will return again near the end of David's story (2 Sam 24). For now, it is significant for the legitimization of David's undertakings that he is explicitly authorized by God's prophet.[6] On the other hand, Saul's exploits have been delegitimized by the prophet Samuel. Saul disobeys God's prophet while David obeys God's prophet. As the story moves on, Yahweh will continue to direct David through prophets and other oracular means (e.g., 1 Sam 23:2–4). Saul, however, receives no prophetic word, as Samuel no longer visits him (1 Sam 15:35) and even when Saul decides to inquire of God, Yahweh will not answer him (1 Sam 28:6). This status of being cut off from prophetic oracles probably contributes to the manic king's violent response to news of David's successful inquiry of Ahimelek in the next episode.

The Slaughter of the Priests (22:6–19)

The scene then changes to Gibeah, where Saul sits with all the trappings of royal power. Saul hears that David and his men have returned to Judah and begins to berate his Benjamite entourage, accusing them of conspiring against him. Saul's paranoia has grown to the point that he is alienating those who are faithful to him. Saul asks them if they think David would treat them better than he has, giving them more "fields and vineyards" or better positions in the army (22:7). Saul is hinting that siding with David would be against their best interests. Saul accuses them of having no concern for him and hiding the fact that Jonathan has made a covenant with David (22:8). Saul continues to avoid using David's name, instead referring to him as the "son of Jesse"

---

4. Klein, *1 Samuel*, 223.

5. Some believe that Hereth is a variant of Horesh (1 Sam 23:15, 18–19), which is often thought to be not too far from Hebron. Klein, *1 Samuel*, 223. Alternatively, McCarter proposes the forest of Hereth is near Keilah (cf. 23:1–2). McCarter, *I Samuel*.

6. R. P. Gordon, *I & II Samuel: A Commentary* (Grand Rapids: Regency Reference Library, 1986), 173.

(22:7, 8, 13). Saul's servants appear to be dumbfounded at the accusations and have nothing to say in response.

Seeing an opportunity for advancement, Doeg steps forward and tells of "the son of Jesse's" visit to Nob (following Saul's disparaging nomenclature for David). Significantly, Doeg refers to Ahimelek as "the son of Ahitub." In case the reader missed Doeg's patronymic reference, both the narrator (22:11) and Saul (22:12) refer to Ahimelek as "son of Ahitub." While Ahitub is far from a main character in the story, he is the son of Eli's wicked son, Phineas, and of the Elide line (1 Sam 14:3). This reference to Ahimelek's Elide heritage recalls the threatening prophecies of the unnamed man of God in 1 Samuel 2, which predicted that "no one in your family will ever reach old age" (1 Sam 2:32). While the events that are about to follow are horrid and disturbing, they nevertheless facilitate the prophetic word's fulfilment.

Doeg correctly notes that Ahimelek gave David provisions and Goliath's sword, but Doeg also claims that Ahimelek "inquired of the LORD" for David (22:10). The story in chapter 21 makes no mention of any inquiry of Yahweh for David. Perhaps Doeg knew that Ahimelek's inquiring of Yahweh on David's behalf would have infuriated Saul the most and so he fabricated this part of his testimony. As we have seen, Saul was obsessed with ritual guidance and insurance of success, and the last time Saul inquired of Yahweh, in the presence of another son of Ahitub (14:3), he received no answer (14:37).

Saul proceeds to have Ahimelek and the other men in his family "who were the priests at Nob" brought to him at Gibeah. Saul charges the priest with conspiracy for giving David provisions, a weapon, and inquiring of God for him (22:13). Ahimelek denies the charge of conspiracy and defends his actions on account of David's known loyalty to Saul, his status as the king's son-in-law and bodyguard, and David's impeccable reputation (22:14). The translation of Ahimelek's response (22:15) to the accusation of inquiring of God for David is difficult and has been interpreted in different ways. The NIV translates it as "Was that day the first time I inquired of God for him? Of course not!" (22:15), which would reveal a prior relationship between the priest and David. However, the Hebrew reads more easily as a *denial* of his inquiring for David that day as seen in the KJV's rendering, "Did I then begin to inquire of God for him? Be it far from me" (similarly, NKJV, ASV, WEB). Seeing as the narrator made no reference to any inquiry to God on David's behalf in the story, Ahimelek's denial makes the most sense here. It was a trumped-up charge against him.

Significantly, Doeg does not offer any details of Ahimelek's interactions with David, which may have acquitted the priest before Saul. After all, David told the priest lies as a pretext for his help—that he was on mission for the king

(21:2), that his men were sanctified and awaiting him (21:2, 5), and that he didn't bring a weapon due to the urgency of the king's mission (21:8). If Doeg told Saul about this, it would have supported Ahimelek's story that he was not knowingly conspiring with David against Saul.

With no evidence to support his judgment, other than Doeg's word against Ahimelek's, Saul interprets the priest's actions as conspiratorial and sentences him and his whole family to death. Saul orders his guards to kill the priests of Yahweh, but they refuse. This is not the first time that Saul's orders have been ignored. Back in chapter 14 after Jonathan had been instrumental in bringing deliverance to Israel from the Philistines, Saul ordered his own son's death for eating during a fast that Saul had proclaimed, but his order was disobeyed (14:44–45). Now another similarly irrational order is resolutely disobeyed by Saul's own guards.

In response to the guard's refusal to kill the priests, Saul orders Doeg to kill them. Being an Edomite and not a Yahwist, Doeg presumably would not have the same religious qualms about killing Yahweh's priests as did Saul's retinue. Doeg complies and slaughters eighty-five priests. Furthermore, though not explicitly ordered to do so, Doeg practically subjects Nob to the ban (*herem*), killing everything that lived, including women, children, infants, and the animals (see Listen to the Story in 1 Sam 15). Ironically, Saul had refused to do exactly this to the Amalekites when so ordered by Samuel in chapter 15, but he allows (or perhaps orders) this massacre in the case of Yahweh's priests and the priestly town of Nob. Nothing could more clearly demonstrate Saul's demonic ways than the events of this chapter.

Abiathar's Escape (22:20–23)

One of Ahimelek's sons, Abiathar, escapes the slaughter of the priests of Nob and flees to join David. His choice to flee to David is likely because he was aware that his father Ahimelek was in league with him. When Abiathar informs him of Saul's massacre of the priests, David blames himself on account of the fact he knew that Doeg was there that day and knew that Doeg would report what he saw to Saul. Presumably, David thought that the lies he told the priest (and, since he was listening, Doeg) would have provided plausible deniability, preventing Saul from viewing the priest as knowingly complicit in his escape and acquit him before the king. He did not predict that Doeg would not corroborate his story or the extent to which madness had gripped the rejected king. David offers no excuses but humbly takes the full blame for the death of the priests. David then urges the priest to stay with him and promises protection, seeing as they now have the same enemy. As the story continues, Abiathar's arrival will prove beneficial for David as he carries with him an ephod for inquiring of Yahweh (cf. 1 Sam 23:6, 9; 30:7–8). David now has priestly and prophetic (Gad) support.

LIVE the Story

The Fulfilment of the Prophetic Word

The story of the slaughter of the priests of Nob furthers one of the major themes in the larger story—the fulfilment of the prophetic word. In fact, the structure of the history running from Joshua–2 Kings is arranged according to the promise and fulfillment of the word of Yahweh. These books were written under the conviction that God's word actually determines the timetable of Israel's future. The author(s) trusted in the historically effective authority of God's word. Throughout the history, the word of Yahweh appears in various ways: a prophetic oracle, a curse or a blessing, a vow, or an oracle of judgment. Many times the word predicts victory over enemies (Josh 6; Judg 4; 1 Sam 30:1–20), or miracles in nature (Josh 3:8, 14–17; 10:12–14; 1 Kgs 17:1, 7; 2 Kgs 4:16–17), or deaths (Judg 9:16–57; 2 Kgs 1:16–17).

Most times the fulfillment of the word occurs in the same story in which the promise occurred. Many other promises, however, are not fulfilled in the same narrative in which they appear. For example, the prophecy regarding the death of Eli's wicked sons in 1 Samuel 2:27–36 is not fulfilled until 1 Samuel 4:1–11. Less often, but just as clearly, the word of Yahweh takes many years to be fulfilled. For example, the declaration that Yahweh will take the kingdom away from Saul and give it to one of his "neighbors" (1 Sam 15:28) is not fulfilled until much later in 2 Samuel 5:3.

In 1 Samuel 22, we see another long-awaited fulfillment with the prophecies against the house of Eli (1 Sam 2:27–36) fulfilled with the slaughter of the Elide priests of Nob. Yet, even this is not the entire fulfillment of this prophetic word, as the anonymous man of God in 1 Samuel 2 declared that God would replace Eli's priestly line with a "faithful priest." Here in 1 Samuel 22 there remains a priest of Eli's line, Abiathar, who will aid David in his fugitive wanderings and later be listed with Zadok as David's priest (2 Sam 15:24–36), but at present there is no move toward replacing his line with a different priestly line. In fact, this prophecy is not completely fulfilled until 1 Kings 2:26–27, 35 with the removal of the last of Eli's line from the priesthood and the installation of Zadok.[7]

---

7. Helga Weippert, "Histories and History: Promise and Fulfillment in the Deuteronomistic History," in *Reconsidering Israel and Judah: Recent Studies on the Deuteronomistic History*, ed. Gary N.

Even at this point, however, we can see four important aspects of Yahweh's word.

1. The reliability and inviolability of the word. The virtual destruction of the house of Eli by Saul in 1 Samuel 22 underscores this. In the larger story, this should lead the reader to expect a similar certainty attached to Samuel's word concerning the future of the house of Saul (1 Sam 13:14; 15:26, 28).

2. The word of God is causative. Just as God spoke the universe into existence (Gen 1), so in this story his word makes things happen. The fulfillment of the word against the Elide house through Saul's slaughter of the priests only occurred because of another prophetic oracle by Gad that commanded David to return to Judah (22:5).[8] Only when David obeys Gad's prophetic word does Saul hear about David's whereabouts (22:6) and convene his conspiracy tribunal which results in the destruction of the Elide house.

3. The fulfillment of Yahweh's word is multi-faceted. Rather than having a monolithic view of prophecy, which allows only one possible meaning or fulfillment, we can see in our story that there are often multiple stages in the fulfillment of the word. A prophecy can be *partially* fulfilled for a time before it is *ultimately* fulfilled at a much later time. This is a significant perspective on prophecy, as many of the messianic prophecies Christ fulfills are not completely fulfilled yet.

   For example, the well-known messianic prophecy from Isaiah 9, often read at Christmas time due to its incorporation into Handel's *Messiah*, reads:

> For to us a child is born,
> > to us a son is given,
> > and the government will be on his shoulders.
> And he will be called
> > Wonderful Counselor, Mighty God,
> > Everlasting Father, Prince of Peace.
> Of the greatness of his government and peace
> > there will be no end.
> He will reign on David's throne
> > and over his kingdom,
> establishing and upholding it

Knoppers and J. Gordon McConville; Sources for Biblical and Theological Study (Winona Lake, IN: Eisenbrauns, 2000), 47–61.

8. Bodner, *1 Samuel*, 237.

> with justice and righteousness
> from that time on and forever.
> The zeal of the LORD Almighty
> will accomplish this.
>   (Isa 9:6–7)

These verses, however, are never quoted or appealed to in the New Testament as fulfilled prophecies about Christ. But the passage in Isaiah begins:

> In the past he humbled the land of Zebulun and the land of Naphtali, but in the future he will honor Galilee of the nations, by the Way of the Sea, beyond the Jordan—

> The people walking in darkness
> have seen a great light;
> on those living in the land of deep darkness
> a light has dawned.
>   (Isa 9:1–2)

This portion of Isaiah 9 *is* quoted in the New Testament in Matthew 4:15–16:

> Land of Zebulun and land of Naphtali,
> the Way of the Sea, beyond the Jordan,
> Galilee of the Gentiles—
> the people living in darkness
> have seen a great light;
> on those living in the land of the shadow of death
> a light has dawned.

Significantly, the section with its promise of the son reigning on David's throne, with the government on his shoulders, is *not* quoted. Likely, the reason this is not explicitly referenced in Matthew is because the prophecy is yet to be fulfilled. After all, immediately after citing Isaiah 9:1–2, the next verse in Matthew reads, "From that time on Jesus began to preach, 'Repent, for the kingdom of heaven has come near'" (Matt 4:17). In other words, the fulfillment has begun—the Son will reign—not now, but it is near. The reign of the Son (i.e., the kingdom) is near. The prophetic word is often fulfilled in partial ways before a complete future fulfillment.[9]

---

9. Arnold, *1 & 2 Samuel*, 314.

4. Yahweh's word is often fulfilled through unexpected and, sometimes, evil agents. In 1 Samuel 22 Saul, the demonic king, unwittingly fulfills the prophecy against the Elide house, as does the Edomite Doeg. It can be disturbing to think of this aspect of prophecy. How can one who appears more wicked (Saul and Doeg) carry out the judgment of a prophecy on another who appears more righteous (Ahimelek)? This is an inscrutable question in many ways and one with which the prophets themselves wrestled. Habbakuk asked a similar question regarding God's use of Babylon (a wicked people) to punish his own people of Judah. The prophet writes; "Why are you silent while the wicked swallow up those more righteous than themselves?" (Hab 1:13). But just as Saul is under judgment and his days are numbered, so the Babylonians would be judged (Hab 2:15–16).

God works through unexpected means to fulfill his word. Yet, this does not remove the culpability of Saul or Doeg from their actions any more than Babylon was absolved of its evil actions against Judah (Isa 13). In the same vein, Judas' wicked betrayal of Jesus fulfilled the prophetic word (John 13:11; cf. Ps 41:9), but he was still culpable for his actions. As Jesus states "The Son of Man will go just as it is written about him. But woe to that man who betrays the Son of Man! It would be better for him if he had not been born" (Mark 14:21). In sum, God works through the actions of the wicked and the righteous to fulfill his word (cf. Acts 4:27–28). But one thing is certain: God's word *will* be fulfilled.

The Army of the Marginalized

In contrast to Saul, who is surrounded by the wealthy and powerful, in this story David begins to be surrounded by the marginalized and disenfranchised at the cave of Adullam.[10] Yet it is this ragtag band of the marginalized that David commands and leads to continual victory (e.g., 1 Sam 23:5; 27:8–9) as the story moves forward, while Saul's professional army and political power fall to irrelevance and destruction. This story serves as an excellent illustration of God calling the marginalized rather than the powerful and the rich. As we noted earlier in chapter 2, throughout Scripture we see God taking special interest in the weak, the downtrodden, and the vulnerable. As James writes:

---

10. Saul clearly implies he has given his fellow Benjamites land and powerful positions when he questions them as to whether they think David would treat them so well in 1 Sam 22:7–8. As Brueggemann (*First and Second Samuel*, 158) writes, "Perhaps [1 Sam 22:2] stands as a counterpoint to [1 Sam 22:7]. In v. 2 it is the marginal and indebted, those without land, who gather around David." Cf. Bodner, *1 Samuel*, 234.

Listen, my dear brothers and sisters: Has not God chosen those who are poor in the eyes of the world to be rich in faith and to inherit the kingdom he promised those who love him? (Jas 2:5)

Contrary to the principles of the world, this is the way God builds his kingdom. Similar to what we see in Jesus' ministry, which attracted the marginalized (Mark 1:32–34),[11] the foundation of David's kingdom is not the wealthy and powerful. While Samuel predicted the king would take the best of everything for himself (1 Sam 8:11–17), here David's nascent kingdom begins with the sidelined, the ostracized, and the excluded coming to him willingly. David will not be "a king such as all the other nations have" (1 Sam 8:5).

The beginning of David's kingdom reminds us that God's kingdom is not built on worldly principles. As Paul writes:

Brothers and sisters, think of what you were when you were called. Not many of you were wise by human standards; not many were influential; not many were of noble birth. But God chose the foolish things of the world to shame the wise; God chose the weak things of the world to shame the strong. God chose the lowly things of this world and the despised things—and the things that are not—to nullify the things that are, so that no one may boast before him. (1 Cor 1:26–29)

First Samuel 22 is ripe for theological reflection on the nature of God's kingdom and the grace he has shown in calling us to be a part of it.

---

11. Brueggemann, *First and Second Samuel*, 156.

CHAPTER 21

1 Samuel 23:1–29

 LISTEN to the Story

¹When David was told, "Look, the Philistines are fighting against Keilah and are looting the threshing floors," ²he inquired of the LORD, saying, "Shall I go and attack these Philistines?"

The LORD answered him, "Go, attack the Philistines and save Keilah."

³But David's men said to him, "Here in Judah we are afraid. How much more, then, if we go to Keilah against the Philistine forces!"

⁴Once again David inquired of the LORD, and the LORD answered him, "Go down to Keilah, for I am going to give the Philistines into your hand." ⁵So David and his men went to Keilah, fought the Philistines and carried off their livestock. He inflicted heavy losses on the Philistines and saved the people of Keilah. ⁶(Now Abiathar son of Ahimelek had brought the ephod down with him when he fled to David at Keilah.)

⁷Saul was told that David had gone to Keilah, and he said, "God has delivered him into my hands, for David has imprisoned himself by entering a town with gates and bars." ⁸And Saul called up all his forces for battle, to go down to Keilah to besiege David and his men.

⁹When David learned that Saul was plotting against him, he said to Abiathar the priest, "Bring the ephod." ¹⁰David said, "LORD, God of Israel, your servant has heard definitely that Saul plans to come to Keilah and destroy the town on account of me. ¹¹Will the citizens of Keilah surrender me to him? Will Saul come down, as your servant has heard? LORD, God of Israel, tell your servant."

And the LORD said, "He will."

¹²Again David asked, "Will the citizens of Keilah surrender me and my men to Saul?"

And the LORD said, "They will."

¹³So David and his men, about six hundred in number, left Keilah and kept moving from place to place. When Saul was told that David had escaped from Keilah, he did not go there.

¹⁴David stayed in the wilderness strongholds and in the hills of the Desert of Ziph. Day after day Saul searched for him, but God did not give David into his hands.

¹⁵While David was at Horesh in the Desert of Ziph, he learned that Saul had come out to take his life. ¹⁶And Saul's son Jonathan went to David at Horesh and helped him find strength in God. ¹⁷"Don't be afraid," he said. "My father Saul will not lay a hand on you. You will be king over Israel, and I will be second to you. Even my father Saul knows this." ¹⁸The two of them made a covenant before the Lord. Then Jonathan went home, but David remained at Horesh.

¹⁹The Ziphites went up to Saul at Gibeah and said, "Is not David hiding among us in the strongholds at Horesh, on the hill of Hakilah, south of Jeshimon? ²⁰Now, Your Majesty, come down whenever it pleases you to do so, and we will be responsible for giving him into your hands."

²¹Saul replied, "The Lord bless you for your concern for me. ²²Go and get more information. Find out where David usually goes and who has seen him there. They tell me he is very crafty. ²³Find out about all the hiding places he uses and come back to me with definite information. Then I will go with you; if he is in the area, I will track him down among all the clans of Judah."

²⁴So they set out and went to Ziph ahead of Saul. Now David and his men were in the Desert of Maon, in the Arabah south of Jeshimon. ²⁵Saul and his men began the search, and when David was told about it, he went down to the rock and stayed in the Desert of Maon. When Saul heard this, he went into the Desert of Maon in pursuit of David.

²⁶Saul was going along one side of the mountain, and David and his men were on the other side, hurrying to get away from Saul. As Saul and his forces were closing in on David and his men to capture them, ²⁷a messenger came to Saul, saying, "Come quickly! The Philistines are raiding the land." ²⁸Then Saul broke off his pursuit of David and went to meet the Philistines. That is why they call this place Sela Hammahlekoth. ²⁹And David went up from there and lived in the strongholds of En Gedi.

Listen to the Text in the Story: Exodus 28:30; Leviticus 8:8; Numbers 27:21; Judges 6; El-Amarna Letters (EA 280, 289, 290)

This chapter begins with the Philistines attacking the Israelite border town of Keilah. It appears it was a fortified city, as Saul refers to it as "a town with gates and bars" (1 Sam 23:7). Keilah is likely to be identified with Khirbet Qila, located about eight miles northwest of Hebron, though it has yet to be excavated. Several letters from El-Amarna mention Keilah.[1] The ruler of Keilah writes of his having "to make war against Keilah" then claims, "I have made war (and) I was successful; my town has been restored to me" (EA 280).[2] In another text, Keilah is accused of making trouble and the governor of Jerusalem, Abdu-Heba, requests military aid be sent (EA 289–290). Thus, these texts underscore the precariousness of Keilah as a border town and "attest to the frequently changing status of Keilah and other border towns."[3]

In the crisis at Keilah in 1 Samuel 23, the Philistines were "looting the threshing floors" (v. 1). In ancient agricultural societies like Israel, threshing floors were often attacked because they were not well defended and the loss of grain greatly weakened the enemy. Warfare often included the looting and destruction of agricultural production and commodities. For example, in Judges 6:3–6 Israel's enemies frequently targeted farms and livestock, which "greatly impoverished" the Israelites (Judg 6:6).

Before David moves to deliver Keilah, he first inquires of Yahweh. David's ability to do so is directly related to his acquiring of the ephod at the end of last chapter (1 Sam 22:20–23). In ancient Israel the ephod was often used as an oracular device whereby priests could determine the will of Yahweh (Exod 28:30; Lev 8:8; Num 27:21; cf. 1 Sam 30:7–8), and to "inquire of the LORD" was a technical phrase for asking for an oracle of God, usually expecting either a yes or no answer. It was commonplace in the ancient Near East to consult one's god(s). For example, an ancient Hittite text records such requests, "Do you, O god, approve a campaign this year for His Majesty on the Dumatta front?"[4] Going forward, David is careful to consult Yahweh before important decisions (e.g., 1 Sam 30:7; 2 Sam 2:1; 5:19).

EXPLAIN the Story

In this chapter we see David acting like a faithful king of the land despite being on the run from the current king, Saul. Upon hearing that the Philistines were attacking Keilah, an Israelite city, David inquires of God for direction and is told to attack the Philistines, and he thereby saves the city. When Saul hears of David's location, he heads out with his army to besiege David at

---

1. Though at that time (fourteenth century BC) it was called Qiltu, it is likely the biblical town of Keilah. Cf. Long *1 Samuel*, 362.

2. *ANET*, 487.

3. Long *1 Samuel*, 362.

4. R. H. Beal, "Hittite Military Organization," *CANE*, 545–554. Cited in Long, *1 Samuel*, 363.

Keilah, causing David and his men to head to the wilderness. Despite searching "day after day," God does not allow Saul to find David. When David is in the desert of Ziph, Saul's son, Jonathan, visits David and once again they covenant together. The people of Ziph, however, report David's whereabouts to Saul, and the king closes in on David and his men. Before he catches them, Saul is forced to withdraw from his pursuit due to another Philistine raid. Though not explicitly stated, the reader gets the impression that through the Philistine aggression God has again rescued David from Saul's hand.

David at Keilah (23:1–13)

The chapter begins with David hearing of a Philistine attack on the city of Keilah. David's initial reaction, to defend the city from the foreign aggressor, is like that of a good king (cf. 1 Sam 9:16). Before acting, David first inquires of God for direction, underscoring the benefit of having Abiathar as an ally, as the priest had brought the ephod with him (23:6). Unlike Saul's previous inquiring of Yahweh (14:37), which received no response, here God responds to David and encourages him to take action to deliver Keilah. A second divine enquiry provides assurance of victory to David's men who were reticent of taking action. In response, David and his men obediently went to Keilah, saved the city, and prevailed against the Philistines.

Saul's spy network again serves him well, as he hears that David was in Keilah. David's deliverance of the city exposed his location. As Klein observes, "Instead of rejoicing in the salvation which Yahweh had given to Keilah, Saul tried to take advantage of David's tactical mistake."[5] Here we see a window into Saul's delusional thoughts as he interprets this news as "God" delivering David into his hands (1 Sam 23:7). Despite his rebellion against the prophetic word of Samuel, despite his inability to successfully inquire of God, and despite his murder of Yahweh's priests, now Saul somehow thinks God is operating on his behalf.

Saul proceeds to muster the entire army to besiege David and his men (23:8). Of course, this is not the first time Saul had successfully mustered the Israelite forces. In the past, however, the musters were to defend Israel from foreign aggression (1 Sam 11:7–8; 1 Sam 13:3–4). Now the manic king musters the army *not* to meet a foreign aggressor but to attack his most faithful military leader, who had just delivered an Israelite city from a foreign aggressor. Saul's change in priorities is clear. His obsession over David now overrides his proper duty as king to protect his country, and now he misuses "the armies of the living God" (17:26) for his own selfish and paranoid purposes. He is set

---

5. Klein, *1 Samuel*, 230.

to besiege an Israelite city and even "destroy the town" (23:10) on account of his obsession with David.

While Saul's information network avails him in this chapter, David's intelligence services are superior in that he has access to divine information through the ephod brought by Abiathar.[6] When David hears of Saul's approach, he again inquires of God to verify the intel he has received. David asks two things in the first inquiry: (1) whether the citizens of Keilah would turn him over to Saul and (2) whether Saul will come to Keilah. God's initial answer "he will" (23:11) seems to only respond to the second question, leading David to inquire of God a second time, asking again whether the citizens of Keilah will turn him and his men over to Saul (23:12). God answers in the affirmative. Despite his having saved the town from the Philistines, facing a siege, Keilah *would* hand David over to Saul. Therefore, David and his men, now six hundred in number (up significantly from the four hundred of last chapter), leave Keilah and began moving from place to place, leading Saul to abandon his plan to besiege Keilah.

David in the Wilderness (23:14–29)

From Keilah, David and his men begin an itinerant existence, moving from place to place. Though Saul relentlessly pursued them, God did not allow the rejected king to find him (23:14). Despite Saul's inability to locate David, his son Jonathan appears to have no trouble finding him, and he meets with David in the wilderness. Jonathan helps David find "strength in God." What exactly this phrase means is not explained, but given that Jonathan reassures David that Saul will not "lay a hand" on him and that he will be king, it would seem Jonathan is reminding David of his anointing and God's hand in David's life. Here Jonathan clearly concedes the kingship to David, though he notes he will be "second" in command in his kingdom (23:17). This is the first we have heard of Jonathan's anticipated high role in David's future kingdom. Previously, Jonathan made David promise to preserve his family (20:14–15) but not to secure him an influential role in the coming kingdom. David appears to agree with the proposal, as the two friends once again make a covenant before Yahweh before Jonathan returns home. Sadly, Jonathan never does take his place in David's kingdom, as his untimely death at the hand of the Philistines prevents it (1 Sam 31:2).

In his encouragement to David, Jonathan claims that even his father "knows" that David will be king (23:17). The truth of his statement is backed up in the larger story, as Saul has already been told by Samuel that his kingdom

---

6. Bodner, *1 Samuel*, 242.

is at an end and that a "neighbor" who is "better" than he will inherit the throne (1 Sam 15:28). Yet Saul has resisted the prophetic word and continues to pursue David regardless. Saul is on a mission to change his fate. On the one hand, he knows David will become king; on the other, he does all he can to prevent this from happening. As Saul struggles against the divine will, his madness grows.

After making the covenant with David, Jonathan leaves for home. One may question why Jonathan does not stay with David if he is so sure of David's eventual success. Perhaps he thinks he might be more useful elsewhere? Regardless, after his departure the Ziphites (the inhabitants of the wilderness wherein David hides) send Saul an offer to hand over David to him. This time Saul is slow to move on the intel, perhaps as his last mustering of the army to go to Keilah did not bear fruit in this regard. Now the rejected king wants the Ziphites to first find out more information about David's hiding spots, and then he will go "with" them to pursue David. The Ziphites agree and go out to find David "ahead of Saul" (23:24).

Eventually Saul and his men join the hunt and are closing in on David and his men when news comes of a Philistine raid on Israel which makes Saul give up his pursuit of David (23:27), allowing David to escape (23:29). Though the narrator does not make an explicit statement in this regard, one gets the impression that God is behind the Philistine distraction (cf. 23:14). Due to the close call, the place was named Sela Hammahlekoth, which means in Hebrew "rock of escape/separation." David and his men then went to En Gedi, an oasis along the western shores of the Dead Sea.

LIVE the Story

Relying on Divine Guidance

In this passage, a clear juxtaposition between David and Saul is presented, that of human guidance and divine guidance. Saul's extensive reliance on human intelligence services is emphasized in this chapter as Saul is informed of David's location in Keilah (23:7) and then of David's presence in the wilderness (23:19). Saul requests further reconnaissance by the Ziphites (23:22) before he joins them in the pursuit of David. In contrast to Saul's reliance on human espionage, David relied on divine guidance through Abiathar and the ephod. This text provides a good opportunity for reflection on the contrast between divine and human guidance.

David's access to Abiathar and the ephod, however, is not the whole story, as Saul previously had other ephod-bearing priests with him (1 Sam 14:3).

In fact, as we have seen, Saul was quite concerned with obtaining divine guidance throughout the story thus far. Saul sought prophetic help in finding his father's donkeys (1 Sam 9:6–7); he kept an ephod-bearing priest nearby in his battle with the Philistines (1 Sam 14:3); he inquired of Yahweh as to whether to pursue the Philistines (1 Sam 14:37); he cast lots to obtain divine guidance as to who the "sinner" was who was to blame for God not answering his inquiry (14:41–42); and the charge that Ahimelek inquired of Yahweh for David seemed to be what infuriated Saul the most in his treason tribunal (22:13–16). Saul clearly was concerned with divine guidance, though it eluded him.

So, what was the difference between David's reliance on divine guidance and Saul's obsession with ritualistic divine guidance? I would suggest the difference is one of obedience. David submits himself to the prophetic word and obeys. Saul, on the other hand, has disobeyed God's prophetic words delivered by Samuel (e.g., 1 Sam 13:8–13; 15:1). In other words, Saul *did* receive clear divine words, but he didn't like what he heard. Samuel clearly told Saul that God had rejected him, but Saul continued to live in disobedience. When Saul did not hear what he wanted to hear, he continued to go his own way. Rather than having an attitude of submission to the divine will, Saul wanted divine confirmation that his *own* will was correct.

Sometimes, as Christians, our praying can be similar to Saul's inquiring of God. Our prayers can amount to something like, "Lord bless *my* plans—but don't change them (as I know my plans are right before I even come to pray to you)."[7] When we pray "show me your will," we do not really mean it but just want God to ease our conscience about something and are asking that God's will become like ours. The error in this approach is the *difference between God being God and our trying to use God as a diviner.* Similarly, we may pray about something but do not want God to take over the matter and instead pray all around it—dodging the issue.[8] Such prayer is a refusal to submit to God.

In reflecting on this story, Saul's example can serve as a reminder that our disposition toward God need be one of submission. Before further divine guidance can be obtained from God, obedience to what has already been revealed is first required. As Christians, we do not need to seek further guidance for situations that are already addressed in God's written Word. For example, a Christian need not seek further guidance about whether they should steal, kill somebody, or commit adultery, as these are explicitly dealt with in the Ten Commandments. David's example in this story, however, can reassure us that God does not leave us without guidance when we need it. While we no longer

---

7. William M. Anderson, "How May I Find out the Will of God?," *BSac* 103 (1946): 97.
8. Ibid.

have access to the Urim and Thummim of the priestly ephod or (usually) God directing us in an audible voice, we do have access to something those in Bible times did not—God's written Word and the indwelling of the Holy Spirit. Just as God was *with* David, so Immanuel, *God-with-us*, is with us as his Spirit indwells all believers, and he has left us with his magnificent word to guide us. As we submit and live in obedience to his revealed Word and walk in faith and trust in him, he will lead us through the hard times in our lives.

LISTEN to the Story

¹After Saul returned from pursuing the Philistines, he was told, "David is in the Desert of En Gedi." ²So Saul took three thousand able young men from all Israel and set out to look for David and his men near the Crags of the Wild Goats.

³He came to the sheep pens along the way; a cave was there, and Saul went in to relieve himself. David and his men were far back in the cave. ⁴The men said, "This is the day the LORD spoke of when he said to you, 'I will give your enemy into your hands for you to deal with as you wish.'" Then David crept up unnoticed and cut off a corner of Saul's robe.

⁵Afterward, David was conscience-stricken for having cut off a corner of his robe. ⁶He said to his men, "The LORD forbid that I should do such a thing to my master, the LORD's anointed, or lay my hand on him; for he is the anointed of the LORD." ⁷With these words David sharply rebuked his men and did not allow them to attack Saul. And Saul left the cave and went his way.

⁸Then David went out of the cave and called out to Saul, "My lord the king!" When Saul looked behind him, David bowed down and prostrated himself with his face to the ground. ⁹He said to Saul, "Why do you listen when men say, 'David is bent on harming you'? ¹⁰This day you have seen with your own eyes how the LORD delivered you into my hands in the cave. Some urged me to kill you, but I spared you; I said, 'I will not lay my hand on my lord, because he is the LORD's anointed.' ¹¹See, my father, look at this piece of your robe in my hand! I cut off the corner of your robe but did not kill you. See that there is nothing in my hand to indicate that I am guilty of wrongdoing or rebellion. I have not wronged you, but you are hunting me down to take my life. ¹²May the LORD judge between you and me. And may the LORD avenge the wrongs you have done to me, but my hand will not touch you. ¹³As the old saying goes, 'From evildoers come evil deeds,' so my hand will not touch you.

[14]"Against whom has the king of Israel come out? Who are you pursuing? A dead dog? A flea? [15]May the LORD be our judge and decide between us. May he consider my cause and uphold it; may he vindicate me by delivering me from your hand."

[16]When David finished saying this, Saul asked, "Is that your voice, David my son?" And he wept aloud. [17]"You are more righteous than I," he said. "You have treated me well, but I have treated you badly. [18]You have just now told me about the good you did to me; the LORD delivered me into your hands, but you did not kill me. [19]When a man finds his enemy, does he let him get away unharmed? May the LORD reward you well for the way you treated me today. [20]I know that you will surely be king and that the kingdom of Israel will be established in your hands. [21]Now swear to me by the LORD that you will not kill off my descendants or wipe out my name from my father's family."

[22]So David gave his oath to Saul. Then Saul returned home, but David and his men went up to the stronghold.

Listen to the Text in the Story: 1 Samuel 15:27; 18:3–4

As noted earlier in the commentary, in the book of Samuel robes often carry added symbolic significance. In Samuel 15, when Saul tore Samuel's robe, the prophet declared that it symbolized the kingdom being torn away from the rejected king (15:27). In 1 Samuel 18, when Jonathan gave his robe to David, it symbolized his giving up his claim on the throne and willingly handing it over to David.[1] This, along with ancient Near Eastern evidence (see Listen to the Story in 1 Sam 18), shows that a robe can symbolically signifiy the royal status of its bearer. This must be kept in mind when David decides to cut a piece off Saul's royal robe in the present chapter.

EXPLAIN the Story

After David's narrow escape from Saul in the last chapter, we now see Saul's narrow escape from David. Following his campaign against the Philistines, Saul is informed of David's location and takes three thousand men with him to search for David. During his search, Saul takes a bathroom break in the very same cave where David and his men were hiding. David's men interpret

---

1. Cf. 1 Kgs 11:29–31 where another garment symbolizes the kingdom of Israel as well.

this turn of events as God saying to David that he would have his enemy delivered into his hands. However, rather than attack Saul, David chooses to simply cut off a corner of Saul's robe without Saul noticing. Yet, even this action pricks David's conscience due to his reverence for Saul being Yahweh's anointed one. When Saul leaves the cave, David goes out and calls out to Saul. David tries to convince him that he is not out to harm him, producing the portion of his robe he had cut off as proof. Saul responds somewhat repentantly, admitting his bad treatment of David and acknowledging not only David's righteous character but also his destiny to be king of Israel. Like his son Jonathan, Saul also asks David to swear he will spare the life of his descendants when he becomes king, to which David agrees. Despite the apparent reconciliation, however, Saul and David again part ways. After all, David had enough experience with Saul's double-dealing ways than to trust him with his life.

Saul Continues His Pursuit (24:1–3)

This chapter is the first of two golden opportunities David has to kill Saul, but he is unwilling (the second opportunity is found in ch. 26). This has led some commentators to suggest the two stories are derived from the same historical memory of one event.[2] Regardless of the merit of such speculation, in its final form the two episodes form bookends to chapter 25 and the three chapters together function to bring into relief David's increasingly complex character, to which we will return later. The last chapter ended with Saul being forced to call off his pursuit of David due to another Philistine raid. This chapter begins with Saul returning from fighting the Philistines and again being informed about David's location. Again, Saul's intelligence network appears quite proficient, correctly identifying his location in the desert of En Gedi (cf. 23:29), an oasis along the western shores of the Dead Sea and rife with rocky cliffs and caves (perfect for hiding). Saul chooses three thousand "able" men from "all Israel" to search for David (24:2), thus outnumbering him five to one (23:13). It is significant that Saul chose men not just from Benjamin but from "all Israel." Given what was to occur in this chapter, having witnesses from "all Israel" would likely go a long way in the later support of "all Israel" for David (2 Sam 5:3).

The "Crags of the Wild Goats" (24:2) is not a clear designation, though ibex are known to have lived near En Gedi (and still do to this day). In a cave near this location, Saul stops to use one of the caves as a lavatory. It just so happens that the very cave Saul chooses for a latrine is already occupied by David

---

2. E.g. Brueggemann, *First and Second Samuel*, 166.

and his men. Saul stays near the mouth of the cave to do his business while David and company "were far back in the cave" (24:3). While no narratorial comment is made, one gets the feeling that this royal stop is providential.

The Word of Yahweh and Cutting the Corner of Saul's Robe (24:4–7)

When David's men saw this amazing turn of events, with the king caught with his pants down (literally), they reference a word from Yahweh which said, "I will give your enemy into your hands for you to deal with as you wish" (24:4). The problem is that nowhere in the story have we come across such a word from God or similar prophetic oracle to David. Perhaps this is simply David's men drawing out perceived implications of David's anointing by the prophet Samuel. Alternatively, it is possible that the verb "spoke/said" should be translated in the present tense.[3] In other words, the verse could be rendered as something like the NLT's, "Today the LORD is telling you, 'I will certainly put your enemy into your power, to do with as you wish.'" As Auld explains, "the men may have been urging David to recognize the facts in front of his face: seeing Saul delivered defenseless before them should be tantamount to hearing a divine utterance."[4] A third option is that David's men completely fabricated this divine word. After all, the men likely wanted Saul dead. As Bodner explains:

> The group that gathers around David, we recall from 22.2, are distressed, discontent, and in debt. These are men, therefore, who have every reason to want Saul liquidated—and given their various states of debt and distress, probably they are not above fibbing. If Saul is destroyed, so are their criminal records.[5]

In response to this claim of prophetic fulfilment, David covertly approaches the indisposed king and cuts off a corner of his robe. Whether the robe had been removed for the purposes of relieving himself or whether David was so silent as to cut off the corner while the king was wearing it is unclear (I suspect the former was the case).[6]

As noted in the Listen to the Story section above, in the book of Samuel robes have had significant symbolic meaning. So, when David cuts a piece off Saul's royal robe here, it was a way of symbolically indicating his power over the kingdom. David's actions cause his conscience to be pricked, leading

---

3. As suggested by Auld, *I & II Samuel*, 275.
4. Ibid.
5. Bodner, *1 Samuel*, 251.
6. Klein speculates that perhaps Saul fell asleep "while answering the call of nature." Klein, *1 Samuel*, 239.

him to regret his covert alteration of Saul's robe and to forbid his men from attacking the king. This is an important moment in David's characterization. He had an opportunity, interpreted by his men as a divinely ordained opportunity, to be rid of his enemy and take the throne of Israel. After all, he was anointed to the office by no less than the prophet Samuel himself. Yet David's respect for God's anointing stayed his hand. In David's theological perspective, since God had installed Saul as king it was up to God to remove him from the throne. David would have no direct part in it. By cutting off a corner of Saul's robe, David symbolically made a move to take the kingdom from Saul directly. David had no intention to usurp Saul himself. Thus, David's actions in cutting off the edge of Saul's robe did not align with his convictions that the succession to the throne would be carried out by Yahweh, not himself.

Commentators have also pointed out the self-serving nature of David's words about the prohibition of touching Yahweh's anointed.[7] After all, David is also Yahweh's anointed, so the rule that no one may harm the anointed one works in David's favor. This is especially relevant when we realize he is addressing the men who were just claiming that Yahweh wanted David to kill the anointed one. Better to have the policy of never killing anointed ones.

David Addresses Saul (24:8–22)

In a daring move, after Saul exits the cave, David follows and calls out to him. Though he is now exposed, David takes the opportunity to talk some reason into the king (though clearly Saul is anything but reasonable). David urges Saul to realize that he is not out to get him and offers the piece of robe in his hand as evidence. If he were really out to kill Saul, he would already be dead. David pleads innocence in regard to any charges of wrongdoing Saul may have against him. While David does appeal to Yahweh to avenge the wrongs done to him and deliver him from Saul's hand, David swears he will not hurt Saul in any way.

Saul responds first by confirming that it is really David addressing him. It is unclear whether this is because David had bowed to the ground when Saul first turned to see him (24:8) or whether David is a long way off from Saul at this point, which seems likely (better to keep some distance between himself and the manic king). Saul's unbalanced nature comes to the fore once again as he first weeps loudly (remember that initially in 1 Sam 16:21 Saul "loved" David) then admits his bad treatment of David as well as David's righteous actions and character. What is more, just as Jonathan told David (23:17), Saul now admits that he knows David will be king. In light of this, Saul, like

---

7. E.g., Polzin, *Samuel and the Deuteronomist*, 210.

Jonathan, pleads for the life of his descendants when David takes the throne (24:21). As noted earlier, in the ancient world when one dynasty replaced another it was standard practice to destroy anyone who might have a claim to the throne. Though he owed nothing to the king by way of friendship or loyalty, David accedes to the request and so swears (24:22).

At this Saul returned home, but David and his men stayed in the desert as fugitives. Despite Saul's acknowledgment of David's future regency, David was not fool enough to join with the king at this point. Saul's word could not be relied upon. David had enough experience with the double-dealing ways of Saul to prevent him from taking the king at his word. After all, Saul does not even claim he will stop pursuing David here and thereby give David back his freedom. He simply acknowledges that David will one day reign over Israel.

 LIVE the Story

Spiritual Discernment

In this story when Saul entered into the cave where David was hiding with his men, his men interpreted the event as a divine opportunity for revenge. In fact, they referenced a prophetic word virtually claiming that God was saying to kill Saul now. David faced a difficult decision that required real spiritual discernment. Was God really saying what David's men claimed?

Regardless of one's theological tradition, this story of David in the cave with Saul is relevant for present-day believers. Sometimes in our lives we may be in situations where a fellow Christian(s) claims to know God's will for us. Some may even explicitly claim that they have a "word from God" for you to follow. Alternatively, many of us will be faced with a situation in our life that might be interpreted as a God-ordained sign that we should take a certain action. In other words, two important issues are brought into relief here: situations where you must judge a "word" that a fellow believer may give you; and situations where you must interpret events and opportunities as to whether they are giving you divine direction to take certain actions.

Judging a "Prophetic Word"

As regards to judging a fellow believer's "word from God" for you, it must first be recognized that no (prophetic) word would ever go against God's explicit will as found in the Scriptures. For an extreme example, a word that encourages/commands one to commit adultery would obviously be unacceptable since adultery is barred in the Ten Commandments. Strange as it seems, some self-proclaimed modern prophets have actually made such pronouncements (like David Koresh, leader of the "Christian" cult called the Branch Davidians in the early 1990s, who took some of the wives of his followers as his own).

The New Testament urges believers to test prophetic words rather than simply obey them. Paul writes: "Do not quench the Spirit. Do not treat prophecies with contempt but test them all; hold on to what is good; reject every kind of evil" (1 Thess 5:19–22). Similarly, 1 Corinthians 14:29 tells us that prophetic words should be judged by others: "Two or three prophets should speak, and the others should weigh carefully (discern/judge) what is said." The standard for testing is clearly Scripture as Paul asserts that Scripture is made for "teaching, rebuking, correcting and training in righteousness" (2 Tim 3:16).

Another important factor in judging a "prophetic word" is the inner witness of the Holy Spirit (Rom 8:16; 1 John 5:6). Jesus told believers that the Spirit would "guide you into all the truth" (John 16:13; cf. 1 John 2:20). In this story David's response to the prophetic word was not in step with the witness of the spirit, as his conscience pricked him following his cutting the corner of Saul's robe (24:5). As discussed above, while his act showed great restraint, it *was* a way of implying he was taking the kingdom from Saul. Thus, his actions here were born of self-interest. The actions conflicted with David's convictions about God's plan for him. David was trusting in God to give him the kingdom and was not out to take it from Saul. David's conscience struck him because he realized what he did was wrong. Thus, the supposed prophecy his men spoke led him to do something that went against his convictions.

It is not always easy to distinguish between the spirit's voice and our own selfish desires. In order to not be deceived by our own sinful hearts, it is important to examine our motives (to see if we are seeking our own interests or God's) and reaffirm our willingness to submit to God's will no matter what. When David felt convicted, he realized his selfish motives in the matter and submitted himself once again to God's will. He affirmed that God had anointed Saul (1 Sam 24:6) and put Saul into God's hands rather than his own. Furthermore, David's submission to the divine will can be seen in his subsequent action of leaving the security of the cave and showing himself to Saul. This demonstrated his great faith in God's plan for his life. David believed so strongly that God was going to give him the kingdom that he took his life in his hands and exposed himself to his enemy. David affirms his yieldedness to Yahweh's will when he said to Saul, "May the LORD judge between you and me. And may the LORD avenge the wrongs you have done to me, but my hand will not touch you" (24:12).

Discerning Divine Opportunities

On the other hand, many Christians regularly interpret the turn of events or opportunities presented as divine guidance to take a particular action. This often entails interpreting opportunities or what may otherwise appear to be coincidence as a sign confirming or disconfirming what one thinks the will of God is regarding a particular decision. For example, when I am given a new job opportunity, should I interpret this as God calling me to change careers or positions? Or could it be meant to confirm that I am a valuable or skilled employee? Or could it be there to confirm that I need to stay where I currently work? Should I necessarily draw out a divine message at all from the opportunity?

Living life and discerning God's will takes wisdom and we are urged as Christians to be "making the most of every opportunity" (Eph 5:16). James 4:15 encourages Christians to be humble in our decisions and planning in life and say, "If it is the Lord's will, we will live and do this or that." Apparently, we should not always expect certainty regarding which path to take or regarding which choice is clearly God's will for us. In the book of Esther, when the Jewish people were going to be annihilated by Haman, Esther's uncle Mordecai urges Esther to act on their behalf but does not tell her with certainty that it is because God has ordained her to do so at this point. Instead he says, "*who knows* but that you have come to your royal position for such a time as this?" (Esth 4:14, emphasis added). This perspective expresses a biblical position on interpreting events and opportunities. It expresses some humility. It does not claim full knowledge of God's will in the matter, but it does, in faith, suggest a divine possibility.[8] As Christians, we must always remember to "test and approve what God's will is" (Rom 12:2) and to live life with humility and faith (Rom 12:3).

---

8. Cf. 1 Sam 14:6 and the similarity wtih Jonathan's view that "perhaps LORD will act . . . ."

LISTEN to the Story

¹Now Samuel died, and all Israel assembled and mourned for him; and they buried him at his home in Ramah. Then David moved down into the Desert of Paran.

²A certain man in Maon, who had property there at Carmel, was very wealthy. He had a thousand goats and three thousand sheep, which he was shearing in Carmel. ³His name was Nabal and his wife's name was Abigail. She was an intelligent and beautiful woman, but her husband was surly and mean in his dealings—he was a Calebite.

⁴While David was in the wilderness, he heard that Nabal was shearing sheep. ⁵So he sent ten young men and said to them, "Go up to Nabal at Carmel and greet him in my name. ⁶Say to him: 'Long life to you! Good health to you and your household! And good health to all that is yours!

⁷"'Now I hear that it is sheep-shearing time. When your shepherds were with us, we did not mistreat them, and the whole time they were at Carmel nothing of theirs was missing. ⁸Ask your own servants and they will tell you. Therefore be favorable toward my men, since we come at a festive time. Please give your servants and your son David whatever you can find for them.'"

⁹When David's men arrived, they gave Nabal this message in David's name. Then they waited.

¹⁰Nabal answered David's servants, "Who is this David? Who is this son of Jesse? Many servants are breaking away from their masters these days. ¹¹Why should I take my bread and water, and the meat I have slaughtered for my shearers, and give it to men coming from who knows where?"

¹²David's men turned around and went back. When they arrived, they reported every word. ¹³David said to his men, "Each of you strap on your sword!" So they did, and David strapped his on as well. About four hundred men went up with David, while two hundred stayed with the supplies.

¹⁴One of the servants told Abigail, Nabal's wife, "David sent messengers from the wilderness to give our master his greetings, but he hurled insults at them. ¹⁵Yet these men were very good to us. They did not mistreat us, and the whole time we were out in the fields near them nothing was missing. ¹⁶Night and day they were a wall around us the whole time we were herding our sheep near them. ¹⁷Now think it over and see what you can do, because disaster is hanging over our master and his whole household. He is such a wicked man that no one can talk to him."

¹⁸Abigail acted quickly. She took two hundred loaves of bread, two skins of wine, five dressed sheep, five seahs of roasted grain, a hundred cakes of raisins and two hundred cakes of pressed figs, and loaded them on donkeys. ¹⁹Then she told her servants, "Go on ahead; I'll follow you." But she did not tell her husband Nabal.

²⁰As she came riding her donkey into a mountain ravine, there were David and his men descending toward her, and she met them. ²¹David had just said, "It's been useless—all my watching over this fellow's property in the wilderness so that nothing of his was missing. He has paid me back evil for good. ²²May God deal with David, be it ever so severely, if by morning I leave alive one male of all who belong to him!"

²³When Abigail saw David, she quickly got off her donkey and bowed down before David with her face to the ground. ²⁴She fell at his feet and said: "Pardon your servant, my lord, and let me speak to you; hear what your servant has to say. ²⁵Please pay no attention, my lord, to that wicked man Nabal. He is just like his name—his name means Fool, and folly goes with him. And as for me, your servant, I did not see the men my lord sent. ²⁶And now, my lord, as surely as the LORD your God lives and as you live, since the LORD has kept you from bloodshed and from avenging yourself with your own hands, may your enemies and all who are intent on harming my lord be like Nabal. ²⁷And let this gift, which your servant has brought to my lord, be given to the men who follow you.

²⁸"Please forgive your servant's presumption. The LORD your God will certainly make a lasting dynasty for my lord, because you fight the LORD's battles, and no wrongdoing will be found in you as long as you live. ²⁹Even though someone is pursuing you to take your life, the life of my lord will be bound securely in the bundle of the living by the LORD your God, but the lives of your enemies he will hurl away as from the pocket of a sling. ³⁰When the LORD has fulfilled for my lord every good thing he promised concerning him and has appointed him ruler over Israel, ³¹my lord will

not have on his conscience the staggering burden of needless bloodshed or of having avenged himself. And when the LORD your God has brought my lord success, remember your servant."

³²David said to Abigail, "Praise be to the LORD, the God of Israel, who has sent you today to meet me. ³³May you be blessed for your good judgment and for keeping me from bloodshed this day and from avenging myself with my own hands. ³⁴Otherwise, as surely as the LORD, the God of Israel, lives, who has kept me from harming you, if you had not come quickly to meet me, not one male belonging to Nabal would have been left alive by daybreak."

³⁵Then David accepted from her hand what she had brought him and said, "Go home in peace. I have heard your words and granted your request."

³⁶When Abigail went to Nabal, he was in the house holding a banquet like that of a king. He was in high spirits and very drunk. So she told him nothing at all until daybreak. ³⁷Then in the morning, when Nabal was sober, his wife told him all these things, and his heart failed him and he became like a stone. ³⁸About ten days later, the LORD struck Nabal and he died.

³⁹When David heard that Nabal was dead, he said, "Praise be to the LORD, who has upheld my cause against Nabal for treating me with contempt. He has kept his servant from doing wrong and has brought Nabal's wrongdoing down on his own head."

Then David sent word to Abigail, asking her to become his wife. ⁴⁰His servants went to Carmel and said to Abigail, "David has sent us to you to take you to become his wife."

⁴¹She bowed down with her face to the ground and said, "I am your servant and am ready to serve you and wash the feet of my lord's servants."

⁴²Abigail quickly got on a donkey and, attended by her five female servants, went with David's messengers and became his wife. ⁴³David had also married Ahinoam of Jezreel, and they both were his wives. ⁴⁴But Saul had given his daughter Michal, David's wife, to Paltiel son of Laish, who was from Gallim.

Listen to the Text in the Story: Deuteronomy 17:17; 1 Samuel 15:12

There are some different textual witnesses concerning the location to where David moves at the beginning of this chapter. The traditional Hebrew text says that David went to the desert of Paran, which the 2011 NIV follows. However, Paran is in the far south of Judah, a good distance from Maon, where the following events of the chapter take place. This, along with ancient Greek versions of this text that read "the desert of Maon" in place of Paran, leads many scholars (and the 1984 NIV) to translate following the Greek (e.g., NLT).[1] This makes the most sense in the story, as David claims to have spent some time in the vicinity of Nabal (25:7), which Nabal's men corroborate (25:15–16). If he had been dwelling in Paran and just arrived at Maon, it would appear to contradict this fact.

Near Maon is Carmel, which should not be confused with the more famous Mount Carmel (e.g., 1 Kgs 18) in the northern coastal region of Israel. This southern Carmel is about eight miles southeast of Hebron and probably should be identified with Khirbet el-Kirmil. Earlier in the story, we were told that Saul had erected a monument to himself in Carmel (1 Sam 15:12). Saul's claim on the area, therefore, may explain Nabal's hostility to David in this story.[2]

EXPLAIN the Story

Following the death of Samuel, David moves to the desert of Maon where he encounters a wealthy landowner named Nabal and his intelligent and beautiful wife, Abigail. David sends messengers to Nabal requesting food in payment for the protection David had provided for his shepherds and flocks, but the surly Nabal refused and instead offered insults. This led David to move to avenge himself on Nabal by killing him and all males of his household. Fortunately, David's planned revenge is successfully prevented by Abigail's intervention, wherein she offered the food that her husband had refused to share and reminded David to not avenge himself. Furthermore, Abigail expressed loyalty to David and her faith that God will install him as king over Israel. David accepted Abigail's intervention and withdrew from his planned attack. When Abigail returned and told her husband what had happened, he had a cardiac event of some kind and died soon thereafter. Subsequently, David took Abigail as his wife.

The Death of Samuel (25:1)

This chapter begins with the death of the prophet Samuel and the response of "all Israel" assembling and mourning for him. Given the importance of Samuel in the story so far, the brevity of this notice is striking. The last judge

---

1. E.g., Auld, *I & II Samuel*, 293; McCarter, *I Samuel*, 388; Baldwin, *1 and 2 Samuel*, 146; Hans Wilhelm Hertzberg, *1 and 2 Samuel: A Commentary* (Philadelphia: Westminster, 1965), 198.
2. Long, *1 Samuel*, 369.

of Israel is gone, and we are left with only monarchs. The death of the prophet may have stirred something in David, as following Samuel's passing David begins to be more aggressive. Perhaps David had assumed the prophet would be there when he was finally crowned king and the death of Samuel was cause for rethinking his passive stance. Regardless, the burial of Samuel occasioned David's move to a new location.

Nabal and Abigail (25:2–3)

David's move to Maon put him in the vicinity of a wealthy landowner named Nabal. In Hebrew Nabal literally means "fool." If the name were not enough, the narrator further describes Nabal as "surly and mean in his dealings" (25:3). What is more, this is in contrast to his wife, Abigail, who is said to be "intelligent and beautiful" (25:3). Both characters will live up to their initial descriptions later in this story.

David's Request (25:4–9)

Nabal is said to own three thousand sheep and was shearing them in Carmel (25:2). David hears about the shearing and sees an opportunity. He sends ten men to meet Nabal and give the most elaborate well wishes recorded in the Bible. (The greeting wishes *shalom* to Nabal and his house *three* times.) Furthermore, and to the point, David's men request provisions be given to them on account of their good treatment of Nabal's shepherds in the recent past. Specifically, they ask them to give them "whatever you can find" (25:8). Seeing as this was a festive time as they were presently shearing the sheep, there would have been much on hand.

It is unclear how exactly David's men serviced Nabal's shepherds, as they only mention that they did not mistreat them or steal anything from them. This is not exactly something that seems worthy of payment. As one scholar writes:

> Nabal actually owed David nothing. He had not contracted for David's protection. It is difficult to escape the conclusion that, in fact, the only threat to Nabal's flocks had been David himself. Surely, Nabal did not owe David payment for a theft not committed.[3]

This has led some to see David's request as extortion or racketeering.[4] Gordon and Rendsburg, however, point out that in the ancient Near East this was a common practice. By protecting Nabal's shepherds and flock, David

---

3. Mark E. Biddle, "Ancestral Motifs in 1 Samuel 25: Intertextuality and Characterization," *JBL* 121 (2002): 637.

4. E.g., Green, *How Are the Mighty Fallen?*, 397.

had full rights to impose "protection money" as he was "entitled to Nabal's tribute."[5]

This may have been accepted practice in the ancient Near East, but it still does not reflect too well on David. While in my judgment, accusations of mafia-like extortion go too far, David's appeal to the practice of protection money reflects actions not unlike "the other nations." Remember, Israel had requested a king "as all the other nations" (1 Sam 8:5) and Samuel had warned them that such a king would take, take, take (1 Sam 8:11–17), concluding with the note that he will "take a tenth of your flocks" (1 Sam 8:17). By playing by the accepted rules of the game, David is acting like a king "as all the other nations" (1 Sam 8:5).

Nabal's Response (25:10–11)
In response to the extremely polite and legitimate request by David's men that they be given some provisions, Nabal refuses the request and, like Saul before him, refers to David as "son of Jesse," a pejorative term (1 Sam 20:27, 30, 31; 22:8, 13). In fact, it seems likely that Nabal is actually a supporter of Saul. After all, this sheep shearing is taking place in Carmel, the same place where Saul had built a monument to himself (15:12), and he accuses David of being one of many rebellious servants who "are breaking away from their masters these days" (25:10).

David's Response to Nabal (25:12–13)
When David is told of Nabal's response, David instructs his men to strap on their sword, and he does so himself. Just as his greeting to Nabal earlier mentioned *shalom* three times, now "sword" is mentioned three times.[6] While in the last chapter David showed restraint in not harming Saul, such restraint is not present here. Lest we think that Nabal's refusal to provide food for David was a matter of life and death, David leaves two hundred men to stay behind to guard the supplies they already had (25:13). David's quick move to war comes as a surprise.

The Intervention of Abigail (25:14–35)
One of Nabal's servants realized that his master was putting them all in grave danger, so he went and told Abigail, Nabal's wife. The servant corroborated

---

5. Cyrus Herzl Gordon and Gary Rendsburg, *The Bible and the Ancient Near East* (New York; London: Norton, 1997), 189.

6. Though this is missed in some translations, "sword" appears three times as 1 Sam 25:13 reads, "each man strap on his *sword.* And each man strapped on his *sword.* And David also strapped on his *sword*" (my translation; similarly, ESV, NRSV, JPS, KJV).

David's story of protecting Nabal's shepherds and asked Abigail to do something before it was too late. Abigail proves herself as wise as initially described, taking a generous amount of food and bringing it to David without her husband's knowledge. As she approaches David, the narrator tells us that David had just finished declaring that he was going to kill all the males of Nabal's household. Unlike the restrained David we have seen before, David is ready to kill many due to the rudeness of their master. Slaughtering the house of Nabal would not only have been wrong due to the innocent bloodshed, but it would have undermined his support from Israelites in the area. As Birch writes, "One could hardly imagine the later crowning of David at Hebron if he had wiped out the entire household of a prominent Calebite."[7] As noted earlier, Nabal is in the same area where Saul had built a monument to himself, possibly hostile territory for David. Slaughtering Nabal's house was unlikely to encourage support for his regency.

Providentially, God spares David through the intervention of Abigail. Unlike her husband, Abigail shows great humility and respect when she meets David, bowing and falling at his feet (25:23–24). She begins by insulting her husband and declaring him wicked and a fool (as his name means fool, this is a pun). Further, Abigail seems to wish her husband death when she says, "may your enemies and all who are intent on harming my lord be like Nabal" (25:26). This, along with her closing line that David "remember" (25:31) her when his kingdom is established, suggests that Abigail was attempting to join David—without her husband.[8]

Abigail next points out the gift she has brought and expresses her faith that God is going to make David king, so he should avoid avenging himself. She further alludes to David's victory over Goliath with a sling (25:29) and pleads for David's forgiveness. Interestingly, she reminds David that God had kept him from "bloodshed and from avenging yourself with your own hands" (25:26), apparently displaying knowledge of the events that occurred in the cave of En Gedi (1 Sam 24).

Abigail's speech must have been an eye opener for David, as he realizes how close he was to blowing it. David responds with praise to God for sending Abigail to keep him from bloodshed and avenging himself. What is more, he assures Abigail that he will no longer attack but will grant her request.

The Death of Nabal (25:36–38)

Abigail returns to her husband and finds him holding a drunken banquet, so she decides not to tell her husband about what happened until the morning

---

7. Birch, "Books of Samuel," 1168.
8. Bodner, *1 Samuel*, 267.

after when he was sober (and possibly hung over).[9] When told about what transpired the night before, Nabal's "heart failed him and he became like a stone" (25:37). What exactly happened is unclear, though it appears he had a heart attack or stroke and entered into a coma, dying soon thereafter. David did not need to avenge himself on Nabal. Yahweh himself "struck" Nabal instead (25:38).

David Takes Abigail as Wife (25:39–44)

Upon hearing the news that Nabal had died, David praised God for keeping him from wrongdoing and avenging him. In a somewhat surprising move, David then sends word to Abigail asking her to marry him, to which Abigail quickly and humbly agrees. As Nabal was a prominent figure in the area, it is possible (though not certain) that Abigail, or David, inherited his extensive properties. Either way, his marriage to Abigail may have helped secure the support of the area for David.

The chapter closes noting that this was David's third wife. As you will recall, David first married Saul's daughter Michal, though here it is noted that Saul since gave her away to another man (1 Sam 25:44). Subsequently, David had married Ahinoam of Jezreel, and now he had taken Abigail as wife. While no narratorial judgment is explicitly laid on David's polygamy here, Deuteronomy 17:17 famously commanded that an Israelite king "must not take many wives." While David's three wives (thus far) pale in comparison to the number of wives 1 Kings 11:1–3 ascribes to his son, Solomon, (seven hundred wives and three hundred concubines), it is at least a step in the wrong direction (cf. 2 Sam 3:2–5; 5:13; 11).

LIVE the Story

Saint and Sinner

In this story we see a less-than-ideal David. While he showed remarkable restraint in the previous chapter when he refused to harm Saul (and even regretted the symbolic action he undertook regarding the kingdom), now David loses his temper and sets out to avenge himself. What is more, Nabal did not seek to kill David, as had Saul, but merely insulted him and was unwilling to share his food with him. David's quick leap to judge, jury, and executioner does not reflect well on him. Of course, we should not be surprised to see David as a mixture of sinner and saint, "for all have sinned and

---

9. This could be interpreted as either merciful (letting him have one last worry-free night of wine) or cruel (adding insult to injury—telling him when he is hungover).

fall short of the glory of God" (Rom 3:23). Seeing David's flaws, however, illustrates the struggles with living a life of faith. Just as David struggled to do the right thing here and let his temper and pride get the better of him, so in our lives we will struggle with these vices.

In this story, David was about to make a very bad choice that would have likely had negative consequences for the future king. Slaughtering the house of a prominent man would have negatively affected the support of the people in the area and marred David's otherwise innocent rise to the throne, as he would have incurred bloodguilt. This text reminds us of the danger of making choices based on our pride and letting our anger get out of hand. Seeing David's struggle with pride, anger, and making right decisions allows us to see God's grace in his life and, most importantly for our lives, serves as a reminder that God is gracious to us, too.

God's Preventative Grace

The story also illustrates God's preventative grace in providentially guiding his children away from sin. God used Abigail to remind David of his principles, and David responded by praising God that he had sent Abigail (25:32) and prevented him from incurring bloodguilt and avenging himself. Thus, this passage is cause for reflection on God's work in our lives to preserve us from sin. This side of eternity we will never know the extent of God's providence in our lives that has steered us from sin. Furthermore, David's struggle with Nabal illustrates the truth of 1 Corinthians 10:13 that "No temptation has overtaken you except what is common to mankind. And God is faithful; he will not let you be tempted beyond what you can bear. But when you are tempted, he will also provide a way out so that you can endure it." Here in 1 Samuel 25 we see David tempted to sin by avenging himself, but God providing a way out through Abigail and her timely gifts and wise counsel.

Trusting God with Our Future

Finally, this story illustrates the act of fully trusting God with our future. Abigail reminds David that God was going to make him "a lasting dynasty" (25:28) and that David was not to avenge himself. As one scholar writes, in 1 Samuel 25 "David learns not to seek revenge or seize power with his own hand, but rather to depend on God and on God's timing."[10] While our sinful nature may want to act out in pride and anger to take revenge, we must leave our desire for vengeance with God. As God says, "It is mine to avenge; I will repay" (Deut 32:35; cf. Rom 12:19). After all, David was not the only

---

10. Arnold, *1 & 2 Samuel*, 346.

one to patiently wait for God to fulfill his word.[11] A later anointed one and "son of David," Jesus, "when they hurled their insults at him, he did not retaliate; when he suffered, he made no threats. Instead, he entrusted himself to him who judges justly" (1 Pet 2:23), and we are called to "follow in his steps" (1 Pet 2:21).

---

11. Ibid., 348.

CHAPTER 24

1 Samuel 26:1-25

 LISTEN to the Story

¹The Ziphites went to Saul at Gibeah and said, "Is not David hiding on the hill of Hakilah, which faces Jeshimon?"

²So Saul went down to the Desert of Ziph, with his three thousand select Israelite troops, to search there for David. ³Saul made his camp beside the road on the hill of Hakilah facing Jeshimon, but David stayed in the wilderness. When he saw that Saul had followed him there, ⁴he sent out scouts and learned that Saul had definitely arrived.

⁵Then David set out and went to the place where Saul had camped. He saw where Saul and Abner son of Ner, the commander of the army, had lain down. Saul was lying inside the camp, with the army encamped around him.

⁶David then asked Ahimelek the Hittite and Abishai son of Zeruiah, Joab's brother, "Who will go down into the camp with me to Saul?"

"I'll go with you," said Abishai.

⁷So David and Abishai went to the army by night, and there was Saul, lying asleep inside the camp with his spear stuck in the ground near his head. Abner and the soldiers were lying around him.

⁸Abishai said to David, "Today God has delivered your enemy into your hands. Now let me pin him to the ground with one thrust of the spear; I won't strike him twice."

⁹But David said to Abishai, "Don't destroy him! Who can lay a hand on the LORD's anointed and be guiltless? ¹⁰As surely as the LORD lives," he said, "the LORD himself will strike him, or his time will come and he will die, or he will go into battle and perish. ¹¹But the LORD forbid that I should lay a hand on the LORD's anointed. Now get the spear and water jug that are near his head, and let's go."

¹²So David took the spear and water jug near Saul's head, and they left. No one saw or knew about it, nor did anyone wake up. They were all sleeping, because the LORD had put them into a deep sleep.

[13]Then David crossed over to the other side and stood on top of the hill some distance away; there was a wide space between them. [14]He called out to the army and to Abner son of Ner, "Aren't you going to answer me, Abner?"

Abner replied, "Who are you who calls to the king?"

[15]David said, "You're a man, aren't you? And who is like you in Israel? Why didn't you guard your lord the king? Someone came to destroy your lord the king. [16]What you have done is not good. As surely as the LORD lives, you and your men must die, because you did not guard your master, the LORD's anointed. Look around you. Where are the king's spear and water jug that were near his head?"

[17]Saul recognized David's voice and said, "Is that your voice, David my son?"

David replied, "Yes it is, my lord the king." [18]And he added, "Why is my lord pursuing his servant? What have I done, and what wrong am I guilty of? [19]Now let my lord the king listen to his servant's words. If the LORD has incited you against me, then may he accept an offering. If, however, people have done it, may they be cursed before the LORD! They have driven me today from my share in the LORD's inheritance and have said, 'Go, serve other gods.' [20]Now do not let my blood fall to the ground far from the presence of the LORD. The king of Israel has come out to look for a flea—as one hunts a partridge in the mountains."

[21]Then Saul said, "I have sinned. Come back, David my son. Because you considered my life precious today, I will not try to harm you again. Surely I have acted like a fool and have been terribly wrong."

[22]"Here is the king's spear," David answered. "Let one of your young men come over and get it. [23]The LORD rewards everyone for their righteousness and faithfulness. The LORD delivered you into my hands today, but I would not lay a hand on the LORD's anointed. [24]As surely as I valued your life today, so may the LORD value my life and deliver me from all trouble."

[25]Then Saul said to David, "May you be blessed, David my son; you will do great things and surely triumph."

So David went on his way, and Saul returned home.

Listen to the Text in the Story: Genesis 10:15; 23:3; 1 Samuel 24–25

This is the second of two stories where David has a golden opportunity to eliminate Saul but refuses to do so. After David's experiences last chapter, wherein God himself dealt with his enemy, Nabal (25:38), David thought better of taking action himself and again waits on God to deal with Saul. While in 1 Samuel 24 Saul was caught unawares relieving himself in a cave, this time it is Saul's deep sleep that allows David's approach.

When David looks for volunteers to accompany him into Saul's camp, one of the men he asks is "Ahimelek the Hittite" (26:6). The Hittites are a famous ancient people whose empire dominated Syria-Anatolia in the fourteenth–thirteenth centuries BC—so much so that the land of Syria was sometimes referred to as "the Hittite country" (Josh 1:4). However, other people called the Hittites were Canaanite peoples, so named after their epyonmous ancestor, Heth (sometimes referred to as "the sons of Heth" in the Hebrew; e.g., Gen 23:3, 5, 7, 10. Cf. ASV, KJV), who is said to be a son of Canaan (Gen 10:15). Most references to the Hittites in the Old Testament refer to the second group, the Canaanite Hittites, and not the great nation that founded the Hittite empire of old. Ahimelek is not the only Hittite who was part of David's loyal soldiers, as the more well-known Uriah the Hittite will figure prominently in the story in 2 Samuel 11 of David's sin with Bathsheba, Uriah's wife.

EXPLAIN the Story

Given another opportunity to kill Saul, David once again refuses to harm Saul out of respect for Yahweh's anointing. Instead, he takes Saul's royal spear and water jug from his sleeping side. Unlike the previous time, David's conscience does not strike him for his actions, even though the spear was a symbol of Saul's royal power and taking it was a symbolic act of taking the throne. Instead, David uses his stolen items to again show Saul that he is not out to kill him. Once again Saul admits his wrongdoing and affirms David's blessed future. The two part ways for the last time. David continued life as an exile, and Saul returned to his home.

The Hunt Continues (26:1–4)

For the second time the Ziphites come to Gibeah to inform Saul of David's location. What is more, David is hiding in the exact same spot—"on the hill of Hakilah" near "Jeshimon" (23:19; 26:1). Since Saul is at Gibeah and not out pursuing David, it may indicate that after the incident at the cave (1 Sam 24) Saul had in fact stopped pursuing David. But when the Ziphites inform him that David was at the same hiding spot where Saul nearly caught David before (1 Sam 23:25–29), Saul cannot resist. Once again the manic king sets out with a large force to pursue David.

Unlike the last encounter in this area, where David's meeting with Saul was accidental (as Saul chose David's cave as a toilet), this time David takes the initiative. When Saul camps nearby (with his army encamped around him), David sends scouts to confirm Saul's location, and then David proceeds to enter Saul's camp by night, taking "Abishai son of Zeruiah, Joab's brother" with him. This is the first mention of Abishai in the story, but he will become a fairly prominent character. It is also the first mention of Joab, who will be a main character in 2 Samuel. Abishai later becomes one of David's top soldiers (2 Sam 23:18), who is lauded for his mighty exploits in battle (2 Sam 21:16–17; 23:18–19) and proves to be hotheaded and always ready to deal out death (2 Sam 16:19; 19:21).

David Enters Saul's Camp (26:5–12)

We are not told why David decided to enter the enemy camp or what his objective was, but remarkably he and Abishai manage to get through the entire camp to where the king was sleeping without being detected. Once again David is given a golden opportunity to take out Saul, and Abishai perceives that this is due to God's work. This is confirmed by the narrator, who tells us that Yahweh put Saul and his company into a "deep sleep" (26:12). Others in the Old Testament were put into a "deep sleep" by God, such as Adam (Gen 2:21), Abraham (Gen 15:12), and Daniel (Dan 8:18).

Abishai wants to use the opportunity to kill Saul himself but David forbids it, noting that harming Yahweh's anointed would bring guilt on Abishai. While David clearly hopes for Saul's demise (26:10), he leaves it to Yahweh to bring it about. Instead, David takes Saul's spear and his water jug before they leave.

David Addresses Abner (26:13–26)

Having successfully completed their heist, David moves away from the camp, putting some space between him and Saul, then he calls out not to Saul but to his general, Abner, who does not recognize David. Why exactly he addresses Abner instead of Saul is not clear, though given David's former role as "captain" of Saul's bodyguard (1 Sam 22:14), David may be pointing out that he was a more loyal and effective protector to Saul than Abner. Furthermore, this address to Abner may show David's reticence to attack Yahweh's anointed *even verbally*. After all, David continues to use deferential language of Saul, calling him lord, king, and, referring to himself as servant (or flea). On the other hand, David uses this opportunity to verbally assault the rest of the Saulide power present with the king.

David proceeds to charge Abner with negligence in protecting his liege, offering evidence of the danger Saul was in by pointing out that his spear and water jug are gone. What is more, David says that Abner and his men deserve a death sentence (26:16)! Ironically, Abishai's brother, Joab, will later carry out this death sentence, murdering Abner, much to the chagrin of David (2 Sam 3:27). Abishai's presence here, when the future king pronounced judgment on Abner, may put Joab's later actions in a bit of a different light.

Saul recognizes David's voice and responds to his call. David asks Saul why he pursues him, questioning whether someone has incited Saul against him. David further laments that Saul's pursuit is driving him away from his homeland of Israel (26:20), which would force him to "serve other gods" (26:20). This is an odd statement but it reflects a common ancient Near Eastern understanding that gods dwelt or were concerned with local areas and could only be worshiped in their own land. This thinking is seen in 2 Kings 17:26–27, where the Assyrians had repopulated northern Israel with non-Israelites but sent priests there to teach the new inhabitants how to worship "the god of the land" (2 Kgs 17:27). David's statement implies that Yahweh was the God of the land of Israel and leaving the land would prevent him worshiping Yahweh. This type of theology seems quite problematic for Yahweh's anointed one, though we should realize David did have a limited theological understanding. What is more, this does not reflect the theology of the narrator, who clearly did not view Yahweh as limited to Israel, having plagued both Egyptians and Philistines in their homeland. Furthermore, 26:19 makes it clear that it is not David saying this but other people ("they . . . have said, 'Go, serve other gods'"). David is not saying he *would* worship another god. However, David's statement may reveal that he planned on leaving Israelite territory, which he will do next chapter (27:1).

Saul confesses that he has "sinned" and even asks David to come back with him, promising he will never again try and harm him. This is the second time in the book that Saul confesses that he has sinned. The first time was after the Amalekite incident in 1 Samuel 15 where Saul failed to obey God's orders to kill the animals and Amalekite king. Seeing as Saul's repentance in that chapter seemed empty at best, David's lack of trust in taking Saul at his word seems wise.

David will not go back with Saul, though he allows Saul to send a servant to come retrieve his royal spear—but *not* the water jug. Some have speculated that the water jug may not have been worth returning either because of its lack of value or the fact it was in the hands of an enemy, for which reason the king would never drink from it again (in case of poison).[1] Another possibility is that, like the piece of Saul's robe cut off in 1 Samuel 24, David was keeping it as evidence of his having spared Saul's life.[2]

---

1. Klein, *1 Samuel*, 259.
2. Bodner, *1 Samuel*, 282.

This is actually the last time Saul and David will meet. When they part ways for the last time Saul adds one more blessing on David, "May you be blessed, David my son; you will do great things and surely triumph" (26:25). Interestingly, there is no mention of David becoming king or his coming kingdom, unlike Saul's confession at the cave (1 Sam 24:20). Whether this shows some reticence on Saul's part to admit his dynasty is doomed or not, we cannot be sure. Nevertheless, Saul's words provide yet another endorsement of David, which the reader is getting used to hearing (cf. 20:16; 22:14; 23:17; 24:20; 25:28–30).

This second golden opportunity to kill Saul reveals some development in David's character. In chapter 24 when David cuts off the corner of Saul's robe, his conscience pricks him for doing so. As discussed in the commentary for that chapter, the robe represented the kingdom, and in cutting off part of it David was symbolically making a move to take the kingdom from Saul. David, however, repented of this action due to his conviction that God was giving him the kingdom. Conversely, in the present story David's conscience does *not* prick him, despite the fact he takes Saul's royal spear, which is significant symbolically. Saul's spear has appeared throughout the story as a clear symbol of his royal power (e.g., 1 Sam 22:6). Taking the spear would be akin to cutting off the corner of the royal robe, if not even more clearly symbolic of taking Saul's royal power. The lack of conviction by his conscience in this instance reveals some development in David's character. After all, why did David enter the camp in the first place? What was his objective? It seems clear he set out to send Saul a message. While he repented of this objective last time, this time he sets out to do just that. Still, David seems resolved to never actually strike Saul. He will not use violence to take the kingdom but trusts that Yahweh will arrange Saul's demise one way or another (26:10).

LIVE the Story

The Unseen Hand of Yahweh

In the chance encounter at the cave in 1 Samuel 24, where David and his men are in the same cave Saul had chosen for a latrine, the reader was likely to guess that the meeting was providential but was not explicitly told so by the narrator. In 1 Samuel 26, however, the narrator explicitly informs the reader of God's involvement. God had put Saul and his camp into a deep sleep. But David is never told this. Abishai surmises such, but neither of them knows the deep sleep is miraculous. David still had to operate without certain knowledge and to act in faith. This is typical of the life of faith. As Hebrews declares, "faith is confidence in what we hope for and assurance about what we do not see" (Heb 11:1). David had affirmed his faith that God will work out his rise to the throne and that he need not struggle to take the kingdom. David, however, was in the dark about the "deep sleep" that fell on Saul and his army. David lived by faith and not by sight. This is a good reminder to us as Christians that this is the way life is the vast majority of the time. We do not necessarily see God's hand explicitly at work in our present circumstances, but we, in faith, live trusting God with our lives. We are not alone in this limited perspective. Even David himself did not see the extent of God's work in his life. Like David, we must live in faith, despite not seeing.

The Lord Rewards Faithfulness

In David's speech to Saul he declares, "The LORD rewards everyone for their righteousness and their faithfulness" (1 Sam 26:23). Rather than taking this opportunity to eliminate his rival to the throne, David chose to spare Saul. On the basis of this conviction that Yahweh rewards righteousness, David trusts that Yahweh will deliver him. This speaks to Christians today of the need for holy living. Many times in life there appear to be shortcuts to success, if only we would compromise our principles. In such instances, it is important to remember David's words that God rewards faithfulness. Like David, we must trust God with our security and success. Furthermore, our trust in God need not be based on our own righteousness but on the righteousness imputed to us through Jesus Christ. We live holy lives in honor of the one who makes us holy.

Looking to Christ

In this story we see David, the anointed one, as a type of Christ. Just as David refused to force his way to the throne, so Jesus Christ, though he was fully God and had authority over everything (Col 1:15–17), did not force his way. As David humbly called himself a "servant" (26:18), so Christ became like a servant (Phil 2:6–7). As David was convinced that God "rewards everyone for their righteousness and faithfulness" (26:22), so Jesus "entrusted himself to him who judges justly" (1 Pet 2:23). As David trusted God would reward his act of righteousness, so God rewarded Jesus' act of righteousness, as Paul writes, "one righteous act resulted in justification and life for all people" (Rom 5:18).

CHAPTER 25

1 Samuel 27:1-28:2

LISTEN to the Story

¹But David thought to himself, "One of these days I will be destroyed by the hand of Saul. The best thing I can do is to escape to the land of the Philistines. Then Saul will give up searching for me anywhere in Israel, and I will slip out of his hand."

²So David and the six hundred men with him left and went over to Achish son of Maok king of Gath. ³David and his men settled in Gath with Achish. Each man had his family with him, and David had his two wives: Ahinoam of Jezreel and Abigail of Carmel, the widow of Nabal. ⁴When Saul was told that David had fled to Gath, he no longer searched for him.

⁵Then David said to Achish, "If I have found favor in your eyes, let a place be assigned to me in one of the country towns, that I may live there. Why should your servant live in the royal city with you?"

⁶So on that day Achish gave him Ziklag, and it has belonged to the kings of Judah ever since. ⁷David lived in Philistine territory a year and four months.

⁸Now David and his men went up and raided the Geshurites, the Girzites and the Amalekites. (From ancient times these peoples had lived in the land extending to Shur and Egypt.) ⁹Whenever David attacked an area, he did not leave a man or woman alive, but took sheep and cattle, donkeys and camels, and clothes. Then he returned to Achish.

¹⁰When Achish asked, "Where did you go raiding today?" David would say, "Against the Negev of Judah" or "Against the Negev of Jerahmeel" or "Against the Negev of the Kenites." ¹¹He did not leave a man or woman alive to be brought to Gath, for he thought, "They might inform on us and say, 'This is what David did.'" And such was his practice as long as he lived in Philistine territory. ¹²Achish trusted David and said to himself, "He has become so obnoxious to his people, the Israelites, that he will be my servant for life."

²⁸:¹In those days the Philistines gathered their forces to fight against

Israel. Achish said to David, "You must understand that you and your men will accompany me in the army."

[2]David said, "Then you will see for yourself what your servant can do."

Achish replied, "Very well, I will make you my bodyguard for life."

Listen to the Text in the Story: 1 Samuel 21:10–15; 28; Mari Letters; El Amarna Letters

In this chapter, somewhat surprisingly, David chooses to return to the Philistine king Achish in Gath, where David had sought refuge once before (1 Sam 21:10–15). The last time he was there the Philistines had recognized him and, fearing for his life, David had to feign insanity in order to escape. Presumably, David's fear is alleviated on this second trip to Philistia, likely due to his being accompanied by six hundred loyal soldiers. The reputation of David and his army was such that Achish would not want to quarrel with them.

As surprising as David's decision might be to the reader, his strategy reflects common practices in the ancient Near East wherein disenfranchised people would often hire themselves out as a paramilitary asset in order to obtain land.[1] Scholars have pointed to several examples that show a similar pattern to David in leading a group of mercenaries en route to their eventual taking of power. An Amorite named Zimri-Lim (eighteenth century BC), Idrimi of Alalah (fourteenth century BC), Abdi-Aširta of Amurru, and Rib-Addi of Byblos (fourteenth century BC) all led groups of mercenaries "in their struggle to seize power or recover their lost power."[2] The mercenaries in these contexts were called *'apiru* (or Habiru), a term designating "outlawed people who had fled their sovereigns. They had no lands. Instead they wandered in groups as marauders or rented their services as mercenaries to warlords."[3] Recalling that the six hundred men with David were those who had fallen out with Saulide rule ("those who were in distress or in debt or discontented," 1 Sam 22:2), in this story David acts something like an *'apiru* warlord.

In ancient times, the motivations of such mercenaries were not purely for economic gain but also due to grievances they had against their former sovereign.[4] Given that the Philistines knew of the rivalry between Saul and

---

1. N. P. Lemche, "David's Rise," *JSOT* 10 (1978): 12–14.

2. Daniel Bodi, "The Story of Samuel, Saul, and David," in *Ancient Israel's History: An Introduction to Issues and Sources*, Richard S. Hess and Bill T. Arnold, ed. (Grand Rapids: Baker Academic, 2014), 215.

3. Ibid., 219.

4. Long, "1 Samuel," 375.

David (having quoted the song, "Saul has slain his thousands, and David his tens of thousands," 1 Sam 21:11), it seems likely the Philistines would know of Saul's relentless pursuit of David and likely thought that revenge against Saul was part of David's motivation in joining them. The Philistines may have wanted to take advantage of having the archenemy of Israel's king on their side. One way or the other, David successfully settles in Gath with king Achish.

EXPLAIN the Story

This is the first of five chapters chronicling David's sojourn in the land of the Philistines (1 Sam 27–31). It begins with David displaying doubts regarding his sure future as king of Israel. Fearing he will be killed by Saul if he remains in Israel, David again leaves Israelite territory to take refuge with the Philistines. Though he had once tricked Achish before by feigning madness (1 Sam 21:10–15), he now is welcomed by the Philistine king and given a city of his own. David lived among the Philistines for sixteen months, spending his time attacking Judah's enemies but telling Achish he had attacked Israelite territories. These lies so fooled the Philistine king that he was convinced David would always be loyal to him since he could never go back to Israel after attacking his own people. Achish is so convinced of David's loyalty he enlists David to fight alongside of him as the Philistines set out to attack Israel. While David agrees to fight, his response can be taken two ways, leaving the reader to suspect that David will betray the Philistine king in battle, finally showing the king his true colors.

David Immigrates to Philistia (27:1–7)

After showing such faith in letting Yahweh sort out his future and in being unwilling to kill Saul or take the kingdom with force, David now begins to harbor serious doubts as to whether he will survive long enough to be crowned king in Israel. Last chapter David seemed sure Saul would die at Yahweh's behest, telling Abishai, "the LORD himself will strike him, or his time will come and he will die, or he will go into battle and perish" (26:10). Now, David worries that Saul might kill him before Yahweh arranges Saul's demise. In response, David decides to leave Israelite territory and settle in Philistia so that Saul will stop hunting him.

As David had hoped, when Saul hears of David's immigration to Gath, he stops pursuing him (27:4). Perhaps in light of this new reality, David proceeds to request that Achich give him "one of the country towns" to live in rather than staying in Gath with the king. Since Saul was no longer pursuing him,

David would rather dwell away from the watchful eye of Achish. The Philistine king agrees and gives him Ziklag. Interestingly, Ziklag is listed in the book of Joshua as allotted to the Israelite tribes of Simeon and Judah (Josh 15:31; 19:5), though we are never told that they ever conquered the town. In other words, David is continuing Israel's conquest. The narrator then notes that Ziklag has been a Judean town ever since (1 Sam 27:6), thus making it the first (but not the last) foreign city appropriated into Judah by David.

David's Raids (27:8–12)

Having successfully acquired a Philistine town as base of operations, David proceeds to spend his extensive Philistine sojourn raiding the towns of Israel's enemies. The Geshurites are Israelite enemies (Josh 13:2) in the south. Girzites are not mentioned elsewhere but were likely Israelite enemies also in the southern region. The Amalekites, who had attacked Israel shortly after the exodus (Exod 17:8–16), are long-time enemies of Israel. Of course, the reader will remember that God sent Saul to attack the Amalekites before, but he failed to completely destroy them as ordered (1 Sam 15). Thus, we see David's raids continue to show how David fights "the battles of the LORD" (cf. 1 Sam 18:17; 25:28).

Knowing that his actions were a risky proposition, David was very careful not to leave alive any eyewitnesses who could report to Achish the identity of their attacker. Further, when questioned by the Philistine king as to his activities, David would tell him that he was attacking Judah or Judah's allies, much to the delight of Achish, who logically concluded that David's actions against his homeland would prevent him from ever returning to his people and would make David Achish's servant for life.

The Philistine-Israelite War (28:1–2)

Inevitably the Philistines prepared for another war against Israel. Achish was so convinced of David's loyalty that he demands that he and his men join him in the army. This puts David in a very awkward position. Thus far he has managed to fool Achish that he was loyal to Philistia while at the same time attacking Judah's enemies. Now he is being asked to go to war against his own people.

David's response to Achish is somewhat ambiguous. He tells Achish: "Then you will see for yourself what your servant can do" (28:2). What exactly is meant by these words is unclear. David no doubt intends it to be understood by Achish that he will be amazed at how well David will serve him in the coming battle. To the reader, however, the words likely suggest that finally Achish will see what David is really up to. After all, David has been lying to

Achish this whole time about his activities and whom he was spending his days attacking. By joining in the Philistine ranks, will David prove to be Philistia's biggest enemy? Will David work against them from within? It is not clear what David's plan is, but Achish trusts David and appoints him to be his bodyguard.

LIVE the Story

Doubt in the Life of a Believer

As mentioned above, David's fear that Saul may soon kill him if he stayed in Israel seems to betray some doubt in David's mind as to Yahweh's plan for him. In the previous chapters, David had expressed his faith in Yahweh's timing and given Saul over to Yahweh to avenge rather than stretch out his own hand against him. David's reticence to strike Saul was clearly rooted in his conviction that Yahweh was delivering the kingdom to David and that God would deal with Saul. Now David expresses explicit doubt in Yahweh's effectiveness, speculating that Saul will kill him if he remains in Israel.

On the human side of the equation, this doubt seems logical. Saul had the entire Israelite army at his disposal, while David was limited to six hundred men who were not necessarily soldiers (1 Sam 22:2). On the divine side of the equation, David himself had pointed out that Yahweh delivers without "sword or spear" (1 Sam 17:47), and Yahweh was on his side. Yet David now takes extraordinary measures in immigrating to Philistia to live with Israel's enemies. How we should understand this is subject to some debate. Some commentators think David's move to Philistia showed his faith. Arnold writes, "Though not stated by the narrator, we may assume from the characterization of David elsewhere that he takes action [that is, his leaving of Israel for Philistia] in the assumption that God will intervene on his behalf."[5] Other scholars have thought this action reflected poorly on David. Lemche writes, "we have in ch. 27 a tacit criticism of David as seen by the fact that David's decision to seek refuge among the Philistines is described as David's own idea without divine approval (expressed by means of oracles)."[6] I suggest, however, that David's actions do not merit censure as Lemche claims (as most decisions in life do not come with explicit divine approval), but neither should we understand his move to Philistia as an act of faith. David was human, and in a moment of doubt he made what seemed like the best decision he could at the time. This doubt should not be equated with sinful unbelief.

Some types of doubt clearly are sinful. For example, the serpent in the

---

5. Arnold, *1 & 2 Samuel*, 363.
6. Niels Peter Lemche, "David's Rise," *JSOT* 10 (1978): 13.

garden displays a rebellious doubt when he questions, "Did God really say, 'You must not eat from any tree in the garden?'" (Gen 3:1).[7] Another culpable form of doubt can be seen in the Gospels where the stubborn Pharisees are unwilling to be persuaded in the face of miracles and other evidence of Jesus' messiahship (Matt 12:38–42; Mark 6:6).

Furthermore, in 2 Thessalonians 2:10–12, Paul talks about those who display doubt through "an inability to interpret the evidence due to wilful immorality."[8] King Saul is a good example of this. Despite all the clear words from God regarding his future, he obstinately refused to believe God's word. As we will see in the next chapter, Saul is so obstinate he even goes as far as to consult a witch rather than take God at his word (1 Sam 28:7).

On the other hand, some doubt stems not from sin but simply from lack of faith, wherein a person longs to believe but struggles to trust God's word completely (cf. Matt 14:31; 28:17). This can be clearly seen in the story in Mark 9 of the man with the demonized son who was mute. When Jesus emphasized the importance of belief, the man answered, "I do believe; help me overcome my unbelief!" (Mark 9:24).

Other types of doubt arise from apparent contradictions between a believer's present experience and God's Word. Having moments of doubt or being of two minds about what we understand to be God's will are not uncommon experiences among believers. The clearest example of this is in the book of Job, where Job's experience of suffering as a righteous man contrast with statements in Scripture about the protection of the righteous and the suffering of the wicked (e.g., Deut 11:26–28; Prov 16:17). Similarly, in 1 Samuel 27, David finds a contradiction between his present experience and the words of Yahweh's prophet in anointing David to be king. Saul's continued reign appears to contradict David's having been anointed king by Samuel. Samuel's death (1 Sam 25:1) may have been particularly discouraging in that regard, as David may have assumed the prophet would be around for his coronation.

Significantly for our own lives of faith, the story in 1 Samuel 27 has much to teach us about God. First, it is clear that God does not abandon believers when they doubt but instead encourages them. While some think of God as a taskmaster who is looking for us to fail and ready to punish all failure, God is not in the business of simply punishing doubters. God's modus operandi is to support doubters and encourage those of weak faith. When the father of the demonized child in Mark 9 confessed his struggle to believe, Jesus still healed his son, thus encouraging his faith. In 1 Samuel 27, when David moved to

---

7. D. J. Tidball, "Doubt," in *The New Dictionary of Biblical Theology*, ed. T. Desmond Alexander and Brian S. Rosner (Leicester/Downers Grove: InterVarsity Press, 2000), 209.

8. Ibid.

Philistia due to his doubt, God did not depart from David but continued to bring him success. This can be seen in how David's plan succeeded perfectly. David hoped that if he moved to Philistia Saul would stop chasing him (27:1), and that is exactly what happened (27:4). Furthermore, God's continued blessing in David's life can be seen in how Achish welcomes him and even gives him a city of his own.

A second lesson we can learn about God here is that even when we lack faith, God is faithful. In 1 Samuel 27, when David doubted, God continued to work in his life and to use David to aid God's people. In his self-imposed exile David attacked the enemies of Israel and captured territory that Israel was supposed to have captured in the conquest. Further, in a positive contrast with Saul's failure to kill all the Amalekites in 1 Samuel 15, when David attacks the Amalekites, he does not spare any of them (1 Sam 27:8–9). In other words, despite David's doubt, God was faithful to his anointed one and used David to fulfill the mission of Israel's king. Analogously, we can expect that God will not abandon us, despite our weak faith or doubt, but for the sake of his anointed one, Jesus Christ, God will be faithful to his call on our lives and continue to use us for his good pleasure (Phil 2:13). While the Scriptures continually encourage faith and belief and we pray that doubts will be overcome as we move toward Christian maturity, God is a God of grace and does not abandon those of us who struggle with complete faith but instead encourages and supports us. Thankfully, the God who commands us to "Be merciful to those who doubt" (Jude 22) is exceedingly merciful on his doubting children.

CHAPTER 26

1 Samuel 28:3-25

 LISTEN to the Story

³Now Samuel was dead, and all Israel had mourned for him and buried him in his own town of Ramah. Saul had expelled the mediums and spiritists from the land.

⁴The Philistines assembled and came and set up camp at Shunem, while Saul gathered all Israel and set up camp at Gilboa. ⁵When Saul saw the Philistine army, he was afraid; terror filled his heart. ⁶He inquired of the LORD, but the LORD did not answer him by dreams or Urim or prophets. ⁷Saul then said to his attendants, "Find me a woman who is a medium, so I may go and inquire of her."

"There is one in Endor," they said.

⁸So Saul disguised himself, putting on other clothes, and at night he and two men went to the woman. "Consult a spirit for me," he said, "and bring up for me the one I name."

⁹But the woman said to him, "Surely you know what Saul has done. He has cut off the mediums and spiritists from the land. Why have you set a trap for my life to bring about my death?"

¹⁰Saul swore to her by the LORD, "As surely as the LORD lives, you will not be punished for this."

¹¹Then the woman asked, "Whom shall I bring up for you?"

"Bring up Samuel," he said.

¹²When the woman saw Samuel, she cried out at the top of her voice and said to Saul, "Why have you deceived me? You are Saul!"

¹³The king said to her, "Don't be afraid. What do you see?"

The woman said, "I see a ghostly figure coming up out of the earth."

¹⁴"What does he look like?" he asked.

"An old man wearing a robe is coming up," she said.

Then Saul knew it was Samuel, and he bowed down and prostrated himself with his face to the ground.

¹⁵Samuel said to Saul, "Why have you disturbed me by bringing me up?"

"I am in great distress," Saul said. "The Philistines are fighting against me, and God has departed from me. He no longer answers me, either by prophets or by dreams. So I have called on you to tell me what to do."

¹⁶Samuel said, "Why do you consult me, now that the LORD has departed from you and become your enemy? ¹⁷The LORD has done what he predicted through me. The LORD has torn the kingdom out of your hands and given it to one of your neighbors—to David. ¹⁸Because you did not obey the LORD or carry out his fierce wrath against the Amalekites, the LORD has done this to you today. ¹⁹The LORD will deliver both Israel and you into the hands of the Philistines, and tomorrow you and your sons will be with me. The LORD will also give the army of Israel into the hands of the Philistines."

²⁰Immediately Saul fell full length on the ground, filled with fear because of Samuel's words. His strength was gone, for he had eaten nothing all that day and all that night.

²¹When the woman came to Saul and saw that he was greatly shaken, she said, "Look, your servant has obeyed you. I took my life in my hands and did what you told me to do. ²²Now please listen to your servant and let me give you some food so you may eat and have the strength to go on your way."

²³He refused and said, "I will not eat."

But his men joined the woman in urging him, and he listened to them. He got up from the ground and sat on the couch.

²⁴The woman had a fattened calf at the house, which she butchered at once. She took some flour, kneaded it and baked bread without yeast. ²⁵Then she set it before Saul and his men, and they ate. That same night they got up and left.

Listen to the Text in the Story: Exodus 22:18; Leviticus 19:31; 20:27; Deuteronomy 18:9–12; 1 Samuel 13:8–14; 15:1–23; 22:6–19; Ritual to Counteract Sorcery (Hittite); Ritual Against Domestic Quarrel (Hittite); Middle Assyrian Laws A 47; Protocol of a Necromancy

This story of Saul at Endor completes Saul's tragic journey from rebellion to witchcraft as foreshadowed by Samuel's words to Saul in 1 Samuel 15:23:

> For rebellion is like the sin of divination,
>   and arrogance like the evil of idolatry.
> Because you have rejected the word of the LORD,
>   he has rejected you as king.

In this chapter we see Saul desperate for divine guidance but receiving nothing but silence from God. As readers, however, we are not unaware of why Saul is getting the divine silent treatment. Saul has been living in rebellion against God. Despite his desperate desire for divine revelation, God has already revealed his will to Saul. When Samuel was alive he told Saul clearly what he was to do, but Saul disobeyed (cf. 1 Sam 13:8–14; 15:1–9). In response to this disobedience, God clearly informed Saul that he was revoking his kingship (13:13–14; 15:23). But rather than let go of the throne, Saul refused to submit to God's decision and stubbornly held on to the kingship. In his rebellion Saul continually attempted to kill God's chosen anointed one and even killed all Yahweh's priests (1 Sam 22). Yet, now Saul desperately seeks God's guidance. Ironically, when Samuel appears to him at the medium's house in Endor, Saul says he wants Samuel to "tell me what to do" (28:15). God had already told Saul what to do, but Saul has disobeyed.

We are told at the beginning of this pericope that Saul had "expelled the mediums and spiritists from the land" (28:3). We are not told why Saul had taken action against the necromancers, but these actions were in keeping with the prohibitions in Mosaic law (Lev 19:31; 20:27; Deut 18:9–12). Although Saul had shown himself quite disobedient to God's word, Saul *was* very zealous for ritual. Perhaps his penchant for ritual and divine guidance led to his adhering to laws concerned with divinatory practices.

Magic (including necromancy) and sorcery were widely practiced in the ancient Near East. In Mesopotamia a clear distinction was made between black magic performed by a sorcerer/ess (Akkadian *kaššapu* and *kaššaptu*) and white magic performed by authorized practitioners.[1] Similar to the Bible's condemnation of sorcery as a capital offense (e.g., Exod 22:18), in Mespotoamian texts sorcery merited execution, though white magic was deemed beneficial to society. For example, a Middle Assyrian law says, "If either a man or a woman should be discovered practicing witchcraft, and should they prove the charges against them and find them guilty, they shall kill the practitioner of witchcraft."[2]

Necromancy in ancient Mesopotamia often included "rubbing salves on the necromancer's face or skulls or figurines as temporary houses for the spirit which was being summoned up."[3] Though 1 Samuel 28 doesn't give such

---

1. Scurlock, "Magic (ANE)," *ABD* 4:465.

2. Middle Assyrian Laws A 47. Quoted from Roth, *Law Collections*, 172. In Mesopotamia, actual charges against concrete individuals were uncommon, and anti-witchcraft rituals were performed instead. But sometimes "legal proceedings were initiated and actual people were brought to trial as alleged witches." Daniel Schwemer, "The Ancient Near East," in *The Cambridge History of Magic and Witchcraft in the West: From Antiquity to the Present*, ed. David J. Collins (Cambridge University Press, 2015), 45.

3. J. A. Scurlock, "Magic (ANE)," *ABD* 4:465.

details concerning the medium's ritual, a distinctive feature in Hittite texts is the role of an "old woman"[4] in the rituals, which perhaps provides a parallel to the "woman" in 1 Samuel 28:8–25, though she is not described as "old" here.

EXPLAIN the Story

Here, in the last days of Saul, we see him progress from using orthodox Israelite ritual in divinatory ways to going all the way to utilizing witchcraft. With battle against Philistia looming and Saul's attempts to inquire of God not working, he seeks out a medium who consults with the dead. Although the medium is located behind enemy lines, Saul disguises himself and risks his life to visit her in order to talk once more to Samuel. When Samuel actually appears, he tells him that God has rejected him and will give the kingdom to David. What is more, Samuel informs Saul that he and his sons will die the next day. Scared to death Saul falls to the ground, exhausted. The witch persuades him to eat and prepares an exceptional meal for him before he leaves. One gets the feeling it is the last meal Saul ever eats.

On the Brink of War (28:3–7)

This section begins with once again noting that Samuel was dead. While Saul and Samuel hadn't been on speaking terms since chapter 15, his death makes clear that Saul had no access to further guidance from this prophet. Saul had also expelled the mediums and spiritists (28:3). Both of these pieces of information prove vital in understanding Saul's reaction to the fast approaching war with the Philistines. Ironically, Saul's desperation and fear lead him to contravene his own prohibition on divination.

The Philistines camp for war at Shunem, a northern Israelite town located in Issachar near Jezreel (Josh 19:18). Philistine penetration this far north in Israel shows the seriousness of the situation. In response to the enemy's movements, Saul once again gathered "all Israel" and set up his base camp at Gilboa. Gilboa is not mentioned elsewhere in the Bible but was on the opposite side of the Jezreel valley facing Shunem. When Saul saw the army, however, he was terrified (1 Sam 28:5), and he wanted to ensure his success through obtaining a divine oracle or some other ritualistic sign, leading Saul to inquire of Yahweh. We are not told exactly how he inquired of God, but we are told that no prophet spoke to him, no priest gave him divine guidance through the use of the Urim and Thumim (see Listen to the Story in chs. 13–14), and God did not send Saul a revelatory dream.

---

4. *ANET* 347, 350–351; cf. *KUB* 1.16+ reverse iii // iv 66–70.

As we have seen in the story thus far, Saul is very superstitious and obsessed with ritualistic insurance of signs of success. In fact, Saul inclines toward using orthodox Israelite ritual in ways close to sorcery and divination. What is ironic about Saul's progression is that as he leans toward divinatory practices, Yahweh refuses to answer him.[5] Now, when orthodox Israelite rituals fail him, Saul is desperate. Despite having expelled the mediums from Israel (1 Sam 28:3), Saul asks his attendants to find him a medium so he can inquire of her (28:7). Saul has gone *all the way* this time. He has gone from using proper Israelite institutions as divinatory aids to seeking out actual witchcraft.

Somewhat surprisingly, given that Saul had expelled all the mediums, his attendants know the location of such a medium. The medium lived in Endor, a town that according to Joshua 17:11–12 was assigned to the tribe of Manasseh but was never conquered by Israel and remained a Canaanite city. This, along with the fact that this woman was a medium (which Deut 18:9 lists as one of the detestable ways of the Canaanite nations), suggests she was likely a Canaanite. Unlike David, who was currently in the business of capturing towns (e.g., Ziklag) left unconquered at the conquest (1 Sam 27), Saul was not attempting to conquer the town but actually going to Canaanites for spiritual guidance.

The Medium at Endor (28:8–11)

One problem with the witch's location being in Endor was that it was north of Shunem, making it behind enemy lines. Saul's willingness to take such a risky journey shows not only his desperation but the inordinately high value he placed on supernatural guidance. The location of Endor was likely one of the reasons that Saul left in the secrecy of night and disguised himself for his journey.

It is important to note the symbolic significance of Saul taking off his royal robes and putting on other clothes. As we have seen, robes have had significant meaning throughout Saul's reign. In 1 Samuel 15:27–28, when Saul accidentally tore Samuel's robe, it was symbolic of God taking the kingdom from him. When Jonathan gave his garment to David, it signified his acceding the throne to David (1 Sam 18:4). When Saul stripped himself of his robes and prophesied before Samuel at Ramah (1 Sam 19:24), it symbolized the divestment of his kingship. Now here in Saul's last hours he voluntarily strips himself of his royal robes and disguises himself, symbolizing the sure loss of his kingship.

Upon arrival at Endor, Saul commanded the medium to "*Consult* a spirit for me" (28:8, emphasis added). The word translated "consult" (Hebrew *qsm*) means "to use divination" or "witchcraft." This is the third time this word is used in 1 Samuel. The first occurrence was in 1 Samuel 6:2 when the

---

5. Polzin, *Samuel and the Deuteronomist*, 218.

Philistines consulted their "diviners" (Hebrew *qsm*) to see what they should do with the ark of the covenant that was plaguing them. Thus, in Saul's request for divination, Saul was acting just like a pagan Philistine.[6] The second occurrence of "divination" (Hebrew *qsm*) in the book was when Samuel rebuked Saul for his failure to obey the prophetic word, informing the king that his "rebellion is like the sin of divination" (1 Sam 15:23). Samuel's indictment turns out to have been clear foreshadowing, as Saul now participates in actual divination.

Saul asks the medium to bring up for him "the one I name" (28:8). The wording of Saul's request is somewhat suspenseful since the reader as of yet has not been told exactly what Saul is up to. Whom will he request to be brought up? The medium, however, was hesitant to accede to his request due to Saul's own ban on mediums and spiritists in the land and her worry that this was a sting operation in order to catch her in the act. In keeping with his superstitious character and his penchant for uttering oaths, Saul swears by Yahweh's life that the woman would not be punished for fulfilling his request. As Bergen points out, "Saul's oath invoked the Lord to grant immunity to one who broke the Lord's command—it turned God against himself. Such an oath was not only foolish but actually blasphemous."[7] However, Saul's oath somehow reassured the woman, and, ready to proceed, she asked Saul who she was to bring up for him. At last the reader is told that Saul wants Samuel brought up from the dead.

The Séance (28:12–19)

To be sure, this is one of the most bizarre texts in Scripture. A straightforward reading of the text is that of a successful séance where a prophet of God is called up from the dead. Yet, there is much debate over what actually transpires here. Does the woman actually bring Samuel up from the dead? Or was the woman (or an evil spirit) impersonating him? Or did God himself bring Samuel up for this last prophetic word against Saul?

In the ancient Near Eastern world, the power of necromancy was not questioned. Even biblical texts themselves do not necessarily discount its reality but instead condemn its practice (cf. Lev 19:31; 20:6; 27; Deut 18:11). Thus, it is possible that the text presents the medium as able to call up Samuel from the dead through witchcraft. It seems unlikely, however, that evil powers could command the righteous dead to appear from the grave, since they were in the care of God.

Another possibility is that the medium, like all mediums, was merely

---

6. As Auld writes, "Saul is desperately using Philistine means to cope with his Philistine foe." A Graeme Auld, "1 and 2 Samuel," in *Eerdmans Commentary on the Bible*, ed. Dunn and Rogerson (Grand Rapids: Eerdmans, 2003), 228.

7. Bergen, *Samuel*, 266.

impersonating Samuel. After all, Saul could not see Samuel, only the woman could (28:3). Presumably then, the speech of Samuel was mediated by the woman herself. Further, Samuel's speech to Saul was nothing new but simply reiterated what Samuel was known to have said in the past. As Smelik explains:

> This was no real prophecy, because it consists only of facts that are well known to everybody, like the rejection of Saul, because of his attitude towards Amalek, and the anointment of David. And one did not need to be a prophet to predict that Saul would perish soon. The woman actually recognized Saul from the beginning, noticed his fear, and understood what the issue of the battle against the Philistines would be. So it was not difficult for her to feign this prophecy, and have success with it.[8]

After all, this is what these charlatans did. They took from the knowledge they had of the dead person and attempted to use it to fool their customers that they were in fact in contact with the dead.

On the other hand, it must be noted that the biblical text does say the woman "saw Samuel" (28:12), so the plain sense of the text is that Samuel *was* truly present. But if evil powers could not command the righteous dead, then it must be that Samuel appeared not due to the power of necromancy but due to the power of God who brought Samuel there for one last prophetic indictment. After all, no séance ritual is described, but the request for Samuel immediately results in the appearance of the prophet. As Klein writes, "Samuel beats the woman at her own game by coming up as a prophet of the living God before she could conjure up a dead ghost."[9] In fact, at Samuel's appearance the woman screams in terror (28:12), which suggests she did not achieve these types of results in her practice. She was as surprised as the reader that Samuel actually shows up.

That God would allow Samuel to come from the dead in the context of a pagan ritual is not completely uncharacteristic. After all, in 1 Samuel 6 God allowed the plan of the Philistine priests and diviners to be successful in ridding themselves of the ark, despite its pagan superstition. Furthermore, in the New Testament, God used the astrology of the Magi to bring them to Jesus (Matt 2:1–12). As early church father John Chrysostom wrote, "the heathen only believe in predictions of their kind of mantic, so God makes use of it in order to reach them, however abominable pagan mantic is to Him."[10]

For some reason, when the medium saw Samuel, she knew that her visitor was none other than King Saul (28:12). Perhaps Saul's unusual height

8. Klaas A. D. Smelik, "The Witch of Endor: I Samuel 28 in Rabbinic and Christian Exegesis Till 800 AD," *VC* 33 (1979): 163–64.

9. Klein, *1 Samuel*, 271.

10. Quoted in Smelik, "The Witch of Endor," 175.

(1 Sam 10:23), despite his disguise, had made her suspicious to begin with. As noted, Saul could not see Samuel but only the woman, as he asks her, "What do you see?" (28:13). The woman's response in 28:13 has been variously translated. The 2011 NIV says she sees "a ghostly figure," while the 1984 NIV translated it as "a spirit." The Hebrew actually reads the word for "god/s" (*elohim*) here, making the NLT's translation of "I see a god coming up out of the earth" quite literal. Perhaps the woman's description of what she saw reflects her "pagan belief that Samuel had become a 'god'—a spirit-being possessing capabilities beyond those of mortals—following his death."[11]

Saul asked the woman what the heavenly being looked like and she described him as "an old man wearing a robe" (28:14), which Saul immediately recognized was Samuel. Saul then bowed down before him, face to the ground—an interesting change of affairs. In the past, Saul had refused to submit to Samuel's word; now in his moment of utter desperation he displays complete obeisance to the prophet. This is a classic case of too little, too late.

When Samuel asks Saul why he has brought him up from the dead, Saul explains the situation of the eminent war with the Philistines and Yahweh's silence on the matter, concluding with "So I have called on you to tell me what to do" (28:15). At this point we might ask, what did Saul want to know? It seems like Saul's attempts at divination are not a search for knowledge as much as they are an attempt to get his own way. Saul wanted to know what he could do to hold on to the kingship. Samuel responds by reiterating what he already had told Saul: "The LORD has done what he predicted through me. The LORD has torn the kingdom out of your hands" (1 Sam 28:17). Saul already knew the answer—he just didn't like it. He was trying to change the divine will and get his own way.

Samuel then proclaims that God was giving the kingdom to David. This is the first time this was said openly to Saul. Earlier Samuel had said God was giving "it to one of your neighbors" (15:28), but he did not name names. Samuel then predicts Saul's death, saying that "tomorrow you and your sons will be with me" (28:19). By saying "with me" the prophet means in the grave—they will die. The death of Saul and his sons on the same day recalls the death of Eli and his sons on the same day (1 Sam 4). As Bodner writes:

> This suggests that Eli's backward fall (from his throne) anticipates the fall of Saul, and the demise of both their houses. Samuel's grave words transport the reader back to the future, as the two dynastic houses of Saul and Eli will play no part in Israel's long-term leadership.[12]

---

11. Bergen, *Samuel*, 268.
12. Bodner, *1 Samuel*, 300.

Saul's Last Meal (28:20–25)

At the prediction of his death Saul falls down in terror, completely exhausted. At this point we are told he was also fasting, which as we saw in 1 Samuel 14:24 was another way Saul attempted to ensure success or gain divine favor. Saul's hunger must have been evident, as the woman then insists that Saul eat something so he can journey home. Though Saul at first refused, the women and Saul's own attendants prevail and convince him to eat. Ironically, "It was the voice of the woman and his servants he obeyed (v 23) and not the voice of Yahweh (v 18)."[13]

In an odd closing scene, Saul's last meal is prepared by the hands of the witch, who not only baked fresh bread for the occasion but actually slaughtered (literally "sacrificed") a "fattened calf" (28:24). Presumably the witch's sacrifice was a pagan sacrifice, adding to Saul's culpability. The significance of the sacrifice within the story of Saul is apparent. Just as Saul's illicit sacrifice elicited his rejection as king (1 Sam 14), so one final illicit sacrifice (a pagan sacrifice performed by a witch) precedes the end of Saul's reign. This witch's meal becomes Saul's last meal. As with all last meals "it contains an inherently curious paradox: marking the end of a life with the stuff that sustains it seems at once laden with meaning and beside the point."[14] So, Saul's last meal may hint at divine compassion, or it could be a perverse occasion showing the emptiness of divination and its fruits.

After Saul and his men eat, they leave the same night. The immediate departure was no doubt a relief to the witch (who seemed anxious for them to go in 28:22) and a necessity for Saul and his attendants to keep their nocturnal mission a secret.

LIVE the Story

Obedience and Hearing from God

Saul's life can be a sobering lesson for us today. Just as Saul's cries to God seemed to fall on deaf ears, sometimes in our lives we may have a similar experience. When it seems that we can not get through to heaven, or when it seems the Bible fails to speak to us, the example of Saul should cause us to examine our lives and see if we too have spurned God's will or are living in rebellion against him.

Sometimes we may pray to God for direction, "Lord what do you want

---

13. Klein, *1 Samuel*, 272.

14. Brent Cunningham, "Last Meals," *Laphams Quarterly*; http://www.laphamsquarterly.org/death/last-meals?page=all

me to do?" God may speak to us about a sin in our life or something he wants us to do. For example, God may say "forgive your brother or sister." Instead of obeying, however, we may continue to harbor unforgiveness and then return to God and say, "Lord what do you want me to do?" God again speaks to us about forgiving them, yet we may return to God again and again asking for direction and offering other service to him ("I'll tithe! I'll attend church regularly!") even though we already know what God requires of us. If we, like Saul, continue to live in rebellion against God's will, we may begin to find our prayers fall on deaf ears. If it seems like you cannot hear from God—obey.

Instead of obeying, Saul lived in rebellion against God. Samuel referred to rebellion being like divination (1 Sam 15:23). Divination desires an independence from God, not a submission to him. Rather than submitting to God, witchcraft lives in rebellion and seeks a substitute for true religion. As we have seen, Saul prioritized orthodox Israelite religious rituals like sacrifice, casting lots, and fasting but did so in divinatory ways. Now at the beginning of chapter 28, he sought God by all orthodox means—dreams, Urim, and prophets—but did so in his rebellion and refusal to obey God's prophetic word regarding the end of his kingship. Thus, even his participation in orthodox spiritual activities showed his rebellion as he attempted to use them toward divinatory ends.

Similarly, if we as Christians live in rebellion against God, even our participation in orthodox spiritual activities may become contaminated. Our worship can edge closer to being like divination. We may sing passionately at church, but if we continue to harbor rebellion against what God has asked us to do, our worship may subtly become a way whereby we may attempt to manipulate God to do our will. We may pray continually for God to show us what to do, but unless we obey when God speaks, our prayers may become like witchcraft in its attempt to try and manipulate God to get our own way or to change his mind regarding what he asked us to do.

The life of Saul can teach us a vital lesson. God does not exist to do what we want him to do. Conversely, we are to do what he would have us do. We must submit ourselves to do his will. God wants our obedience first, not sacrifice or religious observance. Of course, all of us are flawed sinners. None of us will obey perfectly in our walk with God, but his grace is available for our weaknesses. As John writes: "If we confess our sins, he is faithful and just and will forgive us our sins and purify us from all unrighteousness" (1 John 1:9). Our relationship with God is not based on our own righteousness but on his grace. However, a refusal to submit to God's will or outright rebellion against what we know to be his will damages our close fellowship with him.

If we claim to have fellowship with him yet walk in the darkness, we lie and do not live by the truth. But if we walk in the light, as he is in the light, we have fellowship with one another, and the blood of Jesus, his Son, purifies us from all sin. (1 John 1:6–7)

LISTEN to the Story

¹The Philistines gathered all their forces at Aphek, and Israel camped by the spring in Jezreel. ²As the Philistine rulers marched with their units of hundreds and thousands, David and his men were marching at the rear with Achish. ³The commanders of the Philistines asked, "What about these Hebrews?"

Achish replied, "Is this not David, who was an officer of Saul king of Israel? He has already been with me for over a year, and from the day he left Saul until now, I have found no fault in him."

⁴But the Philistine commanders were angry with Achish and said, "Send the man back, that he may return to the place you assigned him. He must not go with us into battle, or he will turn against us during the fighting. How better could he regain his master's favor than by taking the heads of our own men? ⁵Isn't this the David they sang about in their dances:

"'Saul has slain his thousands,
        and David his tens of thousands'?"

⁶So Achish called David and said to him, "As surely as the LORD lives, you have been reliable, and I would be pleased to have you serve with me in the army. From the day you came to me until today, I have found no fault in you, but the rulers don't approve of you. ⁷Now turn back and go in peace; do nothing to displease the Philistine rulers."

⁸"But what have I done?" asked David. "What have you found against your servant from the day I came to you until now? Why can't I go and fight against the enemies of my lord the king?"

⁹Achish answered, "I know that you have been as pleasing in my eyes as an angel of God; nevertheless, the Philistine commanders have said, 'He must not go up with us into battle.' ¹⁰Now get up early, along with your master's servants who have come with you, and leave in the morning as soon as it is light."

[11]So David and his men got up early in the morning to go back to the land of the Philistines, and the Philistines went up to Jezreel.

[30:1]David and his men reached Ziklag on the third day. Now the Amalekites had raided the Negev and Ziklag. They had attacked Ziklag and burned it, [2]and had taken captive the women and everyone else in it, both young and old. They killed none of them, but carried them off as they went on their way.

[3]When David and his men reached Ziklag, they found it destroyed by fire and their wives and sons and daughters taken captive. [4]So David and his men wept aloud until they had no strength left to weep. [5]David's two wives had been captured—Ahinoam of Jezreel and Abigail, the widow of Nabal of Carmel. [6]David was greatly distressed because the men were talking of stoning him; each one was bitter in spirit because of his sons and daughters. But David found strength in the LORD his God.

[7]Then David said to Abiathar the priest, the son of Ahimelek, "Bring me the ephod." Abiathar brought it to him, [8]and David inquired of the LORD, "Shall I pursue this raiding party? Will I overtake them?"

"Pursue them," he answered. "You will certainly overtake them and succeed in the rescue."

[9]David and the six hundred men with him came to the Besor Valley, where some stayed behind. [10]Two hundred of them were too exhausted to cross the valley, but David and the other four hundred continued the pursuit.

[11]They found an Egyptian in a field and brought him to David. They gave him water to drink and food to eat—[12]part of a cake of pressed figs and two cakes of raisins. He ate and was revived, for he had not eaten any food or drunk any water for three days and three nights.

[13]David asked him, "Who do you belong to? Where do you come from?"

He said, "I am an Egyptian, the slave of an Amalekite. My master abandoned me when I became ill three days ago. [14]We raided the Negev of the Kerethites, some territory belonging to Judah and the Negev of Caleb. And we burned Ziklag."

[15]David asked him, "Can you lead me down to this raiding party?"

He answered, "Swear to me before God that you will not kill me or hand me over to my master, and I will take you down to them."

[16]He led David down, and there they were, scattered over the country-side, eating, drinking and reveling because of the great amount of plunder they had taken from the land of the Philistines and from Judah. [17]David

fought them from dusk until the evening of the next day, and none of them got away, except four hundred young men who rode off on camels and fled. [18]David recovered everything the Amalekites had taken, including his two wives. [19]Nothing was missing: young or old, boy or girl, plunder or anything else they had taken. David brought everything back. [20]He took all the flocks and herds, and his men drove them ahead of the other livestock, saying, "This is David's plunder."

[21]Then David came to the two hundred men who had been too exhausted to follow him and who were left behind at the Besor Valley. They came out to meet David and the men with him. As David and his men approached, he asked them how they were. [22]But all the evil men and troublemakers among David's followers said, "Because they did not go out with us, we will not share with them the plunder we recovered. However, each man may take his wife and children and go."

[23]David replied, "No, my brothers, you must not do that with what the LORD has given us. He has protected us and delivered into our hands the raiding party that came against us. [24]Who will listen to what you say? The share of the man who stayed with the supplies is to be the same as that of him who went down to the battle. All will share alike." [25]David made this a statute and ordinance for Israel from that day to this.

[26]When David reached Ziklag, he sent some of the plunder to the elders of Judah, who were his friends, saying, "Here is a gift for you from the plunder of the LORD's enemies."

[27]David sent it to those who were in Bethel, Ramoth Negev and Jattir; [28]to those in Aroer, Siphmoth, Eshtemoa [29]and Rakal; to those in the towns of the Jerahmeelites and the Kenites; [30]to those in Hormah, Bor Ashan, Athak [31]and Hebron; and to those in all the other places where he and his men had roamed.

Listen to the Text in the Story: Numbers 31; Joshua 22; 1 Samuel 15; 21:10–15; 28; Deeds of Suppiluliuma as Told by His Son, Mursili II

Following Saul's nocturnal visit with the witch at Endor, the narrative returns to David, who had been asked to fight in the Philistine army against his own people (1 Sam 28:1). The narrative of chapters 29–30 are out of chronological order with 28:3–25 and are a flashback of sorts. After all, chapter 29 begins with David marching out with the Philistines on their way to Jezreel (29:11), which is where the Philistine army already was in 1 Samuel 28:4 (Shunem is on the north side of the Jezreel valley). Further, in the last chapter Samuel had predicted that Saul would die the next day, but several days are narrated in chapters 29–30 (e.g., 30:1). This is not too unusual in ancient historiographical narratives, and other examples are easily found (see Introduction).

The chapter begins with David being relieved of his duties in the Philistine army. Divisions in the Philistine camp have already been foreshadowed earlier in the story, with David's first trip to Achish in 1 Samuel 21:10–15 displaying some bad blood between the Philistine king and his servants (Achish complained of having a house full of "madmen" in 1 Sam 21:15). In that earlier story, Achish's servants recalled and recited the victory song said of David, "Saul has slain his thousands, and David his tens of thousands" (1 Sam 21:11). In the present story the song is again recalled (1 Sam 29:5), and despite king Achish vouching for David, he is not allowed to proceed to battle with the Philistines.

Both the Amalekites' plundering of Ziklag and David's recovery of the plunder in this story reflect an ancient Near Eastern mindset regarding the spoils of war. In the ancient Near East, victors in battle were entitled to the spoils of war, though spoils were not to be the reason to go to war in the first place.[1] Given that the Amalekites here attacked a city devoid of an army (or perhaps any men at all), given that David and his men were absent, their plundering and burning of Ziklag would have been viewed as especially heinous. David's recovery of the spoil and his distribution of it afterwards is in line with customs found in some ancient Near Eastern texts, wherein spoils of war were sometimes returned to their original owners who had lost them in a previous battle. This was especially the case with allies who had lost such property to a common enemy. For example, the Hittite king Suppiluliuma, who when "in the booty he found objects that, perhaps in a previous war, had been robbed from the Hittites, he restored them to the former owners."[2] In another instance, Suppiluliuma fought against the enemies of Ugarit and gave the plunder he acquired to the king of Ugarit as a present.[3] This practice might be analogous to David's giving a portion of his plunder to the elders of Judah (1 Sam 30:26). After all, the slave whom David finds informs him that the Amalekites had also raided Judahite territories.

Furthermore, David's assertion that both those who fought in the battle and those who stayed behind receive a portion of the spoils of war was in keeping with practices reflected earlier in the Bible (e.g., Num 31:27; Josh 22:8). Ironically, while Saul's failed Amalekite campaign led to his disqualification as

1. Long, *1 Samuel*, 386.
2. V. Korošec, "The Warfare of the Hittites: From the Legal Point of View," *Iraq* 25 (1963): 162.
3. David Elgavish, "The Division of the Spoils of War in the Bible and in the Ancient Near East," *ZABR* 8 (2002): 272.

king (1 Sam 15), as we were reminded again in 28:18, David's successful campaign against the Amalekites here demonstrates his qualifications as a capable king, obedient to God's commands and whose actions are equitable and just.

EXPLAIN the Story

Chapter 28 had explained that Saul was facing a fateful battle with the Philistines. Chapters 29–30 explain why David will not be present for that battle. As David was heading out to the battle with Achish (as ordered in 28:1), some Philistine commanders object to David's presence, thinking he might betray them in battle (28:4), forcing David and his men to leave the Philistine camp. David and his men return to Ziklag and find the city razed by the Amalekites, who also had taken their wives and families prisoner. Every man was overwhelmed with grief and mutiny was brewing. Distressed, David found strength in God and inquired of Yahweh. God answered David and assured him of the success of the rescue mission. With the help of an abandoned slave, David and his men successfully rescue their families. Following the battle, David shared some of their plunder with the land of Judah. Thus, chapters 28 and 29–30 contrast David and Saul. As Saul is failing to lead his people (instead visiting a witch), David is delivering Judah from its enemies and finding strength in his God. Saul's failure as king and David's legitimation could not be clearer.

Relieved of Duty in the Philistine Army (29:1–11)

In case the reader thought that perhaps David was with the Philistines when they camped at Shunem (28:4–5), the flashback in chapter 29 now explains that David was *not* present and why he was discharged from the Philistine army. The chapter begins with David accompanying Achish, just as the Philistine king asked in 28:1. Although Achish was convinced of David's loyalty to him, the Philistine military commanders refuse to let David come to the battle lest he betray them and take "the heads of our own men" (29:4). Of course, their concern is legitimate. It wouldn't be the first time David had relieved a Philistine of his head (Goliath), and the song recounted by the Philistine commanders in 29:5 actually commemorated that exact event (cf. 18:6–8).

Achish concedes the point to the Philistine commanders (though he is still convinced of David's loyalty to him) and asks David to leave the Philistine camp. Achish appears to feel bad about the decision and attempts to soften the blow to David by employing the name of Yahweh (29:6) and blaming the "Philistine rulers" (29:7) instead of the military commanders who actually demanded this. The rulers were the true political power in Philistia. The "commanders" were military leaders and, as such, subject to the kings. In other words, Achish's explanation to David was like saying "its out of my hands, David! The decision was made above my pay grade," when in fact it was not the Philistine rulers who made the decision (which he would be obligated to obey); it was the military commanders. After all, Achish was a king, not an officer in the army.

At this David objects and emphasizes his loyal service to Achish and seems incredulous as to why he cannot accompany him to battle (29:8). Again, the reader is left to decide whether David is actually attempting to be allowed to continue with the Philistine army into battle or whether this was for show. Did David genuinely seek to go into battle so that he could betray the Philistines and fight them from within their ranks? Or was David happy to be discharged but attempting to hide his true feelings through this false protest? It is difficult to decide. In fact, David's words could be taken two ways when he says, "Why can't I go and fight against the enemies of my lord the king?" (29:8), since it is not necessarily clear who "my lord the king" is. It could mean Achish, or it could mean Saul (or Yahweh). Regardless of his protest, David is not allowed to continue with the army to the battlefront.

Achish continues to show himself gullible and naïve with his over-the-top affirmation of David's loyalty to him "as pleasing in my eyes as an angel of God" (29:9). He is not suspicious of David one little bit. Nevertheless, David is told to leave first thing in the morning. Thus, David returns to Ziklag while the Philistine army goes on to Jezreel (where they will encamp at Shunem as narrated in 28:4). Thus, the story explains how and why David was *not* with the Philistine army when it clashes with Israel, resulting in the death of Saul.

Ziklag Pillaged (30:1–8)

When David and his men return home to Ziklag, they find their city burned by the Amalekites. The Amalekite action may have been payback for David's earlier raids on them (27:8), though since David left no survivors in his raids (27:9) it is unclear how they would know against whom they should retaliate. Luckily for David and his men, the Amalekites did not follow the same extermination policy as David (27:9) but instead had taken captive the inhabitants—including their wives and children. At this, David and his men wept, and David was especially distressed because some of his men blamed him for the situation and were considering stoning him.

In response to this difficult and stressful situation, the text says that David "found strength in the Lord his God." This is in direct contrast to Saul, who, in a stressful situation, found no solace in God but sought out a witch. The juxtaposition is strengthened by the choice of words here. The narrator tells us in 30:6 that David was "greatly distressed" (Hebrew *tsarar*), and Saul says in 28:15, "I am in great distress" (again, Hebrew *tsarar*). The contrast between Saul and David is very clear. Like Saul, David inquired of God, but unlike Saul, God answers him. While God did not answer Saul by Urim (28:6), David has access to the ephod with the Urim and Thummim through the priest Abiathar. (Of course, Saul had cut off his access to such spiritual guidance when he had the priests slaughtered [22:17–18], driving the last remaining priest, Abiathar, to David.) Thus, when David inquires of Yahweh as to whether he should pursue the raiding party and rescue the captives, God answers him clearly and ensures him that he will be successful (30:8).

The Rescue (30:9–20)

With divine assurance of success secured, David and his six hundred men set out to rescue the captives. However, after travelling about fifteen miles (at Besor), some of the men become too fatigued to continue the pursuit. Seeing as the entire group had traveled over fifty miles in their journey home to Ziklag from the Philistine camp at Aphek, the whole group was no doubt fatigued. Nevertheless, two hundred men are too exhausted to go on and instead stay behind with the supplies while the other four hundred continue the pursuit. David and his men then happen upon an Egyptian slave abandoned by his Amalekite owner. David does not treat him like a slave but gives him an extensive meal (complete with a dessert of fig cake and raisin cakes!). David's mercy here leads to some key intel as to the whereabouts of their enemy. The slave informs them that it was the Amalekites who had raided them (up till now David was unaware of who the raiding party was). Furthermore, the slave agrees to lead them to the Amalekite camp.

When David arrives at the camp, the Amalekites are celebrating their successful raids and their plunder in a drunken party—a perfect time for David to attack. In an exceptionally long but remarkably effective battle, David and his men successfully rescued all the prisoners and slaughtered all the Amalekites save "four hundred young men" (30:17) who escaped on camels. The escape of merely "four hundred" probably underscores the fact that David and his men were severely outnumbered (as the entire Davidic army was a mere four hundred) but victorious nonetheless. The escape of the four hundred camel riders also prevents the complete elimination of the Amalekites, who will resurface later in this story (2 Sam 1) and in later biblical books (like the book of Esther, where Haman is of Amalekite descent).[4] In addition to routing the enemy, David captured all the Amalekite livestock as plunder and brought it back with them. In fact, they paraded it in front of them as they returned,

---

4. Bodner, *1 Samuel*, 313.

shouting, "This is David's plunder" (30:20). As one commentator has observed: "A youthful reader—one reared in a modern democracy—could be forgiven for wondering if this is the ancient Near Eastern equivalent of a campaign trail."[5]

Distributing the Plunder (30:21–31)

Ironically, while Saul's failed Amalekite campaign led to his disqualification as king (1 Sam 15), as we were reminded again in 28:18, David's successful campaign against the Amalekites here demonstrates his qualifications as a capable king, obedient to God's commands and whose actions are equitable and just. On the way back to Ziklag, the four hundred came across the two hundred who had been too fatigued to continue. Some of David's men, who are characterized as "evil" and "troublemakers," determine that those who did not fight with them did not deserve to share in the plunder. David intervenes and decrees that all will share in the plunder, regardless of whether they stayed with the supplies or went into battle. David's rationale for this is that the plunder was a blessing from God. Yahweh had given them the plunder, protected them, and gave them success in battle (30:23). Furthermore, in an act befitting a king, David makes his decision the official policy in Israel from then on (30:25). As Birch asserts: "David boldly decides the issue and claims an authority that anticipates his kingship."[6]

David's regal actions and generosity are further displayed in his decision to give some of the plunder to various areas in Judah where he had "friends" (30:26) or where he and his men had sojourned (30:30). These magnanimous actions no doubt strengthened his influence in the region and helped pave the way for his being crowned king in Hebron of Judah not long thereafter (2 Sam 2:4). While Samuel had warned the people that what would characterize the king would be his continual taking from the people (1 Sam 8:11–18), David shows he is not such a king but is instead a generous giver to the people.

LIVE the Story

Faith and Works

In this story we see how David, in an extremely stressful situation, "found strength in the LORD his God" (30:6). As noted in the comments above, a clear contrast with Saul is made in that when David is "greatly distressed" (30:6) he strengthens himself in God, but when Saul is "in great distress" (28:15) he seeks out a medium to consult. What further distinguishes David from Saul

---

    5. Ibid.
    6. Birch, "Books of Samuel," 1194.

are the implications of the phrase "found strength in the LORD his God," as the Hebrew words for "found strength" in this instance include a reflexive component wherein David "strengthens himself."[7] That is, David is indeed strengthened by Yahweh, but David is involved in the process. God does not just reach down and sovereignly strengthen David. David's own faith and will play an important role. In faith, David seeks God and is strengthened as a result.

Just as David's strengthening involved his initiative along with God's work, so also the rescue mission itself demonstrates this. David receives a word from God that he will be successful in the rescue mission, but at the same time David undertakes the mission with human strength and military tactics. This combination of God's work and David's work is analogous to Paul's famous statements in Philippians 2:12–13 that encourage us "to work out your salvation" but asserts that "it is God who works in you."[8] Similarly, in Ephesians 2:8–10 Paul notes that we are saved "through faith" and "not by works" but declares that we are created to "do good works" nonetheless. Life with God is not just reliance on God but actions rooted in faith. As James puts it, "faith by itself, if it is not accompanied by action, is dead" (Jas 2:17).

The Source of Strength

This text also calls for theological reflection on the source of our strength as Christians. When we are put through the wringer, so to speak, where do we find inner strength? Does our faith in God strengthen us or do we rely on tangible signs or demand supernatural guidance or assurance to comfort us? As we have seen, in an incredibly stressful situation David "found strength in the LORD his God" (30:6). It is important to note that David is strengthened in God (30:6) *before* he receives any divine word (30:8) from the Lord. He had not yet been assured that he would recover his family from the Amalekites. It is only *after* David has strengthened himself in God that he inquires of the Lord through Abiathar and receives divine assurance of his success. David is *not* strengthened through supernatural assurance of his success but through Yahweh himself. This is an important point. David's faith in God strengthened him, not a promise of a successful rescue.

God is not a means to an end; God is the end. A. W. Tozer once wrote, "God being who He is must always be sought for Himself, never as a means toward something else."[9] Often Christians can end up viewing God as a means to get what they want out of life. They think coming to Jesus will improve

---

7. Arnold, *1 & 2 Samuel*, 389.

8. Brueggemann, *First and Second Samuel*, 202. Arnold, *1 & 2 Samuel*, 393.

9. A.W. Tozer, "God Must Be Loved for Himself," chapter 13 of *Man, the Dwelling Place of God*; http://www.worldinvisible.com/library/tozer/5j00.0010/5j00.0010.14.htm

their marriage, make them more successful, or help their self-esteem, etc. In this way God becomes a means to an end rather than him being the end himself. This perspective is not only selfish but is in fact idolatrous. God is not there to provide things whereby we can be satisfied; God himself is what satisfies! As the Westminster Shorter Catechism states, humanity's "chief end is to glorify God, and to enjoy him forever."[10] Jesus said he had come "that they may have life, and have it to the full" (John 10:10). But this full life is none other than relationship with God. As Jesus later states, "this is eternal life: that they may know you, the only true God, and Jesus Christ, whom you have sent" (John 17:3). A full life does not mean one full of wealth, notoriety, and security. A full life is knowing God. God is what fulfills. God is what strengthens. He is not a means to an end—he is the chief end of everything.

A Generous New Kingdom

David's generosity in having all share alike in the plunder, despite some having stayed with the supplies (30:23–24), recalls Jesus' parable in Matthew 20:1–16 where the landowner chooses to pay all his workers the same despite having worked differing amounts of time.[11] While those who worked harder complained, the landowner defended his right to be generous. In fact, the landowner's words could be placed on the mouth of David in our story here. "Don't I have the right to do what I want with my own money? Or are you envious because I am generous?" (Matt 20:15). After all, prior to meeting up with the two hundred who stayed behind, David's men had been shouting "this is David's plunder." If it were David's, he could do as he saw fit with it.

With David, a new kingdom was coming, one that was to be different than kings "like all the other nations," which only took from the people (1 Sam 8:11–18). David's kingdom embraced the disenfranchised, as seen in how "those who were in distress or in debt or discontented" (22:2) were welcomed as valued citizens. David aided the oppressed, such as the Egyptian slave whom he fed even before they knew he was an asset in their pursuit (30:11–12). David generously shared God's blessings (30:23) with all, regardless of the extent of their involvement; whether they stayed with the supplies (30:24) or simply lived in Judah (30:26–31). In this way the new kingdom of David, the anointed one, foreshadowed the kingdom of God, wherein God shares his grace to all who embrace the kingdom of his Anointed One, Jesus. We receive this grace not on the basis of merit (Titus 3:5–7) but on the basis of our relationship with the Anointed One, Jesus Christ.

---

10. Westminster Shorter Catechism; http://www.reformed.org/documents/wsc/index.html?_top=http://www.reformed.org/documents/WSC.html

11. Brueggemann, *First and Second Samuel*, 205.

LISTEN to the Story

¹Now the Philistines fought against Israel; the Israelites fled before them, and many fell dead on Mount Gilboa. ²The Philistines were in hot pursuit of Saul and his sons, and they killed his sons Jonathan, Abinadab and Malki-Shua. ³The fighting grew fierce around Saul, and when the archers overtook him, they wounded him critically.

⁴Saul said to his armor-bearer, "Draw your sword and run me through, or these uncircumcised fellows will come and run me through and abuse me."

But his armor-bearer was terrified and would not do it; so Saul took his own sword and fell on it. ⁵When the armor-bearer saw that Saul was dead, he too fell on his sword and died with him. ⁶So Saul and his three sons and his armor-bearer and all his men died together that same day.

⁷When the Israelites along the valley and those across the Jordan saw that the Israelite army had fled and that Saul and his sons had died, they abandoned their towns and fled. And the Philistines came and occupied them.

⁸The next day, when the Philistines came to strip the dead, they found Saul and his three sons fallen on Mount Gilboa. ⁹They cut off his head and stripped off his armor, and they sent messengers throughout the land of the Philistines to proclaim the news in the temple of their idols and among their people. ¹⁰They put his armor in the temple of the Ashtoreths and fastened his body to the wall of Beth Shan.

¹¹When the people of Jabesh Gilead heard what the Philistines had done to Saul, ¹²all their valiant men marched through the night to Beth Shan. They took down the bodies of Saul and his sons from the wall of Beth Shan and went to Jabesh, where they burned them. ¹³Then they took their bones and buried them under a tamarisk tree at Jabesh, and they fasted seven days.

Listen to the Text in the Story: Judges 9; 1 Samuel 11; 13–15; 28:4; Records of Ashurbanipal

The story now returns to Saul's last day and the fateful battle with the Philistines that was predicted by Samuel. In 1 Samuel 28:4, we were told that the Philistines were camped at Shunem on one side of the Jezreel valley and that Saul had assembled the Israelite army at Gilboa on the other side of the valley. However, when the battle report begins this chapter, the Philistines are slaughtering the Israelites not in Shunem or in the valley but on Mount Gilboa, showing that the Philistines are clearly dominating the battle and the Israelites were retreating.

Furthermore, the Hebrew of the opening sentence implies that this action (fighting against Israel) was happening simultaneously with the action in the previous chapter.[1] In other words, it could be translated, "the Philistines were [currently] battling against Israel." This is significant because the narrative again is juxtaposing David and Saul. While David is successfully defeating Israel's age-old enemy, the Amalekites, Saul is being defeated by Israel's current archenemy, the Philistines. Furthermore, while David successfully rescues his family from the enemy, Saul's family is about to be killed by the enemy. As we noted last chapter, David's actions were building up a foundation for his kingdom, but here Saul's kingdom is about to end.

The death of Saul in this story should be read in light of the larger story of Israel. Significantly, Saul's request that his armor-bearer kill him parallels the request by King Abimelech in Judges 9. Abimelech had been wounded and asked his armor-bearer to kill him (9:24), to which his armor-bearer obliged. The allusion to the death of Abimelech does not reflect well on Saul as Abimelech was clearly a very wicked king (Judg 9:23–24, 56).

An interesting parallel to Saul's death is found in a text by the Assyrian King Ashurbanipal, wherein a Babylonian king named Nabu-bel-shumate, enemy of Ashurbanipal, acts similarly to Saul when confronted with his own defeat. The text reads, Nabu-bel-shumate "commanded his own shield-bearer, saying: 'Cut me down with the sword.' He and his shield-bearer ran each other through with their iron girdle daggers."[2] What is more, the suicide of this Babylonian king was, like Saul, probably to avoid being tortured by the enemy. Evidence of such intent can be seen in the treatment of both Saul's and Nabu-bel-shumate's cadavers after their suicides. Just as the Philistines decapitate Saul (1 Sam 31:9) and hang his body on display (1 Chr 10:10), so the Assyrian king boasts of Nabu-bel-shumate: "I did not give his body to

---

1. As Diana Edelmen explains: "Grammatically, the phrase has the force of a circumstantial clause and represents an action that occurred simultaneously with the previous action, so that the Philistine–Israelite battle is thereby placed on a contemporaneous chronological plane with David's Amalekite operation." Diana V. Edelman, *King Saul in the Historiography of Judah*, JSOTSup 121 (Sheffield: Sheffield Academic, 1991), 279; Bodner, *1 Samuel*, 316–317. Cf. Klein, *1 Samuel*, 287.

2. Luckenbill, *ARAB* 2.312§815.

be buried. I made him more dead than he was before. I cut off his head and hung it on the back of Nabu-kata-sabat, (his) twin brother."[3]

Despite the sympathy with which one might view Saul's suicide, its presentation here does not reflect well on the fallen king. Though some have viewed it as brave or noble (i.e., a refusal to let the enemy have the pleasure of defeating him), there is little evidence to suggest it was viewed this way in ancient Israel. While other cultures (e.g., Greece, Japan) clearly viewed suicide as gallant and dignified, it had no such connotations in Israel. After all, when Job suffered so intensely, suicide is never brought up as an option either by Job or his friends.[4] Therefore, from an Israelite perspective, Saul's suicide continues his negative characterization to the end. In fact, the suicide again shows Saul's "concern for his 'image.'"[5] The stated reason that Saul wants to die before the Philistines get to him has been translated by the NIV as his fear they would "abuse me" (31:4). However, other translations render the Hebrew as "make sport of me" (NRSV, JPS, RSV). Saul was so concerned about his image that he could not bear to be humiliated and made fun of. This would go along with his character as we have seen so far. In chapter 15, after failing to implement the ban on Amalek, Samuel tells Saul God has taken away the kingdom (15:28), but Saul responds by asking Samuel "please honor me before the elders of my people and before Israel" (15:30). He clearly is more concerned about what he looks like in front of the elders than what God thinks of him. Saul's concern with his honor is in keeping with ancient Mesopotamian thought on suicide, which was primarily viewed "as a means of retrieving honor."[6]

More significantly, Saul's suicide reflects poorly on him in that it again shows his impatience and unwillingness to bow to the divine will. As Polzin explains:

> Perhaps Saul's final sin is more tragic than his earlier sins: as he impatiently took matters into his own hands in chapters 13 and 15, and impatiently tried to force God's hand in chapter 14, Saul one last impatient time refuses to let the LORD's providence run its course and takes matters into his own hands by ending his life.[7]

Would it have not been nobler to continue fighting Israel's enemy against all odds? Would it have not been more valiant to bring down even *one* more Philistine soldier (or at least wound one) rather than take one's own life? Add to this the fact that Saul's act did *not* prevent the Philistines from making

---

3. Ibid.

4. Polzin, *Samuel and the Deuteronomist*, 271, n. 16.

5. Edwin M. Good, *Irony in the Old Testament* (Philadelphia: Westminster, 1965), 78.

6. Jo Ann Scurlock, "Death and the Afterlife in Ancient Mesopotamian Thought" in *CANE* (New York: Scribner's Sons, 1995), 1890.

7. Polzin, *Samuel and the Deuteronomist*, 224.

sport of him, as his head, body, and armor were all used to this end (31:9–10). Saul's suicide was pointless. What is more, Saul's final act confirmed him as a rebel and defiant to God's word to the end.

Yet despite his ignominious end, Saul's grand beginning is also recalled in this story. Back in 1 Samuel 11 Saul's first military action as king was to save Jabesh Gilead from the Ammonites. Now with their once-savior fallen, the men of Jabesh Gilead will act in kind. Despite his failed reign as king, his intial good deeds as king result in the rescue of Saul's corpse from the hands of the enemy.

EXPLAIN the Story

The tragic story of Saul comes to an end in this chapter with a fateful battle with the Philistines. Though the reader knows that Saul's sin has led him here, his tragic death still evokes pity. No longer pursuing David, Saul dies in a vain effort to perform his royal duty of defending Israel. Dominating the battle, the Philistines pursue the king, killing Saul's sons and critically wounding him. With the enemy closing in, Saul takes his own life by falling on his sword. The next day, when the battle was over, the Philistines found Saul's body and cut off his head and stripped him of his armor. In celebration of their victory, they displayed Saul's armor in a temple and hung his decapitated body on the wall of Beth Shan. When the inhabitants of Jabesh Gilead, whom Saul had rescued in his first battle as king, heard about what happened to the bodies of Saul and his sons, they stole them back and brought them to Jabesh and mourned them. The actions of Jabesh Gilead here remind the reader of the high point in Saul's kingship, where he acted like the king he was supposed to be (1 Sam 11). However, at the same time, the memory of the deliverance of Jabesh underscores the heights from which Saul had fallen, making his story that much more tragic.

Saul's Last Battle (31:1–7)

Narration begins with the battle in full swing. With the Philistines having the clear upper hand, they concentrate on Saul and his sons. The royal sons are killed first and their names are listed somewhat matter-of-factly, given that Jonathan was a prominent character and David's best friend. Jonathan proved himself a man of faith in 1 Samuel 14:1–14 and covenanted with David for the protection of his progeny. Sadly, his prediction that he would be David's second in command (23:17) will never come to pass. This terse notice of his death adds to the tragedy of their deaths, but it begins to fulfill Samuel's post-mortem prophetic word (28:19). Saul's fourth son, Ishbosheth, was not killed in the battle and later will briefly serve as Saul's successor (2 Sam 2–4).

As the pursuit continued, Saul gets critically wounded and gives up all hope of escape. Thinking that he is soon to be taken by the enemy, he asks his armor-bearer to kill him in order to avoid being "abused" (NIV) or "made sport of" (NRSV, JPS) by the Philistines (31:4). The mention of the armor-bearer here reminds us of Saul's first mentioned armor-bearer—David (1 Sam 16:21). The actions of this armor-bearer are similar to Saul's first armor-bearer in that, like David, he refuses to kill Saul. The reason given is that the armor-bearer was "terrified." Was he terrified of the battle in general, or was he terrified of striking down Yahweh's anointed one? Regardless, upon his refusal to obey the king, Saul falls on his own sword, taking his own life.

Seeing Saul dead and, perhaps, like his fallen king, wary of being abused at the hand of the enemy, Saul's armor-bearer falls on his own sword and takes his own life as well. It is a very tragic day for Israel, as the narrator sums up, "Saul and his three sons and his armor-bearer and all his men died together that same day" (31:6). Samuel's prophecy had been fulfilled (28:19).

Conspicuously missing from this battle is any mention of Saul's general, Abner. The reader will recall David calling out Abner for failing to protect Saul in the past (26:14–16), and now when the king needed him most, he is nowhere to be found. David had pronounced a death sentence on him earlier (26:14–16) for failing to protect Saul when David stole his spear and water. How much more when the king has actually been killed? Furthermore, Abner will continue to be an important and powerful character in the narratives to come (cf. 2 Sam 2–3).

News of the death of the king and his sons spreads quickly, leading the inhabitants of nearby Israelite towns (both across the Jezreel valley, north of the Philistine camp, and those across the Jordan River) to abandon their homes and flee from the war, which allowed the Philistines to take over their cities. While the king was supposed to deliver Israel from the hand of the Philistines (1 Sam 9:16), Saul's tenure as king comes to an abysmal end, with Philistines annexing Israelite towns and slaughtering the Israelite army.

The Remains of Saul and his Sons (31:8–13)

Following a battle, soldiers would go around and strip the dead of valuables and weapons. In doing so, the Philistines came across Saul and his three sons on Mount Gilboa. Seeing as it took them until the next day to find them, Saul's worry about the Philistines finding him so quickly that he took his own life now seems premature. On the other hand, his worry that they might "abuse" him *was* well founded. First, they cut off his head and strip off his armor.

Ironically, the word to "strip off" here in Hebrew was used previously in the story when Jonathan took off his robe and gave it to David (18:4) and when Saul took off his clothes when prophesying before Samuel and the prophets (19:24), both of which had symbolic undertones. Now finally, Saul's robe/kingdom is stripped off, though it was not Saul willingly setting it aside to conform to God's will; it was the Philistines who strip it off his cold, dead body.

The Philistines proclaim the good news of his demise throughout Philistia and in their idolatrous temples. They take Saul's armor as a war trophy and placed it in a temple of Ashtoreth (31:10). Furthermore, they take Saul's decapitated body and hang it to a wall in Beth Shan. Displaying the enemy's corpse for ridicule and exposure to wild animals was not uncommon at the time (cf. 1 Sam 17:43–44). There is no mention here of what became of Saul's head, but the book of Chronicles tells us that it was hung up in the temple of Dagon (1 Chr 10:10).

The people of Jabesh Gilead, whom Saul had rescued from the Ammonites in his first royal battle (1 Sam 11), remembered Saul's valiant deliverance and set out to put a stop to the shameful use of Saul's body by the Philistines. Under the secrecy of night, they marched from Jabesh Gilead to Beth Shan, a trip of about thirteen miles, to where the bodies of Saul and his sons were hanging on a wall and recovered the cadavers and brought them to Jabesh. In Jabesh they cremated the bodies, buried the bones, and mourned them by fasting for a whole week. Cremation is not otherwise known in ancient Israel, and its implementation here may have been due to the extreme decayed state of the corpses, which prevented normal burial. The brave actions of the men of Jabesh Gilead help the reader to recall the high point of Saul's leadership in Israel at the commencement of his reign, when Saul acted like the king he was supposed to be (1 Sam 11). In this way, it forms a fitting end to Saul's tragic story. On the one hand, "Saul is dignified in death by the remembrance of his moment of glory."[8] On the other hand, the memory of the deliverance of Jabesh shows the depths to which Saul had sunk, making his story that much more tragic. How far the mighty have fallen (2 Sam 1:19).

 LIVE the Story

From Jabesh to Gilboa: A Theological Reflection on Saul's Epic Fail
On the somber occasion of Saul's final demise, the reader is left to reflect on the career of Israel's first king. Chosen by God to deliver Israel from the Philistines (1 Sam 9:16), Saul had a lot going for him. He was impressive to

---

8. Murphy, *1 Samuel*, 284.

behold and noted for his great height (10:23). As Samuel said, "Do you see the man the LORD has chosen? There is no one like him among all the people" (10:24). He was anointed by the spirit, even prophesying with the prophets (10:10). The spirit changed him into a better man (10:6). He had the backing of Israel's last judge and principal prophet (10:1, 24) and was chosen publicly by lot (10:21). His career began impressively with a successful rallying of Israel to come to the aid of the besieged men of Jabesh Gilead and the defeat of the Ammonites (1 Sam 11). Subsequently, support for his reign was reaffirmed through acclamation (11:14–15). Saul was poised for success. Who could have predicted how far he would fall and how fast?

Explaining the tragic fall of Saul poses some difficult theological questions for some readers. Since God was the one who chose Saul to be king (Saul initially did not even seek the office), and Saul failed so miserably, did God set up Saul for a fall? Did God fate Saul to fail? Was Saul something of a victim of God?[9] After all, God sent Saul an evil spirit (1 Sam 16), and he stopped answering Saul (1 Sam 28:6) and instead continually answered David and supported him.

Some have suggested Saul's main problem was "his self-depreciation and his concern for his status with the people."[10] Saul was "small in [his] own eyes" (15:17) and clearly had issues with his pride. Further, Saul was superstitious. His faith consisted of reliance upon signs and supernatural guidance, and he lacked trust in God. The story, however, makes it clear that Saul's main problem was his unrepentant disobedience. This disobedience was rooted in his pride and his superstition. The culpable role of his superstition is seen in how it led him to violate God's clear commands. Instead of waiting to offer the sacrifice as commanded, Saul thought it more important to seek God's pleasure by offering the sacrifice before the battle (1 Sam 13:13).[11] Then, in chapter 15, instead of completely killing the Amalekite animals as God commanded, superstitious Saul thought it better to offer them to God as a sacrifice (1 Sam 15:11–23). The role of pride in his fall is seen in chapter 15, where instead of obeying God, Saul built a "monument in his own honor" (15:12). Instead of pleading for forgiveness, he asks the prophet to "honor [him] before the elders" (15:30). Due to his disobedience in chapter 13, Saul is told his dynasty will not continue after him. Due to his disobedience in chapter 15, Saul is told that he has been rejected as king altogether and that God has given the kingdom to one of his neighbors who was "better" than him (15:27–28).

---

9. E.g., David M. Gunn, *The Fate of King Saul: An Interpretation of a Biblical Story*, JSOTSup, 14 (Sheffield: JSOT Press, 1980), 111.

10. J. Cheryl Exum, *Tragedy and Biblical Narrative: Arrows of the Almighty* (Cambridge: Cambridge University Press, 1992), 17.

11. As Exum writes, "Saul seeks to gain divine favor before battle, but instead loses it for all time." Ibid., 29.

Those who find Saul to be a victim of God have suggested that the critical issue is not why Saul was rejected, as Saul clearly disobeyed, but "why there is no forgiveness."[12] After all, David will later commit sinful acts that seem worse than Saul's initial disobedience. Saul sacrificed early and failed to completely kill the Amalekites, but David committed adultery with a faithful soldier's wife and then had the soldier killed to cover it up (2 Sam 11). Which sin was worse? If David received forgiveness, why not Saul? A close reading of the story, however, reveals that the difference between Saul and David is repentance.

In chapter 13, when Samuel confronts him on his sin, Saul defends his actions, offering excuses and even subtly blaming Samuel (13:11–13). In chapter 15, when Samuel confronts him on his sin saying, "Why did you not obey the LORD?" (15:19), Saul denies the charges saying, "But I did obey the LORD!" (15:20). Saul defends his actions as correct (15:20–21). Saul's lack of repentance here is made clear in how, at the end of chapter 15, we are told that Samuel is grieved and that God himself feels regret (15:35), but Saul expresses no sorrow or obvious regret over the events. He is unrepentant to the end.

On the other hand, when David is caught in sin he quickly repents. David does not attempt to shift the blame away from him like Saul.[13] David's response to Nathan's prophetic indictment about his sin was to admit he had "sinned against the LORD" (2 Sam 12:13). Even before David is confronted with his sin in 2 Samuel 24, David is quick to repent and takes full responsibility, asking God for forgiveness (2 Sam 24:10).

Furthermore, not only does Saul fail to repent, he stubbornly digs in his heels and lives in outright rebellion against the prophetic word. When God informs Saul that God has taken away his kingdom, Saul does not relinquish the kingdom but instead holds on to it at all costs. For example, Samuel clearly informed him that "The LORD has torn the kingdom of Israel from you *today*, and has given it to one of your neighbors better than you" (15:28, emphasis added). The kingdom was no longer his. (The prophet says, "today"!) Yet Saul defied the word of the LORD and held on to his throne. Though Saul apparently never sought the kingship to begin with, in rebellion to the prophetic word, he holds on to the kingship desperately from here on out.

Some interpreters read against the grain of the text and think that Saul "displays heroic greatness in his refusal to acquiesce in the fate prophesied by Samuel, taking extraordinary steps to hold on to his kingdom. A lesser man . . .

---

12. Ibid., 40.

13. As Boda notes: "Saul's repentance only comes after seeking to manipulate the prophet Samuel and appears to have as its goal saving face before the elders. David's follows immediately after the confrontation by the prophet Nathan" (*A Severe Mercy: Sin and Its Remedy in the Old Testament*, Siphrut 1 [Winona Lake, IN: Eisenbrauns, 2009], 156 n. 23).

might merely accept his destiny. Saul, however, wrestles against it."[14] This is not the biblical view, however. Saul's wrestling against God's will is *not* admirable. It does *not* show greatness but rebellion. It is this rebellion that is the key to his downfall.

To be sure, in response to Saul's rebellion God sends an evil spirit to torment him (1 Sam 16) and refuses to answer Saul (1 Sam 28:6). But we must remember this is in response to his unrepentant heart and defiance of the prophetic word. Instead of repenting and bowing to the divine will, Saul attempts to thwart God's word. He continually tries to kill Yahweh's anointed, David. Saul has all Yahweh's priests at Nob slaughtered (1 Sam 22). It is no wonder that Samuel tells Saul that "the LORD has departed from you and become your enemy" (28:16). While we can entertain some sympathy for Israel's first king, his downfall is clearly due to his defiance of the prophetic word and an unrepentant heart. God's actions against Saul and in support of David must be seen in this light. God is not being capricious or unfair in his actions. Saul is not a victim of God's "dark side" while David happens to be lucky and get God's good side.

In 1 Corinthians, Paul notes that Old Testament stories are "examples and were written down as warnings for us, on whom the culmination of the ages has come. So, if you think you are standing firm, be careful that you don't fall!" (1 Cor 10:11–12). So, Saul's story serves as a cautionary tale for Christians today. Saul's story of his epic fail from the heights of Jabesh to the depths of Gilboa serve as a warning about the dangers of unrepentant sin and the impact our choices have on our life. The story does not simply affirm that we must *do better* than Saul. It is not simply a call to *be more moral* than Saul. The story illustrates the need for repentance. We, like Saul, are flawed characters. Like Saul we may be prideful, superstitious, and pigheaded. We all have sinned and fall short (Rom 3:23). However, Saul's story reminds us of our need to repent. We will never get it all right. We may never live a fully sinless life. But we can, like David, be quick to repent. God's mercy is there for all to claim. That is the good news. That is the gospel, as evidenced in David's life. Though David had his own epic fails, God's mercy extended to him in his repentance. God's mercy is available to all who would, in humility, repent and believe.

---

14. Exum, *Tragedy and Biblical Narrative*, 41.

CHAPTER 29

2 Samuel 1:1–27

 LISTEN to the Story

¹After the death of Saul, David returned from striking down the Amalekites and stayed in Ziklag two days. ²On the third day a man arrived from Saul's camp with his clothes torn and dust on his head. When he came to David, he fell to the ground to pay him honor.

³"Where have you come from?" David asked him.

He answered, "I have escaped from the Israelite camp."

⁴"What happened?" David asked. "Tell me."

"The men fled from the battle," he replied. "Many of them fell and died. And Saul and his son Jonathan are dead."

⁵Then David said to the young man who brought him the report, "How do you know that Saul and his son Jonathan are dead?"

⁶"I happened to be on Mount Gilboa," the young man said, "and there was Saul, leaning on his spear, with the chariots and their drivers in hot pursuit. ⁷When he turned around and saw me, he called out to me, and I said, 'What can I do?'

⁸"He asked me, 'Who are you?'

"'An Amalekite,' I answered.

⁹"Then he said to me, 'Stand here by me and kill me! I'm in the throes of death, but I'm still alive.'

¹⁰"So I stood beside him and killed him, because I knew that after he had fallen he could not survive. And I took the crown that was on his head and the band on his arm and have brought them here to my lord."

¹¹Then David and all the men with him took hold of their clothes and tore them. ¹²They mourned and wept and fasted till evening for Saul and his son Jonathan, and for the army of the LORD and for the nation of Israel, because they had fallen by the sword.

¹³David said to the young man who brought him the report, "Where are you from?"

"I am the son of a foreigner, an Amalekite," he answered.

¹⁴David asked him, "Why weren't you afraid to lift your hand to destroy the LORD's anointed?"

¹⁵Then David called one of his men and said, "Go, strike him down!" So he struck him down, and he died. ¹⁶For David had said to him, "Your blood be on your own head. Your own mouth testified against you when you said, 'I killed the LORD's anointed.'"

¹⁷David took up this lament concerning Saul and his son Jonathan, ¹⁸and he ordered that the people of Judah be taught this lament of the bow (it is written in the Book of Jashar):

> ¹⁹"A gazelle lies slain on your heights, Israel.
>   How the mighty have fallen!
> ²⁰"Tell it not in Gath,
>   proclaim it not in the streets of Ashkelon,
> lest the daughters of the Philistines be glad,
>   lest the daughters of the uncircumcised rejoice.
> ²¹"Mountains of Gilboa,
>   may you have neither dew nor rain,
>   may no showers fall on your terraced fields.
> For there the shield of the mighty was despised,
>   the shield of Saul—no longer rubbed with oil.
> ²²"From the blood of the slain,
>   from the flesh of the mighty,
> the bow of Jonathan did not turn back,
>   the sword of Saul did not return unsatisfied.
> ²³Saul and Jonathan—
>   in life they were loved and admired,
>   and in death they were not parted.
> They were swifter than eagles,
>   they were stronger than lions.
> ²⁴"Daughters of Israel,
>   weep for Saul,
> who clothed you in scarlet and finery,
>   who adorned your garments with ornaments of gold.
> ²⁵"How the mighty have fallen in battle!
>   Jonathan lies slain on your heights.
> ²⁶I grieve for you, Jonathan my brother;
>   you were very dear to me.
> Your love for me was wonderful,

> more wonderful than that of women.
> [27]"How the mighty have fallen!
>   The weapons of war have perished!"

Listen to the Text in the Story: Leviticus 18:22; 20:13; 1 Samuel 18:1–4; 20:1–42; 23:15–18; 1 Samuel 31; The Fight for the Throne (Esarhaddon); Gilgamesh

Though we are now in a new biblical book, 1–2 Samuel are really one literary work (see Introduction). Furthermore, the first four chapters of 2 Samuel continue the literary unit that began back in 1 Samuel 16 and concerns David's rise to the throne in place of Saul. This literary unit is not completed at the end of 1 Samuel but only concludes when David is crowned king of all Israel in 2 Samuel 4.

With Saul gone, Israel lacked a king. While the narrative thus far has clearly argued that David is Yahweh's anointed and should be Israel's new king, it was not an opinion unanimously accepted at the time. Normally, the successor to the throne would first be sought among the previous king's heirs. In Saul's case, seeing as three of his sons died on the battlefield with him, there are limited choices. Furthermore, at this point the power of the government lay with the head of the Israelite army, Abner. The first four chapters of 2 Samuel are concerned with the succession to the throne and how David comes to be crowned king in Saul's place.

As noted previously, the syntax of 1 Samuel 31:1 implied that the fateful events on Mount Gilboa were simultaneous with David's campaign against the Amalekites and the rescue of his family. This is confirmed here and we are now told that David only returned to Ziklag after the death of Saul. In reading this opening chapter of 2 Samuel, it is important to keep in mind the story told in the closing chapter of 1 Samuel. According to the narrator, in 1 Samuel 31:4–5 Saul committed suicide. Yet here in 2 Samuel 1 an Amalekite messenger claims to have killed Saul himself, though he claims that Saul was wounded and near death (2 Sam 1:9). In light of the contradiction between 1 Samuel 31 and the Amalekite's story, the deceit of the Amalekite is obvious.

David's reaction to Saul's death is unexpected in many ways, given the hostility Saul had shown toward him. This is brought into relief by an Assyrian text wherein the new crown prince Esarhaddon, who was to inherit his father's throne despite being the youngest heir, hears that his elder brothers were attempting to take the throne. Upon hearing the news, Esarhaddon initially reacts similarly to David: he claims he "cried out 'Woe!' rent my princely robe and began to lament loudly."[1] Unlike David, however, he set out to fight his brothers, who fled into exile. Unlike David who sought to show kindness to his rival's family members, Esarhaddon killed his brothers' families and followers.

After hearing of the death of Saul and Jonathan, David offers poetic lamentation. Such laments are known from the ancient Near East, with the most well known coming from the epic of Gilgamesh as the hero, Gilgamesh, mourns his dead friend Enkidu. A sample of his lament reads:

> Hear me, O elders [and give ear] unto me! It is for Enkidu, my friend,
>   that I weep, Moaning bitterly like a wailing woman.
> The axe at my side, my hand's trust,
> The dirk in my belt, the shield in front of me, My festal robe, my richest
>   trimming—An evil demon rose up and robbed me!
> O my younger friend, thou chasedst
> The wild ass of the hills, the panther of the
> steppe! Enkidu, my younger friend, thou who chasedst
> The wild ass of the hills, the panther of the steppe![2]

Most notable about David's lament for Jonathan in our modern context is his claim that Jonathan's love was "more wonderful than that of women" (2 Sam 1:26), which leads some to suggest that they had a homosexual relationship.[3] Along these lines some have even attempted to explain Saul's hatred of David, including his attempts to kill him with his spear, as due to homophobia.[4] However, the homosexual interpretation is difficult to defend. First, Old Testament attitudes toward homosexuality (e.g., Lev 18:22; 20:13) would argue against it, given that the narrative is attempting to portray David in a positive light as the chosen of God to be king in Israel. Second, David clearly had many heterosexual relationships in the story (two wives so far). Third, the Hebrew word used for love here (*ahabah*) usually does not have sexual connotations. It is used of our love for God (e.g., Deut 6:5) and God's love for his people (e.g., Isa 63:9; Jer 31:3), and Saul himself is said to love David using this word (1 Sam 16:21). Most importantly, in the context of a covenant, the word has important political connotations.[5] Seeing as David

---

1. *ANET*, 289.

2. Ibid., 88.

3. E.g., Tom Horner, *Jonathan Loved David: Homosexuality in Biblical Times* (Philadelphia: Westminster, 1978), 20, 26–28, 31–39. 415–17. Cf. David M. Gunn, *The Story of King Saul*, JSOTSup 14 (Sheffield: University of Sheffield Press, 1980), 93.

4. David Jobling, et al., *1 Samuel*, BO (Collegeville, MN: Liturgical Press, 1998), 161–65.

5. J. A. Thompson, "Significance of the Verb Love in the David-Jonathan Narratives in 1 Samuel," *VT* 24 (1974): 213–214. Arnold, *1 & 2 Samuel*, 413. Cf. Frank Moore Cross, *From Epic to Canon: History and Literature in Ancient Israel* (Baltimore: Johns Hopkins University Press, 1998), 9.

and Jonathan twice cut covenants together (1 Sam 18:1–4; 20:16), the use of this word seems most appropriate and it is likely that "this part of the poem is referring to the depth of that covenant relationship."[6]

Finally, as Alter points out, "The bond between men in this warrior culture could easily be stronger than the bond between men and women."[7] Interestingly, the story of Gilgamesh once again provides light on David's lament. In the ancient Babylonian story, King Gilgamesh is told in a dream he would meet a friend who he would match in strength and love like a woman.[8] In that story, he meets Enkidu (whom Gilgamesh later laments after his death, as noted above), and they become the best of friends but do not have a sexual relationship of any kind. Thus, as Arnold writes, in Gilgamesh to love a man like a woman was "a rhetorical expression of the great depth of friendship experienced between Gilgamesh and his friend, Enkidu."[9]

The greatest error in the homosexual interpretation is the reading in of our present culture's concerns and mores into that of an ancient culture. There is a world of difference between them. In fact, Nissinen writes of homosociability in the ancient Near East, "which permits even intimate feelings to be expressed" between men without implying anything sexually and points to other examples in ancient literature (e.g., Achilles and Patroclus).[10] Reading into this text a homosexual relationship misses the close intimate bond that David and Jonathan shared, expressed through loyalty, covenant, and friendship—not sexuality.

EXPLAIN the Story

After David returned to Ziklag from his successful rescue mission and attack on the Amalekites, an Amalekite arrives and tells David of Saul's and Jonathan's deaths. The man claims he found Saul mortally wounded and had killed him at Saul's own request. What is more, the Amalekite brings with him Saul's crown and royal armband. Since the reader already knows what happened on that fateful day, the Amalekite is clearly lying, probably in hopes of receiving a reward from David. Instead, David has him killed for striking the LORD's anointed. David and his men mourn Saul and Jonathan, and David utters a

---

6. Arnold, *1 & 2 Samuel*, 413.

7. Alter, *The David Story*, 201.

8. See Susan Ackerman, *When Heroes Love: The Ambiguity of Eros in the Stories of Gilgamesh and David*, Gender, Theory, and Religion (New York: Columbia University Press, 2005)

9. Arnold, *1 & 2 Samuel*, 414.

10. Martti Nissinen, *Homoeroticism in the Biblical World: A Historical Perspective* (Philadelphia: Fortress, 1998), 53–56.

lament. Like the earlier stories that showed how David did not participate in the battle against Saul, this story exonerates David from any guilt in his path to becoming king. Though David came to be in possession of the crown and royal armband, he had no part in taking it from the king, as he was far away in Ziklag. The story further explains how God "crowned" David king through the unwitting actions of a lying Amalekite.

David Hears of the Death of Saul and Jonathan (1:1–16)

On their third day back, a man from Saul's camp arrives with dust on his head and torn clothes—standard evidences of mourning (e.g., Gen 37:34; Josh 7:6; 1 Sam 4:12). The appearance of mourning likely is a pretense, however, and does not reflect the actual state of this messenger (e.g., 2 Sam 3:31). The man explains that he had "escaped from the Israelite camp," that Israel had suffered a defeat, and that Saul and Jonathan had died. No doubt this news created mixed emotions in David. The death of Saul would mean David could return to Israel at long last. But the death of Jonathan would have caused him great grief. Furthermore, the defeat of Israel would have grieved David further.

David inquired as to how he came by this information, and the man begins to tell a version of events that contradicts what is recorded in 1 Samuel 31. First, he says, "I happened to be on Mount Gilboa" (v. 6). This already seems unlikely. As Alter writes, "Does one accidentally stumble onto a battlefield while the killing is still going on? A more likely scenario is that the Amalekite came onto the battlefield immediately after the fighting as a scavenger . . . ."[11] Second, the man claims he came upon Saul "leaning on his spear with the chariots and their drivers in hot pursuit" (2 Sam 1:6). No mention is made of Saul being wounded by archers (1 Sam 31:3), and it seems unlikely that chariots were pursuing Saul on the mountainous territory of Gilboa (besides which, chariots were usually armed with spears, not bow and arrow).[12] The man also says nothing of Saul committing suicide (1 Sam 31:4). He claims Saul was leaning on his spear, but lest we think that perhaps the man came across Saul after having attempted to commit suicide, it is important to note that Saul used his sword (1 Sam 31:4), *not* his spear to kill himself (besides which, a spear is far too tall to fall on for such purposes). The man instead claims that Saul requested he kill him because he was in "the throes of death" but "still alive" (1:9).

According to this man's story, when he offered Saul assistance, Saul first asked him who he was and he informed the king that he was an Amalekite.

---

11. Alter, *The David Story*, 196.
12. Yigael Yadin, *The Art of Warfare in Biblical Lands in the Light of Archaeological Studies* (New York: McGraw-Hill, 1963), 250.

Since David has just returned from a battle with Amalekites who had kidnapped his family, this may have added to his hostility to this Amalekite bearer of evil news.

As evidence of the veracity of his story, the Amalekite had brought with him Saul's crown and royal armband (1:10). Though the crown was likely a lighter crown than what was likely used in a coronation (e.g., 2 Sam 12:30), it still conveyed royalty. The armband is otherwise unknown in Israel, but Egyptian and Assyrian kings are portrayed with bands or bracelets on their arms.[13] This account of how David came into possession of the royal crown and armband served an important purpose in the story in that it exonerates David from wrongdoing. Just as the account of David's campaign against the Amalekites in 1 Samuel 29–30 explains that David could not have partaken in the battle that killed Saul, so this story of the Amalekite bringing the crown to David explains that David did not take it for himself.

This lying Amalekite no doubt thought he would be rewarded for his deeds, but he had gravely misunderstood David. Rather than rejoicing over Saul's death, David and his men tear their clothes and mourn and weep (1:11–12). David's actions might even surprise the reader, seeing as David had hoped for such an outcome for Saul. David had earlier predicted that "the LORD himself will strike [Saul], or his time will come and he will die, or he will go into battle and perish" (1 Sam 26:10). But now that it has occurred, David is overcome with sorrow and grief. Of course, the greatest part of the sorrow was likely due to Jonathan's death, which David had not envisioned (cf. 1 Sam 23:17).

After relaying his story to David, David further asked the man where he came from. The man had already mentioned he was an Amalekite in his story; however, now he identifies himself as the son of a foreigner (Hebrew *ger*), an Amalekite. "Foreigner" (Hebrew *ger*) is a technical term for a resident alien, or someone of foreign origin living in Israel. Because of his status as a resident in the land, David holds him accountable.[14] Seeing as he lived in the land of Israel, he should have known to never strike Yahweh's anointed one (1:14). David responds by ordering one of his men to kill the Amalekite man, and he declares that his blood was on his own head since he said, "I killed the LORD's anointed." Technically speaking, the Amalekite did not say this. He never referred to Saul as the anointed one. He merely said, "I stood beside him and killed him" (v. 10). However, David puts the language of Yahweh's anointed into his (dead) mouth. This clearly drives home the point that Yahweh's anointed is off-limits. No one can strike the anointed one without acquiring

---

13. J. B. Pritchard, ed., *The Ancient Near East in Pictures Relating to the Old Testament* (Princeton: Princeton University Press, 1954), nos. 441–42, 617, 626.

14. A. A. Anderson, *2 Samuel*, WBC 11 (Dallas: Word, 1989), 8.

guilt. Seeing as David is Yahweh's anointed, the message was not only very applicable to his audience but also could be viewed as self-serving.

David's Lament (1:17–27)

While we have seen David's musical abilities displayed in the story so far (1 Sam 16:18, 23; 18:10), here we see the first glimpse of David's poetic prowess. Later, of course, he will be known for his songs (2 Sam 23:1), and many poems in the biblical book of Psalms are attributed to him (Pss 3–9; 11–41; 51–65; 68–70; 86; 101; 103; 108–110; 122; 124; 131; 133; and 138–145).

In case the reader thought David's response to news of the royal deaths was all show or pure political posturing, David delivers an intimate lament over the fallen soldiers that reveals his heart. As Brueggemann points out, "We as spectators have been so caught up in the struggle between Saul and David that we might miss what Saul's death means to Israel."[15] The death of the king at the hands of the enemy was a sorrowful and disillusioning time for any nation. Despite the fact that Saul had been seeking to take David's life, David now shows love for his enemy, honoring him publicly.

Like any funeral dirge, the poem uses hyperbolic language, metaphors, and similes. The poem continually contrasts the past (the deceased's lives) and present (the loss). In keeping with the tradition of not speaking ill of the dead, the poem speaks so highly of the departed that its content might appear to contradict the earlier narratives about Saul; but, that is part of its genre as a funeral poem. The lament repeats the refrain, "how the mighty have fallen," in verses 19, 25, and 27, which divides the poem into sections (vv. 19–24 and 25–27) and forms an inclusio that sets off the beginning and ending of the poem.[16]

The poem forbids the news be told in Philistia lest the enemy gloat. Of course, in reality, the news was reported throughout Philistia (1 Sam 31:9) and their gloating included the displaying of the royal corpses as trophies of war (1 Sam 31:10). The poem addresses Gilboa, the hill on which the king and princes were killed. David utters a curse on Gilboa for not protecting Saul, calling for it to become a barren landscape—a poetic call for the land to mourn the loss of these great warriors. Such language is found in the prophetic books (e.g., Jer 4:28; 12:4; Amos 1:2).[17]

The poem further recalls the heroics of Saul and his son and praises their effectiveness in battle (1:22). The lyrics recall the best of times, when both Saul and Jonathan were "loved and admired" and their strength and speed

---

15. Brueggemann, *First and Second Samuel*, 214.
16. Anderson, *2 Samuel*, 15.
17. Ibid., 18.

unmatched (1:23). As they were so united in life, David notes that their death together was somewhat fitting.

While the daughters of the Philistines were forbidden from rejoicing over the occasion (1:20), the daughters of Israel are commanded to weep (1:24). Israelite women were clearly the ones to memorialize events in song (1 Sam 18:7). David points to the affluence of these women ("clothed . . . in scarlet and finery," 1:24). Despite how we have seen that Saul's regency did not seem to improve the fate of Israel, David attributes the wealth of Israel to Saul's leadership and urges all to remember how much they owe to their fallen king.

The remainder of the lament (1:25–27) remembers Jonathan, David's dear friend. In fact, the lament concludes without mentioning the king again. This is especially striking when we remember that David commanded the lament be taught to the people of Judah (v. 18). Clearly the greatest grief for David was in the loss of Jonathan. David notes their dear friendship and their shared love as superior to even the love of a wife (1:26). Though the poem was to be made public, this portion is incredibly intimate. While earlier portions called on others to grieve, now David expresses his personal loss on his own.

LIVE the Story

How the Mighty Fall

The opening line of the lament (1:19a) has been translated by the NIV as, "a gazelle lies slain on your heights, Israel," yet most translations (e.g., ESV, NRSV, NLT, 1984 NIV) render, "The glory of Israel" rather than "a gazelle." To be sure, the Hebrew word can be translated as "gazelle" or "beauty, honor."[18] Choosing "gazelle" could make sense given the later reference in the poem to the speed of Saul and his son (1:24) and how Asahel is later compared to a gazelle due to his swiftness (2 Sam 2:18). However, "splendor" or "honor" makes the most sense in this context, as kings were to be the outstanding representative of the people.

The word rendered "on your heights" by the NIV is a Hebrew word (*bamah*) that is usually translated "high places" (e.g., 1 Kgs 3:4; 14:23; 2 Kgs 17:11) and denotes cultic places of worship located on high places (hills, mountains) where illegitimate sacrifices were offered, often to false gods.[19] While the word can also refer to a height on a mountain or a ridge, given the prominence of the theme of the cultic "high places" (Hebrew *bamah*) in the history of the Israelite monarchy, the reference has a double meaning.

---

18. BDB, 840.

19. P. H. Vaughan, *The Meaning of 'Bāmâ' in the Old Testament: A Study of Etymological, Textual and Archaeological Evidence*, SOTSMS 3 (Cambridge: Cambridge University Press, 1974).

While Saul and Jonathan did die on a mountain ridge (a high place), reference to the "glory of Israel" being slain on a "high place" (i.e., illegitimate cultic place of worship) would have tremendous significance for those reading this story in the exile. As explained in the introduction, the book of Samuel is part of the great history work of Joshua–2 Kings, which was only completed during the exile. One of the main overall messages of the history was to explain *why* Israel ended up in exile. The theme of the high place (Hebrew *bamah*) focuses on Israel's cultic sins and how they continually followed other gods, worshiping them on the high places, rather than worshiping Yahweh at the Jerusalem temple. Later kings of Israel are continually criticized for not destroying the high places (1 Kgs 12:32; 15:14; 22:43; 2 Kgs 12:3; 14:4; 15:4; 16:4; 17:9, 11, 29, 32; 21:3). The only kings who do destroy the high places are Hezekiah (2 Kgs 18:4) and Josiah (2 Kgs 23:5, 8, 13, 19–20). In other words, while David's lament here clearly mourns the fall of Saul in David's time, the words chosen also foreshadow the later fall of Jerusalem at the hands of Babylon. The "high places" allude to the reason the nation went into exile—Israel's perpetual idolatrous sin.[20] In this lament of the fall of the king, the fall of the entire community is foreshadowed.

Seeing as Old Testament "examples ... were written down as warnings for us, on whom the fulfillment of the ages has come" (1 Cor 10:11), Saul's "epic fail" is a cautionary tale for Christians today regarding the importance of repentance. Similarly, the allusion to the fall of Judah into exile serves as a warning for the church today. Just as Saul superstitiously craved divine assurances of success and even fell into outright pagan religion (1 Sam 28), so the nation continually fell into pagan idol worship, craving the assurance of prosperity and fertility offered by the false gods of Canaan. Canaanites worshiped gods like Baal, who were fertility gods/goddesses, and their faith was basically a materialist religion. Their focus was to worship these gods in order to ensure the prosperity of their cattle and harvests. So, too, we modern Christians can be tempted by the gods of our society today and crave the false offer of prosperity and success offered by the high gods of materialism and consumerism. We too must remember this lament. Remember Paul's warning, "if you think you are standing firm, be careful that you don't *fall!*" (1 Cor 10:12, emphasis added). *How the mighty have fallen!* Paul urges Christians to put away "deceitful desires" (Eph 4:22). Just as Israel was deceived, so we can potentially fall on the "high places" of materialistic desires. But our struggle

---

20. Robert Polzin, *David and the Deuteronomist: A Literary Study of the Deuteronomistic History. Part Three: 2 Samuel*, Indiana Studies in Biblical Literature (Bloomington: Indiana University Press, 1993), 16; Anderson, *2 Samuel*, 17; Keith Bodner, *Power Play: A Primer on the Second Book of Samuel* (Toronto: Clements, 2004), 21.

is not on our own. Paul immediately encourages his readers in the next verse, "No temptation has overtaken you except what is common to mankind. And God is faithful; he will not let you be tempted beyond what you can bear. But when you are tempted, he will also provide a way out so that you can endure" (1 Cor 10:13). God is faithful so that we can be, too.

Love of Enemies

David's deep grief expressed over the death of Saul and his public honoring of the fallen king display an amazing magnanimity. How David was able to forgive Saul for ruining his life is astonishing. Saul had repeatedly tried to kill him, he had taken David's wife and given her to another man (1 Sam 25:44), and he had forced David into exile with the despised Philistines (1 Samuel 27). Nevertheless, not only does David forgive his enemy, he shows love to the end in publically honoring him and commanding that his lament over Saul be taught to all the people (1:18).

This passage is a good illustration of the biblical principle of loving your enemy. The concept is found in Proverbs 25:21: "If your enemy is hungry, give him food to eat; if he is thirsty, give him water to drink." Paul quotes this proverb in Romans 12:20 and adds:

> Do not repay anyone evil for evil. . . . Do not take revenge, my friends, but leave room for God's wrath, for it is written: "It is mine to avenge; I will repay," says the Lord. (Rom 12:18–19)

David's actions are clearly in line with this apostolic exhortation. David repaid Saul's evil with good as Saul himself said to David, "you have repaid me good, whereas I have repaid you evil" (1 Sam 24:17, NRSV). David refused to take revenge on Saul despite having opportunity to do so (1 Sam 24, 26).

The proverbs further caution us: "Do not gloat when your enemy falls; when they stumble, do not let your heart rejoice" (Prov 24:17). David's lament in chapter 1 serves as a great example in this regard. Rather than rejoicing at Saul's defeat, David mourns his loss. Enemy love is to be one of the hallmarks of a Christian. Jesus commanded his disciples, "Love your enemies, do good to those who hate you" (Luke 6:27; cf. Matt 5:43–44). David's forgiveness of Saul here illustrates just this type of enemy love. May we, like David, forgive our enemies and show love to those who persecute us.

Of course, as David's own life shows, he did not always practice enemy love (e.g., 1 Kgs 2:8), and we will no doubt fail at this from time to time. But thanks be to God that it is not through our own righteousness that we have been forgiven. Our forgiveness through Christ's death on the cross, however, was not cheap, and it urges us to forgive as we have been forgiven (Matt 6:14;

Eph 4:32). But in important ways through his lament in 1 Samuel 1, David prefigures the later Son of David who forgave his persecutors and prayed for his enemies on the cross (Luke 23:34). Thus, we can hope in this Anointed One, Jesus Christ, that we too will find forgiveness of sins, though we were once his enemies (Rom 5:10).

LISTEN to the Story

¹In the course of time, David inquired of the LORD. "Shall I go up to one of the towns of Judah?" he asked.

The LORD said, "Go up."

David asked, "Where shall I go?"

"To Hebron," the LORD answered.

²So David went up there with his two wives, Ahinoam of Jezreel and Abigail, the widow of Nabal of Carmel. ³David also took the men who were with him, each with his family, and they settled in Hebron and its towns. ⁴Then the men of Judah came to Hebron, and there they anointed David king over the tribe of Judah.

When David was told that it was the men from Jabesh Gilead who had buried Saul, ⁵he sent messengers to them to say to them, "The LORD bless you for showing this kindness to Saul your master by burying him. ⁶May the LORD now show you kindness and faithfulness, and I too will show you the same favor because you have done this. ⁷Now then, be strong and brave, for Saul your master is dead, and the people of Judah have anointed me king over them."

⁸Meanwhile, Abner son of Ner, the commander of Saul's army, had taken Ish-Bosheth son of Saul and brought him over to Mahanaim. ⁹He made him king over Gilead, Ashuri and Jezreel, and also over Ephraim, Benjamin and all Israel.

¹⁰Ish-Bosheth son of Saul was forty years old when he became king over Israel, and he reigned two years. The tribe of Judah, however, remained loyal to David. ¹¹The length of time David was king in Hebron over Judah was seven years and six months.

¹²Abner son of Ner, together with the men of Ish-Bosheth son of Saul, left Mahanaim and went to Gibeon. ¹³Joab son of Zeruiah and David's men went out and met them at the pool of Gibeon. One group sat down on one side of the pool and one group on the other side.

¹⁴Then Abner said to Joab, "Let's have some of the young men get up and fight hand to hand in front of us."

"All right, let them do it," Joab said.

¹⁵So they stood up and were counted off—twelve men for Benjamin and Ish-Bosheth son of Saul, and twelve for David. ¹⁶Then each man grabbed his opponent by the head and thrust his dagger into his opponent's side, and they fell down together. So that place in Gibeon was called Helkath Hazzurim.

¹⁷The battle that day was very fierce, and Abner and the Israelites were defeated by David's men.

¹⁸The three sons of Zeruiah were there: Joab, Abishai and Asahel. Now Asahel was as fleet-footed as a wild gazelle. ¹⁹He chased Abner, turning neither to the right nor to the left as he pursued him. ²⁰Abner looked behind him and asked, "Is that you, Asahel?"

"It is," he answered.

²¹Then Abner said to him, "Turn aside to the right or to the left; take on one of the young men and strip him of his weapons." But Asahel would not stop chasing him.

²²Again Abner warned Asahel, "Stop chasing me! Why should I strike you down? How could I look your brother Joab in the face?"

²³But Asahel refused to give up the pursuit; so Abner thrust the butt of his spear into Asahel's stomach, and the spear came out through his back. He fell there and died on the spot. And every man stopped when he came to the place where Asahel had fallen and died.

²⁴But Joab and Abishai pursued Abner, and as the sun was setting, they came to the hill of Ammah, near Giah on the way to the wasteland of Gibeon. ²⁵Then the men of Benjamin rallied behind Abner. They formed themselves into a group and took their stand on top of a hill.

²⁶Abner called out to Joab, "Must the sword devour forever? Don't you realize that this will end in bitterness? How long before you order your men to stop pursuing their fellow Israelites?"

²⁷Joab answered, "As surely as God lives, if you had not spoken, the men would have continued pursuing them until morning."

²⁸So Joab blew the trumpet, and all the troops came to a halt; they no longer pursued Israel, nor did they fight anymore.

²⁹All that night Abner and his men marched through the Arabah. They crossed the Jordan, continued through the morning hours and came to Mahanaim.

> ³⁰Then Joab stopped pursuing Abner and assembled the whole army. Besides Asahel, nineteen of David's men were found missing. ³¹But David's men had killed three hundred and sixty Benjamites who were with Abner. ³²They took Asahel and buried him in his father's tomb at Bethlehem. Then Joab and his men marched all night and arrived at Hebron by daybreak.

Listen to the Text in the Story: 1 Samuel 11:1–15; 25; 27:7; 30:26–31; 31:11–13

The death of Saul (1 Sam 31), though tragic and lamented by David, meant that at long last, after spending sixteen months in Philistine territory (1 Sam 27:7), David is able to return home and finally be crowned king. We are not told what exactly led the men of Hebron to anoint David king, though David was clearly well known throughout the land as a man of valor who led many victories over their enemies (e.g., 1 Sam 16:18; 18:6–7, 30). As well, David was from Bethlehem of Judah, and it is likely that some in Judah knew of his having been anointed king by Samuel, seeing as the anointing was performed with an audience (1 Sam 16:13). In the period since David was forced to flee his home, however, much has happened that contributes to his being crowned king. First, of course, Saul had died, and there was the need for a new leader. Second, David had in fact already been performing the duties of a king for Judah during his sojourn in Philistia. He had fought Judah's enemies (1 Sam 27:8) and even shared the spoils of his victories with Hebron and other Judahite towns (1 Sam 30:26–31). Finally, some have suggested the fact that David's wives were prominent women from the area. Ahinoam was from Jezreel (not the well-known valley in the north), a town near Carmel in Judah (Josh 15:55–56). Abigail was the widow of Nabal, a prominent Calebite chieftain (1 Sam 25:2–3) from Carmel (not the mountain range in northern Israel), just southeast of Hebron. Hebron itself was a Calebite town (cf. Josh 15:13–14; Judg 1:20), making Abigail's Calebite connections important.[1]

EXPLAIN the Story

After hearing of Saul's death and inquiring of God, David returns to Israel and lives in Hebron, where he is anointed king over Judah. When David was told that Saul had been buried by the Jabesh Gileadites, he sends messengers

---

1. For more on the political importance of David's wives, see Jon D. Levenson and Baruch Halpern, "The Political Import of David's Marriages," *JBL* 99 (1980): 507–18.

to them, thanking them for their deeds and also informing them that he has been anointed king in Saul's stead. Meanwhile, Abner, Saul's general, had made one of Saul's remaining sons, Ish-Bosheth, king over northern Israel. With a civil war brewing, Abner and Ish-Bosheth's men meet with Joab and David's men at Gibeon. What begins as something of a combat game between young men from each side turns into an outright battle of Joab and his men defeating Abner and his troops. In battle, Joab's brother, Asahel, was killed by Abner while pursuing the general. In response, Asahel's brothers, Joab and Abishai, pursued Abner until Abner finally talked them out of continuing the battle. In the end, the battle was a clear victory for David's kingdom, with Joab and David's men having killed 360 of Abner's men, while losing only twenty of their own.

The Return to the Land of Israel (2:1–3)

Before returning, David inquires of Yahweh, asking whether he should settle in Judah. David receives positive confirmation and is told specifically to settle in Hebron. When David obediently moves to Hebron, no mention is made of what the Philistine reaction might have been. Given their snubbing of David when they were heading to battle, David's move may have not been too surprising, though Achish would likely have egg on his face. On the other hand, since he was only becoming king of Judah, the Philistines may have still supported David's move at this point, viewing it as continued opposition to Saul's Israel.[2]

Anointed King of Judah (2:4–7)

Once in Hebron, David is anointed king over the house of Judah. Unlike the anointing by Samuel (1 Sam 16), which indicated God's choice and empowerment, this anointing represents the people's support of David as their king.

When David is told the story of how the men of Jabesh Gilead retrieved Saul's body and buried him, in his first act as king David sends messengers to Jabesh to thank them and bless them for their heroic and benevolent actions. David promises to return the favor to them and pledges his support. The message further informs Jabesh that he has been made king in Judah. Seeing as Jabesh is in the northern part of Israel, quite far from the environs of Judah, David's message to Jabesh was clearly extending an olive branch to the community in hopes that they too would accept David as their king. It was an effective strategy. We are not told that the heroic deeds of Jabesh were acknowledged by Abner or Saul's remaining sons. David's recognition of their good deed (along with his public lament of Saul's death) would likely go a long way to winning

---

2. Alter thinks the Philistines "countenanced it as a reasonable act on the part of their vassal opposing the house of Saul." Alter, *The David Story*, 202.

friends in the area. In fact, later on in the story when David's son Absalom attempts to usurp the kingdom from him, Gilead shows loyalty to David (2 Sam 17:27), which suggests David's mission to Jabesh Gilead bore fruit.

Civil War (2:8–32)

While David is solidifying his support as king and has offered to be king over those in Jabesh Gilead, Saul's general, Abner, is making political moves. As the reader will remember, Abner was in charge of Israel's army and was Saul's cousin (1 Sam 14:50). Abner takes Saul's son and "made him king" over Israel. The language here suggests that Saul's son is more of a puppet king than anything, as Abner "*had taken*" him and "*made* him king" (v. 9, emphasis added). The name Ish-Bosheth is given as "Ish-Baal" in Chronicles, and most scholars think Chronicles reflects the original form of the name. This is not to say that Saul was a Baal worshiper. In Hebrew *baal* means "lord" and may have been used to refer to Yahweh (e.g., Hos 2:16).[3] In other words, Ish-Baal would mean "man of the lord." However, given that later in Israel's history the name predominantly is used to refer to the pagan god, Baal, the Deuteronomist (or later scribes) probably changed the name to Bosheth, which means "shame" in Hebrew, making "Ish-Bosheth" to mean "man of shame" or "shameful man." The chosen capital for Ish-Bosheth is Mahanaim, a town located in the north and east of the Jordan River, making it quite removed both from Judah and from the territory lost to the Philistines in Saul's final battle.

Ish-Bosheth seems to have only progressively become king of "all Israel," as the text first lists Gilead then other places before noting "all Israel" (v. 9). Rather than viewing "all Israel" as a summary of all these parts, it seems likely there was "a chronological process" involved whereby Ish-bosheth gradually began ruling over these different areas, eventually ruling over all Israel.[4] After all, the text goes on to say he ruled for two years, while David ruled for seven. The discrepancy between the years listed probably reflects the five years Ish-bosheth extended his rule over the different tribes until he ruled "all Israel" for two years.

Contrary to David's coronation, the installation of Ish-Bosheth as king does not mention any public support, anointing, or attempt to get divine approval.[5] Nevertheless, the narrator apparently recognizes Ish-Bosheth as king in that he gives a brief summary of his reign, typical of later summaries (e.g., 1 Kgs 14:21; 22:42). We are told his age at his ascension to the throne (forty)

---

3. John Day, *Yahweh and the Gods and Goddesses of Canaan*, JSOTSup 265 (Sheffield: Sheffield Academic, 2000), 72.

4. Alter, *The David Story*, 204.

5. Arnold, *1 & 2 Samuel*, 434.

and the length of his reign (two years). Of course, this son of Saul never reigns over the whole nation, as David ruled Judah during this time (v. 11).

The bifurcation of the nation under two monarchies threatens a civil war as Abner brings Ish-Bosheth's men to Gibeon to meet David's men. Gibeon is a fairly central location between northern Israel and Judah. We are not told exactly why the meeting was taking place, but presumably, given that there were two competing kings, it was to be the first round of either negotiations or conflict between the two sides. Furthermore, David's appeal to the northern city of Jabesh Gilead as king may have led to Abner's actions. There is a clear aura of distrust as the two groups sit across from each other separated by a pool.

David's men here are said to be under the command of Joab, son of Zeruiah. This is the first time Joab is mentioned, though his younger brother Abishai has appeared in the story before (1 Sam 26:6). From here on out, Joab will prove to be a prominent and very complex character. On the one hand, Joab possesses numerous heroic qualities and proves an eminently able and politically wise soldier who is essential to the establishment and success of David's kingdom. On the other hand, Joab will also prove somewhat treacherous as he reveals himself a shrewd, rebellious general who often disregards David's orders (2 Sam 18:5–14) and undermines the king's authority (2 Sam 3:26–27). Furthermore, at times David appears helpless before his cunning general and ascribes his failure to rein in Joab as due to the wildness of the "sons of Zeruiah" (2 Sam 3:39).

Abner suggests that some of the "young men" on both sides "fight hand to hand" before them. This is similar to Goliath's challenge to Israel, where it is suggested that instead of a battle between entire armies, a smaller representative group would fight (in Goliath's case, one-on-one). Joab agrees to the contest and twelve fighters are counted off for each side (probably to symbolize one for each tribe of Israel, as both sides were arguing for their king to be leader over the whole twelve-tribe nation). Remarkably, all the young men die as each kills his opponent somewhat simultaneously. The place was therefore named "Hekath Hazzurim," which in Hebrew means "the portion of the blades" or "field of the blades."

The death of all combatants in the hand-to-hand combat sport does not lead to any resolution but instead to all-out battle. Not that we should have expected a resolution, as we remember that even when David bested the Philistine champion, an all-out battle ensued (1 Sam 17:52). In the resultant conflict, David's men decisively defeat Abner's men.

The narrator then informs us that three sons of Zeruiah were present that day: Joab, Abishai, and Asahel. Chronicles lists Zeruiah as David's sister (1 Chr 2:13–16), which would make these three men David's nephews. Asahel, known for his speed, persistently pursued Abner. Abner pleaded with Asahel to stop chasing him, as he did not want to kill him. Lest we think Abner had some special affection for Asahel, the reason he did not want to be responsible for his death was clearly because he knew that Asahel's brother Joab was a formidable opponent and would never forgive him (v. 22). Asahel would not be persuaded by Abner's words and as Asahel closed in on him, Abner suddenly put the head of his spear down to the ground with the butt facing up in the air, and Asahel ran into the butt of the spear at high speed, causing the spear to pierce his belly (in Hebrew it is literally "the fifth," translated as the "fifth rib" in the KJV).

Asahel's death clearly shook the soldiers on both sides, as verse 23 says that "every man" stopped at the place where Asahel had died. After all, they were all Israelites, countrymen, and probably many knew each other. Asahel's brothers took up the pursuit of Abner, no doubt with renewed vigor in light of their brother's death. They chased Abner and his men until the sun was setting, when Abner's men rallied behind him and took the high ground and awaited Joab's pursuit. Just as he had pleaded with Asahel, Abner now called out to Joab, pleading with him to stop the pursuit. Unlike his brother Asahel, however, Joab listens to Abner and calls off the chase. While Abner's strategic advantage of the high ground may have come into play here, probably it was Abner's reminder that they are all "Israelites" (v. 26) that led Joab to halt the pursuit. Given that Joab welcomed Abner's call to a ceasefire, it is unlikely he knew of Abner's similar call to Asahel earlier, which may have changed his opinion of Abner somewhat. As we will see, even though Joab blows the trumpet here and ends the conflict, Joab does *not* forget Abner's deed and he is intent on avenging his brother's death (cf. 3:27).

Not taking any chances that the ceasefire might not last, Abner and his men march all night a great distance back to Mahanaim. While Abner retreated, Joab assembled his army and took a roll call. Remarkably, they had lost only nineteen soldiers (v. 30), while they had killed 360 of their enemy (v. 31). Before returning to David at Hebron, they took time to bury Asahel in his hometown of Bethlehem, in his father's tomb. Then, wasting no time, they marched the entire night to arrive at Hebron by morning. Just as Abner did not fully trust Joab to uphold the ceasefire, so Joab didn't trust Abner either.

 LIVE the Story

Servant Leadership

This story juxtaposes two ways of becoming king. David is presented as one who would not even move back to his homeland without divine approval (2:1). Once in Hebron, David is made king by the people. There is no talk of coercion or force used by David to get himself installed as king. David has already won the hearts of the people through his good leadership and good deeds. All this is counter to what is going on in the North. Abner, Saul's powerful general, "takes" Saul's son and "makes" him king. There is no public support mentioned, no inquiring of God, simply a man with military force setting up Ish-Bosheth as king.

This text is cause for reflection on the ways of the world versus the ways of the kingdom. Jesus said anyone who would lead should serve (Mark 10:42–45). This is exactly what David had done so far. He had protected Judah and defeated her enemies. He also had provided for Judah, giving of the spoil he recovered from his battles. When David offers to Jabesh Gilead to be their king, he offers to help them (literally, he will do "good" to them [v. 6]). Rather than the "take, take, take" of the king as predicted by Samuel (1 Sam 8:11–18), in David's kingdom, he offers to serve his constituents.

CHAPTER 31

2 Samuel 3:1–4:12

 LISTEN to the Story

¹The war between the house of Saul and the house of David lasted a long time. David grew stronger and stronger, while the house of Saul grew weaker and weaker.

²Sons were born to David in Hebron:

His firstborn was Amnon the son of Ahinoam of Jezreel;
³his second, Kileab the son of Abigail the widow of Nabal
   of Carmel;
the third, Absalom the son of Maakah daughter of Talmai
   king of Geshur;
⁴the fourth, Adonijah the son of Haggith;
the fifth, Shephatiah the son of Abital;
⁵and the sixth, Ithream the son of David's wife Eglah.

These were born to David in Hebron.

⁶During the war between the house of Saul and the house of David, Abner had been strengthening his own position in the house of Saul. ⁷Now Saul had had a concubine named Rizpah daughter of Aiah. And Ish-Bosheth said to Abner, "Why did you sleep with my father's concubine?"

⁸Abner was very angry because of what Ish-Bosheth said. So he answered, "Am I a dog's head—on Judah's side? This very day I am loyal to the house of your father Saul and to his family and friends. I haven't handed you over to David. Yet now you accuse me of an offense involving this woman! ⁹May God deal with Abner, be it ever so severely, if I do not do for David what the LORD promised him on oath ¹⁰and transfer the kingdom from the house of Saul and establish David's throne over Israel and Judah from Dan to Beersheba." ¹¹Ish-Bosheth did not dare to say another word to Abner, because he was afraid of him.

¹²Then Abner sent messengers on his behalf to say to David, "Whose

land is it? Make an agreement with me, and I will help you bring all Israel over to you."

¹³"Good," said David. "I will make an agreement with you. But I demand one thing of you: Do not come into my presence unless you bring Michal daughter of Saul when you come to see me." ¹⁴Then David sent messengers to Ish-Bosheth son of Saul, demanding, "Give me my wife Michal, whom I betrothed to myself for the price of a hundred Philistine foreskins."

¹⁵So Ish-Bosheth gave orders and had her taken away from her husband Paltiel son of Laish. ¹⁶Her husband, however, went with her, weeping behind her all the way to Bahurim. Then Abner said to him, "Go back home!" So he went back.

¹⁷Abner conferred with the elders of Israel and said, "For some time you have wanted to make David your king. ¹⁸Now do it! For the LORD promised David, 'By my servant David I will rescue my people Israel from the hand of the Philistines and from the hand of all their enemies.'"

¹⁹Abner also spoke to the Benjamites in person. Then he went to Hebron to tell David everything that Israel and the whole tribe of Benjamin wanted to do. ²⁰When Abner, who had twenty men with him, came to David at Hebron, David prepared a feast for him and his men. ²¹Then Abner said to David, "Let me go at once and assemble all Israel for my lord the king, so that they may make a covenant with you, and that you may rule over all that your heart desires." So David sent Abner away, and he went in peace.

²²Just then David's men and Joab returned from a raid and brought with them a great deal of plunder. But Abner was no longer with David in Hebron, because David had sent him away, and he had gone in peace. ²³When Joab and all the soldiers with him arrived, he was told that Abner son of Ner had come to the king and that the king had sent him away and that he had gone in peace.

²⁴So Joab went to the king and said, "What have you done? Look, Abner came to you. Why did you let him go? Now he is gone! ²⁵You know Abner son of Ner; he came to deceive you and observe your movements and find out everything you are doing."

²⁶Joab then left David and sent messengers after Abner, and they brought him back from the cistern at Sirah. But David did not know it. ²⁷Now when Abner returned to Hebron, Joab took him aside into an inner chamber, as if to speak with him privately. And there, to avenge the blood of his brother Asahel, Joab stabbed him in the stomach, and he died.

²⁸Later, when David heard about this, he said, "I and my kingdom are forever innocent before the LORD concerning the blood of Abner son of Ner. ²⁹May his blood fall on the head of Joab and on his whole family! May Joab's family never be without someone who has a running sore or leprosy or who leans on a crutch or who falls by the sword or who lacks food."

³⁰(Joab and his brother Abishai murdered Abner because he had killed their brother Asahel in the battle at Gibeon.)

³¹Then David said to Joab and all the people with him, "Tear your clothes and put on sackcloth and walk in mourning in front of Abner." King David himself walked behind the bier. ³²They buried Abner in Hebron, and the king wept aloud at Abner's tomb. All the people wept also.

³³The king sang this lament for Abner:

> "Should Abner have died as the lawless die?
> ³⁴Your hands were not bound,
> your feet were not fettered.
> You fell as one falls before the wicked."

And all the people wept over him again.

³⁵Then they all came and urged David to eat something while it was still day; but David took an oath, saying, "May God deal with me, be it ever so severely, if I taste bread or anything else before the sun sets!"

³⁶All the people took note and were pleased; indeed, everything the king did pleased them. ³⁷So on that day all the people there and all Israel knew that the king had no part in the murder of Abner son of Ner.

³⁸Then the king said to his men, "Do you not realize that a commander and a great man has fallen in Israel this day? ³⁹And today, though I am the anointed king, I am weak, and these sons of Zeruiah are too strong for me. May the LORD repay the evildoer according to his evil deeds!"

⁴:¹When Ish-Bosheth son of Saul heard that Abner had died in Hebron, he lost courage, and all Israel became alarmed. ²Now Saul's son had two men who were leaders of raiding bands. One was named Baanah and the other Rekab; they were sons of Rimmon the Beerothite from the tribe of Benjamin—Beeroth is considered part of Benjamin, ³because the people of Beeroth fled to Gittaim and have resided there as foreigners to this day.

⁴(Jonathan son of Saul had a son who was lame in both feet. He was five years old when the news about Saul and Jonathan came from Jezreel. His nurse picked him up and fled, but as she hurried to leave, he fell and became disabled. His name was Mephibosheth.)

⁵Now Rekab and Baanah, the sons of Rimmon the Beerothite, set out for the house of Ish-Bosheth, and they arrived there in the heat of the day while he was taking his noonday rest. ⁶They went into the inner part of the house as if to get some wheat, and they stabbed him in the stomach. Then Rekab and his brother Baanah slipped away.

⁷They had gone into the house while he was lying on the bed in his bedroom. After they stabbed and killed him, they cut off his head. Taking it with them, they traveled all night by way of the Arabah. ⁸They brought the head of Ish-Bosheth to David at Hebron and said to the king, "Here is the head of Ish-Bosheth son of Saul, your enemy, who tried to kill you. This day the LORD has avenged my lord the king against Saul and his offspring."

⁹David answered Rekab and his brother Baanah, the sons of Rimmon the Beerothite, "As surely as the LORD lives, who has delivered me out of every trouble, ¹⁰when someone told me, 'Saul is dead,' and thought he was bringing good news, I seized him and put him to death in Ziklag. That was the reward I gave him for his news! ¹¹How much more—when wicked men have killed an innocent man in his own house and on his own bed—should I not now demand his blood from your hand and rid the earth of you!"

¹²So David gave an order to his men, and they killed them. They cut off their hands and feet and hung the bodies by the pool in Hebron. But they took the head of Ish-Bosheth and buried it in Abner's tomb at Hebron.

Listen to the Text in the Story: Deuteronomy 17:17; 1 Samuel 18:20–25; 25:44; 26:5–16; 2 Samuel 2:18–28; Laws of Eshnunna; Middle Assyrian Laws; Code of Hammurabi

In these chapters, we see an end to the Israelite civil war and David finally becomes king of all Israel. In his negotiations with Abner David demands that Michal, Saul's daughter and David's first wife, be returned to him. It is important for understanding this text to realize that David was not demanding something strange. Michal *was* his wife for whom he paid a grotesque bride-price (1 Sam 18:25–27), and he had not divorced her.[1] David was within his legal rights in asking for her back (note that he references the bride-price he had paid in 2 Sam 3:14). Ancient Near Eastern law codes deal with cases of what should be done when a husband has been absent from his wife for an extended period of time. The Laws of Eshnunna and Middle Assyrian Laws

---

1. Anderson, *2 Samuel*, 58.

both legislate that a husband who was taken prisoner by the enemy and was forcibly taken to another land should receive his wife back when he returns (though according to Middle Assyrian Law, in such instances the wife was to wait two years before remarrying).[2] However, the Laws of Eshnunna also legislates that "if a man repudiates his city and his master and then flees, and someone else then marries his wife, whenever he returns he will have no claim to his wife."[3] Similarly, the Code of Hammurabi allows a woman to marry another if her husband is captured and did not leave enough provisions for her.[4] Upon the return of her first husband, however, she will again become his wife (though any children she had from her second husband remain with their father). On the other hand, if the husband "deserts his city and flees," when he returns, "the wife of the deserter will not return to her husband."[5]

Thus, since David was forced to leave the country due to Saul's murderous actions and was *not* a deserter, and in light of ancient Near Eastern law, David had every right to ask for the return of his wife Michal. Of course, Saul probably viewed David as a man who "repudiates his city and his master and then flees" and thus no longer had any claim to his wife.[6] Of course in Middle Assyrian Laws, when a wife was abandoned by her deserting husband, she was allowed "to reside with the husband of her own choice."[7] Yet in Michal's instance, she appeared to have no say in the matter as Saul simply gives her to another man (1 Sam 25:44), probably motivated by his evil intentions toward David. That was not the first time Michal was used by her father in this way, as when we first meet her in 1 Samuel 18 she is used by her father in an attempt to get David killed.

While negotiations with Abner go well in David's view, David's general, Joab, is incensed by them. In light of Abner's killing of Joab's younger brother, Asahel, in the previous chapter, Joab disregards David's political agreements with Abner and takes justice into his own hands.

Any debate over the justice or injustice of Joab's vengeful killing of Abner must take into account the events of the previous chapter. A close reading of chapter 2 reveals that Abner had not murdered Asahel but killed him on the battlefield, which usually does not mean that the family had a legal right to blood vengeance.[8] Later David will say as much in 1 Kings 2:5, where he

---

2. Roth, *Law Collections*, 63§29; 170–71§A45. Cf. Long, *2 Samuel*, 425.

3. Roth, *Law Collections*, 63§30.

4. Ibid., 106 §134.

5. Ibid., 107 §136.

6. Ibid.

7. Roth, *Law Collections*, 63§29; 170–71§A45. Cf. Long, *2 Samuel*, 425.

8. A. Phillips, *Ancient Israel's Criminal Law* (Oxford: Oxford University Press, 1970), 85; Anderson, *2 Samuel*, 61.

states that Joab killed Abner "in peacetime as if in battle." In fact, the reader will remember that Abner clearly did not want to kill Ashahel, twice warning him to call off his pursuit (2 Sam 2:21–22). Asahel's death was somewhat on his own hands in that he would not heed Abner's warning as did his brother Joab, who called off the pursuit at Abner's words (2 Sam 2:26–28). Further complicating things are possible political motives for Joab. If Abner, the powerful general of the northern armies, was to join David's kingdom, it is conceivable that he might replace Joab as top military general.[9] Therefore, Joab's murder of Abner not only avenged Asahel but took out a potential rival.

Interestingly, David had earlier leveled a judgment of execution on Abner for not protecting Saul, saying to Abner, "As surely as the LORD lives, you and your men must die, because you did not guard your master, the LORD's anointed" (1 Sam 26:16). Seeing as Joab's brother, Abishai, was present (1 Sam 26:6–9) when David said this, it is likely that Joab heard of it, perhaps leading him to think David would approve of Abner's death (or at least give Joab some leverage in defending his actions).

EXPLAIN the Story

These chapters explain how David came to rule over not only Judah but all of Israel. During a period of hostilities between the north and south, "David grew stronger and stronger, while the house of Saul grew weaker and weaker" (3:1). David's growing progeny is first listed to demonstrate David's growing strength. Saul's weaknesses are enumerated first through the story of Abner's and Ish-Bosheth's conflicts and then through the stories of their deaths. Amidst the demise of Saul's house, the narrative is sure to demonstrate that David was innocent of all the bloodshed in this transition of power from Saul's house to David. David had no part in the death of Abner, who was killed by Joab in revenge of his brother Asahel (2 Sam 2:23). Similarly, David had no part in the death of Ish-Bosheth, who was murdered by his own men. The tragic events, which enabled David's rise to rule all Israel, were not the result of David's actions. In view of the larger narrative, Yahweh was installing his chosen one as king, and the actions of wicked men served his purpose.

War between Judah and Israel (3:1–11)

The narrative begins with a summary statement of the civil war in Israel between the remainder of Saul's house and David. Though the civil war is said

---

9. Alter, *The David Story*, 213; Victor P. Hamilton, *Handbook on the Historical Books* (Grand Rapids: Baker, 2001), 308.

to have lasted "a long time" (3:1), the narrative chooses not to dwell on the details of the war. Instead, it simply states that David was growing stronger and Saul's house was continually weakening (3:1). To illustrate this trend, the six sons born to David while he reigned in Hebron are listed. In the ancient world, a king with many sons has the best chance to establish a dynasty, and the larger the number of progeny, the greater a king's stability.

It should be noted that each of these six sons have different mothers. David came to the throne with two wives (not including his first wife Michal, who was taken from him by Saul) and now has six. While not uncommon in the ancient world, it was not to be the way of a king of Israel. Deuteronomy 17:17 clearly states that a king of Israel "must not take many wives." Significantly, one of the reasons for the king not taking many wives is that "his heart will be led astray" (Deut 17:17). This is especially relevant given that at least one of David's wives is a foreigner. The mother of his third child, Absalom, is said to be a daughter of "Talmai king of Geshur" (3:3). Geshur is a Transjordanian state in the north, and David's marriage to this foreign princess was likely a tool of diplomacy whereby he established an alliance in the north, near the territory of Saul's house. In ancient times, it was common for kings to marry for political reasons in order to secure foreign allies (after all, the father of the princess would have a personal stake in the success of his son-in-law's kingdom). However, it is precisely foreign wives that lead Solomon, David's successor, astray (1 Kgs 11:3). While not coming near to the magnitude of Solomon's marital sins (as Solomon ended up with seven hundred wives and three hundred concubines), David's multiplication of wives does not reflect well on him here. Furthermore, several of the sons listed will be key players in future tragedies for David's house. Amnon will rape his half sister and then be murdered by her brother (2 Sam 13). Absalom will usurp the throne from his father then be killed by Joab (2 Sam 15–18). Adonijah will claim the throne while the elderly David lies sick in bed, and then he'll be killed by Solomon (1 Kgs 1–2). Thus, this list of sons born in Hebron foreshadows difficult times for the house of David.

While David was strengthening his dynasty in Hebron, Abner "had been strengthening his own position in the house of Saul" (v. 6). We are not told exactly how Abner was strengthening himself, but despite his efforts, internal strife was weakening King Ish-Bosheth's kingdom in the north. The strife begins with the king questioning Abner about his sleeping with Rizpah, one of Saul's concubines. In the books of Samuel and Kings, taking a former king's wife or concubine was like taking symbolic hold of the throne.[10] For example,

---

10. M. Tsevat, "Marriage and Monarchial Legitimacy in Ugarit and Israel," *Journal of Semitic Studies* 3 (1958): 241.

during Absalom's attempt to take the kingship from his father David, Absalom went into David's harem (2 Sam 16:21–22). Similarly, Solomon's brother, Adonijah, requests one of David's concubines to be given him as his wife (1 Kgs 2:17). Solomon interprets this as tantamount to an attempt to take "the kingdom" (2:22). Therefore, Ish-Bosheth's accusation against Abner was a serious one.

It is not clear that Abner was actually sleeping with Rizpah, though his anger at the accusation and stated loyalty to the house of Saul seems to be a denial of the action. Whether innocent of the crime or simply offended at being called to task, Abner responds by completely defecting to David. In fact, Abner claims he will fulfill what Yahweh promised David "on oath" (v. 9). Abner's knowledge of God's promises to David actually incriminates Abner here. After all, he knew of Yahweh's will but had installed Ish-Bosheth as king anyway (2 Sam 2:8–9). Abner's actions thus far have been rebellious.

Furthermore, Abner's claim to be able to deliver the kingdom to David is a bit presumptuous and reveals a very high estimation of himself. After all, Abner goes so far as to claim he will "establish David's throne" (3:10) from "Dan to Beersheba" (Dan is in the far north and Beersheba the far south, so the phrase means the totality of the land of Israel). As we will see, Abner's efforts to transfer the kingdom to David were well under way but were cut short due to his untimely death. Nevertheless, Abner was clearly the real power in northern Israel (see comments on 2 Sam 2:8–9) and was best positioned to deliver on his promise. Ish-Bosheth's lack of real power is reaffirmed here as Ish-Bosheth has nothing to say in response to Abner due to his fear (v. 11).

Abner's Defection (3:12–21)

Abner wasted no time sending messengers to David, offering his support if they could come to an agreement. David was quite willing but demanded that his first wife, Michal, Saul's daughter, be returned to him. Somewhat surprisingly, it is not Abner who arranges this but Ish-Bosheth, again highlighting that Abner was truly in charge.

In a gut-wrenching scene, Michal's second husband, Paltiel, is distraught over losing his wife and follows behind her for a great distance before Abner made him return home. One must feel for Michal in this situation, as she is being used as a pawn, since her return, as the former king's daughter, strengthened David's legitimation as king. We are not told about the reunion between David and Michal. Were both sides eagerly anticipating the day? Earlier in the story we were told that Michal "loved" David (1 Sam 18:20), though we are never told David loved her. Now, on the occasion of their reunion, did Michal's love still burn for David, or did she now miss Paltiel, her husband with whom she may have spent more time with than David (and clearly her new husband loved her)? Was David's love for Michal the reason he demanded her back, or was it more about legal rights or the legitimation she would provide for his bid to rule all Israel? Seeing as David already had at least six other wives, the latter may be the case, but the text is silent on the issue. However, the narrator's focus on the love of Paltiel, evident in his actions here, would seem to purposefully contrast David and juxtapose Paltiel's deep love for Michal with David's dispassionate actions. The inclusion of this brief scene with Paltiel makes David look bad.

Abner further negotiated with the elders of Israel (vv. 17–18) and personally met with the Benjamites (v. 19) to convince them to pledge allegiance to David. Abner then meets with David in Hebron and is welcomed by David with a feast and, upon the conclusion of the negotiation, David sends him away in peace. In fact, the text mentions David sending him off "in peace" three times (vv. 21, 22, 23), clearly stressing David's innocence in regard to the murder of Abner, which follows.

The Murder of Abner (3:22–30)

Just after Abner left David's presence, Joab returned and was told that Abner had been allowed to leave in peace. In response, Joab rebukes David for letting Abner go, implying that David is naïve and claiming that Abner had only come to spy on him and deceive him (v. 25). No response by David is given, perhaps implying Joab's abrupt departure from the king's presence. The lack of response could also reflect David's weakness in the area of Joab, which he himself highlights later (3:39).

Out for blood, Joab devises a plan to murder Abner. First, unbeknownst to David, Joab calls Abner back to Hebron under a pretense of diplomacy. Once in Hebron, Joab takes him aside (3:27) for a private word. It is somewhat surprising that Abner would trust Joab enough to allow a private audience with him, but Abner likely thought he was now under David's protection seeing as he was such a valuable asset to the king. Despite his agreement with David, Joab stabs Abner in the exact same spot where Abner had smote Asahel—the stomach (in Hebrew it is literally "the fifth" translated as the "fifth rib" in the KJV).

When David hears of the murder, he is quick to point out his innocence in the matter and to point out the guilty party, lest anyone think David had Abner killed in order to more easily annex northern Israel into his kingdom. In this case, however, Abner's death only delayed David's takeover of the north and made no sense politically. Nevertheless, some have interpreted David's actions here as protesting too much. That is, they think David *was* complicit in the death of Abner, and the elaborate funeral and lamentation was merely a public relations act to convince the public otherwise. While it is possible to read the text this way, it goes completely against the grain of the text and requires privileging one's skepticism of David over one's trust of the text. The text clearly states that "David did not know" (3:26) that Joab arranged a meeting with Abner. The text clearly states that "the king had no part in the murder of Abner son of Ner" (3:37). Unless we assume the entire fabrication of this story, a faithful reading of this text concludes that David was indeed innocent of Abner's death.

Instead of having Joab punished for the murder, David utters a curse over him and his family. This course of action should be interpreted in light of David's statement in verse 39: "though I am the anointed king, I am weak, and these sons of Zeruiah are too strong for me." In other words, though David was the king, Joab had some measure of independence from David and was uncontrollable. Of course, from another perspective, despite the difficulties of working with Joab, he was also a great asset to David's kingdom. As Kirsch has pointed out, "a hard man can be good to find in the treacherous world in which he lived. Joab . . . was too valuable to the ambitious king of Judah to be sacrificed for the sake of public relations."[11] Thus, rather than take action against Joab, David commits him to Yahweh that he "repay" Joab for "his evil deeds" (v. 39). Later upon his deathbed, however, David apparently grew impatient with Yahweh's judgment on Joab and he commands Solomon to have Joab killed for his murders (1 Kgs 2:5–6).

Abner's Funeral (3:31–39)

In order to emphasize David's innocence and the tragic nature of Abner's death, David arranged a public funeral and mourning for Abner, even commanding the murderer to take part (3:31). Abner is buried in David's royal city of Hebron and he weeps for all to see and even utters a lament. These actions are important for David's future unification of the north and south: "David needs to establish his innocence and to reassure the elders of the north who (like Abner) deal with David that they are not automatically placed in jeopardy."[12] David accomplishes his goal as the people are "pleased" with David's actions and assured of David's innocence in the murder of Abner. Therefore, the way is still open for David to unite the tribes and become king of all Israel.

---

11. Jonathan Kirsch, *King David: The Real Life of the Man Who Ruled Israel* (New York: Ballantine, 2000), 146.

12. Brueggemann, *First and Second Samuel*, 230.

The Murder of Ish-Bosheth (4:1–12)

The death of Abner reverberated throughout Israel, shaking the confidence of King Ish-Bosheth and the populace. Even the king's own men were affected, leading two of them to betray their king and murder him in his sleep. The two men are said to be Beerothites from the tribe of Benjamin (v. 2). Beeroth was a Gibeonite city that had made a covenant with Israel back in Joshua's time (Josh 9:17), though we are told that Beeroth was now a Benjamite city and that its original inhabitants had abandoned the city to live in Gittaim (v. 3). Seeing as Saul's most prominent servants were Benjamites whom Saul had given land for their service (cf. 1 Sam 22:7), it seems likely that some of these Benjamites were given this Gibeonite city as a royal grant by Saul. This may explain why Gibeon had a grudge against the house of Saul (cf. 2 Sam 21).

Before the details of the murderous deed are told, the narrator is sure to point out the existence of another Saulide besides Ish-Bosheth. Jonathan, David's best friend, had a son, Mephibosheth, who had been dropped by his nurse as a baby when they heard of his father's death, and he became disabled. Like the name Ish-Bosheth, it is possible that the name Mephibosheth may be an intentional distortion of the original name. Chronicles gives Jonathan's son the name Merib-Baal (1 Chr 8:34; 9:40), and it seems likely that was the original name. As in the case of Ish-Bosheth, the name likely originally did not refer to the pagan god, Baal, but was used with its generic meaning "lord," possibly in reference to Yahweh. Nevertheless, in the book of Samuel, in order to disparage the false god, Baal, the word "bosheth" (which means "shame" in Hebrew) is substituted for "Baal." Mephibosheth will come back into the story later (2 Sam 9), but for now this notice functions to show that after the death of Ish-Bosheth there will be no other Saulide heir who could take the throne (as his disability would disqualify him as a candidate).[13]

Two of Ish-Bosheth's own men snuck into his house in the middle of the day. Given the ease in which they infiltrate the royal residence, it seems likely the two men were trusted and had somewhat prominent positions. After all, they are said to be "leaders of raiding bands" (v. 2), which sounds quite similar to Joab in Judah, who led raiding parties (2 Sam 3:22).

Entering the house on false pretenses, they murder the king while he slept, cut off his head, and bring it to David, probably thinking they would receive a reward. Clearly these men did not understand David. The two men present their actions as the fulfillment of Yahweh's vengeance against Saul (2 Sam 4:8), but David rejects their theological interpretation and calls it for what it was: two "wicked men" killing "an innocent man in his own house

---

13. Alter, *The David Story*, 218.

and on his own bed" (v. 11). As punishment for their crime, David had them executed. Furthermore, their dismembered bodies were publically displayed (2 Sam 4:12) as a warning to others. David's actions would likely have received approval from those in the north whose king had been killed in such a grisly manner.[14] David further had Ish-Bosheth's head buried with Abner in Hebron.

LIVE the Story

Providence

Throughout chapters 3–4 very little is said about Yahweh's role in the events, as God's promises are fulfilled through the unwitting actions of sinful people. David's chief rivals to the throne are removed through the murderous actions of Joab and the two servants of Ish-Bosheth. Both murders are undertaken for personal reasons—Joab murders Abner to avenge the death of his brother, and the two wicked servants of Ish-Bosheth murder Saul's son to obtain a reward. David and the narrator characterize their actions as evil and those murdered as innocent. Yet, these sinful actions move God's purposes forward.[15]

This text provides a good chance to reflect on God's providence. Providence has been defined as:

> The beneficent outworking of God's sovereignty whereby all events are directed and disposed to bring about those purposes of glory and good for which the universe was made. These events include the actions of free agents, which while remaining free, personal and responsible are also the intended actions of those agents.[16]

While often Christians think of providence in terms of fortunate turns of events that God directs, usually providence involves God's use of human sinful actions.[17] Since all are sinners, when God works through human actions, more often than not God is working through sinful actions. On one hand, the story in 2 Samuel 2–3 clearly portrays the death of David's rivals as due to the evil actions of human beings. On the other hand, we can see God working through these actions to bring about his will and the installation of David as king. Human agency is not denied in favor of divine agency, nor is the reverse. In fact, in response to the murders of Ish-Bosheth, David clearly states that it was Yahweh "who has delivered me out of every trouble" (2 Sam 4:9), even though

---

14. Anderson, *2 Samuel*, 73.
15. Brueggemann, *First and Second Samuel*, 232.
16. Ferguson, et al., *New Dictionary of Theology*, 541.
17. Walton, *Genesis*, 634.

it has been the Philistines who killed Saul, Joab who killed Abner, and now the two Beerothites who kill Ish-Bosheth.

This is not the only case in the Bible of God working through the evil actions of humans to bring about his good purposes. The story of Joseph in Genesis is probably the most famous example. Joseph was sold into slavery due to the jealous actions of his brothers, but later in life Joseph realized that it was really God who "sent" him to Egypt in order to save many people (Gen 45:7). Further, even though the actions were intentionally evil, Joseph declares that "God intended it for good" (Gen 50:20).

Other Bible stories similarly demonstrate God working through evil actions to accomplish his purposes. For example, in Genesis 34, in order to avenge the rape of their sister by a Hivite prince (Gen 34:2), Simeon and Levi kill every male in the Hivite city (Gen 34:25) and take all their wives and children captive (Gen 34:29). While the action was horrific, the result was the prevention of Jacob's family from assimilating with Canaanites by intermarrying with them. This preservation of Jacob's family was instrumental in God preserving his people Israel.

Most significant of all for Christians is the arrest and execution of Jesus of Nazareth, which was carried out through the evil actions of humans to bring about God's good purposes. As Peter states in Acts 2:23–24, "This man was handed over to you by God's deliberate plan and foreknowledge; and you, with the help of wicked men, put him to death by nailing him to the cross. But God raised him from the dead, freeing him from the agony of death, because it was impossible for death to keep its hold on him."

This is not to suggest that God causes humans to do evil. He did not cause Joab to murder Abner, the two Beerothites to kill Ish-Bosheth, Joseph's brothers to sell him into slavery, Jacob's sons to slaughter an entire city, or the Romans to crucify Jesus. God's providence is seen not in causing people to make sinful choices but by working *within* free human choices and weaving them into his own plan. As Block writes: "God is able to incorporate the free activities of human beings into his plan for his own glory and for the salvation of his people"[18] Even when people undertake actions that come from sinful motives, God can still providentially use these choices to fulfill his will.

---

18. Block, *Judges, Ruth*, 210.

LISTEN to the Story

¹All the tribes of Israel came to David at Hebron and said, "We are your own flesh and blood. ²In the past, while Saul was king over us, you were the one who led Israel on their military campaigns. And the LORD said to you, 'You will shepherd my people Israel, and you will become their ruler.'"

³When all the elders of Israel had come to King David at Hebron, the king made a covenant with them at Hebron before the LORD, and they anointed David king over Israel.

⁴David was thirty years old when he became king, and he reigned forty years. ⁵In Hebron he reigned over Judah seven years and six months, and in Jerusalem he reigned over all Israel and Judah thirty-three years.

⁶The king and his men marched to Jerusalem to attack the Jebusites, who lived there. The Jebusites said to David, "You will not get in here; even the blind and the lame can ward you off." They thought, "David cannot get in here." ⁷Nevertheless, David captured the fortress of Zion—which is the City of David.

⁸On that day David had said, "Anyone who conquers the Jebusites will have to use the water shaft to reach those 'lame and blind' who are David's enemies." That is why they say, "The 'blind and lame' will not enter the palace."

⁹David then took up residence in the fortress and called it the City of David. He built up the area around it, from the terraces inward. ¹⁰And he became more and more powerful, because the LORD God Almighty was with him.

¹¹Now Hiram king of Tyre sent envoys to David, along with cedar logs and carpenters and stonemasons, and they built a palace for David. ¹²Then David knew that the LORD had established him as king over Israel and had exalted his kingdom for the sake of his people Israel.

¹³After he left Hebron, David took more concubines and wives in

Jerusalem, and more sons and daughters were born to him. [14]These are the names of the children born to him there: Shammua, Shobab, Nathan, Solomon, [15]Ibhar, Elishua, Nepheg, Japhia, [16]Elishama, Eliada and Eliphelet.

[17]When the Philistines heard that David had been anointed king over Israel, they went up in full force to search for him, but David heard about it and went down to the stronghold. [18]Now the Philistines had come and spread out in the Valley of Rephaim; [19]so David inquired of the LORD, "Shall I go and attack the Philistines? Will you deliver them into my hands?"

The LORD answered him, "Go, for I will surely deliver the Philistines into your hands."

[20]So David went to Baal Perazim, and there he defeated them. He said, "As waters break out, the LORD has broken out against my enemies before me." So that place was called Baal Perazim. [21]The Philistines abandoned their idols there, and David and his men carried them off.

[22]Once more the Philistines came up and spread out in the Valley of Rephaim; [23]so David inquired of the LORD, and he answered, "Do not go straight up, but circle around behind them and attack them in front of the poplar trees. [24]As soon as you hear the sound of marching in the tops of the poplar trees, move quickly, because that will mean the LORD has gone out in front of you to strike the Philistine army." [25]So David did as the LORD commanded him, and he struck down the Philistines all the way from Gibeon to Gezer.

Listen to the Text in the Story: Deuteronomy 17:15–17; 1 Samuel 16:11; 17:34–36; Sargon: The Khorsabad Texts; Memorial Stela of Tukulti-Ninurta

With all legitimate Saulide heirs gone, the road is now paved for David to be crowned king. This is actually initiated by the people, who approach David in his capital at Hebron. The people first acknowledge their kinship with David (their "own flesh and blood"), which is important in light of Deuteronomy 17:15, which demands that the king "must be from among your fellow Israelites. Do not place a foreigner over you, one who is not an Israelite." Thus, as their kin, David qualifies as king. The people also recall how David had led them in the past and reference Yahweh's calling David to the throne. Again, this is in keeping with the law of the king in Deuteronomy 17:15, which demands that the king Israel appoints be "a king the LORD your God chooses." The people also note David's calling to "shepherd" Israel. This is fitting given that David was a literal shepherd before being called to the kingship (cf. 1 Sam 16:11; 17:34–36). In ancient Near Eastern literature, "shepherd" was an epithet used of kings. For example, in the Code of Hammurabi the Babylonian king says, "I am Hammurabi, the shepherd, selected by the god Enlil" [1] and "shepherd of the people, whose deeds are pleasing to the goddess Ishtar."[2] The epithet of shepherd evoked "the image of his responsible care for the population placed in his charge by the deity."[3]

In this story, David conquers Jerusalem and makes it his new capital. What is more, he renames it "the City of David" (2 Sam 5:9). This practice of naming a conquered city or new capital city after the conquering king is evidenced in ancient Near Eastern texts. For example, the Assyrian King Tukulti-Ninurta I (ca. 1243–1207 BC) writes, "I built the great cult centre, my royal dwelling, (and) called it Kār-Tukultī-Ninurta,"[4] which literally translated means "Port of Tukulti-Ninurta." Similarly, the Assyrian King Sargon II (ca. 721–705 BC) conquered the Median city of Harhar and renamed it "Kar-Sharrukin" which, literally translated, means "port of Sargon."[5] Sargon also named his newly built capital after himself, boasting in an inscription, "Sargon, king of the universe, king of Assyria, has built a city, Dur-Sharrukin he has called its name."[6] Dur-Sharrukin literally is translated "Fortress of Sargon."[7] Cities named after the king were often cult-centers and as such their citizens often "enjoyed such privileges as exemption from taxation, military duty, or corevee labor."[8] Such privileges were due to their being "temple cities," which were supposed to be "free of oppression and of obligations toward the government, since it was to be governed by the gods alone."[9] Thus, in an ancient Near Eastern context, David's choice to move the ark of the covenant into his new city in the next chapter (2 Sam 6) and then declare his intentions to build Yahweh a temple (2 Sam 7) follow logically after his calling the city by his own name here (2 Sam 5:9).

1. Roth, *Law Collections*, 77 §Prologue to Laws of Hammurabi; "The Laws of Hammurabi," trans. Martha T. Roth, *COS* 2.131:335–53.

2. Roth, *Law Collections*, 80 §Prologue to Laws of Hammurabi.

3. Ibid., 10.

4. Grayson, *Assyrian Rulers of the Third and Second*, 270, A.0.78.22:39–51.

5. Luckenbill, *ARAB* 2.16§11.

6. Ibid., 2.68§131.

7. Elswhere Sargon refers to it as "my city." Luckenbill, *ARAB* 2.13§29.

8. Long, *2 Samuel*, 435.

9. Moshe Weinfeld, *Social Justice in Ancient Israel and in the Ancient Near East* (Minneapolis: Fortress, 1995), 101.

EXPLAIN the Story

At long last, David is crowned king over all Israel, as all the tribes come to him in Hebron and anoint him king. David's first move as Israel's king is to conquer Jerusalem and make it his new capital. In Jerusalem, David expands his harem and takes more wives and concubines who bear him many children, further securing his dynasty but countermanding God's law that an Israelite king not take many wives. In response to the news of David's kingship, the Philistines attack Israel, but David defeats them. When the Philistines attack a second time, David receives specific direction from Yahweh not to attack head-on but to go behind the enemy and wait until he hears the sound of God's army marching ahead of him. David obeys the word of the LORD and does what the anointed king was meant to do (1 Sam 9:16) and what Saul was unable to do; he defeats the Philistines.

David Crowned King of All Israel (5:1–5)

After the long wait and precarious journey to this moment, David is finally crowned king by "all the elders of Israel" (2 Sam 5:3). In response, David makes a covenant with the people, who reciprocate by anointing him king. Covenants between a king and his people were common in the ancient Near East. Most commonly such a covenant expressed some mutual obligations. The subjects were to show loyalty and obedience to the sovereign, while the king committed to a just rule and protection. This covenant united the two states of Judah and Israel under David.

We are now told that David was thirty years old when he became king of Judah in Hebron. In ancient Israel, thirty is the age where a man is thought to enter his prime, and it was the minimum age for an Israelite to be qualified to work in the tabernacle (Num 4:3). (Interestingly, Luke 3:23 tells us that Jesus was thirty when he began his public ministry.) Together with his years as Judah's king, David reigned for forty years.

David Takes Jerusalem (5:6–16)

David's first move as king of Israel is to establish a new capital city for the unified kingdom. After all, the southern city of Hebron would likely not be deemed suitable by the northerners, making a neutral location—a city that was not part of Judah or northern Israel—ideal. David attacks the Jebusites in their "fortress of Zion." "Zion" is the name for the hill on the southeastern part of the city of Jerusalem but is often used as a synonym for Jerusalem itself. The Jebusites were a holdout Canaanite tribe who were never defeated by Israel in the conquest (cf. Josh 15:63; Judg

1:21).[10] Just as he had done while living in Philistia (1 Sam 27:8–11), David is finishing up the conquest.

The Jebusites trash talk David and his men, warning them that even their weakest citizens—the blind and the lame—could ward off their attack (v. 6). Likely, this Jebusite confidence stemmed from the fact that Jerusalem, due to its elevation, was well positioned from a defensive standpoint. David was undeterred and even threw their taunt back at them, sarcastically calling all who lived in Jerusalem "the blind and the lame" (5:8). The verbal jousting between David and the Jebusites actually gave birth to a proverbial saying that "the blind and the lame will not enter the palace" (5:8). It is not clear exactly what this saying meant. Some have suggested that it refers not to the "palace" but the "temple" (the Hebrew here is the word for "house" and can refer to either meaning), since disabled people were not allowed to serve in the temple (e.g., Lev 21:18). There was no temple at the time, however, so this interpretation seems unlikely.

David clearly had insider knowledge of how to enter the city as he tells his men that in order to take the city, they will have to "use the water shaft" (5:8)—probably a water tunnel whereby they could access the city.[11] How did David know this? While the text does not explicitly tell us, earlier in the story we were told that after killing Goliath, David had taken Goliath's severed head to Jerusalem (1 Sam 17:54). Perhaps this trophy of war was offered to the inhabitants of Jerusalem (who likely also counted the Philistines an enemy) as a way to gain a measure of trust and entry into the city. Regardless of how David knew about Jerusalem's weaknesses, he and his men manage to penetrate the defenses and capture "the fortress of Zion" (5:7).

After conquering the city, David makes it his new capital, residing there and undertaking building projects to enhance the city. We are further told that he was growing more and more powerful because the "LORD God Almighty," more literally "Yahweh of hosts/armies," was with him (v. 10). It is significant that God is here referred to by his old battle name referencing his armies. Before this chapter is over, there will be more references to Yahweh's army with the sound of the marching of God's army in the poplar trees (v. 24).

David's new capital made news in the region, leading the Tyrian king, Hiram, to send craftsmen and materials to build a palace for David. At this David realized that Yahweh had indeed established his kingdom. Significantly,

---

10. Judges 1:8 says that "The men of Judah attacked Jerusalem also and took it. They put the city to the sword and set it on fire," but in light of Judg 1:21 it is evident they did not permanently capture the city.

11. It is also possible that the reference to the water meant that David took control of the city's water supply and forced their surrender, perhaps through a siege.

it says God did this "for the sake of his people Israel" (5:12). This may point to the fact that the kingship was to be for the benefit of Israel, not the reverse. This is counter to how things usually were, where the king benefited from the arrangement more than the people.

In Jerusalem, David expands his harem, taking not only more wives but concubines as well. These women bear David many more children. As noted last chapter, in the ancient world a king with many sons has the best chance to establish a long-lasting dynasty, and the larger the number of progeny, the greater a king's stability. In this regard, David's many offspring bode well for an enduring dynasty. It is important to note, however, that David already had seven wives at this point and has now added many more, along with concubines. While at the beginning of the chapter we saw David lining up well with the Mosaic legislation for the king in Deuteronomy, with his being a native Israelite (v. 1; Deut 17:15b) and chosen by God (v. 2; Deut 17:15a), now David violates the prohibition on Israelite kings taking "many wives" (Deut 17:17). Ironically, just after David has realized that Yahweh had established his kingship and kingdom, rather than trust in Yahweh's provision and adhering to God's law for an Israelite king, David proceeds to establish his kingship the pagan way, by multiplying his harem and male heirs.

War with the Philistines (5:17–25)

When the Philistines hear that David was now king over Israel, their enemy, they are angered. While David was king in Hebron, it appears the Philistines were satisfied with the situation, since David's kingdom was at war with their enemy, Israel. Now that David has been crowned king of their archenemy Israel, however, the Philistines count David as their enemy. The personal nature of the affront can be seen in their going out "in full force" not to attack Israel but to *search* for David (v. 17). It was in the Philistines' best interests to stop the unification of Israel as soon as possible, and taking out their new king would be the best way to accomplish this.

The Philistine manhunt reaches the Rephaim Valley, southwest of Jerusalem—a bold move attacking so close to the new capital. In response, David inquires of Yahweh for direction. Again, we see the character of David who always relies on the Lord. Having received divine backing and assurances, David defeats the enemy at Baal Perazim and ascribed his victory to God "*breaking* out" against his enemies "as waters *break* out" (v. 20). The Hebrew word for "breaking out" is *paraz* and the Hebrew word for the waters "*break* out" is *perez*, coming from the same root as *paraz*. Thus, the name *Peraz*im is a pun on the words.

Significantly, the narrator notes that, in the battle, the Philistines are forced to abandon their idols and that David and his men capture them (v. 21). This is something like a reversal of the situation in previous wars, especially the infamous battle with the Philistines in 1 Samuel 4:1–11 when Israel suffered a terrible defeat and lost the ark of the covenant to their enemy.

When the Philistines attack again, David again inquires of the Lord, but this time instead of simply being given the go-ahead to attack, God gives him a specific battle strategy. Rather than confront the enemy head-on, God tells David to circle behind them and attack the Philistines in front of the poplar trees. Furthermore, they are to wait until they hear the sound of marching, which will be a sign that God had gone ahead to strike the Philistines. The sound of marching is the sound of God's "hosts/armies" who are fighting on behalf of Israel. This miraculous sound of God's heavenly army is similar to the story in 2 Kings 6:17 when God reveals the presence of his heavenly army to Elisha's servant by opening "his eyes" to see "the hills full of horses and chariots of fire all around Elisha." Once God's armies have marched into battle, David attacks, and he defeats the Philistines. David proves himself Israel's legitimate king, doing what Saul was unable to do and doing what the Israelite king was meant to do (1 Sam 9:16)—he rescues Israel from the perennial threat of the Philistines.

LIVE the Story

The Anointed Shepherd

The reference to the responsibility of David, the anointed one (Hebrew *mashiah*), to "shepherd" Israel becomes a theologically significant theme in Scripture. David is actually the only Israelite king referred to as a shepherd in the historical books. God, however, is frequently identified as our shepherd (e.g., Gen 48:15; 49:24; Pss 23:1; 80:1). To get the full significance of the metaphor of the shepherd, we must realize that in ancient times sheep were not simply left out in a fenced field by themselves like they often are today. Instead, the animals were completely dependent on the shepherd. Shepherds protected the flock from predators. Shepherds led their sheep and guided them to find places to graze and water. The life of a shepherd was demanding, as the sheep required constant care and protection (Gen 31:38–40).

The symbolic meaning of a shepherd draws on these aspects of ancient shepherding. Just as sheep were utterly dependent on shepherds, so God's people desperately need a shepherd. God himself is often pictured in this role. He guides his flock, even carrying lambs (Isa 40:11) and seeking out lost ones (Ezek 34:16). David is presented as the ideal shepherd king in the psalms. Psalm 78:70–72 reads:

> He chose David his servant
>   and took him from the sheep pens;
> from tending the sheep he brought him
>   to be the shepherd of his people Jacob,
>   of Israel his inheritance.
> And David shepherded them with integrity of heart;
>   with skillful hands he led them.

Metaphorically, the role of shepherd was to lead the people and care for them (cf. Ezek 34:2–6). Most times in the Old Testament, the image of shepherd is used to critique or denounce leaders who were *not* being good shepherds of God's people (Ezek 34; Jer 25:34–36; Zech 10:2–3; 11:15–17). A good shepherd existed for the good of the sheep, not the other way around. Bad shepherds instead took advantage of the sheep, thinking they were there for their own benefit.[12] Of course, historically, even David failed in his role as Israel's shepherd. In 2 Samuel 12 the prophet Nathan will employ the shepherd metaphor to condemn David for his evil actions concerning Uriah and Bathsheba.

The lack of good shepherds in Israel led to expectations that God would provide a king from David's line who *will* be a good shepherd. As Ezekiel prophesies, "My servant David will be king over them, and they will all have one shepherd. They will follow my laws and be careful to keep my decrees" (Ezek 37:24). The New Testament explicitly presents Jesus as the fulfilment of these Old Testament promises (Matt 2:6). Jesus calls himself the "good shepherd" (John 10:1–18) and speaks of himself as a shepherd in his parables (Luke 15:4–7). While David took his life into his hands in protecting his flock (1 Sam 17:34–35), Jesus surpasses this level of commitment, stating that he will even give his life for his sheep (John 10:11). Hebrews 13:20 refers to Jesus as "the great Shepherd of the sheep," and 1 Peter 2:25 calls him "the Shepherd and Overseer of your souls."

The metaphor of Christ as our shepherd reminds us of our utter dependence upon him. Just as sheep would not last long without a shepherd, we are lost without Jesus. When we think we are self-sufficient and can chart our own course on our own, we need to remember that Christ is our guide. Without him, we are sheep that have lost their way (Isa 53:6). Yet when we find ourselves lost and realize we cannot do it on our own, remembering Christ's role as our shepherd is reason for hope and faith.

Just as the metaphor in the Old Testament was applied to both God and Israelite leaders, so the New Testament applies it both to Christ and Christian leaders. In a post-resurrection appearance, Jesus commands Peter to "feed my

---

12. Brueggemann, *First and Second Samuel*, 238.

sheep" (John 21:15–17). Paul urges the Ephesian elders to "keep watch over yourselves and all the flock of which the Holy Spirit has made you overseers. Be shepherds of the church of God" (Acts 20:28). Peter urges pastors and ministers to be "examples to the flock," not for selfish or monetary reasons but in service to God (1 Pet 5:3–4).

The metaphor of shepherding for Christian ministry has been called the "pivotal analogy" for Christian leadership in the Bible.[13] Remembering a Christian minister's role as shepherd will prevent a view of the ministry as a professional occupation more analogous to running a business than being a spiritual overseer in God's church. With Jesus as role model, we will remember that a minister is there to serve the flock, not the other way around. Christian leaders serve as an example (1 Pet 5:3). Of course, no leader will fulfill the role perfectly, so we remember Christ is the chief shepherd (1 Pet 5:4), and he makes up for our weaknesses. But we are called to be Christ-like in our ministry, relying on the strength he provides.

Zion

In this chapter, Zion appears for the first time in the Bible. Just as David becomes a symbol for ideal kingship and a coming ideal Anointed One, Zion is another theme that carries tremendous theological significance. As mentioned above, Zion is often used as a synonym for the city of Jerusalem and it literally refers to the historical city of Jerusalem. Symbolically, however, as the place where the temple was located, it signifies God's dwelling place (Pss 9:11; 76:2; 132:13). As the capital of Israel, Zion also signifies God's people (Pss 48:11; 97:8; 99:2)—whether a people under judgment (Isa 49:14) or a remnant preserved by God (Ps 102:13; Isa 1:8; 4:2–6). As the home of Israel's king (Ps 2:6), it signifies Davidic kingship and eventually the Messiah (Isa 11:1–16). As the center of God's rule (Ps 110:2), Zion symbolizes the eschatological renewal of the world (Isa 2:2–4) and all creation (Isa 65:25). In contrast to Mount Sinai, Zion symbolizes the new covenant inaugurated by Jesus Christ (Heb 12:22–23).

As David captured historical Zion, the place of the ancient temple, so the Son of David has rescued theological Zion, the church, and has made it his temple (1 Cor 3:16; 6:19; 2 Cor 6:16; Eph 2:21). As God dwelt in Zion, he now dwells in us, his people. As Paul writes, the church is "built on the foundation of the apostles and prophets, with Christ Jesus himself as the chief cornerstone. In him the whole building is joined together and rises to become a holy temple in the Lord. And in him you too are being built together to become a dwelling in which God lives by his Spirit" (Eph 2:20–22).

---

13. Thomas C. Oden, *Pastoral Theology: Essentials of Ministry* (New York: Harper & Row, 1983), 49.

LISTEN to the Story

¹David again brought together all the able young men of Israel—thirty thousand. ²He and all his men went to Baalah in Judah to bring up from there the ark of God, which is called by the Name, the name of the LORD Almighty, who is enthroned between the cherubim on the ark. ³They set the ark of God on a new cart and brought it from the house of Abinadab, which was on the hill. Uzzah and Ahio, sons of Abinadab, were guiding the new cart ⁴with the ark of God on it, and Ahio was walking in front of it. ⁵David and all Israel were celebrating with all their might before the LORD, with castanets, harps, lyres, timbrels, sistrums and cymbals.

⁶When they came to the threshing floor of Nakon, Uzzah reached out and took hold of the ark of God, because the oxen stumbled. ⁷The LORD's anger burned against Uzzah because of his irreverent act; therefore God struck him down, and he died there beside the ark of God.

⁸Then David was angry because the LORD's wrath had broken out against Uzzah, and to this day that place is called Perez Uzzah.

⁹David was afraid of the LORD that day and said, "How can the ark of the LORD ever come to me?" ¹⁰He was not willing to take the ark of the LORD to be with him in the City of David. Instead, he took it to the house of Obed-Edom the Gittite. ¹¹The ark of the LORD remained in the house of Obed-Edom the Gittite for three months, and the LORD blessed him and his entire household.

¹²Now King David was told, "The LORD has blessed the household of Obed-Edom and everything he has, because of the ark of God." So David went to bring up the ark of God from the house of Obed-Edom to the City of David with rejoicing. ¹³When those who were carrying the ark of the LORD had taken six steps, he sacrificed a bull and a fattened calf. ¹⁴Wearing a linen ephod, David was dancing before the LORD with all his might, ¹⁵while he and all Israel were bringing up the ark of the LORD with shouts and the sound of trumpets.

¹⁶As the ark of the LORD was entering the City of David, Michal daughter of Saul watched from a window. And when she saw King David leaping and dancing before the LORD, she despised him in her heart.

¹⁷They brought the ark of the LORD and set it in its place inside the tent that David had pitched for it, and David sacrificed burnt offerings and fellowship offerings before the LORD. ¹⁸After he had finished sacrificing the burnt offerings and fellowship offerings, he blessed the people in the name of the LORD Almighty. ¹⁹Then he gave a loaf of bread, a cake of dates and a cake of raisins to each person in the whole crowd of Israelites, both men and women. And all the people went to their homes.

²⁰When David returned home to bless his household, Michal daughter of Saul came out to meet him and said, "How the king of Israel has distinguished himself today, going around half-naked in full view of the slave girls of his servants as any vulgar fellow would!"

²¹David said to Michal, "It was before the LORD, who chose me rather than your father or anyone from his house when he appointed me ruler over the LORD's people Israel—I will celebrate before the LORD. ²²I will become even more undignified than this, and I will be humiliated in my own eyes. But by these slave girls you spoke of, I will be held in honor."

²³And Michal daughter of Saul had no children to the day of her death.

Listen to the Text in the Story: Exodus 34: 1–9; Joshua 15:9; 1 Samuel 4–7; 18:20–29; Inscriptions of Ashurnasirpal II, Sargon II, and Sennacherib

The last time we saw the ark of the covenant, it was left in Keriath-Jearim (1 Sam 7:1), having been sent there by the people of Beth Shemesh after seventy people were struck dead for looking into it. Here the text notes that the ark is in Baalah of Judah, which appears to be another name for Keriath-Jearim (cf. Josh 15:9; 1 Chr 13:6). Thus, the ark was still resting in the place the story left it in 1 Samuel 7. Now, many years later, David attempts to bring the ark into his new royal city.

To understand the importance of this, the significance of the ark in ancient Israel must be understood. The ark represented God's presence in Israel, and the story so far has spent considerable time chronicling the loss (1 Sam 4–5) and recovery (1 Sam 6–7) of the ark. These stories reveal the anxiety concerning God's presence, or lack thereof, in ancient Israel. If David is successful in bringing the ark to Jerusalem, it would alleviate such anxiety and lead Israel to feel confirmed that Yahweh really is with David. Furthermore, in the ancient world one of the key moments for a king establishing his legitimacy was to build a temple to the patron deity.[1] Of course, this is exactly what David will attempt to do in the next chapter (cf. 2 Sam 7:2), but first he would need the religious item to be housed in the temple. While in pagan cultures temples housed idols, in Israel, with idols forbidden, the ark of the covenant was the key item for a temple.

Some ancient Near Eastern examples are helpful in understanding the story of the ark's journey to Jerusalem in this chapter. Several such texts describe ceremonies wherein a national god is introduced to a new royal city. Along with an invitation to the gods/goddesses to come into the city, sacrifices were offered and a feast held with a large group of citizens participating in the celebration. For example, after constructing his royal city, Assyrian King Ashurnasirpal II (883–859 BC) invited his gods (Ashur and others) to reside there and established celebratory festivals, offering sacrifices and hosting a massive banquet with guests from all over his land. Ashurnasirpal writes, "For ten days I gave them food, I gave them drink . . . (So) did I honor them (and) send them back to their lands in peace and joy."[2]

Similarly, inscriptions from the Assyrian King Sargon II (721–705 BC) narrate how Sargon built his new city, Dur Sharrukin ("Fortress of Sargon"), then invited his gods there and offered sacrifices "amid jubilation and feasting" with many attendees as the gods were brought into the city.[3] Sargon also established "a feast of music" at the time.[4] Inscriptions from another Assyrian King, Sennacherib (704–681 BC), also include the invitation of gods to his new royal city, offering sacrifices, and holding a feast for the populace. Similar to Sargon's celebration, Sennacherib boasts, "I drenched the foreheads of the people of my land with wine, with mead I sprinkled their hearts."[5]

These texts show significant congruence between Israelite and Assyrian cultures in this regard and suggest we should understand 2 Samuel 6:1–19 similarly as narrating David's introduction of Yahweh, as represented in the ark of the covenant, to his new royal city.[6] Like in the Assyrian texts, the ark is brought to the new royal city with jubilation and celebration (2 Sam 6:12), with sacrifices offered (2 Sam 6:13, 17), and a wide swath of the populace participating and being given a generous amount of celebratory sustenance (2 Sam 6:19).

---

1. Cf. Victor Hurowitz, *I Have Built You an Exalted House: Temple Building in the Bible in Light of Mesopotamian and Northwest Semitic Writings*, JSOTSup 115 (Sheffield: JSOT Press, 1992), 171–223.

2. Grayson, *Assyrian Royal Inscriptions* (Wiesbaden: Otto Harrassowitz, 1976) §§A.O. 30:151–54.

3. Luckenbill, *ARAB* 2.37–39 §§ 72, 73, 74.

4. Ibid., 2.39 §§ 74.

5. Ibid., 2.178 §416.

6. McCarter, *II Samuel*, 180.

⚡ EXPLAIN the Story

Having conquered Jerusalem, David now moves to bring the ark to the nation's new capital. Despite the fervent celebration, the attempt to bring the ark to Jerusalem is a failure, as a man named Uzzah is struck by God for grabbing hold of the ark when the oxen pulling its cart stumbled. This incident angers David, and he becomes afraid to bring the ark to Jerusalem. Instead, he leaves it with a Gittite named Obed-Edom, whose household ends up blessed by its presence. At news of this blessing, David again attempts to bring the ark to Jerusalem, this time successfully bringing the ark to his capital and placing it inside a tent there. As the ark was brought in, David danced fervently in worship before God. When David came home, however, his first wife, Michal, expressed her displeasure at his dancing in the presence of the servant girls. David's response reminds Michal that he was chosen to lead Israel—not her father or her family—and that he did not care if he looked foolish in his worship. He danced for God, not other people. The chapter ends sadly noting that Michal never did have children.

The First Attempt to Bring the Ark to Jerusalem (6:1–11)

Having established his new capital city, David proceeds to bring up the ark and thereby symbolically ask God to reside in the city. David did not take the task lightly. He gathers thirty thousand of the best men in Israel to aid in the task. They set the ark on a "new cart," and the massive throng celebrated in musical worship before God. The use of a "new cart" ironically follows the practice of the Philistines in 1 Samuel 6:7, who also set the ark on a "new cart" in order to send it back to Israel. Though this showed an attempt to use the best they had to transport the ark, this method of transport was contrary to Mosaic law, which legislated that the ark be carried, not transported on a cart (Exod 25:12–14; 37:5; Num 4:15, 19; 7:9). Two sons of Abinadab (the man who had housed the ark all these years; cf. 1 Sam 7:1) are assigned to the cart, one in front (Ahio) and the other (Uzzah) guiding the cart. Being Abinadab's sons they were not newcomers to the ark but likely had experience being around it. Nevertheless, when the oxen pulling the cart stumbles, Uzzah reaches out to take hold of the ark and is struck dead by Yahweh for his "irreverent act" (6:7). So memorable was this event that the place was named Perez Uzzah after the tragedy. In Hebrew *perez* means "to break out" or "outburst" so that the name Perez Uzzah means "outburst [on] Uzzah."

Modern readers are not the only ones baffled by this divine action. David himself is both angered and frightened by it. It would seem that Uzzah's transgression was not respecting the holiness of the ark and, more importantly, disprespecting Yahweh who made it sacrosanct. It was well known that the ark was dangerous. After all, the reason the ark came to Baalah was the death of seventy men who had violated its sanctity at Beth Shemesh (1 Sam 6:19). Given that Uzzah must have had some experience with the ark and was tasked with guiding the cart, he would have been aware of normal precautions that should be taken (cf. Num 4:15).[7]

At this, David changes his plans and refuses to take the ark to Jerusalem but instead leaves it with a foreigner, Obed-Edom, the Gittite. Perhaps no Israelites wanted to take the ark after this terrible incident, so it was left with a Philistine.

The Second Attempt to Bring the Ark to Jerusalem (6:12–19)

When David hears that the house of Obed-Edom was blessed by the ark's presence, David decides to give it another shot. This time, rather than transporting the ark on a cart, it is carried by people, which is in alignment with Mosaic law (e.g., Num 7:9), though it is not said whether the carriers were Levites. What is more, in addition to again accompanying the ark with fervent worship, David offers sacrifices near the start of the voyage (v. 13). Furthermore, David dances "with all his might" before God (v. 14) and all the Israelites shout (v. 15). Dancing in worship is encouraged in the psalms as a way of expressing the worshiper's joy (Pss 149:3; 150:4). David also wears a linen ephod, the priestly garb that Samuel wore in Shiloh as a young priest (1 Sam 2:18). The garment normally would cover its wearer with sufficient modesty, though perhaps David's exuberant dancing caused some exposure.[8] The main offense to Michal may not have been actual exposed skin as much as his dance being an undignified action for a king.

As the ark approached Jerusalem, David's first wife, Michal, is watching the procession from indoors. We are not told why she was not outside or participating in the celebration, but her negative attitude may answer that question for us. Significantly, in this chapter she is consistently referred to as "daughter of Saul" (vv. 16, 20, 23) rather than David's wife, which could suggest she was not "behaving as David's wife . . . but as his opponent," as did her father.[9] Michal "despises" David when she sees him dancing. What is interesting is that the narrator says she despises David for dancing and leaping (v. 16). It says nothing there of jealousy because of any female audience (which she later notes as "slave girls" in v. 20) nor of any exposure of his body.

When the ark is finally placed into the tent David had prepared for it,

---

7. Hertzberg, *1 and 2 Samuel*, 279.

8. Anderson, *2 Samuel*, 105.

9. David J. A. Clines, "X, X Ben Y, Ben Y: Personal Names in Hebrew Narrative Style," *VT* 22 (1972): 272; Alter, *The David Story*, 228.

there is a huge celebration, with David sacrificing many burnt offerings to God and all eating together, thanks to David's generous provision of food for the occasion. Given that the ark had tremendous religious meaning for both Judah and northern Israel, David's successful transport of the ark to his new capital of Jerusalem further binds all the tribes to David and his united kingdom.[10] Not only is Jerusalem the political center of the nation, it is now the religious center as well.

Michal's Insult (6:20–23)

On top of the world, David returns to his house to bless his family, but Michal's greeting puts a huge damper on the mood. Her words drip with sarcasm as she tells her husband that he has made a fool of himself. In her view, David has disrobed himself like a "vulgar" person would, and this in front of "the slave girls of his servants" (v. 20). As noted above, when the narrator told us how Michal despised David, it was for his dancing and leaping, making no mention of his exposing himself. This suggests the issue is not so much Michal's jealousy of other women seeing the king exposed as that she despised him for looking so foolish before his subjects. In Michal's proud view, David's exuberant dancing before God was not befitting a king.

David is quick to retort that Michal is in no place to judge what befits a king. Her royal family was rejected by God, and he was chosen to be king instead. As king, he emphasizes that he will "celebrate before the LORD" (v. 21). While Saul may not have freely worshiped the LORD, David intends to do so. More than this, he will worship with even more abandon—regardless of how foolish he may look.

The chapter ends noting that Michal never did have children. There is no explanation given for this sad situation. Did David not have sexual relations with her because of this incident? Did Michal refuse David sexual access because of this? The reader may suspect that God may have been involved (was her barrenness the final step in the rejection of Saul's house?). But either way, sadly, Michal never knew the joy of motherhood.

LIVE the Story

A God Who is Not Safe but Good

The death of Uzzah for touching the ark is a disturbing text for many readers. The fact that he dies instantly for his transgression does not sit well with an

---

10. Anderson, *2 Samuel*, 108.

understanding of God as loving. I would suggest that our problem with the story is not so much the story's problem but our own. Many of our modern Christian worship songs talk of Jesus as a lover, best buddy, or about touching and seeing God. In the Bible, however, this was not the attitude of biblical characters. They understood God's holiness better. When an angel appeared to people in the Bible, most thought they were going to die (Exod 33:20; Judg 13:22; Isa 6:5) because the holy one had seen them and they were sinners. God is not safe. We often, like Uzzah, presume too much and fail to take his holiness seriously.

In the classic children's novel *The Lion, the Witch, and the Wardrobe* by C. S. Lewis, Aslan the lion is an allegory for God. The children who get to know him love him dearly but also are afraid of him. When Lucy is talking with Mr. Beaver about Aslan, she asks him whether Aslan is safe, to which Mr. Beaver replies:

> "Safe?" said Mr. Beaver. "Don't you hear what Mrs. Beaver tells you? Who said anything about safe? 'Course he isn't safe. But he's good. He's the King, I tell you."[11]

Modern Christians often so emphasize God's love and forgiveness that we forget that God is not safe. The Bible says that "the fear of the LORD" is the beginning of both wisdom (Prov 9:10; Ps 11:10) and knowledge (Prov 1:7). Yet, on the other hand, God is good. Sometimes our thinking about God's wrath can lead us to forget this fact. God's holy wrath against sin can lead some to have overwhelming guilt or excessive fear of God to the point where they actually give up their faith rather than live in constant fear and guilt. However, the portrait of God as wrathful against sin must be balanced with the reality of God's patience and forgiveness. While God's anger is real, he is patient, forgiving, and loving. In the Gospels, we see God's love emphasized in sending Jesus to save the world. John 3:16 famously states that "God so loved the world that he gave his one and only Son, that whoever believes in him shall not perish but have eternal life."

Love is what most characterizes God in the Old Testament as well. When God revealed his character to Moses on Sinai he placed God's love and mercy up front saying, "The LORD, the LORD, the compassionate and gracious God, slow to anger, abounding in love and faithfulness" (Exod 34:6). These characteristics are repeated many times throughout the Old Testament (Num 14:18; Neh 9:17; Pss 86:15; 103:8; 145:8; Jonah 4:2; Nah 1:3). For example, Joel 2:13 reads: "Return to the LORD your God, for he is gracious

---

11. C. S. Lewis, *The Lion, the Witch and the Wardrobe* (New York: Macmillan, 1950), 77.

and compassionate, slow to anger and abounding in love, and he relents from sending calamity." Psalm 103:12 similarly rejoices that "as far as the east is from the west, so far has he removed our transgressions from us." God forgives sin. God relents from punishing. Though his anger is real, "his anger lasts only a moment, but his favor lasts a lifetime" (Ps 30:5). The Bible emphasizes that God is forgiving. His mercy outlasts his anger.

On the other hand, the reality of God's anger at sin is an indispensible part of our theology. Without it, we cannot make sense of Christ's death on a cross. The main problem modern Christians have with an angry God is that we do not balance this picture of God with God's patience, forgiveness, and comfort. As Matt Schlimm writes:

> [Christians] too often ignore God's wrath or ignore God's comfort. The Bible we have, however, intertwines the two. . . . The Old Testament is acutely aware of how bad decisions have terrible consequences. It's also aware that God's love persists before, during, and after those consequences.[12]

The story of Uzzah's death is difficult for many modern Christians. But, as noted above, Uzzah's actions did not respect God's holiness; he was aware of the dangerous nature of the ark and should have known better. Yet, God's reaction still seems harsh as Uzzah dies immediately for his transgression. Similarly, in the New Testament Ananias and Sapphira die immediately for their sin (Acts 5:1–11). These stories bother us because most of the time people do not die instantly for their sin, and it seems unfair. However, we must realize that the reason the vast majority of people do not die instantly for their transgression is due to God's patience and mercy. God is gracious and slow to anger. But his anger is real. God's delay in punishments should remind us of God's patience, but instead it often leads us to forget that we must take sin seriously. God's judgment quickly fell on Uzzah. By God's mercy, it usually does not fall on us so quickly. Uzzah's story reminds us that God is not safe; but David's story (e.g., 2 Sam 11–12) and the story of the later Son of David reminds us that God is merciful—so merciful that Jesus "bore our sins in his body on the cross, so that we might die to sins and live for righteousness" (1 Pet 2:24).

Humility in Worship

In Michal's despising of David for his dancing and David's defense of his worship, we see an important theological lesson about corporate worship. Michal ridiculed David for his exuberant dancing. In her view, David had made a fool

---

12. Matthew Richard Schlimm, *This Strange and Sacred Scripture: Wrestling with the Old Testament and Its Oddities* (Grand Rapids: Baker Academic, 2015), 195.

of himself. He did not present as a dignified king. Conversely, David didn't care that people may have viewed him as foolish. David did not put on a show for other people. He danced for God. David was not concerned with looking dignified. He was concerned with worshiping God.

In corporate worship it is easy to become insecure or feel conspicuous about the way we worship. When we sing in church, some of us are not exactly the best singers and we may feel a bit uncomfortable singing in the presence of others. Or perhaps you might lift your hands in worship and consequently feel that someone would notice and think you look rather silly. In this chapter, David was explicitly mocked for his energetic worship, but instead of being embarrassed he committed himself to worship even if he looked even "more undignified" in the future (v. 22). Worship is not about us. We must set aside our pride and focus not on ourselves but on God. David admits his worship might cause him to "be humiliated" even in his own eyes. But worship isn't about saving face or glorifying oneself. Worship is about glorifying and praising God.

On the other hand, worship is not for show. It is not to impress others. In some church traditions some might think they could impress fellow church-goers by excessive enthusiasm or gesturing in worship. Sometimes there is a temptation to look more spiritual than others through the way one participates in corporate worship. This story would speak to that situation as well. It was Michal who thought David was out to impress the "slave girls." Michal did not really understand what was going on. She thought David's worship was for show. As David answered Michal, it was not for other people that he worshiped; he was dancing "before the LORD" (v. 21). This story reminds us that in worship God is the audience, not other people who might be present. Both attempts to save face by excessively restraining oneself in worship or attempts to impress others by showing unbridled and excessive enthusiasm are missing the point. Neither belong in true worship. We are to forget about ourselves and our own self-importance, humble ourselves, and focus on the only One who is worthy of worship.

LISTEN to the Story

¹After the king was settled in his palace and the Lᴏʀᴅ had given him rest from all his enemies around him, ²he said to Nathan the prophet, "Here I am, living in a house of cedar, while the ark of God remains in a tent."

³Nathan replied to the king, "Whatever you have in mind, go ahead and do it, for the Lᴏʀᴅ is with you."

⁴But that night the word of the Lᴏʀᴅ came to Nathan, saying:

⁵"Go and tell my servant David, 'This is what the Lᴏʀᴅ says: Are you the one to build me a house to dwell in? ⁶I have not dwelt in a house from the day I brought the Israelites up out of Egypt to this day. I have been moving from place to place with a tent as my dwelling. ⁷Wherever I have moved with all the Israelites, did I ever say to any of their rulers whom I commanded to shepherd my people Israel, "Why have you not built me a house of cedar?"'

⁸"Now then, tell my servant David, 'This is what the Lᴏʀᴅ Almighty says: I took you from the pasture, from tending the flock, and appointed you ruler over my people Israel. ⁹I have been with you wherever you have gone, and I have cut off all your enemies from before you. Now I will make your name great, like the names of the greatest men on earth. ¹⁰And I will provide a place for my people Israel and will plant them so that they can have a home of their own and no longer be disturbed. Wicked people will not oppress them anymore, as they did at the beginning ¹¹and have done ever since the time I appointed leaders over my people Israel. I will also give you rest from all your enemies.

"'The Lᴏʀᴅ declares to you that the Lᴏʀᴅ himself will establish a house for you: ¹²When your days are over and you rest with your ancestors, I will raise up your offspring to succeed you, your own flesh and blood, and I will establish his kingdom. ¹³He is the one who will build a house for my Name, and I will establish the throne of his kingdom forever. ¹⁴I will be his father, and he will be my son. When he does wrong, I will punish him with a rod wielded by men, with floggings inflicted by human hands. [15]But my love will never be taken away from him, as I took it away from Saul, whom I removed from before you. [16]Your house and your kingdom will endure forever before me; your throne will be established forever.'"

[17]Nathan reported to David all the words of this entire revelation.

[18]Then King David went in and sat before the LORD, and he said:

"Who am I, Sovereign LORD, and what is my family, that you have brought me this far? [19]And as if this were not enough in your sight, Sovereign LORD, you have also spoken about the future of the house of your servant—and this decree, Sovereign LORD, is for a mere human!

[20]"What more can David say to you? For you know your servant, Sovereign LORD. [21]For the sake of your word and according to your will, you have done this great thing and made it known to your servant.

[22]"How great you are, Sovereign LORD! There is no one like you, and there is no God but you, as we have heard with our own ears. [23]And who is like your people Israel—the one nation on earth that God went out to redeem as a people for himself, and to make a name for himself, and to perform great and awesome wonders by driving out nations and their gods from before your people, whom you redeemed from Egypt? [24]You have established your people Israel as your very own forever, and you, LORD, have become their God.

[25]"And now, LORD God, keep forever the promise you have made concerning your servant and his house. Do as you promised, [26]so that your name will be great forever. Then people will say, 'The LORD Almighty is God over Israel!' And the house of your servant David will be established in your sight.

[27]"LORD Almighty, God of Israel, you have revealed this to your servant, saying, 'I will build a house for you.' So your servant has found courage to pray this prayer to you. [28]Sovereign LORD, you are God! Your covenant is trustworthy, and you have promised these good things to your servant. [29]Now be pleased to bless the house of your servant, that it may continue forever in your sight; for you, Sovereign LORD, have spoken, and with your blessing the house of your servant will be blessed forever."

Listen to the Text in the Story: Genesis 12, 15, 17; Exodus 6:7; Leviticus 26:12; 2 Samuel 6; Gudea Temple Cylinder; Sennacherib: The Building Inscriptions; Treaty Between Hattusilis and Rameses II; Hittite Treaties; The Vassal Treaties of Esarhaddon; Legend of King Keret; Treaty between King Hattusilis III and Ulmi-Teshshup

After successfully bringing the ark to his new capital city, David then asks a prophet for permission to build a temple to Yahweh (2 Sam 7:2). That a king should seek divine approval for building a temple is congruent with ancient Near Eastern practice. For example, a text about Gudea of Lagash (ca. 2144–2124 BC), who set out to build a temple, underscores that this was not without divine approval. It reads:

> [I]n order to build the temple of Ningirsu—Gudea brought (these materials) together in his town Girsu. After the god Ninzagga had given him a (pertinent) order, they brought copper for Gudea, the temple-builder . . . after the god Ninsikila had given him a (pertinent) order, they brought great willow-logs, ebony-logs . . . to the ensi, the temple-builder.[1]

Similar to David in 2 Samuel 7, the Assyrian King Sennacherib talks of seeking divine permission to build a temple and receiving confirmation by an "oracle." He writes, "My heart moved me, the command of Shamash and Adad I sought by oracle, a favorable reply they gave me, and commanded (me) to build."[2] David, too, seeks divine permission from the prophet Nathan (in Israel prophets were the ones who delivered oracles).[3] Though he initially received permission (2 Sam 7:3), he is denied permission to build (2 Sam 7:5–7).

In place of divine permission to build a temple, God makes fantastic promises to David and his line (2 Sam 7:8–16). The language used in these amazing promises is actually the language of covenant, clearly showing that God is making a covenant with the house of David. God speaks of David's successor in covenantal terms saying, "I will be his father, and he will be my son" (2 Sam 7:14; cf. Pss 2:7–8; 89:26–27; cf. Heb 1:5). This language is akin to the classic covenant formula, "you will be my people and I will be your God" (cf. Exod 6:7; Lev 26:12; Jer 31:33; Ezek 11:20; 37:23, 27; cf. Isa 54:5–10). Furthermore, God uses covenant terminology when he states, "But my love [*hesed*] will never be taken away from him" (2 Sam 7:15). In the Old Testament, this Hebrew word for "love," *hesed*, is a standard technical term for Yahweh's steadfast love that makes covenants possible. David clearly understands God's promises as covenant, as later in the story he says that God has "made with me an everlasting covenant" (2 Sam 23:5). Other biblical texts also understand Nathan's oracle as a covenant (e.g., Pss 89:28, 34, 39; 2 Chr 13:5; 21:7). For example, Psalm 89:3–4 reads:

---

1. *ANET*, 268.
2. Luckenbill, *ARAB* 2.184–85 §436.
3. Long, *2 Samuel*, 442.

You said, "I have made a covenant with my chosen one,
    I have sworn to my servant David:
'I will establish your line forever,
    and make your throne firm through all generations.'"[4]

Covenant refers to God's act of establishing a relationship with human-kind and is the most common analogy used in the Bible for the relationship between the LORD and his people. Most covenants in the Old Testament are bilateral or conditional in nature. That is, these covenants contained obligations for both parties to the agreement. The Mosaic covenant identified Israel as God's people and Yahweh as their God and granted the people blessings dependent upon their obedience to the stipulations of the covenant (the law of Moses). Some scholars think that the Mosaic covenant was structured on ancient Near Eastern treaties (or covenants) wherein the powerful king (the suzerain) covenanted with a subject people or king (the vassal).[5] In a bilateral suzerainty covenant, the faithfulness of the vassal/weaker party to the terms of the covenant is paramount. If the vassal defaults on required duties, action would be taken against the violating party, which could result in the covenant's termination. The Mosaic covenant is often thought to be a good example of such a treaty between unequal partners. However, while ancient Near Eastern vassal treaties contained virtually no obligations for the suzerain and a multitude of stipulations for the vassal,[6] the Mosaic covenant contained obligations for both sides of the agreement as God promised many blessings attached to the covenant.

Another type of covenant found in the Bible is a promissory covenant. In a promissory covenant, the reliability of the one granting the gifts and making the promises of the covenant is paramount, and it emphasizes the certainty of the promise rather than the necessity of the faithfulness of the vassal.[7] In the Old Testament, covenants are made with Noah, Abraham, Moses, and David. Furthermore, a new covenant is prophesied by Jeremiah (Jer 31), which is fulfilled in the New Testament and the work of Jesus Christ and is for all those who put their trust in him (Heb 9:15, 27–28).

The language used in the Davidic covenant of God being a "father" and the king being a "son" is similar to language used in some ancient Near Eastern texts to describe a patron deity's relationship with a king. For example, the epic of King Keret (or Kirta) refers to the king as the "lad of El" and "son" of the

---

4. The word "covenant" also occurs later in the chapter (Pss 89:28, 34, 39).

5. E.g., *ANET*, 201–6.

6. E.g., *ANET*, 534–41.

7. Cf. P. R. Williamson, "Covenant," in *New Dictionary of Biblical Theology*, ed. Alexander and Rosner (Leicester/Downers Grove, IL: InterVarsity Press, 2000), 419–29.

god El.[8] As well, claims to divine sonship are found in throne names of Syrian kings like Barhadad (known as Ben-Hadad in the Bible; e.g., 1 Kgs 15:18), which means son of (the god) Hadad.[9]

A significant aspect of the Davidic covenant that sets it apart from the Mosaic covenant is its statement of unconditional commitment to the Davidic line as 2 Samuel 7:14–15 states: "When he does wrong, I will punish him with a rod wielded by men, with floggings inflicted by human hands. But my love will never be taken away from him." An interesting parallel to this is found in an ancient Near Eastern treaty between King Hattusilis III and Ulmi-Teshshup which states:

> My Majesty, will [not depose] your son. . . . It may not be taken away from him. If any son or grandson of yours commits an offense, then the King of Hatti shall question him. And if an offense is proven against him, then the King of Hatti shall treat him as he pleases. If he is deserving of death he shall perish, but his household and land shall not be taken from him and given to the progeny of another."[10]

In this example, even if the descendant of the king proves treasonous, the covenant remains valid. The promises to David in 2 Samuel 7, however, exceed those found in this treaty, as no mention of the death of the heir is made, only the punishment "with a rod wielded by men," and continued commitment to David's line is affirmed.

EXPLAIN the Story

After David had successfully brought the ark to the new capital of Jerusalem and a palace had been built for him, David approaches the prophet Nathan to express his desire to build a temple for Yahweh. Initially, Nathan gives his blessing on the project, but God quickly informs the prophet otherwise. David is not to build a temple, though his successor after him will do so. Instead, God makes a covenant with David promising him an enduring dynasty. In fact, despite the future disobedience of David's descendants, God will never remove his covenant. This new covenant creates a tension between the demands of the Mosaic law and the free gift of the Davidic covenant. While both covenants are affirmed in the history, it is the Davidic promises that provide ongoing hope to the original audience who was in exile.

---

8. E.g., *ANET*, 142, 147. Long, *2 Samuel*, 444.

9. See cultic inscription of Ben-Hadad in *ANET*, 655.

10. Beckman, *Hittite Diplomatic Texts*, WAW no. 18B. Quoted in Long, *2 Samuel*, 445.

Furthermore, Yahweh's gracious commitment to David will become the seed-bed not only for messianism but also for the gospel of grace proclaimed in Jesus' name in the New Testament.

The Request to Build a Temple (7:1–3)

Verse one begins by reminding the reader of the context. David "was settled in his palace" (v. 1). David had consolidated his power and been established king of Israel (2 Sam 5:1–3). He had captured and renovated Jerusalem (2 Sam 5:6–9), secured the longevity of his dynasty with the birth of multiple sons in Jerusalem (2 Sam 5:13–16), had a palace built for him (2 Sam 5:11), and successfully brought the ark to his new capital city, Jerusalem (2 Sam 6:17). Furthermore, "the LORD had given him rest from all his enemies" (v. 1), as David's military success against the Philistines showed (2 Sam 5:17–25). As far as human efforts at establishing a dynasty, only one more act could be envisioned—that of building a temple to his God. In the ancient world, this is one of the key moments for a king establishing his legitimacy. It is therefore not surprising that, having done all he can to establish himself as king, David approaches a prophet with his idea of building a temple for God (2 Sam 7:2). It seems likely that after his own grand palace was finished David couldn't help but compare it to the meager tent in which the ark was sitting. David no doubt sought to honor God by building a permanent structure for the ark. Given the context of establishing himself as king, however, the move was likely mingled with somewhat selfish motives.

The prophet Nathan (appearing for the first time in the story) initially replies in the affirmative, telling David, "Whatever you have in mind, go ahead and do it, for the LORD is with you" (2 Sam 7:3). We are frequently told that Yahweh was "with" David (1 Sam 18:12, 14, 28; 2 Sam 5:10).

Building Permit Withdrawn (7:4–17)

Despite Nathan's blessing to proceed, shortly after this (2 Sam 7:4) God informs Nathan that David is *not* to build a temple for him. God gives several reasons for withdrawing the temple building permit. First, unlike David, God has no desire for "a house of cedar" (2 Sam 7:7) or posh palace in which to reside (v. 6a). It is presumptuous to think God is in need of such a structure, as are human kings. Second, God has historically been on the move (as the ark and tent of meeting are portable shrines; v. 6b). Yahweh is a free God, and he will not be confined to one place. Third, God did not ask for David to build the temple (v. 7).

Perhaps the most important reason for denying David's request is Yahweh's concern that it be clear that God is the one who is building David's kingdom and not David's human efforts (v. 12). God's response seems to be cognizant of David's somewhat selfish motivations for building the temple (that it would further legitimize him in the eyes of the people). God emphasizes that *he* will make David's name great—not David himself (v. 9). This is stated explicitly in verse 11, where God counters David's suggestion that he build God a house by saying, "The LORD declares to you that the LORD himself will establish a house for you." God will establish David, and not David's own actions—including the construction of a temple. Here we can see God's concern that the temple does *not* become a means to a selfish, human end.

In other words, in a context of David's best efforts to establish his kingdom, Yahweh counters with an emphasis that he is in need of no such efforts. Not only does God have no need of a temple, there is actually no role for David's works to play here. David's kingdom will actually be established apart from David's own works. It will be established on the basis of God's gracious gift: a covenant of grace given to David.

God then promises that he will "raise up" one of David's sons to be his successor and that God will establish his son's kingdom (v. 12). It is this successor who will build a temple (v. 13). Furthermore, God will establish "the throne of his kingdom forever" (v. 13).

David Responds (7:18–29)

In response to the amazing covenant offered to him, David "went in and sat before the LORD" (v. 18). That is, David goes to the tent he had set up with the ark inside it. Unlike Saul, who rebelled against the prophetic word, David submits to God's word. He does not argue for the right to build the temple. Instead, he expresses gratitude and humility regarding Yahweh's gracious words and promises. He praises God for calling him and recalls his gracious calling of Israel as well. What is more, David does not just end there. He does not just passively receive God's promises either. David aggressively holds God to be true to his word. David boldly implores God to "do as you promised" (v. 25). He calls on God to "keep forever" his promise to him. David even expresses good reason for God to do so, "so that your name will be great forever" (v. 26). David attributes his courage to pray this way to God's amazing promise to build him a house (v. 27). He expresses his trust in God's covenant (v. 28) and closes with an appeal for God's blessing (v. 29).

LIVE the Story

The Davidic Covenant in Salvation History

God's covenant with David looms large on the horizon of biblical salvation history. The most striking aspect of the covenant is its unconditional or promissory nature. Unlike the Mosaic covenant, with its demands of obedience, Nathan's oracle to David involves only obligations on God's behalf toward the recipient, without any explicit reciprocal obligations. This is similar to the Abrahamic covenant which initially hinged only on Abram's willingness to leave his homeland and go to a land God would give him (Gen 12).[11] Even when God ratified his covenant with Abram in Genesis 15, the promises made are promissory, with no stipulations mentioned and Abram's only contribution being "faith" (Gen 15:6). In a later iteration or restatement of the covenant, however, Abraham is called to "walk before me faithfully and be blameless" (Gen 17:1), which suggests a contingent requirement. Further on in the same chapter an explicit stipulation for being in this covenant is given—that of circumcision (Gen 17:10–14). While many would still call the Abrahamic covenant promissory, these stipulations do contrast with the Davidic promises in 2 Samuel 7, which do not contain *any* stipulations whatsoever.[12] This lack of stipulations is most clearly seen in 2 Samuel 7:14–16, where an unequivocal commitment to David's descendent is made:

> When he does wrong, I will punish him with a rod wielded by men, with floggings inflicted by human hands. But my love will never be taken away from him, as I took it away from Saul, whom I removed from before you. (2 Sam 7:14–15)

While Davidic kings, like all Israelites, were obliged to obey Mosaic law, the Davidic covenant as proclaimed in 2 Samuel 7 was *not* contingent on obedience to Mosaic stipulations. Though David's descendants may be punished for their wickedness, they will not be rejected—*ever*. In fact, "forever" is used twice here: "Your house and your kingdom will endure *forever* before me; your throne will be established *forever*'" (2 Sam 7:16, emphasis added).

The origins of messianic hope trace to this divine adoption of (2 Sam 7:14; Heb 1:5) and eternal commitment to David. Nathan's oracle in 2 Samuel 7 was clearly not only for David but also for a future descendant of David. It explicitly mentioned David's son but clearly has in mind future "Davids" as well. Of course, the later history of Israel problematized the Davidic covenant as most of David's descendants were faithless and failed to live up to the standard of their namesake, with only a few Davidic kings being assessed

---

11. As Weinfeld asserts: "Both covenants are diametrically opposed to the Mosaic covenant, in which the people pledge loyalty to God. The Abrahamic and Davidic covenants are then a promissory type while the Mosaic covenant is an obligatory type" ("The Davidic Covenant," in *Interpreter's Dictionary of the Bible: Supplementary Volume*, ed. Keith Crim [Nashville: Abingdon, 1976], 189).

12. As McCarthy asserts, the Davidic covenant "was a kind of covenant which was simply a promise of God and was valid despite anything Israel might do" (*Old Testament Covenant: A Survey of Current Opinions* [Richmond: John Knox, 1972], 47).

positively in Israel's story—and only Hezekiah (2 Kgs 18:3–5) and Josiah (2 Kgs 22:2) are said to do so without reservation.[13] Yet despite the failure of Davidic kings, Israel continued to look to the future for a faithful "David" who would put things right. The New Testament reveals that Jesus Christ was this future Son of David (see Matt 1:1; Acts 13:22–23; Heb 1:5) to whom God has given David's throne (Luke 1:32).

Mosaic and Davidic Covenants in Tension

The promissory nature of the Davidic covenant creates a tension in the story of Israel's history between the requirements of the Mosaic law and the grace of the Davidic promises. How do the Mosaic and Davidic covenants relate? When we consider the original audience of the story, who lived in Babylonian exile, the two themes of the Mosaic and Davidic covenants would both have communicated essential messages. The focus on Mosaic law explained the audience's current situation of exile as due to their disobedience. Jerusalem and her temple were destroyed due to Judah's violations of the Mosaic covenant, *not* because of Babylonian might or the superiority of Babylonian gods. Yahweh was behind the destruction of Jerusalem and the deportation of the bulk of the population into exile (2 Kgs 24:20).

On the other hand, the focus on the promises to David offered hope for the future to the exilic audience. Through these gracious promises to David, hope could be seen beyond the loss of land and beyond the hardships of exile to a future grounded in God's good word. Davidic hope thrived in the exilic period and beyond, as the Davidic promises were the well from which prophetic proclamations of future hope sprang.

The Relationship between Grace and Works in Biblical Faith

In many ways, the Davidic promises are foundational for an evangelical faith based not on works but dependent on God's gracious promise. They are a covenant offered with no stipulations, with right standing in the covenant dependent only upon Yahweh's gracious initiative, that is, something very much like salvation through faith alone.[14] Given the tension it created with the Mosaic covenant and the obvious emphasis on good works in the telling of the history of Israel, this emphasis on grace opens up the question of the relationship between works and faith. This same tension exists not only in the story of Israel's history but more broadly in biblical theology. While the Mosaic covenant emphasized the role of good works in God's salvation, the

---

13. E.g., Asa is positively compared but fails in regard to high places. Cf. 1 Kgs 15:11–14.

14. Brueggemann (*First and Second Samuel*, 257) calls this "a powerful, clear articulation of 'justification by grace.'"

Davidic covenant emphasized God's unconditional grace. Yet, both are part of Scripture. In the New Testament, Paul vehemently asserts that salvation is through faith and not dependent on a believer's good works (Eph 2:8–9). However, the author of James is quick to point out that good works have an important role even in New Testament faith (Jas 2:23). In other words, this is a tension inherent in New Testament faith as well.

This tension can be difficult to live with. In fact, the tension may tempt us to resolve the tension by reading conditionality into 2 Samuel 7 when it is not there. Similarly, we could read into the New Testament gospel of grace a conditionality that concludes that a believer's good works are a contributing factor to their salvation. Attempts to do so are often due to concerns about the dangers inherent in speaking about a gospel of pure grace. In fact, these are similar concerns to those expressed about Paul's gospel—that it might promote antinomianism—causing the apostle to address this twice in one passage:

> What shall we say, then? Shall we go on sinning that grace may increase? (Rom 6:1)

> What then? Shall we sin because we are not under law but under grace? By no means! (Rom 6:15)

While Paul vehemently denies that the gospel would promote the idea of continuing in sin, the nature of the gospel opens itself up to such misunderstanding. Martyn Lloyd-Jones addressed this issue and wrote:

> The true preaching of the gospel of salvation by grace alone always leads to the possibility of this charge being brought against it. There is no better test as to whether a [person] is really preaching the New Testament gospel of salvation than this, that some people might misunderstand it and misinterpret it to mean that it really amounts to this, that because you are saved by grace alone it does not matter at all what you do; you can go on sinning as much as you like because it will redound all the more to the glory of grace. That is a very good test of gospel preaching. If my preaching and presentation of the gospel of salvation does not expose it to that misunderstanding, then it is not the gospel.[15]

Despite the dangers of a gospel of grace, the Davidic covenant speaks against an antinomian understanding of the gospel. Though God offered an unconditional covenant to David in 2 Samuel 7, this did not mean Israel could

---

15. David Martyn Lloyd-Jones, *Romans: Exposition of Chapter 6, the New Man* (Edinburgh: The Banner of Truth, 1974), 8–9.

sin with impunity. The conclusion to 2 Kings taught that this was not the case, as the harsh realities of exile drove home the reality of judgment.

Furthermore, the Davidic covenant would speak against an approach that would resolve the works/grace tension by emphasizing grace and thereby conclude that *all* people are therefore justified and all will be saved (universalism). The specificity of the Davidic covenant militates against such universalism. The covenant is offered *only* through David and his descendant/the Son. It is *not* a universal covenant with all of humanity. David's descendant is given a unique relationship with God that will facilitate divine blessing (Ps 72:17). Yahweh himself will be this Son's father (2 Sam 7:14; Ps 2:7), and God's unmerited, unconditional favor is offered through the Son of David and through no other. For "salvation is found in no one else, for there is no other name under heaven given to mankind by which we must be saved" (Acts 4:12).

LISTEN to the Story

¹In the course of time, David defeated the Philistines and subdued them, and he took Metheg Ammah from the control of the Philistines.

²David also defeated the Moabites. He made them lie down on the ground and measured them off with a length of cord. Every two lengths of them were put to death, and the third length was allowed to live. So the Moabites became subject to David and brought him tribute.

³Moreover, David defeated Hadadezer son of Rehob, king of Zobah, when he went to restore his monument at the Euphrates River. ⁴David captured a thousand of his chariots, seven thousand charioteers and twenty thousand foot soldiers. He hamstrung all but a hundred of the chariot horses.

⁵When the Arameans of Damascus came to help Hadadezer king of Zobah, David struck down twenty-two thousand of them. ⁶He put garrisons in the Aramean kingdom of Damascus, and the Arameans became subject to him and brought tribute. The LORD gave David victory wherever he went.

⁷David took the gold shields that belonged to the officers of Hadadezer and brought them to Jerusalem. ⁸From Tebah and Berothai, towns that belonged to Hadadezer, King David took a great quantity of bronze.

⁹When Tou king of Hamath heard that David had defeated the entire army of Hadadezer, ¹⁰he sent his son Joram to King David to greet him and congratulate him on his victory in battle over Hadadezer, who had been at war with Tou. Joram brought with him articles of silver, of gold and of bronze.

¹¹King David dedicated these articles to the LORD, as he had done with the silver and gold from all the nations he had subdued: ¹²Edom and Moab, the Ammonites and the Philistines, and Amalek. He also dedicated the plunder taken from Hadadezer son of Rehob, king of Zobah.

¹³And David became famous after he returned from striking down eighteen thousand Edomites in the Valley of Salt.

[14]He put garrisons throughout Edom, and all the Edomites became subject to David. The LORD gave David victory wherever he went.

[15]David reigned over all Israel, doing what was just and right for all his people. [16]Joab son of Zeruiah was over the army; Jehoshaphat son of Ahilud was recorder; [17]Zadok son of Ahitub and Ahimelek son of Abiathar were priests; Seraiah was secretary; [18]Benaiah son of Jehoiada was over the Kerethites and Pelethites; and David's sons were priests.

Listen to the Text in the Story: Ruth 4:21–22; 1 Samuel 8:11–18; 22:3–4; Annals of Thutmose III; Black Obelisk of Shalmaneser III

In the ancient world, when one nation defeated another nation but did not actually annex it to become part of the victor's country, the conquering king would impose payments of tribute on the subject people. Tribute enriched the victorious nation and drained the economy of the defeated people in order to prevent future revolts. Tribute is the subject of much boasting in ancient Near Eastern texts. For example, the Pharaoh Thutmose III (ca. 1479–1425 BC) boasts of his defeating Megiddo and how the chieftains of the conquered people brought tribute: "Now [all] the chieftains . . . bore their tribute of silver, gold, lapis lazuli and copper, bearing grain, wine, cattle and flocks for the army of his majesty."[1] Many examples of the Assyrians receiving tribute from conquered peoples can be found in Assyrian sources, including a depiction on the Black Obelisk of Shalmaneser showing the Israelite king, Jehu (or his messenger), bringing tribute to Shalmaneser III (ca. 858–824 BC) and bowing at the Assyrian monarch's feet.[2] The relevant portion of the text of the Black Obelisk reads: "The tribute of Jehu (*Ia-u-a*), son of Omri (*Hu-um-ri*); I received from him silver, gold, a golden *saplu*-bowl, a golden vase with pointed bottom, golden tumblers, golden buckets, tin, a staff for a king, (and) wooden *puruhtu*."[3]

EXPLAIN the Story

Following God's amazing promises to David in the previous chapter and his promise to give him rest from his enemies (7:11), this chapter chronicles

---

1. "The Annals of Thutmose," translated by J. K. Hoffmeier, *COS* 2.2.2A:12.
2. The Black Obelisk can be viewed online; http://www.britishmuseum.org/research/collection_online/collection_object_details.aspx?objectId=367012&partId=1
3. *ANET*, 281.

David's successful defense of Israel against their enemies. Unlike Saul, who constantly struggled with the Philistines, David defeats not only the Philistines but the Moabites, Zobahites, Arameans, Edomites, Ammonites, and Amalekites. David's unparalleled success is explicitly attributed to God, who gave David victory "wherever he went" (v. 14). Furthermore, David also deals with his own people fairly, exercising a just rule over Israel, with the help of his government officials. The army was there for national security, the civil servants were there for daily needs of the people, and the priests served the people in their spiritual relationship with God. David's kingdom serves as the model for all future Israelite kings.

David Defeats Israel's Enemies (8:1–4)

This chapter opens chronicling David's military success against Israel's enemies, including various details of his victories. First, we are told that David defeats the Philistines and takes Metheg Ammah from Philistine control. (The location of Metheg Ammah is uncertain and it is not attested elsewhere in Scripture.) While the text does not say that David made Philistia subject to him, it does say he subdued them. This suggests he did not take over Philistine territory per se, but he definitely ended Philistine domination over Israel, something Saul was unable to do.

Next, we are told of David's defeat of Moab. Seeing as David previously had friendly relations with the Moabites, even bringing his family there for safety when Saul was pursuing him (1 Sam 22:3–4), and that David's own grandmother (Ruth) was a Moabitess (Ruth 4:21–22), the hostilities are somewhat surprising. We are not told the context in which he defeated them. Had the Moabites attacked the new king or had David invaded Moab? Regardless, we are told in the aftermath of the battle that David killed two-thirds of the prisoners, using a measuring method otherwise unknown. Some have speculated that the reason for this mass execution may have been that it was simply too many slaves for Israel to accommodate, though it seems more likely the slaughter was meant to be a deterrent.[4] Through this Moab was not only subdued but made subject to Israel. In fact, the text explicitly says they brought David "tribute" (see discussion of "tribute" above). Moab's subjugation to Israel lasted for a long time, as 2 Kings 3:4 tells us that the Moabites continued to pay tribute of sheep and wool to Israel long afterwards.

David's defeat of Hadadezer is narrated next. Here Hadadezer is called king of Zobah, which was an Aramean city situated south of Hamath and north of Damascus. Historians, however, suggest that Hadadezer, here called the son of

---

4. Anderson, *2 Samuel*, 132.

Rehob, was associated with the city of Beth Rehob (cf. 2 Sam 10:6) and was the leader of a military coalition in southern Aram (also known as Syria).[5] By defeating Hadadezer, David in effect took over all the territories controlled by that coalition, which made this a significant step toward establishing David's empire.

The occasion of Hadadezer's defeat at David's hands was when he set out to "restore his monument at the Euphrates River" (v. 3). It is unclear whether this should be translated as "restore his monument" (NIV) or "strengthen his control [of the area]" (NLT), as the Hebrew word, literally "hand" (*yad*), may refer to a person's authority or can indicate a monument with a royal inscription (e.g., 1 Sam 15:12; 2 Sam 18:18). Regardless of how it is translated, it basically describes the same circumstances. Restoring a monument implies that the Aramean king was out to recover lost territory in the area (thus, the large army accompanying him).

As a result of the battle, David captured twenty-seven thousand prisoners along with one thousand horses. Since the Israelites up to this point in their history did not have much use for cavalry, due to the fact that most of their fighting was in mountainous areas, David saw little use for the horses they captured.[6] Therefore, David hamstrung nine hundred of the captured horses in order to prevent their use against him in the future. Furthermore, the fact that David did not take the horses for himself complies with the law for the king in Deuteronomy where it is legislated that an Israelite king "must not acquire great numbers of horses for himself" (Deut 17:16). From this perspective David's actions reflect well on him.

Excursus: Ethical Issues

David's treatment of Moabite prisoners of war and the captured war horses can be quite shocking to modern readers who would, for good reason, consider them war crimes and unnecessary acts of cruelty. In reading the story today, it is important to remember that David lived in a time far removed from our own. In David's time there were no "Geneva conventions" regarding the treatment of prisoners of war or PETA[7] movements advocating for the ethical treatment of animals. It also must be remembered that war was not an Israelite invention and that their waging of war fell in line with standards

---

5. Abraham Malamat, "A Political Look at the Kingdom of David and Solomon and Its Relations with Egypt," in *Studies in the Period of David and Solomon and Other Essays: Papers Read at the International Symposium for Biblical Studies, Tokyo, December, 1979*, ed. Tomoo Ishida (Winona Lake, IN: Eisenbrauns, 1982), 196.

6. Alter, *The David Story*, 237.

7. People for the Ethical Treatment of Animals.

for their times.[8] It is a mistake to attempt to judge the actions of the ancients by the standards of our own time. In David's case, what is problematic to the modern reader was actually something that ancient readers took as evidence that God really was with David in his battles.[9] This is precisely what is emphasized in this chapter, where we are twice told that this success was due to God giving David "victory wherever he went" (vv. 6, 14). David's ability to dominate Israel's enemies showed God's presence with him.

David Plunders the Enemy (8:5–15)

David's defeat of Hadadezer's forces led to a battle with the Arameans of Damascus who, as members of his political bloc (or perhaps one of his vassals), came to his aid. As a result of this military aggression, David killed twenty-two thousand Arameans, put his own military garrisons in Damascus, and, like he had done to the Moabites, subjected the Arameans to Israel. Lest the reader forget the source of David's success, the narrator reminds us that it was God who gave David victory (v. 6).

As the ancient adage notes, "the enemy of my enemy is my friend," so too when the king of Hamath, who was an enemy of the Arameans, heard of David's defeat of Aram, he sent his son to congratulate him and sent David many gifts. David in turn took the gifts and dedicated them to God. In fact, we are told that this was David's regular practice and that he had done so with the precious metals previously captured in his wars with Israel's enemies. Remembering that the law for the king in Deuteronomy 17:17 forbade an Israelite king from collecting "large amounts of silver and gold," David's dedication of these precious metals to God was in keeping with this law and reflects well on him. Furthermore, we are told in the book of Chronicles that, although David was forbidden from building the temple, the king began stockpiling materials for its construction (1 Chr 22:3, 5, 14). Perhaps this accumulation of silver and gold dedicated to God was the beginning of this preparation for the temple.

David's fame (literally in Hebrew the text says he makes a "name") is further increased by his massive defeat of the Edomites in the Valley of Salt (which is of uncertain location, though doubtless near the Dead Sea). Then the narrator again repeats that David's success was due to God giving David victory wherever he went (v. 14; cf. v. 7).

Finally, David's reign is assessed by the narrator and praised for "doing what was just and right for all his people" (v. 15). The terms used here, "just" and "right," are frequently used as characteristics of what Israelite kingship should

---

8. Anderson, *2 Samuel*, 135.
9. Arnold, *1 & 2 Samuel*, 498.

be like (e.g., Isa 9:7; Ps 72:1–4). The prophets also call for these characteristics ("just" and "right") to be the hallmark of Israelite leadership (Isa 5:7; Amos 5:6, 24).[10] In light of this, the assessment of David's administration at this point sets out an ideal upon which all later Israelite kings will be judged.

David's Government Officials (8:16–18a)

The chapter closes with a list of David's officials of state, which consists of three pairs of leaders. There are two military leaders, Joab and Benaiah. Joab is head of the Israelite forces, and Benaiah is over "the Kerethites and Pelethites," who were a foreign mercenary force who served David as his bodyguard (cf. 2 Sam 23:23).[11] There are two civil leaders, Jehoshaphat (the recorder) and Seraiah (the secretary). There are also two religious leaders, the priests Zadok and Ahimelek. Possibly this dual structure was intended to reduce the power accumulated by a single individual.[12] Rather than being an abusive monarchy like the type Samuel warned (1 Sam 8:11–18), David's administration displays equitable treatment of the people and extraordinary effectiveness (especially as compared to the reign of his predecessor). In summary, this chapter shows that David's rule provided equitable administration and national security. Through Yahweh's anointed one, Israel experiences a taste of the kingdom of God.

Epilogue? David's Sons as Priests (8:18b)

At the very end of this chapter there is a concluding note wherein David's sons are said to serve as priests. This is somewhat surprising given that David's sons, as non-Levites, would not qualify to be priests. Furthermore, we do not see David's sons ever referred to in this way again, nor do we see them fulfilling such duties. Therefore, some understand them to be "royal advisors" (NIV 1984), "priestly leaders" (NLT), or "chief ministers" (ASV). Given that two priests were already listed (Zadok and Ahimelek), it seems odd that David's sons would be listed separately if they were indeed priests in the same way as these Levitical priests. What is more, when Chronicles reproduces this list of officials, it lists the duties of David's sons as "chief officials" (1 Chr 18:17), and the Greek translation of the Old Testament, the Septuagint (LXX), similarly called them "court rulers" (using the Greek word *aularchai*). It may be, therefore, that David's sons served in the religious establishment in some sort of minor way (like a royal chaplain) or were simply some sort of official.

---

10. Brueggemann, *First and Second Samuel*, 263.

11. The Kerethites (Cretans) and Pelethites (possibly a variant of 'Philistines') probably originated with the migration of the Sea Peoples from the Aegean area (near Greece) near the beginning of the eleventh century BC.

12. Anderson, *2 Samuel*, 136.

That being said, the word "priest" (in Hebrew *kohen*) *is* used here, and it is difficult to explain away. Therefore, it may be possible that the narrator is hinting at David's hubris even after this otherwise laudatory chapter. After all, we have seen inappropriate nepotism raise its head before in this story. The priest Eli had sons appointed priests who proved wicked and immoral (1 Sam 2:22). The prophet Samuel had his sons appointed to high levels of leadership, but they proved corrupt (1 Sam 8:1–3). Perhaps here we see a glimpse of David's pride in appointing his sons as priests to serve alongside the official priests. After all, David had dedicated a tremendous amount of precious metals to God and therefore to the hands of the priests. David's appointment of his sons as priests of a sort may have been a way of making sure he had a say in the use of these riches.[13] Regardless, we will see later in this story that the king's sons do become the cause of much hardship for David.

God Fulfills Promises

One of the key takeaways from this chapter is an affirmation that God keeps his promises. This especially comes to the fore when we read it in light of the previous chapter. In 2 Samuel 7, God made some fantastic promises to David, including making his name great (2 Sam 7:9), giving rest from his enemies (2 Sam 7:11), and establishing the Davidic dynasty forever (2 Sam 7:11–13). In 2 Samuel 8 we see the first two promises already being fulfilled. First, David has unparalleled success defeating Israel's enemies on all sides. Second, the making of a great name for David (translated as "became famous" by the NIV) is explicitly referenced in connection to his defeat of Edom (v. 13). These nearly immediate fulfilments of the promises of the Davidic covenant lead the reader to expect that God will indeed fulfill the promise of a perpetual dynasty for David.

What is more, reading this story in light of the larger story of Israel, David's military success also demonstrates that God fulfills his promises to Abraham. David's conquests expand the borders of Israel nearly to the extent promised to Abraham when God said, "To your descendants I give this land, from the Wadi of Egypt to the great river, the Euphrates" (Gen 15:18). David's defeat of Hadadezer was at the river Euphrates, and his defeat of Edom and Philistia both were in the far south nearest Egypt. Thus, through David's success, God was bringing about the fulfilment of the Abrahamic covenant. The Israelite

---

13. Polzin, *David and the Deuteronomist*, 93–94.

borders finally reflect the Abrahamic promises in the days of Solomon where we are told that "Solomon ruled over all the kingdoms from the Euphrates River to the land of the Philistines, as far as the border of Egypt" (1 Kgs 4:21).

In other words, this story encourages faith in God's promises. Throughout the Bible, God's promises are at the heart of his grace and love directed to his people. Nevertheless, many of the promises given in the Old Testament failed to find fulfilment for a long time. But stories like the story of David here encouraged God's people to faith that God would, one day, fulfill his promises to his people—despite what the present looked like or the seemingly long period between promise and fulfillment. God has shown that he is a promise keeper.

In the New Testament, it is revealed that Jesus Christ is the fulfilment of the promises of God in the Old Testament. For example, in Galatians, Paul points back to God's promises to Abraham as fulfilled by Jesus Christ. The promise to Abraham that "all peoples on earth will be blessed through you" (Gen 12:3; 18:18; 22:18; 26:4) was ultimately only fulfilled through Jesus who "redeemed us in order that the blessing given to Abraham might come to the Gentiles through Christ Jesus, so that by faith we might receive the promise of the Spirit" (Gal 3:14).

The New Testament also looks back to the promises to David as being fulfilled in Christ. In Matthew's genealogy of Christ, Jesus is called "the son of David, the son of Abraham" (Matt 1:1). When Jesus preaches about the "kingdom of God," he speaks of a fulfillment of the promises to the Davidic kingdom. In fact, the Gospels are the stories of how God ultimately fulfilled the promises he made in the Old Testament.

Yet, not all the promises of God have been fulfilled. For example, in Hebrews 2:8 the writer points out that even though God promised to put everything under Jesus' feet (i.e., subject to his control), "yet at present we do not see everything subject to him." That is, there are still some promises of God not yet fulfilled. However, by remembering that God is a faithful promise keeper, just as we see God fulfilling his promises in David's reign here in 2 Samuel 8, we can trust that he will ultimately be faithful to his promises.

The story of David is illustrative of God's faithful character. David was promised to be king of Israel, yet it did not happen overnight. David was nearly killed many times and lived through many trials and exile before arriving at 2 Samuel 8. So we must remember that God's promises, though sure to be fulfilled, may not always be filled according to our preconceived timeline. He is faithful and we must have faith that he will deliver on his word. God keeps his promises.

LISTEN to the Story

¹David asked, "Is there anyone still left of the house of Saul to whom I can show kindness for Jonathan's sake?"

²Now there was a servant of Saul's household named Ziba. They summoned him to appear before David, and the king said to him, "Are you Ziba?"

"At your service," he replied.

³The king asked, "Is there no one still alive from the house of Saul to whom I can show God's kindness?"

Ziba answered the king, "There is still a son of Jonathan; he is lame in both feet."

⁴"Where is he?" the king asked.

Ziba answered, "He is at the house of Makir son of Ammiel in Lo Debar."

⁵So King David had him brought from Lo Debar, from the house of Makir son of Ammiel.

⁶When Mephibosheth son of Jonathan, the son of Saul, came to David, he bowed down to pay him honor.

David said, "Mephibosheth!"

"At your service," he replied.

⁷"Don't be afraid," David said to him, "for I will surely show you kindness for the sake of your father Jonathan. I will restore to you all the land that belonged to your grandfather Saul, and you will always eat at my table."

⁸Mephibosheth bowed down and said, "What is your servant, that you should notice a dead dog like me?"

⁹Then the king summoned Ziba, Saul's steward, and said to him, "I have given your master's grandson everything that belonged to Saul and his family. ¹⁰You and your sons and your servants are to farm the land for him and bring in the crops, so that your master's grandson may be

provided for. And Mephibosheth, grandson of your master, will always eat at my table." (Now Ziba had fifteen sons and twenty servants.)

[11]Then Ziba said to the king, "Your servant will do whatever my lord the king commands his servant to do." So Mephibosheth ate at David's table like one of the king's sons.

[12]Mephibosheth had a young son named Mika, and all the members of Ziba's household were servants of Mephibosheth. [13]And Mephibosheth lived in Jerusalem, because he always ate at the king's table; he was lame in both feet.

Listen to the Text in the Story: 1 Samuel 20:14–17; 2 Samuel 4:4; 8:1–14

One of the keys to understanding this story is to remember the covenant David made with Jonathan before he died. Back in 1 Samuel 20, Jonathan had David take an oath (1 Sam 20:17) to show "kindness like the LORD's kindness" (1 Sam 20:14), not only to him but to his descendants. Jonathan said, "do not ever cut off your kindness from my family—not even when the LORD has cut off every one of David's enemies from the face of the earth" (1 Sam 20:15). This is exactly the context of our story in 2 Samuel 9. David has defeated all his enemies (2 Sam 8), and now he sets out to "show kindness" (9:1). To show "kindness" (Hebrew *hesed*) is covenant terminology referring to fulfilling one's obligations agreed to in a covenant, and the term is used three times in this chapter (v. 1, 3, 7). In fact, when David asks Ziba, Saul's former servant, about any surviving Saulides he expresses his intent to show "God's kindness" (2 Sam 9:3), which is very close to Jonathan's wording in his request that David show "kindness like the LORD's kindness" (1 Sam 20:14). In other words, this chapter presents David as a man of his word as he attempts to fulfill his vow to his dear friend Jonathan.

Another earlier part of the story now shows itself important. Back in 2 Samuel 4 we were told how David's best friend, Jonathan, had a son named Mephibosheth, who had became permanently disabled when he was dropped by his nurse as a baby when she heard about Saul and Jonathan's death (2 Sam 4:4). Though it seemed like an unnecessary aside at the time, now the story picks up Mephibosheth's story once again as David sets out to fulfill his promise to his fallen friend.

Some interpreters question David's motives for aiding Jonathan's son and suggest it was mainly a self-interested act. First, aiding a surviving Saulide could be politically advantageous and help keep the loyalty of the northern tribes, who had been loyal to Saul's son before his death. Second, David's acts of "kindness" here could simply be to ease his guilty conscience for being instrumental in the death of the Saulides. Third, allowing Mephibosheth to eat at his table could be a way of keeping tabs on the Saulide family. All of these speculations, however, go against what the text actually says. First, the story has made abundantly clear that David was completely innocent in the death of Saul, so there was no guilty conscience to appease. Second, the text emphasizes that David's acts of kindness were motivated by his covenant with Jonathan (vv. 1, 7), not for reasons of surveillance of a rival or for political propaganda. While among sinful humans no act is completely selfless and some mixed motives may have been present in David, the overriding concern for David here is clearly his wish to keep his promise to his dear friend.

EXPLAIN the Story

In this chapter, David seeks to fulfill the vow he made to his dearly departed friend, Jonathan, to take care of his descendants (1 Sam 20:14–16). David inquires of Saul's former servant, Ziba, and discovers that a son of Jonathan is still alive, though he is lame in his feet. David sends for him and restores his family's land holdings to him and even invites him to eat at the royal table with David's own children. Thus, David shows he is true to his word to Jonathan as he keeps his promise and shows kindness to Jonathan's son, Mephibosheth.

David Fulfills His Vow to Jonathan (9:1–13)

After David expressed his desire to show kindness to surviving Saulides, Saul's former servant, Ziba, is brought before the king, and he informs David that a son of Jonathan still lives, though he is "lame in both feet" (v. 3). Some suggest that Ziba mentions the disability right away because he fears David would kill any remaining Saulides, but Mephibosheth's disability likely would disqualify him from any claim to the throne and perhaps spare him from any purge of rivals.[1] However, David made his intentions to "show kindness" explicit (v. 1), so this seems unlikely. Perhaps Ziba was simply reporting what he knew about Mephibosheth (or Ziba was attempting to undermine Mephibosheth's value in David's eyes so that Ziba could continue to be in charge of his old master's house).

David is told that Jonathan's son is living in the house of a man named Makir, who will reappear later in the story to help David when he is on the run from Absalom (17:27–29). Makir lives in Lo Debar, a Transjordanian

---

1. Brueggemann, *First and Second Samuel*, 267; Arnold, *1 & 2 Samuel*, 509.

city near Mahanaim, where Saul's son, Ish-Bosheth, had his temporary capital (2 Sam 2:8). The fact that Mephibosheth was not living on Saulide property probably points to its having been appropriated by the crown. In other words, though Ziba appears to have been in charge of Saul's former estate, he did not own it (which explains why David has the power to give it to Mephibosheth).[2] Thus, the gift to Mephibosheth was a royal land grant, as evidenced by the fact it could also be taken away from him later (see 2 Sam 16:4).

David has Mephibosheth brought to Jerusalem. When Jonathan's son arrives, he respectfully bows to the ground before the king. Keeping in mind that Mephibosheth is disabled, his bowing to the ground may have proved quite difficult. As Fokkelman observes, "The scene is poignant; we observe the cripple bowing to the ground with all the difficulty and pain that that entails."[3] It was doubtless a stressful situation for the Saulide, who probably was fearful that David sought him out to kill him. After all, it was commonplace in the ancient world for a king from a new line to kill all the remaining descendants of the previous dynasty (e.g., 1 Kgs 15:29; 16:11; 2 Kgs 10:6–7). His bowing probably underscores his fear of the situation (after all, we are not told Ziba bowed in this way).[4]

Upon his arrival, David calls him by his name, Mephibosheth (v. 6). As we noted in our commentary on 2 Samuel 4, the name Mephibosheth may be an intentional distortion of the original name, Marib-Baal (the name used for him in 1 Chr 8:34; 9:40). In order to disparage the false god "Baal," the word "bosheth" (which means "shame" in Hebrew) is substituted for "baal." Probably sensing Mephibosheth's nervousness, David immediately reassures him that he brought him here to show him kindness for the sake of his father (v. 7) and explains that he is restoring all of Saul's land to Mephibosheth, making him quite rich. Furthermore, Mephibosheth is granted the privilege of eating at the royal table with David and his own sons.

Mephibosheth shows great humility at David's gracious offer (v. 8). David then calls for Ziba and tells him that he and his sons (and servants) will farm the land for Mephibosheth (who was lame and likely couldn't do the hard work of farming). Lest the reader think this was a hardship for Ziba, the narrator informs us that the man had fifteen sons and twenty servants—a very sizeable crew for the task. Ziba agrees to do as David commanded and David fulfills his vow to Jonathan by showing God's kindness to Mephibosheth.

---

2. Tryggve N. D. Mettinger, *Solomonic State Officials: A Study of the Civil Government Officials of the Israelite Monarchy*, ConBOT 5 (Lund: Gleerup, 1971), 85; Anderson, *2 Samuel*, 141.

3. J. P. Fokkelman, *Narrative Art and Poetry in the Books of Samuel: A Full Interpretation Based on Stylistic and Structural Analysis: Vol. 1, King David (II Sam. 9–20 & I Kings 1–2)* (Assen, The Netherlands: Van Gorcum, 1981), 29.

4. Alter, *The David Story*, 241.

The chapter ends noting that Mephibosheth had a son of his own, named Mika. Due to David's kindness to Jonathan's son, his line will live on and Mika now has a bright future ahead of him. He now belongs to a rich household with many servants ("all the members of Ziba's household were servants of Mephibosheth," v. 12), living in the capital city of Jerusalem. The final line of the chapter, however, again notes Mephibosheth's disability, which might be intended to once more contrast the destinies of the Saulide house with the Davidic house. As Alter writes:

> This notice at the end about Mephibosheth's disability also underscores the continuing antithesis between the fates of the house of Saul and the house of David: King David came into Jerusalem whirling and dancing before the LORD; the surviving Saulide limps into Jerusalem, crippled in both legs.[5]

Be that as it may, mercy is also shown to the Saulides. Despite what the proverbial saying declared back in 2 Samuel 5:8, that "the blind and the lame will not enter the palace," a "lame" man now eats regularly with the king in "the palace" due to the covenant loyalty of God's anointed.[6]

 LIVE the Story

Keeping Your Word

It is said that words are cheap while actions are of most value. Making a promise is easier than actually following through and keeping the promise, as it often ends up involving more difficult circumstances and actions than initially imagined. In this story, David had every reason not to keep his word in this instance. An heir to the throne of the previous monarchy could have been viewed as a threat, as Mephibosheth knew well. Furthermore, reestablishing the heir with the former king's land holdings and servants would run counter to political logic that would rather keep rival lines impoverished (if one were to leave them alive in the first place).[7] Furthermore, David's own self-expressed hatred for the lame and the proverbial saying barring the lame from the king's palace (2 Sam 5:8) would have also made keeping his word here more difficult—as he would have had to eat crow. Yet David goes out of his

---

5. Ibid., 243.

6. Sternberg muses at the possibility that "Mephibosheth's lameness [is] only designed to show David so resolved to keep faith with the dead Jonathan that he will have the son dine at his table regardless of his own proverbial aversion for the lame" (*The Poetics of Biblical Narrative: Ideological Literature and the Drama of Reading* [Bloomington: Indiana University Press, 1985], 339).

7. Baldwin, *1 and 2 Samuel*, 227.

way to keep his word and honor his covenant made with his dear friend Jonathan, despite the difficulties or embarrassments in doing so. In this instance, David is a good example for us to emulate when we are tempted to default on promises due to perceived difficulties of follow through.

God Keeps His Word

Although David makes good on his word in this story, this is not to say that David is always an ideal model. Just as from time to time all of us sin, lie, and fail to keep all of our promises, David will falter later in the story (with some of his failures being perhaps even grander than our own failures). However, David's faithfulness at this point is encouraging to believers not simply as an example we can emulate but as a reminder that Jesus is utterly faithful. Remember that David is God's anointed one (Hebrew *mashiah*) and that due to the failures of later Davidic kings, messianic expectations looked forward to another Anointed One—one who would not fail. So, we look to our Anointed One, Jesus Christ, who, unlike David, always keeps his promises and is faithful to his covenant.

So, when we see David, as God's anointed one, showing mercy and compassion and honoring his covenant, we can be encouraged. David here serves as a type of Christ, the Anointed One and long-awaited Son of David. As David was faithful to his covenant here, so Christ is faithful to the new covenant sealed by his blood shed for us. Due to his faithfulness to his covenant, David showed mercy on his former enemy, the rejected line of Saul. In the same way, Jesus, through the covenant established by his death and resurrection, shows mercy on sinners who were previously God's enemies (Rom 5:10). While later in the story David will actually default on this covenant with Jonathan and take away what he had given to Mephibosheth, due to his being deceived by Ziba (2 Sam 16:1–4), the later Son of David, Jesus Christ, will never default on his covenant. His is the "eternal covenant" (Heb 13:20) and Christ himself its "guarantor" (Heb 7:22).

LISTEN to the Story

¹In the course of time, the king of the Ammonites died, and his son Hanun succeeded him as king. ²David thought, "I will show kindness to Hanun son of Nahash, just as his father showed kindness to me." So David sent a delegation to express his sympathy to Hanun concerning his father.

When David's men came to the land of the Ammonites, ³the Ammonite commanders said to Hanun their lord, "Do you think David is honoring your father by sending envoys to you to express sympathy? Hasn't David sent them to you only to explore the city and spy it out and overthrow it?" ⁴So Hanun seized David's envoys, shaved off half of each man's beard, cut off their garments at the buttocks, and sent them away.

⁵When David was told about this, he sent messengers to meet the men, for they were greatly humiliated. The king said, "Stay at Jericho till your beards have grown, and then come back."

⁶When the Ammonites realized that they had become obnoxious to David, they hired twenty thousand Aramean foot soldiers from Beth Rehob and Zobah, as well as the king of Maakah with a thousand men, and also twelve thousand men from Tob.

⁷On hearing this, David sent Joab out with the entire army of fighting men. ⁸The Ammonites came out and drew up in battle formation at the entrance of their city gate, while the Arameans of Zobah and Rehob and the men of Tob and Maakah were by themselves in the open country.

⁹Joab saw that there were battle lines in front of him and behind him; so he selected some of the best troops in Israel and deployed them against the Arameans. ¹⁰He put the rest of the men under the command of Abishai his brother and deployed them against the Ammonites. ¹¹Joab said, "If the Arameans are too strong for me, then you are to come to my rescue; but if the Ammonites are too strong for you, then I will come to rescue you. ¹²Be strong, and let us fight bravely for our people and the cities of our God. The LORD will do what is good in his sight."

¹³Then Joab and the troops with him advanced to fight the Arameans, and they fled before him. ¹⁴When the Ammonites realized that the Arameans were fleeing, they fled before Abishai and went inside the city. So Joab returned from fighting the Ammonites and came to Jerusalem.

¹⁵After the Arameans saw that they had been routed by Israel, they regrouped. ¹⁶Hadadezer had Arameans brought from beyond the Euphrates River; they went to Helam, with Shobak the commander of Hadadezer's army leading them.

¹⁷When David was told of this, he gathered all Israel, crossed the Jordan and went to Helam. The Arameans formed their battle lines to meet David and fought against him. ¹⁸But they fled before Israel, and David killed seven hundred of their charioteers and forty thousand of their foot soldiers. He also struck down Shobak the commander of their army, and he died there. ¹⁹When all the kings who were vassals of Hadadezer saw that they had been routed by Israel, they made peace with the Israelites and became subject to them.

So the Arameans were afraid to help the Ammonites anymore.

¹¹:¹In the spring, at the time when kings go off to war, David sent Joab out with the king's men and the whole Israelite army. They destroyed the Ammonites and besieged Rabbah. But David remained in Jerusalem.

²One evening David got up from his bed and walked around on the roof of the palace. From the roof he saw a woman bathing. The woman was very beautiful, ³and David sent someone to find out about her. The man said, "She is Bathsheba, the daughter of Eliam and the wife of Uriah the Hittite." ⁴Then David sent messengers to get her. She came to him, and he slept with her. (Now she was purifying herself from her monthly uncleanness.) Then she went back home. ⁵The woman conceived and sent word to David, saying, "I am pregnant."

⁶So David sent this word to Joab: "Send me Uriah the Hittite." And Joab sent him to David. ⁷When Uriah came to him, David asked him how Joab was, how the soldiers were and how the war was going. ⁸Then David said to Uriah, "Go down to your house and wash your feet." So Uriah left the palace, and a gift from the king was sent after him. ⁹But Uriah slept at the entrance to the palace with all his master's servants and did not go down to his house.

¹⁰David was told, "Uriah did not go home." So he asked Uriah, "Haven't you just come from a military campaign? Why didn't you go home?"

¹¹Uriah said to David, "The ark and Israel and Judah are staying in tents, and my commander Joab and my lord's men are camped in the open

country. How could I go to my house to eat and drink and make love to my wife? As surely as you live, I will not do such a thing!"

¹²Then David said to him, "Stay here one more day, and tomorrow I will send you back." So Uriah remained in Jerusalem that day and the next. ¹³At David's invitation, he ate and drank with him, and David made him drunk. But in the evening Uriah went out to sleep on his mat among his master's servants; he did not go home.

¹⁴In the morning David wrote a letter to Joab and sent it with Uriah. ¹⁵In it he wrote, "Put Uriah out in front where the fighting is fiercest. Then withdraw from him so he will be struck down and die."

¹⁶So while Joab had the city under siege, he put Uriah at a place where he knew the strongest defenders were. ¹⁷When the men of the city came out and fought against Joab, some of the men in David's army fell; moreover, Uriah the Hittite died.

¹⁸Joab sent David a full account of the battle. ¹⁹He instructed the messenger: "When you have finished giving the king this account of the battle, ²⁰the king's anger may flare up, and he may ask you, 'Why did you get so close to the city to fight? Didn't you know they would shoot arrows from the wall? ²¹Who killed Abimelek son of Jerub-Besheth? Didn't a woman drop an upper millstone on him from the wall, so that he died in Thebez? Why did you get so close to the wall?' If he asks you this, then say to him, 'Moreover, your servant Uriah the Hittite is dead.'"

²²The messenger set out, and when he arrived he told David everything Joab had sent him to say. ²³The messenger said to David, "The men overpowered us and came out against us in the open, but we drove them back to the entrance of the city gate. ²⁴Then the archers shot arrows at your servants from the wall, and some of the king's men died. Moreover, your servant Uriah the Hittite is dead."

²⁵David told the messenger, "Say this to Joab: 'Don't let this upset you; the sword devours one as well as another. Press the attack against the city and destroy it.' Say this to encourage Joab."

²⁶When Uriah's wife heard that her husband was dead, she mourned for him. ²⁷After the time of mourning was over, David had her brought to his house, and she became his wife and bore him a son. But the thing David had done displeased the LORD.

Listen to the Text in the Story: Exodus 20; 1 Samuel 8:20; 1 Samuel 11:1–11; 26:6; Treaty between Hattusilis and Rameses II

The chapter begins by noting the death of the king of the Ammonites and how the king's son took the throne after him. The Ammonites were situated across the Jordan from Jerusalem and their capital city was Rabbah (present day Amman, the capital of Jordan). When David hears of the Ammonite king's passing, he sends a delegation to express his sympathy to the new king, Hanun, son of Nahash. The reader will remember Nahash as the malevolent king who besieged Jabesh Gilead back in 1 Samuel 11. In one sense, Nahash was the enemy of Saul so that the adage "the enemy of my enemy is my friend" could apply here. Nahash, however, was also the enemy of all Israel and was very cruel (cf. 1 Sam 11:2). Regardless, it appears that David had made a covenant with Nahash sometime in the past. The references to showing "kindness" (Hebrew *hesed*) in verse 2 point to a covenant relationship, as "kindness" (*hesed*) is covenant terminology. It is likely David made an agreement with Nahash when he was on the run from Saul (or perhaps when he was at war with Ish-Bosheth). The pact would likely have agreed on mutual nonaggression benefiting both sides. An example of such a treaty is found in the parity treaty between Hattusilis (king of Hatti) and Rameses II (Pharaoh of Egypt), wherein both kings agreed "to mutual nonaggression, mutual defense, extradition of fugitives, and even assistance in cases of contested royal accession."[1] The point of the treaty is "to cause that good peace and brotherhood occur between us forever."[2] Evidently, the treaty between Hattusilis and Rameses was actually a renewal of a treaty that had existed between Hatti and Egypt in the time of their fathers, and the extant treaty is reaffirming its terms.[3] Similarly, upon the death of Nahash, David is likely setting out to reaffirm the terms of the treaty (showing "kindness" with the new king).

As noted in the commentary on 1 Samuel 26, the Hittites mentioned in the book of Samuel were Cannanite peoples, said to have descended from their ancestor, Heth (Gen 10:15; 23:3). Some speculate that the Hittites may have been hired as mercenaries (like David's use of other foreign mercenaries; cf. 2 Sam 15:18; 23:23). It is likely that Hittites married into Israel during the period of the judges so that their descendants lived among Israelites. In 1 Samuel 26:6 we see that David had Hittites among his men, with Ahimelek the Hittite mentioned there. Now in this chapter, we see another Hittite

---

1. Long, *2 Samuel*, 455.

2. *ANET*, 199.

3. The relevant section of the treaty reads: "As to the traditional regulation [the pre-existing treaty] which had been here in the time of Suppiluliumas [Hattusili's grandfather] . . . as well as the traditional regulation which had been in the time of Muwatallis, the Great Prince of Hatti, my father, I seize hold of it. . . . Behold, Ramses Meri-Amon, the great ruler of Egypt, seizes hold of [it] . . . . We seize hold of it, and we act in this traditional situation" (*ANET*, 200).

among David's men. This Hittite appears to be a man of great integrity and will later be listed as one of David's best soldiers (2 Sam 23:39).

EXPLAIN the Story

Like the last chapter, David again sets out to show "kindness" to someone he had a covenant with, but this time his gracious gesture is met with hostility instead of thankfulness. When David sent some of his men to Ammon to express his sympathy at the passing of the Ammonite king, the Ammonites suspect David's delegation of spying, humiliate them, and send them back. After hearing the Ammonite's had enlisted the support of Arameans, David sends the whole army under Joab's command and they handily defeat their enemies. When the Arameans regroup, David himself leads out "all Israel" to victory against them. As a result, the Aramean kings made peace with Israel and were subjugated. This left only the Ammonites and their capital city of Rabbah to conquer. However, while Joab led an army to take Rabbah, David decides to stay at home. At home, David observes a beautiful woman bathing on a nearby rooftop. David inquires about her and takes her and sleeps with her. Upon finding out she is pregnant from their encounter, David calls Uriah, her husband, back from the Ammonite war and attempts to get him to go home to sleep with his wife. When Uriah refuses to return home, David sends a letter to Joab by Uriah's hand instructing him to have Uriah killed in battle at the hand of the enemy. Once the deed is done, David takes Bathsheba as his wife. David seemingly has gotten away with adultery and murder, but God was displeased.

The Sympathy Delegation (10:1–5)

The chapter begins by noting the death of the king of the Ammonites and David sending a sympathy delegation to the new Ammonite king. David's sympathy delegation, however, is viewed as suspicious by the Ammonite commanders, who convince Hanun that David was really spying out their land. Hanun agrees with his commanders' suspicion and in response mistreats David's messengers, a surprising move given that messengers were usually treated respectfully (even with immunity), similar to foreign diplomats today. The humiliating treatment of shaving off half of their beards probably referred to shaving off one side of the face and not just shortening the beard. Seeing as a full beard was a sign of manhood and was a point of pride, this was very embarrassing for the men. David understood this and so allows them to wait until their beards have grown back before returning home (v. 5). In addition to the unwanted haircut, the Ammonites also made unwanted wardrobe alterations, causing the messengers to have their buttocks exposed.

The Ammonite War (10:6–14)

Furthermore, while the Israelite envoy's facial hair was growing back, the Ammonites hired an Aramean army from areas that David had already defeated—Beth Rehob and Zobah. As we saw in chapter 8, Zobah was the center of power in southern Aram with its king Hadadezer, the leader of a powerful military coalition (cf. 2 Sam 8:3–5). The Ammonites also secured troops from Maakah and Tob (v. 6). Maakah was a little Aramean nation between Mount Hermon and Gilead, and Tob was a small city-state in Gilead, about 12 miles southeast of Galilee.

David sends Joab and "the entire army" to meet the Ammonite threat. The Ammonites were set to defend their city gate (probably the city of Rabbah), while the hired Arameans were set up away from the city "in the open country" (v. 8). As a result, Joab had two different battle lines to engage. Joab took the best troops with him to attack the Arameans and left the rest of the men under the command of his brother, Abishai, to attack the Ammonites with plans for either group to come rescue the other if need be. Joab encourages his brother to fight bravely but also, in a rare faith-filled moment for Joab, puts the final outcome in Yahweh's hands, asserting that "The Lord will do what is good in his sight" (10:12).

It turned out that neither brother needed the aid of the other as Joab easily bested the Arameans, causing Abishai's foe, the Ammonites, to retreat inside their city (probably Rabbah). When the Ammonites retreated, Joab led the army home rather than putting the city to siege—probably either because he did not have sufficient means to begin a long siege or because they had taken casualties in the war.[4]

Renewed Hostilities (10:15–19)

The Arameans, however, did not take defeat well and regrouped. This time Hadadezer gets involved and sends the commander of his army, Shobak, with them, along with reinforcements. The reader will remember Hadadezer as the king soundly defeated by David in chapter 8. Therefore, this offensive was not only a response to the Aramean defeat at the hands of Joab but was also an Aramean rebellion against their suzerain (or overlord), David.

When David hears of the plot, he joins in the fray and brings "all Israel" with him (v. 17). With David in charge, the Arameans fair no better and again flee before Israel. What is more, David kills Hadadezer's commander, Shobak. As a result of the battle, all the kings who were subject to Hadadezer "made peace" with Israel and were subjugated. Thus, the battle had long-range consequences, as the kingdom centered in Zobah would no longer be the dominant

---

4. Arnold, *1 & 2 Samuel*, 522.

center in Aram, as it is eclipsed by Damascus from here on out.[5] The defeat of Aram, of course, also meant that they no longer aided the Ammonites (v. 19), which was a significant step forward for Israel's national security.

These wars with the Ammonites and the Arameans expanded the influence and boundaries of Israel considerably. By squelching the rebellion of the Arameans after their subjugation in chapter 8, David proved his kingdom was for real. Israel was the dominant military power in the region now. With the Arameans no longer supporting Ammon, the way was paved for an attack on the Ammonite capital city of Rabbah (2 Sam 12:26–31). However, before the final victory occurs, tragic events occur in Jerusalem.

What follows in chapter 11 is the great turning point of the entire story of David. Up until now, David's career had been nearly flawless. His kingdom was established, his enemies vanquished, and his relationship with God secured in an amazing covenant. It appeared nothing could slow him down. After chapter 11, however, David's story becomes one of frequent troubles, calamities, and disasters. All of these misfortunes trace back to David's choices here in 2 Samuel 11.

David's Absence from the Final Battle with Ammon (11:1)

While the defeat of the Arameans has opened the door to a final defeat of Ammon, David chooses to remain in Jerusalem instead of leading his troops in their final victory against Ammon. David's absence is highlighted as unusual by the narrator because it was "spring," which was the normal time that "kings go off to war" (11:1). The end of the rainy season was in March, making ideal conditions for war in the ancient Near East.[6] David instead sent Joab and the army to finish off Ammon and finally put their capital city, Rabbah, to siege. Had David become too complacent? Had his regular victories led him to a false confidence and a neglect of his duties? After all, it was the duty of "a king to lead us and to go out before us and fight our battles" (1 Sam 8:20). As one commentator notes, "the irony, of course, is that David stays home, and rather than defend his subjects, he abuses them (i.e., Bathsheba and her family)."[7]

The Adultery (11:2–5)

Idle hands are the devil's workshop. This could be illustrated well here, as David is not only failing to lead his troops into battle, he is taking a mid-day

---

5. Ibid.

6. Some interpret the phrase in Hebrew literally as "the turn of the year," indicating it was the one-year anniversary of the Ammonite war. E.g., P. Kyle McCarter, *II Samuel*, AB 9 (Garden City, NY: Doubleday, 1984), 285. However, most (like the NIV) take it as the "turn" from winter to spring, which was the traditional time for war.

7. Arnold, *1 & 2 Samuel*, 523.

nap. In fact, as Alter points out, normally "a siesta on a hot spring day would begin not long after noon," so when we are told that David rose up from his nap in the evening, it means that "this recumbent king has been in bed an inordinately long time."[8] What is more, David is walking around the roof of the palace. It is possible that David's bed may have been located on the roof, just as Saul slept on a roof of a house in his visit with Samuel (1 Sam 9:25).[9] Whether he slept there or was simply walking on the roof, due to his elevation David would have had a good view of nearby houses and yards. From his vantage point David sees a woman bathing. The woman is described as *very* beautiful, a somewhat unique expression in the Old Testament. Three other women are described as beautiful in the Old Testament: Rebekah (Gen 26:7), Vashti (Esth 1:11), and Esther (Esth 2:7).[10] Only Bathsheba is described as "*very* beautiful" (2 Sam 11:2, emphasis added).[11]

David then sends a servant to find out information about the woman he saw. To the point, David finds out that the woman is married and that she is the wife of Uriah the Hititte. While we have not heard of Uriah as of yet, he is later listed as one of David's best soldiers (2 Sam 23:39), making David's actions all the more deplorable. While described as a Hittite, Uriah had a good Israelite name that means "Yahweh is my light," which indicates either that he was born in Israel or that he had changed his name.[12] Thus his Hittite heritage should not be held against him.

David is also told who Bathsheba's father was. This is a bit unusual since most married women were simply identified by their husbands and no longer by their father. Her father is said to be Eliam, who is also later listed as one of David's best soldiers (2 Sam 23:34). Furthermore, Eliam is said to be "son of Ahithophel the Gilonite" (2 Sam 23:34), who is later described as one of David's wisest counselors (2 Sam 15:12; 16:23). Since Uriah, Eliam, and Ahithophel were such prominent members of David's kingdom, he undoubtedly already knew the family and likely Bathsheba as well. After all, the servant actually reports the information in the form of a question, "Isn't this Bathsheba, the daughter of Eliam and the wife of Uriah the Hittite?" (NIV 1984). Though the NIV 2011 has changed the rendering, the interrogative aspect is clear in

---

8. Alter, *The David Story*, 250.

9. Anderson, *2 Samuel*, 153.

10. In Hebrew "*tobat mareh*" is literally "good of appearance" (or "good looking.") While we are also told about Abigail and Tamar's attractiveness, different Hebrew words are used in those instances (in 1 Sam 25:3 Abigail is said to be "*yephat toar*" ("fair of form") and in 2 Sam 14:27 Tamar is said to be "*yephat mareh*" ("fair of appearance").

11. That is, with the modifier "very" (Hebrew *meod*) attached to the phrase. Of course, Esther is described as "lovely of form and beautiful of appearance" (Esth 2:7).

12. Anderson, *2 Samuel*, 153.

the Hebrew. The servant's report is clearly a rhetorical question—one that assumed David knew who she was. Furthermore, the interrogative aspect of the servant's response would seem to be "an implicit warning designed to stir the conscience of the king regarding the identity of the woman who happens to live next door to him."[13]

Despite her married status and the fact she comes from an important family, David sends messengers to "take" Bathsheba (translated as "to get her" in the NIV). The use of the word "take" here reminds the reader of Samuel's warnings to the people (1 Sam 8:11–18) that a king would "take, take, take." Their sons (1 Sam 8:11), their daughters (1 Sam 8:13), and their wealth and livelihood (1 Sam 8:14–15) are all up for grabs with a king on the throne. Up to this point in the story, David has not been a taker. He has been a receiver, as God has blessed him with all he needs. Now, however, something has changed. "Now he is in control. He can have whatever he wants, no restraint, no second thoughts, no reservations, no justification. He takes simply because he can. He is at the culmination of his enormous power."[14] David takes Eliam's daughter, the wife of Uriah.

The sexual encounter is tersely described. "She came to him, and he slept with her" (11:4). What choice did she have? He was in a position of power and she a lowly woman. After the narrator describes the sexual encounter, however, it is disclosed that she was "purifying herself from her monthly uncleanness" (11:4b). That is, she had just finished menstruating and was following the relevant purity laws (Lev 15:19–24). Most important for this story is to note that Bathsheba was clearly *not* pregnant before this adulterous encounter with the king. Furthermore, the days following menstruation are often the most likely time for a woman to get pregnant.

After the adulterous tryst, "she went back home" (v. 4). Perhaps in David's mind the relationship was over. However, Bathsheba conceives and sends word to David that she is pregnant.

The First Attempted Cover Up (11:6–13)

The king quickly sets out to cover up his sin and sends word to his general to send Bathsheba's husband, Uriah the Hittite, home from the battlefront. The text doesn't tell us what excuse was given by either David or Joab for Uriah's furlough or whether Uriah was suspicious of anything. The likely reason given for the leave from battle was to inform the king how the siege of Rabbah was proceeding (11:7). Of course, as we will see later in the chapter (11:19), a simple "messenger" would suffice rather than sending one of David's best warriors (2 Sam 23:39) home to report. Of course, the real reason for Uriah's

---

13. Bodner, *David Observed*, 92.
14. Brueggemann, *First and Second Samuel*, 273–74.

presence would be so that Uriah could appear to father the child Bathsheba currently carried.

After questioning Uriah about the battlefront, David sent Uriah back to his house to "wash [his] feet" (11:8). In the ancient Near East, washing one's feet could simply be just that—washing one's feet with water. After all, sandals were standard fare, and after a journey feet were dirty. However, in Hebrew "feet" also can be a euphemism for the genitals. The reader will recall David's encounter with Saul in the cave where Saul entered the cave to "cover his feet" (1 Sam 24:3; i.e., relieve himself). In this case, David's suggestion to Uriah to go home and wash his feet seems to imply sex. After all, he probably would have had his feet literally washed at the palace in preparation for dining with the king. Furthermore, later in the story Uriah knows exactly what David meant when he says, "How could I go to my house to eat and drink and make love to my wife?" (11:11). While the "washing your feet" idiom is lost on modern readers, it was crystal clear to Uriah. Uriah, however, does *not* go home to "wash [his] feet" (11:8) but instead sleeps at the entrance to the royal palace with David's servants (11:9).

The events narrated thus far imply that there had been witnesses to the nefarious goings-on in the palace. David sent someone to inquire about Bathsheba. He then ordered someone to bring her to the palace. Once there, she was brought through the palace and up to David's room. It seems very likely that the witnesses and these "servants" with whom Uriah spends the night might be one and the same. Did these servants tell Uriah that his wife had been to visit the palace?

When David is told that Uriah did not go home, he again speaks to him (who, if he was not already suspicious at this point now "might wonder how David knew [that he did not go home], or why David cared").[15] David attempts to get him to go home by implying that Uriah deserves the break (11:10). Uriah makes it clear he has no intention of going home and his response is damning to David. Uriah notes first that the ark and Israel and Judah live in tents and that Joab and the king's men were also presently camping on the battlefield. As we know, the ark resides in a tent (cf. 2 Sam 7:1), though David had wanted to build a temple for it. The national army was encamped ready to go into battle, as were Joab and his men. How could Uriah, in good conscience, enjoy all the comforts of home when so many are roughing it in tents for Israel's cause? This is extremely pious of Uriah, who wants to show solidarity with the troops in battle. At the same time, his objection is also quite condemning of the king, as David is living in a palace while all Israel (and the ark) are in

---

15. Ibid., 275.

tents. Furthermore, Uriah explicitly acknowledges that David had been trying to get him to go "and make love" to his wife (11:11), and he adamantly refuses. While not mentioned here, it appears that Israelite practice was that soldiers abstain from sexual relations during a war (cf. Deut 23:9–10; 1 Sam 21:4; cf. Lev 15:16–18), making David's request of Uriah doubly deplorable.

In the end, it is difficult to know whether Uriah suspected the adultery and therefore refused to go home, or whether he was simply too pious to go enjoy the comforts of home when his fellow soldiers were at war. It could be that initially he was unaware but did not go home for reasons of solidarity with the troops, but then in his night spent with the servants was informed of the adultery and therefore refused to play along with the king's incessant requests to sleep with his wife.[16] Either way, Uriah refuses to go home and be with his wife. Ironically, this "is the one thing powerful David cannot have, much as he wants it!"[17]

Desperate for Uriah to sleep with his wife in order to cover up his adultery, David makes Uriah stay for another day (11:12) and gets him drunk (11:13) in hopes that in his inebriated state he would go home and sleep with his wife. Uriah, however, again fails to go to his house and again stays at the palace with the servants. As one commentator has put it: "Uriah drunk is more pious than David sober."[18]

The Second Attempted Cover Up: The Murder (11:14–25)

Unable to get Uriah to sleep with his wife and desperate to cover up his adultery no matter the cost, in his mind David is left with only one option—Uriah must die. Rather than sully his own hands, David decides to let the Ammonites kill him. In other words, David pulls a chapter out of Saul's playbook, who had tried to use Israel's enemy to kill David (1 Sam 18:7). To this end, David composes a letter to Joab ordering the general to send Uriah to the most dangerous place in the battle and then abandon him so that he would fall at the hand of the enemy (11:15). What is more, David sends the note by the hand of Uriah himself (11:14). The fact that the letter got to Joab would seem to reflect well on Uriah, who, out of respect for his king and his commander, did not read it. Of course, it could have been sealed, or it is possible that Uriah could not actually read. Either way, ironically Uriah delivers his own death warrant to his executioner.[19]

Joab's actions in response to the instructions are very interesting. David had

---

16. Alter, *The David Story*, 253.
17. Brueggemann, *First and Second Samuel*, 275.
18. Peter R. Ackroyd, *The Second Book of Samuel: Commentary*, The Cambridge Bible Commentary, New English Bible (Cambridge; New York: Cambridge University Press, 1977), 102.
19. Anderson, *2 Samuel*, 155.

said to put Uriah in the most dangerous spot and then abandon him to die. Joab, however, seems to be aware that David's plan would look very suspicious. After all, how could you suddenly command everyone to abandon a fellow soldier without arousing suspicion? Instead, similar to David's suggestion, Uriah is sent where "the strongest defenders were" (11:16), near the wall of the besieged city, but he is not sent there alone, as fellow soldiers are sent with him. The key difference is that rather than abandoning Uriah to his death, Joab orchestrates the death of several Israelites in the cover-up, which would look far less suspicious. Furthermore, the main reason for their death, being too close to the city wall, is more plausible.

Joab sends "a full account of the battle" to David (11:18) via messenger. Joab warns the messenger that David may get angry at the news of the many battle casualties and that he might question the tactic of getting too close to the wall. If this happens, Joab advises the messenger to tell David that Uriah is dead. The messenger, perhaps wary of the king's anger—who has a reputation for shooting the messenger in the past (cf. 2 Sam 2, 4)—puts his own spin on the message of Joab, emphasizing that they approached the wall due to their success in driving back the Ammonites from out "in the open" toward the city gate (11:23). Furthermore, rather than wait for the king to get angry about the report, the wise messenger ends his message reporting the death of Uriah (11:24).

In response, David sends a message back to Joab "to encourage" him, telling him not to "let this upset you" (v. 25). Literally, in Hebrew David says to Joab, "don't let this deed be evil in your eyes." David suggests this should not be a big deal because "the sword devours one as well as another" (11:25). Unbeknownst to the messenger, this last phrase was likely "an implicit admission that Joab's revision of David's orders was necessary."[20] On another level, it was likely the duplicitous justification for Uriah's death that David was holding on to in order to alleviate his own guilty conscience.

David's dismissive reaction to the deaths of these Israelite soldiers contrasts his reactions to untimely deaths earlier in the story. When his political and military rivals, Saul and Abner, were killed, David showed intense grief and publicly mourned them (2 Sam 1:11–27; 3:31–39). Yet here, when his own loyal soldiers die, David shows no grief and does not mourn.[21]

The Aftermath of the Affair (11:26–27)

When Bathsheba hears of her husband's death she mourns him (11:26). Presumably, this was a genuine sorrow. Her world had irrevocably been changed and she was powerless to stop it. She had no choice in the matter, as David's

---

20. Alter, *The David Story*, 255.
21. Arnold, *1 & 2 Samuel*, 530.

men "took" her to the palace and she, being a powerless woman, was forced to sleep with the most powerful man in the land. What is not known is whether she knew of David's hand in her husband's death. The account of his death was quite plausible and probably did not attract much suspicion. It is possible that she may not have suspected David in this regard, especially if she was unaware of Uriah's visit to the palace shortly before his demise.

David does not take her as his wife until "the time of mourning was over" (11:27). It does not say that Bathsheba was done mourning, only that the official time of mourning was completed. While the length of this period is not specified, other texts would suggest a period of seven days (Gen 50:10; Jdt 16:24).[22] From the king's perspective (and likely Bathsheba's), time was of the essence. The couple had to marry very soon or it would become apparent that she was pregnant before their marriage while her husband was off at war. Conceivably, the delivery of the child could be viewed as premature, but people could count to nine months quite easily, and the time from the initial adultery to when Bathsheba realized she was pregnant was a bit too long for the months to add up correctly (never mind the time it took to bring Uriah in, send him back, then have him killed).

In the end, it would appear that at the human level David got away with it. He had managed to successfully cover up his adultery and not only take his mistress as his wife (perhaps making it look like a benevolent act in taking in a fallen soldier's widow) but have a new son born to him. However, the chapter ends with an ominous note: God was displeased (literally in Hebrew it says, "the thing was evil in Yahweh's eyes"). Through the entire scheme, David had forgotten his God and was clearly more concerned with his own lusts and preserving his own image than with breaking God's law. The description of David's deeds being "evil in Yahweh's eyes" (v. 27, author's translation) completely contrasts with David's own words to Joab about the deed. In verse 25 David tells the messenger to tell Joab, "don't let this deed be evil in your eyes" (NIV translates, "Don't let this upset you"). As one commentator has observed, David's "perceptions of reality are not congruent with Yahweh's perception."[23]

LIVE the Story

The Anatomy of a Great Fall

It is striking to me to see how quickly and how far David has fallen. Not long before this, David had shown incredible restraint with his predecessor and

---

22. Anderson, *2 Samuel*, 155.
23. Brueggemann, *First and Second Samuel*, 279.

refused to take the kingdom for himself, instead patiently waiting for God to deliver it. When Saul had been killed, David mourned his passing. Once king, David had brought the ark to Jerusalem and worshiped God with abandon. David had sought to build a temple for God and graciously received an amazing unconditional covenant from God in response. David further showed great character in keeping covenant with Jonathan, despite the political risks, by caring for Mephibosheth. David had defended Israel's national security and defeated all their enemies. David had risen to near absolute power and notoriety in Israel as Yahweh's anointed one, who was acting like an Israelite king was supposed to. Even in the previous chapter, David successfully defeated the Aramean threat and was poised to conquer the Ammonites. Suddenly, it would seem, David falls hard here in chapter 11 and will never completely recover.

David's sudden fall, however, is not as sudden as first appears. Looking back on the story of David, we have seen cracks in his armor. As noted previously, David had been multiplying wives. When he was crowned king, he had two wives already (three if we count Michal). At Hebron he married at least four more women (2 Sam 3:3–4). After he became king of all Israel at Jerusalem we read that "David took more concubines and wives" (2 Sam 5:13). The mention of concubines before wives is unusual and the narrator was likely emphasizing them for a reason. While in the ancient world, having many wives made sense in order to secure many male heirs or to secure international allies, taking concubines is another matter. While some overlook these dalliances as part and parcel of the life of kings, David was clearly breaking the Mosaic law for kings (Deut 17:17). Furthermore, this points to a significant lust problem within David. Now, with his kingdom settled and the majority of his enemies vanquished, David had become the most powerful man in Israel and could take whatever he wanted. When he saw a woman of unusual beauty bathing on a rooftop, he *took* her (breaking yet another Mosaic law—Deut 5:18—committing adultery).

In his brilliant fictional book, *The Screwtape Letters*, C. S. Lewis presents a senior devil named Screwtape writing to his nephew demon, Wormwood, and instructing him on how to lead people to sin. The satirical letters provide unique insights into the life of faith and human struggle with temptation. In one instance Screwtape writes:

> It does not matter how small the sins are provided that their cumulative effect is to edge the man away from the Light and out into the Nothing. . . . Indeed the safest road to Hell is the gradual one—the gentle slope, soft underfoot, without sudden turnings, without milestones, without signposts.[24]

---

24. C. S. Lewis, *The Screwtape Letters; with, Screwtape Proposes a Toast* (San Francisco: Harper SanFrancisco, 2011), 61.

The road to David's fall here in 2 Samuel 11 was paved with "small" sins in the past. Despite the grand success that was David's career up to this point, his weaknesses in the area of lust were left unchecked, and their cumulative effect is realized in chapter 11. In the Sermon on the Mount, Jesus points out the small sins that were often overlooked by teachers of the day. While it was well known to not "murder" (Matt 5:21) or "commit adultery" (Matt 5:27), Jesus points out the sin that occurs prior to these big sins—the sin of anger precedes murder (Matt 5:21–22) and the sin of lust precedes adultery (Matt 5:27).

In the New Testament, Paul explains that the stories in the Old Testament "happened to them as examples and were written down as warnings for us, on whom the culmination of the ages has come" (1 Cor 10:11). David's tragic fall should be sobering to Christians, and his story should be viewed as a serious warning. As Paul goes on to write in the next verse: "So, if you think you are standing firm, be careful that you don't fall!" (1 Cor 10:12). No one appeared more secure at this point in the story than David. If anyone appeared to be standing firm, it was Yahweh's anointed one. Yet, how quickly he fell, and when he fell, he fell hard. David coveted another man's wife, committed adultery, and finally murdered her husband—breaking three of the Ten Commandments (Exod 20).

If it could happen to David, it could happen to you. It could happen to me. In the New Testament, James talks about how temptation leads to sin, warning that "each person is tempted when they are dragged away by their own evil desire and enticed" (Jas 1:14). Here David's lust problem, evident in his taking of many wives and concubines, entices him to lust after Bathsheba. James goes on to say that "then, after desire has conceived, it gives birth to sin" (Jas 1:15a), so David took Bathsheba and slept with her. Finally, as James notes, "sin, when it is full-grown, gives birth to death" (Jas 1:15b), and the final result of David's sin was not only the death of Uriah but the death of his son (see the next chapter) born out of the adultery.

Paul further writes, "No temptation has overtaken you except what is common to mankind. And God is faithful; he will not let you be tempted beyond what you can bear. But when you are tempted, he will also provide a way out so that you can endure it" (1 Cor 10:13). Paul asserts that there is always "a way out." There is always a way to "endure" temptation. In this story, David had many opportunities to do the right thing. When first tempted, he could have looked away from the bathing woman. Second, he could have left and joined in the Ammonite war, as a king was supposed to do. Third, he could have yielded to the veiled warning given by his servant who said, "Isn't this Bathsheba daughter of one of David's key men and wife of one of his best soldiers?" Fourth, even after the adultery, he could have simply confessed his sin. He could have publicly confessed if necessary. But instead of choosing repentance and confession, David chose cover-up and murder. There were many other ways out, but David only perceived one way of saving face.

This reminds us that the point to standing up under temptation is not to save face. The point is to avoid sin, to be forgiven, and to restore relationship—even if that requires that we look weak. It is well known that secret sins have much greater power than overt sin. Secret sins left unconfessed fester and can gain particular power over us. When sin is confessed, it loses its power. If David had confessed his sins, he would have avoided compounding his guilt with the sin of murder(s). As we will see in the coming chapters, the cost of David's sins was great. Though receiving divine forgiveness, the consequences of his sins reverberated for years to come. This text should move us to be on short accounts with God. Confess our sin to God regularly. God is faithful and makes a way out of temptation. Nevertheless, continually ignoring sin or covering it up will eventually lead us to our own grand fall.

LISTEN to the Story

¹The LORD sent Nathan to David. When he came to him, he said, "There were two men in a certain town, one rich and the other poor. ²The rich man had a very large number of sheep and cattle, ³but the poor man had nothing except one little ewe lamb he had bought. He raised it, and it grew up with him and his children. It shared his food, drank from his cup and even slept in his arms. It was like a daughter to him.

⁴"Now a traveler came to the rich man, but the rich man refrained from taking one of his own sheep or cattle to prepare a meal for the traveler who had come to him. Instead, he took the ewe lamb that belonged to the poor man and prepared it for the one who had come to him."

⁵David burned with anger against the man and said to Nathan, "As surely as the LORD lives, the man who did this must die! ⁶He must pay for that lamb four times over, because he did such a thing and had no pity."

⁷Then Nathan said to David, "You are the man! This is what the LORD, the God of Israel, says: 'I anointed you king over Israel, and I delivered you from the hand of Saul. ⁸I gave your master's house to you, and your master's wives into your arms. I gave you all Israel and Judah. And if all this had been too little, I would have given you even more. ⁹Why did you despise the word of the LORD by doing what is evil in his eyes? You struck down Uriah the Hittite with the sword and took his wife to be your own. You killed him with the sword of the Ammonites. ¹⁰Now, therefore, the sword will never depart from your house, because you despised me and took the wife of Uriah the Hittite to be your own.'

¹¹"This is what the LORD says: 'Out of your own household I am going to bring calamity on you. Before your very eyes I will take your wives and give them to one who is close to you, and he will sleep with your wives in broad daylight. ¹²You did it in secret, but I will do this thing in broad daylight before all Israel.'"

¹³Then David said to Nathan, "I have sinned against the LORD."

Nathan replied, "The LORD has taken away your sin. You are not going to die. [14]But because by doing this you have shown utter contempt for the LORD, the son born to you will die."

[15]After Nathan had gone home, the LORD struck the child that Uriah's wife had borne to David, and he became ill. [16]David pleaded with God for the child. He fasted and spent the nights lying in sackcloth on the ground. [17]The elders of his household stood beside him to get him up from the ground, but he refused, and he would not eat any food with them.

[18]On the seventh day the child died. David's attendants were afraid to tell him that the child was dead, for they thought, "While the child was still living, he wouldn't listen to us when we spoke to him. How can we now tell him the child is dead? He may do something desperate."

[19]David noticed that his attendants were whispering among themselves, and he realized the child was dead. "Is the child dead?" he asked.

"Yes," they replied, "he is dead."

[20]Then David got up from the ground. After he had washed, put on lotions and changed his clothes, he went into the house of the LORD and worshiped. Then he went to his own house, and at his request they served him food, and he ate.

[21]His attendants asked him, "Why are you acting this way? While the child was alive, you fasted and wept, but now that the child is dead, you get up and eat!"

[22]He answered, "While the child was still alive, I fasted and wept. I thought, 'Who knows? The LORD may be gracious to me and let the child live.' [23]But now that he is dead, why should I go on fasting? Can I bring him back again? I will go to him, but he will not return to me."

[24]Then David comforted his wife Bathsheba, and he went to her and made love to her. She gave birth to a son, and they named him Solomon. The LORD loved him; [25]and because the LORD loved him, he sent word through Nathan the prophet to name him Jedidiah.

[26]Meanwhile Joab fought against Rabbah of the Ammonites and captured the royal citadel. [27]Joab then sent messengers to David, saying, "I have fought against Rabbah and taken its water supply. [28]Now muster the rest of the troops and besiege the city and capture it. Otherwise I will take the city, and it will be named after me."

[29]So David mustered the entire army and went to Rabbah, and attacked and captured it. [30]David took the crown from their king's head, and it was placed on his own head. It weighed a talent of gold, and it was set with

precious stones. David took a great quantity of plunder from the city [31]and brought out the people who were there, consigning them to labor with saws and with iron picks and axes, and he made them work at brickmaking. David did this to all the Ammonite towns. Then he and his entire army returned to Jerusalem.

Listen to the Text in the Story: Exodus 22:1; 1 Samuel 22:5; 2 Samuel 7; 10:1–14

An undisclosed amount of time passes, though it could not be yet nine months as Bathsheba has yet to deliver David's child born of adultery. While David may have thought he had successfully concealed his sin, God sends a prophet to the king. This is the third time God has sent a prophet to David in the story. When David had fled to Moab from Saul, God directed him to return to Judah through the prophet Gad (1 Sam 22:5). When David asked to build God a temple, God made a covenant with David through the prophet Nathan (2 Sam 7). However, not since the days of Samuel had God sent a prophet to rebuke an Israelite king for his sin. So, when the prophet came to David, the king may not have been wary of his presence.

This chapter also continues the ongoing war with Ammon that has been raging since Hanun's repudiation of David's sympathy delegation (2 Sam 10). Now, the final capture of the Ammonite capital city of Rabbah is in sight, but rather than being another glorious victory for David, his sin casts a pall over the achievement.

EXPLAIN the Story

While David had thought he had gotten away with adultery and murder, Yahweh sends his prophet to confront the king. Though David confesses his sin against God and Nathan informs him of God's forgiveness, serious consequences are predicted. First, his son born through adultery will die. When the child falls ill, David desperately pleads for his child's life, fasting and praying unceasingly. When the child dies, much to the surprise of his attendants, David ceases his petitioning, explaining that since the child is dead there is no reason to continue praying for him. Despite the tragedy, a note of hope is sounded in the birth of a second son to David and Bathsheba, Solomon.

The chapter ends with the final capture of the Ammonite city of Rabbah. Having taken the city, Joab sent word for David to join the army so that he can take credit for its capture. David obeys and brings the army to Rabbah and captures it. While this would normally be a happy victory story for the king, the indictment of Nathan hangs over the scene. While David receives accolades from his public, his son has died and the prophet has predicted perilous times ahead for the once great king of Israel.

The Prophet Confronts the King (12:1–6)

In response to David's heinous sins, God sends Nathan the prophet to confront the king. The confrontation is not initially direct, with Nathan instead telling him a story of a rich man stealing and killing a poor man's sheep. Perhaps comfortable that he had gotten away with everything and due to his uniformly positive interactions with prophets thus far, David was naively unsuspecting that in the parable the prophet was speaking about the king.

The parable underscores the depravity of David's actions by contrasting the states of the victim and the perpetrator. The rich man had "a very large number of sheep and cattle" (v. 2) while the poor man had one little lamb who was like a child to him. As one commentator puts it, "the one who has practically everything takes away the only treasured possession of the one who has next to nothing."[1] This presents the rich man of despicable character and his act as particularly deplorable.

Several significant words serve to link the previous story of David's sinful actions to the parable.[2] In chapter 11 David "sends" Joab to battle (11:1), and here God "sends" the prophet Nathan (12:1). David "walks" on his rooftop (11:2), while in the parable a "traveler" (literally in Hebrew a "walker") visits the rich man (12:4). Both stories use the words "to eat" and "to drink" (11:13; 12:3). The poor man's lamb is said to be like "a daughter" to him (12:3), and Bathsheba is said to be "daughter of Eliam" (11:3). Furthermore, David "lies" (Hebrew *shakab*) with Bathsheba (11:4) and the poor man "lies" (Hebrew *shakab*) with his lamb at night (12:3). Most significantly, the rich man "takes" (Hebrew *laqah*) the lamb from the poor man, just as David "takes" (Hebrew *laqah*) Bathsheba (2 Sam 11:4).

Nathan's parable is an ingenious way of getting the king to level judgment against himself. After all, given that David was once a shepherd, the image of a poor man with a lamb would have resonated with him and led him to identify with the poor man in the story rather than the rich one. Having been drawn into the story, David "burned with anger" and declared that the rich man "must die!" and also pay restitution "four times over" (vv. 5–6). What is more, David castigates the man for doing "such a thing" and having "no pity."

1. Anderson, *2 Samuel*, 162.
2. Hamilton, *Handbook*, 333.

As we saw last chapter David did "such a thing" but told Joab to not let it "upset you" (2 Sam 11:25), though the chapter concluded by noting that the thing "displeased the LORD" (2 Sam 11:27). What is more, at the news of the deaths of the Israelite soldiers (not just Uriah) who died in David's cover-up, David showed no pity.

David's judgment that the rich man must payback "fourfold" to recompense the poor man for the loss of his sheep is in keeping with Israelite law, which requires a thief to repay "four sheep" for the theft of one sheep (Exod 22:1). As the narrative progresses, however, there might be a further irony to David's judgment, as David loses four of his sons: (1) his unnamed son with Bathsheba (12:18); (2) Ammon is killed by Absalom (13:29); (3) Absalom is killed by Joab (18:14–15); (4) Adonijah is killed by Solomon (1 Kgs 2:25). Is this a coincidence, or was David's judgment a "self-curse"?[3] Regardless, the word of the LORD is fulfilled. The sword never left his house (v. 10).

You are the Man! (12:7–12)

After David has leveled judgment against the poor man in Nathan's story, the prophet reveals the truth. The story is about David. He is the cruel rich man. In response, God reminds David of how he made him king, rescued him from Saul, and gave him all he needed—including wives—and even the kingdom.[4] Yet David "despise[d] the word of the LORD by doing what is evil" (v. 9).

The punishment for David's sin is meted out in kind. Just as David killed Uriah with the "sword of the Ammonites," so David's house will be forever plagued by "the sword" (v. 10). This prophecy recalls David's message to Joab after Uriah was murdered saying, "the sword devours one as well as another" (2 Sam 11:25) and throws it "back in his face."[5] In keeping with the punishment in kind, just as David took another man's wife, the prophet declares that one "who is close to [David]" will take his wives and violate them. What is more, while David did this in secret (alluding to his cover-up), this will happen in broad daylight. This prophecy is sadly fulfilled when his son Absalom will enter David's harem and "slept with his father's concubines in the sight of all Israel" (2 Sam 16:22).

The prophetic pronouncement on his sin suddenly creates tension in the story between the prophetic word Nathan brought to David in chapter 7. Nathan's first prophetic word promises rest from enemies (7:11), a great name

---

3. Bodner, *Power Play*, 112. The Jewish Talmud (Yoma 22B) understood the fourfold restitution as fulfilled in the fate of David's children.

4. The reference to David receiving Saul's wives likely refers to David's supplanting of Saul's house, not to his having married Saul's wives. So Brueggemann, *First and Second Samuel*, 281. Contra Levenson and Halpern, "Political Import of David's Marriages," 507–18.

5. Alter, *The David Story*, 259.

(7:9), and an eternal dynasty (7:13). Nathan's second prophetic word to David warns of calamity "out of [his] own household" (12:11), continual violent strife (the sword) within his house (12:10), and terrible times ahead (12:11–12). This leads the reader to wonder about the promise of an eternal dynasty. Was this now revoked as Saul's was revoked before him (1 Sam 15:10–31)? After all, Samuel told Saul that had he been obedient God "would have established your kingdom over Israel for all time" (1 Sam 13:13). Was David's dynasty now at risk?[6] For now the question is not answered, and the tumultuous times that follow all threaten to answer it in the affirmative.

David's Response (12:13–25)

At this David confesses his sin. Given David's passion for God shown in his enthusiastic worship earlier in the story (2 Sam 5), one might have expected a bit more from the king here. David's confession at the prophetic indictment, however, is viewed more positively when compared to that of his predecessor, Saul. When Samuel confronted Saul about his sin saying, "Why did you not obey the LORD? Why did you pounce on the plunder and do evil in the eyes of the LORD?" (1 Sam 15:19), Saul denied his sin replying, "I did obey the LORD" (1 Sam 15:20). Eventually Saul does confess that he sinned, but he also offers excuses. He says, "I have sinned. I violated the LORD's command and your instructions. I was afraid of the men and so I gave in to them" (1 Sam 15:24). David's straightforward confession of sin is a massive improvement on Saul's duplicitous shenanigans.

What is more, compared with later Israelite kings, David's repentance reflects quite well on him. For example, when the later King Jehoiakim receives a written prophetic indictment from the prophet Jeremiah, rather than repent, the king burns the prophetic writings (Jer 36:23–24).[7] Sadly, this royal defiance of God's word was not uncommon (cf. 1 Kgs 18–19; 20:34–43; 22; 2 Kgs 1:1–9; 17:13–17; Isa 7). Furthermore, it is worth noting that in the ancient world kings did *not* have to confess to prophets. Court prophets in the ancient Near East generally addressed a king to assure them of success, perhaps warn of some danger, or at most to request that the king perform a cultic act of some sort. By and large their prophecies concerned the well-being and warfare of the king.[8] Kings were not obligated to obey prophets, and prophets could be imprisoned or killed if they displeased the king and his court (e.g., in 1 Kgs 22:27 one of Yahweh's prophets is imprisoned by the king for negative

---

6. Arnold, *1 & 2 Samuel*, 533.

7. Bodner, *Power Play*, 113.

8. Martti Nissinen, et al., *Prophets and Prophecy in the Ancient Near East*, WAW 12 (Atlanta: Society of Biblical Literature, 2003), 17.

prophesying). In other words, David does not repent simply because he has no other option at having been confronted with his sin.[9]

While the text does not elaborate on David's state of mind in repenting, seeing as David has shown great passion for his God in the past, it seems in keeping with his character that his repentance is genuine. This is further supported by the reaction of Nathan to David's confession of sin, as immediately after David's confession the prophet announces that God forgives him and that the king will not die. David's genuine repentance is met with God's merciful forgiveness. In Israelite law, a person guilty of David's crimes was worthy of death (e.g., Lev 20:10), yet God proves himself exceedingly merciful here.

David's sin, however, is not without consequence. Though his life is spared, the son born to him and Bathsheba will die. Significantly, in v. 15 Bathsheba is still referred to as "Uriah's wife." While at first glance this penalty may seem fortuitous for the king, any parent would know that this was not the case. It is a common proverbial saying that a parent should never have to bury their child. Yet this is what this prophetic oracle meant to David. He was going to have to bury his son. This is not getting off lightly. For myself, I would sooner forfeit my own life than see my child die. Having my child die in place of me—for sin that I committed—would be a fate worse than death.

It is no wonder that David began a week of pleading with God for his child's life. He dressed in sackcloth, slept on the ground, and refused to eat despite the pleading of his attendants to do so. When the child dies on the seventh day of the illness, David's attendants worry that David may snap, but instead David cleans himself up and goes to the "house of the LORD" (probably the tent housing the ark) to worship. Remember, David has been pleading with God to spare his child for seven days straight. When the child dies—which means that God denied his request—David worships God. He worships the God who let his son die, the God who ignored David's impassioned pleas. This speaks to David's character and his heart toward God. David worships God, not because he answered his prayer. David worships in spite of the death of his son, which David firmly believed God could have prevented.

What is more, further baffling his attendants, David eats and returns to normal life. When asked about this change David explains that before the child died, he knew there was a chance God could be gracious and heal the child, but now that he is gone, there is no more point to the pleading. David's final remark, "I will go to him, but he will not return to me" (v. 23), reveals that his son's death causes David to reflect on his own mortality.[10]

Just as his attendants were baffled at David's lack of mourning after the

---

9. Brueggemann, *First and Second Samuel*, 282; Arnold, *1 & 2 Samuel*, 534.
10. Alter, *The David Story*, 262.

death of his child, so is the reader. As we have seen, David has shown great capacity for grief and mourning. He has mourned the deaths of Saul (2 Sam 1:11–12) and Abner (2 Sam 3:31–35), and he will later mourn the deaths of other sons (2 Sam 13:36–37; 18:33–19:4).[11] Why does he not mourn this child after his death? We are not told and can only speculate. David never ceases to surprise.[12]

Despite the tragedy of the lost child, this is not the end of the story. After the death of the baby, Bathsheba again conceives and another son, Solomon, is born. Significantly, Bathsheba is now called David's wife (rather than the wife of Uriah). Furthermore, we are told that Yahweh loves Solomon and that, due to this love, God gives him the name Jedidiah (meaning "friend of Yahweh" or "beloved by Yahweh") through the prophet Nathan. While Yahweh's love for this new child suggests a hopeful future for David's house (and the fact that Solomon will be the next king), the ominous predictions of the sword and the future peril that his wives will face augur a darker side to this future.

The Capture of Rabbah (12:26–31)

The story now returns to the war with the Ammonites and the final victory over their capital city of Rabbah. It is possible that the defeat of Rabbah actually occurred before the previous pericope about the birth of Solomon; however, sieges in the ancient world often lasted years (e.g., 2 Kgs 17:5; 25:1–2), so this is not certain. As you probably remember, the Ammonite conflict began in chapter 10 with David featuring prominently in the victories before abdicating his role in the war in 2 Samuel 11:1. As a result, instead of David defeating the Ammonites, his general, Joab, does. In fact, we are first told by the narrator in verse 26 that Joab captured "the royal city" (though translated by the NIV as "captured the royal citadel," most translations render "royal city," cf. NRSV, ESV, KJV, ASV, JPS). However, in order to not have the victory attributed to him, Joab sent for David to come and capture the city so that the king will get credit for the victory. This creates some ambiguity as to what actually happens. Who really captured Rabbah? In addition to the narrator, Joab also claims to have conquered it in verse 27 saying, "I have taken the city of water" (though the NIV translates this as its "water supply," most translations translate "city of water," cf. NRSV, ESV, KJV, ASV, JPS). Joab apparently wants David to know that *he* has captured the city. This may be a move by the general to show David who holds the real power in Israel.[13] This likelihood is increased by the way in which Joab practically *orders* David to

---

11. Anderson, *2 Samuel*, 164.
12. Alter, *The David Story*, 261.
13. Ibid., 264.

come to Rabbah. We have seen David and Joab come into conflict earlier in the story with the death of Abner in 2 Samuel 2–3, and the king and general will butt heads again in the near future (2 Sam 14). Joab, however, is shrewd and provides a great service to David here in allowing his king "a public success when he surely needed it to stop the gossip at court."[14]

In response, David brings the rest of the army and gets credit for the victory, taking the crown from the Ammonite king's head. David is also credited with taking a vast amount of plunder and enslaving many of the Ammonites. Despite the victory and spoils taken, the victory seems hollow after all that has happened and Nathan's ominous prophecy of chapter 12. From a worldly perspective, David's throne looks secure and his success unmitigated; however, from God's perspective things have taken a wrong turn and will never be the same again.

LIVE the Story

The Nature of Sin and Forgiveness

The story of the prophet Nathan confronting David about his sin underscores important aspects of a biblical view of sin and forgiveness. The prophet underscores that David's sin was not just against humans but against God himself. Nathan declares that in sinning David "despised" God's word (v. 9), "despised" God himself (v. 10), and showed "utter contempt for the Lord" (v. 14). It is easy to forget this aspect of sin. We may only really acknowledge that our sin is against other people (perhaps leading us to think that sins of the mind are really "victimless crimes" or not really sin at all). The story here in 2 Samuel 12 reminds us that sin is first and foremost against God. This theocentric aspect of sin is also brought out in Psalm 51, which is connected to our chapter, as the superscription reads, "A psalm of David. When the prophet Nathan came to him after David had committed adultery with Bathsheba." The psalmist acknowledges to God, "Against you, you only, have I sinned and done what is evil in your sight" (Ps 51:4). This is not to say that David's action was not against people. To be sure, sin affects other people, directly and indirectly, as acknowledged in Nathan's prophetic indictment (v. 9). But ultimately sin is an offense against a holy God. This perspective does not lessen an offense. In fact, "the intent is perhaps to heighten the sense of offense by acknowledging that ultimately violations of the covenant are offenses against God himself and are judged by divine sanction rather than

---

14. Brueggemann, *First and Second Samuel*, 284.

societal acceptance or disapproval alone."[15] Sin is first and foremost an offense against God. David's brief confession in this story, "I have sinned against the LORD" (2 Sam 12:13), shows this theocentric perspective.

This story also provides an opportunity for reflection on forgiveness. Given the disturbing nature of David's sin, it can be difficult to understand how the king's brief, one-line confession of sin results in God immediately forgiving him. David's confession of sin appears to lack apology. It lacks any pleading for forgiveness. It lacks any bargaining or offer to do some type of penance in exchange for forgiveness. There is no promise to never do it again. There are no outward gestures to show his sorrow or convince the prophet of the genuineness of his repentance. How can such a simple confession result in forgiveness like this?

First, regarding David's brief confession, it should be remembered that "The LORD does not look at the things people look at . . . but the LORD looks at the heart" (1 Sam 16:7), and in a confession God looks for "a broken spirit; a broken and contrite heart" (Ps 51:17). David was clearly broken, and God saw his heart in his simple confession. Second, though God's quick forgiveness of David's despicable sin is surprising to me, God's mercy and forgiveness should *not* be surprising—it is one of God's defining characteristics! In Exodus 34, when God reveals his character to Moses, God declares that he is "the compassionate and gracious God, slow to anger, abounding in love and faithfulness, maintaining love to thousands, and forgiving wickedness, rebellion and sin" (Exod 34:6–7). In fact, this description of the divine character in Exodus 34 is something like the Old Testament confession of faith, or creed, as can be seen in how it is frequently referenced or alluded to throughout the Old Testament (cf. 2 Chr 30:9; Neh 9:17; Pss 86:15; 103:8; 111:4; Joel 2:13; Jonah 4:2). God is all about forgiveness. He is known for his mercy, graciousness, and forgiveness of sin.

My initial disapproval of God's quick forgiveness of David is similar to Jonah's anger at God's forgiveness of Nineveh.[16] Nineveh was the capital of Assyria, a nation known for its war crimes and particularly cruel ways of dealing with other nations. In particular, Assyria had been incredibly brutal with the Israelites. Assyrian artwork depicts many of the awful war crimes perpetrated against Israel.[17] Yet, when the Assyrians repent, God instantly

---

15. Gerald Henry Wilson, *Psalms*, NIVAC (Grand Rapids: Zondervan, 2002), 773.

16. Arnold, *1 & 2 Samuel*, 543–544.

17. E.g., the Lachish reliefs depict Israelites impaled on stakes, Assyrian tents filled with the heads of Israelites, and Israelite heads on a stake. See http://www.reclaimingthemind.org/blog/2010/07/top-ten-biblical-discoveries-in-archaeology-10-assyrian-lachish-reliefs/. Other Assyrian reliefs depict them skinning people, dismembering corpses, and other horrible war crimes. See http://www.ancient.eu/Ashurnasirpal_II/

forgives them. God's mercy on Assyria angers Jonah. How could God forgive such an evil nation who had done such terrible things to God's people?

Contrary to this righteous indignation, I must confess that when *I* sin and *I* ask for forgiveness, I generally do not have the same level of disapproval. Rather, God's forgiveness of my sin is much appreciated and welcomed. Similarly, when Jonah is forgiven for disobeying God's command to preach to Nineveh, Jonah praises and thanks God (Jonah 2:9). My qualms about God's forgiveness of a sinner do not extend to my own circumstances, as I am quite biased toward myself.

My misgivings about the quick forgiveness granted to David probably reveals that I misunderstand something about God's forgiveness. Often when we sin we plead for forgiveness. We might bargain with God. We might promise to do something for him if he would but forgive us. Perhaps we act this way out of a guilty conscience, out of our awareness of our sin and how far we fell. But do we think that we need to convince God to forgive us? Will our vow of good deeds convince God to forgive? Is there a part of us that thinks we can somehow *earn* God's forgiveness? The story of God forgiving David reminds us that God forgives because that is who he is.[18] God forgives us because of what he has done for us, not because of how good we are (Titus 3:5; Eph 2:8–9). God's forgiveness of David at his (albeit brief) confession is consistent with biblical teaching on forgiveness that, "If we confess our sins, he is faithful and just and will forgive us our sins and purify us from all unrighteousness" (1 John 1:9). Our sins are forgiven not on the basis of our convincing God to forgive through our eloquent confession. Our sins are forgiven for the sake of Jesus Christ and what he has done for us (Eph 4:32; 1 John 2:12).

---

18. In his exhaustive study of the theme of sin in the Old Testament, Boda (*Severe Mercy*, 522) has underscored "the importance of the character of God for remedying sin."

CHAPTER 39

2 Samuel 13:1–39

 LISTEN to the Story

¹In the course of time, Amnon son of David fell in love with Tamar, the beautiful sister of Absalom son of David.

²Amnon became so obsessed with his sister Tamar that he made himself ill. She was a virgin, and it seemed impossible for him to do anything to her.

³Now Amnon had an adviser named Jonadab son of Shimeah, David's brother. Jonadab was a very shrewd man. ⁴He asked Amnon, "Why do you, the king's son, look so haggard morning after morning? Won't you tell me?"

Amnon said to him, "I'm in love with Tamar, my brother Absalom's sister."

⁵"Go to bed and pretend to be ill," Jonadab said. "When your father comes to see you, say to him, 'I would like my sister Tamar to come and give me something to eat. Let her prepare the food in my sight so I may watch her and then eat it from her hand.'"

⁶So Amnon lay down and pretended to be ill. When the king came to see him, Amnon said to him, "I would like my sister Tamar to come and make some special bread in my sight, so I may eat from her hand."

⁷David sent word to Tamar at the palace: "Go to the house of your brother Amnon and prepare some food for him." ⁸So Tamar went to the house of her brother Amnon, who was lying down. She took some dough, kneaded it, made the bread in his sight and baked it. ⁹Then she took the pan and served him the bread, but he refused to eat.

"Send everyone out of here," Amnon said. So everyone left him. ¹⁰Then Amnon said to Tamar, "Bring the food here into my bedroom so I may eat from your hand." And Tamar took the bread she had prepared and brought it to her brother Amnon in his bedroom. ¹¹But when she took it to him to eat, he grabbed her and said, "Come to bed with me, my sister."

¹²"No, my brother!" she said to him. "Don't force me! Such a thing should not be done in Israel! Don't do this wicked thing. ¹³What about me? Where could I get rid of my disgrace? And what about you? You would be

like one of the wicked fools in Israel. Please speak to the king; he will not keep me from being married to you." [14]But he refused to listen to her, and since he was stronger than she, he raped her.

[15]Then Amnon hated her with intense hatred. In fact, he hated her more than he had loved her. Amnon said to her, "Get up and get out!"

[16]"No!" she said to him. "Sending me away would be a greater wrong than what you have already done to me."

But he refused to listen to her. [17]He called his personal servant and said, "Get this woman out of my sight and bolt the door after her." [18]So his servant put her out and bolted the door after her. She was wearing an ornate robe, for this was the kind of garment the virgin daughters of the king wore. [19]Tamar put ashes on her head and tore the ornate robe she was wearing. She put her hands on her head and went away, weeping aloud as she went.

[20]Her brother Absalom said to her, "Has that Amnon, your brother, been with you? Be quiet for now, my sister; he is your brother. Don't take this thing to heart." And Tamar lived in her brother Absalom's house, a desolate woman.

[21]When King David heard all this, he was furious. [22]And Absalom never said a word to Amnon, either good or bad; he hated Amnon because he had disgraced his sister Tamar.

[23]Two years later, when Absalom's sheepshearers were at Baal Hazor near the border of Ephraim, he invited all the king's sons to come there. [24]Absalom went to the king and said, "Your servant has had shearers come. Will the king and his attendants please join me?"

[25]"No, my son," the king replied. "All of us should not go; we would only be a burden to you." Although Absalom urged him, he still refused to go but gave him his blessing.

[26]Then Absalom said, "If not, please let my brother Amnon come with us."

The king asked him, "Why should he go with you?" [27]But Absalom urged him, so he sent with him Amnon and the rest of the king's sons.

[28]Absalom ordered his men, "Listen! When Amnon is in high spirits from drinking wine and I say to you, 'Strike Amnon down,' then kill him. Don't be afraid. Haven't I given you this order? Be strong and brave." [29]So Absalom's men did to Amnon what Absalom had ordered. Then all the king's sons got up, mounted their mules and fled.

[30]While they were on their way, the report came to David: "Absalom has struck down all the king's sons; not one of them is left." [31]The king

stood up, tore his clothes and lay down on the ground; and all his attendants stood by with their clothes torn.

³²But Jonadab son of Shimeah, David's brother, said, "My lord should not think that they killed all the princes; only Amnon is dead. This has been Absalom's express intention ever since the day Amnon raped his sister Tamar. ³³My lord the king should not be concerned about the report that all the king's sons are dead. Only Amnon is dead."

³⁴Meanwhile, Absalom had fled.

Now the man standing watch looked up and saw many people on the road west of him, coming down the side of the hill. The watchman went and told the king, "I see men in the direction of Horonaim, on the side of the hill."

³⁵Jonadab said to the king, "See, the king's sons have come; it has happened just as your servant said."

³⁶As he finished speaking, the king's sons came in, wailing loudly. The king, too, and all his attendants wept very bitterly.

³⁷Absalom fled and went to Talmai son of Ammihud, the king of Geshur. But King David mourned many days for his son.

³⁸After Absalom fled and went to Geshur, he stayed there three years. ³⁹And King David longed to go to Absalom, for he was consoled concerning Amnon's death.

Listen to the Text in the Story: Genesis 34; Exodus 22:16–17; Leviticus 18:9, 11; 20:17; 1 Samuel 25; 2 Samuel 12

No sooner has Nathan the prophet predicted dark times for David's family (2 Sam 12:10–11) than it begins to be fulfilled. Understanding the disturbing events narrated in this chapter relies partly on understanding ancient Israelite attitudes toward incest, as revealed in Mosaic law, and legislation surrounding sexual relations outside of marriage. First, it is clear that in Mosaic legislation, sexual relationships between siblings are outlawed (Lev 18:9, 11; 20:17). Even relations between half siblings are forbidden, as Leviticus 18:11 makes clear, "Do not have sexual relations with the daughter of your father's wife, born to your father; she is your sister." Clearly in attacking Tamar, Amnon is guilty of both rape and incest.

Mosaic law surrounding pre-marital sexual relations must also be kept in mind in order to understand this story. For example, Exodus 22:16–17 decrees that when a man sleeps with "a virgin who is not pledged to be married" (Exod 22:16), the man was to take the woman to be his wife. Legislation in

Deuterononmy 22:28–29 similarly legislates marriage in instances of premarital sex and includes instances of rape (Deut 22:28).[1] If the woman who was raped was betrothed, then the rapist was to be executed (Deut 22:25). But in situations where the rape victim is not betrothed to anyone, the rapist is forced to pay fifty shekels of silver (a bride price) to her father and marry her. In fact, in such instances the resulting marriage provides no allowance for future divorce (Deut 22:29). The intent of the law is to prevent a rape victim from being left destitute and outside a family structure for the rest of her life. The reason a rapist must marry his victim was so that she would have access to all his goods and resources for the rest of her life so that she could live with some security. In other words, the law was meant to disempower the rapist and provide care for the victim.[2] This legislation must be kept in mind in interpreting this chapter and we will explain its relevance below.

EXPLAIN the Story

Despite the somewhat encouraging ending to the last chapter with the birth of Solomon and the final defeat of Amnon, this chapter begins to fulfill Nathan's prophetic word to David that "Out of your own household I am going to bring calamity on you" (2 Sam 12:11). First, David's eldest son, Amnon, grows lustfully obsessed with his beautiful half sister, Tamar, who was the full sister of Absalom. Amnon devises a plan to feign illness and have Tamar wait on him. When she does so Amnon rapes her, then kicks her out of his house. When David hears what happened, he is outraged, but does nothing about it. Her brother, Absalom, takes Tamar in, and two years later acts out his revenge and has Amnon killed. While Absalom flees Israel, David mourns Amnon for a long time. The chapter ends noting that eventually David gave up his plans to bring Absalom to justice, having been consoled over Amnon's death.

The Rape of Tamar (13:1–20)

After an undisclosed amount of time, many of David's sons had grown into men and the eldest, Amnon, harbors a lustful obsession over his "beautiful" half sister Tamar. Amnon was born to David's wife, Ahinoam (2 Sam 3:2),

---

1. As with many other Old Testament laws, this law doesn't "represent an ethical ideal, but instead charts a course (limited moves, some compromise, and awareness of the practicalities of life), and a destination (ethical ideals)." Paul S. Evans, "Imagining Justice for the Marginalized: A Suspicious Reading of the Covenant Code (Exodus 21:1–23:33) in Its Ancient Near Eastern Context," in *The Bible and Social Justice*, ed. Cynthia Long Westfall and Bryan R. Dyer, McMaster New Testament Series (Eugene, OR: Wipf & Stock, 2015), 30.

2. For a good discussion of these texts see George Athas, *Deuteronomy: One Nation under God*, Reading the Bible Today Series (Sydney: Aquila Press, 2016), 260–71.

while Tamar and Absalom were children of another wife of David named Maakah, a foreign princess from Geshur (2 Sam 3:3). Amnon's fixation with Tamar was so great the narrator says, "he made himself ill" (13:2). As a virgin daughter of the king, it is possible Tamar was well guarded or usually confined to women's quarters, making it hard for Amnon to act on his obsession. Amnon, however, receives advice from his cousin, Jonadab, son of David's brother Shimeah, who proposes a plan that Amnon pretend to be ill so that his father would allow Tamar to come nurse him back to health. It is unclear whether Jonadab knew that Amnon would assault Tamar, as it is possible Jonadab was just advising a way that Amnon could spend time with Tamar. Regardless, the plan works as David agrees to Amnon's request and orders his daughter Tamar to go to Amnon's house and prepare a meal for him. Ironically, David inadvertently aids Amnon in raping the king's own daughter.

Tamar obeys her father and prepares a meal at Amnon's house, but when she attempts to serve the food Amnon refuses to eat. Instead, Amnon orders everyone to leave and requests that Tamar serve him in his bed, no doubt appealing to his "illness" as the reason for the strange request. Tamar agrees to Amnon's request and brings the food to his bedroom. Instead of letting her serve him, however, Amnon grabs her and demands that she sleep with him.

Tamar refuses and pleads with Amnon not to rape her, warning her attacker that it would "disgrace" her and ruin his reputation forever. Finally, bargaining for her life, she suggests that their father would give her to him as wife if he would only ask (v. 13). It seems quite unlikely that Tamar's claims here are realistic. Would David have allowed two of his children to marry since they had different mothers? As noted above, sexual relations between siblings like this is clearly outlawed in biblical legislation (Lev 18:19). It seems more likely that Tamar is frantically arguing for this possibility even though she knows it is unlikely. She is buying time. She is so desperate to stop her attacker that she fabricates another option for him. After all, earlier we were told that there was nothing Amnon could do to fulfill his obsession for her (v. 2), which seems to contradict the idea that he could have simply asked the king for her hand in marriage. Furthermore, Tamar's statement that "such a thing should not be done in Israel" (v. 12) suggests siblings could *not* marry.

Tamar's arguments fail to convince Amnon from abandoning his planned rape. The deed is narrated briefly, emphasizing the quick and violent nature of the act by using three verbs in a row: "he seized her, he raped her, and he bedded her" (though the NIV does not show this but uses only one English verb and notes Amnon was stronger than Tamar).[3] This use of three verbs

---

3. The last verb is translated "bedded" by Alter (*The David Story*, 269) or "laid her" by Phyllis Trible (*Texts of Terror: Literary-Feminist Readings of Biblical Narratives* [Philadelphia: Fortress, 1984], 46).

to describe the rape is similar to the story of the rape of Dinah in Genesis 34 where the rapist "takes her, beds her, and rapes her" (Gen 34:2, author's translation).

While in the story of Dinah's rape in Genesis 34, the rapist falls in love with his victim after violating her (Gen 34:3), here Amnon, instead of having increased affection for Tamar, now "hated" her—in fact he hated her more intensely than he had lusted after her before the crime (v. 15). This sudden change of heart in Amnon could perhaps be due to the fact that he now realizes the gravity of what he has done and the consequences that could follow (the wrath of Absalom and his father), and the rapist, in some sense, blames his victim.[4]

In his new hatred of Tamar, Amnon adds insult to injury and orders her out of his house. At this Tamar pleads with him that he not force her to leave, which she claims would be a "greater wrong" than the rape itself. While from a modern viewpoint, the chance to get away from your rapist would be welcomed, in this ancient context, this turn of events could result in even further victimizing the victim. Recalling the Mosaic legislation surrounding pre-marital sexual relations discussed above (see Listen to the Text), Amnon's actions here are in clear violation. Amnon is now obliged to provide for Tamar.[5] In that ancient context, marriage would help the young woman gain the security she would need.[6] The man in such instances had no choice but to pay a bride price and marry the woman. Seeing as Tamar is not betrothed to anyone, she wants Amnon to take responsibility and, like the rapist in Deuteronomy 22:28–29, marry her so that she is not left destitute and outside a family structure for the rest of her life.

After having created an elaborate scheme to bring her there against her will, Amnon now sends her away—even locking her out of his house. Amnon's low opinion of Tamar is evident in his command to his servant. Though the NIV translates, "Get this woman out of my sight," the original Hebrew lacks the word "woman," as Amnon literally says "Get this [thing] out of my sight." As one scholar puts it: "For Amnon, Tamar is a thing, a 'this' he wants thrown out. She is trash. The one he desired before his eyes, his hatred wants outside, with the door bolted after her."[7]

In response, Tamar wails loudly and puts ashes on her head like a mourner

---

4. Alter, *The David Story*, 269.

5. Peter Enns, *Exodus*, NIVAC (Grand Rapids: Zondervan 2000), 450.

6. Ibid. The situation legislated in Exod 22:16–17 was not one of rape; however, Deut 22:28–29 does seem to refer to instances of rape and has a similar law (with the man paying a bride price and marrying the girl) but adds the stipulation that the man "can never divorce her as long as he lives" (Deut 22:29).

7. Trible, *Texts of Terror*, 48.

(cf. Esth 4:3; Jer 6:26). What is more, we are told she wore a special robe reserved for the king's virgin daughters and that Tamar now tears it, symbolizing her great loss and serving as a public signal to observers drawing attention to the crime. While Amnon probably wanted his crime covered up (like David covered up his sexual sin before him), Tamar does not let it remain a secret.

When her brother Absalom finds her, he quickly surmises what happened and takes in his hurting sister. The fact that Absalom so quickly guessed who the culprit was could suggest there was already some hostile history between the two brothers.[8] Furthermore, the ease at which Absalom guessed Amnon's involvement casts David in a bad light. If Absalom perceived that Amnon was a threat to Tamar, the king should have realized something was up with Amnon's request for Tamar to wait on him.

In an attempt to comfort his devastated sister, Absalom urges that she not "take this thing to heart" (v. 20), which at first blush seems like pretty empty comfort to a rape victim. Absalom's next words, however, may suggest that Tamar understood him to say he would avenge her. Absalom reminds Tamar that "he is your brother" (v. 20). In other words, "What Absalom may be suggesting is that, were it any other man, I would avenge your honor at once, but since he is your brother, and mine, I must bide my time."[9] Regardless, Tamar lived the life of a "desolate woman" from here on out, living in the house of her brother Absalom. One may wonder why Tamar does not go back to her father's house. Some think it is because a "raped daughter is a reproach to her father's honor; a living reminder of his failure."[10] Her choice to stay with Absalom reflects poorly on the king (but reflects well on Absalom).

When David hears about these terrible events he is "furious" but does nothing. This is surprising given the king's history of being somewhat of a hothead. When David felt affronted by Nabal, he set out with his men to avenge himself by killing all the males from Nabal's house (1 Sam 25:21–22). When the Amalekite reported his "mercy killing" of Saul, David had him killed on the spot (2 Sam 1:14–15). Similarly, when David heard Nathan's parable about the rich man taking the poor man's lamb, he declared a death sentence (2 Sam 12:5). Now, when his own daughter has been raped and shamed, this former man of action does nothing.[11] This probably shows David's morally compromised nerve. Having failed so miserably with his sin with Bathsheba,

---

8. Anderson, *2 Samuel*, 176.

9. Alter, *The David Story*, 271.

10. Jenni Williams, "Adding Insult to Injury? The Family Laws of Deuteronomy," in *Tamar's Tears: Evangelical Engagements with Feminist Old Testament Hermeneutics*, ed. Andrew Sloane (Eugene, OR: Pickwick, 2012), 104.

11. Biblical manuscripts from the Greek textual traditions as well as the Dead Sea Scrolls include a line at this point explaining that David "would not punish his son Amnon, because he loved him,

David now lacks the capacity to act. David's lack of action at the rape of his daughter recalls Jacob's similar inaction when his daughter is raped in Genesis 34. In both cases the inaction of the father sets the stage for "the bloody act of revenge" by the rape victim's brother(s).[12] While the king does nothing, at this point neither does Absalom. His quiet rage, however, is seen in his refusal even to speak with his brother Amnon (v. 22). Absalom "hated" him for violating his sister.

Absalom's Revenge (13:21–39)

Two years pass before Absalom moves to exact revenge on his brother. It is important to remember that Amnon was David's firstborn (2 Sam 3:3) and thus the heir apparent to the throne. This would mean he likely had a body-guard, as did Absalom when he became the heir (2 Sam 15:1), and Adonijah (1 Kgs 1:5), which explains why Absalom waited so long for his revenge. His plan involves using the joyous occasion of sheep shearing to trap his brother. When sheep were sheared it was a time of celebration with feasting, and Absalom not only invites all the kings' sons to attend but even extends a direct invitation to the king himself. It seems likely that Absalom did not actually want David to attend and that the invitation was a ploy to enlist the king's aid in his trap. Knowing the king did not have time for such things, Absalom planned to use his refusal as an occasion to get the king to send Amnon instead. (The invitation would also have likely thrown off any suspicion the king might have of Absalom's intentions in inviting Amnon.) Ironically, as in the rape of Tamar (where David ordered her to attend Amnon), David's unwitting help is instrumental in the carrying out of a wicked plan. With Amnon away from the security of Jerusalem and on Absalom's own estate (where his servants were shearing sheep), the event became a golden opportunity to exact revenge.

Since Amnon was heir apparent to the throne, it is possible that Absalom's motives for murdering Amnon were not solely out of vengeance for Tamar but could also include advancing his route to the kingship. With Amnon gone, he would be next in line. Absalom was technically the third-born son, with Kileab (Abigail's son) being second in line. However, the fact that Kileab is never mentioned after his birth (or in the following narratives concerned with the succession to David's throne) suggests he died earlier than this.[13]

In this chapter, we see many of David's qualities reflected in his children. Like David (1 Sam 16:12), Absalom and Tamar are both good looking (2 Sam

---

for he was his firstborn" (NRSV). However, it seems unlikely this was a part of the original text but was an explanatory note added later.

12. Alter, *The David Story*, 271.

13. Anderson, *2 Samuel*, 49.

13:1; 14:25). Like David (1 Sam 17:45–47), Tamar displays eloquent argumentation (2 Sam 13:12–13). Like David (2 Sam 11), Amnon takes what he lusts after (2 Sam 13). Now, like David before him (2 Sam 11:14–17), Absalom orders his servants to murder for him (2 Sam 13:28–29). However, while many of David's qualities are reflected in his children, his bravery (e.g., 1 Sam 17) is evidently not one of them, as all the king's sons flee at the murder of Amnon (v. 29).

Curiously, while the sons are still on their way home, David receives a report that Absalom had killed all of his sons. This could, of course, have been from an observer who fled even quicker than the sons did (perhaps before realizing only one prince had been killed). Regardless, at receiving the news David is grief stricken. Did the king then remember Nathan's prophecy that "the sword will never depart from your house" (2 Sam 12:10)?

Enter Jonadab, the king's nephew. The reader will remember Jonadab as Amnon's "adviser" who concocted the plan to get Tamar into Amnon's house (v. 3). This time Jonadab steps in to correct the inaccurate report the king had received, reassuring the king that all the king's sons were not dead—only Amnon (and apparently Jonadab was not too bothered by this news). Jonadab, who was described as "very shrewd" (v. 3), seemed to surmise this because Absalom's antipathy toward Amnon was obvious. Of course, if Jonadab knew that Absalom was out to get Amnon, should not the king have seen this as well? This is the second time David's imperceptivity is highlighted in this chapter (cf. 13:20). Jonadab's insight proves correct (as he is sure to point out to the king "just as your servant said" v. 35) as the king's sons arrive in Jerusalem. All are in tears, no doubt mourning their brother and shaken up from the horrifying incident.

Absalom, however, flees Israel and seeks refuge with his grandfather, Talmai, king of Geshur (cf. 2 Sam 3:3), where he remains for three years. The concluding verse has been understood in different ways and is difficult to translate. The NIV understands it to mean that during Absalom's exile David "longed to go to Absalom," but the Hebrew is not so clear. David's "longing" seems to be a longing to bring Absalom to justice, not a father's affectionate longing for his son. A better translation might be, "The king's longing to march against Absalom was spent because he was consoled concerning Amnon's death."[14] This translation is supported from the context. After all, in the next chapter Joab has to trick David into bringing Absalom back (2 Sam 14:1–21), and even after David allowed his return, the king did not even let Absalom see his face but made him go to his own house (2 Sam 14:24). None of this makes

---

14. Similar to McCarter, *II Samuel*, 344 and Alter, *The David Story*, 274.

sense if the king was longing to see Absalom. As Alter concludes, "An abatement of hostility against Absalom rather than a longing for him makes much more sense in terms of what follows."[15] Thus, this concluding statement sets up the next chapter. With this abatement of hostility, David is "ready to be prodded step by step towards a reconciliation."[16]

LIVE the Story

The Reality of Sin and Its Consequences

The story of the rape of Tamar is one of the most troubling texts in Scripture. The pathology of Amnon in assaulting his sister is troubling. The pathos in Tamar's pleas with her attacker, including an offer to marry him, is both moving and disturbing. David's failure to take any action is appalling. As much as we sympathize with Tamar and understand Absalom's yearning for revenge, his plan is cold-blooded murder. What is more, the story doesn't provide any role models which modern Christians should emulate. Amnon's rape, David's failure to act, and Absalom's violence are all horrific. For those who read the Bible expecting inspirational stories, this one may be a bit of a shock, leading the reader to question why it is included in the first place.

What is the point to the story? What does this text want us to do? How can we better live out God's story in light of this story? While the story may not be particularly uplifting or what one might call an inspirational read, it is nonetheless inspired, and there are several aspects of the text worth reflecting upon. First, the story highlights the reality of sin and does not gloss over its horrors. Like the world today, the world of the Bible is full of violence and sin. What is more, God does not appear in the story. Some have noted God's narratival silence in this story, but this silence does not indicate indifference. Divine silence may be viewed as an indictment against the sinful actions that take place. As one writer puts it, "God refuses to take any part in these particular machinations of men."[17] In fact, a high view of Scripture as God's word would suggest that God is not silent. God is voicing Tamar's story through its inclusion in the text.

The inclusion of Tamar's story suggests that occurrences of sexual violence need to be talked about. In fact, some scholars have suggested that this story

---

15. Alter, *The David Story*, 274.
16. McCarter, *II Samuel*, 344.
17. Miriam J. Bier, "Colliding Texts: Reading Tamar (2 Samuel 13:1–22) as a Twenty-First Century Woman," in *Tamar's Tears: Evangelical Engagements with Feminist Old Testament Hermeneutics*, ed. Andrew Sloane (Eugene, OR: Pickwick, 2012), 186.

calls for Christians "to speak up and express outrage at this text. . . . [S]peak into the gaps and speak out in protest. Only by doing so might we ensure that Tamar's voice continues to be heard and is not buried forever in the basement of her brother Absalom's house."[18] In the story, Tamar is courageous and makes a public statement against the violence by tearing her robe and mourning (v. 19). She is not silent, though in that society she was virtually powerless. The church must not be silent on sexual violence, as many of the victims today are similarly powerless. As one study has noted, "In societies where the silence on sexual violence is not broken, abuse of power is not held accountable."[19] Christians must speak out against such sin and aid the voice of the victims. Further, Christians must reflect on what the church's response to sexual violence must be. It is an unpleasant topic, but the Bible refuses to ignore such questions.[20] Instead, the Bible "causes readers to recognize how damaging abuse can be and how it can spark incredibly strong reactions."[21] The devastating effect of sexual violence on people is well known, and, as the body of Christ, the church must care for such victims. We must work to heal those affected by sexual violence.

Second, this story reminds us of the terrible effect sin has on our lives. This story paints a sad portrait of the once mighty king of Israel. The disturbing events of this chapter begin to fulfill Nathan's ominous prophecy (2 Sam 12). While once David was a man of action, he now is paralyzed from acting. While once David did "what was just and right for all his people" (2 Sam 8:15), now David is unable to do the right thing. David's inability to function as Israel's ideal king is directly tied to his sin. Though David had been forgiven of his sin (2 Sam 12:13), his failures have led to a situation where he was no longer able to govern justly. This text serves as a warning about the long-term effects of sin, not only on our lives but on the lives of those around us.

The close connection between these events and the prophetic indictment in the previous chapter may lead the reader to wonder about God's role in these terrible events. Was Tamar's rape *intentionally* part of God's purpose in disciplining David for his sin?[22] Nathan's prophetic word to David, however, says nothing about Tamar or a rape. Clearly, in the story it is the lust and violence of Amnon that causes it to happen, and it is David's lack of action

---

18. Ibid., 188.

19. Denise Ackermann, "Tamar's Cry: Rereading an Ancient Text in the Midst of an HIV/AIDS Pandemic," in *Character Ethics and the Old Testament: Moral Dimensions of Scripture*, ed. M. Daniel Carroll R and Jacqueline E. Lapsley (Louisville: Westminster John Knox, 2007), 196.

20. Deuteronomy 22:26 says of rape, "This case is like that of someone who attacks and murders his neighbor," equating rape to murder.

21. Schlimm, *Strange and Sacred Scripture*, 65–66.

22. Bier, "Colliding Texts," 182.

that exacerbates the problem. The free choice of human characters in the story are to blame, *not* God. While sin brings consequences, we cannot lay the blame for them at the feet of God. Instead, we remember that God too was a victim of human violence when Jesus died on the cross for sinners. Rather than blaming God for the evil in the world, we recognize the great lengths to which God went to rid the world of evil and to deal with sin once and for all. We look to Jesus "who gave himself for our sins to rescue us from the present evil age, according to the will of our God and Father" (Gal 1:4).

LISTEN to the Story

¹Joab son of Zeruiah knew that the king's heart longed for Absalom. ²So Joab sent someone to Tekoa and had a wise woman brought from there. He said to her, "Pretend you are in mourning. Dress in mourning clothes, and don't use any cosmetic lotions. Act like a woman who has spent many days grieving for the dead. ³Then go to the king and speak these words to him." And Joab put the words in her mouth.

⁴When the woman from Tekoa went to the king, she fell with her face to the ground to pay him honor, and she said, "Help me, Your Majesty!"

⁵The king asked her, "What is troubling you?"

She said, "I am a widow; my husband is dead. ⁶I your servant had two sons. They got into a fight with each other in the field, and no one was there to separate them. One struck the other and killed him. ⁷Now the whole clan has risen up against your servant; they say, 'Hand over the one who struck his brother down, so that we may put him to death for the life of his brother whom he killed; then we will get rid of the heir as well.' They would put out the only burning coal I have left, leaving my husband neither name nor descendant on the face of the earth."

⁸The king said to the woman, "Go home, and I will issue an order in your behalf."

⁹But the woman from Tekoa said to him, "Let my lord the king pardon me and my family, and let the king and his throne be without guilt."

¹⁰The king replied, "If anyone says anything to you, bring them to me, and they will not bother you again."

¹¹She said, "Then let the king invoke the Lord his God to prevent the avenger of blood from adding to the destruction, so that my son will not be destroyed."

"As surely as the Lord lives," he said, "not one hair of your son's head will fall to the ground."

[12]Then the woman said, "Let your servant speak a word to my lord the king."

"Speak," he replied.

[13]The woman said, "Why then have you devised a thing like this against the people of God? When the king says this, does he not convict himself, for the king has not brought back his banished son? [14]Like water spilled on the ground, which cannot be recovered, so we must die. But that is not what God desires; rather, he devises ways so that a banished person does not remain banished from him.

[15]"And now I have come to say this to my lord the king because the people have made me afraid. Your servant thought, 'I will speak to the king; perhaps he will grant his servant's request. [16]Perhaps the king will agree to deliver his servant from the hand of the man who is trying to cut off both me and my son from God's inheritance.'

[17]"And now your servant says, 'May the word of my lord the king secure my inheritance, for my lord the king is like an angel of God in discerning good and evil. May the LORD your God be with you.'"

[18]Then the king said to the woman, "Don't keep from me the answer to what I am going to ask you."

"Let my lord the king speak," the woman said.

[19]The king asked, "Isn't the hand of Joab with you in all this?"

The woman answered, "As surely as you live, my lord the king, no one can turn to the right or to the left from anything my lord the king says. Yes, it was your servant Joab who instructed me to do this and who put all these words into the mouth of your servant. [20]Your servant Joab did this to change the present situation. My lord has wisdom like that of an angel of God—he knows everything that happens in the land."

[21]The king said to Joab, "Very well, I will do it. Go, bring back the young man Absalom."

[22]Joab fell with his face to the ground to pay him honor, and he blessed the king. Joab said, "Today your servant knows that he has found favor in your eyes, my lord the king, because the king has granted his servant's request."

[23]Then Joab went to Geshur and brought Absalom back to Jerusalem. [24]But the king said, "He must go to his own house; he must not see my face." So Absalom went to his own house and did not see the face of the king.

[25]In all Israel there was not a man so highly praised for his handsome

appearance as Absalom. From the top of his head to the sole of his foot there was no blemish in him. ²⁶Whenever he cut the hair of his head—he used to cut his hair once a year because it became too heavy for him—he would weigh it, and its weight was two hundred shekels by the royal standard.

²⁷Three sons and a daughter were born to Absalom. His daughter's name was Tamar, and she became a beautiful woman.

²⁸Absalom lived two years in Jerusalem without seeing the king's face. ²⁹Then Absalom sent for Joab in order to send him to the king, but Joab refused to come to him. So he sent a second time, but he refused to come. ³⁰Then he said to his servants, "Look, Joab's field is next to mine, and he has barley there. Go and set it on fire." So Absalom's servants set the field on fire.

³¹Then Joab did go to Absalom's house, and he said to him, "Why have your servants set my field on fire?"

³²Absalom said to Joab, "Look, I sent word to you and said, 'Come here so I can send you to the king to ask, "Why have I come from Geshur? It would be better for me if I were still there!"' Now then, I want to see the king's face, and if I am guilty of anything, let him put me to death."

³³So Joab went to the king and told him this. Then the king summoned Absalom, and he came in and bowed down with his face to the ground before the king. And the king kissed Absalom.

¹⁵:¹In the course of time, Absalom provided himself with a chariot and horses and with fifty men to run ahead of him. ²He would get up early and stand by the side of the road leading to the city gate. Whenever anyone came with a complaint to be placed before the king for a decision, Absalom would call out to him, "What town are you from?" He would answer, "Your servant is from one of the tribes of Israel." ³Then Absalom would say to him, "Look, your claims are valid and proper, but there is no representative of the king to hear you." ⁴And Absalom would add, "If only I were appointed judge in the land! Then everyone who has a complaint or case could come to me and I would see that they receive justice."

⁵Also, whenever anyone approached him to bow down before him, Absalom would reach out his hand, take hold of him and kiss him. ⁶Absalom behaved in this way toward all the Israelites who came to the king asking for justice, and so he stole the hearts of the people of Israel.

⁷At the end of four years, Absalom said to the king, "Let me go to Hebron and fulfill a vow I made to the LORD. ⁸While your servant was

living at Geshur in Aram, I made this vow: 'If the Lord takes me back to Jerusalem, I will worship the Lord in Hebron.'"

⁹The king said to him, "Go in peace." So he went to Hebron.

¹⁰Then Absalom sent secret messengers throughout the tribes of Israel to say, "As soon as you hear the sound of the trumpets, then say, 'Absalom is king in Hebron.'" ¹¹Two hundred men from Jerusalem had accompanied Absalom. They had been invited as guests and went quite innocently, knowing nothing about the matter. ¹²While Absalom was offering sacrifices, he also sent for Ahithophel the Gilonite, David's counselor, to come from Giloh, his hometown. And so the conspiracy gained strength, and Absalom's following kept on increasing.

¹³A messenger came and told David, "The hearts of the people of Israel are with Absalom."

¹⁴Then David said to all his officials who were with him in Jerusalem, "Come! We must flee, or none of us will escape from Absalom. We must leave immediately, or he will move quickly to overtake us and bring ruin on us and put the city to the sword."

¹⁵The king's officials answered him, "Your servants are ready to do whatever our lord the king chooses."

¹⁶The king set out, with his entire household following him; but he left ten concubines to take care of the palace. ¹⁷So the king set out, with all the people following him, and they halted at the edge of the city. ¹⁸All his men marched past him, along with all the Kerethites and Pelethites; and all the six hundred Gittites who had accompanied him from Gath marched before the king.

¹⁹The king said to Ittai the Gittite, "Why should you come along with us? Go back and stay with King Absalom. You are a foreigner, an exile from your homeland. ²⁰You came only yesterday. And today shall I make you wander about with us, when I do not know where I am going? Go back, and take your people with you. May the Lord show you kindness and faithfulness."

²¹But Ittai replied to the king, "As surely as the Lord lives, and as my lord the king lives, wherever my lord the king may be, whether it means life or death, there will your servant be."

²²David said to Ittai, "Go ahead, march on." So Ittai the Gittite marched on with all his men and the families that were with him.

²³The whole countryside wept aloud as all the people passed by. The king also crossed the Kidron Valley, and all the people moved on toward the wilderness.

²⁴Zadok was there, too, and all the Levites who were with him were carrying the ark of the covenant of God. They set down the ark of God, and Abiathar offered sacrifices until all the people had finished leaving the city.

²⁵Then the king said to Zadok, "Take the ark of God back into the city. If I find favor in the Lord's eyes, he will bring me back and let me see it and his dwelling place again. ²⁶But if he says, 'I am not pleased with you,' then I am ready; let him do to me whatever seems good to him."

²⁷The king also said to Zadok the priest, "Do you understand? Go back to the city with my blessing. Take your son Ahimaaz with you, and also Abiathar's son Jonathan. You and Abiathar return with your two sons. ²⁸I will wait at the fords in the wilderness until word comes from you to inform me." ²⁹So Zadok and Abiathar took the ark of God back to Jerusalem and stayed there.

³⁰But David continued up the Mount of Olives, weeping as he went; his head was covered and he was barefoot. All the people with him covered their heads too and were weeping as they went up. ³¹Now David had been told, "Ahithophel is among the conspirators with Absalom." So David prayed, "Lord, turn Ahithophel's counsel into foolishness."

³²When David arrived at the summit, where people used to worship God, Hushai the Arkite was there to meet him, his robe torn and dust on his head. ³³David said to him, "If you go with me, you will be a burden to me. ³⁴But if you return to the city and say to Absalom, 'Your Majesty, I will be your servant; I was your father's servant in the past, but now I will be your servant,' then you can help me by frustrating Ahithophel's advice. ³⁵Won't the priests Zadok and Abiathar be there with you? Tell them anything you hear in the king's palace. ³⁶Their two sons, Ahimaaz son of Zadok and Jonathan son of Abiathar, are there with them. Send them to me with anything you hear."

³⁷So Hushai, David's confidant, arrived at Jerusalem as Absalom was entering the city.

Listen to the Text in the Story: 2 Samuel 11, 13

As explained in the commentary above, 2 Samuel 13 ends not with David longing to see Absalom as the NIV translation suggests but noting that David's desire to march against Absalom (in response to his killing of Amnon) and bring him to justice had abated because he had been "consoled concerning Amnon's death" (2 Sam 13:39). So, 2 Samuel 14 opens with David's heart still being "against Absalom" (2 Sam 14:1). The NIV has understood this verse as saying that David's attitude toward Absalom was a longing "for Absalom" (v. 1). The Hebrew, however, would suggest that the king's heart was "against Absalom." David still held hard feelings for his son who had killed David's beloved firstborn.

In order to better understand the defection of David's trusted counselor, Ahithophel, to Absalom's cause, it is important to recall the story of David's adultery with Bathsheba and murder of Uriah back in 2 Samuel 11. As noted in the commentary there, Bathsheba's father was said to be Eliam (2 Sam 11:3), and Eliam is later said to be the son of Ahithophel the Gilonite (2 Sam 23:34). In other words, this makes Ahithophel Bathsheba's grandfather. It seems likely, therefore, that Ahithophel may have had motivation to end David's kingship as retribution for the way David killed his grandson-in-law and mistreated his granddaughter. Ahithophel's specific advice to Absalom in the next chapter also hints at this motivation (2 Sam 16:21). Clearly the effects of David's sin continue to haunt him, as the defection of Ahithophel to Absalom's side strengthens Absalom's position considerably.

EXPLAIN the Story

Chapter 13 ended with David abandoning his desire to march against Absalom for murdering Amnon. Now Joab devises a plan to bring back Absalom by enlisting the aid of a "wise woman" (v. 2) who brings a fictional scenario to David to persuade him. Even though David sees through the ruse and discerns that Joab was behind it, the king agrees to allow Absalom to return, though he confines him to his own house. Unsatisfied with his lack of access to the palace, Absalom twice calls on Joab to approach the king for him, but Joab does not answer him. Finally, after Absalom burns Joab's fields in order to get his attention, Joab approaches the king for Absalom and David agrees to see Absalom. Pardoned by the king, Absalom then begins his long-term plan to ascend the throne. First, Absalom acquires a significant bodyguard contingent to accompany him. Second, he tells those seeking justice that David would not hear their case but that he would if he were king. Third, Absalom would always embrace and kiss any who tried to bow before him. After four years of gaining public support, Absalom arranged to be made king in Hebron by his supporters. When David hears of the widespread support for Absalom, he and his entire household flee from Jerusalem, leaving only ten concubines to mind his house. When David hears that his top advisor, Ahithophel, had defected to Absalom, David prays for God to intervene. In answer to his prayer, David happens upon one of his other advisors, Hushai, who agrees to remain in Jerusalem and serve as David's inside man and sabotage Ahithophel's advice to Absalom.

Joab and the Wise Woman (14:1–22)

Joab has always been a man of action, with keen insight into the political machinations in Israel. He has been wrong in the past (interpreting Abner's meeting with David as espionage in 2 Sam 3:24–25) but usually had a good grasp of things (like devising a more believable cover-up for Uriah's death in 2 Sam 11:15–17 or having David take the credit for the defeat of Rabbah in 2 Sam 12:27–28). Once again, at the beginning of this chapter Joab displays keen insight in his discerning of the king's disposition toward Absalom and what the popular stance on the matter was.

Joab realizes that David's heart was still against Absalom and he wants to change this. It is not clear why Joab wanted Absalom back, but given Joab's clear concern for the security of the monarchy (and the way in which Joab's ruse is composed), it was likely because Joab realized that there was popular support for bringing back the prince and Joab wanted David to be seen in a favorable light.

The wily general enlists the aid of a "wise woman" from Tekoa and devises a ruse to convince David to bring back his exiled son. Tekoa is a city some ten miles from Jerusalem, which would mean David would likely not recognize her.[1] The woman is to pretend to be in mourning and tell the king a fictional tale of her two sons, one of whom killed the other, leaving the rest of the family angry with the murderer to the point where they would kill him in retribution. The woman pleads for the life of the murderer, and David grants her request.

In response, the woman asks that the king "pardon" her and her family and that David "be without guilt" (14:9). This suggests that the woman is willing to bear the guilt of the king, who in protecting the exiled son was actually interfering with the rights of the "avenger of blood" to kill the murderer.[2]

When David accedes to her request, the woman turns his judgment against him, saying, "When the king says this, does he not convict himself" (14:13). In other words, by offering protection to her son, the king should, in fairness, offer it to his own exiled son. This suggests that during the time Absalom had been in exile David had been somewhat in the role of the "avenger of blood" (v. 11) in longing to march against Absalom (13:39; 14:1), while the "people of God" (v. 13) had wanted to bring Absalom back.[3]

---

1. Some have suggested Tekoa is associated with wisdom, given that this "wise woman" hails from there, as does the prophet Amos. However, this idea is too speculative to be helpful.

2. Anderson, *2 Samuel*, 187.

3. Ibid., 188.

Surprisingly, even after turning the story on the king, the woman stays in character and goes back to her story, pretending the situation with her fictional son was real and that it was the reason for her approaching the king (14:15). However, after the woman had applied it directly to David and Absalom, the cat was out of the bag—so to speak. The king is not so easily fooled and does not buy her story and correctly discerns that Joab is behind it.

The woman responds with flattery, telling the king he has full knowledge of the happenings in Israel. This, of course, was already seen to be untrue in how David did not suspect that Amnon was out for Tamar (as Absalom surmised easily in 2 Sam 13:20) or that Absalom hated Amnon and was plotting his death (as Jonadab surmised easily in 2 Sam 13:32). David's ignorance will also be underscored in the very next chapter as Absalom undertakes subversive activities right under David's nose (2 Sam 15:1–6).[4]

Remarkably, even though David knows the whole story was a means to trick him into bringing Absalom back, the king agrees to allow Joab to do so. David was not deceived, so his change of mind was not based on his being tricked by the wise woman. Instead, David has been persuaded to act in this way. The key part of her argument seems to be her assertion that God "devises ways so that a banished person does not remain banished from him" (v. 14). This theological perspective persuades David to act similarly in regard to Absalom's case.[5] This theme of exile and return that the woman references becomes one of the main themes that 2 Samuel 14–20 will explore, especially in terms of whether or not God "will bring David back to Jerusalem."[6]

In response to the woman, David addresses Joab directly, as the general must have been present during the woman's performance. The king agrees to his request and orders him to bring back Absalom.

The Return of Absalom (14:23–27)

Although Joab was allowed to bring back Absalom, David refused to give him an audience but instead had Absalom sent to his own house. David had not "longed to see Absalom" but apparently still had hard feelings towards his son

After his return, the narrator tells us of Absalom's famous good looks, including his spotless skin and prolific hair growth. Like today, with widespread adoration lavished on good-looking actors, actresses, and public figures, Absalom's winning looks led to his popularity in Israel. Just as Saul's striking

---

4. As Alter (*The David Story*, 279) writes, "there is much in the land about which he knows nothing."

5. Steven Thatcher Mann, *Run, David, Run! An Investigation of the Theological Speech Acts of David's Departure and Return (2 Samuel 14–20)*, Siphrut 10 (Winona Lake, IN: Eisenbrauns, 2013), 69–70.

6. Ibid., 29.

looks (1 Sam 9:2) and towering height (1 Sam 10:23–24) impressed the people, Absalom's appearance contributed to his popularity. We are also told of Absalom's own children—three sons and a daughter. Significantly, we are only told the daughter's name—not the sons—as she was clearly named after Absalom's sister, Tamar, underscoring his affection for her. Like her aunt, she is said to be "a beautiful woman" (v. 27). Later, in 2 Samuel 18:18, we find out that Absalom had no sons, which suggests that they may have died quite young.[7] (The fact that the sons are not named here could also suggest their early deaths.)

Absalom Gains an Audience with the King (14:28–33)

Two years pass and still Absalom had not met up with his father (again, underscoring David's anger over Absalom killing David's firstborn). Apparently dissatisfied with the situation, Absalom twice attempts to get Joab to go to the king for him, but Joab refuses. This is somewhat surprising, seeing as Joab went out of his way to get Absalom back in the first place. Perhaps Joab was satisfied having the heir back in the land but did not want to again try and approach the king for more favors. Alternatively, Joab may have thought better of the usefulness of Absalom and therefore was reluctant to assist him further.

In order to get Joab's attention, Absalom has his servants burn the general's field. Again, we see Absalom's willingness to use any means necessary to get what he wanted. The arson is successful, as Joab responds and finally agrees to go to the king for Absalom. Despite its success in getting Joab's attention, the arson incident was probably not soon forgotten by Joab, who later is instrumental in Absalom's demise. In response, David summons Absalom, and father and son are reconciled at last, with David kissing his son. This reconciliation, however, may have been only one way, with Absalom harboring a grudge against his father for excluding him for so long.[8]

Winning the Hearts of the Israelites (15:1–12)

Having received a full pardon and having his freedom restored, Absalom sets out to undermine David and take his throne. He begins by riding in a chariot drawn by horses, with an escort of fifty men—a clear claim to royal status. Absalom clearly thought he was a big deal. Of course, this is in keeping with what he learned about him last chapter and how he would cut his hair every year and have it weighed. Absalom not only had a lot of hair, he had a big head. Later on, his brother, Adonijah, similarly will ride in a chariot and

---

7. Or perhaps were killed due to Absalom's rebellion.

8. As Alter (*The David Story*, 282) observes, the reconciliation "clearly gives Absalom no satisfaction, as his initiative of usurpation in the next episode strongly argues."

secure fifty men to run ahead of him in his bid for the throne (1 Kgs 1:5). Ironically, Absalom and Adonijah are acting like the king that Samuel warned Israel about saying, "This is what the king who will reign over you will claim as his rights: He will take your sons and make them serve with his chariots and horses, and they will run in front of his chariots" (1 Sam 8:11). Needless to say, this does not reflect well on them.

Absalom's most subversive activities involved interfering with the justice system in Israel. When a citizen came to Jerusalem with a case to be heard by the king, Absalom would meet them first and tell them that the king could not hear their case but that they were in the right. Reminiscent of modern politicians on the campaign trail, Absalom would tell them that if he were king he would side in their favor and that he would always hear everyone's case and make sure there was justice for all. This all sounds great, but in reality Absalom would not make an ethical judge. First, there is no indication by the narrator that such cases really could not be heard in David's court, as Absalom was telling these litigants. No doubt, with the presence of his large entourage, he appeared to be an authoritative figure, so litigants probably assumed he was telling the truth. The fact that Absalom rose early in the morning to meet complainants before they reached the king suggests that Absalom was actually preventing these people from receiving justice. Just as we have seen in the past, Absalom will go to great lengths to get what he wants, even if it means, as in this case, hurting other people.

Absalom further ingratiated himself to the people by not allowing people to bow to him out of respect. Instead, when they went to bow, he would embrace them and kiss them. Absalom wanted to appear to be the "people's man" and not an aloof royal who would curry acts of deference and worship. This is ironic given that he had gone to great lengths to appear important in the people's eyes, riding a horse-drawn chariot and arranging for fifty men to run ahead of him (on top of the hair weighing ceremony). The fact that David appears ignorant of Absalom's rise reflects poorly on the monarch. How could he not be aware of Absalom's posturing when he traveled around on a chariot with fifty men running before him?

Absalom has proved himself a patient man. He had plotted revenge for two years before murdering Amnon; now we are told he worked subversively against David for four years before overtly moving against him. Confident he had garnered enough support to make a play for the throne, Absalom put his plan in place. He would go to Hebron, the traditional center of the Judean state and where David was first crowned king (2 Sam 2:4), and be acclaimed king there. Despite his pardon from his crimes, however, it appears Absalom still had to ask David to journey to Hebron. In order to secure permission,

Absalom tells his father of a vow he made to Yahweh. Here Absalom appears to break the third commandment (taking Yahweh's name in vain), as he falsely references a vow to Yahweh. In keeping with his character thus far, Absalom will stop at nothing to get what he wants.

David is apparently unsuspecting of his son and he gives him his blessing to go to Hebron. This decision again shows that, unlike what the wise woman of Tekoa said in the last chapter (2 Sam 14:19), the king is unaware of what is going on in his kingdom. This is even more clear since this is the second time (2 Sam 13:24–27) Absalom had deceitfully made a request of the king that David granted (the first resulted in the murder of Amnon).

Absalom secretly arranges for supporters to come to Hebron and, in order to throw off suspicion, brings along two hundred men from the capital who were not known to be his supporters and were not privy to Absalom's plans. Absalom, however, had covertly arranged an enthronement ceremony, complete with him offering sacrifices and David's top counselor, Ahithophel the Gilonite, in attendance. The two hundred Jerusalemite innocents would find themselves caught up in the sedition and likely be forced to participate.

David and His Household Flee (15:13–37)

When word of Absalom's coup reaches the king, he finally takes action. Despite his perpetual passivity since his sin with Bathsheba, we now see flashes of his "old self."[9] David decides to flee Jerusalem out of concern not only for his own safety but the safety of all in the city. In a decision that will come back to haunt him (2 Sam 16:21), David leaves ten concubines to take care of his palace. This may show David's hope that he shall return one day, but it also facilitates the fulfillment of part of Nathan's ominous prophetic word (2 Sam 12:11).

Throughout the story of David's departure, we see tremendous loyalty expressed to David, which contrasts clearly with the betrayal of his own son. First, his officials express total commitment to David (v. 15), then Ittai the Gittite commits to follow David to the death if necessary (v. 21). Furthermore, we are told "the whole countryside" (v. 23) wept at David's departure. Possibly this loyalty was isolated mostly in Jerusalem, or perhaps the report of the people's loyalty to Absalom was overstated. Either way, in an unprecedented move the king abandons his capital city.

The king and his company leave southwards, toward the wilderness of the Negev. Evidently, the priests accompany the king and bring the ark of the covenant along with them (v. 24). David, however, sends them back to

9. Fokkelman, *King David*, 177.

Jerusalem with the ark. If we recall the great joy David found in bringing the ark to Jerusalem, we can appreciate the difficulty David likely had in sending away the ark. What is more, this action shows that David did not regard the ark as a palladium that ensures success, as did Israel years ago against the Philistines (1 Sam 4:3–5), with devastating consequences. Despite David's sinful past and despite his present weaknesses, David's faith in Yahweh has not abated. David does not attempt to manipulate God through his use of the ark. Instead, in an astounding confession of faith, David puts himself and his future in God's hands when he says,

> If I find favor in the LORD's eyes, he will bring me back and let me see it and his dwelling place again. But if he says, "I am not pleased with you," then I am ready; let him do to me whatever seems good to him. (15:25–26)

David is resigned to God's will. He would rather have access to the ark and worship in God's sanctuary but leaves that in God's hands. He trusts his future to God. He therefore sends the priests and their sons back with the ark. David, however, hopes to hear from them and informs them he will wait their communications "at the fords in the wilderness" (probably some well-known locations where people crossed the Jordan valley).[10]

One cannot help but feel for David as he climbs the Mount of Olives in tears as his chickens come home to roost. How far David had fallen from being an ideal monarch with God on his side, victoriously extending his influence and territory, to being a refugee on the run from his own son. He has hit rock bottom. But it is at this low point that David expresses his full trust in God and his total submission to God's will.

When David is told that his top advisor, Ahithophel, has defected to Absalom's side, David prays that God would prevent Ahithophel from properly counseling Absalom. In a remarkable answer to prayer, almost immediately after praying, David comes upon one of his other advisors, Hushai the Arkite (a clan from Benjamin; cf. Josh 16:2), at the place "where people used to worship God" (v. 32). In Hushai, David is given an opportunity to thwart Ahithophel's role in Absalom's court. David asks Hushai to return to Jerusalem and pretend to join Absalom in order to sabotage Ahithophel's advice. Further, Hushai is to spy on Absalom's palace and send back information through the priest's sons.

As it happens (one suspects as God makes it happen), Hushai arrives back at Jerusalem just as Absalom arrived there; in other words, just in time for the ruse to work. Since Hushai's story was that he did not go with David but was

---

10. Anderson, *2 Samuel*, 201.

defecting to Absalom, his presence in Jerusalem was necessary to corroborate his story. If Hushai had arrived after Absalom, it would have looked suspicious.

 LIVE the Story

A God Who Brings Exiles Back

The wise woman's appeal to the nature of God as one who "devises ways so that a banished person does not remain banished from him" (14:14) brings up the prominent biblical theme of exile. The theme is seen initially in Genesis where the first man and woman are exiled from their home in the garden in Eden (Gen 3:24). In the next chapter, Cain is cursed to wander in exile (Gen 4:11–14). Later, the builders of Babel are exiled from their land (Gen 11:1–9). Abraham leaves his home in Ur (Gen 11:30–12:9) to enter the promised land only to go into brief exile in Egypt, followed by his exodus back to the promised land (Gen 12:10–20). The theme surfaces again as Jacob goes into exile in fear of the wrath of his brother Esau (Gen 28–32) but then eventually returns to the land (Gen 33). Joseph is exiled to Egypt (Gen 37), and his father Jacob and his brothers follow him there (Gen 30). Eventually these descendants are enslaved (Exod 1:8–14) and only return to the promised land through *the* exodus.

As we have seen in David's story, he experiences exile (e.g., 1 Sam 27:7) due to the murderous intentions of Saul and now again due to Absalom's coup d'état. Later on in Israel's story, after the division of the Israelite kingdom, the northern kingdom of Israel is eventually exiled by Assyria (2 Kgs 18:9–12), and the southern kingdom of Judah is exiled to Babylon (2 Kgs 24–25). The exiled Babylonian community, authorized by Cyrus of Persia, then returns to the land with leaders such as Sheshbazzar (Ezra 1:8, 11), Zerubbabel (cf. Hag 1:12; Ezra 3:2, 8), Ezra, and Nehemiah (e.g., Ezra 7:6, 10; Neh 8:9).

The theme of exile resonates in many ways with the state of the church today and has been appropriated by many scholars as a helpful analogy for reflection on the relationship of the church to the postmodern culture of the West.[11] Just as those in exile find themselves in a "hostile, alien environment where the predominant temptation is assimilation,"[12] so the modern church

---

11. E.g., Ralph W. Klein, *Israel in Exile: A Theological Interpretation* (Philadelphia: Fortress, 1979); Stanley Hauerwas and William H. Willimon, *Resident Aliens: A Provocative Christian Assessment of Culture and Ministry for People Who Know That Something Is Wrong* (Nashville, TN: Abingdon, 1989); Walter Brueggemann, *Cadences of Home: Preaching among Exiles* (Louisville: Westminster John Knox, 1997).

12. Walter Brueggemann, "Disciplines of Readiness," in *Occasional Paper No. 1*, Theology and Worship Unit, Presbyterian Church (Louisville: Presbyterian Church [USA], 1989), 6.

finds itself in a largely hostile environment and is pressured to assimilate to the dominant culture.

The parallels between the theme of exile and the experiences of the modern church bring into relief the importance of God's character as one who brings exiles back. This character trait of God is referenced by the wise woman in 2 Samuel 14:14, and it was this aspect of her speech that struck a chord with David. Though David saw through the woman's story and perceived it was a ruse concocted by Joab, the theological argument was still persuasive to the anointed king. After all, he himself had experienced God's bringing back the exile first hand.

This characteristic of God as one who brings back exiles is brought out in Deuteronomy 30:1–4 where God asserts:

> When all these blessings and curses I have set before you come upon you and you take them to heart wherever the LORD your God disperses you among the nations, and when you and your children return to the LORD your God and obey him with all your heart and with all your soul according to everything I command you today, then the LORD your God will restore your fortunes and have compassion on you and gather you again from all the nations where he scattered you. Even if you have been banished to the most distant land under the heavens, from there the LORD your God *will gather you and bring you back*. (emphasis added)

Similarly, God proclaims in Jeremiah:

> "I will be found by you," declares the LORD, "and *will bring you back* from captivity. I will gather you from all the nations and places where I have banished you," declares the LORD, "and *will bring you back* to the place from which I carried you into exile." (Jer 29:14, emphasis added; cf. Isa 11:11–12)

This theological perspective of God being one who brings back exiles underscores David's faith in God's character and his submission to God's will (e.g., 2 Sam 15:25–26).

God's disposition to bring back exiles can be a source of hope for the church, which may be discouraged with their role in the world today. The Bible reminds us that we are in the world but not of it (John 17:16). In many ways Christians live in exile, in that we are not *truly* home. We belong, but it is a qualified belonging. In many respects we are still "foreigners and strangers on earth" (Heb 11:13), but we believe in a God who brings exiles back (2 Sam 14:14). This aspect of God's character provides a secure hope for our future. But unlike exiles who long to return to the way it was, we are looking forward to a new home. As the writer of Hebrews notes: "If they had been thinking of the country they had left, they would have had opportunity to return. Instead, they were longing for a better country—a heavenly one" (Heb 11:15–16). We all as one body await our bridegroom to be revealed, that one day we may all live together in the heavenly Jerusalem and hear the words, "Look! God's dwelling place is now among the people, and he will dwell with them. They will be his people, and God himself will be with them and be their God" (Rev 21:3).

God Exalts the Humble

David had forgotten about God in the recent past. This can be seen in his neglect of the king's role in fighting Israel's battles (2 Sam 11:1), in his adultery with Bathsheba, and in the murder of her husband. David had forgotten that he was God's man (that is, a man after God's own heart), chosen and anointed by Yahweh. Now, as David hits rock bottom, David once again submits himself to God's will saying, "let [God] do to me whatever seems good to him" (v. 26).

Sadly, just like in David's life, it often takes hitting rock bottom for us to "let go and let God"—to give up our own ambition, to give our life over to God and his plan for our lives. Ironically, it is at such a low state that God moves on people's behalf. The Bible says that God opposes the proud but gives grace to the humble (Jas 4:6; cf. Prov 29:23). While David felt self-sufficient, he forgot God and fell into sin. When David realizes his need, however, God moves on his behalf.

David's submission to God's will displays his deep faith in God. Just as David allowed Absalom to return home due to his belief that God brings exiles back (2 Sam 14:14), so David's submission to God's will here was likely informed by this theological conviction. David was trusting himself to a God whose character he could trust. David was willing to place his life in the mercy of such a God. If we, like David, know God's character, we will be willing to trust him. If we remember he is full of mercy, compassionate, and forgiving, we will submit to his will, even in difficult circumstances.

Answered Prayer

Another laudable aspect of David's faith comes through in this story when, in the midst of this terrible trial, David hears that his top advisor, Ahithophel, has defected to Absalom's side. Though he was already in tears, rather than despairing or cursing, David prays. David prays for God to frustrate Ahithophel's advice. In a fantastic answer to this prayer, David miraculously meets Hushai almost immediately after uttering his prayer. Furthermore, it is significant that he meets this trusted advisor at the summit of the Mount of

Olives, where people worshiped God. David prayed and God answered. The superscription to Psalm 3 actually situates the psalm in the time of David's flight from Absalom and it fittingly describes David's mindset. The psalmist cries, "LORD, how many are my foes! How many rise up against me!" (Ps 3:1), which fits with David's situation in 2 Samuel 15. But as the psalmist writes, "I call out to the LORD, and he answers me from his holy mountain" (Ps 3:4), so David cried out to God on the Mount of Olives (2 Sam 15:31) and received an immediate answer to prayer (2 Sam 15:32)—God answers David on his holy hill (at the place people worshiped).

Though God sent Hushai in answer to David's prayer, that was not the end of it. Despite submitting to God's will and praying for God's help, when God answers by sending Hushai to him, David takes steps to have his prayer answered. As Alter writes: "Theologically, Hushai is the immediate answer to David's prayer. Politically, David seizes upon Hushai as the perfect instrument to thwart Ahithophel's counsel."[13] There is a pairing here of divine help and human effort. As Brueggemann writes: "David is indeed thinking, planning, and scheming. That does not cancel out his enormous faith, however. He does entrust himself to God, but such trust does not entail mindlessness or resignation."[14]

This is a good reminder for Christians today regarding the role of prayer in our lives. Like David, we need to submit to God's will. We need to bring to God all of our requests. But this submission and reliance on prayer should not negate our own efforts to live the Christian life. In Colossians 4:3–4, Paul requests prayer from the church saying, "pray for us, too, that God may open a door for our message, so that we may proclaim the mystery of Christ, for which I am in chains. Pray that I may proclaim it clearly, as I should." Note the two aspects of faith here. Pray *God* will give an opportunity so that *we* can act. Paul prays for an open door (God's part) so that he can preach, and preach well (Paul's part). While as Christians we must pray continually (1 Thess 5:16–18; Eph 6:18), our reliance on God should not paralyze us from action.

David's Departure and the Passion of the Christ

The story of David's departure from Jerusalem has significant resonances with the story of Christ's passion in the Gospels. In fact, one commentator has viewed the story as "Prefiguring the passion of another anointed King centuries later."[15] Just as David ascended the Mount of Olives troubled in spirit

---

13. Alter, *The David Story*, 289.

14. Brueggemann, *First and Second Samuel*, 304.

15. Ronald F. Youngblood, "1, 2 Samuel," in *Expositor's Bible Commentary*, ed. F. E. Gaebelein (Grand Rapids: Zondervan, 1992), 3:995.

(2 Sam 15:30), so Jesus would do so (Luke 22:44). Just as David's exile from Jerusalem was a spectacle wherein the anointed one was scorned and disgraced, so the later Anointed One would suffer outside the city (Heb 13:12) and have scorn heaped on him (Matt 27:29, 31; Mark 15:20; Luke 18:32). Just as people wept as David departed from Jerusalem (2 Sam 15:23), though popular support was against him (2 Sam 15:13), so people would weep at Jesus' journey outside Jerusalem with his cross (Luke 23:27), though popular support was against him (as they had cried for his crucifixion; Luke 23:23). Just as David hoped for his deliverance (2 Sam 15:25) but submitted himself to God's will even if it meant his death (2 Sam 15:26), so Jesus would pray for deliverance but submit to the divine will, even to the death (Matt 26:39; Mark 14:36; Luke 22:42). Just as David's followers expressed undying loyalty and faithfulness to him, Jesus' followers so expressed fidelity to him on nearly the same *exact* spot (Matt 26:30, 33, 35). Though unlike David's followers, Jesus' disciples would fail in their fidelity, sleeping at the time of prayer (Matt 26:40, 43) and eventually abandoning him (Matt 26:56). Most significantly, David's ordeal was precipitated by his own sins, while Jesus suffered not for his own sins but the sins of others. The later Son of David eclipsed David (Matt 12:6) in every way and truly fulfilled the role of the ideal Anointed One who would deliver his people (Luke 1:69).

CHAPTER 41

2 Samuel 16:1–17:29

 LISTEN to the Story

¹When David had gone a short distance beyond the summit, there was Ziba, the steward of Mephibosheth, waiting to meet him. He had a string of donkeys saddled and loaded with two hundred loaves of bread, a hundred cakes of raisins, a hundred cakes of figs and a skin of wine.

²The king asked Ziba, "Why have you brought these?"

Ziba answered, "The donkeys are for the king's household to ride on, the bread and fruit are for the men to eat, and the wine is to refresh those who become exhausted in the wilderness."

³The king then asked, "Where is your master's grandson?"

Ziba said to him, "He is staying in Jerusalem, because he thinks, 'Today the Israelites will restore to me my grandfather's kingdom.'"

⁴Then the king said to Ziba, "All that belonged to Mephibosheth is now yours."

"I humbly bow," Ziba said. "May I find favor in your eyes, my lord the king."

⁵As King David approached Bahurim, a man from the same clan as Saul's family came out from there. His name was Shimei son of Gera, and he cursed as he came out. ⁶He pelted David and all the king's officials with stones, though all the troops and the special guard were on David's right and left. ⁷As he cursed, Shimei said, "Get out, get out, you murderer, you scoundrel! ⁸The LORD has repaid you for all the blood you shed in the household of Saul, in whose place you have reigned. The LORD has given the kingdom into the hands of your son Absalom. You have come to ruin because you are a murderer!"

⁹Then Abishai son of Zeruiah said to the king, "Why should this dead dog curse my lord the king? Let me go over and cut off his head."

¹⁰But the king said, "What does this have to do with you, you sons of Zeruiah? If he is cursing because the LORD said to him, 'Curse David,' who can ask, 'Why do you do this?'"

[11]David then said to Abishai and all his officials, "My son, my own flesh and blood, is trying to kill me. How much more, then, this Benjamite! Leave him alone; let him curse, for the LORD has told him to. [12]It may be that the LORD will look upon my misery and restore to me his covenant blessing instead of his curse today."

[13]So David and his men continued along the road while Shimei was going along the hillside opposite him, cursing as he went and throwing stones at him and showering him with dirt. [14]The king and all the people with him arrived at their destination exhausted. And there he refreshed himself.

[15]Meanwhile, Absalom and all the men of Israel came to Jerusalem, and Ahithophel was with him. [16]Then Hushai the Arkite, David's confidant, went to Absalom and said to him, "Long live the king! Long live the king!"

[17]Absalom said to Hushai, "So this is the love you show your friend? If he's your friend, why didn't you go with him?"

[18]Hushai said to Absalom, "No, the one chosen by the LORD, by these people, and by all the men of Israel—his I will be, and I will remain with him. [19]Furthermore, whom should I serve? Should I not serve the son? Just as I served your father, so I will serve you."

[20]Absalom said to Ahithophel, "Give us your advice. What should we do?"

[21]Ahithophel answered, "Sleep with your father's concubines whom he left to take care of the palace. Then all Israel will hear that you have made yourself obnoxious to your father, and the hands of everyone with you will be more resolute." [22]So they pitched a tent for Absalom on the roof, and he slept with his father's concubines in the sight of all Israel.

[23]Now in those days the advice Ahithophel gave was like that of one who inquires of God. That was how both David and Absalom regarded all of Ahithophel's advice.

[17:1]Ahithophel said to Absalom, "I would choose twelve thousand men and set out tonight in pursuit of David. [2]I would attack him while he is weary and weak. I would strike him with terror, and then all the people with him will flee. I would strike down only the king [3]and bring all the people back to you. The death of the man you seek will mean the return of all; all the people will be unharmed." [4]This plan seemed good to Absalom and to all the elders of Israel.

[5]But Absalom said, "Summon also Hushai the Arkite, so we can hear what he has to say as well." [6]When Hushai came to him, Absalom said,

"Ahithophel has given this advice. Should we do what he says? If not, give us your opinion."

[7]Hushai replied to Absalom, "The advice Ahithophel has given is not good this time. [8]You know your father and his men; they are fighters, and as fierce as a wild bear robbed of her cubs. Besides, your father is an experienced fighter; he will not spend the night with the troops. [9]Even now, he is hidden in a cave or some other place. If he should attack your troops first, whoever hears about it will say, 'There has been a slaughter among the troops who follow Absalom.' [10]Then even the bravest soldier, whose heart is like the heart of a lion, will melt with fear, for all Israel knows that your father is a fighter and that those with him are brave.

[11]"So I advise you: Let all Israel, from Dan to Beersheba—as numerous as the sand on the seashore—be gathered to you, with you yourself leading them into battle. [12]Then we will attack him wherever he may be found, and we will fall on him as dew settles on the ground. Neither he nor any of his men will be left alive. [13]If he withdraws into a city, then all Israel will bring ropes to that city, and we will drag it down to the valley until not so much as a pebble is left."

[14]Absalom and all the men of Israel said, "The advice of Hushai the Arkite is better than that of Ahithophel." For the LORD had determined to frustrate the good advice of Ahithophel in order to bring disaster on Absalom.

[15]Hushai told Zadok and Abiathar, the priests, "Ahithophel has advised Absalom and the elders of Israel to do such and such, but I have advised them to do so and so. [16]Now send a message at once and tell David, 'Do not spend the night at the fords in the wilderness; cross over without fail, or the king and all the people with him will be swallowed up.'"

[17]Jonathan and Ahimaaz were staying at En Rogel. A female servant was to go and inform them, and they were to go and tell King David, for they could not risk being seen entering the city. [18]But a young man saw them and told Absalom. So the two of them left at once and went to the house of a man in Bahurim. He had a well in his courtyard, and they climbed down into it. [19]His wife took a covering and spread it out over the opening of the well and scattered grain over it. No one knew anything about it.

[20]When Absalom's men came to the woman at the house, they asked, "Where are Ahimaaz and Jonathan?"

The woman answered them, "They crossed over the brook." The men searched but found no one, so they returned to Jerusalem.

²¹After they had gone, the two climbed out of the well and went to inform King David. They said to him, "Set out and cross the river at once; Ahithophel has advised such and such against you." ²²So David and all the people with him set out and crossed the Jordan. By daybreak, no one was left who had not crossed the Jordan.

²³When Ahithophel saw that his advice had not been followed, he saddled his donkey and set out for his house in his hometown. He put his house in order and then hanged himself. So he died and was buried in his father's tomb.

²⁴David went to Mahanaim, and Absalom crossed the Jordan with all the men of Israel. ²⁵Absalom had appointed Amasa over the army in place of Joab. Amasa was the son of Jether, an Ishmaelite who had married Abigail, the daughter of Nahash and sister of Zeruiah the mother of Joab. ²⁶The Israelites and Absalom camped in the land of Gilead.

²⁷When David came to Mahanaim, Shobi son of Nahash from Rabbah of the Ammonites, and Makir son of Ammiel from Lo Debar, and Barzillai the Gileadite from Rogelim ²⁸brought bedding and bowls and articles of pottery. They also brought wheat and barley, flour and roasted grain, beans and lentils, ²⁹honey and curds, sheep, and cheese from cows' milk for David and his people to eat. For they said, "The people have become exhausted and hungry and thirsty in the wilderness."

Listen to the Text in the Story: 2 Samuel 12:10–12; Correspondance de Baḫdi-Līm (Mari Archives)

Texts from ancient Mari have brought to light the importance of donkeys as symbolizing royalty in ancient Syria-Palestine (specifically Northwest Semitic tribes). In one text an official from Mari named Baḫdi-Līm recommends that a tribal chieftain named Zimri-Lim enter the city on a donkey rather than a horse: "You are king of the Haneans [= seminomads] and, only secondarily, king of the Akkadians. May my lord not ride on horses! Let it be only in a chair (drawn by) mules that my lord may ride and honor his royal head!"[1] Donkeys were also important symbols of royalty in Israelite traditions. In Judges 5:10 Israelite commanders are said to ride donkeys, and David's sons all ride donkeys/mules (2 Sam 13:29). When Solomon is proclaimed the new king in Israel he rides on

---

1. Jean R. Kupper, *Correspondance de Baḫdi-Lim, préfet du palais de Mari,* ARM 6 (Paris: Imprimerie Nationale, 1954), 76:20–24. Cited in Daniel Bodi, "Chapter 6: The Story of Samuel, Saul, and David," in *Ancient Israel's History: An Introduction to Issues and Sources,* ed. Richard S. Hess, and Bill T. Arnold (Grand Rapids: Baker, 2014), 212.

David's donkey (1 Kgs 1:38). The prophet Zechariah also describes the messiah riding a donkey (Zech 9:9–10; cf. Matt 21:2–7; John 12:14–15).

In this chapter Ziba, Mephibosheth's servant, brings David donkeys carrying food and victuals for the exiled king. In light of the symbolic significance of donkeys in that ancient context, Ziba's use of donkeys here underscores his expression of loyalty to David and the legitimizing of David as Israel's king.

This chapter continues to fulfill the prophecy of Nathan against David after his great sin with Bathsheba. The prophet had predicted, "Out of your own household I am going to bring calamity on you," calamities that have been unfolding over the last three chapters (the rape of Tamar, the murder of Amnon, etc.). Now, Nathan's prophecy that "I will take your wives and give them to one who is close to you, and he will sleep with your wives in broad daylight" (2 Sam 12:11) comes to fulfillment as Absalom, "one who is close to [David]," takes David's concubines and sleeps with them "in the sight of all Israel" (2 Sam 16:22).

EXPLAIN the Story

As the story of David's exile from Jerusalem continues, he encounters two men of the house of Saul, Ziba (Saul's former steward who now served Mephibosheth) and Shimei (who was from the same clan as Saul). Ziba brings food and donkeys for David and his men, claiming that Mephibosheth decided to stay in Jerusalem in hopes he would be made king in David's stead. David takes him at his word and subsequently awards Ziba all that Mephibosheth owned. Shimei, on the other hand, curses David and hurls stones and dirt at him, alleging that David was getting his just deserts for shedding much blood of the Saulide house. Though Abishai offers to kill Shimei for his cursing, David refuses and commands them to leave Shimei alone, as he leaves open the question of whether Shimei was sent by God or not. Finally, David and his men arrive at their destination exhausted from the journey. In the meantime, back in Jerusalem, Hushai follows David's orders and becomes an advisor for Absalom. Ahithophel then advises Absalom to sleep with David's remaining concubines in order to strengthen the resolve of the people toward him. Absalom follows his advice, unwittingly fulfilling Nathan's prophecy of 2 Samuel 12:11. Ahithophel secondly advises that he lead an army to attack David immediately while tired from his journey and that he kill only David, allowing the rest to live and serve Absalom. Providentially, Absalom asked for a second opinion from Hushai, who proceeded to convince Absalom to delay an attack and lead the army himself. In answer to David's prayer, Absalom decided to follow Hushai's advice. Hushai sends word to David warning him to cross the Jordan out of danger. On hearing that his advice was rejected, Ahithophel returned home and hanged himself. In the Transjordan, David stayed at Mahanaim, the former capital city of Saul's son Ishbosheth. Absalom brought the Israelite army now under Amasa's command and camped nearby, ready for battle. With battle looming, David receives further provisions from the unlikely source of three prominent men who each had good reason to be hostile to David, revealing God's work on David's behalf.

David Encounters Two Saulides (16:1–14)

Not long after encountering Hushai and sending him on his mission, David meets Ziba, Saul's former steward who now served Jonathan's son Mephibosheth. Ziba had brought with him a great deal of food and refreshments for David and his men, as well as donkeys to ride. Ziba's motivation is unclear. It could be he was simply very loyal to David. Alternatively, it could be that Ziba saw a chance to promote himself by slandering Mephibosheth. David appears somewhat surprised by Ziba's presence and asks where Mephibosheth was. Ziba tells David that Mephibosheth chose to stay in Jerusalem (rather than follow David) in hopes that he would be made king by the Israelites. Ziba's claim seems quite unlikely, as there was little reason Mephibosheth would think that Absalom's rebellion would result in the restoration of a Saulide to the throne. Furthermore, later on Mephibosheth will deny these charges and claim that Ziba had lied to David. Regardless, at this point David takes Ziba at his word and gives him all that Mephibosheth owned as reward for his faithfulness. In doing so, David appears to go back on his covenant made with Jonathan in 1 Samuel 20:15 that David would "not ever cut off [his] kindness from [Jonathan's] family."

Next, as David neared the town of Bahurim, east of Jerusalem, David comes upon another former Saulide supporter, Shimei, who was of the same clan as Saul. This Saulide utters curses at David and hurls stones and dirt at him, alleging God was giving Absalom the kingdom due to David's shedding Saulide blood. Shimei may be implicating David in the deaths of Saul and Jonathan and/or the deaths of Abner (2 Sam 3:31–39) and Ishbosheth (2 Sam 4:5–12). The narrative, however, has clearly shown that David had nothing to do with the deaths of Saul and his sons, who had died at the hands of the Philistines (1 Sam 31) while David was still back in Ziklag (1 Sam 30), or with the deaths of Abner (who Joab killed against David's wishes) or Ish-Bosheth (who was killed by two former soldiers of Saul who murdered him asleep in his bed).

Another possibility is that Shimei refers to David's handing over seven sons of Saul to be killed by the Gibeonites in 2 Samuel 21:1–9. (The story from

2 Sam 21 clearly takes place earlier in David's reign and could have occurred before Absalom's rebellion.) If this is the case, David could have been viewed as culpable (though God had initiated the punishment of Saul's house), leading him to entertain the possibility Shimei's curse was really from God. Of course, David really did have blood on his hands—the blood of Uriah the Hittite and those Israelite soldiers who also perished in the scheme to murder him (2 Sam 11:17). Perhaps David's guilty conscience leads him to entertain the possibility that Shimei's curse was heaven sent.

The cursing of Israel's leaders is forbidden in the law of Moses (Exod 22:28), though it seems unlikely the offer of Abishai (Joab's brother) to relieve Shimei of his head for his slander was as motivated out of concern for Mosaic legislation as by his hotheaded temper. After all, the sons of Zeruiah are known for such violence. On an earlier occasion, Abishai requested permission to pin Saul to the ground with his spear (1 Sam 26:8), and the cold-blooded murder of Saul's general, Abner, is attributed to both Abishai and his brother Joab (2 Sam 3:30). David, however, forbids retaliation, leaving open the possibility that Shimei may have been sent by God. Furthermore, David hopes that God may have pity on David due to the cursing. Finally, when David and his people arrive at their destination they are utterly exhausted. They are "weary and the battle has not yet begun."[2]

The War of the Counselors in Jerusalem (16:15–17:14)

While David and his company were fatigued from their flight, David's plan to thwart the advice of Ahithophel begins to unfold as David's confidant, Hushai, meets with Absalom. With Absalom in control of Jerusalem and the palace, Hushai is one of David's few supporters in the capital. Husahi greets Absalom saying, "long live the king!" which could be viewed as ambiguous since the name of the king is not mentioned (compare 1 Kgs 1:25 and the shout "Long live King Adonijah!"). Absalom is understandably wary of trusting a turncoat and proceeds to question Hushai as to why he had abandoned David. Hushai's flattering answer, that he served the one "chosen by the LORD, by these people, and by all the men of Israel" (v. 18), is nearly as ambiguous as his initial greeting, seeing as David was the one chosen by Yahweh and the people. Absalom, however, seems to miss the ambiguity, likely because in the end Hushai speaks plainly, saying to Absalom, "Just as I served your father, so I will serve you" (v. 18). Hushai's deceptive words along with flattery convince the usurper of Hushai's resolve to serve Absalom.

Returning to the business at hand, Absalom then asks Ahithophel's for advice on how to proceed. Ahithophel's initial advice that Absalom sleep with David's concubines seems very strange to a modern reader. However, as noted in the commentary on 2 Samuel 3, in ancient times it was sometimes thought that taking a former king's wife or concubine was tantamount to symbolically taking the throne. This underlies Ishbosheth's anger at Abner for sleeping with Saul's concubine (2 Sam 3:7). Similarly, Solomon's brother, Adonijah, requests one of David's concubines to be given him as wife (1 Kgs 2:17), which Solomon equates with an attempt to take "the kingdom" (2:22). Here Absalom is attempting to take the kingdom, so taking the king's concubines proclaimed to the people that he was king. Ahithophel explains the action in that it will make him "obnoxious" to David and that it will strengthen the resolve of his supporters.

More might be going on, however, than simply solidifying the support of the people. If Ahithophel was so insightful, it is likely he knew David's disposition toward his children. As we have seen, David did not punish Amnon for his violent rape of Tamar (2 Sam 13:21). Furthermore, after Absalom's rebellion is put down, David wanted no harm to come to his son (18:5, 12). Ahithophel probably realized that if the rebellion failed, David could very well reconcile with Absalom but still kill his treasonous allies.[3] So the counsel to sleep with David's concubines was probably "of a 'bridge burning' nature."[4] In other words, Absalom's taking the king's concubines created "a complete and irreversible break" with his father.[5] There was no going back.

Ahithophel's advice to sleep with David's concubines may also reveal a personal agenda wherein he avenged David's affair with his granddaughter Bathsheba. As Bergen writes:

> For Ahithophel personally, the scheme must have seemed like a particularly satisfying application of the Torah's *lex talionis* [eye for an eye]. . . . David had had unlawful sexual relations with Ahithophel's granddaughter at the royal palace in Jerusalem, though she was married to another; so now, unlawful sexual relations with David's harem would take place at the same palace—only in this case the retributive act would be ten times greater than the original offense, and in public![6]

Absalom follows Ahithophel's advice. A tent is pitched on the roof of the palace so that everyone would know what was going on. Ironically, David's sin began on the roof of the same palace from where he lusted after Bathsheba.

---

3. Keith Bodner, "Motives for Defection: Ahithophel's Agenda in 2 Samuel 15–17," *SR* 31 (2002): 67.

4. Ibid.

5. Anderson, *2 Samuel*, 214.

6. Bergen, *Samuel*, 411.

This connection reminds the reader that this terrible turn of events sadly fulfills the prophetic word of Nathan (2 Sam 12:11). Of course, a son taking his father's wife is explicitly forbidden in Mosaic law (Lev 18:8; 20:11; Deut 22:30), so the deed casts Absalom in a bad light to say the least.

The narrator then notes that Ahithophel's advice was so reliable that both David and Absalom equated its dependability with a divine oracle from God. In other words, if Absalom decided to not follow Ahithophel's advice, it would be almost a miracle! Of course, as we quickly see in the story, that is exactly what happens.

Ahithophel next advises that a military contingent be sent to attack David immediately while he is weary and weak. Given that the narrator had informed us that David and his men were "exhausted" from their journey, Ahithophel's advice seems wise. Furthermore, Ahithophel suggests that *he* rather than Absalom lead the army against David. This would appear wise from several angles. First, it would prevent the king from being put at mortal risk in the battle (and later in the story Absalom's choice to lead the army *does* lead to his death). Second, it would allow David to be killed without Absalom being personally implicated. The usurping son killing his father would likely not sit well with all citizens, and Absalom would have plausible deniability were he to allow Ahithophel to do his dirty work. Finally, Ahithophel counsels that they kill *only* David. Pragmatically, this makes sense in order to gain the support of the other people and bring them back to Absalom's side. Why alienate such a large contingent of Israelites? With the king dead, the remaining Israelites will doubtless rally to Absalom.

As wise as this advice is on one level, on another it betrays a personal agenda. First, it seems rather odd that a counselor like Ahithophel lead an army on a mission to assassinate the king.[7] Given that Ahithophel's granddaughter, Bathsheba, was violated by the king and his grandson-in-law, Uriah, was murdered by the king, we can see Ahithophel's motivation here. After all, Ahithophel plans to personally kill *only* David.

As expected, following the comment about the reliability of Ahithophel's advice, his plan is received well by Absalom and Israel's elders. Then, in a surprising move, Absalom decides to also hear the advice of David's confidant, Hushai, who begins by noting that Ahithophel's advice is not good "this time" (v. 7). That is, most often his advice is to be followed, making this a rare occurrence. Then Hushai successfully dissuades Absalom and his court to reject Ahithophel's advice by emphasizing the battle prowess of David and his men and suggesting that David would not even be camping with his troops

---

7. Mauchline, *1 and 2 Samuel*, 279.

but be hidden elsewhere. Furthermore, Hushai suggests that David might attack them first (from his hiding place) and cause rumors to circulate that Absalom was losing the war. Ironically, in his advice given supposedly to help Absalom, Hushai manages to praise David's abilities as a soldier and remind his enemies that he is a mighty warrior. In fact, Hushai paints a picture of David that contrasts with current reality. As Alter writes:

> This image of David as the constantly wakeful, elusive guerilla leader scarcely accords with the figure David has cut in the last several years of reported narrative—sleeping through the long afternoon while his army fights in Ammon, sedentary in his palace while internecine struggle goes on between his own children.[8]

Contrary to Ahithophel, Hushai instead advises that Absalom first muster all of Israel and lead them into battle *himself*, killing not only David but all of his men as well (describing the putative victory with rhetorical flourish). Hushai's suggested strategy appeals to the glory-seeking Absalom, who probably relished the idea of leading the entire army into battle. The fledgling king may also have liked the idea of eliminating those faithful to David, especially Joab, with whom he had problems in the past (2 Sam 14:29–32).

Hushai's plan, however, clearly served David's interests. First, the call to muster the entire army would buy David some much-needed time. Second, unlike the plan of Ahithophel, Hushai's plan puts Absalom directly in harm's way. Shockingly, Absalom rejects Ahithophel's wise counsel and follows Hushai's proposed strategy instead. In case the reader missed the miraculous nature of this turn of events, the narrator explicitly states that this was Yahweh's doing and that God planned to "bring disaster on Absalom" (2 Sam 17:14).

Hushai Sends Word to David (17:15–29)

Hushai then tells the priests what happened in Absalom's court and asks them to send word to David to cross the Jordan immediately rather than spend the night where they were. This advice seems to assume that Absalom *will* follow Ahithophel's advice to march against David immediately. Perhaps Hushai was unsure whether Absalom would follow Hushai's advice after all and wanted to take extra measures in case.

The method of informing David was very covert, with a female servant being sent to the sons of the priests. Presumably, a female servant would be less suspicious than a male servant since valuable information like this would not so easily be entrusted to a female in an ancient patriarchal society. Despite

---

8. Alter, *The David Story*, 298.

the clandestine nature of the operation, someone spotted the priests' sons, causing them to hide in a well at a house in Bahurim. Given that Bahurim was Shimei's hometown (1 Kgs 2:8) and the place where Shimei came out cursing David and his company, the favor shown David's spies here could be due to David's humble reaction to Shimei, which impressed the locals. David's spies not only hid in the well of a house in Bahurim, but the women of the house also covered for them. Thus, David was successfully warned and he and his company crossed the Jordan to safer grounds.

Ahithophel, however, does not take rejection well. When he learns that his advice was not taken, he hangs himself. Perhaps the wise counselor knew that failure to take his advice would result in David winning back the throne and that at that point his life would be forfeit due to his treason (though David actually ends up granting amnesty to those involved in the rebellion). Still, it seems odd he would kill himself before he knew for sure that the rebellion had failed. Perhaps this reveals that "the success of the coup was not his main concern."[9] After all, if his defection from David concerned personal revenge over the treatment of his granddaughter (Bathsheba), then the rejection of his plan wherein he would personally "strike down only the king" (17:3) meant that his sole purpose in joining the conspiracy was gone. With his "private ambition to destroy David" thwarted, he now despaired and took his own life.[10]

Having crossed the Jordan, David went to Mahanaim, Ish-Bosheth's former capital city during his short-lived rival kingdom to David (2 Sam 2–3). In Mahanaim, locals brought David and his company victuals and supplies. Somewhat surprisingly, given Israel's recent war with Nahash's son, King Hanun of Ammon, another son of Nahash (probably Hanun's brother), brings David supplies here, perhaps remembering David's earlier covenant with Nahash (2 Sam 10:2). Makir of Lo Debar, former Saulide supporter (who was Mephibosheth's guardian; cf. 2 Sam 9:3–6), also supplies David and his men. Finally, a Gileadite named Barzillai also brings supplies for David and his company. Later in 2 Samuel 21:8 we learn that "Barzillai the Meholathite" was the father of five sons whom David handed over to the Gibeonites to be executed for Saul's bloodguilt. If this Barzillai is the same person, then this is once more a surprising source of blessing. (In 2 Sam 21 Barzillai is called a Meholathite, which means "from Meholah," a place in Gilead, and the Barzillai here is from Gilead.) So, David goes to what was once hostile territory (Mahanaim, the former capital of a rival kingdom to David) and receives gifts from men who had previously been enemies of David or had good reason to be hostile to him. The reader should see these unlikely turns of events as from the Lord.

---

9. Bodner, "Motives for Defection," 73.
10. Ibid.

At this point Absalom musters his army and crosses the Jordan, choosing Amasa as general over the army instead of Joab. Amasa, as it turns out, was Joab's cousin (with Amasa's father having married the sister of Joab's mother), so perhaps Absalom was emulating David's choices in his royal duties.

LIVE the Story

Patient Endurance

David's character shown in his endurance of Shimei's wrongful cursing and his refusal to retaliate is a good illustration of patient endurance under suffering. Jesus commands Christians to "bless those who curse you" (Luke 6:28) and to not retaliate against those who attack (Matt 5:39; Luke 6:29). The early church fathers saw David in this instance as a model of such patient endurance. Augustine writes, "With this patience holy David endured the insults of one abusing him, and, though he could easily have wreaked vengeance on him," and Ambrose of Milan comments, "when Shimei the son of Gera reviled him, David was silent; and although he was surrounded with armed men he did not return the abuse, nor seek revenge."[11]

As the story shows, David's refusal to retaliate pays off as his spies are given safe harbor in Shimei's hometown of Bahurim (17:18). David's turning the other cheek likely made an impression on the locals and contributed to their aiding his spies. In the end, David was more concerned with God's view of his actions than the locals of Bahurim. David was willing to submit to God's judgment as "he unquestioningly accepts that Yahweh's judgment is just."[12] David hopes God might pity him due to the cursing, that "Yahweh may yet balance the curse of Shimei with a blessing."[13] David's hope is in line with the Psalmist who prays, "Look on my affliction and my distress and take away all my sins" (Ps 25:18). Both David and the psalmist hope that patient endurance rather than retaliation will result in God's favor—and God's favor means more than any human help.

God's Providence

Again we see in this story that important events unfold that rely on daring and brilliant human action but at the same time are the work of God. Hushai's countermanding of Ahithophel's wise advice can be seen as the result of his brilliant rhetoric. David's confidant appeals to Absalom's pride (suggesting he lead out the army himself) and employs rhetorically persuasive grand

---

11. Franke, *Joshua, Judges, Ruth, 1–2 Samuel*, 375.
12. Anderson, *2 Samuel*, 207.
13. Ibid.

metaphors (that he gather an army "as numerous as the sand on the seashore" then "fall on him as dew settles on the ground," vv. 11–12) to influence Absalom and his court. Commentators have noted the brilliance of his speech, and its effectiveness is clear, with Absalom and all the men of Israel favoring his advice over Ahithophel's. Yet at the same time, the true reason that Absalom and his court choose Hushai's advice is clearly stated by the narrator: "For the LORD had determined to frustrate the good advice of Ahithophel in order to bring disaster on Absalom" (v. 14). While Hushai's brilliant rhetoric was obviously persuasive, in the end Absalom and his court chose to follow Hushai's advice "because God has commanded it."[14] Somehow God is involved, though no "overt divine action" is described, leading us to see "complementary causation" in this incident.[15] In the mystery of God's providence, the brilliant rhetorician Hushai and God are *both* key players in Absalom's downfall.

The story gives us a good chance to reflect on a biblical view of providence. Biblical providence is not the same as fatalism. Fatalism is a pagan idea that is popular today through astrology (which was also prevalent in the ancient world). Fatalism sees human actions as irrelevant because the history of humanity is written in the stars. Instead "[human] free actions are free no longer, since the horoscope's predictions (unlike the prophet's) make no allowance for personal response."[16] Providence, on the other hand, includes free human actions, though it puts them within God's higher purposes. God's frustrating Ahithophel's advice included the brilliant rhetorical speech of Hushai.

The story also speaks against the idea of chance ruling the universe. David happens upon Hushai (15:31) just as he prays for God to frustrate Ahithophel's advice (15:32). Absalom inexplicably calls for Hushai's advice (17:5) even though he and his court had already decided that Ahithophel's advice was good (17:4). These turns of events could be viewed as mere chance, but the narrator clearly states God's involvement (17:14). Biblical providence asserts that God directs history and, within his direction, free human actions are integrated and incorporated. Thus, providence is a source of hope for those of us living in a fallen world.[17]

Prefiguring the Betrayal of Jesus

As noted last chapter, there is much in David's departure from Jerusalem that resonates with Jesus' passion narratives in the Gospels. These resonances continue here. Like Jesus, when David "was abused, he did not return abuse;

---

14. Brueggemann, *First and Second Samuel*, 313.

15. Halpern, *David's Secret Demons: Messiah, Murderer, Traitor, King*, 46.

16. Ferguson et al., *New Dictionary of Theology*, 541.

17. Ibid., 542.

when he suffered, he did not threaten; but he entrusted himself to the one who judges justly" (1 Pet 2:23 NRSV). David refused to allow retaliation for Shimei's words and actions. Instead he entrusted himself to God, relying on God's faithfulness in the face of Shimei's curse, and he submitted himself to God's will (2 Sam 15:25–26). Just as David rebuked his loyal follower (Abishai) for wanting to kill Shimei in defense of David, so Jesus had to rebuke his loyal follower (Peter) for taking up the sword in defense of Jesus (Matt 26:52). Just as David said that the Lord was behind Shimei's assault (2 Sam 16:11), Jesus similarly claimed that God was behind the assault in the garden ("Put your sword away! Shall I not drink the cup the Father has given me?" John 18:11).

Another distinct parallel is found between Ahithophel and Judas Iscariot, in their betrayals of David and Jesus and their suicides. Just as Ahithophel was a trusted counselor of David who betrayed him to those who would kill him, so Judas Iscariot was a trusted disciple (John 13:29) who betrayed the Son of David to his death. Many of the locations mentioned in David's flight from Jerusalem and Jesus' passion narrative are the same. Both David and Jesus ascend the Mount of Olives and there learn of the betrayal (David is told by a messenger while Jesus is betrayed with a kiss).[18] Both traitors advise the enemies of the anointed one in Jerusalem—Ahithophel in the king's palace and Judas at the temple (Luke 22:4). Finally, both Ahithophel and Judas (Matt 27:5) hang themselves after betraying the anointed one. What is more, they kill themselves *before* the fruits of their betrayal are completed (Judas before the crucifixion and Ahithophel before Absalom's army marched against David). As Ackroyd argues, "the narrative of Jesus' passion is deeply enriched with such Old Testament allusion and analogy."[19]

---

18. McCarter, *II Samuel*, 389. Though of course, Jesus was earlier aware that Judas would betray him (John 6:71).

19. Ackroyd, *Second Book of Samuel*, 162.

LISTEN to the Story

¹David mustered the men who were with him and appointed over them commanders of thousands and commanders of hundreds. ²David sent out his troops, a third under the command of Joab, a third under Joab's brother Abishai son of Zeruiah, and a third under Ittai the Gittite. The king told the troops, "I myself will surely march out with you."

³But the men said, "You must not go out; if we are forced to flee, they won't care about us. Even if half of us die, they won't care; but you are worth ten thousand of us. It would be better now for you to give us support from the city."

⁴The king answered, "I will do whatever seems best to you."

So the king stood beside the gate while all his men marched out in units of hundreds and of thousands. ⁵The king commanded Joab, Abishai and Ittai, "Be gentle with the young man Absalom for my sake." And all the troops heard the king giving orders concerning Absalom to each of the commanders.

⁶David's army marched out of the city to fight Israel, and the battle took place in the forest of Ephraim. ⁷There Israel's troops were routed by David's men, and the casualties that day were great—twenty thousand men. ⁸The battle spread out over the whole countryside, and the forest swallowed up more men that day than the sword.

⁹Now Absalom happened to meet David's men. He was riding his mule, and as the mule went under the thick branches of a large oak, Absalom's hair got caught in the tree. He was left hanging in midair, while the mule he was riding kept on going.

¹⁰When one of the men saw what had happened, he told Joab, "I just saw Absalom hanging in an oak tree."

¹¹Joab said to the man who had told him this, "What! You saw him? Why didn't you strike him to the ground right there? Then I would have had to give you ten shekels of silver and a warrior's belt."

¹²But the man replied, "Even if a thousand shekels were weighed out

into my hands, I would not lay a hand on the king's son. In our hearing the king commanded you and Abishai and Ittai, 'Protect the young man Absalom for my sake.' ¹³And if I had put my life in jeopardy—and nothing is hidden from the king—you would have kept your distance from me."

¹⁴Joab said, "I'm not going to wait like this for you." So he took three javelins in his hand and plunged them into Absalom's heart while Absalom was still alive in the oak tree. ¹⁵And ten of Joab's armor-bearers surrounded Absalom, struck him and killed him.

¹⁶Then Joab sounded the trumpet, and the troops stopped pursuing Israel, for Joab halted them. ¹⁷They took Absalom, threw him into a big pit in the forest and piled up a large heap of rocks over him. Meanwhile, all the Israelites fled to their homes.

¹⁸During his lifetime Absalom had taken a pillar and erected it in the King's Valley as a monument to himself, for he thought, "I have no son to carry on the memory of my name." He named the pillar after himself, and it is called Absalom's Monument to this day.

¹⁹Now Ahimaaz son of Zadok said, "Let me run and take the news to the king that the LORD has vindicated him by delivering him from the hand of his enemies."

²⁰"You are not the one to take the news today," Joab told him. "You may take the news another time, but you must not do so today, because the king's son is dead."

²¹Then Joab said to a Cushite, "Go, tell the king what you have seen." The Cushite bowed down before Joab and ran off.

²²Ahimaaz son of Zadok again said to Joab, "Come what may, please let me run behind the Cushite."

But Joab replied, "My son, why do you want to go? You don't have any news that will bring you a reward."

²³He said, "Come what may, I want to run."

So Joab said, "Run!" Then Ahimaaz ran by way of the plain and outran the Cushite.

²⁴While David was sitting between the inner and outer gates, the watchman went up to the roof of the gateway by the wall. As he looked out, he saw a man running alone. ²⁵The watchman called out to the king and reported it.

The king said, "If he is alone, he must have good news." And the runner came closer and closer.

²⁶Then the watchman saw another runner, and he called down to the gatekeeper, "Look, another man running alone!"

The king said, "He must be bringing good news, too."

27The watchman said, "It seems to me that the first one runs like Ahimaaz son of Zadok."

"He's a good man," the king said. "He comes with good news."

28Then Ahimaaz called out to the king, "All is well!" He bowed down before the king with his face to the ground and said, "Praise be to the LORD your God! He has delivered up those who lifted their hands against my lord the king."

29The king asked, "Is the young man Absalom safe?"

Ahimaaz answered, "I saw great confusion just as Joab was about to send the king's servant and me, your servant, but I don't know what it was."

30The king said, "Stand aside and wait here." So he stepped aside and stood there.

31Then the Cushite arrived and said, "My lord the king, hear the good news! The LORD has vindicated you today by delivering you from the hand of all who rose up against you."

32The king asked the Cushite, "Is the young man Absalom safe?"

The Cushite replied, "May the enemies of my lord the king and all who rise up to harm you be like that young man."

33The king was shaken. He went up to the room over the gateway and wept. As he went, he said: "O my son Absalom! My son, my son Absalom! If only I had died instead of you—O Absalom, my son, my son!"

Listen to the Text in the Story: 2 Samuel 14

The details of the final demise of Absalom at the hands of Joab in this chapter recall events narrated earlier in the story in 2 Samuel 14. The reader will recall that it was Joab who orchestrated Absalom's return from exile (2 Sam 14:1–23) only to have Absalom undertake a coup d'état. What is more, shortly after returning to Israel, despite all Joab had done for him, Absalom repaid the favor by burning Joab's fields (2 Sam 14:30). While the text does not explicitly connect Joab's actions against Absalom in this chapter with these earlier stories, it seems most likely that Absalom's previous interactions with Joab supply significant background for the story here. What is more, 2 Samuel 14 also provides important background material for the role in which Absalom's great hair plays in his demise. The scene in this chapter is ripe with irony, as Absalom's excessive hair was a pronounced source of pride for him (see 2 Sam 14:26) but now becomes the source of his undoing.

EXPLAIN the Story

With Absalom's attack looming, David organizes his troops and prepares for war. Though he intended to march out with his troops, his commanders talk him out of it, and David stays in the city while Joab, Abishai, and Ittai go out with the army. Before they leave, David gives explicit orders to his commanders to treat Absalom gently (an order of which all the troops were aware). When the battle commences, David's troops defeat Absalom's army, but despite David's orders Absalom is killed. As he rides on his mule, Absalom's long hair gets tangled in the branches of a tree, leaving him hanging there as his royal steed abandons him. When Absalom is found, Joab has him killed, disregarding David's command. Absalom is buried in the forest, and the Israelites flee, ending the insurrection. When David is informed of the victory, he is most concerned about the status of his son. When he is told of Absalom's demise, David is distraught and mourns his son, wishing he had died in his stead.

Battle Plans (18:1–5)

The chapter begins with David's men poised for battle. Thanks to food and supplies given by Shobi, Makir, and Barzillai (2 Sam 17:27–29), David's army was now refreshed. Thanks to the work of Hushai, who had bought David extra time by convincing Absalom not to attack immediately as per the advice of Ahithophel (2 Sam 17:6–13), David and his men have a chance to organize themselves for battle. David divides the army into three divisions, as was Israelite custom (cf. Judg 7:16; 9:43; 1 Sam 11:11; 13:17). In command of the divisions are Joab, Abishai, and Ittai the Gittite (cf. 2 Sam 15:19–22). When David informs them that he himself will march into battle with them, his men disagree with the strategy due to David's being such a high value target. Perhaps in light of Ahithophel's plan (of which they were aware; cf. 2 Sam 17:21) to focus on killing only David, the men insist that David stay behind in the city, to which David agrees. It is also possible that the men knew that David could be a liability in the battlefield due to his conflicting feelings toward Absalom and the rebels. Regardless, David agrees to remain behind. Before the army leaves, however, David gives explicit orders to his commanders to not harm Absalom, an order heard by the entire army. This is a difficult order for the troops. How can one put down the rebellion but save the chief rebel?

The Battle (18:6–18)

The battle is tersely narrated, with David's men routing Absalom's army, resulting in great casualties. The narrator notes that not all of the fatalities were the result of David's forces, as more men died as a result of the difficulties of fighting and fleeing in the rugged terrain of the forest than by the sword (soldiers fleeing may have become tangled up in the brushwood or perhaps killed each other in the confusion and dark of the forest). While certainly not bloodless, the narrator is emphasizing that David's troops did not set out to cause great bloodshed (note Joab's calling off the battle once Absalom is killed). After all, "it is important for a king who has lost power and needs to regain it not to alienate too many of his citizenry."[1]

This cryptic notice of nature's involvement in the battle is further explicated by Absalom's death. As the would-be king was riding along on his mule, his head gets stuck in tree branches, probably due to his voluminous amount of hair. So stuck was he that he was left hanging from the tree while his mule carried on without him. Some have pointed out that a mule is a royal mount.[2] The sons of the king all fled on mules when Absalom killed Amnon (2 Sam 13:29), and later in the story David will have Solomon ride on his own mule to show he is to be king (1 Kgs 1:33, 38, 44). Thus, when Absalom loses his mule here, he symbolically loses his royal seat and his kingdom.[3]

When one of David's men sees Absalom's predicament, he reports it to Joab, who castigates him for not killing Absalom on the spot (for which Joab claims he would have handsomely rewarded him). The man, however, informs Joab he would not lay a hand on Absalom for any price, since it would violate the king's explicit order. The man further accuses Joab of dissembling with his promise of reward, saying that the general would actually have distanced himself from the act and that he would have been left to take the fall for the death of the king's son.

Joab does not respond to the man's accusation but takes matters into his own hands, hurling three "javelins" (in Hebrew, *shebet*) at Absalom while he hung helplessly from the tree. The Hebrew word (*shebet*) translated "javelin" by the NIV means a blunt wooden rod (elsewhere translated staff, club), usually used in the context of corporal punishment of a disobedient child (cf. Prov 10:13; 13:24; 22:15; 26:3; 29:15).[4] The use of wooden rods here suggests two things. First, literally, the picture is of Joab knocking Absalom out of the tree using wooden rods (hitting him in the "heart" can also mean in the chest area)—*not* killing Absalom. After all, if Joab intended to stab him, a sword or spear would have been preferable. Furthermore, it was likely politically

---

1. Antony F. Campbell, *2 Samuel*, FOTL 8 (Grand Rapids: Eerdmans, 2005), 159.

2. Charles Conroy, *Absalom Absalom!: Narrative and Language in 2 Sam 13–20*, AnBib 81 (Rome: Biblical Institute Press, 1978), 60.

3. Ibid.; Alter, *The David Story*, 305.

4. The word "rod" (*shebet*) is also used in reference to God punishing Israel by using other nations (e.g., Isa 10:5; 10:24).

advantageous for Joab to be able to say he did not personally kill David's son. Besides which, the text makes it clear Absalom was alive at this point, with Joab's armor-bearers actually killing him (cf. 1 Sam 14:13).

Second, the use of wooden rods may metaphorically imply the application of the disciplinary rod (that David failed to apply) to Absalom for his disobedience. Proverbs 13:24 states, "Whoever spares the rod (*shebet*) hates their children, but the one who loves their children is careful to discipline them." Interestingly, the word "spares" (Hebrew *hasak*) from Proverbs 13:24 also appears here as Joab "halted" (Hebrew *hasak*) the people from continuing the battle. In fact, only Proverbs 13:24 connects these two words from this passage.[5]

Proverbs 13:24	2 Samuel 18:14, 16
Whoever spares (*hasak*) the rod (*shebet*) hates their children, but the one who loves their children is careful to discipline them.	[Joab] took three javelins (*shebet*) . . . . Joab halted (*hasak*) them [the troops]

Before Joab's actions, David had called on the army to treat his son gently (v. 5). As Auld comments:

> Calling off the pursuit compounds Joab's inversion of the gentle treatment commanded by David for Absalom. But the fact that he does not hold back his [rods] from the badly behaved son, though he does hold back his forces, may again serve to show Joab in a better light than his master.[6]

As in the story of the census in 2 Samuel 24, where the general tries to talk David out of implementing his sinful act (2 Sam 24:3), Joab may be viewed positively here.[7]

On another level, Joab's killing of Absalom is par for the course for the shrewd Israelite general who has defied the king in the past when he thought it best for the kingdom. Back in 2 Samuel 2, Joab had killed Abner (against David's wishes), a politically advantageous act, as it effectively put an end to Ish-Bosheth's rival kingdom and at the same time distanced David from Abner's death (which would have been a barrier for David's unification of the kingdom afterwards). Of course, Joab's motives were mixed on that occasion, as his main motivation was to avenge Abner's killing of Joab's brother, Ashahel. Like the killing of Abner, the death of Absalom, from a political perspective, was the right move (though it was against David's wishes), squelching the

---

5. Auld, *I & II Samuel*, 543.
6. Ibid.
7. Ibid.

insurrection in one swift stroke. Again, as in Abner's case, the king did not have to get his hands dirty in the action, which would go a long way to bring the tribes back to David. The similarities also make the reader wonder about Joab's motives in this case (as noted above in the Listen to the Story section).

With the leader of the insurrection killed, Joab sounds the trumpet for his troops to withdraw from combat. This move recalls Ahithophel's counsel to kill the king then withdraw, leaving the rest of the troops alive (only in this case, the king is Absalom). Joab doubtless hoped that as Ahithophel said, "The death of the man you seek will mean the return of all" (2 Sam 17:3). That is, given that the army they were fighting was composed of Israelites, the death of Absalom would hopefully result in the enemy again becoming David's subjects. When Absalom is buried in a pit in the forest with a great mound of rocks piled over his corpse, the rest of the Israelites flee to home, as Joab had hoped. This, of course, is not a proper burial, which would be to entomb the deceased in the family grave (cf. 2 Sam 2:32). Instead, this burial implies the dead man was cursed. Deuteronomy 21:22–23 states that someone hanging on a tree was cursed and calls for a quick burial. The notorious Achan was similarly buried in Joshua 7:26, as were Canaanite kings defeated under Joshua (Josh 8:29; 10:27).

With a large pile of rocks forming his burial monument in the forest, the narrator finds this an appropriate point to inform us that Absalom had earlier erected a monument to himself in the King's Valley (cf. Gen 14:17) by reason of his lack of a male heir to carry on his name. Ironically, Saul is the only other Israelite king to make a monument for himself (1 Sam 15:12).[8] While Absalom's claim to have no sons here appears to contradict 2 Samuel 14:27, which informs us he sired three sons, it need not be so. First, Absalom may have created the monument before his sons were born. Second, and more likely, the children may have died in infancy, as suggested by the fact they are not named and how the story makes no reference to his heirs who could have been viewed as a threat going forward. The reference to his self-named monument sadly ends his story. Absalom had always showed great concern for his fame and reputation, so this closing note on his attempt to secure a pillar for his legacy is appropriate. Ironically, instead of his envisioned grand monument, Absalom is left with a pile of rocks in the forest.

Informing the King (18:19–33)

The chapter closes with messengers being sent to David to inform him of the outcome of the battle. Zadok's son, Ahimaaz, who had earlier successfully

---

8. Bodner, *Power Play*, 183.

delivered Hushai's warnings to David (2 Sam 17:17–21), asks for permission to inform David of the victory. Joab initially denies the request, aware that David would not take it as good news due to the death of Absalom and sends a Cushite messenger instead. Undeterred, Ahimaaz pleads with Joab for permission to go to the king as well, to which Joab conceded. Ahimaaz proved himself a speedier messenger as he outruns the Cushite messenger.

Back at Mahanaim, David is sitting between the inner and outer gates to the city (ancient Israelite cities often had double walls) awaiting news of the battle. While David sits, his watchman climbs to the roof and spies a messenger running to them. Given that it is a lone messenger and not a group (which would suggest soldiers fleeing from the enemy), David discerns that the messenger bears good news. The watchman then spies a second messenger behind the first and then identifies the first as Ahimaaz due to the way he was running (evidently Ahimaaz had a particular running style or was known for his speed). Confident in Ahimaaz's character, David is sure the news is good. Of course, it is not logical that Ahimaaz's reputation as a good man will mean that the news he brings is good. As Alter notes, David's comment here "suggests that the desperately anxious David is grasping at straws. . . . it shows us just how desperate he feels."[9]

Ahimaaz reports the victory, ascribing it to Yahweh. Without commenting on the good news, David instead asks Ahimaaz about Absalom's status. Clearly the king was most concerned about his son and not the victory. At this point Ahimaaz feigns ignorance, claiming that he only saw some confusion when he left and was unaware of what it was. Since we have seen that Joab himself mentioned Absalom's death to Ahimaaz, it is clear Ahimaaz is not telling the truth at this point. No doubt aware of how David has treated bearers of bad news in the past (2 Sam 1:6–10; 4:7–8), Ahimaaz chooses to allow another messenger to inform the king of his son's passing. When the Cushite messenger finally informs David of Absalom's death, David is distraught and retreats to a private room to grieve, lamenting that he wished he had died in his stead.

LIVE the Story

Pride Comes Before a Fall

The conclusion to the story of Absalom provides an amazing picture of the destructiveness of the sin of pride. From the beginning, Absalom's pride has been seen in his concern with his image and reputation. We are told he was

---

9. Alter, *The David Story*, 309.

"highly praised" for his good looks (2 Sam 14:25) and that he would weigh his hair when he cut it each year and announce it to show off his virility to his admirers.[10] Absalom utilized a chariot and horses, complete with fifty men, to run ahead of him in order to impress the Israelites and make a claim to royalty.

Absalom's pride becomes a snare to him as Hushai's flattery (2 Sam 16:18) blinds Absalom from Hushai's real motives. Furthermore, Hushai's bad advice (which countered Ahithophel's wise advice) was likely accepted by Absalom due to the way it played on his ego. Hushai suggested that Absalom himself ride out with a great army, leading them to battle (2 Sam 17:11)—painting a picture of Absalom participating in a glorious battle (2 Sam 17:12–13). Absalom's thirst for glory and prestige was his undoing. Now, in his final moments, ironically what had been such a source of pride for Absalom, his great locks of hair, became the source of his undoing. We could hardly ask for a better illustration of how pride ensnares us.

The Bible places tremendous emphasis on the sin of pride and its antithesis, humility. Instead of depending upon God, pride depends upon the self, due to an excessive assessment of one's own capabilities. Many ancient Christian thinkers (e.g., Augustine, Aquinas, and Dante) place pride as the deadliest sin and the preeminent of all vices.

Throughout Old Testament wisdom literature (and the Psalms), pride is ubiquitously condemned. Proverbs 16:18 could be speaking directly of Absalom when it says, "Pride goes before destruction, a haughty spirit before a fall." Proverbs 16:5 declares that "The LORD detests all the proud of heart. Be sure of this: they will not go unpunished" (cf. Prov 21:4). Furthermore, the story of the fall of Absalom could be a narrative portrayal of the truth of Proverbs 18:12 which states, "Before a downfall the heart is haughty, but humility comes before honor." In 2 Samuel 15–18, we see Absalom's heart become increasingly proud, but David humbling himself. When David departed from Jerusalem, the king showed his humility by covering his head (cf. Jer 14:3–4; Esth 6:12), going barefoot (cf. Isa 20:3–4), and weeping (2 Sam 15:30). As Proverbs 3:34 states, God "shows favor to the humble" (cf. Ps 138:6), which can be seen in how God graciously answered David's prayer to frustrate the wisdom of Ahithophel (2 Sam 15:31).

The New Testament also condemns pride and underscores humility as a virtue. Jesus called himself "humble in heart" (Matt 11:29), while Proverbs 3:34 is quoted in James 4:6 (cf. 1 Pet 5:5), declaring that "God opposes the proud but shows favor to the humble," urging the reader to "humble

---

10. One commentator notes that "Absalom was so proud of [his hair] that he announced its weight after his annual barbering." See Craig E. Morrison, *2 Samuel* (Collegeville, MN: Liturgical Press, 2013), 192.

yourselves before the Lord, and he will lift you up" (Jas 4:10). Just as David humbled himself before God and submitted to God's will, saying, "let him do to me whatever seems good to him" (2 Sam 15:26), so 1 Peter 5:6 urges Christians to "humble yourselves, therefore, under God's mighty hand, that he may lift you up in due time."

Whether it is in our ministry, our family relationships, or personal friendships, pride is detrimental to human flourishing. Furthermore, God's grace is given to the humble while pride is associated with "the same judgment as the devil" (1 Tim 3:6). As Christians, we must continually humble ourselves before God, submit to his will, and wait on his grace.

CHAPTER 43

2 Samuel 19:1–43

 LISTEN to the Story

¹Joab was told, "The king is weeping and mourning for Absalom." ²And for the whole army the victory that day was turned into mourning, because on that day the troops heard it said, "The king is grieving for his son." ³The men stole into the city that day as men steal in who are ashamed when they flee from battle. ⁴The king covered his face and cried aloud, "O my son Absalom! O Absalom, my son, my son!"

⁵Then Joab went into the house to the king and said, "Today you have humiliated all your men, who have just saved your life and the lives of your sons and daughters and the lives of your wives and concubines. ⁶You love those who hate you and hate those who love you. You have made it clear today that the commanders and their men mean nothing to you. I see that you would be pleased if Absalom were alive today and all of us were dead. ⁷Now go out and encourage your men. I swear by the LORD that if you don't go out, not a man will be left with you by nightfall. This will be worse for you than all the calamities that have come on you from your youth till now."

⁸So the king got up and took his seat in the gateway. When the men were told, "The king is sitting in the gateway," they all came before him.

Meanwhile, the Israelites had fled to their homes.

⁹Throughout the tribes of Israel, all the people were arguing among themselves, saying, "The king delivered us from the hand of our enemies; he is the one who rescued us from the hand of the Philistines. But now he has fled the country to escape from Absalom; ¹⁰and Absalom, whom we anointed to rule over us, has died in battle. So why do you say nothing about bringing the king back?"

¹¹King David sent this message to Zadok and Abiathar, the priests: "Ask the elders of Judah, 'Why should you be the last to bring the king back to his palace, since what is being said throughout Israel has reached the king at his quarters? ¹²You are my relatives, my own flesh and blood. So why

should you be the last to bring back the king?' ¹³And say to Amasa, 'Are you not my own flesh and blood? May God deal with me, be it ever so severely, if you are not the commander of my army for life in place of Joab.'"

¹⁴He won over the hearts of the men of Judah so that they were all of one mind. They sent word to the king, "Return, you and all your men." ¹⁵Then the king returned and went as far as the Jordan.

Now the men of Judah had come to Gilgal to go out and meet the king and bring him across the Jordan. ¹⁶Shimei son of Gera, the Benjamite from Bahurim, hurried down with the men of Judah to meet King David. ¹⁷With him were a thousand Benjamites, along with Ziba, the steward of Saul's household, and his fifteen sons and twenty servants. They rushed to the Jordan, where the king was. ¹⁸They crossed at the ford to take the king's household over and to do whatever he wished.

When Shimei son of Gera crossed the Jordan, he fell prostrate before the king ¹⁹and said to him, "May my lord not hold me guilty. Do not remember how your servant did wrong on the day my lord the king left Jerusalem. May the king put it out of his mind. ²⁰For I your servant know that I have sinned, but today I have come here as the first from the tribes of Joseph to come down and meet my lord the king."

²¹Then Abishai son of Zeruiah said, "Shouldn't Shimei be put to death for this? He cursed the LORD's anointed."

²²David replied, "What does this have to do with you, you sons of Zeruiah? What right do you have to interfere? Should anyone be put to death in Israel today? Don't I know that today I am king over Israel?" ²³So the king said to Shimei, "You shall not die." And the king promised him on oath.

²⁴Mephibosheth, Saul's grandson, also went down to meet the king. He had not taken care of his feet or trimmed his mustache or washed his clothes from the day the king left until the day he returned safely. ²⁵When he came from Jerusalem to meet the king, the king asked him, "Why didn't you go with me, Mephibosheth?"

²⁶He said, "My lord the king, since I your servant am lame, I said, 'I will have my donkey saddled and will ride on it, so I can go with the king.' But Ziba my servant betrayed me. ²⁷And he has slandered your servant to my lord the king. My lord the king is like an angel of God; so do whatever you wish. ²⁸All my grandfather's descendants deserved nothing but death from my lord the king, but you gave your servant a place among those who eat at your table. So what right do I have to make any more appeals to the king?"

²⁹The king said to him, "Why say more? I order you and Ziba to divide the land."

³⁰Mephibosheth said to the king, "Let him take everything, now that my lord the king has returned home safely."

³¹Barzillai the Gileadite also came down from Rogelim to cross the Jordan with the king and to send him on his way from there. ³²Now Barzillai was very old, eighty years of age. He had provided for the king during his stay in Mahanaim, for he was a very wealthy man. ³³The king said to Barzillai, "Cross over with me and stay with me in Jerusalem, and I will provide for you."

³⁴But Barzillai answered the king, "How many more years will I live, that I should go up to Jerusalem with the king? ³⁵I am now eighty years old. Can I tell the difference between what is enjoyable and what is not? Can your servant taste what he eats and drinks? Can I still hear the voices of male and female singers? Why should your servant be an added burden to my lord the king? ³⁶Your servant will cross over the Jordan with the king for a short distance, but why should the king reward me in this way? ³⁷Let your servant return, that I may die in my own town near the tomb of my father and mother. But here is your servant Kimham. Let him cross over with my lord the king. Do for him whatever you wish."

³⁸The king said, "Kimham shall cross over with me, and I will do for him whatever you wish. And anything you desire from me I will do for you."

³⁹So all the people crossed the Jordan, and then the king crossed over. The king kissed Barzillai and bid him farewell, and Barzillai returned to his home.

⁴⁰When the king crossed over to Gilgal, Kimham crossed with him. All the troops of Judah and half the troops of Israel had taken the king over.

⁴¹Soon all the men of Israel were coming to the king and saying to him, "Why did our brothers, the men of Judah, steal the king away and bring him and his household across the Jordan, together with all his men?"

⁴²All the men of Judah answered the men of Israel, "We did this because the king is closely related to us. Why are you angry about it? Have we eaten any of the king's provisions? Have we taken anything for ourselves?"

⁴³Then the men of Israel answered the men of Judah, "We have ten shares in the king; so we have a greater claim on David than you have. Why then do you treat us with contempt? Weren't we the first to speak of bringing back our king?"

But the men of Judah pressed their claims even more forcefully than the men of Israel.

Listen to the Text in the Story: 2 Samuel 9; 16:1–6

With the death of Absalom and the defeat of his rebellion, David can now return to Jerusalem. The king's journey back to Jerusalem recalls important scenes from earlier in the story. When David had fled from Jerusalem (2 Sam 16:1–4), Ziba, the steward of Saul's grandson Mephibosheth, had brought the king provisions, claiming that Mephibosheth had defected to Absalom's side. Now, as David returns to his capital city, he encounters both Ziba and Mephibosheth. As well, while departing Jerusalem, David had been cursed by Shimei (2 Sam 16:5–6). Now as David returns, Shimei again shows up, this time to apologize and offer his loyalty. Given an opportunity for revenge and restitution, David must negotiate between these options and securing the loyalty of the entire nation.

EXPLAIN the Story

After the rebellion was put down, Joab is told that David was mourning the leader of the rebellion, his son Absalom. Joab confronts David and castigates him for his actions, which had taken the joy of victory away and caused the troops to despair. Persuaded by Joab, David finally went out to see the troops. Meanwhile, the aftermath of the civil war unfolds as the Israelites debate bringing David back as king. En route to Jerusalem, three meeting scenes are narrated that display David's peacemaking and magnanimous character. First, David forgives Shimei, who had previously cursed him in his exile. Second, he pardons Mephibosheth (for not joining him in his exile). Third, David offers royal residence to Barzillai, who had supplied him with provisions in his exile. Still en route to the capital, David and his Judahite company meet the men of Israel who quarrel with them about why Judah was escorting the king back when they had first spoke of bringing David back. Though the civil war was over, civil unrest persists in Israel.

Joab Confronts David (19:1–8)

With victory won, David's men should be elated. Instead, the troops are despondent because their king was mourning the death of the leader of the rebellion—his son Absalom. When Joab is told, he privately confronts David about the gravity of his actions. Again, we see Joab's insightful political side. Unlike David, Joab saw the precariousness of the situation. If David did not encourage his troops, he could lose their support. In his speech, Joab employs a generous amount of hyperbole (e.g., David hates his troops) to wake David from his grief-induced inertia, making vitriolic allegations of the king in order to inform him how his mourning is being interpreted by the troops. Joab warned David that if he didn't encourage the troops, it would be worse than Absalom's rebellion for him. In response, David finally goes out and makes a public appearance. The troops were so craving an approving word from the king that when they heard David was there, they all came to him. David's speech is not narrated, giving the impression that David only grudgingly consented to Joab's demands.

The Return of the King (19:9–40)

While David is giving his long-overdue victory address to the troops, the narrative switches to the situation with the Israelites who had all gone home after the death of Absalom. Remembering how David had brought peace to the land by defeating the Philistines, the Israelites debate whether to bring David back as king.

When David hears about the talk in Israel about bringing him back as king, he sends messengers to Judah asking them to take the initiative on the matter, since he is a Judahite like them. By appealing to Judah in this way, David seems to be taking advantage of the jealousy between Judah and the northern tribes. Given that Absalom was installed as king in Hebron of Judah (2 Sam 15:10), David was also likely concerned to win back the support of his own tribe after their backing of Absalom's insurgency.

David's magnanimous ways continue in his message to Amasa, whom Absalom had made general over his army and who had led the opposing forces in the rebellion. David not only forgives his treason but promises to make him Israel's general in Joab's stead. David's motivation for this offer could be due to the fact that Amasa was an influential man, so that such an offer was needed to secure Judah's support. However, given Joab's defiance of David's orders regarding protecting Absalom ("nothing is hidden from the king," 2 Sam 18:13) and the general's vitriolic rebuke of the king during his grief, the reader suspects that David was fed up with his general, and the appointment of Amasa was somewhat an act of revenge in this regard. Regardless, David's appeal to Judah is successful and the men of Judah are on board with the plan.

As David and his men begin their return and go as far as the Jordan River, who shows up but Shimei with a thousand Benjamites (including Saul's former steward, Ziba). The reader will remember Shimei as the one who cursed David and showered him and his men with rocks and dirt as they departed Jerusalem (2 Sam 16:5–6). Obviously aware of how his earlier actions may have serious consequences now that David is back in power, Shimei bows to David, confesses his sin, and apologizes profusely.

In character as always, Abishai suggests Shimei be executed for his earlier actions (after all, when Shimei was cursing earlier, Abishai wanted to decapitate him). As he did in the earlier incident, David rebukes Abishai, once again disparagingly addressing the "sons of Zeruiah." Given that only one son of Zeruiah is present, David's use of the plural "sons" may hint at his anger at Joab's killing of Absalom. David wisely knew that in order to consolidate his power and maintain the support of all the tribes, the granting of amnesty was required. After all, the majority of the nation had just recently conspired against him. Were David to execute all who participated, there would be few left to rule. Therefore, David promises that Shimei will not be killed. David, however, does not forget Shimei's cursing, as later on his deathbed David will ask Solomon to kill Shimei on that account (1 Kgs 2:8–10). David's statement, "Should anyone be put to death in Israel today?" (v. 22), recalls a similar statement by King Saul after an Israelite victory wherein he declares, "No one shall be put to death today, for this day the LORD has rescued Israel" (1 Sam 11:13). Perhaps David's similar judgment would help to win over the former Saulide supporters (one thousand Benjamites) present in this instance.

Yet another prominent character shows up to meet David at the Jordan as well—Mephibosheth, son to David's (deceased) best friend Jonathan, with whom David had arranged to eat at his table in perpetuity (2 Sam 9). The reader will remember that when David fled Jerusalem, Ziba, Mephibosheth's steward, met David along the way, bringing him supplies (2 Sam 16:1–2), but Mephibosheth himself did not show up. Ziba had told David (2 Sam 16:3) that Mephibosheth had stayed in Jerusalem in hopes of gaining the throne (as an heir of the Saulide dynasty). Now Mephibosheth has a chance to defend himself to David in person.

David immediately asks him to account for his absence, to which Mephibosheth replied that he had attempted to go with David but was betrayed by Ziba. Mephibosheth reminds David that he is lame in his feet and therefore could not accompany David on foot but claims that he was attempting to arrange a donkey for transport when Ziba betrayed him. He does not say exactly what Ziba did, but it seems likely that Ziba left without him and took the very donkey on which Mephibosheth planned to ride. After all, when Ziba met David on his way out of Jerusalem, Ziba had "a string of donkeys saddled" with him (2 Sam 16:1). Mephibosheth further expresses his gratefulness to David for all he had done for him and makes no claim for anything further from the king.

While the narrator does not explicitly state whether Ziba or Mephibosheth was telling the truth here, the narrative presentation suggests Mephibosheth was speaking honestly. First, Ziba's claim that Mephibosheth thought Absalom's coup would result in him reclaiming the Saulide throne is very unlikely. Given Absalom's ambition and widespread popularity, there would be no reason for Mephibosheth to have hopes of becoming king. Second, the narrator notes that Mephibosheth had not groomed himself or even laundered his clothes the whole time that David had departed Jerusalem until now. Such actions would not reflect an attempt to take the throne for himself, wherein proper grooming and a show of power would be requisite. Instead, it showed solidarity with David and a mourning of his departure from Jerusalem. Third, Mephibosheth's story of a failed attempt to go with David, being prevented by his disability and Ziba's taking of his donkey, is quite plausible. Ziba had the most to gain in all of this. He used the occasion to try and move up at the expense of Mephibosheth (and did possess saddled donkeys when he met David). Fourth, even after David gives back half of his property to Mephibosheth, he seems uninterested in keeping them and is most grateful that David is safe. Conversely, when David gave Ziba all Mephibosheth's property, Ziba took them readily (2 Sam 16:4). All this would seem to underscore the good character of Mephibosheth.

It is unclear whether or not David is convinced by Mephibosheth. He cuts off Mephibosheth from speaking further and rules that he and Ziba will split the fields. It would seem David is unsure of whom to trust and cuts his losses by having them split the land. Alternatively, it could be that David believes Mephibosheth but does not want to alienate Ziba in an effort keep his support of the throne. After all, Ziba has fifteen sons and twenty servants who (along with their families) constitute a large contingent of support for David. What is more, Ziba is presently accompanied by one thousand Benjamites—an even bigger support base. By giving half to both parties here David may hope to retain the support of all involved. Thus, David is again showing good political savvy, though he may be shirking his responsibility to his covenant he made with Mephibosheth's father, his best friend Jonathan (1 Sam 20:15).

Yet another meeting at the Jordan is narrated before the king crosses back into the land. This time it is Barzillai, who supplied provisions for David in his exile (2 Sam 17:27). We are now told that Barzillai is quite elderly. In thanks for his support, David asks him to come to Jerusalem with him where he would provide for him. Barzillai, however, respectfully declines, and instead asks that David take Kimham with him in his stead. Presumably Kimham is one of his sons, as in his dying days David asks that Solomon allow the sons of Barzillai to eat at his table (1 Kgs 2:7). David agrees and, when he finally crosses the Jordan, Kimham accompanies him.

Tribal Unrest (19:41–43)

Tribal rivalries come to the fore as a quarrel arises between the men of Judah and men from the other tribes of Israel. First, we are told that "all the troops of Judah" and "half the troops of Israel" brought David over the Jordan (v. 40). Despite the fact they both participated, the disparity in the representation of the tribes, with Judah having a disproportional presence, becomes an issue of dispute. This is not the first time there have been petty tribal disputes between the northern and southern tribes (e.g., Judg 8:1; 12:1). Though the questions are posed to the king, it is the men of Judah who answer them, defending their actions as due to their kinship relations with him (since David was from Judah). Israel counters that they have a greater claim on the king due to their greater number of tribes. The issue seems to be one of who gets credit for David's return and thus benefits from the king's favor. The chapter ends with the squabble continuing, and Judah vehemently arguing its case, which sets the stage for the defection of many Israelites in the next chapter. Though the Israelite civil war was over, civil unrest persists.

LIVE the Story

Hearing Hard Truths

When Joab confronts the king about his reaction to the victory over the rebellion it is a very difficult time for David. The king is grieving the loss of his son. Likely, it is more than that. David has seen his chickens come home to roost and was likely aware of the role he played in the disastrous string of events that led there. The anointed one was now paralyzed by grief and regret. He has retreated into a private room and is inconsolable. Enter Joab. Joab's speech has been described as a "verbal assault on David"[1] and that it has been said that "Joab talks tougher than even Nathan (2 Sam 12:1–15)."[2] How hard it was for David to hear his words, yet how necessary. David had ceased to act as a king. He neglected his troops and stopped leading his people. He needed a loud voice to wake him from his stupor. Sometimes in our life we will need to hear such a voice. Sometimes we need an "intervention."

One practice that is used to reach people who struggle with addiction to alcohol and/or drugs is an "intervention." Such an intervention involves family members, friends, or other significant figures in the addict's life meeting with the addict (often arranging an unexpected meeting) to attempt to show them their need for help. Addicts frequently are in denial about their habit and do

---

1. Alter, *The David Story*, 313.
2. Brueggemann, *First and Second Samuel*, 325.

not seek treatment. Usually this is because they do not realize the negative effects that their addiction has on not only themselves but other people in their lives. An intervention is needed to make the addict make changes before things get worse.

In many ways, Joab's confrontation with David here resembles an intervention. David was grieving deeply and lost in his mourning and regret. Joab had to shake David out of it and make him see how his actions were negatively affecting not only his own situation as king but the future of the kingdom. If he did not change, he would lose everything.

The Bible frequently urges its readers to be open to criticism. Proverbs notes that "Whoever heeds discipline shows the way to life, but whoever ignores correction leads others astray" (Prov 10:17). Furthermore, the one who "heeds correction shows prudence" (Prov 15:5). God clearly uses others to speak into our lives. The wise and humble person will listen.

While the merits of Joab's confrontation are easy to see, the fact that he had killed David's son, explicitly contravening David's orders, would have made Joab's words that much harder to hear. While we do not know for sure whether David knew who killed his son at this point, David knew Joab well and likely surmised that Joab, if he did not do the deed himself, at least let it happen. After all, as the young man who refused to kill Absalom said in the chapter before, "nothing is hidden from the king" (2 Sam 18:13).

Sometimes in our lives we will hear difficult words that we really need to listen to. Further, like in the case of Joab and David, the person speaking the words to us may be a deeply flawed individual (is there any other type?). The person may have caused us much pain or betrayed us in the past. Yet, God may use them to tell us what we need to hear at that time. Hopefully, like David in this story, we will be humble enough to hear such words and apply them to our lives. May we be one "who heeds life-giving correction" and so "be at home among the wise" (Prov 15:31).

CHAPTER 44

2 Samuel 20:1-26

 LISTEN to the Story

¹Now a troublemaker named Sheba son of Bikri, a Benjamite, happened to be there. He sounded the trumpet and shouted,

> "We have no share in David,
>   no part in Jesse's son!
> Every man to his tent, Israel!"

²So all the men of Israel deserted David to follow Sheba son of Bikri. But the men of Judah stayed by their king all the way from the Jordan to Jerusalem.

³When David returned to his palace in Jerusalem, he took the ten concubines he had left to take care of the palace and put them in a house under guard. He provided for them but had no sexual relations with them. They were kept in confinement till the day of their death, living as widows.

⁴Then the king said to Amasa, "Summon the men of Judah to come to me within three days, and be here yourself." ⁵But when Amasa went to summon Judah, he took longer than the time the king had set for him.

⁶David said to Abishai, "Now Sheba son of Bikri will do us more harm than Absalom did. Take your master's men and pursue him, or he will find fortified cities and escape from us." ⁷So Joab's men and the Kerethites and Pelethites and all the mighty warriors went out under the command of Abishai. They marched out from Jerusalem to pursue Sheba son of Bikri.

⁸While they were at the great rock in Gibeon, Amasa came to meet them. Joab was wearing his military tunic, and strapped over it at his waist was a belt with a dagger in its sheath. As he stepped forward, it dropped out of its sheath.

⁹Joab said to Amasa, "How are you, my brother?" Then Joab took Amasa by the beard with his right hand to kiss him. ¹⁰Amasa was not on his guard against the dagger in Joab's hand, and Joab plunged it into his belly, and his intestines spilled out on the ground. Without being stabbed again, Amasa died. Then Joab and his brother Abishai pursued Sheba son of Bikri.

¹¹One of Joab's men stood beside Amasa and said, "Whoever favors Joab, and whoever is for David, let him follow Joab!" ¹²Amasa lay wallowing in his blood in the middle of the road, and the man saw that all the troops came to a halt there. When he realized that everyone who came up to Amasa stopped, he dragged him from the road into a field and threw a garment over him. ¹³After Amasa had been removed from the road, everyone went on with Joab to pursue Sheba son of Bikri.

¹⁴Sheba passed through all the tribes of Israel to Abel Beth Maakah and through the entire region of the Bikrites, who gathered together and followed him. ¹⁵All the troops with Joab came and besieged Sheba in Abel Beth Maakah. They built a siege ramp up to the city, and it stood against the outer fortifications. While they were battering the wall to bring it down, ¹⁶a wise woman called from the city, "Listen! Listen! Tell Joab to come here so I can speak to him." ¹⁷He went toward her, and she asked, "Are you Joab?"

"I am," he answered.

She said, "Listen to what your servant has to say."

"I'm listening," he said.

¹⁸She continued, "Long ago they used to say, 'Get your answer at Abel,' and that settled it. ¹⁹We are the peaceful and faithful in Israel. You are trying to destroy a city that is a mother in Israel. Why do you want to swallow up the LORD's inheritance?"

²⁰"Far be it from me!" Joab replied, "Far be it from me to swallow up or destroy! ²¹That is not the case. A man named Sheba son of Bikri, from the hill country of Ephraim, has lifted up his hand against the king, against David. Hand over this one man, and I'll withdraw from the city."

The woman said to Joab, "His head will be thrown to you from the wall."

²²Then the woman went to all the people with her wise advice, and they cut off the head of Sheba son of Bikri and threw it to Joab. So he sounded the trumpet, and his men dispersed from the city, each returning to his home. And Joab went back to the king in Jerusalem.

²³Joab was over Israel's entire army; Benaiah son of Jehoiada was over the Kerethites and Pelethites; ²⁴Adoniram was in charge of forced labor; Jehoshaphat son of Ahilud was recorder; ²⁵Sheva was secretary; Zadok and Abiathar were priests; ²⁶and Ira the Jairite was David's priest.

Listen to the Text in the Story: 1 Samuel 9:1; 2 Samuel 16:22; 19:3; Code of Hammurabi

No sooner had the rebellion been defeated than a new one arises. This time a Benjamite named Sheba son of Bikri instigates the insurgence. Some have suggested that Sheba's father "Bikri" may be "Becorath" named in Saul's genealogy back in 1 Samuel 9:1.[1] If this is the case, then Sheba was actually Saul's relative and this may partly explain the zeal with which he moves against David.

Upon returning home, David has to deal with the mess Absalom left behind. Given Absalom's sexual assault of the concubines who had remained in Jerusalem (2 Sam 16:22), David decides to cloister these women, though he provides for them. In effect, David treated them like widows or as wives who were now unfit to serve as wives. In the Babylonian code of Hammurabi, such a wife was allowed to be replaced, but the husband had to "continue to support her as long as she lives."[2] Most commentators think that David's actions here were due to the taboo status of the concubines after Absalom's actions.[3] Another possibility is that David is taking steps to move away from standard royal practices of the ancient Near East with their large harems and back toward the Israelite ideal (Deut 17:17).[4] We will return to this question below.

EXPLAIN the Story

The tribal unrest explodes in this chapter as a troublemaker named Sheba leads a defection of the northern tribes from supporting David. After his return to Jerusalem, David sets out to squelch the new rebellion. David first sends for Amasa, whom David had set over the army in Joab's place, but Amasa fails to report to duty on time. David then sends Abishai (not Joab) in charge of the army to pursue Sheba. Along the way they meet Amasa, and Joab kills Amasa in cold blood. With his rival dead, Joab leads the army against Sheba besieging the city in which he was hiding. Before the city fell, a wise woman from the city negotiates a somewhat peaceful end to the conflict, having Sheba's head thrown out to Joab from their city wall. At this Joab calls off the troops and all return home. Having squelched the rebellion, Joab returns to David in Jerusalem and remains head of the army.

---

1. John Bright, *A History of Israel*, 4th ed. (Louisville: Westminster John Knox, 2000), 210. Long, *2 Samuel*, 472.

2. *ANET*, 172 §148.

3. Alter, *The David Story*, 322.

4. Brueggemann, *First and Second Samuel*, 330. Arnold (*1 & 2 Samuel*, 605) speculates it could even be "an act of repentance."

A New Rebellion (20:1–2)

No sooner had Absalom's rebellion been defeated than a new one is formed. A "troublemaker" named Sheba is present during the dispute between the northern tribes and the men of Judah that concluded last chapter. Sheba blows a trumpet and calls for the northern tribes to desert David (v. 2), leaving only the men of Judah, who bring David back to Jerusalem from the Jordan (v. 2). The uneasy alliance of the nation and the divisions that went back to Ish-Bosheth's short-lived rival kingdom to David (consisting of the northern tribes) once again come to the fore. Sheba's cry that "We have no share in David . . ." is a drastic reversal of the ten shares in David that the tribes had vehemently claimed just a few verses before (2 Sam 19:43). Sheba's rallying cry is picked up again after Solomon's death, when the northern tribes once again defect from the Davidic throne (1 Kgs 12:16). David faces the challenge of uniting the very tribes who were recently allied together against him under Absalom. Sheba's rebellion, however, was probably a more localized defection, not nationwide like Absalom's, as the fact that the rebellion is squelched without any battles suggests.

Cloistering the Concubines (20:3)

Before dealing with the rebels, David first deals with his concubines whom he had left behind in his departure from Jerusalem and with whom his late son Absalom had sexually assaulted (2 Sam 16:22). The king puts them under house arrest and never has sexual relations with them again, though he provides the other necessities of life. Regardless of the rationale for David doing so (see Listen to the Story above), confining the victims of Absalom's sexual assault under lock and key only adds insult to their injury. David's action here may betray his low view of women, as Hamilton comments:

> What a contrast between how David treats men and women! Shimei, who openly cursed the king, is forgiven (19:16–23). Mephibosheth, who earlier may have been disloyal to David, receives back half of his estate (19:24–30). But ten anonymous women who have never done anything disloyal to David are placed under lock and key, held incommunicado, and denied a future except for three meals a day and a bed to sleep on at night.[5]

Preparing for Battle (20:4–7)

Next, David sets out to squelch the new rebellion, first sending for his newly appointed general, Amasa, to muster the men of Judah for battle. Amasa, however, was tardy in his duties, leading David to send Abishai after the rebels

---

5. Hamilton, *Handbook*, 357.

instead. Abishai is made head over what was previously Joab's contingent (called Absishai's "master's men" in v. 6). The fact that in the next verse the narrator refers to them as "Joab's men" (v. 7) hints that despite his demotion, Joab is still in charge.

The Murder of Amasa (20:8–13)

En route to find Sheba, Abishai's forces encounter the tardy Amasa. At this point, we find out that Joab had also accompanied the troops. With resonances of the murder of Abner (2 Sam 3:27), Joab makes pretence of a friendly greeting before killing the unsuspecting victim. Joab's dagger would have been strapped to his left side for easy access with the right hand. As Joab stepped out to greet Amasa, he let his weapon fall out to the ground. Joab then feigned to kiss Amasa, taking his beard with his "right hand"—the hand that normally would wield a sword—then grabbing the fallen dagger with his left hand and stabbing his naïve cousin in the belly. Distracted by Joab's affectionate gesture with his right hand, "Amasa was not on guard against the dagger in Joab's hand" (v. 10), since it was the left hand that wielded the weapon (recalling Ehud's left-handed stabbing of Eglon in Judg 3:21).

The murder is cold blooded. Yet, it is little surprise that Joab would not take David's promotion of Amasa (to the rank Joab had held since David's rise to the throne) sitting down. At the same time, Amasa *was* the head of the army of the rebellion against David under Absalom (2 Sam 17:25), so Joab likely thought it not only a politically expedient act but perhaps even the right thing for the kingdom. In Joab's view, while amnesty may be granted common soldiers and ordinary citizens, military leaders of the rebellion should not be held guiltless.

Stabbing him only once, Joab leaves Amasa in the middle of the road, bleeding out for all to see, while he and his brother Abishai pursue Sheba. Joab purposefully does not finish Amasa off with another blow but instead prolongs his suffering for all to see. In fact, Joab does not even pause to rally the troops, probably because he is quite assured of their loyalty. After all, with Amasa "wallowing in his blood in the middle of the road," who wouldn't be motivated to follow Israel's fierce general? Instead, one of Joab's men calls for those loyal to Joab *and* David to follow Joab. Loyalty to one implies loyalty to the other.

The troops press on following the sons of Zeruiah, but the gory, dying, Amasa lying in the middle of the road is a distraction and slows the army's progress due to rubbernecking soldiers. Treating Amasa as nothing but an inconvenient, inanimate object, the soldier solves the problem by dragging the dying soldier into a field and covering him with a garment.

The End of the Rebellion (20:14–22)

Sheba, the ringleader of the rebellion, is now holed up in the town of Abel Beth Maakah, a city about four miles west of Dan.[6] Joab and his forces besiege the city and begin to knock down its wall when a wise woman calls out from the city, wishing to negotiate. In contrast to the low view of women seen in the cloistering of David's concubines, here a female character saves the day, ending the rebellion and preventing needless bloodshed. While in this instance Joab's solution is tearing down the city walls (and destroying the city if need be), this wise woman comes up with an alternative. She first eloquently explains to Joab the value of the city to Israel, calling it "a mother in Israel." Given that towns in the Bible are frequently referred to as "daughters" (e.g., 2 Kgs 19:21; Isa 10:30; 23:12 Jer 46:1), the metaphor suggests this town's prominence. The wise woman thus asks Joab why he intends to destroy "the LORD's inheritance" (v. 19). Joab vehemently denies the charge and explains his mission, declaring that if they simply hand over Sheba, the army would withdraw. The woman agrees to the terms and has the head of the rebel leader thrown to Joab from the city wall. True to his word, Joab withdraws from the siege and all return to their home. The ease at which the city gives up Sheba suggests his support was not that widespread or had wavered considerably.

The Davidic Administration (20:23–26)

In the end, David's attempts to oust Joab from his position over the army failed. Having eliminated his rivals, Joab is firmly in charge of the Israelite army. David seems powerless to rein in his general and no solution for the impasse is in sight. In the not too distant future, the antipathy between David and Joab will result in Joab supporting Adonijah in his attempt to take the throne (1 Kgs 1:25) and David ordering Solomon to have Joab killed (1 Kgs 2:5–6).

The final note in this chapter lists key leaders in the Davidic administration, paralleling the list in 2 Samuel 8:16–18. This is really the concluding note in the story that stretched from 2 Samuel 9–20, indicating that David was again established and the threats are over.[7] While Joab is over the army, as in the earlier administration list, Benaiah is now said to be in charge of the Kerethites and Pelethites, professional soldiers who were a powerful force in Israel. In fact, Benaiah's support of Solomon (1 Kgs 1:38) was a key factor in his rise to the throne, trumping the support of Joab for Adonijah (1 Kgs 1:25). Though David allowed Joab to return to his role as Israel's general, Benaiah's new role may show the king taking steps to limit Joab's influence in the future.

---

6. Anderson, *2 Samuel*, 241.
7. Brueggemann, *First and Second Samuel*, 332.

LIVE the Story

The Right Relationship to the King

In this story, we have seen the tribes of northern Israel and Judah argue over their relationship to the king. Judah boasts of its close kinship with David, since he was from Judah (2 Sam 19:42). The tribes of northern Israel boast that due to their larger size they have "ten shares in the king" and thus "a greater claim on David" (2 Sam 19:43). At the heart of this squabble is a flawed understanding of the relationship between Israel and its king. Judah and Israel here act like the king was there to do what they wanted. The argument over who had a greater claim on David was tantamount to arguing over whether the king had a greater obligation to one party or the other. Neither side reveals an attitude of obligation *to* the king. Both sides forgot that the king was appointed by God, and neither side acknowledged the fact that the king was Yahweh's anointed. Earlier in his career David had shown great respect for the anointing when he refused to raise his hand against Saul. How quickly both Judah and Israel forgot this and rebelled against Yahweh's anointed. Now both sides seek the reinstallment of the king for self-serving reasons.

This shouldn't be too surprising. After the failure of Absalom's rebellion against David, the people showed little in the way of remorse or repentance. Just as the nation had been quick to follow Absalom, ignoring David's God-given role as Yahweh's anointed, so they are quick to follow Sheba. When the people felt that the king was not living up to their expectations, the people felt free to disown him and rebel against him. Israel saw the king as being first and foremost obligated *to* them and their felt needs. Rebellion against God's anointed one, however, was really rebellion against God.

Seeing as Jesus Christ is the Anointed One who fulfilled Davidic hopes, the relevance of this passage for Christians today is fairly straightforward. In the Gospels, Jesus often received similar treatment to David. People were excited about Christ's message initially. Crowds followed him when he fed them (John 6:26). Many were excited about his coming kingdom until they realized it was of a different nature than they had hoped for (i.e., not a military insurrection against Rome). Wide support was shown Jesus as the Son of David on Palm Sunday (John 12:13), only days before they turned against him and had him crucified, pledging allegiance instead to the Roman emperor (John 19:15).

While it is easy to point the finger regarding the unfaithfulness of Israel to its messiah, we must examine our own relationship with Jesus. Just as Israel acknowledged that David was their savior from the Philistines (2 Sam 19:9), so Christians acknowledge that Jesus is their Savior. However, just as Israel was slow to show obedience to David as their king (2 Sam 19:41–20:2), so we are often slow to acknowledge Jesus as Lord of our lives. As Israel sought to leverage their relationship with David to their own advantage, so we can similarly try and leverage our relationship with Jesus. But just as sure as Israel owed allegiance to David as Yahweh's anointed, we owe obedience to Jesus, God's Anointed One (*mashiah*). Will we, like Israel, abandon Jesus if we feel he has failed to live up to our expectations? Will we, like Israel, think that Jesus is somehow obligated to give us what we want? Such attitudes toward the Anointed One forget that Jesus is not only our Savior, but our Lord. We owe allegiance to our king—not the other way around.

A correct posture towards God's anointed is clearly presented in the second psalm, where rebellion against the Davidic throne is poetically described. "Why do the nations conspire and the peoples plot in vain? The kings of the earth rise up and the rulers band together against the LORD and his anointed" (Ps 2:1–2). Just as Sheba declared he had "no share in David" and commanded Israel to abandon him (2 Sam 20:1), so the people in Psalm 2 declare their rebellion (v. 3). The psalm's admonitions are instructive. The psalmist commands:

> Serve the LORD with fear
>   and celebrate his rule with trembling.
> Kiss his son, or he will be angry
>   and your way will lead to your destruction,
> for his wrath can flare up in a moment.
>   Blessed are all who take refuge in him. (Ps 2:11–12)

To "kiss the son" is a show of respect to the king, who is in one sense the son of God (cf. 2 Sam 7:14). Respect and obedience is due the king, not manipulation or the making of demands. As Christians, we must daily lay down our selfishness and self-interested view of our relationship with Jesus. We must live lives of surrender and obedience to our Lord. Yet, the psalm reminds us that those who seek and honor him *will* find refuge. That is the good news. Just as God provided the king to deliver Israel, so Christ will deliver us. "Blessed are all who take refuge in him" (Ps 2:12).

LISTEN to the Story

¹During the reign of David, there was a famine for three successive years; so David sought the face of the LORD. The LORD said, "It is on account of Saul and his blood-stained house; it is because he put the Gibeonites to death."

²The king summoned the Gibeonites and spoke to them. (Now the Gibeonites were not a part of Israel but were survivors of the Amorites; the Israelites had sworn to spare them, but Saul in his zeal for Israel and Judah had tried to annihilate them.) ³David asked the Gibeonites, "What shall I do for you? How shall I make atonement so that you will bless the LORD's inheritance?"

⁴The Gibeonites answered him, "We have no right to demand silver or gold from Saul or his family, nor do we have the right to put anyone in Israel to death."

"What do you want me to do for you?" David asked.

⁵They answered the king, "As for the man who destroyed us and plotted against us so that we have been decimated and have no place anywhere in Israel, ⁶let seven of his male descendants be given to us to be killed and their bodies exposed before the LORD at Gibeah of Saul—the LORD's chosen one."

So the king said, "I will give them to you."

⁷The king spared Mephibosheth son of Jonathan, the son of Saul, because of the oath before the LORD between David and Jonathan son of Saul. ⁸But the king took Armoni and Mephibosheth, the two sons of Aiah's daughter Rizpah, whom she had borne to Saul, together with the five sons of Saul's daughter Merab, whom she had borne to Adriel son of Barzillai the Meholathite. ⁹He handed them over to the Gibeonites, who killed them and exposed their bodies on a hill before the LORD. All seven of them fell together; they were put to death during the first days of the harvest, just as the barley harvest was beginning.

¹⁰Rizpah daughter of Aiah took sackcloth and spread it out for herself

on a rock. From the beginning of the harvest till the rain poured down from the heavens on the bodies, she did not let the birds touch them by day or the wild animals by night. ¹¹When David was told what Aiah's daughter Rizpah, Saul's concubine, had done, ¹²he went and took the bones of Saul and his son Jonathan from the citizens of Jabesh Gilead. (They had stolen their bodies from the public square at Beth Shan, where the Philistines had hung them after they struck Saul down on Gilboa.) ¹³David brought the bones of Saul and his son Jonathan from there, and the bones of those who had been killed and exposed were gathered up.

¹⁴They buried the bones of Saul and his son Jonathan in the tomb of Saul's father Kish, at Zela in Benjamin, and did everything the king commanded. After that, God answered prayer in behalf of the land.

¹⁵Once again there was a battle between the Philistines and Israel. David went down with his men to fight against the Philistines, and he became exhausted. ¹⁶And Ishbi-Benob, one of the descendants of Rapha, whose bronze spearhead weighed three hundred shekels and who was armed with a new sword, said he would kill David. ¹⁷But Abishai son of Zeruiah came to David's rescue; he struck the Philistine down and killed him. Then David's men swore to him, saying, "Never again will you go out with us to battle, so that the lamp of Israel will not be extinguished."

¹⁸In the course of time, there was another battle with the Philistines, at Gob. At that time Sibbekai the Hushathite killed Saph, one of the descendants of Rapha.

¹⁹In another battle with the Philistines at Gob, Elhanan son of Jair the Bethlehemite killed the brother of Goliath the Gittite, who had a spear with a shaft like a weaver's rod.

²⁰In still another battle, which took place at Gath, there was a huge man with six fingers on each hand and six toes on each foot—twenty-four in all. He also was descended from Rapha. ²¹When he taunted Israel, Jonathan son of Shimeah, David's brother, killed him.

²²These four were descendants of Rapha in Gath, and they fell at the hands of David and his men.

Listen to the Text in the Story: Joshua 9; 1 Samuel 15; 22:11–19

An important background text to this story is found in Joshua 9, which narrates the story of how a foreign people, the Gibeonites, found a place in Israel through their deceiving Joshua and the Israelites. As a result of their successful ruse, Israel "made a treaty of peace with them to let them live" (Josh 9:15).

Furthermore, Gibeon was given a formal role in Israel being "woodcutters and water carriers for the assembly, to provide for the needs of the altar of the LORD" (Josh 9:27). Thus, as we read of Saul's slaughter of the Gibeonites, we must realize that his malevolent actions directly contradicted Israel's oath recorded in Joshua 9. As the Gibeonites explain, they had been "decimated" and no longer even had a "place anywhere in Israel" (2 Sam 21:5). It is ironic that Saul showed such "zeal" (v. 2) to kill these foreigners who had been promised safety and security in Israel, but he had refused to annihilate the Amalekites who had been condemned to death by God directly (1 Sam 15). Was his zeal here an attempt to make up for his disobedience regarding the Amalekites? Some have suggested that the slaughter of the Gibeonites may be connected to the slaughter of the priests at Nob (1 Sam 22:11–19).[1] Given the cultic role the Gibeonites had (being woodcutters and water carriers for the altar), this is possible but definitely not clear. Others have suggested that Saul had wished to make Gibeon his capital and so was ridding the area of the Gibeonites.[2] With little evidence either way, it is difficult to decide. Regardless, Israel was still paying for Saul's mistakes.

EXPLAIN the Story

David is faced with a difficult decision when a three-year long famine ravages the land. After much prayer, Yahweh informs David that the famine was due to Saul's killing of the Gibeonites. In response, David summons the Gibeonites who demand that seven sons of Saul be handed over for public execution. David agrees and hands over the men (though he spares Mephibosheth, Jonathan's son). After their execution, Rizpah, mother of two of the men killed, mourns them and defends their corpses from wild animals. When David hears of Rizpah's actions, he gives the bodies of the seven Saulides, along with Saul and Jonathan, a proper burial in their ancestor's grave in Benjamin, at which God answers the prayers for the land. The second half of the chapter notes how David's men defeated four other gigantic Philistines who were descended, like Goliath, from Rapha in Gath.

The Epilogue

The last four chapters of 2 Samuel form something of an epilogue and should not be understood as continuing the narrative forward after Sheba's revolt.

---

1. Hertzberg, *1 and 2 Samuel*, 382.
2. Klaus-Dietrich Schunck, *Benjamin: Untersuchungen Zur Entstehung Und Geschichte Eines Israelitischen Stammes*, BZAW 86 (Berlin: Töpelmann, 1963), 131–138.

Instead, they describe incidents that occurred sometime during David's reign but are not placed within the main narrative chronologically. It seems likely they occurred sometime in the middle of David's reign. These final four chapters are structured concentrically:

> A ch 21—David intercedes during a time of calamity
>> B ch 21—a list
>> C ch 22—a song/poem
>> C¹ ch 23—a song/poem
>> B¹ ch 23—a list
> A¹ ch 24—David intercedes during a time of calamity

The Gibeonite Famine (21:1–14)

The first part of the epilogue concerns David's actions during a prolonged famine. In light of Shimei's accusation that David was guilty of shedding Saulide blood (2 Sam 16:7), this story may have been included to rebut such a view. According to this chapter, David clearly was responding to divine guidance and did not seek the deaths of these Saulides himself.

A more suspicious reading of this story is possible and has been suggested by some.[3] Though the narrative on the surface level exonerates David for the deaths of the Saulides, some think that in reality David took advantage of the opportunity of a long famine to have the remaining Saulides killed (eliminating potential threats to his throne). For this reading to be possible, it is necessary to understand God's words to David in verse 1 as not being authentic. Instead, since only David received the private word from God, it is questioned whether it was truly a divine oracle and not a "piece of Davidic fabrication."[4] As well, it is suggested that Saul was a "scrupulously religious man who is unlikely to evoke such bloodguilt."[5] Though such a reading is possible, it is very unlikely for the following reasons. First, throughout the books of 1–2 Samuel when the narrator says, "The LORD said," it has always been a true word of the Lord (1 Sam 3:11; 8:7, 22; 10:22; 16:1, 2, 7, 12; 23:2, 11; 2 Sam 2:1; 5:19). The narrator does not lie. Second, Saul's supposed religious scruples did not keep him from slaughtering the priests at Nob, so persecuting Gibeonites is consistent with Saul's compunctions. For these reasons, the suspicious reading of this story is to be rejected.

This is not to say that the narrative is not functioning as a defense of the Davidic monarchy. As noted in the introduction, some scholarship has

---

3. Ibid., 336–38.
4. Ibid., 337.
5. Ibid.

suggested that the book of Samuel functioned as an apology for the Davidic monarchy, defending it against charges that David usurped the throne from Saul, killed off his heirs, and unlawfully became king. The story here in 2 Samuel 21 clearly functions in this way, as it explains that David did not seek the deaths of Saul's sons.

David prays to God about the lengthy famine, and Yahweh tells him the famine was due to Saul's slaughter of the Gibeonites. In response to the grave situation, David summons the Gibeonites to ask them what he can do to make things right. The Gibeonites ask for seven of Saul's descendants to be killed and their bodies exposed before Yahweh in Saul's hometown of Gibeah. David agreed to their request; however, he spared Mephibosheth, Jonathan's son, due to his promise to Jonathan (1 Sam 20:15).

The type of execution referred to here is unclear. Some ancient Greek and Aramaic translations of the text suggest crucifixion, and the Syriac version understands it to be a sacrifice. The names of the victims are listed along with the names of their mothers. Surprisingly, given that the previous verse notes that David spared Mephibosheth, a man named Mephibosheth is listed among those who were executed by the Gibeonites. The Mephibosheth who was killed, however, is said to be the son of Saul's concubine, Rizpah, not the son of Jonathan. Thus, it would appear that Jonathan named his son after his half brother.

The five sons of Merab, Saul's daughter, were also handed over for execution. Here we learn that Merab was married to a son of Barzillai, who appears to be the same man who supported David during Absalom's rebellion (2 Sam 19:31–32), making his loyalty to David remarkable.[6] After the executions, with the bodies of the victims exposed to the elements, Rizpah, mother of two of the victims, mourns her sons and stays with the bodies, defending them from carrion birds and animals. Rizpah's concern for the dead bodies of her children remind David of the gruesome end that met the bodies of Saul and Jonathan, who were similarly exposed by the Philistines (1 Sam 31:9–12). The reader will recall that the men of Jabesh Gilead had valiantly retrieved their bodies from the Philistines, burned them, and buried them under a tree in Jabesh (1 Sam 31:11–13). Inspired by Rizpah's actions, David had the bones[7] of Saul and Jonathan taken from Jabesh Gilead, along with the remains of

---

6. In 2 Sam 17, Barzillai is said to be from Rogelim in Gilead. Here in ch. 21, Barzillai is called a Meholathite, which means "from Meholah" in Gilead. Given that both are from Gilead and share a name otherwise unique in Scripture, it seems likely they are the same individual.

7. Though their bodies were burned by the men of Jabesh Gilead, bones are not completely burned to ashes. Even a modern cremation leaves bones that are ground to ash, which is what is returned to the family afterwards.

Saul's sons whom the Gibeonites had killed and had them buried in the tomb of Saul's father in Benjamin. At this, God answered prayers for the land.

Four More Giants (21:15–26)

The chapter concludes with a note of how in addition to Goliath, whom David had killed, David's men killed four other gigantic men from Gath. While the heights of these men are not noted, they are said to descend from Rapha, which is a variant form of the Hebrew word most commonly translated "giants"—Rephaim or Rephaites (e.g., Deut 3:11, 13. For more on giants see commentary on 1 Samuel 17). Their great size is also implied by the weight of their weapons (vv. 16, 19). One of these gigantic men also had an abnormality of having six fingers on each hand and six toes on each foot. The size and strength of the enemy must have made their defeat quite memorable, which explains the addition of this historical note to the narrative.

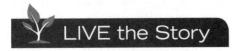

LIVE the Story

Divine Displeasure

Does God really manipulate the weather to punish sin? Can natural disaster be due to the sinful actions of human beings? The connection between the famine and Saul's bloodguilt fits with the mindset in the ancient world that saw natural disasters as being due to divine displeasure. This chapter, however, is not unique in the Bible in suggesting this, as natural disaster *is* tied to God's pleasure or judgment elsewhere (e.g., Deut 11:13–14; Jer 4:22–26; Ezek 14:21). For example, Amos 4:6–9 explicitly states that God used famine to chastise his people.

> "I gave you empty stomachs in every city
> and lack of bread in every town,
> yet you have not returned to me,"
> declares the LORD.
> "I also withheld rain from you
> when the harvest was still three months away.
> I sent rain on one town,
> but withheld it from another. . . .
> yet you have not returned to me,"
> declares the LORD.

Clearly God can and has used natural disasters as a way of reaching people, calling them to repentance and chastising them for their sin. So, what do we do today when there is a famine, a tornado destroys a town, forest fires cause the evacuation of a city, or farmers lose their crops? Unfortunately, some sincere and well-meaning believers have attempted to interpret modern natural disasters as evidence of God's displeasure or attributed them to the sin of the disaster victims. A sad example is the terrible Hurricane Katrina that ravaged New Orleans in 2005. Some Christians suggested that the reason for the disaster was that New Orleans was a hub for jazz music (which some viewed as evil), was notably immoral (as home to the notorious Mardi Gras festival), or in some other way deserved God's punishment in a special way. This conclusion, however, is based purely on human speculation. To counter this suggestion, some have pointed out that New Orleans's French Quarter, the area known for its jazz music, Mardi Gras celebrations, nightclubs, etc., was one of the least affected by the hurricane due to its being on higher ground. In fact, the hardest hit areas of the city were the most impoverished. If the hurricane was judgment for these "sins," then God missed his target and drowned the poor instead.

Furthermore, despite the fact that some biblical passages clearly connect disasters to God's chastisement, the Bible makes clear this is *not* always the case. In the book of Job, Job is described as perfectly righteous, yet his cattle (Job 1:16) and children (Job 1:18–19) die due to natural disasters. While God was clearly sovereign over what happened to Job, the natural disasters were *not* due to either the sin of Job or that of his children. Sadly, Job's "friends" concluded that the disasters that befell Job were due to his (Job 11:6) and his children's sin (Job 8:4). In Luke 13:4, Jesus references a disastrous event where a tower fell, killing some people, but he rebuts the idea that the victims died because they were somehow "more guilty than all the others living in Jerusalem" (Luke 13:4). Furthermore, Jesus notes that God "causes his sun to rise on the evil and the good, and sends rain on the righteous and the unrighteous" (Matt 5:45). That is, when there is famine, it does not mean the people have been more sinful than others, and when there is rain it is not because people have been more righteous than others.

In light of this, rather than attempting to pronounce judgment on victims of natural disaster, Christians should realize that we are not in a position to explain such disasters in this way. Given our ignorance, it is impossible to authoritatively decide or discern that the reason behind such natural disasters is human sin, either individual or communal. Attempting to do so could put us in the same category as Job's friends, who incurred God's wrath for their error in judgment (Job 42:7). Though we believe in a sovereign God, on this side of eternity we can never fully know why these things happen, and we should reserve judgment until we know better.

Did God Require the Death of Saul's Sons?

While the text clearly says that the famine was due to Saul's murderous actions against Gibeon, should we understand the slaying of Saul's sons as being what God actually wanted? Before concluding that God required the death of Saul's sons, it should be pointed out that it was David who asked the Gibeonites what needed to be done—he was *not* told to do so by God. Furthermore, it was not God who revealed that Saul's sons should be killed; it was the vengeful request of the Gibeonites.

Of course, the context of the executions must be kept in mind. The Gibeonites claim that Saul had so persecuted them that they had been "decimated" and claimed to "have no place anywhere in Israel" (v. 5). If we take the statement at face value, then Saul's crimes against them were terrible indeed. Yet, we must be careful not to equate human vengeance with God's justice. The Gibeonites probably called for all the sons of Saul to die in order to wipe out his family entirely. This is not exactly an eye-for-an-eye justice, since the Gibeonites were not entirely wiped out by Saul. So, their demand for the death of the seven sons was flawed and should not be viewed as equal to God's justice. As in the case of all justice carried out by human beings, it is always mingled with injustice.

Significantly, the impaling of Saul's sons before the Lord does not have the desired affect of ending the famine. So, we get no indication that God desired the death of Saul's children. The actions that precipitate God's answering prayers for the land are David's burial of Saul, Jonathan, and the Saulides slain by the Gibeonites. This could imply that it was not the execution of the seven Saulides that appeased God but the proper care of the remains of Saul, Jonathan, and the victims of the Gibeonite revenge. Though God was clearly displeased with Saul's actions against Gibeon, even sending a famine in response, God's concern for the proper burial of the remains of Saul and his house distance God from the call for their deaths. Perhaps God wanted the Saulides to make amends with the Gibeonites. Perhaps their execution was not what God had in mind at all. In the absence of a clear word from the narrator on the matter, the interpreter should be wary of concluding that God required the execution of the Saulides and that their deaths satisfied his demands, leading him to heal the land. God's concern for the victims' burial may suggest that God was not pleased with their execution. Rather than seeing this story as a textbook example of God's punishment of the wicked, God's concern for the victims' burials here could instead be used as an example of God's merciful heart.

CHAPTER 46

2 Samuel 22:1–23:39

 LISTEN to the Story

¹David sang to the Lord the words of this song when the Lord delivered him from the hand of all his enemies and from the hand of Saul. ²He said:

> "The Lord is my rock, my fortress and my deliverer;
> ³my God is my rock, in whom I take refuge,
> my shield and the horn of my salvation.
> He is my stronghold, my refuge and my savior—
> from violent people you save me.
> ⁴"I called to the Lord, who is worthy of praise,
> and have been saved from my enemies.
> ⁵The waves of death swirled about me;
> the torrents of destruction overwhelmed me.
> ⁶The cords of the grave coiled around me;
> the snares of death confronted me.
> ⁷"In my distress I called to the Lord;
> I called out to my God.
> From his temple he heard my voice;
> my cry came to his ears.
> ⁸The earth trembled and quaked,
> the foundations of the heavens shook;
> they trembled because he was angry.
> ⁹Smoke rose from his nostrils;
> consuming fire came from his mouth,
> burning coals blazed out of it.
> ¹⁰He parted the heavens and came down;
> dark clouds were under his feet.
> ¹¹He mounted the cherubim and flew;
> he soared on the wings of the wind.
> ¹²He made darkness his canopy around him—

the dark rain clouds of the sky.
¹³Out of the brightness of his presence
    bolts of lightning blazed forth.
¹⁴The LORD thundered from heaven;
    the voice of the Most High resounded.
¹⁵He shot his arrows and scattered the enemy,
    with great bolts of lightning he routed them.
¹⁶The valleys of the sea were exposed
    and the foundations of the earth laid bare
at the rebuke of the LORD,
    at the blast of breath from his nostrils.
¹⁷"He reached down from on high and took hold of me;
    he drew me out of deep waters.
¹⁸He rescued me from my powerful enemy,
    from my foes, who were too strong for me.
¹⁹They confronted me in the day of my disaster,
    but the LORD was my support.
²⁰He brought me out into a spacious place;
    he rescued me because he delighted in me.
²¹"The LORD has dealt with me according to my righteousness;
    according to the cleanness of my hands he has rewarded me.
²²For I have kept the ways of the LORD;
    I am not guilty of turning from my God.
²³All his laws are before me;
    I have not turned away from his decrees.
²⁴I have been blameless before him
    and have kept myself from sin.
²⁵The LORD has rewarded me according to my righteousness,
    according to my cleanness in his sight.
²⁶"To the faithful you show yourself faithful,
    to the blameless you show yourself blameless,
²⁷to the pure you show yourself pure,
    but to the devious you show yourself shrewd.
²⁸You save the humble,
    but your eyes are on the haughty to bring them low.
²⁹You, LORD, are my lamp;
    the LORD turns my darkness into light.
³⁰With your help I can advance against a troop;

with my God I can scale a wall.
31"As for God, his way is perfect:
    The Lord's word is flawless;
    he shields all who take refuge in him.
32For who is God besides the Lord?
    And who is the Rock except our God?
33It is God who arms me with strength
    and keeps my way secure.
34He makes my feet like the feet of a deer;
    he causes me to stand on the heights.
35He trains my hands for battle;
    my arms can bend a bow of bronze.
36You make your saving help my shield;
    your help has made me great.
37You provide a broad path for my feet,
    so that my ankles do not give way.
38"I pursued my enemies and crushed them;
    I did not turn back till they were destroyed.
39I crushed them completely, and they could not rise;
    they fell beneath my feet.
40You armed me with strength for battle;
    you humbled my adversaries before me.
41You made my enemies turn their backs in flight,
    and I destroyed my foes.
42They cried for help, but there was no one to save them—
    to the Lord, but he did not answer.
43I beat them as fine as the dust of the earth;
    I pounded and trampled them like mud in the streets.
44"You have delivered me from the attacks of the peoples;
    you have preserved me as the head of nations.
People I did not know now serve me,
    45foreigners cower before me;
    as soon as they hear of me, they obey me.
46They all lose heart;
    they come trembling from their strongholds.
47"The Lord lives! Praise be to my Rock!
    Exalted be my God, the Rock, my Savior!
48He is the God who avenges me,

who puts the nations under me,
    ⁴⁹who sets me free from my enemies.
You exalted me above my foes;
    from a violent man you rescued me.
⁵⁰Therefore I will praise you, LORD, among the nations;
    I will sing the praises of your name.
⁵¹"He gives his king great victories;
    he shows unfailing kindness to his anointed,
    to David and his descendants forever."

^{23:1}These are the last words of David:

"The inspired utterance of David son of Jesse,
    the utterance of the man exalted by the Most High,
the man anointed by the God of Jacob,
    the hero of Israel's songs:
²"The Spirit of the LORD spoke through me;
    his word was on my tongue.
³The God of Israel spoke,
    the Rock of Israel said to me:
'When one rules over people in righteousness,
    when he rules in the fear of God,
⁴he is like the light of morning at sunrise
    on a cloudless morning,
like the brightness after rain
    that brings grass from the earth.'
⁵"If my house were not right with God,
    surely he would not have made with me an everlasting covenant,
    arranged and secured in every part;
surely he would not bring to fruition my salvation
    and grant me my every desire.
⁶But evil men are all to be cast aside like thorns,
    which are not gathered with the hand.
⁷Whoever touches thorns
    uses a tool of iron or the shaft of a spear;
    they are burned up where they lie."

⁸These are the names of David's mighty warriors:
Josheb-Basshebeth, a Tahkemonite, was chief of the Three; he raised
his spear against eight hundred men, whom he killed in one encounter.

⁹Next to him was Eleazar son of Dodai the Ahohite. As one of the three mighty warriors, he was with David when they taunted the Philistines gathered at Pas Dammim for battle. Then the Israelites retreated, ¹⁰but Eleazar stood his ground and struck down the Philistines till his hand grew tired and froze to the sword. The Lord brought about a great victory that day. The troops returned to Eleazar, but only to strip the dead.

¹¹Next to him was Shammah son of Agee the Hararite. When the Philistines banded together at a place where there was a field full of lentils, Israel's troops fled from them. ¹²But Shammah took his stand in the middle of the field. He defended it and struck the Philistines down, and the Lord brought about a great victory.

¹³During harvest time, three of the thirty chief warriors came down to David at the cave of Adullam, while a band of Philistines was encamped in the Valley of Rephaim. ¹⁴At that time David was in the stronghold, and the Philistine garrison was at Bethlehem. ¹⁵David longed for water and said, "Oh, that someone would get me a drink of water from the well near the gate of Bethlehem!" ¹⁶So the three mighty warriors broke through the Philistine lines, drew water from the well near the gate of Bethlehem and carried it back to David. But he refused to drink it; instead, he poured it out before the Lord. ¹⁷"Far be it from me, Lord, to do this!" he said. "Is it not the blood of men who went at the risk of their lives?" And David would not drink it.

Such were the exploits of the three mighty warriors.

¹⁸Abishai the brother of Joab son of Zeruiah was chief of the Three. He raised his spear against three hundred men, whom he killed, and so he became as famous as the Three. ¹⁹Was he not held in greater honor than the Three? He became their commander, even though he was not included among them.

²⁰Benaiah son of Jehoiada, a valiant fighter from Kabzeel, performed great exploits. He struck down Moab's two mightiest warriors. He also went down into a pit on a snowy day and killed a lion. ²¹And he struck down a huge Egyptian. Although the Egyptian had a spear in his hand, Benaiah went against him with a club. He snatched the spear from the Egyptian's hand and killed him with his own spear. ²²Such were the exploits of Benaiah son of Jehoiada; he too was as famous as the three mighty warriors. ²³He was held in greater honor than any of the Thirty, but he was not included among the Three. And David put him in charge of his bodyguard.

²⁴Among the Thirty were:
Asahel the brother of Joab,

Elhanan son of Dodo from Bethlehem,
[25]Shammah the Harodite,
Elika the Harodite,
[26]Helez the Paltite,
Ira son of Ikkesh from Tekoa,
[27]Abiezer from Anathoth,
Sibbekai the Hushathite,
[28]Zalmon the Ahohite,
Maharai the Netophathite,
[29]Heled son of Baanah the Netophathite,
Ithai son of Ribai from Gibeah in Benjamin,
[30]Benaiah the Pirathonite,
Hiddai from the ravines of Gaash,
[31]Abi-Albon the Arbathite,
Azmaveth the Barhumite,
[32]Eliahba the Shaalbonite,
the sons of Jashen,
Jonathan [33]son of Shammah the Hararite,
Ahiam son of Sharar the Hararite,
[34]Eliphelet son of Ahasbai the Maakathite,
Eliam son of Ahithophel the Gilonite,
[35]Hezro the Carmelite,
Paarai the Arbite,
[36]Igal son of Nathan from Zobah,
the son of Hagri,
[37]Zelek the Ammonite,
Naharai the Beerothite, the armor-bearer of Joab son of Zeruiah,
[38]Ira the Ithrite,
Gareb the Ithrite
[39]and Uriah the Hittite.
There were thirty-seven in all.

Listen to the Text in the Story: Genesis 49; Deuteronomy 32; 1 Samuel 2:1–10

Including a poem at the end (or near the end) of a narrative is common elsewhere in the Bible (e.g., Jacob's poetic last words in Gen 49 and Moses' Song in Deut 32). In the books of Samuel, a song/poem is placed near both the beginning and the end of the work, with the song of Hannah (1 Sam 2:1–10) paralleling David's song here in many ways (see commentary on ch. 2). While Hannah's song looked forward to these same events prophetically, David's song now looks back on them from a triumphant perspective.

EXPLAIN the Story

Chapter 22 records a song that David wrote, praising God for delivering him from his enemies. The song seems to reflect on the whole David story. Throughout the song, David credits God with his success and expresses his complete reliance on him. David further declares that he has been faithful to his God and has lived righteously, viewing God's work on his behalf as reward for this. The conclusion to David's song looks to the future, recalling the covenant Yahweh made with David through the prophet Nathan (2 Sam 7) and its promise that God will show covenant love (Hebrew *hesed*) to his anointed (Hebrew *mashiah*) forever (v. 51). The Davidic covenant is again brought to the fore in David's last words, a prophetic poem recorded at the beginning of chapter 23. The recollection of the Davidic covenant at the end of David's story causes the reader to look to the future for its fulfillment.

Chapter 23 concludes with a list of David's mighty men, providing some amazing anecdotes from Israelite military history wherein these formidable soldiers undertook amazing feats. Remarkable for his absence is Joab, David's long-serving general, who is not mentioned. This is perhaps due to the perennial conflicts the king had with his wily general. Most remarkable for his inclusion in the list is Uriah the Hittite, whom David had murdered after committing adultery with his wife. Despite the celebratory nature of the chapter, David's failings are not forgotten even here.

The Introduction to David's Song (22:1)

The exact dating of this song (which is also recorded in Ps 18) is unclear. It ascribes its composition to when God saved David from "all his enemies and from the hand of Saul." Some scholars believe the song goes back to David, while others think it has been secondarily attributed to him. All acknowledge that the Hebrew used in the poem contains many archaic expressions, pointing to its antiquity, so its composition was obviously much earlier than the final completion of the book by an exilic writer (see introduction). While I think it likely that the song came from David himself, either way, in the context of the book David is clearly the speaker. Being situated at the end of the book suggests it is a reflection over David's entire story and the many times he escaped from or triumphed over his foes.

God's Deliverance (22:2–20)

David likens God's protection to that of a rocky crag, like the rocky hideouts in which he hid from Saul and his men. David says, "The LORD is my rock" (v. 2) using the Hebrew word *sela* for rock, the same word used in 1 Samuel 23:25 when David flees from Saul and goes "down to the *rock*." David further says, "God is my rock" (v. 3), using a different Hebrew word for rock, *tsur*, which is the same word used in 1 Samuel 24:2 for the place where David hid from Saul (translated there as "crag" in the NIV). The metaphor of God as "rock" is used commonly in the psalms to stress God as a source of protection. This protective aspect is further accentuated by also calling God his "shield" (v. 3).

David calls God "the horn of my salvation" (v. 3). Drawing on the image of an animal's horn (which served as their weapon and indicated their power), horns symbolized strength and power in the ancient Near East. Using this image, David acknowledges that it was God's power that delivered him. In a way, David sums up the song saying that his deliverance was due to the fact he "called to the LORD" (v. 4).

David reflects on his experiences as tantamount to being drawn toward death, employing imagery of death as unruly waves that pull one under water or as ropes and snares inexorably dragging one down. Only his cry to God saved him. God is pictured as hearing from his temple (v. 7). Given that there was no temple at the time, likely the author viewed God as in his heavenly temple (the pattern of which the earthly temple was meant to reflect).

God's deliverance is then described in terrifying theophanic imagery. Creation reels at God's approach, resulting in earthquakes (v. 8), volcanic eruptions (v. 9), and thunderstorms (v. 10). Through the storms God rides on a cherub (v. 11), a creature elsewhere described as having wings and being a composite creature with different parts of their bodies being from different animals and sometimes having human faces (cf. Exod 25:20; 1 Kgs 6:24; Ezek 10:8, 20; 41:18–19). God's work on the psalmist's behalf is metaphorically described in storm imagery with dark clouds (v. 12), lightning (v. 13), thunder (vv. 14–15), flooding (vv. 16–17), and wind (v. 16).

David's Innocence (22:21–28)

In the song, David declares that God moved on his behalf because of his righteousness (v. 21), his obedience to God's laws (vv. 22–23), and his keeping himself from sin (v. 24). David attributes this to the principle that God repays people in kind. Reading this part of the song in the context of David's story results in some dissonance. In light of his adultery with Bathsheba and his murder of Uriah, how can David say he has lived righteously and kept himself from sin? Due to this incongruity, some have suggested these verses smack of "self-righteousness" rather than righteousness.[1] Are these words "hypocritical"?[2]

I would suggest that the inscription to this song, which attributes its composition to the occasion of God's deliverance of David from Saul, explains the incongruity. David's actions toward Saul were characterized by "righteousness" and "cleanness of hands." David refused to harm Saul, even when golden opportunities to do so were presented (cf. 1 Sam 24:4–6; 26:29). On one such occasion David similarly declared his innocence, stating that he was not "guilty of wrongdoing" (1 Sam 24:11). Saul himself acknowledged the truth of David's claim saying, "You are more righteous than I" (1 Sam 24:17), and predicted that Yahweh would reward David for his righteous actions (1 Sam 24:19). On another occasion where David refused to kill Saul, David's words to Saul are quite close to the words of this song when he says: "The LORD rewards every one for their righteousness and faithfulness. The LORD delivered you into my hands today, but I would not lay a hand on the LORD's anointed" (1 Sam 26:23). David's innocence regarding Saul has been made clear in the preceding narratives and is reflected in the words of this song. It is unlikely the psalm is meant to suggest that David was claiming to have never sinned. The sin of David was clearly narrated. The connection between his sin and his later failures and crises as king was clearly underscored by the prophet Nathan (2 Sam 12:9–12). The reader can see the truth of this song in David's life. The Lord does not only reward righteousness in kind, he humbles the proud (v. 28). When David was proud, God brought him low.

The Secret of David's Success (22:29–46)

David ascribes his military prowess (vv. 30. 34–37) and success in battle (vv. 38–46) to God alone. The reference to David's enemies calling on Yahweh (v. 42) implies these enemies were Israelites. Thus, here the song reflects the context of David being hunted by fellow Israelites Saul and his men, though it also fits with later parts of David's story (the Israelite civil wars or Absalom's coup d'état). Even though his enemies called on Yahweh, he did not answer them (v. 42).

David concludes noting how God has "preserved" him as "the head of nations" (v. 44). Reading this in light of David's story, the reader will recall David's defeat of Philistia, Amalek, Aram, Ammon, and Edom (2 Sam 8:11–15). The psalmist further notes that he is served by foreigners (vv. 44–45), perhaps recalling the Kerethites and Pelethites who faithfully served David.

---

1. D. M. Gunn and Danna Nolan Fewell, *Narrative in the Hebrew Bible* (Oxford: Oxford University Press, 1993), 124.

2. Hamilton, *Handbook*, 364.

Concluding Praise (22:47–51)

The song returns to where it began, praising God as rock and savior and the one who installed him as king and sustained his throne. The final verse, however, recalls the Davidic covenant. Just as Hannah's song in 1 Samuel 2 concluded with a reference to God's anointed one (Hebrew *mashiah*), so this song ends referencing the "anointed" (Hebrew *mashiah*). The song proclaims that God shows his anointed one his "unfailing kindness" (Hebrew *hesed*), using the standard technical term for Yahweh's covenant love and recalling the covenant made between God and David in 2 Samuel 7. Thus, the song puts all of David's success in the context of his covenant with David. Given the clear failures of David seen in the story since 2 Samuel 11, recalling God's promises here is significant. After all that had transpired and how far David had fallen, one might have wondered whether the covenant was still valid. True to his word, God punished David "with a rod wielded by men" (2 Sam 7:14), but God's covenant love (Hebrew *hesed*) "will never be taken away from him" (2 Sam 7:15). Despite David's sin and failures, the Davidic covenant still stands, as it is based not on David's actions but God's *hesed*. Furthermore, the reference to the covenant looks to the future. It mentions not only David but also "his descendants" who will receive this unfailing kindness (*hesed*) "forever." This leads Christians to read this reference as pointing to God's Anointed One (*mashiah*), Jesus, through whom we obtain blessing through his covenant.

David's Last Words (23:1–7)

Chapter 23 begins with what it calls David's "last words," though David does make a deathbed speech to Solomon in 1 Kings 2:1–9. This poem stands together with David's song of the last chapter as the epicenter of the concentric structure of the appendices (see comments on the structure of the epilogue in the commentary on ch. 22). At the heart of the structure both express a theological perspective on the David story, focusing on God's central role in the story. Both poems emphasize that Israel was delivered and sits secure due to God's initiative and his gracious work on the anointed's behalf.

These poetic last words are explicitly introduced as inspired prophecy. Later biblical books will explicitly refer to David as a prophet, with the book of Chronicles referring to him as a "man of God" (2 Chr 8:14), the same prophetic term used for Moses (Deut 33:1; Josh 14:6), Samuel (1 Sam 9:6–8), and other prophets (e.g., 1 Sam 2:27; 1 Kgs 13:1; 2 Kgs 5:8). David is further called "anointed by the God of Jacob" and the "hero" of Israel's songs. The last phrase could also be rendered, "Israel's delightful singer of songs," and reflect

David's reputation for composing songs rather than his being the subject of Israel's songs.[3]

The oracle given to David extols a ruler who is righteous and fears God (vv. 3–4), setting up Yahweh's moral expectations for his anointed.[4] David then goes on to assert that his house is like this with God, as evidenced by the "everlasting covenant" God made with him, echoing Nathan's prophetic word to David in 2 Samuel 7:14–16. God's word is sure and he will be faithful to his promises to David. This covenant guarantees David's deliverance and satisfaction (v. 5). David contrasts his standing with that of the wicked, who are cursed like thorns and destined for flames.

David's final words remind the reader of the royal ideal and contrasts it with "evil men" (literally from the Hebrew "[sons of] Belial"). The righteous are secure with an everlasting covenant, while the wicked are destined for destruction. After the great failings of David and his sons, the poem expresses hope that Israel's king can be God's agent despite human shortcomings.[5] As the story continues into the book of Kings, all future Israelite kings are measured by the Davidic ideal (e.g., 1 Kgs 15:3, 11; 2 Kgs 14:3; 16:2; 18:3; 22:2), though many will prove to be wicked.

David's Mighty Men (23:8–39)

This historical appendix lists the most powerful men who served David, and it includes some remarkable anecdotes about their exploits. The inclusion of such a list shows a somewhat democratic tendency, which goes against ancient Near Eastern kingship ideals where all victory is attributed to the king, not his warriors (as usually only the king is listed as the triumphant warrior).[6] Three of David's elite soldiers were in a league of their own, called "the Three," and verses 8–11 give their names and provide some amazing anecdotes regarding their military achievements. Despite the clear attribution of heroism to the men themselves, the narrator is sure to point out God was behind their success, twice noting that "the LORD brought about a great victory" (v. 10, 12).

Below "the Three" was an elite group called "the Thirty," within which there were three top soldiers. These three soldiers risked their lives to fulfill David's nostalgic wish that he could have a drink from the well of his hometown in Bethlehem. David's refusal to drink the liquid was out of respect for their lives, which they risked in obtaining it. Pouring it out to God implies that

---

3. This last phrase was translated in the first edition of the NIV as "Israel's singer of songs" and has been traditionally translated as "the sweet psalmist of Israel," which reflects David's reputation as a psalmist and musician.

4. Brueggemann, First and Second Samuel, 347.

5. Birch, "Books of Samuel," 1370.

6. Brueggemann, First and Second Samuel, 348.

only God is worthy of such a gift. Presumably it would also have discouraged others from similarly risking their lives for such a petty thing. The fact that these men did so showed the great loyalty that David inspired in his men.

Chief of these three top soldiers of the thirty was Abishai, Joab's brother (v. 18). It is said his fame equaled that of the three, that he was honoured above them and even became their commander, though he was not included in that elite group of the three. Abishai's command of the three can be seen back in 2 Samuel 20:6 when David put Abishai in charge of the army, which presumably included the three. Another soldier of fame was Benaiah, who is also said to be as famous as the three, though he was not included in that elite group. Nevertheless, he was given command of David's bodyguard (cf. 2 Sam 20:23).

The chapter concludes by listing the names of the other mighty men. Most notable for his absence is Joab, son of Zeruiah. In fact, even Joab's armor bearer makes the list (2 Sam 23:37). Some speculate that his absence was due to his status of being above all those in the list. In light of the larger story, however, it seems likely that Joab is excluded from the list due to his perennial conflicts with the king and perhaps the way in which he was ultimately found traitorous and killed by Benaiah and his elite soldiers for supporting the insurrection of Adonijah (1 Kgs 2:28–34).

The list ends on a sober note, listing none other than Uriah the Hittite as one of David's mighty men. That he occurs last in the list is not accidental but is intended to be noticed by the reader. Thus, even in a list celebrating the exploits and strength of David's men, his infamous sin is not forgotten. The nostalgic idealism such a list could inspire in the reader is somewhat muted with Uriah's mention. In keeping with the somewhat democratic function of the list, Uriah's name reminds the reader of the dangers of royal power unchecked and not wielded "in the fear of God" (2 Sam 23:3).

LIVE the Story

The Role of Christian Leaders

Though Israel experienced deliverance from their enemies during David's reign, David's song acknowledges that, in reality, it was God who actually brought the deliverance and protection (2 Sam 22:2–3). The king, while instrumental in defeating their enemies, was really God's instrument. The king called upon God, and he answered (2 Sam 22:7). God brings about surprising salvation even when things look their worst (2 Sam 22:5–6). The success and personal talents of the king were actually gifts of the Lord (2 Sam 22:33–43), and he is the one who is worthy of receiving the glory for them.

In the list of David's mighty men, even the great achievements of the three are also put into perspective as the text twice mentions that "the LORD brought about a great victory" (2 Sam 23:10, 12). It was not the heroism of men, great as it was, that brought success to Israel—it was God (Ps 20:7). Thus, while the books of Samuel chronicle the rise of kingship in Israel and the achievements of their greatest king, it was really God who is the sovereign in Israel.

This passage is a good reminder not to put our leaders on a pedestal. The greatest Christian leaders are merely servants of God. Their effectiveness and success are really due to God's initiative and his work on our behalf. A good leader will recognize this. All glory is to be given to God, without whom none of us could lead or minister in his church. In light of David's amazing accomplishments, he could have taken credit for his victories, but instead he credits his success to God alone. So those in leadership should remember who deserves the credit for their accomplishments.

The Call to Faithfulness

David's song also encourages believers to take faithful living seriously. The psalmist asserts that God responds to human behavior in kind. Believers' faith is met with God's faithfulness, their righteousness with God's deliverance (vv. 26–27). Similarly, God saves the humble but humbles the proud (v. 28). This aspect of God's dealings with humanity are accentuated in the book of Proverbs, which asserts that: "The eyes of the LORD are everywhere, keeping watch on the wicked and the good" (15:3) and that "The LORD is far from the wicked, but he hears the prayer of the righteous" (15:29). David's last words similarly extol the merits of righteous leadership (2 Sam 23:3–4) and even assert that God's covenant with David (2 Sam 23:5) would not have been possible if his house was like that of "evil men" (2 Sam 23:6–7). Similarly, in the New Testament Paul writes of God's dealing with us in kind: "If we died with him, we will also live with him; if we endure, we will also reign with him. If we disown him, he will also disown us" (2 Tim 2:11–12). Believers in both the Old Testament and the New Testament are continually admonished to serve faithfully (e.g., Matt 5:16; Eph 5:10; Jas 2:14–17; Heb 13:16).

Pointing to the Gospel

The problem, however, is that the Bible also affirms that no one is righteous (Ps 14:3; 53:3; Rom 3:10). All fall short of God's standard and so do not merit God's salvation. The key to understanding this dynamic relationship with God is the acknowledgment of the psalmist in 2 Samuel 22 that all he has is from God. Deliverance, protection, talents, success—all of these are due to God's gracious giving. David himself could not continue to point to his own righteousness after he failed so miserably and sinned so heinously. Yet, David's song points to the gospel in that God "shows unfailing kindness to his anointed" (2 Sam 22:51). God shows his covenant love to his anointed—not due to their sinlessness but due to his gracious covenant. Through this covenant God promises to show his kindness "forever" (2 Sam 22:51). David's last words also underscore the perpetual and sure nature of the covenant, explicitly calling it "an everlasting covenant, arranged and secured in every part" (2 Sam 23:5).

Just as David's success was due to God's gracious covenant, so a believer's standing is due solely to our being in covenant relationship with God's anointed (*mashiah*), Jesus the Messiah. On the basis of this relationship and our standing in the covenant, just as David prayed and was delivered (2 Sam 22:4), so we pray for God to act on our behalf, and he hears. Going back to Paul's admonition to faithfulness in 2 Timothy 2:11–12, although the apostle notes the importance of faithfulness, the saying concludes on a positive note stating, "if we are faithless, he will remain faithful, for he cannot disown himself" (2 Tim 2:13). Our salvation is not dependent upon our faithfulness but on the faithfulness of Christ.

Pointing to the Messiah

In fact, the concluding reference in David's song to the Davidic covenant and God's covenant with his anointed (*mashiah*) enables a messianic reading of chapter 22. Originally it is David, Yahweh's anointed (*mashiah*), who sings the song. A messianic reading of the song, however, has the Messiah, Jesus, singing verses 22–25. Jesus is the one who could *truly* say:

> [21]"The LORD has dealt with me according to my righteousness;
>   according to the cleanness of my hands he has rewarded me.
> [22]For I have kept the ways of the LORD;
>   I am not guilty of turning from my God.
> [23]All his laws are before me;
>   I have not turned away from his decrees.
> [24]I have been blameless before him
>   and have kept myself from sin.
> [25]The LORD has rewarded me according to my righteousness,
>   according to my cleanness in his sight.
>   (2 Sam 22:21–25)

The New Testament tells us that Jesus "had no sin" (2 Cor 5:21; cf. 1 John 3:5). He "is holy, blameless, pure, set apart from sinners" (Heb 7:26). Jesus can truly say that God rewarded him for his righteousness, with no irony or qualification. Jesus meets Yahweh's moral expectations of his anointed, ruling "in righteousness" and "in the fear of God" (2 Sam 23:3).

The good news is that "just as through the disobedience of the one man the many were made sinners, so also through the obedience of the one man the many will be made righteous" (Rom 5:19). Through our standing as Christians in the covenant with God's Messiah, with his righteousness imputed to us, we who are righteous through Christ can pray the psalm as well. We can now share in David's experiences of deliverance. The same God who saved David is our God. He saves not only the king but all who call on his name. We can trust in his promise to show "unfailing kindness" to us forever.

CHAPTER 47

2 Samuel 24:1–25

 LISTEN to the Story

¹Again the anger of the LORD burned against Israel, and he incited David against them, saying, "Go and take a census of Israel and Judah."

²So the king said to Joab and the army commanders with him, "Go throughout the tribes of Israel from Dan to Beersheba and enroll the fighting men, so that I may know how many there are."

³But Joab replied to the king, "May the LORD your God multiply the troops a hundred times over, and may the eyes of my lord the king see it. But why does my lord the king want to do such a thing?"

⁴The king's word, however, overruled Joab and the army commanders; so they left the presence of the king to enroll the fighting men of Israel.

⁵After crossing the Jordan, they camped near Aroer, south of the town in the gorge, and then went through Gad and on to Jazer. ⁶They went to Gilead and the region of Tahtim Hodshi, and on to Dan Jaan and around toward Sidon. ⁷Then they went toward the fortress of Tyre and all the towns of the Hivites and Canaanites. Finally, they went on to Beersheba in the Negev of Judah.

⁸After they had gone through the entire land, they came back to Jerusalem at the end of nine months and twenty days.

⁹Joab reported the number of the fighting men to the king: In Israel there were eight hundred thousand able-bodied men who could handle a sword, and in Judah five hundred thousand.

¹⁰David was conscience-stricken after he had counted the fighting men, and he said to the LORD, "I have sinned greatly in what I have done. Now, LORD, I beg you, take away the guilt of your servant. I have done a very foolish thing."

¹¹Before David got up the next morning, the word of the LORD had come to Gad the prophet, David's seer: ¹²"Go and tell David, 'This is what the LORD says: I am giving you three options. Choose one of them for me to carry out against you.'"

¹³So Gad went to David and said to him, "Shall there come on you three years of famine in your land? Or three months of fleeing from your enemies while they pursue you? Or three days of plague in your land? Now then, think it over and decide how I should answer the one who sent me."

¹⁴David said to Gad, "I am in deep distress. Let us fall into the hands of the LORD, for his mercy is great; but do not let me fall into human hands."

¹⁵So the LORD sent a plague on Israel from that morning until the end of the time designated, and seventy thousand of the people from Dan to Beersheba died. ¹⁶When the angel stretched out his hand to destroy Jerusalem, the LORD relented concerning the disaster and said to the angel who was afflicting the people, "Enough! Withdraw your hand." The angel of the LORD was then at the threshing floor of Araunah the Jebusite.

¹⁷When David saw the angel who was striking down the people, he said to the LORD, "I have sinned; I, the shepherd, have done wrong. These are but sheep. What have they done? Let your hand fall on me and my family."

¹⁸On that day Gad went to David and said to him, "Go up and build an altar to the LORD on the threshing floor of Araunah the Jebusite." ¹⁹So David went up, as the LORD had commanded through Gad. ²⁰When Araunah looked and saw the king and his officials coming toward him, he went out and bowed down before the king with his face to the ground.

²¹Araunah said, "Why has my lord the king come to his servant?"

"To buy your threshing floor," David answered, "so I can build an altar to the LORD, that the plague on the people may be stopped."

²²Araunah said to David, "Let my lord the king take whatever he wishes and offer it up. Here are oxen for the burnt offering, and here are threshing sledges and ox yokes for the wood. ²³Your Majesty, Araunah gives all this to the king." Araunah also said to him, "May the LORD your God accept you."

²⁴But the king replied to Araunah, "No, I insist on paying you for it. I will not sacrifice to the LORD my God burnt offerings that cost me nothing."

So David bought the threshing floor and the oxen and paid fifty shekels of silver for them. ²⁵David built an altar to the LORD there and sacrificed burnt offerings and fellowship offerings. Then the LORD answered his prayer in behalf of the land, and the plague on Israel was stopped.

Listen to the Text in the Story: Exodus 30:12; Numbers 22; 1 Samuel 4–5; 6:19; 2 Samuel 6:7; 21:1–14

This concluding narrative begins with "anger of the LORD" burning against Israel "again" (v. 1). Given the way this story is separated from the larger story of David, it is unclear when we should situate it chronologically. God's displeasure with Israel has been seen several times throughout the story (e.g., 1 Sam 4–5; 6:19; 2 Sam 6:7). The most likely backdrop to this narrative, however, is the story of the famine and the Gibeonites in 2 Samuel 21:1–14. Recalling the concentric structure of the concluding appendices of chapters 21–24 (see commentary on 2 Sam 21), this story of the sinful census is the counterpart to the story in 2 Samuel 21:1–14. In both stories, sin has caused God's displeasure, leading him to punish Israel, but David intervenes to stop the punishment. The first story concerns the guilt of the Saulide house (21:1) and the second the guilt of the Davidic house (24:17).[1] Furthermore, both stories conclude with God answering "prayer in behalf of the land" (2 Sam 21:25; 24:25).

EXPLAIN the Story

Following David's song crediting God with all of his success (2 Sam 22) and the list of mighty men on whom David relied and through whom the Lord brought deliverance (2 Sam 23:10, 12), the books of Samuel close with a story of David initiating a census to see how many able-bodied men he could use in a war. Similar to the famine which resulted from Saul's sins, David's sin here results in another national calamity as a plague ravages Israel. Unlike Saul, however, David quickly repents of his sin, and when God sends a prophet to David, he obeys him. As David obediently builds a new altar to the Lord in Jerusalem, God permanently stopped the plague and listened to David's prayer for the land. What is more, the new altar will become the location of the temple.

The Census (24:1–10)

This enigmatic story leaves the reader with many questions. Why is God angry with Israel? What is sinful about the census? Why does God incite David to take a census if it is sinful? While fully satisfying answers to all of these questions may not be possible, I would suggest the following.

Why is God Angry at Israel? The simple answer is—the text does not say. Given the biblical teaching of the sinfulness of humans, however, this is not a huge difficulty for interpreting the passage. The writer has chosen not to focus on what it was that caused God's anger to arise against his people.

---

1. Polzin, *David and the Deuteronomist*, 211.

Why is the Census Sinful?[2] It must be remembered that censuses were taken for military purposes, as made clear by David's order to "enroll the fighting men" (v. 2) and Joab's eventual report that "reported the number of the fighting men" (v. 9). Given that in Israelite theology "the LORD does not save by sword and spear; for the battle is the LORD's" (1 Sam 17:47) and that "nothing can hinder the LORD from saving by many or by few" (1 Sam 14:6), David's inquiry to find out the size of his army suggests he was turning away from reliance on God to human military might. Thus, the census displayed David's lack of faith and a proud reliance on his own resources. This also fits the literary context with the list of David's mighty men immediately preceding the story (2 Sam 23:8–39). With warriors such as these, it would be easy to feel self-sufficient. The taking of a census of all the fighting men in Israel would bolster this pride in the formidable fighting force at his command.

Why Would God Incite David to Take a Census? In this story, due to his anger at Israel for an unspecified sin, God incites David to do a second sin in order to punish Israel for the first (unspecified) sin. God's actions here could be somewhat of a stumbling block to a modern believer, though they are not unique in the Bible. This is quite similar to the story in 1 Kings 22 where God sets out to punish Ahab for his sin by having the prophets lie to him (1 Kgs 22:23) in order to get him to go into battle and be killed.[3] In 2 Samuel 24, however, the focus is on the culpability of the one incited (David), something ignored in 1 Kings 22.

Another biblical story wherein God commands someone to do something then gets angry at them for doing it is found in Numbers 22, where the pagan seer Balaam is solicited by Moabites who attempt to hire him to curse Israel. Balaam initially declines the Moabites' offer because God had told him

---

2. An important intertext here is Exod 30:12, which underscores a connection between census taking and plagues. It reads: "When you take a census of the Israelites to count them, each one must pay the LORD a ransom for his life at the time he is counted. Then no plague will come on them when you number them." Thus, it could be that David did not implement the census properly (collecting the ransom money from each person enlisted), resulting in a plague. Joab's objection, however, does *not* seem to imply a connection between censuses and plagues or argue that they should be careful to collect the ransom money if they count the people. Instead, Joab seems to imply that the actual taking of a census in this instance was wrong (not just the method of taking the census). Cf. Paul S. Evans, "Let the Crime Fit the Punishment: The Chronicler's Explication of David's 'Sin' in 1 Chronicles 21," in *Chronicling the Chronicler: The Book of Chronicles and Early Second Temple Historiography*, ed. Paul S. Evans and Tyler F. Williams (Winona Lake, IN: Eisenbrauns, 2013), 65–80.

3. The parallel passage in 1 Chr 21 actually has Satan instead of God's anger as the initiator, reading "Satan rose up against Israel and incited David to take a census of Israel" (1 Chr 21:1). It would appear that the author of Chronicles saw the role of Satan as a divine intermediary in this situation, similar to the "lying spirit" who volunteers for the job of deceiving Ahab in 1 Kgs 22:21–22. See Paul Evans, "Divine Intermediaries in 1 Chronicles 21: An Overlooked Aspect of the Chronicler's Theology," *Bib* 85 (2004): 545–58.

not to go (Num 22:13). The Moabites returned again, however, and offered Balaam a substantial amount of money to go with them (Num 22:17). At this Balaam again informed the Moabites that he would not go unless God bade him but told the men to wait and see if God would let him go (Num 22:19). Surprisingly, God then tells Balaam to go with the Moabites (Num 22:20). Shockingly, when Balaam goes, God gets "angry" at Balaam for going and sends an angel to kill him along the way (Num 22:22). Upon seeing the angel, Balaam confesses his sin (Num 22:34) and God then tells him what he should do. In other words, in both the stories of Balaam (Numbers 22) and David's census (2 Sam 24): (1) God commands someone (Balaam/David) to do something; (2) God then gets "angry" at them for doing it; (3) God sends an angel to punish them; (4) they confess their sin; and (5) God then instructs them on what they are to do.

Given these significant similarities, perhaps the key to understanding the puzzling action of God in inciting David to take a census is to be found in the Balaam story. Balaam had already heard clearly from God that he was *not* to go with the Moabites, yet when they came back and offered him substantial remunerations for his services, Balaam did not turn them away but waited to see if God would let him go. Why would Balaam secondguess God's initial word and wait for a second word to see if he had changed his mind? Greed. Balaam hoped that God might change his mind so that he could avail himself of the substantial stipend that would come his way if he went with the Moabites. As 2 Peter 2:15 notes, Balaam "loved the *wages* of wickedness" (emphasis added). Thus, when God gives his permission for Balaam to go, God is testing him, giving him what he wants in order to see if he would follow his desires or do what he knew was right.[4]

Analogously, in 2 Samuel 24 God incites David to take a census because David had already forgotten to rely on God for national security and was instead proudly finding security in his army. David's pride in his own strength as king had led him away from his reliance on God, leading God to incite him to bolster his pride in his forces by taking a census (see Live the Story below).

Despite Joab's objections (v. 3), David goes through with the census. The census takes over nine months to complete and then, after the final numbers are listed for the king, David's conscience strikes him (v. 10). The only other time this happened was back when David's conscience struck him for cutting off the corner of Saul's robe in the cave (1 Sam 24:5). At that time, David's crisis of conscience concerned his taking the initiative in gaining the kingdom rather than relying on God (see commentary on 1 Sam 24). Similarly, in

---

4. Roy Gane, *Leviticus, Numbers*, NIVAC (Grand Rapids: Zondervan, 2004), 693.

2 Samuel 24, David's heart pricks him when he again attempts to rely on his own strength rather than trust God. In response to these pangs of conscience David fully repents of his actions, saying he has "sinned greatly" and incurred "guilt," further calling the census "a very foolish thing" (v. 10). This is the second time in the larger story where David has confessed sin, though in the first instance (2 Sam 12:13) it took the confrontation of a prophet to get him to do so. David appears to have learned to respond to his conscience once again as he did in his days gone by (e.g., 1 Sam 24:5), and he repents *before* being confronted on his sin. Though his pride led him to sin, his spiritual sensitivity led to his repentance—even before he was confronted by the prophet and before the terrible consequences of his sin began.

The Choice of Punishments (24:11–14)

In response to David's repentance, God sends the prophet Gad to him. We last saw Gad when the king was staying in Moab and he told David to return to Judah (1 Sam 22:5). This time the prophet presents David with three punishment options: three years of famine, three months of fleeing his enemies, or three days of plague. The punishments are of diminishing nature going from years, to months, to days. It is somewhat odd for David to be offered different options for punishment of sin. Was this a test of some sort? Regardless, in response to the presented options, David chooses God. He does not specifically pick one of the options, though he clearly rejects the second—pursuit by his enemies. While we could guess that perhaps David had seen enough of being pursued by enemies (with his fleeing the pursuit of both Saul and Absalom), his choice of falling into God's hands instead of a human enemy is due to his understanding of God as merciful (v. 14). So, whether it be famine or plague, David leaves it in God's hands, trusting in God's mercy.

The Plague (24:15–25)

In response, the least of the three punishments is implemented: instead of years of famine or months of war, a plague. The effects of the plague are disastrous, with seventy thousand dying as a result. In the end, David's trust in God's mercy, however, is well placed. The plague appears to last less than a day rather than the three days originally specified, as God halts the plague before it reaches Jerusalem. It is stopped not due to any response by David or anyone else but simply because God "relents." God is merciful and halts the plague on his own accord.

The plague is delivered through the agency of an angel, and, when it is halted, the angel is at a Jebusite threshing floor. The reader will recall that

Jebusites were the original inhabitants of Jerusalem, and the threshing floor is presumably in Jerusalem or its outskirts. The later book of Chronicles will make clear that the threshing floor was the same location where Solomon's temple was to be built, and this story is told there (1 Chronicles 21) to explain the divine choice of this spot for the temple.

Continuing the portrayal of David as a complex character, in this chapter David makes a terrible mistake but also passionately repents. Though he begins with a concern about his own military might (thus, the census), he now shows a deep concern for his subjects, asking God to punish him and his family instead of the people (v. 17).

In response to David's repentance, the prophet Gad commands David to build a new altar to God on that very threshing floor. When the owner of the threshing floor, Araunah, sees the king and his entourage coming, he bows and offers to give it to David. David turns down the offer, however, on the principle that sacrifices must cost the one offering them something.

Upon the successful completion of the altar and the offering of sacrifices, God permanently stops the plague and answers David's prayers for the land. This recalls the conclusion to the story of the famine and the Gibeonites, which is the counterpart to this chapter in the concentric structure of these concluding appendices, with both saying God "answered prayer in behalf of the land" (2 Sam 21:25; 24:25).

With this, the books of Samuel come to a close. The story began with a barren wife praying to God (1 Sam 1:11) and worshiping (1 Sam 1:24) in Shiloh, and now ends with a king praying to God (2 Sam 24:17) and worshiping (2 Sam 24:25) in Jerusalem. As Birch has commented, "Worship as the final act of this story is the appropriate recognition of divine reality working in and through human history."[5] Throughout the stories between these events we have seen prophets, kings, and generals seemingly shape the history through their actions. Yet for all their power and machinations, it has always been God who directed events. Thus, this conclusion is fitting.

LIVE the Story

Sacrifices are Costly

As noted above, David's refusal to take the threshing floor from Araunah as a gift is based on the principle that sacrifices must be costly. This expresses a profound truth about the nature of sacrifice. A gift to God is not a sacrifice if

---

5. Birch, "Books of Samuel," 1383.

it costs the worshiper nothing. Any such gift would render worship "cheap" and "meaningless."[6] This principle is still relevant for believers today.

Often what gets given to churches or charities is that which the giver did not need: the giving of pocket change into the offering plate; donations of used goods to charity that the giver no longer needs; gifts that really cost nothing. Such gifts lack any self-denial on our part—or any real sacrifice. Yet a biblical view of giving demands sacrificial giving. In Old Testament law, it was the first fruits that belonged to God. In the book of Malachi, God rebukes Israel's priests for offering sick animals as sacrifices. The prophet writes:

> "By offering defiled food on my altar. . .you offer blind animals for sacrifice, . . .you sacrifice lame or diseased animals. . . . Try offering them to your governor! Would he be pleased with you? Would he accept you?" says the LORD Almighty. (Mal 1:7–8)

God does not want gifts that are perfunctory. In Isaiah 29:13, God laments that "[t]hese people come near to me with their mouth and honor me with their lips, but their hearts are far from me. Their worship of me is based on merely human rules they have been taught" (cf. Matt 15:8–9). True sacrifice that God receives and blesses is a sacrifice that costs something.

God and Temptation

The book of James clearly denies God the role of tempter, saying, "When tempted, no one should say, 'God is tempting me.' For God cannot be tempted by evil, nor does he tempt anyone; but each person is tempted when they are dragged away by their own evil desire and enticed" (Jas 1:13). The story in 2 Samuel 24 is no different. As we noted above, in this story of the census David is actually "dragged away" into sin by "his own evil desire" for independence and his pride. Yet God was clearly involved. Elsewhere in Scripture, we see that God at times gives people "over to their stubborn hearts to follow their own devices" (Ps 81:12). In the New Testament, Paul notes that sometimes "God sends them a powerful delusion so that they will believe the lie and so that all will be condemned who have not believed the truth but have delighted in wickedness" (2 Thess 2:11–12). When one is defiantly determined to sin, sometimes God gives them over to their sin and its consequences (cf. Rom 1:28).

A helpful analogy might be a fight between spouses. Let's say a husband has expressed interest in doing something that has deeply offended his wife. So offended is his wife that she says, "Go ahead! Do it!" What she really means

---

6. Arnold, *1 & 2 Samuel*, 647.

is "You do that and I'll be so upset you will regret this big time." His wife in reality *does not* want her husband to do it but does not want to be seen as difficult in trying to control her husband. She would really like the husband to say on his own, "I'm not going to do that." But the husband is perhaps so obsessed with his desire to do it that he does not hear the truth of his offense. Instead, he thinks his wife is actually giving him permission to do what he wants to do. Perhaps similarly, in 2 Samuel 24 God is saying to David "Go ahead. Do it. You think you're that great. Go ahead, do it without me. You think you can rely on your own strength. Try it, and we'll see what happens."

I have to admit that the idea of God giving me over to my sin is a scary scenario. There is, however, reason to be encouraged. First, the Bible clearly says that in each temptation God makes a way of escape: "God is faithful; he will not let you be tempted beyond what you can bear. But when you are tempted, he will also provide a way out so that you can endure it" (1 Cor 10:13). Even in our story in 2 Samuel 24 we can see this as God uses an unlikely character, Joab, to warn David and give him an out (2 Sam 24:3)—although David did not listen to him. Second, even when we ignore warnings and plunge headlong into sin, God is merciful. After all, God halts the plague (2 Sam 24:16) even before David builds the altar to stop it. Third, David's example shows us it is never too late to repent. Though the sin was already committed, David's quick repentance mitigated its consequences. Fourth, penitent sinners are not just forgiven but are given further opportunities to serve in the kingdom. After his repentance, David successfully intercedes for the people (2 Sam 24:17). Not only this, God uses David to secure the site for the temple: "In the context of a national disaster of his own making, David is able to turn that catastrophe into the occasion for a permanent divine blessing upon Israel."[7]

In this story, God was faithful to his eternal covenant with David (2 Sam 7), punishing him temporarily for his sin (2 Sam 7:14) but restoring him and never taking away his covenant love (2 Sam 7:15). As participants in the new covenant with Christ, the Son of David, how much more can we be assured of God's commitment to us? The punishment of our sin has been paid, forgiveness is available, and God graciously uses us flawed believers for his glory!

---

7. Gary N. Knoppers, "Images of David in Early Judaism: David as Repentant Sinner in Chronicles," *Bib* 76 (1995): 469.

Scripture Index

Numbers

Deuteronomy

1 Kings

2 Kings

Luke

John

Subject Index

541

Author Index